Demi-Tasse and Mrs. Grundy

By
JOSEPHINE VAN DE GRIFT

Helen Josephine Van de Grift

This book is a work of editorial thoughts originally written by my great-grandmother, Helen Josephine Van De Grift Rigby, during the mid-1920's and before the time of the Great Depression and Second World War. She wrote of her moments during the roaring 20's jazz era, of speakeasys, prohibition and her thoughts on whether or not to wear corsets. Through her stories, she gives glimpses to that time period and those local folks she encountered in her day to day life, including her married life and mother to Mary (my grandmother). To the best of my ability, accuracy has been given to any names, characters, businesses, organizations, places, events, and incidents. Great care has been taken with names specifically. Minor misspellings may be present due to reduced legibility of old newspaper clippings. Regarding censorship or political correctness: words or phrases that may have had a different or colloquial meaning in the 1920's than of present day are not omitted as to keep the integrity of the original articles, as well as her thoughts on topics such as war, sexism, and racism, all continual rampant issues alive today. As the saying goes, *"Those who cannot remember the past are condemned to repeat it."* ... *George Santayana*. Extensive effort has gone into ensuring the reliability of the information in this book; however, the publisher makes no warranty, express or implied, with respect to the material contained herein.

Demi-Tasse and Mrs. Grundy
Copyright © 2019 by Josephine Van De Grift and Kristin Carter-Groulx

ISBNs
978-0-9880861-3-5 (Hardback – Case Laminate)
978-0-9880861-6-6 (Paper)
Released on Christmas Day 2019
Kindle and EPUB editions forthcoming

Authors, American--Biography
Van De Grift, Josephine, 1894-1927—Biography

See also: Vandegrift Rigby, Helen Josephine
See also: Van De Grift Rigby, Helen Josephine

With thanks given to The Akron Beacon Journal, Akron, Ohio for the original publication of these enclosed compiled and transcribed stories.

Copy Editors: John Carter and Nathan Mulcahy. Cover design by Moonspinner Designs. Text composition in the Garamond, French Script and Nickelodeon typefaces. The Tenth Muse Logo is inspired from paintings of Edward Robert Hughes (1851-1914).

Published by The Tenth Muse Books (Ottawa/Vancouver, Canada // © 2019
@BooksMuse

Demi-
Tasse
and
Mrs.
Grundy

By
JOSEPHINE
VAN DE GRIFT

A biography and collection of stories

from 1924-1927 of writer

Josephine Van De Grift,

my great-grandmother

by Kristin Carter-Groulx

The Tenth Muse Books

~The Table of Contents~

A   well-loved   writer   in   her   day, Josephine Van De Grift, later known as Mrs. William Rigby, began her writing career early in her teen years. She went on to become a successful society page editor for the Akron Beacon Journal in Akron, Ohio between 1924-1927, when she passed away suddenly at the age of 32 after childbirth complications. Her passing devastated her readers. Her followers begged her husband Bill to one day make a book of all her stories, but none was ever made – until now.

Almost a century later, her great-granddaughter, Kristin (née Carter) Groulx, also a writer, historian and genealogist, has taken the time to thumb through saved newspaper clippings and put them to paper in one book for Josephine's beloved readers to see and remember her by.

Included in this book are also compiled notes and words by John Carter, first-born and oldest son of Josephine's only daughter, Mary.

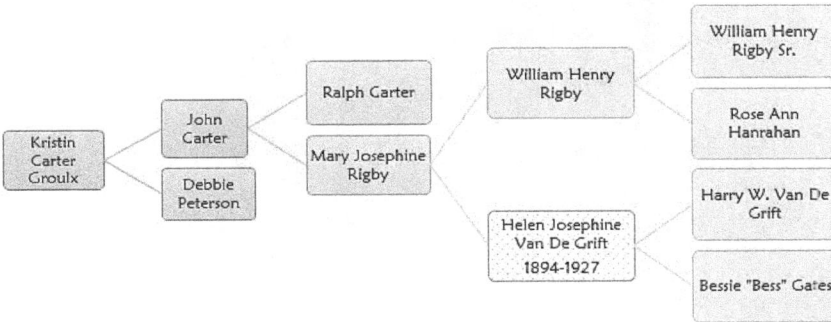

Josephine Van De Grift

- Kristin Carter Groulx
  - John Carter
    - Ralph Carter
    - Mary Josephine Rigby
      - William Henry Rigby
        - William Henry Rigby Sr.
        - Rose Ann Hanrahan
      - Helen Josephine Van De Grift 1894-1927
        - Harry W. Van De Grift
        - Bessie "Bess" Gates
  - Debbie Peterson

Mary Rigby

for Mary Jo
(Josephine's daughter)

Chapter I.

MEETING

JOSEPHINE

meeting Josephine

Josephine in 1914, age 20

HELEN JOSEPHINE VAN DE GRIFT (sometimes spelled Vandegrift, Vandegriff or Van Degrift) was born January 7th in the year 1894 in Shelbyville, Shelby County, Indiana to Harry W. Van De Grift and Bess Gates. Her father's "Vandegrift" ancestry links back to Dutch roots and "Adams," her paternal grandmother's maiden name links back to North Carolina (unsure where in Europe previously before their family immigrated to the U.S.). We do know there is a link by marriage to Frances "Fanny" Matilda Vandegrift to Scottish author Robert Louis Balfour Stevenson on the Vandegrift side. It is well known that Robert Louis Stevenson was inspired by his wife, whom he called his writer's muse. She too was a published writer.

On her maternal ancestry side, her mother, Bess's "Gates" (also Getz) family links back to Baden-Württemberg, Germany, and her maternal grandmother's family tree surname of "McGarr" came from Ireland.

Josephine was Harry and Bess's only child, as her mother passed away a short time later when Jo was only 5 years old. After that passing, the family moved from Indiana to Ohio.

On the 1900 census Jo is recorded living with Bess's sister Helen and listed as her niece. Living at 611 Mechanic, in Shelbyville, Indiana with the Geysie family (her aunt and uncle). It is later told through a story in one of her articles that she was named in exchange for a new baby carriage by her aunt Helen and uncle Joseph (her namesake becoming Helen Josephine upon her birth). She was very close to the Geysie family following the death of her own mother.

Harry remarried Matilda "Tillie" Liedke, a native of Sandusky, Ohio, when Jo was 10 years old. Their marriage was on July 28, 1904 in Essex, Ontario, Canada, due north across the big Lake from Sandusky to Canada.

This marriage did not create any new siblings for Jo. Instead it was her mother's siblings that Josephine called her sisters, rather than her aunts. Bess's sisters included Maggie, Helen, and Alta, whom Jo references in several of her stories as her own sisters.

By the 1910 census, Jo is living with her father and step-mother, Matilda, on 223 Crosby st. in Akron, Ohio.

71	223	294	357	Vandegrift, Ashby			Head		M	W	38	M	2	5
72				Matilda			Wife	W F	7	W	38	M	1	5
73				Helen J.			Daughter		7	W	15	S		

Josephine c. 1910, age 15 or 16, seated in front.
We are unsure whom she is with – however comparing the adjacent graduating class picture, she is with a close school friend from Central High School in Ohio, shown in that image standing two persons to the right of her.

A Talented Pianist and Musician

In the class of 1914, she graduated from Central High School in Akron, Ohio. This newspaper from January 10, 1914 with the headline **Central High School Has Large Class for January Graduation** shows the names of the graduating class from Central High School on January 16, 1914, including "Helen Josephine Vande Grift, 223 Crosby street, Latin."

JANUARY GRADUATING CLASS OF CENTRAL HIGH SCHOOL

Commencement exercises were held Friday evening for the January class of Central High school. Those receiving diplomas are: Dorothy M. Bard, Mary Luetta Billow, Laurence C. Botsford, Ernest R. Bridgwater, Hesper Merriam Buckingham, Katherine Jane Caswall, Helen Elizabeth Conger, Ruth Mary Duncan, Carl F. Fowle, Edna A. Gauthier, Mina A. Gauthier, Charles E. Goth, Rayburn W. Hemphill, Esther Irene Howarth, Jesse D. Jackson, Carey Victor Kendall, Leo Kohn, Hazel Marguerite Mc-Connell, Emily Sperry Means, Donald M. Northrup, Helen Burdett Pfautz, Hazel M. Putt, Eva Delight Ritter, Reginald Robert Sanderson, Mary Margaret Apley, Arthur D. Brennan, William Leonard Curtice, Gertrude Irene Ellis, Clarence E. Freedaman, Forest K. Goodman, Odette Elizabeth Hastings, Elreta May Hawk, Carl L. Hunsicker, Harvey Peterson, Mary Elizabeth Reid, Edna Lillian Reinhold, Albert C. Bentschler, Ruth Marie Sender, Marguerite Louise Washer, Olive Maria White, Bessie D. Williford, Sophie A. Schott, Walter L. Scott, Karl G. Siedschlag, Marion Edward Snyder, John Perry Teeple, Helen Josephine Vandegrift, Marion S. Virtue, Ruth Elizabeth Wager, Gladys Varian Walter, Dorothy A. White, Elizabeth Louise Wilcox, Emory Lewis Zink, Lucretia Morar, Walter C. Wilhelm.

A note from the July 5, 1914 paper states:

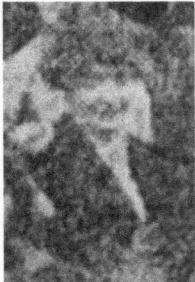

"Another attractive guest in town for the summer is Miss Helen Josephine VanDegrift of Akron, O., who has come to be with her aunt and uncle, Mr. and Mrs. W. S. Mitchell, 1818 North Alabama street, for several months. Miss VanDegrift was graduated last month from the Akron High School, where she was an honor student. She is a talented pianist."

In the previous note, reference to 1914 and her living with her aunt and uncle, she is living with her late mother's sister, Sarah "Maggie" (née Gates) who married William S. Mitchell. They lived in Indiana and had no children of their own. On the 1880 census for Maggie, she is listed as crippled at age 14.

During 1915 – 1919 she attended Buchtel (now Akron) University, participated in the Buchtel Orchestra including doing concerts around Summit County, and graduated in 1919.

(image): **BUCHTEL ORCHESTRA PLAYS FOR CHILDREN**
The Buchtel College orchestra under the direction of Prof. F. D. Sturtevant, will give a concert Sunday afternoon at the Children's Home.

Members of the orchestra are Sol H. Mackman, Wendeli Arnold, Eugene Haas, Eugene Hauenstein, Cyril Smith, Glen Williams, Edward Otis, Robert Michel and Miss Josephine Van der Grift.

She taught music at home for two years prior to becoming an editor. Her first articles in the Beacon Journal were related to music recitals and concerts.

BUCHTEL ORCHESTRA PLAYS FOR CHILDREN

The Buchtel College orchestra under the direction of Prof. F. D. Sturtevant, will give a concert Sunday afternoon at the Children's Home.

Members of the orchestra are Sol H. Mackman, Wendeli Arnold, Eugene Haas, Eugene Hauenstein, Cyril Smith, Glen Williams, Edward Otis, Robert Michel and Miss Josephine Van der Grift.

In a later article of "Demi-Tasse and Mrs. Grundy" from September 9, 1926, she jests with her husband Bill that if she lost 30 pounds, he would buy her a grand piano. She then goes on to tell of her love of the piano and how beautiful they are, but "not the latest upright ones that force you to shove them against a wall to hide the backs of them."

"I think 30 pounds would be a great plenty. What do you say now – 30 pounds – one grand piano."

She frequently talked about pianos, especially about wanting to buy a grand piano. In her New Year's Resolutions from January 1927 (7 months before she passed away) she promises doing just that, buying a grand piano. Her love of music plays continuously throughout her articles, from talking about various composers of Classical music, to types of musical instruments, to purchasing gifts of music for special someones, to her infant daughter playing with a wooden spoon on a tin plate to make a drum.

I have learned from speaking with my father, that throughout his mother's life, Jo's daughter Mary also loved to play piano and played quite well.

⸻ ❧❦◆❧❦ ⸻

A Writer in Bloom

By the 1920 census, Jo is living at 999 West Exchange Street in Akron, Ohio, listed as single, living as a "lodger" in the household of Clyde and Ada Miller. Her occupation is listed as "Society editor, newspaper." Several articles with her name in the byline are featured in the Beacon Journal newspaper between 1920 – 1924 (though articles appear by her as early as 1918). It wasn't until later that she gained the opportunity for her own column.

Her occupation:
Society Editor | Newspaper

During this time, she also wrote several plays and stories, and gained a fascination with theatre and reviews, including Charlie Chaplin's "The Kid" and Mary Pickford's "The Love Light."

From January 18, 1921 (image):

ALLEN THEATER, HOTEL MARNE BLDG.

NOW SHOWING
MARY PICKFORD – IN – "THE LOVE LIGHT"

Josephine Van De Grift in The Beacon Journal says: "Mary is again lovely, and feminine, and very, very alluring. The characters are distinct and finely drawn and the story on the whole convincingly narrated."

NO ADVANCE IN PRICES

Continuous Performance From 10 A. M.

Josephine's name on a movie review of Chaplin's "The Kid"

From March 19, 1921 (image):

TOMORROW
BEGINNING 2ND WEEK
"GRAND PICTURES SEASON"

CHARLES CHAPLIN – IN – "THE KID"

"The world's greatest and the world's newest great are starred in 'THE KID,' which opened the Grand Pictures Season at the Waldorf and Empress theatres." – Beck, The Akron Press.

"Jack Coogan * * * is the worthiest of sidekicks in playing the role of the kid. * * * The association of these two in the rankest and blissfulest of poverty is one of the most delightful domestic arrangements that has yet come to us." – Josephine Van de Grift, Beacon Journal

Everywhere you go the main topic of conversation is "THE KID." In the restaurants, on the street corners, the youngsters at school, club meetings and society gatherings ----you can't afford to miss this wonderful 6 Reels of Joy!

In August 1922, she won an amateur playwright competition with her play "The Lonely Road" entitling her to enter Dr. George Pierce Baker's "Harvard 47 Workshop" in September of that same year. She had planned on traveling to Harvard University in Boston, Massachusetts to do just that as shown in the following 1922 news clippings.

(image): **Manuscript Section**
A meeting of the manuscript section of the Civic Drama association has been called by Mrs. Ellwood B. Spear, leader of the section, for Tuesday evening, August 1, in the assembly room of the Y. W. C. A. Mrs. David Leslie Brown and Josephine Van de Grift will read original manuscripts.

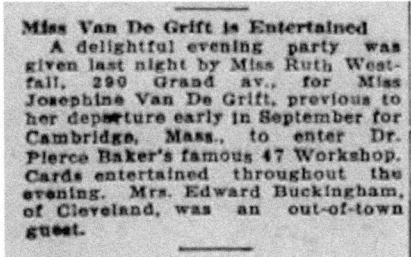

(image): **Miss Van De Grift is Entertained**
A delightful evening party was given last night by Miss Ruth Westfall, 290 Grand av., for Miss Josephine Van De Grift, previous to her departure early in September for Cambridge, Mass., to enter Dr. Pierce Baker's famous 47 Workshop. Cards entertained throughout the evening. Mrs. Edward Buckingham of Cleveland, was an out-of-town guest.

(image): **Afternoon Tea**
Honoring Miss Josephine Van de Grift, 620 E. Buchtel av., who is leaving the middle of September for Boston, where she will enter the "Harvard 47 Workshop," and Miss Lucille Long, a popular young contralto, Mrs. W. C. Beckwith, 202 Twin Oaks rd., entertained at an informal afternoon tea today. Eight intimate friends were received.

(image): **Club to Honor Miss Van De Grift**
From the Business Women's club today comes announcement of dates for three evening entertainments in the form of a Chautauqua course, as a compliment to Miss Josephine Van De Grift, successful contestant for entrance to Dr. Baker's 47 Workshop at Harvard college.

Club to Honor Miss Van De Grift

From the Business Women's club today comes announcement of dates for three evening entertainments in the form of a Chautauqua course, as a compliment to Miss Josephine Van De Grift, successful contestant for entrance to Dr. Baker's 47 Workshop at Harvard college.

Thursday, Sept. 21, Miss Van De Grift will open the course with two original sketches. She will also read her play, "The Lonely Road," that won her the scholarship. Miss Edith Sadler will direct a "Vaudeville Show" on Saturday night, Sept. 20, and Miss Jane Bowman will present an original series of "Adventures in New York," in verse.

About 200 tickets for the course will be placed on sale at Collins Drug Store, 135 S. Main st., also at 529 Akron Savings & Loan building. Reservations for the affairs should be made with Mrs. Elsie Gilbert, at the latter address.

Thursday, Sept. 21, Miss Van De Grift will open the course with two original sketches. She will also read her play, "The Lonely Road," that won her the scholarship. Miss Edith Sadler will direct a "Vaudeville Show" on Saturday night, Sept. 20, and Miss Jane Bowman will present an original series of "Adventures in New York," in verse.

About 200 tickets for the course will be placed on sale at Collins Drug Store, 135 S. Main st., also as 529 Akron Savings & Loan building. Reservations for the affairs should be made with Mrs. Elsie Gilbert, at the latter address.

(image): **Farewell Courtesies**

Complimenting Miss Josephine Van de Grift, 620 E. Buchtel av., who is leaving in the middle of September for Boston, where she will enter the "Harvard 47 Workshop," directed by George Pierce Baker, members of the Business Women's club are sponsoring a pseudo Chautauqua of three programs during August and the early part of September

Farewell Courtesies

Complimenting Miss Josephine Van de Grift, 620 E. Buchtel av., who is leaving the middle of September for Boston, where she will enter the "Harvard 47 Workshop," directed by George Pierce Baker, members of the Business Women's club are sponsoring a pseudo Chautauqua of three programs during August and the early part of September.

Miss Van de Grift will present the first performance, consisting of two original dramatic interpretations, followed by the reading of her Harvard entrance manuscript. An evening of poetry from the versatile pen of Miss Jane Bowman will form the entertainment for the second "Chautauqua" number, while an interesting group of vaudeville numbers, directed by Miss Edith Sadler, will complete the course.

Saturday afternoon, Miss Van de Grift will be honored at a tea given by Mrs. W. C. Beckwith, Twin Oaks rd. Miss Lucille Long, popular young contralto, will be a second honored guest. Saturday night, Miss Mary Wolcott, 101 Burton av., will entertain six couple at the Henry Rudd cottage, West Reservoir, as a farewell courtesy to Miss Van de Grift and to Miss Hesper Buckingham, 840 Bloomfield av., who is leaving the first of September for Cleveland to enter the Western Reserve library school.

Miss Van de Grift will present the first performance, consisting of two original dramatic interpretations, followed by the reading of her Harvard entrance manuscript. An evening of poetry from the versatile pen of Miss Jane Bowman will form the entertainment for the second "Chautauqua" number, while an interesting group of vaudeville numbers, directed by Miss Edith Sadler, will complete the course.

Saturday afternoon, Miss Van de Grift will be honored at a tea given by Mrs. W. C. Beckwith, Twin Oaks rd. Miss Lucille Long, popular young contralto, will be a second honored guest. Saturday night, Miss Mary Wolcott, 101 Burton av., will entertain six couple at the Henry Rudd cottage, West Reservoir, as a farewell courtesy to Miss Van de Grift and to Miss Hesper Buckingham, 840 Bloomfield av., who is leaving the first of September for Cleveland to enter the Western Reserve library school.

The celebrated "Workshop 47" began in 1905, providing a forum for the creation and performance of plays which were developed in Dr. George Pierce Baker's English 47 class at Harvard.

Many of his students' plays exist today in the Harvard Theatre Collection at Harvard's Library. Of his many students, included were Rachel Barton Butler, George Francis Abbott, Samuel Nathaniel Behrman (writer for *The New Yorker*), Thomas Clayton Wolfe, Hallie Flanagan Davis, Edward Brewster Sheldon, and Sidney Coe Howard (author of *Gone With the Wind*). Additionally, notable student Stanley McCandless paved the way for future theatre lighting designers in all aspects of theatrical production.

Dr. Baker was instrumental in the modern-day creation of the Yale School of Drama, after in 1925 Harvard refused to create a playwrighting degree and he moved to Yale University where he remained until his retirement in 1933.

It was on December 10, 1926 The Yale University Theater was dedicated, with 700 seats and was the first of its type. The theater was opened with a student play. Dr. Baker produced the play, "The Patriarch," written by a Yale undergraduate, Boyd Smith and a member of an advanced class in play-writing.

In the article that follows, Josephine talks about her play "The Lonely Road." Just a year later, in May 1923, a silent film came out with the same title and starred Katherine MacDonald *(image)*, but further research proves it is unrelated to Josephine's script.

July 22, 1922, Saturday (image):

Well Known Feature Writer Admitted to Famous Workshop

"Miss Josephine Van de Grift, 620 E. Buchtel av., has the honor of being enrolled in the new class of the famous "Harvard 47 Workshop," under the direction of George Pierce Baker. Membership to this dramatic group is limited to 12, known as "Baker's Dozen," who have had an original manuscript accepted.

For the past three years, Miss Van de Grift has become well known to the majority of Akron people through her feature writings in the Beacon Journal and has gained a large following of friends and admirers.

"The Lonely Road," a one-act play, of pathos and humor the vehicle by which Miss Van de Grift entered the field of her chosen profession, is founded upon real life. It depicts the scene of an aging maiden "all forlorn," waiting for a non de script to make good on the stage. The prodigal hero returns following theatrical failure and the irate father promises him one more chance to retain the heart and hand of his daughter by offering a position in his new grocery store. As the haranguing continues amid the sobs of the patient damsel, a lure in the form of a patent medicine show outside, penetrates the imagination of the dramatic failure. Left alone, the would-be star responds, and makes an exit through an open window replying to the call of the ribald song of the medicine vendor.

Miss Van de Grift will leave for Cambridge the first of September."

A Trip to New York

In September 1922, Josephine decided to become a writer for the Newspaper Enterprise Association (NEA) in New York City. She interviewed several notable persons of the time including stage, motion picture, and vaudeville actor Will Rogers and well known writers Dorothy Parker and Richard Atwater, known for Mr. Popper's Penguins. Among the best of her many stories was an account of a trip to Florida in which she interviewed John D. Rockefeller, Sr. These interviews are in the next chapters to follow.

JOSEPHINE VAN DE GRIFT *(image):*

"As an opportunity to bid Miss Josephine Van De Grift, 620 E. Buchtel av., farewell, prior to her departure tonight for New York City, over 100 friends and members of the business Women's club met at the clubhouse last night to hear her give the opening program of a club Chautauqua series.

Miss Van De Grift read her play, "The Lonely Road," the merits of which entitled her to entrance in Dr. Pierce Baker's 47 Workshop, Harvard university. She also gave an amusing monologue in the form of a "take-off" on activities behind the music counter of a commercial establishment. Both presentations displayed the cleverness and versatility of the author who is well known here. An informal reception in the club rooms followed the entertainment.

Miss Van De Grift, will, in the future, be associated with the Newspaper Enterprise association in New York as a feature writer. She has been connected with the Beacon Journal editorial staff in the same capacity for the last four years."

As of 2019, when this book was written, I have not been able to locate yet the play "The Lonely Road" which she wrote, but I suspect it may exist within the walls of the great Harvard University Library in a book of Dr. Baker's workshop plays.

Photo and article published September 22nd, 1922

Returning Home

By June of 1924, she returned to Akron, Ohio from New York, with an announcement of her arrival on the front page of the Akron Beacon Journal, *(image previous page)* headlining **TALENTED AKRON NEWSPAPER WOMAN TO REALIZE AMBITION IN NEW YORK** with a large photo of Josephine taking center stage of the front page.

(image): **FEATURE WRITER JOINS BEACON JOURNAL STAFF**

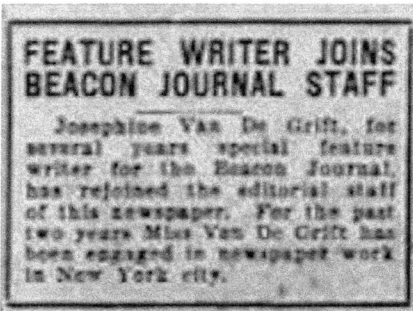

FEATURE WRITER JOINS BEACON JOURNAL STAFF

Josephine Van De Grift, for several years special feature writer for the Beacon Journal, has rejoined the editorial staff of this newspaper. For the past two years Miss Van De Grift has been engaged in newspaper work in New York city.

"Josephine Van De Grift, for several years special feature writer for the Beacon Journal, has rejoined the editorial staff of this newspaper. For the past two years Miss Van De Grift has been engaged in newspaper work in New York city."

Shortly after her return, she began her own syndicated column titled "Demi-Tasse and Mrs. Grundy" which included, among other things, references to her family life at 620 Buchtel Avenue and later, married life and motherhood at 320 Fairy Street.

She was also prominent in social and professional women's clubs including the Business Women's Club, Women's City Club and the Ohio Newspaper Women's Association. Upon moving to New York and working with the NEA, she joined the "Blue Pencil Club of Brooklyn[1]"

---

[1] A literary society in New York in the early 1900's. Its members included author H.P. Lovecraft, present in 1923 when Josephine joined. Others were Hazel Pratt Adams and Ernest A. Dench.

Blue Pencil Club Dinner

The Blue Pencil Club of Brooklyn, whose membership is largely drawn from the Bedford District, held its annual dinner at the Rainbow Restaurant, in Manhattan on Wednesday evening of last week. It was attended by thirty-five members and their friends. Albert M. Adams, the vice-president, presided, and introduced the speaker, James F. Morton, Jr.

The guest of honor was Truman J. Spencer, the Shakespearean lecturer, who gave a delightful talk on early days in amateur journalism, and told many stories of the National Amateur Press Association. Another speaker was Lawrence A. Nixon, who told of the cordial welcome extended to him in different parts of the country by amateurs. He spokt also for the strong sentiment he had for the hobby which meant so much to his father, John T. Nixon, who was a most active amateur journalist.

Miss Josephine Van De Firth, recently of Akron, Ohio, and connected with the Newspaper Enterprise Association, spoke of her hope to join the club in the near future. Others on the program were: Earnest A. Dench, who spoke on "How It Feels To Be An American Citizen." Miss Katherine B. Collier, on "The Highbrow in Amateur Journalism," Otto P. Knack on "The Lowbrow in American Amateur Journalism."

March 3, 1923, Saturday (*image*):

BLUE PENCIL CLUB DINNER

The Blue Pencil[2] Club of Brooklyn, whose membership is largely drawn from the Bedford District, held its annual dinner at the Rainbow Restaurant, in Manhattan on Wednesday evening of last week. It was attended by thirty-five members and their friends. Albert M. Adams, the vice-president, presided, and introduced the speaker, James F. Morton, Jr.

The guest of honor was Truman J. Spencer, the Shakespearean lecturer, who gave a delightful talk on early days in amateur journalism, and told many stories of the National Amateur Press Association. Another speaker was Lawrence A. Nixon, who told of the cordial welcome extended to him in different parts of the country by amateurs. He spokt [sic] also for the strong sentiment he had for the hobby which meant so much to his father, John T. Nixon, who was a most active amateur journalist.

Miss Josephine Van De Firth [sic], recently of Akron, Ohio, and connected with the Newspaper Enterprise Association, spoke of her hope to join the club in the near future. Others on the program were Ernest A. Dench, who spoke on "How It Feels To Be An American Citizen," Miss Katherine B. Collier, on "The Highbrow in Amateur Journalism," Otto P. Knack on "The Lowbrow in American Journalism." …

Who was Mrs. Grundy?

Mrs. Grundy is a figurative name for a personification of an extreme prudish or conventional woman. The name of Mrs. Grundy originates as an unseen character in

---

[2] Named after a *blue pencil* which is a pencil traditionally used by a copy editor to show corrections on a written copy.

---

the 1798 play *Speed the Plough* by Thomas Morton. Mrs. Grundy's character became well known to the public imagination, with scores of 'Mrs. Grundy's' appearing throughout prose and literature.

According to an article written by Judith Martin known as "Miss Manners" she states "Mrs. Grundy, a character in Thomas Morton's rollicking 1798 hit *Speed the Plough* … was a lady who disapproved of everything, usually because she found scandalous possibilities in innocent actions. It is a liberty to presume that she would have given out dispensations, which would have been quite against her nature."

The thought of having a demi-tasse (A French word for a small cup of strong black tea, coffee, or espresso) with such a character brought a whimsy to the imagination of the reader. Josephine never says directly why she calls her column this, however we can deduce having a sneak peek inside the social aspects of the Akron lifestyle and its people while sipping on our morning cuppa provided the town all sorts of entertainment.

Falling in Love

If books and writing were Josephine's first loves, then it would only seem the perfect fit for her to fall in love with a book shop owner. In the fall of 1924, she met William Henry Rigby at his bookstore which opened on South High Street, about a mile's walk from her home on Buchtel Avenue. Local accounts state she was his first customer.

She mentions Bill by name in her Demi-Tasse column on September 9, 1924, when she walked into his shop to look through Bibles to answer a question with her male peers about who wrote the "Lord's Prayer." Afterwards she and her peers went to a pub where she did not eat, but instead she ordered a 'near beer in a stein' and then proceeded to play dice games of chance. It is unclear if this was the "first" meeting, but she was smitten.

She married him less than a year later on May 12, 1925 in Akron, Ohio, at Akron's oldest church, St. Vincent's. St. Vincent de Paul stands now at 164 West Market Street in Akron and was completed in 1867, so this is the building that Josephine and Bill would have had their ceremony inside of. The very first St. Vincent church, built in 1853, was located near the canal on the west side of Green Street, opposite what is now Wood Street.

Their signatures are shown on their marriage certificate to the bottom right.

local newspaper wedding announcement from 12 May 1925

(image): "A LARGE number of Akron people will be interested in the marriage of Miss Josephine Van de Grift, daughter of Mr. and Mrs. Harry Van de Grift, 620 E. Buchtel av., and William Henry Rigby, son of Mr. and Mrs. William Rigby, Pawtucket, R. I., which took place today at the rectory of St. Vincent's church at 11 o'clock. The marriage ceremony was performed by the Reverend Father Patrick Burke. Mr. and Mrs. Edward Krumeich were attendants.

After the wedding Mr. and Mrs. Rigby left by motor for the east. They will visit in Rochester and Albany, N. Y. Upon returning they will make their home in the Twin Oaks apts.

The bride is a former student of Akron university and well known newspaper woman here. Mr. Rigby is owner of the Rigby Book Shop, 24 S. High st."

(image): **Pippins And Cheese**

"I will make an end to my dinner; there's pippins and cheese to come." – Merry Wives of Windsor.

By JAKE FALSTAFF

PRAYER FOR A NEWLY MARRIED COUPLE

MAY every easy chair you own
Grow prematurely old with use;
From bearing load of banquet food
May all the table legs be loose

May heel –, rints mar the fire-dogs
And curtains with tobacco reek;
May every napkin in the house
Go to the laundry every week

We sing epithalamium today for a colleague and a contributor. Yesterday morning Josephine Van De Grift, our next-door neighbor on this page, and William H. Rigby, the Bill Rigby of this column, were married, and we were happy in the union of two very dear friends. When "Pippins & Cheese" came to the Beacon Journal, there were many readers who did not grasp the idea that it could live in perfect amity on the same page with "Demitasse and Mrs. Grundy," and (now it may be told) the conductors of those two columns laughed together over the letters which were written to one or the other. As for Josephine, we think she is a fine girl, and as for Bill, we think he is a fine fellow, and as for the two of them – they're a dandy couple.

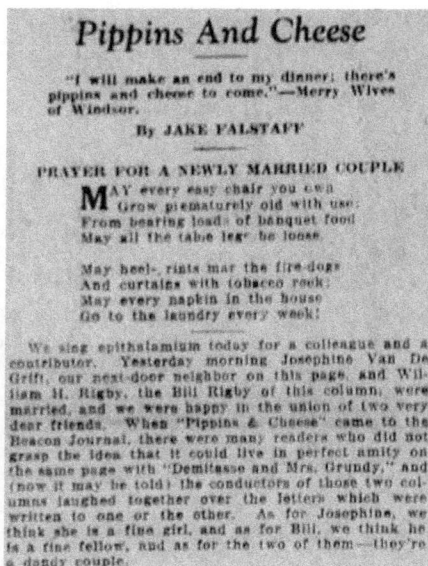

Honeymoon in Canada

Josephine and her new husband, William Rigby, honeymooned in Niagara Falls, Ontario, of which she wrote a column piece in her "Demi-Tasse and Mrs. Grundy" about how disappointed she was in the area being now flanked by factories. She also states her real reason for going was to get into Canada for the "English ale" – and during the times of prohibition, this would have been quite a luxury. However, their arrival did not coincide with the fabled ale shipment, so they settled upon some fine "buttered asparagus."

Typewriters and Tippy Toes

On New Years Eve, December 31st, 1925, she gave birth to her first daughter, Mary Josephine Rigby. Josephine wrote a poem dedicated to her newborn daughter, which was published in the local paper. Concurrently, Mary's name popped up many times in her column.

By 1926, their residence was 320 Fairy Street in Akron, the last residence Josephine would know. This house no longer exists sadly, nor does "Fairy Street," but it is estimated it within a mile's radius around the current Akron public library on Main Street.

Using a map of 1930 showing Fairy Street, we can see its location next to the Grace Public School and is now roughly the area the modern day "Cedar Street" is located. Builders and historians in Akron have stated the actual road which Fairy Street was built on was bulldozed and new streets were placed over the area. I have highlighted the location of the house at 320 Fairy Street by the small grey round dot on the left side of the map. She would have resided here in late 1925 – 1927.

Her Last Story

She gave birth to a son on July 19th, 1927 – however, he was stillborn. Worse still, Josephine underwent complications from this childbirth resulting in the need for multiple blood transfusions for several weeks. Her condition had improved just prior to her final days, along with the morale of her adoring public followers believing in her to pull through and return to her storytelling. Her childbirth complications were not made known to the public and only those close to her knew of the birth of her son.

Josephine was baptised on August 20, 1927, and died the next day on August 21, aged 32 years, 6 months and 24 days. She is buried in Holy Cross Cemetery in Akron.

July 8, 1925, Wednesday (image):

Pippins and Cheese by Jake Falstaff

> Speaking of epitaphs, the finest I have ever heard is the one Josephine Van De Grift has chosen:
> Warte nur, balde ruhest du auch.

"Speaking of epitaphs, the finest I have ever heard is the one Josephine Van De Grift
has chosen:
Warte ur, balde ruhest du auch."

Loosely translated from German reads
"Just wait, soon you will rest too"

Jo's widowed husband, William Rigby went on to remarry a few years later to Ora Ann Carl, the woman who would raise little Mary on a farm in Missouri. The following chapter is his story and hers follows a little later on in Mary's chapter at the end of this book.

Chapter II.

William H. Rigby and His Book Shop

II.
William H. Rigby and his book shop

—⸾⸽⸾◆⸾⸽⸾—

W ILLIAM Henry Rigby was second born (out of ten siblings) in 1889 Pawtucket, Providence, Rhode Island to English and Irish immigrant parents, William Henry Rigby, Sr. from Salford, Lancashire, England and Rose Ann Hanrahan from Clontuskert Parish near Ballinasloe, County Galway, Ireland.

Rose Ann (née Hanrahan) and William Henry "Bill" Rigby Sr.

William H. Rigby attended school in Pawtucket. He is listed in 1910 Pawtucket city index as a clerk, the 1910 Rhode Island census as an apprentice to an automotive shop, and the 1913 city index as moving to Ohio. He is recorded going to Chelsea, Massachusetts at a young age. He loved to travel.

U.S. Army Veteran and falling in love in France

He enlisted in the Army on July 26, 1917 at Columbus Ohio, served as ambulance driver in World War I, and was in Luxembourg in the Christmas of 1918. He was quite fluent with medical terms. He was in the St Mihiel Offensive, the Meuse-Argonne Offensive, and the Army of the Occupation.

While in France, he fell in love, but her parents did not approve as he was Catholic and she was not.

He was discharged July 28, 1919 as a Sergeant, with the WWI Victory Medal. His discharge papers state he had brown eyes, black hair, and was 6'1" in height. After being discharged, he went to Akron, Ohio and worked in a rubber plant from 1920 – 1922.

DID YOU KNOW THAT –

Rigby's own Book Shop!

He worked as a clerk in **Temple Book Store**, last listed in Akron's 1924 city directory. It was located at 64 East Mill Street and operated by Herbert H. Fletcher. Established in 1916, it became a favorite gathering place for the local literati of that period. Patrons and readers included reporters from *The Times* and *The Press*, just a few hundred feet away on South High Street, and from the *Beacon Journal*, then on East Market on Broadway. The name was derived as upon its establishment in 1916, it occupied the first floor of the then-new Masonic Temple.

The next year, the premises were occupied by the Temple Radio Company. A new era of radio had just begun. William opened up his own book store. He owned **Rigby's Book Shop** at 24 South High Street, Akron, Ohio, circa 1924-1930.

She was his first book shop customer!

"At the time Josephine returned from New York, Bill Rigby was opening his book shop on High Street. She was the first customer, and that encounter was her first meeting with the man who was to become her husband."

They were married in May 1925. Josephine continued her work at the Beacon Journal.

As of September 1928, Rigby's Book Shop enlarged to cover also 61 South Main Street proclaiming "our circulating library, of course, will be bigger and better!" To point out that William H. Rigby's bookstore is now the very public spot of the Akron-Summit County Public Library.

Literary Bibliophile

It is said he was definitely of the generation of the roaring 20's. He had letters and pictures of F. Scott Fitzgerald (The Great Gatsby), William McFee, and Edna St. Vincent Millay in his collection. Josephine spoke often of William McFee in her column. In her tribute in the Akron Beacon Journal newspaper, Herman Fetzer said William McFee had asked Josephine to collaborate on a play with him.

---

an

advertisement appearing on 28 September 1926 – to note the referenced, Jake Falstaff the pseudonym of Herman Fetzer) was one of Josephine's nearest and dearest friends and present at the time of her death

Life after Josephine

After the death of his first wife in 1927, the famous Josephine Van De Grift, he remarried Miss Ora Ann Carl, whose family owned a large farm in Missouri.

By 1930, Bill and his new wife moved to Missouri with his daughter, Mary Rigby. Two years later, a daughter Anne Rose Rigby was born in Oklahoma and by 1936, a son, William David was born in Missouri.

In the 1940's, he went to Long Beach, California, where he worked as a Supervisor in the Maintenance Engineering Department at Norton Air Force Base, California (1941 – Jan. 31, 1958).

After retiring, he returned to Mount Vernon, Missouri until the death of his second wife in 1963. He then moved to Lockwood, Missouri, and remained there until his death in 1972 at age 83.

He is buried in Maple Grove Cemetery, Lawrence County, Missouri. His plaque showing, he was a veteran of World War I, SG1 Ambulance Co. 20, Rhode Island.

Chapter III.

New York & The N.E.A.

Interviews

New York & the N.E.A. Interviews

October 1922 – June 1924

JOSEPHINE VAN DE GRIFT

By JOSEPHINE VAN de GRIFT
NEA Service Staff Writer.

Josephine in October 1922, working at the Newspaper Enterprise Association in New York City, NY.

Josephine's byline for the NEA read across countless newspapers nationwide during the years 1922-1924. In that time, she interviewed several famous persons of the era including:

Business magnate and philanthropist John D. Rockefeller, Sr., actor Will Rogers, Charles Garland, Heywood Broun, Dorothy Parker (and the Algonquin Round Table), Tom Daly, Ring Lardner, Tom Sims, Don Marquis, Richard Atwater (Mr. Popper's Penguins), Roy K. Moulton, Josh Wise, Broadway chorus girl Joan Gardner, medium Flora Marian Spore, racing horse Man O'War's younger brother Messenger, Professor Dr. Charles Frederick Kroeh, 14 year old artist savant Herta Zuckermann, and many others.

The New York Newspaper Enterprise Association Interviews:

☞ Interviewing John D. Rockefeller, Sr.

Writer Spends a Week With Rockefeller on Vacation

Woman Writer Spends Week With John D. Rockefeller

Newspaper Writer Spends Week With John D. Rockefeller on a Vacation Trip

GIRL REPORTER DESCRIBES HOW WORLD'S RICHEST MAN WHILES AWAY VACATION AT FLORIDA RESORT

JOSEPHINE's article interviewing John D. Rockefeller, Sr. appeared from February 20-26, 1923 across front page U.S. newspapers nationwide. She walked with him daily to get his take on things, observed him treated as an ordinary neighbor by those at Ormond Beach, and watched him play golf. This was her most well-known interview and was widely talked about for numerous reasons. Notably, she was a woman writer reporter and he was a notoriously famous man. In the 1920's it was quite a big story to report!

(image): **WOULD YOU CHANGE PLACES WITH WORLD'S RICHEST MAN?**

Is being "the world's richest man" really fun? To find out NEA Service assigned Josephine Van de Grift to go to Florida and spend a week with John D. Rockefeller Sr. She noted among his vacation pranks and pastimes:

> He likes to wander alone in the early morning.
> He gives away new dimes to rich and poor alike.
> He takes a daily pummeling from a masseur.
> He wears brown glasses to protect his eyes from sun.

He listens to his valet play hymns on the organ.

He listens to the hotel orchestra recital every Sunday evening.

He refuses to talk with anyone about public questions.

His after-dinner diversion is playing 'Numerics.'

He plays golf daily and tips his pickaninny caddy a dime.

Honestly, now, if that's having a good time you don't have to be a millionaire to enjoy it, do you? What do you say?

Here is that story (1922):

ORMOND BEACH, Feb. 26 – For a week I have been living across the street from the world's richest man; walking with him, brief strolls though they were, talking with him though not officially interviewing him, watching him as he played golf, going to church and musicales, in his wake, getting a picture, intimately, of his play-time life.

So I found out many things about John D. Rockefeller, Sr. Here are two of them that stand out:

He isn't exactly the guarded, coddled Croesus you may imagine. He is being treated here in Ormond as an ordinary neighbor.

There is no fence around his house at the corner of River Road and Beach Road; I can see it from my window in the Ormond Hotel. There are no guards, either. And one morning I met him at the half-light hour of 6 strolling along the bank of Halifax Road, unattended.

It is the stranger in Ormond who ogles him, following, pointing. The people of Ormond accept him casually as their winter neighbor, and he seems to get a lot of fun out of such association.

I FELL into step with Rockefeller on the toll bridge, after he had dug into his pocket for the nickel which Adolf d'Grom, toll-gate keeper, exacts from rich men and reporters alike.

Looking at me keenly, Rockefeller said: "Are you a reporter?"

(And foolish people say age has dimmed the eye, blunted the wits, and dulled the human intuition of this man!)

I admitted my identity and told him many things I wanted to know.

"Well," he smiled, walking along with me (there were no guards about, you must remember!), "I don't think I have anything to say about those things. Instead, won't you accept this?" (And he gave me a shining dime – and another for my mother, when I assured him I wasn't married.)

"We can be friends, can't we?" he said, "without talking about all those things."

HOSE dimes! He gives them to caddies, millionaires, reporters, society ladies, photographers, gardeners, the mayor, chauffeurs, and children. Formerly he dealt in smaller coin. Youngsters here told me he used to give them each a nickel and a penny saying: "Now the five-cent piece is for the bank and the penny is for the church."

Is this an indirect expression from John D. Rockefeller that one-sixth is the proper portion of one's wealth he believes should go to religion and charity?

OHN D. hasn't got a leathery, mummy-like face. His eye is clear, and his skin on close view looks healthy. Yet he undeniably looks much older in his eighty-fourth year than Chancey Depew in his eighty-ninth. Older, too, than General Adelbert Ames, his golf-partner here, who is 88.

Yet he doesn't take a nap in the afternoon as Depew, and many younger men, do. Often he is up before 6, taking a solitary walk if the weather is good.

Breakfast is at 7:30. Usually bacon and eggs, but sometimes a chop. Then a walk in the grounds and a discussion with Head Gardener George Whitlinger about the shrubbery and the prospects for the spring flower beds.

At 10 sharp he appears on the Ormond golf course for eight holes, which he usually does in 50 strokes. He rides to the course and later meets the chauffeur at the eighth hole.

Luncheon is at 1. A long automobile ride, then, and talks with guests. (Always there are guests.) At 7 is dinner, to which a few congenial friends are invited. Bed at 11.

JOHN YORDI is the most important man around the Rockefeller menage, next to John D. himself. Yordi's title is valet. But he is more than that. He is the only known person who can pummel the world's richest man and punch his ribs with impunity.

For this Yordi is a Swiss masseur and a few years ago Rockefeller lured this treasure away from another millionaire. To his deft manipulation is attributed to Rockefeller's good health of recent years.

Next to massage treatments the most important thing is clothes. Yordi prescribes these:

FOR GOLF: Gray woolen trousers, tan silk coat, paper vest, thick shoes, gray woolen cap and white cotton gloves.

FOR RIDING: Black top coat over the golf costume, and a vivid blue muffler.

FOR SUNDAY: Silk hat, Prince Albert coat, gray striped vest, striped trousers, black tie with pearl pin – and a slender cane.

FOR EVENING: Faultless evening wear, with dinner jacket.

Rockefeller does not lean on his cane when he walks. You couldn't call him feeble. The only jangling note in his resplendent church-going costume is in the brown glasses which he always wears in strong sunlight.

THE little colored caddy who enjoys the distinction of carrying Rockefeller's golf clubs and teeing for him answers to the name of "Bunk." The chauffeur pays him at the end of the game, but he always gets a shining dime as a bonus.

THE Rockefeller house sits back only a few yards from River Road, and there is shrubbery along the Beach Road side. Across River Road, down to the river, are his gardens. The house is small and so three other houses have been bought to accommodate the 20 chauffeurs, gardeners, workmen and servants.

John D. bought his winter home three years ago from a minister. There is no display in it – no wealth of tapestries, paintings, distinctive furniture.

When he took over the house he sent word to his son that he wanted an organ. A letter came asking height of ceilings and statistics like that.

Rockefeller promptly wrote back that he didn't want a church organ, but a simple little affair on which one could grind out a tune occasionally. So such an organ was installed. It cost no more than a good piano.

THE capable John Yordi has an other function besides valet and masseur. He can play the organ; hymns are his specialty.

Home concerts are frequent. Sunday mornings, of course, Mr. Rockefeller attends the little Community Church in Ormond and joins in the service; but each Sunday evening he walks across the Ormond Hotel lobby and listens to the orchestra. His favorite selection is the Barcarolle from "Tales of Hoffman."

At the close of these Sunday evening concerts everybody rises and joins in singing the Communion Doxology. I watched Mr. Rockefeller and he was singing, too.

HOSTESS of the Rockefeller household is Mrs. Jennie Evans, a relative of the late Mrs. Rockefeller. A favorite guest is Betty White, daughter of John White of New York; she has been here with her mother, playing golf with her aged host and getting up musicales at home.

General Ames has played golf with Rockefeller for 20 years.

Another favorite partner is E. M. Johnson, steel manufacturer of New York. Mrs. A. B. Wallace generally walks home with Rockefeller from church. And Dr. John Richmond, pastor of the Community Church, has a standing invitation for a visit every Monday afternoon.

NO guards, I said, surround this old man during his evening play-time of life as he courts Florida's sunny wintertime.

But there is this protection: So averse is Mr. Rockefeller to being quoted, even indirectly, on public questions that he does not discuss such subjects even with friends, and it is an unwritten rule that guests content themselves with anecdotes and small talk; best of all he likes talk of books. And after dinner they join with him in playing "Numerica," a mathematical game of which he is very fond.

Rockfeller and His Pals at Ormond Beach

Here you have the world's richest man, all togged out for his daily round of golf in the Florida sunshine, and beside him Gen. Adelbert Ames, who refuses to defeat him too often, and "Bunk," his caddy, who is the daily recipient of a new dime.

☞ Interviewing Will Rogers

October 15, 1922, Sunday (image):

HUMOR'S SOBER SIDE
Being an Interview With Will Rogers, Another of a Series on "How Humorists Get That Way"

By Josephine Van de Grift

"The best line I ever pulled," says Will Rogers, movie actor, comedian, and virtuso with the lariat, "is this: 'America never lost a war – and she never won a conference."

The line occurs as part of the animated comment upon topics of the day which Rogers is contributing to Ziegfeld's current entertainment in New York.

"But," say Rogers, "the best line is not always the biggest laugh getter. I think the biggest laugh I ever got was this: 'Yeh, I'm one of those movie actors from Hollywood. But I'm an exceptional movie actor. I been married 20 years and I got the same wife I started out with."

The hard labor of being funny, with oRgers [sic], lies in a painstaking perusal of the newspapers. The current murder, the recent international complication, the newest development in the prize ring, all come in for a little deft garnishing at his hands. He frequently reads up on a story for a week or more, he admits, before he attempts to submit a gag on it.

Takes Audience in Confidence

He confides this indebtedness nightly to his audiences. "Id [sic] sure be har [sic] up," he remarks, "if you folks didn't read the papers. Last summer when I was playin' on the roof I had an awful time. The audience was all composed of bootleggrs [sic] and they never read. I'm sure glad to get down with the consumers again."

"A joke," according to Rogers, "has got to have its foundation in truth I [sic] it's going to enjoy the process of getting over to the audience.

"I haven't any use," he says, "for that specific of joke where Pat and Mike come out of a saloon and Pat says to Moke [sic] –. And the saddest experiences of my life are brought about by those fellows who say, 'Say, Rogers, here's a good one I heard the other day. Thought maybe you could use it. There was an Irishman and a Jew –."

"No," says Rogers, "I never told that kind of a joke. I can't even remember 'em. And what's more I never made a wise crack at a mother-in-law. I never told a story that had any swearing in it and at this minute I can't recall that I ever told a story that had any double meaning.

Hates Old Gags

"I haven't got much use for the ordinary run of after-dinner speaking where you memorize a lot of gags six weeks before and then get up and tell 'em.

"I always say just to put me last on the program. Then I get up and run off some stuff on what the other speakers have said. Anybody'd know then that I hadn't made it up before.

"Sure it didn't come easy in the beginning, but I trained my mind to do it. Making jokes is just as hard a business as twirlin' a rope. Only if you learn to twirl a rope once why you know it and that's all there is to it. But makin' jokes goes on forever."

☞ Interviewing Charles Garland[3]

---

[3] Charles A. "Barley" Garland (1899-?), radical son of a Boston millionaire and took his $800,000 share of his father's estate and set up the "American Fund for Public Service" or the "Garland Fund," a philanthropic organization in the U.S. (1922-1941). Garland ran a "love farm" reputed to be where he practiced radical communitarian and "Free Love" ideas in East Middleborough, Massachusetts in the 1920's

---

October 25, 1922, Wednesday (image):

PHILOSOPHY OF MILLIONAIRE

Charles Garland Gives His First Authorized Interview to Woman Writer

By Josephine Van de Grift
NEA Service Staff Writer

MIDDLEBORO, MASS., Oct. 25. – What is his philosophy of life – of marriage, of right and wrong, of labor, of wealth?

Garland has answered these questions for the first time. The man who gave away his fortune to be used in public service, and now lives on his run-down farm near here, gave NEA Service this authorized statement.

I am 23 years old. When I was 20 I entered Harvard. I went to college as a matter of course with no definite idea as to what my future was to be.

But some time during the year I started reading Tolstoy and Plato and was surprised to find out how much more Plate knew than the people who were trying to teach me.

At the end of the first year I left college determined to evolve my own standards and to live by them. All that has happened since has been the result of that determination.

Working Out His Own Problems

I do not pretend that those standards are perfect. I have merely attempted to work out my own problem to my own satisfaction.

I have been asked if it is my purpose to establish a colony of people whose ideals are similar to my own. No such idea has seemed practicable to me thus far.

My 30 acres of farm here are run down. I am trying to bring them to a supporting basis. In the meantime I am using as much of my income as I need. The major portion of it I

GARLAND

But some time during the year I started reading Tolstoy and Plato and was surprised to find out how much more Plato knew than the people who were trying to teach me.

At the end of the first year I left college determined to evolve my own standards and to live by them. All that has happened since has been the result of that determination.

am devoting to the American Fund for Public Service, because I believe that all wealth should be used for social purposes.

I have no wish to fasten my ideas upon anyone else. Each individual should work out his own salvation according to the best of his ability.

The individual should be less subservient to outside authority. The whole idea of right and wrong is based on the mistaken assumption that some one person knows what right is.

Parents Should Revere Children

Education is not a matter of teaching children alone. Grown-ups can learn as much from children as children can from grown-ups. We should have more reverence for children. I do not feel that I own my children.

Marriage is all right for those who believe in it. The only thing that makes marriage sacred is love. Love is the only bond to marriage. If love has ceased marriage becomes what it was in the beginning – merely an outward symbol.

If a man and woman differ on certain things then they should each determine what is best for both. Whatever reports there have been to the contrary, Mrs. Garland and I are still friends. We are trying to do what is best for both of us.

I started farming because I felt the need of doing productive work. Everybody should do constructive work of some kind. If each of us had in mind the doing of useful work rather than the making of money, there would be a much better distribution of labor.

October 24, 1922, Tuesday (image):

NIGHT AT GARLAND'S COTTAGE DESCRIBED

Close-Up of Eccentric Heir to Fortune Who Gave Up All for Ideals

NIGHT AT GARLAND'S COTTAGE DESCRIBED

Close-Up of Eccentric Heir to Fortune Who Gave Up All for Ideals.

BY JOSEPHINE VAN DE GRIFT,
N. E. A. Service Staff Writer.

Middleboro, Mass., Oct. 23.—I have spent a night under the roof of Charles Garland, 23-year-old millionaire, who gave up fortune, wife and children in order that he might be—himself.

His hermit retreat is a reconstructed hen house, divided through the middle and equipped with a stove, a table, a cot, a desk, a lamp and a typewriter.

Here is the oddly assorted family which is seeking to wrest happiness out of Garland's tumbledown farm seven miles out from this picturesque little town:

Garland—tall, clad in a heavy woolen shirt, khaki trousers, woolen stockings and moccasins; a little shaggy mustache, betraying gleaming white teeth when he smiles.

Doris Benson—foster-sister of Garland, sturdily built, hair cut short, clad in knickers and a blue sweater.

Alice Edgerton—friend of Doris and of Garland, blond braid down her back, clad in knickers and green blouse, and using the soft "thee" and "thou" of the Quakers.

poems by Edna St. Vincent Millay under his arm and went to his bed in the barn.

Women Seeking Happiness.

The two women told me they are seeking happiness through this venture of shaking off the trappings of city life and living simply and plainly and close to the soil.

Though shy and wistful, Doris Benson vigorously denied that she agreed wholly with all of Garland's theories.

"Anyway," she said, "each person has to work out those things alone. What I want to learn just now, though, is to be a good farmer."

Alice Edgerton was likewise anxious to learn to be a good farmer as part of the pursuit of happiness.

Almost as picturesque as Garland's has been the career of this friendly-eye young woman who for two years has lived without money. Her clothing has been of the simplest, one skirt, two middies, and the plainest of other garments. Recently she has substituted knickers for the skirt.

Her policy has been to work wherever she was needed in shop, hospital or home, and to ask for such simple things as supplied her wants. Holding such ideas it was natural that she should gravitate eventually to the habitat of Garland, where she has been living quietly for several months until the departure of Garland's wife for Europe again called public attention to the millionaire philosopher.

"At first," she said, "my idea was just to give what I could to others. But then I found out there is something bigger than giving—and that is sharing."

And so the night wore on. She drew out of the desk a little notebook of poems which Garland had written.

By JOSEPHINE VAN DE GRIFT,
N. E. A. Service Staff Writer.

Middleboro, Mass., Oct. 23. – I have spent a night under the roof of Charles Garland, 23-year-old millionaire, who gave up fortune, wife and children in order that he might be – himself.

His hermit retreat is a reconstructed hen house, divided through the middle and equipped with a stove, a table, a cot, a desk, a lamp and a typewriter.

Here is the oddly assorted family which is seeking to wrest happiness out of Garland's tumbledown farm seven miles out from this picturesque little town:

Garland – tall, clad in a heavy woolen shirt, khaki trousers, woolen stockings and moccasins; a little shaggy mustache, betraying gleaming white teeth when he smiles.

Doris Benson – foster-sister of Garland, sturdily built, hair cut short, clad in knickers and a blue sweater.

Alice Edgerton – a friend of Doris and of Garland, blond braid down her back, clad in knickers and green blouse, and using the soft "thee" and "thou" of the Quakers.

There Was Laughter

As I stumbled across the darkness the lights from the reconstructed chicken house shone warm and yellow. A blond girl was sitting on the cot hugging her knees contemplatively. A tall dark man was reading something out of a book. There was laughter. They greeted me kindly.

"If folks would only get to know us," said the Quakeress.

As we sat and talked Miss Edgerton suddenly said:

"Hast thee been fed?"

And so while some argued and others listened, she built a brisk little fire in the range and plied me with hot chocolate and soup left from supper, and fresh brown bread. These persons who have figured so in the news are just like other persons, it seems, only, perhaps, a little kinder.

Over on the couch Doris Benson continued her contemplative stare.

"She's thinking about gas engines," explained Miss Edgerton. "Barley (the family name for Garland) was explaining the car to her all afternoon but she can't get it through her head." Doris was contrite.

Garland smiled at her indulgently. Every few minutes he would reach over to light a fresh cigarette from above the lamp. Behind the lamp were two rows of books, all the dialogues of Plato, all the works of Tolstoy, Well's "Outline of History," "The Outline of Science," a volume of Ibsen's plays, a work of Edward Carpenter, other books combining poetry, history and science.

Between cigarettes Garland leaned back in his chair offering occasional observations.

"Jung and Freud and the rest were given to interpreting everything through the medium of sex," he said. He didn't know but what some other medium would do as well.

He hadn't read "Tertium Organum" but meant to. Understood it was a meaty book. He wished more people would read Edward Carpenter.

Once he jumped up to get Webster's definition of pathological. Then he led an animated discussion as to the exact relation between pathos and disease.

Afterward he took a volume of poems by Edna St. Vincent Millay under his arm and went to his bed in the barn.

Women Seeking Happiness

The two women told me they are seeking happiness through this venture of shaking off the trappings of city life and living simply and plainly and close to the soil.

Though shy and wistful, Doris Benson vigorously denied that she agreed wholly with all of Garland's theories.

"Anyway," she said, "each person has to work out those things alone. What I want to learn just now, tough, is to be a good farmer."

Alice Edgerton was likewise anxious to learn to be a good farmer as part of the pursuit of happiness.

Almost as picturesque as Garland's has been the career of this friendly-eye young woman who for two years has lived without money. Her clothing has been of the simplest, one skirt, two middies, and the plainest of other garments. Recently she has substituted knickers for the skirt.

Her policy has been to work wherever she was needed in shop, hospital or home, and to ask for such simple things as supplied her wants. Holding such ideas it was natural that she should gravitate eventually to the habitat of Garland, where she has been living quietly for several months until the departure of Garland's wife for Europe again called public attention to the millionaire philosopher.

"At first," she said," my idea was just to give what I could to others. But then I found out there is something bigger than giving – and that is sharing."

And so the night wore on. She drew out of the desk a little notebook of poems which Garland had written. Some of them savored remarkably of Walt Whitman, although Garland, she assured me, had not read a line of Whitman until recently.

Eventually we, too, turned in and the last yellow light was blotted out in the little reconstructed chicken house where a drama of considerable proportions is being played.

A kitten, until recently a derelict of the Boston streets, when to sleep on the foot of the bed.

A NIGHT UNDER GARLAND'S ROOF
Close-Up Of Millionaire Philosopher

By JOSEPHINE VAN de GRIFT

☞ Interviewing Heywood Broun

Humor's Sober Side!

Being the First of a Series of Interviews With Humorists on "How They Get That Way"

October 5, 1922, Thursday (image):

Humor's Sober Side!

Being the First of a Series of Interviews With Humorists on "How They Get That Way"

By Josephine Van de Grift

"There was once an actor who opened in a new play," says Heywood Broun, New York columnist and critic, whose deft comments have from time to time aroused the ire of theatrical managers.

(By JOSEPHINE VAN DE GRIFT)
"There was once an actor who opened in a new play," says Heywood Broun, New York columnist and critic, whose deft comments have from time to time aroused the ire of theatrical managers.
"His acting was the worst I ever saw and I said so. The actor sued me for libel but he lost the case. Pretty soon he bobbed up in another play. The night of the opening his lawyer came over to me and said

"His acting was the worst I ever saw and I said so. The actor sued me for libel but he lost the case. Pretty soon he bobbed up in another play. The night of the opening his lawyer came over to me and said 'Now look here, if you lambast this man again, he may have cause to say you are prejudiced against him.'

"Well, it looked to me as though there might be some basis for the lawyer's notion, so that night after I had seen the play I merely wrote that the man's acting was not up to his usual standard.

"That," says Broun, "I consider to be my best line."

First Aids for Humorists

Broun likes puns: thinks they're perfectly legitimate, and admits he's been under obligations to 'em more than once. Also to the familiar quotation.

"When you get stuck," he says, "there's nothing like, 'It's a long worm that has no turning' or something similar to get you out of a tight place.

"Of course a humorist has all kinds of aids. There's Heywood 3rd now – when he was about two years old he made all kinds of good copy.

"But Heywood 3rd is four and a half now and I could see I was getting to be like those parents that go around button-holing folks and saying, 'Say, my kid got off a good one the other day – '

HEYWOOD BROUN

so I haven't used Heywood 3rd so much. The other day though – " Broun checked himself suddenly.

"And then there's the fellow who comes up and says, 'Oh, by the way, Broun, I thought of something good the other day. Of course I haven't got it worked out exactly but I thought you could pep it up and use it.' So you see there's always something bobbing up to soften the hard labor of the humorist."

Can't Write Verse

Before Broun became a critic and columnist he was a writer of sports and he still reports ball games and occasional news stories in an effort to counteract the rather artificial influence of the theater.

In his column he endeavors to introduce the serious as well as the humorous.

❧ ✦ ☙

☞ Interviewing Dorothy Parker (and the Algonquin Round Table)

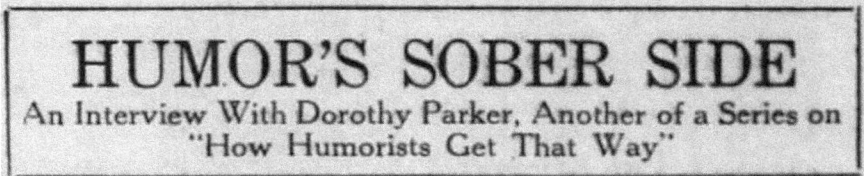

HUMOR'S SOBER SIDE
An Interview With Dorothy Parker, Another of a Series on "How Humorists Get That Way"

November 5, 1922, Sunday (image):

Dorothy Parker Says It's Not All Fun To Be Funny

By JOSEPHINE VAN DE GRIFT

Being a woman humorist, Dorothy Parker, dramatic critic for Ainslee's Magazine, and free lancer for the Saturday Evening Post, Life and others, specializes in last words.

Miss Parker wouldn't specialize in words at all, she says, were it not for the howling wolf immediately outside the door of her little office in the New York Metropolitan Opera House. The building, however, is given over considerably to vocal studios so it may not be the world that is driving Miss Parker to industry.

So far as her verse is concerned her methods, she admits, have a certain kinship to those of that clever chap you met when you were just out of high school who wrote you one

Dorothy Parker Says It's Not All Fun To Be Funny

By JOSEPHINE VAN DE GRIFT

Being a woman humorist, Dorothy Parker, dramatic critic for Ainslee's Magazine, and free lancer for the Saturday Evening Post, Life and others, specializes in last words.

Miss Parker wouldn't specialize in words at all, she says, were it not for the howling of the wolf immediately outside the door of her little office in the New York Metropolitan Opera House. The building, however, is given over considerably to vocal studios so it may not be the wolf that is driving Miss Parker to industry.

So far as her verse is concerned her methods, she admits, have a certain kinship to those of that clever chap you met when you were just out of high school who wrote you one time from Peoria that he had a momentous question to ask. He mooned on about this question for nine pages until you got all thrilled and were dead certain it was a proposal. At the top of page 10 he came right out with it and wanted to know if you thought it was time to change his winter underwear.

Miss Parker's system is to work up to a high pitch of emotion or even tears with what would be good poetry anyway and then destroy it all with a devastating last line.

"Everything I've ever written looks wretched to me," she says, "but here is one I dislike rather less than the rest:

SONG IN A MINOR KEY

There's a place I know where the birds swing low,
And wayward vines go roaming,
Where the lilacs nod and a marble god
Shines pale in scented gloaming.
And at sunset there comes a lady fair
Whose eyes are deep with yearning
By an old, old gate does the lady wait
Her own true love's returning.
But the days sweep by, and the lilacs die,
And the trembling birds seek cover;
Yet the lady stands, with cool white hands,
Outstretched to greet her love.
And it's there she'll stay till one shadowy day,
A monument they'll grave her,
She will always wait by that same old gate —
The gate her true love gave her.

"I don't know whether I'm really a humorist or not," she maintains, "but if I am, you can put it down that it's nothing but pure unalloyed blood sweating. I don't mind the poetry so much — it's a regular jigsaw puzzle and as an infant I took great satisfaction in tiddledy-winks and pigs-in-poke. But I'd rather sweep streets than write prose. I was two year, off and on, writing "An Apartment House Anthology." It was accepted within a week which was the only mitigating circumstance.

"The other side – being commissioned to write – is just as bad. Every once in a while, when the office rent comes due and the ice box springs a leak – again – and B'-rer Wolf opens his teeth and starts yapping at Li'l [sic] Dorothy, it so happens that Life will send in word that thay're [sic] betting out a special number on bed springs in three weeks and to have something bright and snappy for it.

"And you say, 'Oh joy, here's summat [sic] for the plumber!' And you sit down before your typewriter – and sit and sit and sit. And the moon goes up and the stars come out – and you sit and sit and sit.

DOROTHY PARKER

Interviewing Don Marquis

HUMOR'S SOBER SIDE
Being an Interview With Don Marquis, of a Series on "How Humorists Get That Way"

October 21, 1922, Saturday (image):

Humor Doesn't Come Easy for the Columnist

Don Marquis Says It Takes Him 50 Hours to Write a Bunch of Stuff the Reader Finishes in Seven Minutes

By JOSEPHINE VAN DE GRIFT

Christopher Morley, who runs a column on the New York Evening Post says that the best line that Don Marquis, who runs a column on the New York Tribune, ever pulled is this:

"Publishing a book of poems is like dropping a rose leaf down the Grand Canyon and waiting for the echo."

Marquis wrote the line eight years ago after he had published a book of poems. Some time later Morley published a book of poems whereupon he recalled Marquis' line and pronounced it good.

The hard labor of being funny, according to Don Marquis, whose name is pronounced as it is spelled, lies in digging up stuff that will appeal to a variety of readers. The young gentleman in the purple dressing gown and the amber cigaret holder is going to be intrigued about that perfectly ripping allusion to the stars and Haig and Haig, whereas Imogene, the beautiful manicure girl, prefers the one about "Spring, gentle spring."

"Wherefore," says Marquis, "at the beginning of my career as a columnist, about ten years ago, I set about creating a diversity of characters. The first of these was Hermoine, representing the type of young woman who was going in for Freud and 'deep stuff.' Then there was Archie, the trained cockroach, Fothergill Finch, poet and parlor anarchist, Captain Peter Fitzurse, descended from Reginald Fitzurse who killed Thomas a'Becket, Aunt Susan Huckleberry, the prude and the Old Soak who talks about liquor more than he drinks.

Humor Doesn't Come Easy for the Columnist

Don Marquis Says It Takes Him 50 Hours to Write a Bunch of Stuff the Reader Finishes in Seven Minutes

By JOSEPHINE VAN DE GRIFT

Christopher Morley, who runs a column on the New York Evening Post says that the best line that Don Marquis, who runs a column on the New York Tribune, ever pulled, is this:

"Publishing a book of poems is

DON MARQUIS

like dropping a rose leaf down the Grand Canyon and waiting for the echo."

"All these imagine, have their following.

"Being funny is just another case of doing time at hard labor. The other day I got an idea, worked on till 10 o'clock, threw it away, got up at 5 o'clock, worked on it, threw it away, worked on it again and finally had to use it because I needed to fill up space. But I didn't like it even then.

"Yeh – sometimes I spend 50 hours on a column. And the fellow on the subway reads it through in seven minutes and throws it in the ash can.

"I wonder," he says to his wife, "what these here funny fellows do with all their spare time."

☛ Interviewing Tom Daly

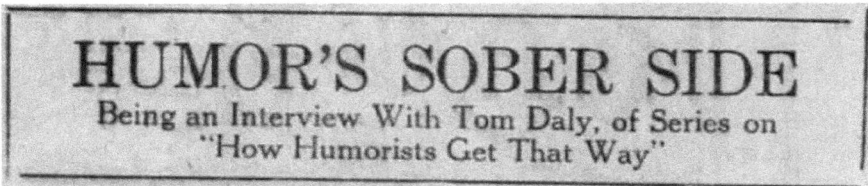

HUMOR'S SOBER SIDE
Being an Interview With Tom Daly, of Series on "How Humorists Get That Way"

November 21, 1922, Tuesday (image):

DIALECT IS CHARM OF THE HUMOR OF TOM DALY'S POETRY

Josephine Van De Grift Interview Famous Irish Philosopher

By JOSEPHINE VAN DE GRIFT

NEA Service Staff Writer.

"Whadya mean, 'How hard it is to be funny?' demands Tom Daly, columnist for the Philadelphia Record and after-dinner speaker.

"If the proposition is addressed to humorous speakers rather than to writers the answer is: it isn't hard at all. The difficulty consists in continuing to be funny through, say, a half hour's talk without making yourself ridiculous, or otherwise a nuisance.

"Every speaker has at least one 'laugh getter' but no man can be sure, until he feels out his audience, how all the other little tricks in his bag may be fitted in. So, it isn't hard to be funny but it IS hard to be funny continuously.

TOM DALY

" ' I vonder,' said the other and the first said, 'Ve go ask him.'

"So they ran after the traveler as hard as they could pelt, and finally catching up to him, the spokesman said, 'mister, didn't you mean the noodle factory?'

" ' Certainly, noodle factory, macaroni factory, where they make all those things. Where is it?'

" 'Vell, ve don't know vare dot is also.' "

"The best laugh getter? Customs and conditions change, but this is a sure-fire gag:

"A dozen years ago Charles M. Schwab told this to me as typical of German thoroughness:

"A traveling salesman, sez [sic] he, got off a train at Souse Besslehem one morning and, starting up the tracks with his suit case, overtook a couple of Pennsylvania Dutch.

"'Pardon me,' says he, 'but do you know where the macaroni factory is?'

"'Meckroni [sic] factory?' echoed one, looking at his companion, 'did you know vare iss [sic] it? No, ve [sic] don't know vare iss [sic] it.'

"The traveler thanked them and went on his way.

"Presently one Dutchman looked at the other and said, 'I vonder [sic] didn't he mean der noodle factory?'

"'I vonder,' said the other and the first said, 'Ve go ask him.'

"So they ran after the traveler as hard as they could pelt, and finally catching up to him, the spokesman said, 'Mister, didn't you mean the noodle factory?'

"'Certainly, noodle factory, macaroni factory, where they make all those things. Where is it?'

"'Vell, ve don't know vare dot iss also.'"

<hr/>

☞ Interviewing Ring Lardner

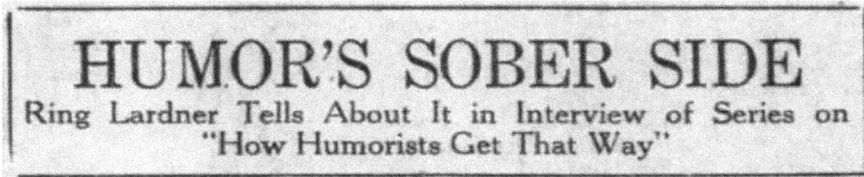

HUMOR'S SOBER SIDE
Ring Lardner Tells About It in Interview of Series on "How Humorists Get That Way"

October 18, 1922, Wednesday (image):

HUMOR'S SOBER SIDE

Ring Lardner Tells About It in Interview of Series on "How Humorists Get That Way"

By JOSEPHINE VAN DE GRIFT

NEA Service Staff Writer.

Back in 1914 there was, as things go, a world series. Stories on the world series were written by various well-known ball players and published in the newspapers. Then somebody began kicking up a little trouble.

"Those stories aren't written by ball players at all," he said, "somebody else writes them and then the ball player signs his name."

A young sport writer who was working on the Chicago Tribune got an idea. "It mightn't go bad," he reflected, "if I'd writer up these games the way a busher'd really write them up."

Which was the way that Ring Lardner became a humorist.

<hr/>

Lardner endeavored to tell about it on the fourth day of the world series recently completed. The place was that retreat immediately beneath the grand stand where newspaper men congregate to tell how it all might have been avoided and to eat – principally to eat.

Lardner, whose countenance, if not sad, at least suggest a deeply introspective turn of mind, sat down upon the chair which three waiters proffered him.

"There's really nothing – " he began

"Some chicken and salad, sir?"

Lardner waved the man away gently. "There's nothing to it, you see, you just stand around and listen to the ball players talk – "

The waiter hopped from one foot to the other. "Some cold Virginia baked ham, sir, or some sliced chicken? A little celery now – "

Lardner gazed atthe [sic] man kindly.

"No thank you," he said. "I've just had breakfast." The waiter went away dubiously.

"You see you just stand around and listen to the ball players talk. That's the way I got to calling it the world serious. Then you pick up a few other expressions like a – "

Another waiter flurried by, "A biscuit Tortoni, sir?"

said a whisky Tortoni. You just pick up some expressions." he continued. "like 'a 1-2 wit," or 'this monking around' or 'why and the dickens' or—"

A joyful screech came from somewhere on the side lines. "Oh, it's Mister Lardner, oo-hoo, hello, Mr. Lardner."

Lardner rose and tipped his hat punctiliously. Then he sat down again. "You pick up a few expressions like that, and then maybe you see a letter where 'especially' is written 'a specially' and 'corps' is spelled 'corpse' and pretty soon, if you bear it all in mind, the thing's done for you Nothing hard, you know, just—"

From somewhere in the offing came a rich buttery voice.

"Batteries for today will be—"

Lardner struggled to his feet. "My most quoted line? Well, I suppose it's 'You know me, Al.' but it doesn't mean a thing, you know, it doesn't."

Lardner relapsed into melancholy.

"Oh," he murmured, "I thought you said a whisky Tortoni. You just pick up some expressions," he continued, "like 'a 1-2 wit,' or 'this monking [sic] around' or 'why and the dickens' or – "

A joyful screech came from somewhere on the side lines. "Oh, it's Mister Lardner, oo-hoo, hello, Mr. Lardner."

Lardner rose and tipped his hat punctiliously. Then he sat down again. "You pick up a few expressions like that, and then maybe you see a letter where 'especially' is written 'a specially' and 'corps' is spelled 'corpse' and pretty soon, if you bear it all in mind, the thing's done for you Nothing hard, you know, just – "

From somewhere in the offing came a rich buttery voice.

"Batteries for today will be – "

Lardner struggled to his feet. "My most quoted line? Well I suppose it's 'You know me, Al,' but it doesn't mean a thing, you know, it doesn't."

<hr>

☛ Interviewing Tom Sims

HUMOR'S SOBER SIDE

Being an Interview With Tom Sims, on "How Humorists Get That Way"

October 17, 1922, Tuesday (image):

HUMOR'S SOBER SIDE

Being an Interview With Tom Sims, in a series on "How Humorists Get That Way"

By JOSEPHINE VAN DE GRIFT

NEA Service Staff Writer.

Every once in a while an idea will start jogging along, headed for no place in particular, and after awhile, it gets sort of careless like, it'll have a collision with another idea. The result is what is sometimes known as a wise crack according to Tom Sim whose column, "Tom Sims Says," has regaled readers of several hundred newspapers for the past year.

"By sheer accident," he says, "I may learn that skirts are longer. Then I see in the paper that coal is getting shorter. How stranger, Watson, give me the typewriter! And hitting on all two fingers I hammer out, "This winter's schedule calls for longer skirts and shorter coal. The women, have more sense than we thought.'

"One pay day while cussing because I had to work late I hit on 'All work and no play makes jack'

This proved to be one of my most quoted lines.

"Another time I profited from a balling out by an extra grouchy traffic cop. It was, 'A grouch is a man who thinks the world is against him — and he's right.

"Back I the subconscious sits the memory of a dog scratching a flea. A newy [sic] married friend whispers that he'd like to borrow a dollar until the ghost walks. The result is, 'Nowadays the only two who can live as cheaply as one are a flea and a dog.'

"I believe the inside workings of my job could be divided into three parts. In the first part you gather up all the news and incidents of the day. In the second you place all the familiar quotations and puns. In the third you have everything you can possibly learn about human nature.

"Then you stir them up. If the news of the day rises to the top you get such lines as, 'Chicago bandit attacked two policemen but both escaped.'

"If puns are mixed with the news you may get, 'May we call the Dardanelles desperate straits? Thanks.' If familiar sayings come up you just twist one and have, 'Back in the trenches by Christmas' is Europe's slogan.'

"I do not know which of my lines I like the best. I met one of mine that I liked in a comic strip the other day: 'Many a baby pretends to sleep to make its father quit singing.'"

☞ Interviewing Richard Atwater

RICHARD ATWATER

lowing his friends' generously offered advice."

October 21, 1922, Saturday (image):

HUMOR'S SOBER SIDE

By JOSEPHINE VAN DE GRIFT

NEA Service Staff Writer.

Circus clowns are popularly supposed to go through their antics with breaking hearts and humorists are, in reality, very serious-minded men with persistent twinges of melancholia according to Richard Atwater, whose column, "From Pillar to Post," is a part of the daily constitutional of readers of the Chicago Post.

"I have always supposed," he declares, "that the one thing in all the world to be guarded against in running a 'funny' column is trying to be funny.

"Several years' study of the best columnists' output long ago convinced me none of them ever succumbed to such a failing; if there was an occasional error of this sort in the work of the masters, I put it down to a momentary headache.

"As for myself I have always been serious-minded and cannot understand so perverted an ambition. The only real difficulty in following the otherwise serene tranquility of a columnists' quiet existence lies in the necessity that daily confronts him of following his friends' generously offered advice."

BY JOSEPHINE VAN DE GRIFT
NEA Service Staff Writer

Circus clowns are popularly supposed to go through their antics with breaking hearts and humorists are, in reality, very serious-minded men with persistent twinges of melancholia according to Richard Atwater, whose column, "From Pillar to Post," is a part of the daily constitutional of readers of the Chicago Post.

"I have always supposed," he declares, "that the one thing in all the world to be guarded against in running a 'funny' column is trying to be funny.

"Several years' study of the best columnists' output long ago convinced me none of them ever succumbed to such a failing; if there was an occasional error of this sort in the work of the masters, I put it down to a momentary headache.

"As for myself I have always been serious-minded and cannot understand so perverted an ambition. The only real difficulty in following the otherwise serene tranquility of a columnists' quiet existence lies in the necessity that daily confronts him of fol-

---

☞ Interviewing Roy K. Moulton

HUMOR'S SOBER SIDE
Being an Interview With Roy K. Moulton, Another of Series on "How Humorists Get That Way"

October 22, 1922, Sunday (image):

HUMOR'S SOBER SIDE

Being an Interview With Roy K. Moulton, Another of Series on "How Humorists Get That Way"

By JOSEPHINE VAN DE GRIFT

NEA Service Staff Writer.

"There's nothing like a little daily stint of 10,000 words or so to give a columnist an appetite.

This from Roy K. Moulton, whose spacious apartment overlooking the Hudson is a concrete testimonial that humor pays. And pays and pays.

Not that Moulton sets any margin to his daily output. Sometimes it amounts to considerably more than 10,000 words – sometimes it is less. But set end to end and mounted stick by stick the array of words is bound to be imposing. One week, for instance, it amounted to six stories on a bankers convention, three base ball stories, two stories for magazines and 12 columns for daily and Sunday papers.

Moulton's system is to keep three typewriters going with a story on each typewriter. He works on one story until he strikes a snag whereupon he progresses to the next.

Occasionally he employs a stenographer at which times it is his custom to pace up and down the room with a newspaper and dictate such items as the following: What do you think of the Turkish atrocities? I don't know, I never smoked one.

says, "my best earnings for the first week amounted to $23. I was about three years getting established and then things began coming better. In 1919, for instance, I did about $45,000 worth of outside work, which netted me almost $300 in cash. The opportunities to spread one's talent about are boundless."

Moulton ordinarily begins setting up exercises on the typewriter at 9 o'clock and along about 6 o'clock he is willing to call it a day. Occasionally he takes a run into the mountains. And comes back the next day.

The paragraph will be duly published and the next day Moulton will hear it on the street car. Three days later he will hear it in a vaudeville house, a week later a magazine will quote it as coming from an editor in Georgia, and four days later Mrs. Moulton will rush home to relate that she saw it in the movies.

All in all several million persons will enjoy Moulton's little quip at the expense of the cigaret manufacturers.

Which is one of the compensations of being a humorist.

To revert to the spacious apartment overlooking the Hudson. Humor, in Moulton's case did not always pay.

"When I was trying to break into New York about eight years ago," he says, "my best earnings for the first week amounted to $23. I was about three years getting established and then things began coming better. In 1919, for instance, I did about $45,000 worth of outside work, which netted me almost $300 in cash. The opportunities to spread one's talent about are boundless."

Moulton ordinarily beings setting up exercises on the typewriter at 9 o'clock and along about 6 o'clock he is willing to call it a day. Occosionally [sic] he takes a run into the mountains. And comes back the next day."

☞ Interviewing Christopher Morley

HUMOR'S SOBER SIDE
Being an Interview With Christopher Morley, Another of Series on "How Humorists Get That Way"

October 19, 1922, Thursday (image):

HUMOR'S SOBER SIDE

Being an Interview With Christopher Morley, Another of Series on "How Humorists Get That Way"

Christopher Morley, whose cogitations upon men and manners under the heading, "The Bowling Green," are issued daily from his little office in the New York Evening Post building, protests that it embarrasses him to be called a humorist.

of Verse, Shakespeare, Walt Whitman and Boswell's Life of Johnson— I'd go into any newspaper office in the world and guarantee to turn out good editorials.

"Being a columnist? Oh, well of course, that's simple, too. All you need is enough material to last you three days and after that the contributors run it for you.

"The best line I ever wrote? "Received payment.'"

"I fell just like one of those bugs," he says, "that has lain snug and cozy under a nice cool rock for a couple of years. Then suddenly somebody lifts the rock and all at once he feels sore of exposed.

"Of course, anyone who runs a column, I suppose, lays himself open to the accusation of being a humorist. I wish I were.

"I think a humorist is the most useful creature in the world. But being a mere columnist has its compensations, too. You form some wonderful human contacts like that of Jedediah Tingle, for instance. (Jedediah Tingle is the unknown philanthropist who makes a business of mailing checks to the people who please him. He once maield [sic] one to Morley).

"The drawback, says Morley, "is that five nights out of six I go home feeling like I'd like to jump off the cliff – that I've desecrated every friendship and blasted my reputation.

"A newspaper editor – now that's a job for you! I'd like to be a newspaper editor. He's got the whole dignity of the paper behind him and he gets away with a lot of tosh.

"With four books – The Home Book of Verse, Shakespeare, Walt Whitman and Boswell's Life of Johnson – I'd go into any newspaper office in the world and guarantee to turn out good editorials.

"Being a columnist? Oh, well of course, that's simple, too. All you need is enough material to last you three days and after that the contributors run it for you.

"The best line I ever wrote? "Received payment.'"

☞ Interviewing Josh Wise

HUMOR'S SOBER SIDE
Josh Wise Tells About It in Interview of a Series on "How Humorists Get That Way"

JOHN W. RAPER

to a hard, hard shell.

He admits, though, that he thinks that line about Abraham Lincoln freeing the colored man and his son, Robert, being president of the Pullman company is pretty good.

October 17, 1922, Tuesday (image):

HUMOR'S SOBER SIDE

Josh Wise Tells About It in Interview of a Series on "How Humorists Get That Way"

By Josephine Van de Grift

"Heaven help the poor stenographer the boss looks after the good one," once remarked Josh Wise whom Cleveland landlords and tax collectors know more intimately as John W. Raper.

But neither heaven nor the boss is disposed to help the humorist, says Raper. He further adds that some of his best lines like "The woman who marries a man to reform him has a steady job for life," he thought up all by himself without any assistance from anybody.

If it had ever occurred to him, though, that there was anything heard [sic] about being unny [sic] he'd have given over his job long ago, says Raper.

"What do I know about hard labor?" he asks. "Of course it's just plain luck but I never served a sentence in my life.

65

"And I never held a political job in nation state or municipality. So what do I know about hard labor?

'I migh [sic] draw on my imagination and fool some folks that I don't think I know any more about it than I do. But drawing on one's imagination is hard labor and I have no desire to come into contact with it either socially or commercially.

"And besides I have formed for hard labor a great contempt, based on hearsay, I admit, and I should not like to dignify it even by discussing it."

Whereupon Mr. Raper withdrew into a hard, hard shell.

He admits, though, that he thinks that line about Abraham Lincoln freeing the colored man and his son, Robert, being president of the Pullman company is pretty good.

☞ Interviewing Joan Gardner

January 11, 1924, Friday (image):

Broadway Beauty Who Weds for Love, Not Money, Blasts Popular Illusion

Joan Gardner, Broadway beauty, who wed Boston man for home.

By Josephine Van de Grift

NEA Service Staff Writer

NEW YORK, Jan. 11. – Another Broadway bubble has burst. Chorus girls aren't marrying millionaires any more.

As witness, Joan Gardner whose five feet eight inches of loveliness has nightly been taking its way through a musical comedy called "Kid Boots."

Joan up and got married New Year's eve and then she promptly penned a note to her boss giving him the customary two weeks' notice. Joan was, so the note said, through with the stage for good.

"Ah," said the boss sarcastically, "another millionaire with a penchant for chorus girls. You'll be back in two weeks."

And a story to the effect that a chorus girl had married a millionaire was duck soup, as the saying goes, for the show's press agent.

But the boss – and the press agent – it seems, were wrong. For Joan's bridegroom was just plain Edward T. Hall from Boston. He's 28 years old and has something to do with the business office of a firm that makes machinery. Not so poor, you understand, but not so rich, either.

And Joan doesn't want to be a rich man's bride. She wants to put on fudge apron and make codfish cakes and all the other things for which Boston's famous.

"A year ago it was different," she says. "That was when I was a school girl out in Spokane, Wash. One day I met Ina Claire, the actress, at a party, and she said I was a Follies type and offered to put in a word for me with Mr. Ziegfeld.

Broadway Beauty Who Weds for Love, Not Money, Blasts Popular Illusion

Joan Gardner, Broadway beauty, who wed Boston man for home.

"Well I got a job in the Follies and I was all excited but the glamour soon left. When you're in the show business you don't have time to meet the people you'd like to meet, you don't get a chance to do the things you'd like to do.

"Most of the show girls I've met aren't happy. They want to get married and settle down."

Which explains why within the next few days, Joan Gardner will disappear from the bright lights of Manhattan and become plain Mrs. Edward T. Hall of Boston.

Has a chance of being happy?

Well here are the records of some other show girls who married men that were far from being millionaires:

Annabelle Whitford, one of the most beautiful Follies girls ever known, married the stage electrician. After seven years or so they're still happy.

Ina Claire married a newspaper man, so did Kay Laurel.

Mildred Richardson, the most beautiful chorus girl of 1915, married the stage manager of the Follies.

Dolores, still famous as a stage beauty, married a business man not unduly wealthy.

Justine Johnson, of the 1916 Follies, married the business manager of a motion picture company.

"In fact," says Flo Ziegfeld, who knows a lot about such things, "I can't think of any Follies girl that ever married a millionaire.

"There was a Geneva Mitchell who eloped and came back to say she'd married a millionaire, but the 'millionaire' turned out to be a youngster who's wealthy elatives [sic] were sending him through Yale.

Jessie Reed married Dan Caswell, but Caswell had little in his own right. He merely had wealthy relatives. Later they were divorced.

"And while English chorus girls are commonly reputed to marry titles I know of only one American girl who did so – Jessica Brown, who married the Earl of Northesk.

"No, most chorus girls marry for love, they marry poor men and they're generally happy."

Obviously this does not include a little chorus girl who made her debut 22 years ago in a piece called "The Wild Rose." People who remember back to that time say that with her long curls over her shoulders she was the loveliest thing they ever saw.

Her name was Evelyn Nesbit.

☛ Interviewing Flora Marian Spore[4]

February 20, 1923, Tuesday (image):

Spirits Reveal Future of the World In An Interview

By JOSEPHINE VAN DE GRIFT
NEA Service Staff Writer

NEW YORK, Feb. 20. – I have just interviewed the spirits of the "other world." I asked them about war and peace and the future of nations and they answered me.

This through the medium of Flora Marian Spore, young psychic whose powers have amazed scientific investigators for the past three years. Although she never had a drawing lesson in her life, Miss Spore creates pictures which are said to show an art a hundred years in advance of the times. She says she does it under the guidance of dead masters; that spirits have dictated fairy stories to her while others are urging her to buy a piano that they may play for her. They talk to her all the time, she says.

So I went to ask her if she could get the spirits to discuss the future of the world. She said she could.

The interview took place in Miss Spore's studio in Greenwich Village. There was nothing mysterious about it – no darkened room, no trances, no awe-inspiring trappings. I sat upon the couch. Miss Spore, clad in artist's smock and knickers, her feet thrust in high-heeled satin pumps, sat upon a chair.

The interview began:

"Ask them what will be the outcome of the Ruhr invasion."

There was a moment's silence, then the answer came:

"France will not return defeated. She will get what she wants. But she will get more trouble than she has already."

---

[4] Flora May Spore (later Marian Spore Bush) (1878-1946) was a dentist, painter, spiritualist, philanthropist and writer. She married industrial tycoon Irving T. Bush. Harry Houdini was fascinated by her artwork and said "I have never excluded the possibility of supernatural intervention from my belief."

"Will Germany turn Bolshevik?"

"Germany already has taken up thoughts from the far north. She will use these thoughts to bind herself closer but she will remain always separate. She will never be a monarchy again. She will always be ruled by many people instead of one."

"Will there be a Russian-German alliance?"

"There will be strong business relations between Germany and Russia but distrust of each other will keep them separate. Business relations will be stronger after a while than now."

"Will there be a Russian-Turkish alliance?"

"Russia will desert Turkey. Turkey slinks away like a fallen foe."

"Will there be a Christian-Mohammedan war?"

"Not in the way you mean. There will never be a religious war."

"What will happen in the Balkans?"

"Dissension, dissension, dissension. Some countries will be annihilated. Others will feed on these and grow."

MISS FLORA MARIAN SPORE, PAINTING ONE OF HER SPIRIT PHOTOGRAPHS.

"What part will the United States play in world affairs from now on?"

"America will be alone with every nation at her throat. There will be a bitter war. She will never rise to her former splendor. Sooner than people say war can come, it will come, like a blow in the dark."

"What part will the Orient play in world affairs?"

"Japan will play a large part. China will rise. She will be one of the strongest nations of the world. In the end she will dominate by her wisdom. Japan will hold on by her military strength rather than by brains. She will always have to be reckoned with."

"Will a world leader arise?"

"There will be no one leader. There will never be universal peace. Each nation must protect itself. The one best protected will lead."

"Is there any possibility of a British-French war?"

"France already hates England but the war that is coming will be a world war."

"What will be the outcome of the Bolshevist experiment in Russia?"

"Before the rivers of spring open Russia will have internal war. We cannot tell whether it is this year or the next."

At this point I considered the interview ended. But not so the spirits.

"Ask her," they said, speaking through Miss Spore, "whether she wants to know about capital and labor."

"Yes," I said.

"Tell her," they said, "there will never be a war between capital and labor. They will continue to struggle but conditions will be better. The war will bind them together. Does she want to know about prohibition?"

"Yes," I said.

"The country will never be openly wet again. There will be some secret – secret – ('they do not seem to know the word for bootlegging', explained Miss Spore) – there will be some secret – it will rise to its zenith and then it will be put down."

And so the interview esded [sic].

Interviewing racing horse Man O'War's younger brother, Messenger

MAN O' WAR'S YOUNG BROTHER REGARDED AS A GREAT COLT

Proud Owner Has Refused $125,000 for Him— Bound to Do Well in Coming Turf Classics If His Legs Do Not Go to the Bad Again.

By Josephine Van de Grift.
N. E. A. Service Staff Writer.

New York, April 14.—I've just been over to see Man o' War's younger brother.

Messenger is his name and August Belmont, who sold Man o' War for $5,000, has refused an offer of $125,000 for Messenger.

In reality, Man o' War's to blame. Belmont bred both horses, but when Man o' War was scarcely more than a frisky colt Sam D. Riddle came along and offered $5,000 for him. Belmont thought it a good offer and took it. Then Man o' War started breezing over the tracks, cleaned up $249,000 for his new master and became one of the famous racers of history.

April 15, 1923, Sunday (image):

MAN O' WAR'S YOUNG BROTHER REGARDED AS A GREAT COLT

Proud Owner Has Refused $125,000 for Him – Bound to Do Well in Coming Turf Classics If His Legs Do Not Go to the Bad Again

By JOSEPHINE VAN DE GRIFT
NEA Service Staff Writer

NEW YORK, April 14. – I've just been over to see Man o' War's younger brother.

Messenger is his name and August Belmont, who sold Man o' War for $5,000, has refused an offer of $125,000 for Messenger.

In reality, Man o' War's to blame. Belmont bred both horses, but when Man o' War was scarcely more than a frisky colt Sam D. Riddle came along and offered $5,000 for him. Belmont thought it a good offer and took it. Then Man o' War started breezing over the tracks, cleaned up $249,000 for his new master and became one of the famous racers of history.

Belmont made no outer show of this chagrin, but when Harry Whitney came along recently and offered $100,000 for Messenger Belmont refused the offer, and when someone later increased the offer to $125,000 Belmont still refused.

Is Messenger expected to excel the record of his distinguished elder brother?

HAS UNUSUAL DISPOSITION

Messenger has a gentle eye, a slim ankle, and his coat is the color of a rich coffee frappe. His disposition, however, is still more a source of bewilderment to his trainer, Louis Feustel.

"Take the blinders off him," says Feustel, "and he'll lope along like an old cow. Put 'em on, and he'll race along for all he's worth."

Messenger, overhearing this, flicked his tail lazily in the direction of his trainer.

The manner in which the hundred thousand dollar colt puts in his time is a matter of extreme solicitude to the stable boys at Belmont park who are grooming him for the coming races.

GETS EVERY ATTENTION

At 5 o'clock Messenger is awakened gently and fed some very special crushed oats. At 9:30 he is saddled and bandaged and taken out for an hour's run on the track.

Clockers perched along the fence report that he has made thus far a quarter of a mile in 26, and a half mile in 57.

At 10:30 he is rubbed down and cooled and given fresh water to drink and at 11 he is fed. After dinner his legs are wrapped with cold water bandages. Toward evening he is taken out and walked while his stall is leveled and fresh hay (special cut California variety) is put in for the night.

Such is the daily schedule of the prized darling of the track.

Messenger's legs, slender and brown, are the principal source of worry to Louis Feustel.

In his first race at Saratoga last August Messenger distinguished himself by coming in third. In the second race he came in fifth. The third race he won, making the three-quarter mile in 1:11 3-5.

Then Messenger kicked one of his own legs and went bad. All the months since have been spent in getting those slender brown members back into shape. If they do and all goes as it should –

Well, Messenger has already been entered for the Belmont stakes, which happen to be the tidy little sum of $50,000. The Preakness stakes are a similar amount and with the generally large stakes put up at the three Kentucky races Messenger stands a fair chance of cleaning up at least $250,000 for his owner.

IS NOT FOR SALE

"Messenger is not for sale," says August Belmont. "My interest in him is not a gambler's interest, for I never bet on the horses.

"But Messenger has every chance of making good. He was sired by Fair Play, who was also the sire of Man o' War. He shows all the physical qualifications of the champion. My hope is that he will become one of the famous race horses of America.'"

And Belmont ought to know. Besides Man o' War, he has bred Fair Play, Hourless, Friar Rock, Mad Hatter and other famous racers.

Interviewing Professor Dr. Charles Frederick Kroeh

Oldest Prof. Quite Modern

November 10, 1923, Saturday (image):

Oldest Prof. Quite Modern

By JOSEPHINE VAN DE GRIFT

HOBOKEN, N. J. – For 54 years Dr. Charles Frederick Kroeh has been a professor, spending 52 of the years here at Stevens Institute of Technology.

In this time he has earned his A. M., Sc. D., among numerous other degrees, and the reputation of being one of the oldest and most highly esteemed educators in the country.

He has trained more than 2500 students. He has written numerous text books, memoirs, scientific and technological reports. He has been one of the pillars of Stevens, rambling, old-fashioned structure, where men and boys come to learn how to dam up waterfalls and build bridges over 'em.

And never, never, except for an occasional stenographer, or somebody's private secretary has there been a flutter of petticoats down its halls.

"Heigho," said we to ourselves, "here's a veteran professor in a musty, venerable, old school. We'll tell him a few things."

"What," we demanded, seeking out Prof. Kroeh in his office, "do you think of the flapper?"

Prof. Kroeh settled his beard above his waistcoat and beamed.

"The flapper, my dear young woman," he returned, "is a work of art. For pictorial purposes she is far superior to the girls of 1871."

He DID know what a flapper was. We were crestfallen but endeavored not to show it.

"Well, then," we puzzled, "what about 'Yes, We Have No Bananas'?"

"That song," returned the professor, "Is only slightly more silly than 'Sally in Our Alley' and some others that I used to sing when I was a boy."

"Do you play mah-jongg?"

The professor looked bored.

"I understand the rules of the game, but raising chickens is more my fancy."

"You attend the modern dances, of course?"

"Oh yes," said the professor, "not, you understand, that I take part in them any more. This jumping up and down like a wooden Indian is, to my mind, very poor taste. 'The Blue Danube' is my idea of a real dance.

We were getting desperate.

"How do you like," we queried, "this new 'la garconne' bob?"

"Oh," he said, "you mean that peculiar hair dress, (illegible) at the back and puffed out over the ears, that the girls are wearing? The waitress who brought me my luncheon the other day had hers done that way and I must say it was quite becoming."

We made our last desperate effort.

"Did you know," we demanded hoarsely, "that Fanny Brice[5] had her nose altered?"

The professor rallied.

"No!" he cried delightedly, "not really."

"Yes," we chanted. We cavorted, we capered. We beamed on the professor. At last we'd been able to tell him something!

PROFESSOR CHARLES FREDERICK KROEH

---

[5] Fanny Brice was born as Fania Borach (1891-1951) and was an American singer and actress. Brice was portrayed on Broadway in the 1964 musical *Funny Girl* starring Barbra Streisand.

Scribblings of Youth Startling Art World

December 29, 1923, Saturday (image):

Scribblings of Youth Startling Art World

By JOSEPHINE VAN DE GRIFT

NEW YORK – Remember those scrawlings you used to make on old cracker boxes and the kitchen wall and the barn door?

Maybe if anybody had taken the trouble to preserve them they would have carried a valuable lesson on to posterity, for children possess an unconscious art that is priceless and that is as worthy of preservation as the works of Rembrandt, Holbein and all the rest.

So says Professor Franz Cizek of Vienna and to prove it he is sending to this country hundreds of pictures, paintings and wood cuts made by the children of Austria.

Almost all of the drawings were made by youngsters under 15 years of age. And not one of them ever had what is ordinarily termed an art lesson.

Miss Francesca M. Wilson, an English woman who "discovered" Professor Cizek and who is accompanying the exhibit to this country, tells of how these tiny Viennese children, many of them undernourished and ragged, forget want
and hunger while they riot with paint pots and scissors.

"Perhaps 70 children," she says, "are turned loose in a room at once. The room is filled with drawing paper, pencils, pain, colored papers, beads, modeling clay, blocks of wood and carving implements.

"Nobody tells the children what to do, for Professor Cizek believes that each child will select what is best suited to his temperament.

"Soon the room is quiet. Karl is cutting a soldier and his horse out of black paper. Hedda is painting an old peasant woman with a basket of apples. Josef is modeling his grandfather out of clay.

"Once in two weeks or so Professor Cizek assigns a set subject to the children. After they have worked a while the pictures are hung up and criticized. This is the nearest that the children have ever come to having an art lesson."

These pictures have attracted praise in various parts of Europe and they are now to be given an extended showing at the Metropolitan Museum of Art after which they traven to various cities in the United States.

And do these children, in later years, become capable artists?

"Many of them," says Miss Wilson, "but Professor Cizek is rarely interested in a child after he is 15 years old."

"Children," he declares, "work with a natural feeling which is spoiled when they grow up and begin to think. The art of childhood is a thing apart and should be preserved as a thing apart."

PAINTING MADE BY HERTA ZUCKERMANN, 15 YEARS OLD.

The children, on the other hand, frequently look with scorn upon their early efforts after they have grown older and have gone to sophisticated art schools.

Herta Zuckermann, for instance, who at the age of 15, painted the lovely child represented here, has now, at the age of 17, nothing but disdain for her early effort.

praise in various parts of Europe and they are now to be given an extended showing at the Metropolitan Museum of Art after which they will traven to various cities in the United States.

And do these children, in later years, become capable artists?

"Many of them," says Miss Wilson, "but Professor Cizek is rarely interested in a child after he is 15 years old."

"Children," he declares, "work with a natural feeling which is spoiled when they grow up and begin to think. The art of childhood is a thing apart and should be preserved as a thing apart."

The children, on the other hand, frequently look with scorn upon their early efforts after they have grown older and have gone to sophisticated art schools.

Herta Zuckermann, for instance, who at the age of 15, painted the lovely child represented here, has now, at the age of 17, nothing but disdain for her early effort.

Chapter IV.

Huldah Benson & 'Getting on The Stage of New York'

Huldah Benson & 'Getting on the Stage of New York'

GETTING ON THE STAGE

Girl Reporter Poses as "Greenhorn" to Try Her Hand at ...

This is the sixth of a series of six stories by Josephine Van de Grift describing how she, posing as a country girl, sought to get on the stage in New York.

By JOSEPHINE VAN DE GRIFT
NEA Service Staff Writer

NEW YORK.—Although stage people are very kind it seems they, to, have their little cliques.

An actor who has a line to say as, "Madam, did you ring?" will never get on intimate terms with a super with no line at all.

Consequently those of us who constituted the "atmosphere" for Paradise" were lonesome. I think this was why Katie clung to me.

It was while we were having supper together before the evening performance that I found out about Katie.

Katie was 17. Her mother had

Miss Van deGriff.

DURING the course of my findings doing research about Josephine working for the NEA as a service staff writer in New York, I found she was hired on for a six-part series to become "Huldah Benson," 23 year-old aspiring actress from Akron, O., and get a part on stage in New York during November and December 1922.

An artist also sketched an accompanying cartoon to go with each of the six parts of the series. The artist is unknown.

Josephine's ruse as Huldah was so successful, the editors decided to also put stage and screen actress, Madge Kennedy, also through the same route and see if she could land a part.

This story titled "Getting on the Stage in New York" ran in several newspapers nationwide.

Part 1:

Girl Reporter Starts Account Of Trials in Stage Job Hunt

(image): "**EDITOR'S NOTE**: - Every year the lure of the footlights draws hundreds of girls to New York. Most of them are without funds, many without talent and all without experience.

EDITOR'S NOTE:—Every year the lure of the footlights draws hundreds of girls to New York. Most of them are without funds, many without talent and all without experience.
These girls are drawn from all parts of the country.
Some return disillusioned to their homes. Others are not again heard from. Those who return rarely tell of their experiences.
To learn what obstacles and pitfalls are encountered by these girls, Josephine Van de Grift was assigned to go through the same experiences any girl would undergo in seeking a stage job in the metropolis.
Miss Van de Grift has written the true story of what befell her. The first article appears today.

These girls are drawn from all parts of the country.

Some return disillusioned to their homes. Others are not again heard from. Those who return rarely tell of their experiences.

To learn what obstacles and pitfalls are encountered by these girls, Josephine Van de Grift was assigned to go through the same experiences any girl would undergo in seeking a stage job in the metropolis.

Miss Van de Grift has written the true story of what befell her. The first article appears today."

N EW YORK, – At half past eight I took my traveling bag in my hand, walked into the Pennsylvania station and brought up by a desk marked "Travelers' Aid."

"I – I've come to New York to go on the stage," I faltered, "and I'm wondering if you could help me."

The two women conferring at the desk looked up quickly. The inspection which they gave me was shrewd but kindly. After a moment one spoke.

"I shouldn't be surprised," she smiled. "In just what way did you want us to help you?"

"Why – I don't know exactly. I thought maybe you could tell me where to go. Don't they have theatrical agencies here in New York?"

The woman who had smiled – she was Mrs. C. B. White, I was to learn later – came from behind the desk.

"Of course there are but I don't happen to know about them. I think they would have definite information over at headquarters, though. Haven't you had any theatrical experience?"

"No – I just thought I'd like to go on the stage."

"Oh. And how long have you been in New York?"

"I just got in from Akron, O."

Here the other woman – Mrs. Leffler – spoke up.

"Well, I'm certainly glad you came to us. I think we can play the part of big sister to you. Mrs. White is just going over to headquarters and you can go along with her."

And so we went to headquarters. It proved to be a remodeled house on Lexington ave., and here I was put into the hands of Miss Katherine McGovern, alert and likewise kind but with a disturbing habit of seeming to know a great deal more than one was telling her.

To her I gave the history of my life as I had carefully prepared and rehearsed it. I was Huldah Benson and I was 23 and I had left home in Akron, O., to go on the stage. No, I hadn't any brothers or sisters and my mother was dead. Had I ever worked before?

I Brought up by a Desk Marked "Travelers' Aid"

Oh yes, I had given music lessons once and I used to sell records in a piano company back home. Did my father want me to leave home? No, he didn't exactly.

"But Huldah," queried Miss McGovern, "what ever put it into your head that you wanted to go on the stage?"

"Oh, I don't know. I was always crazy about the theater and I knew a fellow once that was an actor."

"And because you once knew a man that was an actor you come here, without experience, and expect to get a job where even professionals are having a hard time of it!"

I admitted that such was the case.

Miss McGovern did not argue. Instead she said the most sensible thing in the world.

"Well, we'll try to help you get the job you want, and if that doesn't turn up, you'll be willing to do something else for a while, won't you? Keep in touch with us and we'll help you all we can. In the meantime you'll have to see about getting yourself a room, Over at the Y. W. C. A. now –"

But a room was not what I was seeking just then. On the pretext that I had had no breakfast and was hungry I got away. When I returned three hours later it was with the announcement that I had found a place to stay and had come for my bag.

During the next few days a Travelers' Aid worker called every day at the address I had given to find out whether I was all right and had located a job. They also wired to Akron, O., to find out whether everything there was as if I had told them.

If a girl really were all alone in a big city – what a blessed thing the Travelers' Aid could be!

In the meantime I had started in quest of a job.

TOMORROW: My experiences in the booking agencies.

<hr />

$\mathcal{P}art$ 2:

Trials of Visiting Theatrical Booking Offices for Job, Told

EDITOR'S NOTE—This is the second of a series of six stories by Josephine Van de Grift describing how she, posing as a country girl, sought to get on the stage in New York.

NEW YORK, – The most immediate aid that comes to the service of the young woman in search of a job on the stage in the classified telephone directory marked: "Theatrical Managers and Producers."

Not that I found this out right away. The Travelers' Aid at the Pennsylvania Railroad station had been very kind in the matter of lodging, meals, advice and pure unalloyed friendship.

But I had learned nothing definite as to how I was going to get on the stage. To the Travelers' Aid at the Grand Central Station I put my query in somewhat different form:

"Do you have a list of reputable theatrical agencies?"

The lady at the desk didn't but she thought I might get such a list at the Theater Guild.

There in a little crow's nest I found a girl, plump and pleasant. No, the Theater Guild didn't have such a list but from the telephone directory she selected two agencies that she assured me were all right. I then had recourse to the telephone book myself and made a list of some 30 or so theatrical managers and agencies.

The list began imposingly enough with David Belasco[6]. It ended with Sam Scribner,[7] producer of burlesque.

Then began a heart-breaking tour of the agencies.

Then began a heart-breaking tour of the agencies. I would poke my head through a door hoping vaguely that a producer or a manager, sitting inside, would observe that I had a certain spirituelle cast of countenance, would hop from his chair and say:

"Ah, the very type I've been looking for," and bear me off to triumph. Instead I would find a score or more people sitting in chairs about the wall. They would look at me critically and then relapse into their own introspections.

After a while, when the chairs were all filled and a number of us were standing, a bobbed-haired blond would come out and say, "Nothing today. No, I'm sorry, but there's nothing today for any of you," and we would all get up and file out.

This happened again and again. At the managerial offices it was no better. No, Mr. Belasco and his whole staff were away. He wouldn't be doing anything for several months yet.

Mr. Cohan had a couple of shows in rehearsal but the casts were all filled. In six weeks there might be something –.

No, So-and-So's shows were all closing – he'd had rotten luck, he wouldn't be doing anything until after Christmas.

---

[6] David Belasco (1853-1931) American theatre producer, impresario, director and playwright. His theatre was called Belasco Theatre, located at 111 West 44th st. in Manhattan, New York.

[7] Samuel Alexander Scribner (1859-1941) American circus and burlesque impresario. He switched to burlesque in the late 1890's when he sold his circus to Barnum & Bailey.

I marveled, though, at the kindness everyone manifested. At the Packard agency[8] there was one whom they called Miss Mason. It was a pleasure to be turned down by Miss Mason.

"No, dear, nothing for you today"; "I'm sorry, dear, but you're too tall for the part." "No, nothing today, dear. If you'd only been here three days ago."

"Oh, Mr. Gordon, how are you after your illness? No, there's nothing today but there might be something next week. I'll let you know."

It was Miss Mason who sent me in to an inside office to be registered by Mr. Packard. Mr. Packard was well set up and a little gray and he had nice eyes.

I felt I liked Mr. Packard although our conversation was limited to details I had given weary times before: That I was Huldah Benson, 23, five feet four inches tall, that my hair was blond and my eyes were gray.

"Any experience?" said Mr. Packard.

"None," I said sadly. "Would it help any if they knew I could play the piano?"

"It might," said Mr. Packard, "how much do you weigh?"

"A hundred and forty – five pounds in my coat."

"Well," said Mr. Packard, "that may not be a disadvantage, but never can tell where the lightning will strike."

I took courage. On the way out I met Inez.

The next installment: I talk with Inez, the girl who tried to come back.

Part 3:

---

[8] Packard's Theatrical Exchange and Agency, operated ca. 1894 – aft1922, and located in West 28th st. New York.

"HULDA" WARNED TO GIVE UP DESIRE TO GO ON STAGE

EDITOR'S NOTE—This is the third of a series of six stories by Josephine Van de Grift describing how she, posing as a country girl, sought to get on the stage in New York.

NEW YORK, – Inez – I'll omit her last name although she told me readily – was the type I know now belongs to the steady tramp, tramp, tramp, to the theatrical agencies. She had snap to her clothes.

The day before I had noticed a girl with snap. She had on a blue suit with white collars and cuffs and a fur thrown carelessly across her shoulders.

Then I saw the waist line of her suit was high – where they were wearing them three years ago – her blouse was of cheap material and evidently home-laundered, her fur was old and much brushed, her shoes were cracked but highly polished, her white kid gloves had been carefully mended.

How many months of tramping she had done in that little blue suit I forebore to guess. But she was immaculate. And she had style.

So did Inez. Her veil was thrown across her hat with an air, her wrap fell from confident little shoulders. She was exquisitely groomed. Without knowing exactly why you looked at her twice. Which was what I did when I came out of Packard's office. Her eyes looked tired.

"Are you just registering here, too?" I asked.

"Yes. You see, it's been ten years since I was on the stage and now I'm trying to come back." For some reason, possibly a desire to tell our troubles, we sank down on two chairs in the anteroom just outside Packard's office door.

"My mother has broken her hip," she explained. "She's an actress, too, so you see I was born in it. I gave it up ten years ago to get married. Now I've put my boy in school and I'm trying to get back."

The door opened and Packard's voice came through. He was ushering out a caller.

"Don't let anybody ever tell you that an agency exists for the actor," he said. "It doesn't. It exists for the manager. If we place a well-known actor at $500 or a thousand a week, that's where we make our money. If we place an amateur at $25 a week, we make just about 30 cents –"

"Are you just registering here, too?" I asked.

"Yes," I said.

The door closed. Inez was still speaking. "– been doing ingenues with Joseph Murphy and then I was with Pauline Boyle.[9] She always said I was the best ingenue she ever had. She's running an agency now. I went over to see her but she couldn't remember me. I talked and talked and after a while she did begin to remember me. The stage is life to my mother, but I wouldn't stick to it if I could do anything else –"

Another door opened. Miss Mason had taken off her glasses, had put on her coat and hat with the evident intention of going out to lunch. The door closed –

"– I'd like to do social service work. I know I could do it because I've brushed up with all kinds of people and I can read character at a glance. But instead of that they want somebody with a college certificate.

She stopped suddenly.

"Are you just trying to break in?"

---

[9] Pauline H. Boyle (1859-August 28, 1948) married to Thomas J. Boyle, theater manager. Debuted in the Boyle Stock Company in Nashville and later became production manager of the Broadway show, *Two Little Sailor Boys*. She also managed several theaters in New York.

She looked at me critically.

"Oh, my dear, the stage is hard. It's hard even on the old-timers. I have a little friend – she was starred last year – this year she's speaking two lines in a road show.

"I have another friend – wonderful talent – she held out for two years, just tramping from one agency to another. They'd tell her to come around in two weeks. Then they'd say the part was just filled. One time they rehearsed four weeks and then the show didn't open.

"Finally she didn't even have car fare to go back and forth. She's got a job at a glove counter now.

"I'd advise you not to go into it, but of course if your heart is set on it –

"Oh, it is," I breathed.

"Well, I'll tell you. John Golden is trying out amateurs this afternoon over at the Little theater."

Over at the Little theater I found 400 persons ahead of me. They crowded the theater, their faces lit up unhealthily by a bunch light which, shone from the apron.

John Golden,[10] Madge Kennedy[11] and P. E. McCoy walked out upon the stage.

Next installment: Filling two jobs from 400 applicants and my experiences at the Hippodrome.

Part 4:

---

[10] John L. Golden (1874-1955) American stage producer, theatre owner and operator, composer, director and writer. He was currently producing "Seventh Heaven" at the Booth Theatre in 1922.

[11] Madge Kennedy (1891-1987) American stage actress

'Huldah' Again Fails To Land Job In Effort To Get On Stage

This is the fourth of a series of six stories by Josephine Van de Grift describing how she, posing as a country girl, sought to get on the stage in New York.

BY JOSEPHINE VAN DE GRIFT.

NEW YORK, – After he had introduced his party and the hand clapping had subsided John Bolden started to speak.

"I had no idea," he said, "that so many would be gathered here. It was merely that I let it be known that I had two understudy roles to let out to amateurs. I wanted some young person with talent and ambition to have a chance just as I longed for a chance 30 years ago."

We are thrilled. Here was a man who had made good. And 30 years ago he had been like us.

"You will agree," Golden continued, "that it would be impossible to try all of you today. So Mr. McCoy[12] will go among you and pick out 15 young men and 15 young women who are types for the roles.

"The rest will have to go home. But we shall take your names and let you know about future tryouts."

Straightway Mr. McCoy came down. Three times I managed to get in his way and three times his eyes rested on me and then passed on without the slightest show of interest. I was only too plainly not of the sort desired.

Saddened, I stood in line until I could dutifully recite my name and qualifications to a blond and bespectacled young woman at a desk in the rear of the stage.

---

[12] P.E. McCoy (…) Stage manager and performer known for roles in Lightnin' (1918) and Suzanne (1910)

Then I stole up into the balcony to watch the try-outs. The rest of the crowd had been shooed out of the house.

It was evidently Helen Mencken's[13] role in "Seventh Heaven" for which Golden was

Then I stole up into the Balcony to watch the tryouts.

permitting the try-outs. As I came up the balcony stairs a young woman was shrieking:

"What are you doing there – you – praying – praying – to a thing you call le bon Dieu. Keep away from me – I know what I'm talking about. For four years I lived with my Chico and believed that we were married –"

The voice of Golden broke in harshly.

"No, no, that won't do at all. You've got a long way to go yet, young lady. Where's that girl with the shamrocks on her hat?"

The girl with the shamrocks came forward. "What are you doing there – you –," she recited, "praying to a thing you call le bon Dieu –" Golden sighted and pronounced it not so bad.

Another girl tried and another and another. Some shrieked, some flung their arms, some acted all up and down the stage. The girl I had picked as the most likely recited her lines in a dull, hopeless monotone. Golden stopped her at the end of the second sentence.

[13] Helen Meinken, stage name is Helen Menken (1901-1966) American actress, whose parents were deaf, so she originally communicated in sign language and did not talk until age 4. She was the first wife of actor Humphrey Bogart. The aforementioned play "Seventh Heaven" debuted in October 1922 at the Booth Theatre, 222 W. 45th st. in New York.

After a while I stole out of the theater. Back of me someone was shrilling, "What are you doing – you –"

Down at the Hippodrome[14] I sought out Sam Watson.[15] Sam used to own "Watson's Barn Yard circus." For seven years he has been doorkeeper at the Hippodrome.

"I've just got to get a job, Mr. Watson," I told him. "I've just got to."

"Mr. Burnside[16] isn't in now," said Sam, "he won't be in till about five o'clock.

"But what am I going to do?"

"You look tired," said Sam. "Go home and get rested and come back tomorrow. You know you ought to look real bright and happy to talk to Mr. Burnside."

"But how does a person ever get on the stage anyway?"

"They do just what you're doing," said Sam. "They go from place to place and just keep it up. We've had girls coming here every day for months."

"But how do they do it?"

"I don't know," said Sam.

* * *

$\mathcal{P}art$ 5:

---

[14] The Hippodrome Theatre operated in New York City from 1905 to 1939 and was located on Sixth av. And West 43rd and 44th streets of the Theater district in Manhattan.

[15] Sam Watson (…) Ran his Farmyard Circus at the Orpheum theater in 1909. An article in the Deseret News on September 15, 1909 interviewed Sam, and he talked of how he trains his animals with kindness instead of whips, and has never used any form of cruelty in his circus. His animals are all his pets. Judging from the picture of him, he has the kindest soul.

[16] Robert Hubberthorne Burnside (R.H. Burnside) (1873-1952) Scottish-American director, composer, producer and writer well known for putting on scores and scores of plays including the Pirates of Penzance, Robin Hood, Trial by Jury & H.M.S. Pinafore

NEW YORK, – The next morning I sought out the offices of Mr. Ziegfeld of the Follies.[17] The elevator man informed me that Mr. Kingston and Mr. Aarons were the casting directors.

Being known to Mr. Kingston and fearing recognition I decided on Mr. Aarons. Within the office I was greeted by Mr. Aarons' colored man, William, who stuck his head out from a little square aperture.

"Is Mr. Aarons in?" I queried.

"He is," said William tersely.

"I want to see him," I said, "about getting a job."

"There is absolutely nothing doing," said William and withdrew haughtily.

Three men who were sitting about the office laughed. I burned. I wanted to kill them.

William's haughtiness had started another day wrong. I tried a half dozen other offices without success.

Eventually I landed in the burlesque district down at 701 Seventh avenue. But neither was there anything doing in burlesque. All burlesque recruiting, it seems, is done in June. The various blond young women were very definite about it. They didn't seem particularly sorry, either.

I went back over some of the beaten track. There I found the same offices, the same attendants with their "nothing today, dear," the same little groups, patient, clean smiling, kind, but looking a little hungry.

---

[17] Florenz "Flo" Edward Ziegfeld Jr. (1867-1932) American Broadway impresario, noted for his series of theatrical revues called "The Ziegfeld Follies" which began in 1907 until his death, and were inspired by the Parisian "Folies Bergére."

There remained one name on my list, a name I had somehow circled around. It was that of Charles Blaney.[18] Dispiritedly I made the climb to Blaney's office. A man was sitting there.

"Do you think," I said, "that you could get me a job carrying a spear or something?"

The man stirred.

"Why, I shouldn't be surprised, Harry, here's a young lady that would like to carry a spear."

"Harry" came in from somewhere down the hall. He looked me over and bethought himself a moment.

"I tell you," he said, "we've got a stock company up in the Bronx that's putting on 'The Bird of Paradise'[19] next week. I think the cast is all filled but if you'd like to super in that – just for the experience, you know –"

Joy mounted to my head and made me dizzy. I sat down abruptly. An hour later I delivered into the hands

JOY MOUNTED TO MY HEAD AND MADE ME DIZZY.

_____

[18] Charles E. Blaney (1866-1944) American actor, producer, and playwright. He produced and acted in first play, A Railroad Ticket, in his hometown of Columbus, Ohio by the time he was 20. He then moved to New York to become a producer for Stair and Havlin, and continued on producing around 200 melodramas, developing stars putting them in stock companies and opening two theaters he built in New York

[19] The Original play "The Bird of Paradise" was written and staged by Richard Walton Tully and performed at Daly's Theatre and Maxine Elliott's Theatre in 1912 for a total of 112 performances.

of James Garey,[20] director of the Blaney Players at the Prospect Theater in the Bronx,[21] a note which stated that in the writer's estimation the bearer was an earnest and dependable young woman who would make good at any task assigned her. It was signed by Harry Blaney.[22]

James Garey was reading a piece of stage script when I handed him the note. He read it carefully.

"All right," he said, "come back tomorrow at one o'clock and we'll make you a beautiful Hawaiian girl."

I ran all the stairs up to the elevated railway. I was happy. I had landed a job. It made no difference that there was no pay attached, no future promised, nothing at all to cling to. Hadn't Harry Blaney said I was dependable and he believed I would make good?

I went back for rehearsal the next day and the next and learned thereby that my duties in "The Bird of Paradise" would be these: Together with something like eight other damsels, also supers, I was to loll upon the stage at the rise of the curtain and give a rousing rendition of "On the Beach of Waikiki."

Following this we were to register joy, grief and disapproval as these sentiments were called for by certain principals in the piece. (Joy at the prospect of food, disapproval at the prospect of work, terror at the eruption of a volcano.)

Some time later we were to sing "Aloha" (until the curtain comes down, now girls, see if you can't remember something) and at the end were to kneel down in the apron of the stage with arms uplifted while the hapless Luana made her way up the side of the mountain.

At the second rehearsal I got on intimate terms with Katie.

TOMORROW: The story Katie told me of stage life and my first – and last – performance.

---

[20] James R. Garey (1861-1943) American actor and director. He wrote several short films during 1916/17, and directed at the Blaney Players at the Prospect Theater in 1922.

[21] The Prospect Theater saw several theaters constructed in its same location over the years. Originally built in 1910, it sat at the crossing of Prospect av. And 160th st. Today an abandoned dilapidated building stands reading "Olympic Theater Concert Hall" on the canopy in its place since it closed in 2006.

[22] Harry Clay Blaney (1876-1964) American actor and writer, and brother to Charles E. Blaney.

Part 6:

Stage Star As a Job-Seeker Rebuffed by Theater Agencies

EDITOR'S NOTE—This is the sixth of a series of six stories by Josephine Van de Grift describing how she, posing as a country girl, sought to get on the stage in New York.

NEW YORK, – Although stage people are very kind it seems they, too, have their little cliques.

An actor who has a line to say as, "Madam, did you ring?" will never get on intimate terms with a super with no line at all.

Consequently those of us who constituted the "atmosphere" for "The Bird of Paradise" were lonesome. I think this was why Katie clung to me.

It was while we were having supper together before the evening performance that I found out about Katie.

Katie was 17. Her mother had been in a hospital six years and Katie had been forced to leave school early. She got a job as nursemaid at $30 a month and then the movie fever struck her.

She entered a "movie school" where you paid $50 for training and then got a job at a fabulous sum. In the school they made films of you.

Later you took the films around and showed them to the managers. If the managers liked them they hired you at a wonderful salary.

Katie had paid $80 and taken her "training." But she had been unable to raise the remaining $20 and the school had refused to give her her "films."

Now, by supering in the stock company Katie hoped to rise to a position of affluence where she could rescue her "films."

"Of course," said Katie, "you know the stock company don't pay you anything at first. You have to be an extra actor for four weeks. Then they give you a line and begin to pay you something."

She produced her make-up kit and gave her nose a dab. It was Katie's joy – that make-up kit.

We went upstairs to get ready for the performance.

There were four of us in the dressing room. The grass skirts popularly supposed to be an indispen-learned, I had learned, were not to be ours. Those had been reserved for the dancing girls.

We went upstairs to get ready for the performance.

We supers were to wear the Mother Hubbards introduced into the islands by the missionaries.

Somebody shoved through the door two tablespoonfuls of brown powder on a cold cream lid and instructed us to cover our faces, necks, arms and legs with it.

I wasted considerable time before I discovered that cold cream had to be applied first. But even if that hadn't happened there would never have been enough to go around. Nobody came to make us up. All that we accomplished was four pale splotchey sunburns and some very black eyebrows.

I had just crawled into my Mother Hubbard when somebody bawled "orchestra" and we piled down on the stage.

Eventually we got settled. "Now girls, sing," rasped out Garey.

We sang. The curtains shot up. I was before the footlights at last.

97

Some time later an individual who had been out in front came back stage.

"You girls' make-up is certainly rotten," he remarked.

The stage was cold. I started to sneeze. Four times stage hands requested me to get out of the way so they could put up a lemon tree or something. My make-up was coming off. I was dirty from lying about on the stage.

It was a long show. When 11:30 came and it was finally over I realized that I was tired and hungry and discouraged. I didn't want to be an actress. I would much rather work in a restaurant. Or anything.

I went upstairs and started piling cold cream and eyebrow pencils into my bag.

"What are you doing that for?" said Katie, "you'll have to use them tomorrow."

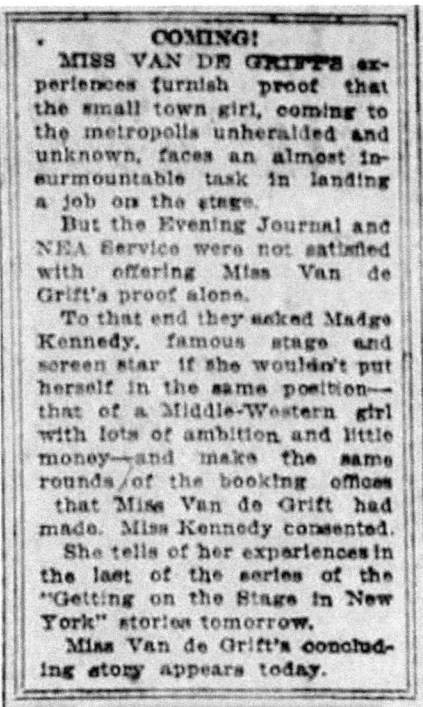

"I know," I said, "but I thought I'd straighten them up a little."

Which, of course, wasn't quite true, for I knew that the stage career of Huldah Benson was over.

After the show:

(image): **COMING!   MISS VAN DE GRIFT's** experiences furnish proof that the small town girl, coming to the metropolis unheralded and unknown, faces an almost insurmountable task in landing a job on the stage.

But the Evening Journal and NEA Service were not satisfied with offering Miss Van de Grift's proof alone.

To that end they asked Madge Kennedy, famous stage and screen star if she wouldn't put herself in the same position – that of a Middle-Western girl with lots of ambition and little money – and make the same rounds of the booking offices that Miss Van de Grift had made. Miss Kennedy consented.

She tells of her experiences in the last of the series of the "Getting on the Stage in New York" stories tomorrow.

EDITOR'S NOTE:—In six stories Josephine Van de Grift has told her experiences in seeking a stage job in New York, posing as a girl from the Middle West. Today, to conclude the series, Madge Kennedy, stage and film star, shows that theatrical agencies do not even recognize real talent when it is masked under old clothes.

BY MADGE KENNEDY
Film and Stage Favorite

Stage Star As a Job-Seeker Rebuffed by Theater Agencies

N EW YORK, – Every year hundreds of girls write to me. The gist of their letters is nearly always the same: "I've got a job out here but I'm not happy. I've always been crazy about the stage and I know I could act if I only got the chance. Please, Miss Kennedy, help me to get on the stage."

Over and over I have had to tell these girls the same thing: "If you have a job, stick to it. The stage isn't what you think it is. There are thousands of girls like you. The one thing awaiting most of them is disillusionment."

Have I known what I was talking about? I always thought so. And now, after an experiment I made I am sure of it.
I got into a blue serge dress, a coat three seasons old, put on a soft sports hat and, forgetting I was Madge Kennedy for the while, I made a tour of the theatrical offices and meekly pleaded for a job.

This is what happened:

Three office boys informed me that their superiors were absolutely inaccessible. An equal number of nice, kind-hearted girls said they were sorry but there wasn't a thin doing – the casts for So-and-So's shows were all filled and he wouldn't be doing anything more until after Christmas.

Madge Kennedy as her admirers see her on stage and screen and (right) in the garb she affected when touring New York agencies in search of a stage job.

Over at the People's Vaudeville agency a number of men were standing about. They looked important and I vaguely hoped that one of them might be a manager or something and would notice me. They did, but it was with absolute indifference.

Timidly I made my plea to the elderly woman behind the desk. But it seems I had come to the wrong office – they were doing no casting there.

I trailed up to the office of Pauline Boyle. It was a very severe person indeed who was presiding over the desk.

"No," she said sternly, "there is nothing – nothing at all."

I looked at her appealingly. I let her have the full benefit of my face, but in the look which she returned to me there was not the slightest flicker of recognition.

My list bore the name of Charles Blaney who, I knew, presided over the destinies of some few stock companies. Certain stock companies in times gone by had been anxious to have me play with them. Nervously, I mounted the stairs to his office. Suppose he would recognize me? Suppose he would say, 'Why, you're Madge Kennedy. What do you mean coming around here asking for a job? Isn't 'Spite Corner' –" What should I tell him?

But my nervousness proved to be without foundation. The very nice man in the office regarded me kindly but without recognition.

"My brother does all the casting around here," he told me. "I think he'll be in about 2 o'clock." You might come back then." And he resumed his conversation with another man.

I turned and went down the stairs.

So – this was it. I was Madge Kennedy whom certain little girls out in the west regarded as a success on the stage and screen.

But Madge Kennedy, without her name, without make-up, without pretty clothes – that was another matter. She might have talent but it would take many weary weeks of trailing from office to office before she would be given a chance to show it.

Altogether I went to some eight or ten agencies (avoiding only one or two where I was certain to be recognized, and not a soul knew me – no one, save a little stenographer in an office that had nothing to do with theatrical agencies.

Those very offices which ordinarily would have been glad to see me looked at my blankly in my plain clothes and said, "Nothing today, dear."

Late in the afternoon I got into my little car and was driven home.

The feeling that had come over me was not one of thankfulness that the little masquerade was over, that I really had a job and was protected and cared for.

It was a great big ache for those thousands and thousands of girls who come to New York and think that some miracle is going to raise them to stardom.

Sometimes, of course, the miracle happens. But again I say, stick to your job: Don't come to New York until you have enough money to last at least two years.

And even then, don't come until you are willing to give to the stage a great deal more than ever will come back to you.

Chapter V.

The

Akron Beacon Journal

The Akron Beacon Journal

J OSEPHINE'S stories might never have been known to the public if it weren't for the chance hiring as society page editor at the Akron Beacon Journal.

An article published September 22nd, 1922 states: "Miss Van De Grift will, in the future, be associated with the Newspaper Enterprise association in New York as feature writer. She has been connected with the Beacon Journal editorial staff in the same capacity for the last four years." This puts her hiring around 1918, and on the 1920 census she writes her occupation as *society page editor — newspaper*.

It was in June of 1924 that she returned to the Akron Beacon Journal rejoining the staff after being in New York for two years as a special feature writer with the NEA. She began her syndicated column "Demi-Tasse and Mrs. Grundy" soon after.

I've included a few articles written between these years that reflect the style of her earlier writing:

The following image is a sample of one of Josephine's early articles in 1920, and alongside an ad about two-piece bathing suits making their first appearance. A true sign of the times!

2 June 1920, Wednesday (seen in image above):

Styles in Literature Have Changed With Times, Says Miss Edgerton

T O those of us who, in our youth, were given to retiring unostentatiously to the wood shed with a copy of "The Discarded Daughter," by Mrs. Emma Dorothy Eliza Nevitte Southworth, under our arm it may come as a distinct shock to learn that 30 years or so ago such a book as "The Changed Brides" and "Cruel as the Grave," "Tried for Her Life" and "The Beautiful Fiend" circulated quite boldly and unblushingly from what has since become our public library.

The fact is sponsored by Miss Pauline Edgerton who Tuesday left that career as Akron's city librarian upon which she embarked thirty years ago. And during these thirty years she has stood back more or less helplessly and seen the styles in heroines change from the pale swooning creature flopping aimlessly on the hero's shirt bosom to the hoyden who tumbles down trees and throws green apples at the minister's high silk hat; from the dear sweet thing who goes about seeing good in everything to the present-day young woman who embark madly on a career and draws on her rubbers to march in the suffrage parade.

Mary Jane Holmes, soul sister to Mrs. Southworth, for whom graves yawned up their dead, writing desks revealed their secrets and consumptive murderers made death bed confessions solely that the Duchess of Cheswick might be united to her beloved Algernon de Montferey, was an Akron visitor at one time and dined at the Edgerton home. She was accompanied by her husband, but the little Pauline, who at that time might have been all of six years, was so lost in admiration of the creator of "Less Rivers" and "Tempest and Sunshine" that she has no recollection of Mary Jane's spouse except that in he shone in pale aureole of reflected glory and red hair.

Growth of The Library

It was when Akron's public library was still a library association, maintained by subscription, and occupied a room on the second floor of the Dime Savings building that Miss Edgerton, being of literary turn acquired from her father, assumed those duties which are now to have their first interruption after 30 years.

The library persisted there for awhile and was then moved to more commodious quarters in what used to be the old Academy of Music. It was just about ready to break out of bounds again when Andrew Carnegie came along with an interesting little financial proposition which resulted in the present library home at E. Market and High sts.

Miss Edgerton accompanied all these peregrinations and house warmings. During all the vicissitudes in popular reading – from E. P. Roe to Gene Stratton Porter, from "Jane Eyre" to "Mary Olivier" she has maintained that high good humor with books and their authors – that sane judgment between what is meat for thought and what is simply hysterics, that has somehow come to be irresistibly bound up with the life of the city. The present library board realized this when they passed the following resolution:

The board of trustees of the Akron public library wishes to acknowledge and thank Miss Pauline Edgerton, retiring librarian, for her many years' of untiring service in the interest of the institution under her care.

For 30 years Miss Edgerton has given her time and labor unstintingly to the library and we feel that many persons in Akron join us in expressing our heartfelt regret at losing her service.

Taking into consideration the adverse conditions, such as lack of fuel, help and financial aid under which the library has carried on its work, Miss Edgerton and her staff has, we feel, accomplished wonderful results."

<hr>

28 October 1921, Friday:

They Used To Talk Of Books And Music, Now It Is Home Brew And "Hootch" Recipes

"I WAS having dinner with some friends the other night," said Ceres. "I've been visiting at their home, I suppose, for 20 years or more. But never before had I been offered anything to drink. I must confess I was startled. And the conversation! It used to be about books, music, plays, politics – things ordinarily considered worth while. Now it was all about home brew. Everybody had a recipe of his own and two or three that he partially remembered from somebody else. They were never a family given to boasting, but now they related with pride that they had five water coolers under preparation in the cellar and three kegs in the attic. Not that I am one given to discussing trivialities –"

Ajax reached up and scratched the spot where his hair was beginning to grow a little thin.

"There was a time dear lady," said he, "when you could drop a box of chocolate dipped cherries or a copy of Emerson's Essays into your pocket and set out to call on some nice sweet girl assured of a successful evening. But now, good Lord, you can't even hook your cane over the hall tree before she demands, "Whaddya got on your hip, old dear." Call her up and tell her you're getting up a little party and right away she wants to know if it's going to be a booze party. The explanation, of course –"

"It's psychology," said Clio, "I know –"

"The history of the world," remarked Phaeton –

"The explanation," said Ajax, buttering a piece of toast and applying a bit of marmalade to it, "is in reality very simple. A woman thrives on sacrifice. When a cocktail could be had for 15 cents it didn't interest her. But now that it entails parting with a Liberty bond and undergoing considerable personal inconvenience, why, nothing else will satisfy her vanity. Of course there's the element of naughtiness, to be considered –"

Clio choked. "Exactly – psychology," she sputtered, "the desire of doing the thing forbidden. And getting away with it. That's the only thing that ails our young people. Astyanax was saying only the other night that the only way we'd ever have prohibition was when we passed a law compelling everybody to drink a quart of whisky a day. I know for a fact that the last summer when I wanted to go to Atlantic City Astyanax wanted to go to Bobcaygeon. I rooted strong for Bobcaygeon and as a result we went to Atlantic City, if more women would only –"

Series of Reactions

"History," said Phaeton, passing his cup for more tea, "is nothing more nor less – no lemon, please – than a series of reactions. To prove it I need go no further back than last week when I was in New York and noted with something akin to melancholy that skirts are now being made ankle length. Consequently I may predict with a fair amount of certainty that the present conditions in which our young people are, ah, weltering, will be succeeded by a period characterized by a reviving interest in petticoats, nut sundaes and the 'Five Little Peppers,'"

"And when that period does come," sighed Clio, "what a comfort it will be to Ceres and me to know that we can turn up our nose at those who weltered, knowing that through it all we kept ourselves unsmirched."

"On tea," murmured Ajax softly, "but why turn up your nose at all, dear lady?"

"Well I'd like to know," demanded Clio hotly, "whether a virtuous woman is not to have any satisfaction at all any more?"

Blames Parents

"It's really the parents' fault," said Ceres. "There's Proserpina, Her oldest girl always had to be in by 11:30 and then she didn't dare to go to bed till she'd been in to see her mother and given an account of herself. But the youngest one – she's only 19 – she rolls in at 2 or 3 o'clock and nobody says a word. The other night her father says to her, 'Seems to me you were pretty well lit up last night,' and she says to him, 'Well, poppa, you were pretty well stewed yourself,'"

"And then there's Oedipus," said Phaeton, "he's been sending his girl to some finishing school in the east, and he just discovered this fall that she'd been learning a lot more about hootch and cigarets than she had about French verbs and cooking. Well, he was for hunting up another school, but the girl cried and said she might as well be dead – she wouldn't have a social chance in the world if she couldn't graduate from a school with a name, and so he had to give in."

"There's just one macaroon apiece," said Clio, "what d'ya say we spin for 'em?"

⸙

26 May 1922, Friday:

Akron Plumber Succumbs To Onset of Muse, Writes Songs and Movie Scenarios

BY day Lewis Harris, 1150 Getz st., cleans out water traps, wipes joints, investigates cisterns, mends leaky bath tubs and performs the duties attendant upon the profession of plumbing.

By night Harris puts aside all thoughts of lead pipe and blow torches and devotes himself to the muse.

Sometimes it's a poem, sometimes it's a short story, sometimes it's a movie – whatever the urge, Harris assails the situation with pad and pencil and a briary pipe. Through his indefatigable industry villainy is again confounded, virtue is rewarded and Roland Merryweather, the son of the poor widow, awaken from his tussle with the bank bandits to find his brow being tenderly bathed by the beautiful daughter of the bank president.

And now Harris is himself being smiled on – by a lady sometimes known as Dame Fortune.

Onset of Verse.

Some weeks ago, while wrestling with a leaky drain, Harris found himself succumbing to an onset of verse. It was about Pauline. "Pauline, Pauline, you are a wonderful queen." It sounded good to Harris. He abandoned the drain pipe and applied himself to composition. Now Pauline has been set to music and found herself a publisher.

A few days ago Harris got word that his movie scenario, "The Gold Dagger," had been accepted by a western producing company.

Now he has high hopes of disposing of his other works. They include a two reel movie, "The Worried Mother," and three short stories, "Unknown Land," "A Trip to Spain," and "A Letter That Was Found."

"It ain't this literary high falutin' that the people want," says Harries, "it's puttin' in the heart interest and the punch that gets you anywhere."

Upon returning from New York after writing for the Newspaper Enterprise Association (NEA) from October 1922 to June 1924, she rejoined the Akron Beacon Journal staff. Her articles were seen as front-page news, but her writing style demanded its own column. It was less than a month before her first "Demi-Tasse & Mrs. Grundy" syndicated column appeared. She continued to add to the paper with front page news articles and her column began in mid-July of 1924.

2 June 1924, Monday (front page article after her time spent in New York as a writer):

"Just Luck" Chorus Four Boys Who Built Winning Plane Meet Models At Last Minute

A BOUT one of the first things a man learns in this life is that he has to take a sporting chance on everything.

For example there's Burdette Sutherland, John Klein, Junior Warley and Allen Paul.

Burdette, John, Junior and Allen were the first four to carry off prizes with their airplane models at the finale of the meet staged under the auspices of the Akron Beacon Journal and Akron chapter of the National Aeronautical association at the armory Saturday afternoon.

And yet when Burdette, John, Junior and Allen toiled into the armory that afternoon with their precious bits of board and string and rubber bands there wasn't one of them who didn't have heavy care tugging at his heart.

Poor in Preliminary

For the airplanes constructed by the four boys had done none too well in the preliminaries. Burdette's airplane had sailed straight up into the air only to fall to earth again with a thud. John's circled about drunkenly. Junior's and Allen's planes just skidded. There was extreme skepticism expressed that say one of the four would make the finale.

But there's something in the air surrounding South high school where all four boys go that makes a man fight in the last ditch. Without a word in anybody mind you, each of the four started Friday night to make new planes for the finale. They didn't have much time but they did have heaps of experience.

Burdette got his plane finished at 10 o'clock Friday night. John finished his at 8:20 Saturday morning. Junior laid a caressing thumb and forefinger along the edge of his super model two hours later and when Allen went without his lunch and made for the armory in the afternoon he was still doubtful whether the glue would hold.

It did. Everything held. It is to be questioned whether at any time anywhere there have been more graceful flights than those made by the last minute inventions of Burdette, John, Junior and Allen.

⚜

12 July 1924, Saturday:

New Book Of Etiquette Just Wonderful For Girls, But My, How It Upsets Many Old Ideas

A T last they've done it – got out a book of etiquette that us working girls can understand.

"It's by Carolyn Nunder and it costs 35 cents – not a cent more than one of those flesh producing crème de menthe frappes. And helpful! My word. Among the subjects it covers are the following:

Umbrellas. Never, never, never does a gentleman carry a lady's umbrella, open or shut, "Unless," says the book of etiquette, "it is in a driving rain when the lady is using both hands to hold her clothes out of the wet and her hat on as well, or when she searches in her wrist bag for something, or stops to take off her gloves or to do anything that requires both hands."

Paragraph Brings Shame

This paragraph brings a blush of shame to the cheek of a young woman who recalls that three years ago she walked out East Market st. under the umbrella of an old gentleman, a perfect stranger, too, who told her that since his wife had died he had to live with his daughter-in-law and she treated him perfectly terrible.

Kissing in public. "As a method of greeting," says the book of etiquette, "kissing in public should not be practiced except among members of the family."

Considering how well the parks are patrolled these days this paragraph is pretty hard on the girl who lives in a hall bedroom and has no family to speak of. On second thought, though, it says, "as a method of greeting."

Calls. "A gentleman on his first call on a lady," says the book of etiquette, "should not remain longer than a half hour. He should not request permission to call again. If his visits are desired he will receive an invitation to dinner or tea."

This is going to be a terrible blow to some of the fireside companions us girls have known. And if they were to observe it, it would ...

* * *

23 July 1924, Wednesday:

St. Bernard Makes Pal of Cat

QUEENIE, at once the most expensive and the most beautiful charge that the county jail has had in a long time, was back in his old quarters Wednesday after a wild burst for freedom.

"You see," said Queenie, when interviewed on the front lawn of the court house, "it was this way."

"To my knowledge I've never done a wrong thing in my life. My father Roger Newfoundland of the Newfoundland Newfoundlands, said to me, stick to your own trail, my boy, and fear not man.

"My being in jail here is purely an accident. I was going along lending to my own business when all at once a woman started to scream and then a man loaded me up in a cart and brought me here.

Wanted To Protest

"At first, I was inclined to protest but when I saw the perfect breeding of Carl Repp, I decided that quality could be found even to country jails and almost immediately I started about making myself useful.

UN JOURN.

EVENING, JULY 23, 1924

St. Bernard Makes Pal of Cat

"It was Alma that got on my nerves. The minute I saw Alma I knew that she was one of those creatures that needed looking after. Such a thin, piddling mew! Such a tail! A child would disdain to pull it.

"I did the best I could for Alma. I invited her to eat out of my dish. She spit at me. I told her she could, if she wished, play with my ear. She stuck up her back at me. I was not used to such treatment. Wherever I have gone I have been a social success.

"And then, toward evening, the inmates of the jail here got in the habit of singing a song about "She's a Girl That Men Forget."

"I, myself, am very fond of music. My father, Roger Newfoundland, used to sing low G in the Ipswich lane quartet. But that song somehow, coupled with Alma's misconstruing of my motives, completed my unhappiness.

Runs Away From Jail

"When Deputy Sheriff Lloyd Lowther, as fine a man as ever lived, God bless him, led me out of the jail for a little air, I broke from behind him and ran and ran.

"I ran and ran and had just gained the railroad tracks when Elton Monagan and Robert Lucas caught up with me in a motorcycle.

"'Come doggie, pretty doggie,' they said. Immediately I melted. I allowed myself to be bundled into the motorcycle cart and brought back to the jail.

"What was my joy upon entering the jail to find Alma waiting for me with tears in her eyes. The minute she saw me she began to purr.

112

"And then to make the moment perfect the jail chorus struck up a new song. It was the "Long, Long Road to Tipperary.""

"Yes, I think I'm going to be very happy here. My friend Lowther says he's going to try to get me a little place in the country – not too big you know – just a sort of gentleman's place.

"In case he is successful I have only one request. It is that Alma may accompany me. She has already intimated that she is willing to go."

Chapter VI.

Demi-Tasse & Mrs. Grundy in The year 1924

Demi – Tasse

- and -

Mrs. Grundy

- by -

Josephine Van de Grift

16 July 1924, Wednesday:

THE American Magazine is urging more and better dinner parties. "If you were getting up an interesting and worth while group to be gathered around a dinner table," it says, "what five men or women out of history or out of present day life would you invite?"

Well, if there's one thing that is more fun than getting up a real dinner party, it is getting up a dinner party on paper. Mr. Crowell's muncher, however, is excessive. He evidently assumes that six persons, five guests and a host constitute the ideal number at dinner.

In reality the ideal dinner party consists of three persons of mellow temperament, three bottles of beer with no questions asked, and two and one-half feet fresh pumpernickel. These should be dropped down in some out of the way tavern where business is not too brisk and it is just barely possible that along about eleven o'clock one of the three might utter an observation worth remembering. Provided any one wanted to remember it.

But to comply with Mr. Crowell's suggestion. If I were getting up a dinner party I'd send my specially engraved stationary to the live ones and I'd pick them as follows:

Fred Sypher. Why I would pick Fred Sypher is a dead secret which the successful hostess should keep to herself.

Tom Reilly. Tom has been rolling cigars for so many years now that all bitterness and rancor have somehow passed him by and all that is left is sweetness and a capital anthology of Irish jokes.

Hervey Minns. Hervey never says anything that anybody would expect anybody to say and besides he knows how to hang a picture.

Col. Horn. Before the colonel lost money on the Horn Stock company he used to make money on a medicine show. Sold snake oil or something and he knows all the tricks.

I. S. Myers. When Tom Reilly ran out of jokes Ike Myers could say, "well now, Tom, that's like the two Irishmen that —"

It will be observed that these five are all men and inclined to be talkative. Naturally they will need good listeners. And so to be their dinner companions I would invite five comely members of the visiting nurses association.

---

17 July 1924, Thursday:

WE ALL of us, I dare say, have our pet methods of testing out the new comer of whom we are not quite certain.

My friend Eleanor Mangum, who is a brilliant musician, used to test out a prospective suitor by playing the piano to him. If he listened quietly he was considered eligible. If he showed a disposition to talk or to move about he might wait in vain for further invitations to Sunday night supper.

Recently I shared an apartment with a young woman who invariably asked a new acquaintance what he thought of Papini's Life of Christ. If he indicated that in his opinion Papini's Life of Christ was a tremendously useless piece of rewriting he was considered a desirable person to cultivate and was allowed to eat wheateas and milk with us at 2 o'clock in the morning.

––––––––––

Jake Falstaff tells me that it is a favorite device of his to ask a person what he thinks of Galsworthy. If the person so under fire declares that Galsworthy is one of his pet abominations he may henceforth consider himself blood brother to Jake Falstaff.

Personally I have always felt that a person who calls a waiter George or who professes to dislike onions is sure, sooner or later, to display appalling flaws of character.

The trouble with these tests is that none of them is infallible. A girl who depends for dates upon the men who approve of her piano playing will probably go stepping into the movies alone, and my friend Eleanor is still unwed. The person who says he abominates Galsworthy or Papini may merely be saying that to cover up the fact he hasn't read them. And many a man who says he dislikes onions is in reality surreptitiously addicted to them on off nights of the week.

––––––––––

There is, however, one test newly arisen which may safely be depended upon at all times. That is the Cross Word puzzle book.

Those who today are experiencing the delights of cross word puzzling are wondering what in the world people did when they didn't have anything to do but go to the movies. Men who formerly were known to be crack hands at bridge now sit up half the night to figure out the intricacies of a 14 lettered word that shall mean "an amphibious boat." The other morning at 3 o'clock an Akron professor gave his wife a prodigious thump in the ribs.

"I have it, Maris," he shouted, "I have it. The word for pest or scoundrel. It's s-c-h-e-l-m, schelm."

––––––––––

Chorus girls who a short time ago would not have given a snap of their garters for history, natural or otherwise, now plough through the encyclopedias looking up synonyms for calcareous lime stone and poisonous South American reptiles.

Naturally in their great enthusiasm they have wanted to pass on the cross word puzzle book to their friends. And these, generally, have proved responsive. Within two days a man who has been inoculated with the cross word puzzle germ may be seen going down the street a thin yellow book before him, a dictionary gripped under either arm. He will go up to an absolute stranger and plead for "a word with seven letters that shall mean 'to absolve.'"

Occasionally, however, a man upon being besought to help in a cross word solution will stare at the enquirer disdainfully.

"Huh," he will query, "whaddya get for doin' all that stuff?"

Such a man has a vulgar soul. He is the sort of person who sends in his name, and yours too, for free booklets and who collects the tops of breakfast food cartons for premiums.

Shun him.

⸺ ❦ ⸺

19 July 1924, Saturday:

NOT so many years ago there presided over the typewriter next to mine a young man with a cheerful bellow. His head was nobly shaped and those who were unaware that he was a struggling newspaper reporter invariably mistook him for an intern in a great hospital. Practically everybody said that some day you would hear from him.

Well, he has been heard from. Demi-Tasse and Mrs. Grundy acknowledges with pleasure the receipt of a letter from its first contributor. He is that same young man that needs to bellow so, he signs himself Le Gosse and he writes as follows:

———

"Many signs point to the inevitable success of your new colyum [sic]. Among them, the following:

"1. The colyumnist [sic] being innocent of matrimonial alliance, can be counted on not to use up any space with little Willie's embarrassing remark when the minister's toupe fell into the soup.

"2. Poetry being evidently "out," the colyum fan foresees unbelievable freedom from that space-filling atrocity: chainverse [sic].

"3. Above all, the colymnist can be trusted never to stoop to the gentle game of "teacher and pupil" in which the pupil says something nice about the teacher and the teacher copies it with comment, and the pupil then reprints the original remarks and the comment in order to comment again – and the whole merrily fills space – merrily for the teacher and pupil, but drearily for the innocent by-stander.

———————

"Success could be doubly assured by the adoption of the following resolutions:

"1. Never to mention a Fischer-Bistos wedding, a man named Taylor who owns a plumbing shop, or the firm of Black & White that sells coal and ice."

"2. Never, on pain of a crack in the demi-tasse and death for Mrs. Grundy, to mention that lowest form of humor: the typographical error.

"3. Etc.

———————

"Since something really constructive is now in order, I submit that an enterprise is best launched by a first annual banquet – so called because the new enterprise will some day be a year old if it lives long enough.

"It is my understanding that the main difficulty with a first annual banquet is that, because of scarcity of membership, it is difficult to crowd the festive board.

"Now, the only person who enjoys a banquet is the speaker and no one ever heard of a speaker refusing his invitation. So I suggest that at your first annual banquet everyone be invited as a speaker.

———————

"To relieve" you of unnecessary headwork, I suggest the following invitation list:

"Gus Wenhart, Joe Sieber, Kyle Ross, the Akron smoke Inspector, Fred Hagloch, Gus Kasch, Bill Clerkin, Frank O'Nell, Bob Noelker, E. L. Martings, and Minnie Ellot.

"I have furnished the list. Now I leave to you the order in which they will speak. Just keep in mind that the first will be last."

———— ❦ ————

21 July 1924, Monday:

ONE MORNING a couple of years ago my boss said to me, "Go out and get a story on this bird McFee."

"Who," I queried, "Is this bird McFee?"

My boss gave me a withering look. Afterwards, "Something people think he's a second Conrad," he explained. "Goes to sea. Writes high brow stuff."

I was so filled with respect at this announcement that I went to the public library. They were out of "Casuals of the Sea" but they had "Allens" and "Captain Macedoine's Daughter," I bolstered myself on these for two days and then I went to see the bird McFee whose first name happened to be William.

He was down polishing the vitals of the ship and when he came up he had on blue overalls and there was a smudge of grease across one cheek. We had a right pleasant time and later we went out someplace for tea where if I recall correctly the bird McFee ate three chocolate eclairs in rapid succession.

The two stories which I wrote on him were immediately consigned to the waste basket and to this circumstance I attribute the fact that we are still friends. But woman's place, asserts McFee, is in the harem, and every once in a while there arrives a letter pounding home the point.

"By the way, how amusing you American woman are," he writes in the latest one, "You buck and rear and gibe at the word 'obey' in the marriage ceremony, obeying a man that is, who works all the time for you, who gives you everything from the skin out to wear, and who thinks all the time about your comfort, but you think nothing of obeying a boss who probably forgets you as soon as he leaves the office."

That the boss does forget is, of course, as it should be. But Mr. McFee has touched upon a theme which it seems to me has never been adequately handled by the fictionists – the devotion of the average working girl to her employer.

————————

I had dinner not so long ago with a business woman who hazarded the guess that at least 80 per cent of the stenographers were in love with their bosses. The boss of course may not be aware of this. If he is aware of it, it should make him a better man.

For to the working girl the boss occupies a position only a little less exalted than God's and certainly more substantial. He has done things. People obey him. He is the source of the working girl's food and clothing and of her long expected raise. Generally he is kind. And at night when the working girl has gone home and has put on her bungalow apron to help do up the dishes and wash out her other pair of silk stockings, the boss, clad in carefully creased evening clothes, is moving among other men of the world, flicking ashes from the end of his cigarette and uttering drawing room witticisms in a well modulated voice.

————————

Or so the working girl fancies. The boss stands for better things. The working girl adores him. I rather imagine she keeps her adoration to herself. It is her one tremendous secret.

Here is a story which O. Henry might have written.

There was a girl who was in love with one of the head men. She was a stenographer in one of those big offices where the typewriters click by battalions.

He was young and attractive and unmarried. She used to pray that some day he would notice her. And at night she would sit up late to put fresh collar and cuffs on her little blue serge dress.

One Saturday night she and a girl friend went for a walk. They were feeling a little giddy, and so they rouged up their faces and applied the eye brow pencil and the lip stick rather freely. And they pulled their hats down over one eye and practiced an exaggerated walk which they had observed on a movie actress. Then they made for Main st.

The second block or so a long low car drew up to the curb. Two men were in it. "Come on, girlies," they called, "hop in and we'll take a ride."

The girl, who had prayed that her boss would notice her, suddenly became aware of a queer feeling. For there he was. And he was noticing her. And he was in a car. And he was asking her to take a ride.

But he hadn't recognized her. He didn't know anything about that girl who for his sake had cut down on her lunches so she could have a marcel wave. And he thought she was one of those — those — And he was that kind of man.

And so she didn't accept the invitation to ride.

Instead she went home and cried about it.

25 August 1924, Monday:

W HEN "Monsieur Beaucaire" was made into a light opera two or three years ago they gave the piece a "happy" ending. In other words they married Beaucaire off to the Lady Mary Carlisle.

Consequently it was with considerable joy that I entered the Orpheum the other day and discovered that in the movie version Beaucaire goes back to France and makes love to Bebe Daniels.

This is as it should be. Any woman with half an eye could have told Beaucaire that Bebe was the girl for him. But you know how men are when you try to tell them anything.

That Lowell Sherman who directed the piece and Rudolph Valentino who stages his come back in it should have made the ending so eminently satisfactory shows that the world isn't such a bad place after all.

But Valentino probably learned a lot about beauties when he was staging his Mineralava contests.

———————

The matter of what constitutes a happy ending is largely a matter of perspective. When Ibsen wrote his "Doll's House" and the piece was produced in a German theater the people went into an uproar because Nora left her husband and children and went out upon her own. The clamor became so great that Ibsen re-wrote the last act and omitted the slamming of the front door. He said that he preferred to do the sacrilege himself than to let somebody else do it.

How would any woman look upon such a proceeding today? "Send Nora back to that dud of a Torvald?" she would query. "I guess not. Let her go out and make her own life and then some day she'll meet some man who is worthy of her."

I can remember that at one time in my life it seemed to me that the summit of happiness would be to marry the grocer's boy and settle down in Sandusky, Ohio. His name, I seem to recall, was Oscar.

———————

A man may be a devoted son, a charming friend, rational in his business, a maker of sensible speeches at the Rotary luncheons and yet when it comes to his love affairs you never can tell.

I met a man only the other day who admitted it. A friend of his had become enamored of one of those bits of fluff that look so well from the fifth row. She despised him and she showed it. She lied to him, sneered at his offerings, told him how much she despised him and openly showed her preference for other men. Still he groveled. And finally when she went off with another man he attached himself to another piece of fluff as near like the first one as possible.

The man to whom I was talking said that he thought this grew from a kink in men's natures that made them try to make up for their other short comings with a blind, unreasoning devotion.

To a woman there will never be any extenuating circumstances. To her it is all plain foolishness on a par with that passage from Samuel Papys in which having gone to the theater, he says: "I sitting behind in a dark place, a lady spit backward on me by a mistake, not seeing me, but after seeing her to be a very pretty lady, I was not troubled at it at all."

———————

Certain dollar-a-year men might consider to their profit the example of a cent-a-year man who died the other day in Columbia, S.C. He was "Uncle" Charles Jaggers born a slave who when still a boy started preaching "from the fence corners" and for 73 years never departed from his last: "Let this mind be in you which was also in Christ Jesus."

He earned the love and respect of white and black alike. With contributions from white friends he established a mission for his people and an old folks' home. He devoted much time to carrying his gospel to prisoners in chain gangs.

At the end of each year he accepted a salary of one cent. His services, he said, belonged to God.

And when he died the other day at the age of 93 the citizens of Columbia paused for 30 minutes to pay the old preacher tribute.

———◆———

9 September 1924, Tuesday:

IT SEEMS that Frank Lahey and John Harvey got into an argument as to who wrote the Lord's Prayer. Frank Lahey said it was Moses, and John Harvey said it was Jesus. So the other night we dropped into a book store ostensibly to buy a book, but in reality to take a peek at a Bible. Frank Lahey wasn't along, but Harry Bengston was. And **William Rigby**, keeper of the store who, it would appear, is a great student of the Bible, explained that so far as technicalities were concerned the Lord's Prayer was written neither by Moses nor by Jesus but by Matthew.

"Dictated but not read," was the way he put it.

This dropping in at the book store was merely one stop in an excursion which I understand Frank Lahey, Harry Bengston and John Harvey take nightly. As I said before Frank Lahey wasn't along and so I was graciously permitted to be the third.

At first there was the tremendous discussion as to where we should eat. This ended, as everybody knew it would, at the Rathskellar and my friends ordered liver and onions. It seems that one time when they were coming home from Cedar Point or maybe it was Niagara Falls they met a pretty girl whose father was a butcher. She asked them did they know what a fine combination liver and onions was and they said no they didn't, but that the next time they ate they would try it. They've been eating liver and onions every night since.

For my own part I dispensed with the liver in a sort of silent protest against pretty girls who turn men's heads and made up for it with some near beer in a stein with a pewter top on it.

After that we went down to Ferbstein's cigar store and shook dice. Harry Bengston made a dollar on 30 cents, and John Harvey made a dollar on, I think, 20 cents. Roots Beer, the little dark fellow who runs the soft drink stand, hung over the counter and watched. It seems that when Frank Lahey is along he always shakes with Roots Beer. And his luck is always very bad. It just goes to show how much better it is to take a girl along with you on such expeditions.

And then we went down to the Ku Klux store on S. Main st. and looked in the windows. On one side there was a whole row of Bibles and under them a banner, "100 per cent American." And on the other side there was some sheet music, "Here's to the Klan," "The Ku Klux Klan March," "It's a Grand Old Flag," and some paper covered books including "Peoria By Gaslight."

But the store was dark. I guess they were all gone to the circus.

And then, having settled the matter as to who wrote the Lord's Prayer, we clung perilously to the edge of the California fruit store and debated whether to go to the East

Market Gardens and watch 'em dance or go down to the Portage coffee room and have coffee. Coffee won.

But it was awfully quiet. T. B. Masterson was up at the counter eating and over in a corner two waitresses were watching a third waitress draw the floor plans of the house she is going to have someday when the rich old gesser [sic] comes in and notices she's the living image of his dead daughter.

John Harvey stretched, threw one leg over the other and flicked the ashes from a cigarette.

"You Americans," he said. "Now out on the street a while ago there was an automobile with 'Howdy' on the front of it. Why do you do that? And these bathing girls. They're stuck up all over the windows. They're even putting up fat bathing girls now. Why do you do it?

"And then wherever you go you see persons getting up on these weighing machines. Now in England no man would ever think of caring how much another man weighed.

"Here's a point. Not so long ago one of your politicians who was running for office was introduced to me. Right away he thrusts his card into my hand. He tells me that he belongs to the Elks and to such and such a club. That he goes to such and such a church, that he is married, that he has three children and I have to listen to what schools they are being educated at. All this to show that he's a fit candidate for office. And then, mind you, he tells me how much he weighs."

Mr. Harvey shook his head. The waitress who had been drawing the house came up.

"Anything else?" she queried.

<hr>

13 September 1924, Saturday:

ONE of the worst cases of insomnia which I have experienced was encountered on Thursday night following the address of Lieut. John A. Macready at the University club. Lieutenant Macready is a young man of attractive, not to say dapper, appearance, his voice is well modulated and he tosses off lightly, as a hero should, the perils of transcontinental aerial flight.

I understand he is recently married.

I think it was this element of romance coupled with peril entering in the young aviator's life which presented the problem with which I wrestled from 11 o'clock until the first faint strains of burnt toast from the house next door were wafted up next morning.

The problem was this:

There's a fellow and he's in love with a girl. The fellow is in the aviation service and he is about to set out on a flight that is almost certain to end in death. He and this girl are terribly stuck on each other and the girl makes a vow that if he is killed she will commit suicide so that they can join each other in the next world.

Well, the fellow goes off and so far as anybody knows he gets killed. They pick up the wrecked plane and parts of his clothing and all of the assistant pilot. But of course the fellow isn't really killed. What has happened is that he has had a terrible accident and has been knocked out of his head and is slowly nursed back to health by Eskimos.

The minute he gets back to his sense you can see what his state of mind would be. All the time that he is toiling back in a telegraph station he is tortured by the thought that the girl believes him dead and has killed herself. But just as he reaches the telegraph station he is struck with a sudden thought. If she has already done the deed a telegram won't help any. He will go back unannounced.

Well he gets back to the home town and staggers up to the University club which is all lit up with bright lights. He goes in and they're having a party. And what do you think it is? The girl who three months ago swore she would kill herself if he died is announcing her engagement to another man.

Now what I want to know is: Should the fellow be sorry she didn't mean what she said or be glad she was alive? Should he claim her for himself or be glad some other fellow was getting her?

Anybody who can answer this question satisfactorily will, contribute considerably to the sleep and repose of this department.

Orlando wants to know if this department knows that the Kind [sic] and Queen of England also made Victrola records. They each made a speech as Victoria day, he says, and then on the other side of the record something was rendered by the Coldstream Guards.

Orlando says that he thinks royalty ought to sing instead of making speeches. On one side of Queen Mary's record he thinks it would be nice if she would sing, "It Aint Gonna Rain No More," (on account of her always carrying an umbrella you know) and for the other side he suggests, "Mama Goes Where Papa Goes."

---

16 September 1924, Tuesday:

I WAS going up to my friend Miriam Beckwith's for luncheon the other day when I met a young man coming down the steps.

"Have you helped the student scholarships?" he queried.

"No," I answered cattishly, "and I don't want to."

The minute I got it out I was sorry. When people talk like that to me I hold it against them for years and years. I turned back with the intention of having a good heart to heart talk with the young man but he had disappeared. I wanted to ask him why he wanted to go to college anyway.

I suppose that for the young man who is planning to be a dentist or a surgeon or a mechanical engineer, there is a perfectly legitimate excuse for going to college. It is his apprenticeship to his trade. But there is a considerable number of us who go to college for an elusive something called Culture. Just before we are graduated from high school a lecture is delivered to us telling why we should go on to college. It is pointed out that college will round us out. The contact with better minds is described as being enormously stimulating. Then too the campus friendships are pointed out as being helpful in later life. It seems that they do almost as much good as belonging to the Elks or the Rotary club.

The boys go away from this lecture convinced that if they give four years to college they will make scads of money later on. The girls argue, at least subconsciously, that by going to college and getting invited into a sorority they will raise their social status and eventually make a better match. "And if Mary Elizabeth doesn't marry," argue Mary Elizabeth's women folks, "she can always teach."

———————

I was one of those who felt that if I didn't get to college, life wouldn't be worth living. I yearned for contact with better minds. And so I went to college. The first better mind that I encountered was that of a young Harvard prodigy who presided over the mathematics department. He was the most obnoxious Harvard prodigy I have ever known. He had an abiding scorn for all who were not as prodigious as he was and disdained to explain anything. The answers were written out on the board and you could take them or leave them. I don't know any more about trigonometry today than I did the day I was born. Back in high school I had loved geometry almost as passionately as I later came to love the Cross Work puzzle book.

———————

Seeing no hope for myself in mathematics I turned to French and English literature and some of the social sciences. I do not blame anyone for my failure in French. It is a language of which I am constitutionally incapable. As for the other things, they were pleasant but I would have gone a great deal further if I had taken an armful of books, a couple of apples and sat down by my own fireside to read. In all my life the books that have meant anything to me were those I read on the outside of school.

Because I was entered as a special student I may not have been entitled to belong to a sorority. I do not know. But I do know that I would never have been asked anyway. I don't remember whether I minded at the time. I probably did.

———————

There were two or three better minds in college that I would have liked to know but they were too busy to give me more than a passing good morning. The friendships that I had were those that I made on the outside and would have had anyway. The books that I read were those I could have read on the outside and would have read anyway.

After two year I left college and went into other things.

The most cultured friends I have had have been a dancer who was brought up in Potsdam and a chorus girl who ran away from a convent when she was in the first year of high school.

My friend Miriam Beckwith who had the full four years of college says that when her small son grows up she expects him to be a great man but that he is not going to college.

⁓

24 September 1924, Wednesday:

"NOW that the pictures of Harvey, Henry and Tom, occupied in the engaging business of accepting moss covered sap buckets from a much annoyed president preparing for a national political campaign, have disappeared from the first pages and the Sunday rotogravure sections," writes Sceptic, "one may reflect on the delightful bit of bosh without being accused of manufacturing a rival product.

———

"For several years, these industrial cronies, Harvey, Henry and Tom, have been spending a week or ten days together on what the press of the nation chooses to call "camping trips." These yearly gatherings have been heralded far and wide as reunions of bosom friends, stealing a few days from the demands of industry and commerce to discuss by the camp fire their mutual problems, whittle sticks and speculate as to 'what the country was comin' to.'

———

"In looking for a suitable location each year, Harvey, Henry and Tom would quite naturally be supposed, to the uninitiated at least, to seek out a quiet, delightfully rustic and peaceful spot where they would be able to shake off the __ and strife attending the manufacture and marketing of balloon tires and flivvers and the consuming efficiency of the scientific laboratory. One could well picture them whiling away the carefree hours under the shade of expensive trees, listening to the mellifluous trickle of the mountain brook over the jagged rocks and the shining body of the brook trout as it darted to the surface in pursuit of an overly careless fly. Yes, one could well picture them, in lazy content, sitting around the camp fire in the evening, inhaling the rarefied mountain air and viewing the striking beauty of a dying sunset.

––––––––––

"But as all illusions are apt to be rudely dispelled in this matter-of-fact age, sadly enough, the picture is not a true one. Instead of finding these three men of large business affairs in some such delightful retreat, beautiful for its proximity to nature in the rough, we discover a setting suspiciously resembling the commercialism and standardization of their own industrial plants.

"For these 'camping trips,' if you have heard them called by that name, bear little resemblance to those you have thought of in considering your ideal vacation. A complete electric light plant supplies excellent reading light to see what sort of 'splay' they got in the New York papers, a mammoth radio set enables them to tune in whenever the conversation lags, hot and cold water is on tap at demand, the food is prepared by an excellent city cook and alert personal servants see to it that Harvey, Henry, and Tom get the same sort of service they are accustomed to on Medina rd., Detroit or East Orange. In fact none of the comforts of city life is lacking, incongruous as they are, or rather supposed to be, on a camping trip.

"True enough, nature is there in a somewhat adulterated form; trees fringe the site, the camp fire burns, a stream is in the offing but the actual essentials of a true holiday, such as every schoolboy has dreamed of, are sadly lacking.

––––––––––

"Just why Harvey, Henry and Tom always have the same conception of a vacation site that appeals to the president, be he Warren or Cat, I must leave to your imagination. Perhaps they are anxious to absorb the views of the nation's chief executive at first hand, free from the restraints of a White House call and then again it may be because the president is usually photographed with his admirers about every 15 minutes and to have your picture taken with the president is good business and the finest kind of advertising. And best of all, it doesn't cost a cent.

––––––––––

"Since all three gentlemen are singularly adept at procuring the maximum amount of press comment on the most trivial of subjects, this idea of swapping ideas with the president away from Washington isn't a half bad one. After all, no other news source holds up quite as well as a president and his doings.

"Leopold and Loeb and 'The Wild Bull of the Pampas' may rule page one for a few days at a time but the president of the United States is a far more reliable news source and averages better over the year.

"We are not going to speculate on what Harvey, Henry and Tom talk about with Silent Cal but we are willing to wager a balloon tire against a bathing girl windshield sticker that Cal would a darn sign rather have talked to Senator Sorghum from Rhode Dakota on the general 'outlook for the ticket' in his state. But at any rate, the sap bucket picture occupied a prominent place in the press of the nation and that's about all the vacationists could hope for or possibly even cared about. As for Cal – well that's just part of the hell of running for office; you have to submit to almost anything.

"And we suppose that when Cal is reelected and vacation time rolls around next year, Harvey, Henry and Tom will decide they need a rest from the turmoil of industry and take a 'camping trip.'

"Predicting a location seems superfluous."

I see no need in commenting on "Sceptic's" remarks. After all, you know, I live in Akron.

---

25 September 1924, Thursday:

MR. I. S. CORMAN has picked Andrew Gump as the ideal presidential candidate. While this department is bored by politics, while it feels that no matter who is put into office the country will go on pretty much the same, still it cannot afford to let one statement of Mr. Corman's go unchallenged, namely, that Andrew Gump "does not ask your vote since he knows that you will give it to him willingly."

Has Mr. Corman ever observed the portraits of Mr. Gump? Does he know that Mr. Gump's chin is all Adam's apple? Is he aware that Mr. Gump will never be able to get into golfing togs owing to his inability to wear anything but a wing collar?

What sort of presidential face is this to be looking at one out of a thousand Sunday supplements?

No, notwithstanding his intellectual attainments there are a goodly number of persons who will not vote for Mr. Gump. They are the women of this fair land who feel that first beauty must be served.

This department has no objections to stating what its ideal presidential candidate is like. He is tall, his chin coming just above the brow – not his brow. He is slender, his closely knit figure showing that muscularity which comes only from years of eating at the very best clubs. He was born in a log cabin and spent his youth splitting rails, later matriculating at Harvard and taking a post graduate course at Oxford, (Eng.). During the formative years of his life he wrestled with the commercial world, this contact with the aggressive minds of his time giving him a keenness which is bound, if he is elected, to result in a sound business administration for this country. He is intensely idealistic being shy and retiring and has frequently withdrawn from a directors meeting to curl up in a corner with a good book. He takes two baths a day – a cold shower in the morning and a hot one at night just before getting into his dinner clothes. His favorite quotation is that one from Abraham Lincoln which runs, "God must have loved the common people – he made so many of them," and remembering the circumstances of his own early environment he will sit for hours on a cracker box exchanging anecdotes with the "folks back home." On the other hand the sterling quality of his ancestry is shown in the manner in which he carries a tea cup across a drawing room floor. His clothing, while impeccable in style and cut, has that air of careless ease about it denoting the man whose thoughts are on other things than "sartorial" refinement. Although a Presbyterian in faith he has broad religious views and once amused his friends by remarking that in his opinion a Chinaman had as much chance of getting to Heaven as he did. He uses Pebeco tooth paste and ivory soap and has frequently made the remark "when in doubt order roast beef and apple pie." His favorite books are "When a Man's a Man" by Harold Bell Wright, the Bible and Shakespeare.

I happened to remark this afternoon that I had once been in Paul Terry's studio and my friend Ike Friedman immediately spoke up and said that there were a lot of folks who were just crazy to know how the animaled cartoons for Aesop's Fables are made.

Come to think of it there are a lot of points that I'm not very sure of myself. The girl who took me around the place was the only girl cartoonist in the studio. She was a might pretty girl and a little while later she became Mrs. Paul Terry. As I remember it, it went something like this:

First Paul Terry makes a complete scenario of the fable. He divides the fable into scenes and in each scene he indicates how many motions of each animal are required. The scenario is then cut up into parts and the parts handed out to the cartoonists. In the room I was in about 20 cartoonists were working before their drawing boards.

Suppose one of the cartoonists receives a scene showing a cat tying on an Easter bonnet. He makes his initial drawing of the cat and over it he lays a sheet of tissue paper. On this tissue paper he makes a second drawing identically like the first except that the cat's arms are moved a bit in the directions of her bonnet. Another piece of tissue paper is laid on and the performance is repeated except that the cat's arms are moved a little more. Six drawings in all may be required to get the cat's paws up to her head. When these drawings are flashed rapidly on the screen in succession they give the effect of motion.

It can be seen how that the tissue-paper-copying method is necessary in order that the original proportions of the cat may not vary. After these outlines are completed they are transferred to regular paper and the details blackened in. Then all the scenes are assembled in their order, fastened together and run through a camera and photographed. I don't remember any more how many individual drawings are required for one short fable but as I recall it the number is prodigious. Also I may have slipped on some of the details but I think I have the main idea straight.

Incidentally it seems to me that these fables are about the best thing on the screen today.

—⦁⦁⦁—

2 October 1924, Thursday.

WE were speaking the other day of some of the sentimental notions with which women have saddled themselves.

Probably the most persistent of these is the notion that the noblest thing a woman can do is to bring a child into the world.

Granting that all women are fit for motherhood which they aren't, does the woman who has succeeded in bringing one colicky infant into being think that her work in any way compares with that of the nurse who stills the wailing of 10 colicky infants? Or of the school teacher who gives her life to teaching us our transitive verbs and to hand a scissors with the handle away from us? Or of the music teacher who first shows us that just as surely as the dominant goes to the tonic too will joy succeed sorrow? Or of the old maid who wears her 1854 black serge model another year so the twins down the road can have a baby carriage?

I think not.

———

Another notion is that virtue has something to do with goodness. The very formation of the word virtue shows that it is a man made thing. So far as I have been able to discover virtue had its beginning back in the time when people were beginning not to live in packs. No man wanted to be bringing in rabbit skins to wrap some other man's bye baby bunting in. And so he impressed upon the woman how necessary it was for her to remain faithful to him alone.

It seems to me, seeing that biology is likely to remain uninfluenced by the suffrage vote, that this is an ideal arrangement. But women should remember that it is purely an economic arrangement.

And when some other woman becomes prodigal and throws discretion to the winds they should bestow upon her the same tolerance which they extend to the heiress who gives her all to charity.

———

Another notion is that there is something beautiful about the wife who forgives. And forgives. And forgives. A year or so ago there was a stage play called "Secrets" which has now been made into a movie. In one of the scenes the husband admits the numerous occasions on which he has been unfaithful. And the wife weeps great tears and says, "I know what you want to tell me. You want to tell me that through it all you loved me just the same." And the man says, "Yes."

My friend to whom I was speaking said that this scene made her especially furious. "Can you fancy," she demanded, "a woman getting away with anything like that?"

And it is true. It is such sickly sentimentality as this, expressed in the movies, expressed in the "moral" plays of the stage, expressed in popular literature everywhere, which has given men the notion that no matter what they do women will still forgive and weep and cling.

I think it is Edward Carpenter who has pointed out that in order for the clinging vine to survive it must eventually throttle the sturdy oak in which it so beautifully adheres.

Another notion is that the race must be carried forward and that noble sons must be produced in order to carry on the great work.

I am not at all sure that the race is worth saving. It has produced Fords and airplanes and phonographs and electric lights. But it has not gotten much beyond the jurisprudence of Moses or written a greater play than Oedipus Rex or found out much about the peccadilloes of man that Gautama didn't seem to know.

All our improvement has been along materialistic lines. To be sure we don't burn witches any more but we burn Negroes. We don't cage up cats and roast them alive to exorcise the devil, but some doctors not so long ago poked a dog for five days with sticks to see how long it could go without sleeping.

9 October 1924, Thursday:

WHEN I had occasion to speak with the Rev. Mr. Jones the other day I asked him what he thought of Rupert Hughes' article on "Why I Quit Going To Church." The Rev. Mr. Jones replied that to anyone who knew his Bible the remarks of Mr. Hughes were just simply laughable.

It would seem now however that the Rev. Mr. Jones is either woefully ignorant of the bible himself or that he has deliberately falsified the Bible in order to indulge in a cheap witticism. I refer to his remarks quoted in Wednesday's Beacon Journal on David, Bathsheba and the window shades.

Since Mr. Jones is a stickler for the veracity of the Bible it might not be amiss to call his attention to the fact that God was so little interested in the matter of feminine attire that he created woman with no clothing at all.

And it might not be amiss also to remark to Mr. Jones that if he will keep his thoughts on God and holy things he will not be troubled by whether women are walking on the shady or the sunny side of the street nor by their paucity of petticoats.

So far as the value of a religious revival to the community is concerned it seems to me that if one has a taste for vulgarity and obscenity it is a more honest thing to go to a burlesque house. In a burlesque house one can hear locus remarks, bad jokes and crude English which do not masquerade under the name of religion.

Songs of Love

I love the motormen. They stop the car when they see me running. They leave their places to help the crippled, the blind and the old ladies up the steps. They put on the brakes when they see a puppy playing in the tracks. When they pass another motorman they clang their bells. They are a happy lot. They are swell guys.

I love the conductors. When a kid hasn't got a penny for his transfer they pay it out of their own pockets. They josh the cops. They hold your packages while you hunt for a nickel. They change your five dollar bills and grin. They have to drink cold coffee out of a milk bottle. They help the crippled, the blind and the old ladies off the cars. I bet their kids are glad when they see them coming home.

I love the Traveler's Aid. When you're in a strange town they tell you which hotel you can afford. They help you out with trains and advice and time tables. If you're broke they fix you up. If your heart's busted they fix that up too. And if you're a foreigner and can't speak the language they tag you and telegraph ahead and get you to where you're going.

I love men. You can kid 'em and they take it. They swear and cuss and dig down into their pockets to help somebody out. They get nagged at home and eat their breakfasts in the one arm lunch and never let out a yelp. They crack bum jokes, go to burlesque shows, drink bad hooch and pray to God on the q.t.

I love women. They see some other girl getting the fellow they want and never let slip a sigh. They carry home the pay envelope to the old folks. They fix up the boss's dictation so the world won't know he splits his infinitives. The married ones bake lemon meringue pie so Pa won't get too mad when he sees Johnny's report card. They keep a home and three kids going on a ten dollars a week.

I love Akron. It's paving more streets all the time. It's gone and built beautiful King school. It's got a swell children's home. It gives a lot of people jobs. It's got dandy street cars. It's got a beautiful viaduct except on the top where it's cracking a little. It's surrounded by swell hills good for poetry, painting or wiener roasts. It's got interesting people, like John Durkin and Bill Haynes.

16 October 1924, Thursday:

A MAN and a woman fall in love, with one another and, unwilling to stoop to intrigue, openly declare their affection and elope.

The woman's husband grants her a divorce.

The man's wife grants him a divorce.

There is nothing for the lovers to do now but marry and live happily ever after.

Both are the details of the Hall-Quest-Hart quadrangle.

All four parties in the case have acted honorably. The divorces and remarriage are in perfect accord with the modern notion that two persons who love one another have a right to be together. If "perfect passion" ruled the actions of two of the parties, certainly perfect sanity marked the actions of the discarded mates. They were not wanted. They gave up without struggling. Those members of society who incline to the modern way of looking at things will receive the passionate lovers without comment. The others will soon forget them.

And still one wonders whether the passionate lovers will be happy.

I heard the other day of a similar case. A man and a woman had fallen in love, had divorced their respective mates and had married one another. For a while they were very happy. Then a trouble began to manifest itself. They both recognized it and talked about it frankly. The woman began to have a little gnawing regret that she had brought pain to her first husband. She began to remember little things that they had planned.

The man began remembering little tricks that his first wife had had. He wished he had been kinder to her. He saw, too, that a second wife can be just as irritating as the first.

Gradually it dawned upon them that no love can be perfect which is built upon the unhappiness of another.

There have been those who have argued that a system of free love would avert all the heartaches that men and women cause one another. But I have lived among those who were free lovers and it seemed to me that their troubles were the same as those who had gone to church and been properly blessed.

So long as they were true to one another they were happy. But as soon as the fancy of one began to wander then there were tears, and recriminations and broken hearts.

Generally it was the fancy of the man which wandered first. I do not know whether men are naturally polygamous, or whether they are so large hearted that they can be true to a great many women at once or whether they have merely arrogated to themselves certain privileges.

What I do know is that so long as women cling fiercely to the idea of being faithful to one man, so long as women are handicapped by their natures as women, free love will not solve the problem. It merely takes away the protections which the law has thrown about the woman and her offspring.

I know a young man of considerable fortune who married while still in college. Shortly after his marriage he became imbued with a fierce idealism which included the right to love wherever the fancy led. Today he is living on a farm. In one house is his wife and three children. In another is another woman and her child – hers and his.

The man is a cultured man and is respected by the whole countryside as a good neighbor and a good farmer. He loves both women. The wife does not agree with her husband's notions but she stays with him because she loves him. She is a good sport and tries not to let the other girl see how she suffers. The other girl agrees with the man's theories – in theory. She has borne disgrace and banishment for his sake. But she is jealous of the wife.

And not one of the three is happy.

I sometimes think that human beings would get along better if they attached less importance to love and more importance to work. The animals have their mating seasons and after that they go about the world's business.

I do not know how true this is but I have been told by a surgeon that human beings would not be so heavily laden with sex if they would eat less highly seasoned foods. If they would learn to drink in moderation, if they would exercise more and if they would purge their literature and their theater of its sentimentality.

Certainly this is true: that if one is devoted to one's work, one's work rewards one in proportion.

Devotion to another human being, on the other hand, frequently has the result merely of boring the other human being.

Occasionally it even results in leaving one with only a large and beautiful sack to hold.

⁓ꝫꝫ⟡ꝫ⟡⟡ꝫ ⁓

4 November 1924, Tuesday:

COMPARED with the life of this planet your life and mine is pitifully short. We have at best possibly 20 years to go yet.

We believe, you and I, that there is a God but we do not know whether he is an old man with whiskers or whether he is the thing that makes the atoms whirl.

We do not know whether there is a heaven or whether we shall live after we have died. We do not know where we came from nor why one man is a genius and another joins lodges.

All that we do know is that we are here and that we have each other. Why then should we spend our handful of years in making each other miserable?

The other day as I was on my way to a gathering of the Ku Klux Klan I rode for a time beside a woman who, as women are sometimes known to do, started in telling me her life history. She said that a few years ago she had taken over the management of a hotel which people had said couldn't exist any more on account of prohibition.

"But I took it over anyway," she said, "and I made money out of it."

"But you aren't running it now," I told her.

"No," she said, "I'm not. I gave it up because it didn't give me any time to go to camp meetings. The good of my soul meant more to me than a few paltry dollars."

"The good of my soul" in this woman's case meant an arrogant satisfaction that she was going to heaven and that a lot of poor devils weren't. She was a comely woman and I have an idea that before the camp meetings got hold of her she was kind hearted.

Late that night I slept in the hotel whose management she had abandoned. It was an interesting enough place but I think that if she hadn't gone away to the camp meetings there would have been a mirror in the bathroom.

Now I was born white, Nordic and Protestant but I cannot see why I deserve any special credit for that. I might just as easily have been born black or yellow. And I might have been abandoned on a doorstep and adopted by a family of Seventh Day Adventists.

Over in the vicinity of New York city there is a founding asylum over which for quite a time a battle raged as to whether the children should be brought up Catholic or Protestant. It was finally decided that every other child should be brought up Catholic, every other child Protestant.

It was Heywood Brown, I think, who drew the engaging picture of some little blue-eyed Irish kid leaving that institution when he grew up and joining the Masses and saying," Now I have no prejudices against the Catholics, some of my best friends are Catholics but I really think that when it comes to politics –"

As a matter of fact this talk about the United States of America being a Protestant Christian country is blah. Its status among other countries is that of heathenism pure and simple. The constitution states it plainly. Turkey, following the Moroccan troubles, refused to treat with us until we had convinced her we were not a Christian country.

Considering the things that are done in the name of Christ this is not a particularly hard impeachment.

A few years ago when we were having a war I believed in my innocence that it was only Germans who perpetrated outrages. Later when the war, but not human hate, was over,

I believed that the Ku Klux Klan was made up of ignorant, stupid louts whose passions were being played upon by religious demagogues.

But I know now that we are all alike. I have seen hate in high places as well as low. I have seen it on the faces of women who were the givers of life and on the faces of men who were the takers of life. And it seemed to me that on the whole the givers of life were more vindictive.

In the name of Christ we lynch and kill and ostracize.

In the name of Christ we seek to take bread from the Jew and give it to our Protestant lodge brother.

In the name of Christ we seek to keep down those who are down because we know in our hearts that some day they shall rise and then it shall be we who are lynched and killed and ostracized.

But we are here such a little while. I wish that we might be kinder to one another.

And I wish that that man who called up a while ago for some information to settle a bet would give me that large box of candy that he promised.

---

7 November 1924, Friday:

LAST night "Peter Ibbetson" fell out of the book case and before I put it back I read over again certain parts of the idyllic childhood of Mimsey and Gogo.

I have often wondered why authors delight in drawing childhood as such a happy time. Are there ever any children so happy and so innocent as all that or do authors paint these pictures much as a starving man dreams of food?

Sometimes when they have been in the mood for it I have talked with others about their childhood. They have all told me the same thing. Not for anything would they live it over again. A school teacher told me the other day that no girl ought to be born until she was 21.

For one thing childhood is a time of arrant snobbery. I remember when I started to school in Shelbyville, Ind. there was a little girl there named Anna whose father was spending two years in the penitentiary. This ordinarily would have been enough to damn any child but it so happened that Anna's papa in spite of his misfortune, he was a forger, had so placed his money that his family was comfortably fixed. Anna was the best dressed child in school. Consequently she was petted, pampered and had enough licorice doll babies lavished on her to give her indigestion for life. Whenever she walked home at night there was an admiring bevy of little friends accompanying her, twining their arms around her waist and tying and untying her hair ribbons.

Now over by the railway tracks there was a family of poor whites whose father had stabbed a man and then disappeared. The mother of the poor whites took in washing. Each morning the poor whites came to school and stared, lonely, dirty and big eyes, at the other children. Not for anything would we have played with them. Their father was a criminal. Their mother took in washing.

There was never any talk of what Anna's father had done. Anna lived in a red brick house on the hill and the family had two servants and drove a carriage with two horses. Whenever one of us was invited to Anna's house to play we boasted about it openly.

If children, up until the time they enter their teens, are good at all it is either because they are mighty clever deceivers or that they have singularly unquestioning minds. They may be good because they are afraid of a licking or they may be good because their trust in the superior wisdom of their elders has never been outraged. But of goodness, is, of and by itself they have no inkling.

What they do seem to have is an inordinate desire for justice and this is the thing that makes middle-childhood so painful. A boy of 10 has nothing but his regard for his elders to cling to. He tells a lie and his father takes him out in the wood shed and dusts him for it. But a day, a week or a month later the boy hears his father tell his mother how he has strangely misplaced the gas money when the boy knows all the time that the money went into a poker pot.

Another time the boy extracts a dollar bill from the bureau drawer, blows it in on ice cream cones and suckers for the gang and when he is found out he is threatened with hell fires. But neither that boy's parents nor any other parents can deny at some time having taken part in some such colloquy as this:

"Ms. when're you going to give me back that five dollars?"

"What five dollars?"

"Why that five dollars you took out of my bank to pay the grocery bill with. You said you'd give it right back."

"Well of all things. Didn't Papa and I buy you a new overcoat just last week? The trouble with you is that you're ungrateful. You never appreciate a thing that's done for you."

In such little domestic passes as this is the faith of our childhood broken. And a little while later comes a severe test of our faith in God.

During all of eight years or so we have heard how that God knows all our badness, how if we were to do certain things lightning would flash from heaven and strike us dead.

Along comes a day when in a fit of either despair or braggadocio we decide to put things to a test.

"Oh damn," we cry, "damn it to hell."

And nothing happens.

---

11 November 1924, Tuesday:

THE Romantik when she was a child reading Pilgrim's Progress for the first time used to slip pieces of dried beef between the leaves. She could then read ahead secure in the conviction of at sometimes or other coming upon refreshment and this device, I darn say, helped enormously in getting poor Christian over the hard places.

The other day when the Romantik took Pilgrim's Progress out of the book case to dust it she was surprised to find small bits of those early lunches still clinging to the leaves. I suppose she will always think of Christian in terms of dried beef.

The habit of eating and reading is pretty firmly ingrained in us, having its origin I suppose in the thought that if the mind is being refreshed it is only fair that the body should be strengthened too. But then benefits of the system are not all of them immediate. To those of us who are averse to marking books with pencils a few dried crumbs between a couple of leaves may in after years be the sole means of reconstructing the mood of a book's first reading.

There is that poem in "Alice in Wonderland" where the Duchess explains how she always spanks the baby when he sneezes. There is a little flurry of dried stuff there smelling faintly of tobacco. You remember then. There was a young fellow just home from work. He swung you up on his lap and read to you. That little bit of dried stuff was tobacco from his pipe.

You take up "Little Women." There is a great smudge of grape jelly where Beth lies dying. That is because you cried so hard at that point you forgot what you were eating and the jelly dripped down through the holes in the bread.

In "The Light That Failed" there is a round spot on the page where the girl rips up the painting. That is because you were cooking cabbage that day. You held the book in one hand and in the other hand a long fork to turn the cabbage with. You had just turned the page to where that horrible girl did that horrible thing. You cried out and forgot to put the fork down. The cabbage broth dripped down to the page.

Twenty years from now if I take up "A Story Teller's Story" I will remember how on the Sunday that I read it I sat by the kitchen table and ate hot dogs. I will remember by the round splotches of butter along certain of the leaves [sic].

My friend Grace Brown likes to mark books up with pencils. I took up a book of short stories by Katherine Mansfield which she had the other day and I found certain passages all underlined and crossed. Grace says she likes to do this because in later years it amuses her to see what words and sentences appealed to her as time goes by.

But I would die rather than voluntarily reveal to anyone what parts of a book were the ones that really moved me. I will gladly tell anyone the condition of the family finances or even my age. But words and sentences are something else again – they can reveal terribly intimate things.

That is why I will not mark my own books and yet I love to get hold of a book that some one else has marked. I had such a one from the public library once. It was a copy of "The Autocrat of the Breakfast Table." Along the margins of it some placid soul had gone along writing, "Oh, fie, Dr. Holmes," or, "True indeed, Dr. Holmes."

Can you fancy any thing lovelier than to take up a collection of the writings of Robert Ingersoll published twenty years ago in which one of the earlier ladies of Tallmadge, say, had inscribed her reactions?

I had thought that I couldn't read a book through anymore but I find now that I was wrong. In "A Story Teller's Story" Sherwood Anderson endeavors to reveal himself in four books and an epilogue. It is a thick book but I interrupted the sitting only once.

In the early pages where he tells about his father, and how the family lived in a succession of haunted houses because the rent was free I kept saying to myself, "Yes, you are grinning like a ninny over this now but someday some one will come along who knew the Anderson family and they will tell you that it is all a lie."

In the back part of the book Anderson placidly admits that parts of it are lies but then, he explains, he has lied to get at the essence of truth.

This is one of those things that you think you understand until you try to explain it to some one else.

***

13 November 1924, Thursday:

THE Civic Drama association is putting on "Fashion" in about a week. This is the play which Miss Edgeworth – I think her given name was Maria – wrote back in 1845 as a stirring rebuke to the social apings of her time.

The other night I chanced to pick up certain of the "Miscellanies" of Edgar Allen Poe and came across the following:

"Miss Edgeworth seems to have only an approximate comprehension of 'Fashion,' for she says: 'If it was the fashion to burn me, and I at the stake, I hardly know ten persons of my acquaintance who would refuse to throw on a fagot.'

"There are many who, in such a case (comments Poe) would 'refuse to throw on a fagot' – for fear of smoothing out the fire.'

From which I gather than Maria, like all social castigators, had none too easy a time of it.

When the New York Theater Guild last season put on "Fashion" as a sort of lark, reproducing the painted scenery of the tin fights of 1845 it straightway became the fashion to go see it, but I was at that time either too indolent or too poor – I forget which – to look into the matter for myself.

After I had watched the Civic Drama association going through its production rehearsal over at the Playhouse the other night I felt doubly sorry.

"Fashion," so far as I was then able to make out, concerns the social aspirations of a certain Mrs. Tiffany who is anxious to get her daughter Seraphina married off to a count. That the count is bogus is apparent to the audience from that very moment in the first act when the French maid, coming on to the scene and beholding him, given a startled screech.

The count's true status however does not become apparent to Mrs. Tiffany until along about 11 o'clock in the evening and in the meantime Mr. Tiffany has been almost ruined by the machinations of a wicked business partner, innocence has been pursued and driven beside itself by the enticements of the count, tremendous asides, have been broadcast to the audience, and a great many 100 per cent American truths have been uttered by an honest individual from the backwoods, who in contrast to Mrs. Tiffany, represents those stern values that come from a contact with the soil.

At the conclusion of the piece, the count being put to shame and the rest of the cast being paired off satisfactorily they all assemble in front of the curtain and recite the moral of the play which has been set down in heroic couplets. They may possibly also grasp one another about the waist and dance. I do not know.

There was a time in my life when I yearned to be an actress. This aspiration was stifled by certain combinations of circumstances which it would not help any to go into now. Besides I now think that it would be much pleasanter to be a director.

Miss Joyce Benner is directing "Fashion." Her first duty in this capacity was to cut the piece down from five acts down to three – a really monumental task because practically all the speeches in "Fashion" are just grand.

The next thing was to see about painting the scenery. I do not know the technical names for all those files and drops which constitute the masonry of the stage but when you go to see "Fashion" you will observe that most of the drawing room furniture consists of some highly gilded chairs painted along the front curtain. And you will observe too that the conservatory, so long and so lovingly dwelt upon in the first act, consists of a row of geranium pots painted at the rear.

Miss Benner's next task was to go among her friends and plead with them to search their attics for frocks and breeches of the 1845 period – a task which she is still pretty much engaged in.

And now finally she has to superintend the rehearsals. Superintending rehearsals so far as I have been able to make out, is a great deal of fun. The cast is always just chock full of merriment and no matter how much it may forget its lines it never gets the least bit ruffled but steps out of the wrong wing with the greatest composure in the world.

<hr />

29 November 1924, Saturday:

I HAVE never been one of those who got on particularly well with children and hence I am unable to understand the tremendous pride which overcomes me when, on walking down the street with somebody else's offspring, I perceive that I am being mistaken for their parent.

Something of the sort happened yesterday. I had gone shopping with Steve and Herman, late of the Children's home, and as we were battering our way down the aisle of an Arlington st. car on the homeward trip a perfectly charming woman arose and touched my arm.

"Won't you let me offer you my seat," she said. "I see that you have your children with you and it would be dreadful if you should get separated."

I then perceived that I was being mistaken for the parent not only of Steve and Herman but of two little girls who stood by as well. Flushing with pleasure I shoved Steve and Herman into the seat thus vacated and regarded them surreptitiously from under my hat brim.

Herman, I reflected, I could easily palm off as my own. There was a strong Teutonic strain in us both. But Steve was hopeless. His eyes were dark and his lashes long and curling. The best I could do in a pinch would be to explain that he took after the other side of the family.

As for the two little girls, both of them brunette, they had been recaptured by their mother.

<hr />

This shoving Steve and Herman in to a vacant seat was a thing which I had said I would never, never do. What I should have done was to take it myself or else require Steve and Herman to stand and offer it with a flourish of their cape to some nice old lady with curls. As a matter of fact after I had shoved them into the seat I stood guard over them to see that they didn't budge. Their feet, I reflected, were a great deal tireder than mine or anybody else's in the car. They had gone up and down countless aisles, climbed numberless stairs, been stepped upon, trampled, pushed and battered. When a woman sitting next to Herman showed signs of being annoyed because he sideswiped her with his foot I told him to move over in a loud voice but at the same time I gave her a look.

This being an amateur parent, even for an hour or so, is a severe check to any spinster who has ideas of her own on how to bring up children.

There is the matter of behavior at the table for instance.

I cannot recall that when I was a child the numerous aunts and grandmothers who had a hand in bringing me up ever had any trouble in getting me to eat. I always ate everything in sight and this characteristic has persisted to the present day. I had a cousin, however, who would eat nothing but jam and pickles. The aunts always threw up their hands when this cousin came to visit and declared they didn't know what her mother was thinking of. Taking my cue from these I early resolved that any children I had a hand in bringing up would always eat what was set before them and would learn to use their forks at the age of two.

Yesterday, however, when Steve made a dive for the cubes in the sugar bowl I grossly encouraged him to take four more. And when Herman smeared chocolate all over his chin and later endeavored to make a concoction of his own by mixing the remnant of his ice cream with the remainder of the ice water and then drinking it I was merely relieved that the child was happy.

All in all it is probably a good thing that at least a small percentage of our children fall into the hands of the kind, wise nurses at the Children's home. Else they would never eat their spinach, never drink their milk, would wheedle themselves out of the tooth brush drill and probably go to bed with the wrong kind of prayers.

Today's column is contributed by the 12-B English students of West high school, taught by Miss Cora Bochstahler.

"MUSICIANS are all crazy," wrote someone for the "Demi-Tasse and Mrs. Grundy" column of the Beacon Journal. For that matter nearly everyone is a little off. If a person were normal, had no peculiar habits, pet sayings, or favorite superstitions people would look at him and say "something's the matter with him." So he wouldn't be "all there" to some people, regardless of how he was.

Everyone is "funny" somewhere. "Zupplie," the famous football coach, never comes on the gridiron without his overshoes. When he came onto the field once he saw that the cheering section had been changed and he raised such a howl that before the game started the cheering section was back in its regular part of the bleachers.

So it doesn't matter if the musician is a little crazy, we are all in the same boat and we couldn't be normal to some people no matter how we tried.

HARRY CURNOW.

Good writers have some sort of inspirations. When I have a story to write the only thing I do is to visit a shop window and get my inspiration. Knowing I had a story to write today I went downtown last night and stopping in front of a large department store said, "The next window I come to I will get my inspiration." I approached the next window and lo! It was empty.

WILLIAM ROTHSCHILD.

This is Christmas. It is unusual for one to criticize at this time of year, therefore I will not criticize. I will merely comment. Recently you spoke to a class at West high school and I was one of the audience. Permit me to state, Miss Van De Grift, with apology for my unbridled audacity, that I enjoyed your informal talk a great deal more than your column writing.

Before I had the pleasure of hearing you speak, I had a mental picture of you as an intellectual old maid, plighting your troth to the world through your column, "Demi-

Tasse and Mrs. Grundy." I am happy to say meeting you materially greatly altered my mental picture. That was my impression of you, obtained through your column.

I do not believe your subjects in that column are what they might be. I can't see your point in such themes as "Musicians Oddities" and the like. Your eminent contemporary, O.O. McIntyre, across the column from you, writes timely stories. Your stories are more of the "anytime" type. Do not forget I am merely commenting.

Let me state in conclusion, Miss Van De Grift, that I am for you. I like your style. I do not like your method of production. Write some topics that you think will interest the people, the average person; the editorial page should not be a mirror for the high-brows of intellect.

AMBER ROSENFIELD.

A couple of years ago, newspapers and magazines were vamped with lists of the "ten best books," compiled by famous and infamous persons. Because these individuals jotted down certain books as the best does not imply that they are excessively familiar with them. Suppose, as was suggested by a contributor to Brentano's "Book Chat," we had various people make out a list of the ten books they enjoyed most. A symposium of this sort could not, of course, be successful unless everyone were perfectly honest with himself. A person always tries to put his best foot forward; if you buy two magazines – the "Atlantic Monthly" and "Whiz Bang," you will carry the former so that its respectable cover hides that of the other more disreputable publication (not that anyone ever reads both of those!) It's the same way with this book list. Although you may have enjoyed Ring Lardner or George Ade more than Dickens or Thackeray – "Vanity Fair" is more likely to be on your list than "How to Write Short Stories." It would be a fine thing to feel that most people read and enjoy the classics, but the truth is not so pleasant. I confess that I enjoy a good modern novel more than most of the classics. I said a good modern novel – not Zane Grey or Ethel M. Dell – but, say, "So Big."

SAM POLSKY.

24 December 1924, Wednesday:

"**D**EAR JO: –

(writes H. F.)

"Something must be done for E. G. K., of Douglas st., who wrote to your editor in part as follows:

"I have watched this female writer, but of all her writing I have not found one little grain of food for my brain; it is always destructive, especially to a weak mind.

"Perhaps I can hold out a ray of hope for your editor's pessimistic correspondent. I, too, used to be troubled with a weak mind, and everything that did not agree with my sacred prejudices made me feel like writing letters to editors. The work of persons whose jobs I envied was destructive to it – to my weak mind, you understand – and every time my mind was destroyed in this manner, it grew weaker, until it seemed that the little invalid would soon be gathered into the arms of the angel hand. It was almost too frail for this earth. But I did not despair. I embarked upon a regimen of mental diet and cerebral calisthenics which, together, have made my mind so firm, strong, and healthy that I frequently use it to drive in carpet tacks when the hammer is not readily at hand.

"In the first place, I observed that infants are not fed on sausage and buckwheat cakes, but on milk which has been so diluted and doctored that no cow would recognize, or recognizing, acknowledge it.

"I saw then by analogy that things which were written for intelligent persons was too hearty a diet for Little Eva, as we will henceforth call my fragile mind.

"I therefore began feeding it with literary porridge – such as the poems of Edgar A. Guest, the invaluable essays of Dr. Frank Crane, the sweety orisons of Mardon, certain works of Ella Wheeler Wilcox (the cheerful rather than the yow variety; and the various Pollyanna books.

"For refreshment between these literary meals, I spelled out A-B-C books, and learned that A is for Asp, a small venomous reptile of Egypt in three letters and B is for Bilbo, a sword or rapier in five.

"It was at about this period of my training that I discovered that everything that is contained in a newspaper is not literary pap. There were a few morsels that sat very heavy on my cerebral stomach, even as your column sits upon that of the pitiable E. G. K.

"As I intimated above, I did not content myself with a proper diet for the mind, but exercised it as well. It is well-spoken that the eye is the window of the brain. Remembering this, I used to have my brain stand at its open window for a few seconds and breathe deeply. It was almost intolerable at first, because I saw, thru that window, so many things that it seemed to me terrible to believe. But to a few years I got so that I could use my eyes without shutting off my brain, and my brain without closing my eyes. This, you must admit, was making good progress.

"Little Eva was beginning to grow strong. People who used to pat her curls with a sad look in their eyes began shying off when she snapped at their heels. Often she woke me in the night, shouting, 'Gimme some raw meat, Grrrrrrr!'

"Little Eva – or Beso, as I rechristened her – now entered upon her second stage. She was strong, but hardly refined. She needed a few edges knocked off. She couldn't stand to let a day go past without reading a novel by Theodore Dreiser or D. H. Lawrence. Not that there wasn't plenty of such food for her, but I wanted Beso to grow up to be a pleasant and dignified person. I cannot recount to you all the trials that the young savage gave me. His particular joy was to talk about private jokes in company. Suffice to say that a long period of careful restraint has made it possible for him to appear in evening clothes without looking as if he were the waiter's cousin called in during an emergency, and he was again rechristened, and called Anthony.

"What I have done, E. G. K., can do. It is not necessary for him to be forever the sort of inurbane person who writes in such shockingly bad taste. It cannot be done for him, however. He must do it for himself.

"Of course, if his mind is too far gone in its weakness, the only thing that can be done about it will be to hold a St. Bartholomew's eve for all intelligent persons so that his Little Eva can live in a world adapted to her limitations.

"But, as I say, there is hope."

———

Well it sorta looks as though we might have a white Christmas after all.

31 December 1924, Wednesday:

ONE of those things which seems tremendously to disturb certain persons is the discovery that certain symbols of the church may be interpreted as being symbols of sex.

I was talking the other day with a man who told me of a conversation he had had with a woman who wore, by way of adornment, a small cross on a ribbon about her neck.

"I told her," he said, "that if she understood what that cross really meant she would grind it in the dust under her heel."

To me such action seems a little bit drastic. The cross, for a good many centuries now, has stood as the symbol of suffering. If you care to look at it in the other sense there is hardly anything in the world which has caused quite so much suffering as sex.

There are some who have thought that one way to get away from this suffering was to deliver lectures to school children.

Perhaps they have achieved their purpose. I do not know. I rather doubt it. Such lectures as I have listened to on the subject have been exceedingly materialistic and they were delivered by persons who were utter strangers to me and whom I did not care for in the least.

A few years ago, however, when I was living in the Y.W.C.A. at Chicago I came upon an essay on the matter by so eminently respectable a writer as Ralph Waldo Emerson. I do not remember what the name of the essay was any more and I think that if the old sour drop who kept the library had known it was there she would have chucked both me and it onto Michigan boulevard.

However this essay called to my attention for the first time how innocent a thing sex is and how very widespread.

Mr. Emerson explained for one thing how the north and the south pole are phases of sex, as are also night and day, the ebb and flow of the tide and the systole and disstole of the heart.

He then went on to explain how, without regard to the bodies they were clothed with, minds in their relations to each other, might be either masculine or feminine.

Thus if my mind is leader over yours, then my mind is masculine and yours is feminine. But if some other mind comes along and becomes leader over mine, then that mind is masculine and mine is feminine.

Charles Bragdon in "The Beautiful Necessity" has shown the universality of sex in somewhat the following fashion.

Fire is masculine, water is feminine; the sun is masculine, the moon, feminine; the dominant chord in music is masculine, the tonic, feminine; the verb of a sentence is masculine, the noun, feminine; even numbers are masculine, odd numbers, feminine. In certain foreign countries the death of a man is noted with two tollings of the church bell. When a woman dies the bell is tolled three times.

Mr. Bragdon has likewise explained the principles of In and Yo as used in Japanese art. It has been a long time since I read the book and I may have the terms twisted but, as I recall, vertical lines are masculine and are called Yo. Horizontal lines are feminine and are called In.

Whether you choose to consider a cathedral or a maple leaf you can find the principles of In and Yo manifest.

Mr. Freud of course taught the universality of sex, too, but in somewhat different fashion. Mr. Freud and most other modern writers have gone along on the theory that human beings have minds and bodies but they have ignored what, for lack of a better term, we have chosen to call a soul.

Practically all the modern books I have read on the subject have ignored the fact that most of us like a little beauty along with the more prosaic aspects of the matter.

I think that some day when we have learned to mingle a little of the philosophies of brain, soul and body, all three, we will be quite able to look at a cross without being horrified.

Chapter VII.

Demi-Tasse & Mrs. Grundy in The year 1925

Demi — Tasse

- and -

Mrs. Grundy

- by -

Josephine Van de Grift

<hr>

12 January 1925, Monday:

"HAVE seen loads of shows and been to the opera," writes Eleanor from Gotham. "Went with K —— last Saturday night and talked to him the few moments when he was not on the floor putting on or taking off his galoshes, running out to breathe vapo-rub or something and altogether he was the worst wiggler I've ever sat next to. A plate of jello would have been statuesque in comparison."

Her letter does not state whether K —— used the short intervals of conversation for explaining the story of the opera to her but I take it that he did for K —— I seem to remember, loves music.

Sometimes I think it is better to go to the opera with a man who loves music and then sometimes I think it is better to go to the opera with a man who doesn't love music.

Suppose you have gone to the opera with a man who loves music. You take out your libretto, purchased for 50 cents from a Syrian in a black derby down in the lobby and prepare to find out what it's all about. The man who loves music puts out a restraining hand.

"Now," he says, "you don't have to do that, you don't have to do that at all. I've seen this thing seventeen times and I can easily explain it to you as we go along."

This he proceeds to do to the infinite interest of everybody else for four rows ahead. As the more familiar arias are sung in he insists on whistling them softly or else humming them in a low tone, keeping, if possible, a little ahead of the orchestra in order to show his perfect familiarity with the score.

When he feels that he has been shushed enough he lapses for a time into silence only to rally again with his personal opinion so to what's wrong with the prima donna and how much better Marcella Sombrich did it 20 years ago. This reminds him of a girl down in Louisiana, really an adorable little thing with lots of talent, who is training her voice merely by listening to phonograph records. The man who loves music (illegible – fools?) that this little girl will make her mark in the world some day and he personally is of the opinion that a lot of money is wasted on vocal teachers who couldn't sing if they had to. Those who can, do, those who can't, teach, in his theory.

Between sets he insists on dragging you out over 32 pairs of feet in order that you may saunter with him up and down the corridor and listen to the comments of the foreigners. He feels that the only persons who really appreciate good singing in this country are the foreigners. Indeed he himself often laughingly refers to it as "grand wopera."

The man who doesn't love music almost always takes the sport final along to the opera. As you are getting settled in your seats he remarks, "Well, here I am. You've brought me. I hope you're happy." Occasionally, as the applause strikes his ear, he stirs himself. "Ha," he remarks bitterly, "ha," and returns to a surreptitious contemplation of the latest exploits of Notre Dame. He manages to rattle the paper with peculiar effectiveness just as little Mimi lays dying.

I suppose the ideal person to take along to the opera is a man who loves music but who is very, very old. He can then be relied on to sleep peacefully through the entire performance only waking up to applaud vigorously between acts.

"Dear Josephine: (writes Luke Ulias)

"It's just my dumb luck! Here I've been sitting back all this time nursing my wrath and thinking up mean things to say about this here E.G.K., and now he turns out to be a woman. Isn't that just like a woman? I am pretty much of a roughneck and one of these here 'human animals' and all that, but I hope I am still enough of a Puritan to refrain from jumping on a weak-minded lady.

"Anyhow it all depends upon the point of view. We all know that a tree is green in summer; yet if we view it from a distance it appears to be blue. Now I dare say that if we could view E.G.K. at close range we would find that she is fairly human; and if she could swap coffee and eggs and gossip about the neighbors with you, across the back fence she would discover that you aren't such a bad scout after all.

"Well, there are ladies present and I can't cuss, but I'll do something just as mean. I'll write verse. Hands off, you 'worldsworst' body-snatchers!

"'Tis the voice of the critic: I heard her declare
Josephine Van de Grift's a cinnamon bear.
Her unregenerate friend, poor old Donald Gray,
is a sabre-toothed tiger — just list to his bray.
They're both human animals, the world is an ark;
Bill Bryan's a monkey and I am a lark,
They'll all die and be dead while I'm soaring high:
I'll be tickled to death in the sweet by and by
I will sit on a cloud and sing to my harp:
'Jo's a cinnamon bear and Luke is a carp.'

"By the way, Josephine, Mrs. Ulius is looking for a laundress."

Well, maybe you think I couldn't.

---

9 February 1925, Monday:

THIS department relates with pride that it has swatted the first fly of the season.

It seems to me there ought to be a law against authors having their pictures taken. It was The Saturday Review, I think, which a couple of weeks ago carried a picture of the poet Swinburne. He was wearing some sort of round hat, very much the sort that the Amish farmers wear, and his beard reached nearly to his belt. To one whose conviction has always been that a poet was a person with slightly curling hair and no whiskers who wore a soft shirt tossed carelessly open at the throat the effect was decidedly disillusioning.

Back in the Sunday school days I remember reading a little book of inspirational character called "The Greatest Thing in the World," by Henry Drummond. I was very fond of it and trusted implicitly that if I did as the book directed and read the 13th chapter of 1 Corinthians industriously I would some day become very wise and good. But one Christmas someone gave me a leather bound copy of "The Greatest Thing in the World," which included a picture of Mr. Drummond for the frontlepiece. I was horrified. Mr. Drummond, who spoke so grandly of faith, hope and charity, had mutton chops! I have never been able to read the book since.

I suffered the same shock over H.G. Wells. I think it was reading "God, the Invisible King," which convinced me that Mr. Wells was a tall, spiritual looking person with artistic finger tips. Then someone who knew him sent me his picture, along with a pen picture of him. He was a sort of amiable Kewpie, said my informant, very thick around the waist. The photograph confirmed all this and conveyed the additional information that Mr. Wells affected a thin, walrus-like mustache. Any sentimental notions that I may have entertained died on the spot.

William McFee once showed me a letter that a woman had written him. She had just seen his picture in the book review section of the New York times. "I had no idea you were so ugly," she wrote. She seemed to feel pretty bitter about it.

––––––––––

The worst book which I have read this week is "A Handsome Engineer's Flirtations, or How He Won the Hearts of Girls," by Miss Laura Jean Libbey.

––––––––––

"You know that world-comin'-to-the-end business sort of got on everybody's nerves," writes S.O.S. "Each one of us, when anyone asked, 'What do you think about it?' made the questioner believe we didn't believe anything was goin' to happen, but you know deep down in all your hearts you believed there was a chance. Now, didn't you?

"You know late Friday night we were reading about the end of the world just before going home and it made us jumpy. Having one of Henry's Detroit products and not being selfish we thought our last act should be doing good to our fellowman, and so we picked up a couple of boys to take along with us so they wouldn't have to wait for the owl bus.

"We started home fine, but there is a safety zone platform on W. Market st., and past that is the deceivingest hill imaginable. We got half way up and the ford stopped. It balked just like a mule.

"'She's out of gas,' one of the passengers timidly suggested. 'No,' I answered, 'I'm still breathing.' I was thinking of Gabriel's horn. Then it dawned on me the passenger meant the ford was out of gas. I looked, but the what-you-call-it showed enough to pull up the hill so I turned around and coasted down.

"Something exploded. Then a horn started to blow. I looked for the Portage. It was still standing. Then I looked down Main st. All those buildings were standing, too.

"'You've got a blow-out,' volunteered the passenger.

"I was terribly relieved.

"Coming back the Ford stalled again on the way up the hill to Howard st. We tried operating a wire that goes somewhere down to the vitals of the car, but it only made it worse. We decided to run it alongside the curb. But, Oh, Boy, did you ever notice how many 'No Parking signs there are in Akron? A policeman came up and said she'd have to be moved.

"'She won't go backwards or forwards,' I protested; 'she's out of gas.'

"Well, he said he'd let her stand there a few minutes while we went for gas, but they only sell it in five gallon lots and you have no idea how a five-gallon can can [sic] bump you in the legs.

"I poured the fuel into her and put my foot down, but she wouldn't go. Then I looked for the key. It wasn't there. The passenger gently wondered if I had turned on the spark.

"Well, eventually the Ford wheezed a little and then began hitting on two, then three, then four. I've always wanted to die in bed and so we hurried home and decided to repair the tires Saturday – that is, if there should be any Saturday.

"We did – took the tires off seven different times. And here it is Monday, and we're still living. All I've got to say is that if that lady had been correct in her prophecy and the world had come to an end Friday, I'd have been devilish tired to step into line with the 144,00 elect."

27 March 1925, Friday:

Y OU TAKE two spoonfuls of sugar and one of pulverized coffee. You mix them together in a little copper pot and fill up the pot with water that is boiling. After that you set the pot in a pan of hot sand and leave it there until it bubbles. Then you pour the coffee into a little cup.

———————

I am wondering if all the mystery which seems to lie around and about S. Howard st. will some day straighten itself out as simply as this matter of Turkish coffee.

At any rate three of us – the musician, the fellow who always keeps his collars neat and myself – ascended into one of those coffee houses which line the west side of the street last night and found ourselves in a Greek cabaret.

There were five persons sitting on the platform [sic] three men musicians, a woman in white and a girl in blue. The musicians were playing one of those repetitious things which, I presume, is the oriental equivalent for Turkey in the Straw. After a while the girl in blue arose and made a few short motions with her feet so that you thought she was going to dance. After a moment though you perceived that the dance steps were merely a sort of prelude. Her song over, she took up a saucer and passed among the guests. She was a pretty girl and her smile was friendly. She explained that the song she had just sung was a Greek love song.

The musician complained that the instruments were out of tune.

———————

A waiter with a sort of apron arrangement around his middle came up to see what we would have. He said that his name was Pete and that the rotund individual down in front who was making the coffee was named George. Pete smiled. George, who has very handsome black eyes, smiled so that for a time his eyes disappeared altogether. The musicians joined altogether now in a rousing chorus and the effect was decidedly pleasing.

And now "Feeleep" came by with his basket.

From his basket Feeleep produced cigars, little red boxes which were found to contain perfume, a partially used bottle of toilet water, any number of silk handkerchiefs, a rather musty roll of pasteboard tickets and a mysterious black bag. We purchased cigarets[23] and perfume and then inquired into the contents of Feeleep's black bag. It seemed that for a quarter you purchased three of the pasteboard tickets. Then you reached into Feeleep's black bag and drew out three numbers. If any of the numbers matched the numbers on the tickets you might take your pick of any of the things that were in Feeleep's basket.

We purchased six numbers but my luck with that sort of thing has always been extremely discouraging.

By this time the fellow who always keeps his collars neat and myself were having a grand time. The musician didn't say anything but the look on his face indicated that he would a good deal rather be listening to the Ninth symphony.

Two pretty girls came in and sat down by a little table in the rear of the room. And now, the initial embarrassment worn off, we looked about and perceived everywhere little groups of two and three, talking quietly together and drinking coffee. They were interrupted by a party of some seven or eight happy individuals who stormed up the stairs and took the middle table. The conversation which up till now had been indistinguishable now broke for a while into English. "Hello, Stiv." "Hello, Charlie."

"Stiv" went over and talked for a while to the pretty girls and then he came to our table. It was he who told me how to make Turkish coffee.

And now the musicians took up some wailing tune again. The woman in white came down to the middle of the floor, made a few preliminary dance steps and started to sing. The girl in blue smiled. The leader of the musicians stopped for a moment to cool his tea in the saucer.

"Aren't you happy? Aren't you glad we came?" we demanded of the musician.

The musician said he didn't know.

---

[23] An old spelling of cigarettes, including cigaret for a single one

The fellow who always keeps his collars neat says that Howard st. never bothers him. He thinks it is because he looks and dresses pretty much like the other people down there. But you know that isn't true on account of that little matter of the collars.

For my own part I think I'll always have a funny feeling about Howard st., as though, in spite of everything, I wasn't quite wasted.

<hr/>

1 April 1925, Wednesday:

ALL day long the vacuum cleaner has been standing just outside the Sceptic's door. If Mike were here, the vacuum cleaner would have been put in its proper place long ago, but Mike has gone away on a week's vacation.

Every once in a while I wonder how we got along down here before Mike came. I remember that there was a long succession of colored boys and that one of them had had the foresight to drag an old mattress into the furnace room. Thereafter, whenever you wanted a clean towel or a bar of soap or a mop or a window pried open, or a door nailed shut, you went and looked down in the furnace room. And there, curled up on the mattress as close to the furnace as he could possibly get, you would find the colored boy fast asleep.

Mike keeps us clean and Mike keeps us happy. Early in the morning, before even the first typewriter has begun to click, Mike is down, opening up doors and windows, getting out his broom and pail. And late at night, after all the others have gone home and even the composing room is quiet, it is Mike who straightens up over a leaning tower of waste baskets and bids you good night with earnest inquiries as to the health of your father and mother.

Do you want a dust cloth for your typewriter, Mike has the very thing. Have you misplaced your umbrella, Mike has put it away in a corner for you for safe keeping. Do you need a clean towel, Mike has already put one away for you in the second drawer of your desk.

Mike keeps the soap dishes filled and the waste baskets empty. He polishes the windows and the floors and the desks. He keeps the fires roaring and the water boiling. He hangs pictures and puts new rollers in the chairs. He knows when you have been gypped on the priced of eggs on the market and when you offer to share your peanut brittle with him, he accepts as a gentleman should.

Only once did Mike and I come dangerously near to getting on the outs. It was over the small matter of a mouse.

It was just a baby mouse and Mike was going to toss it carelessly away along with the rest of the rubbish. Having an idea that it might be saved I rapped it carefully in cheese cloth, put it away in a little box and endeavored to feed it milk from the end of a straw.

But the mouse rejected nourishment. Some time during the weekend – I don't know just when – it died. I was away from the office for several days, and it was some time before Mike discovered it.

Mike's contention in the matter was that the mouse – to put it plainly – smelled. My contention was that so small a mouse could not possibly create unpleasantness of any kind, I asked several other persons in the office about it and they said they hadn't noticed anything. Mike was sure that they had, but he felt that they were just too polite to say anything about it. He wound up by demanding what charity there could be in wanting to save a mouse, anyway.

And to this day I don't know.

Mike has two little boys and a little girl, the latter very pretty to my notion, and sometimes he brings them down with him. All three seem to be continually in a state of suppressed explosion.

They want to bounce marbles on the cement floor, and Mike makes them stop, and then they want to write on the typewriter, and Mike makes them stop that. Finally they get behind doors and peek around at one with barely audible giggling.

You might judge at these times that Mike was a very stern parent. But there was a long time when one of the little boys had to lie with his leg in a plaster cast. And there was another long time when the other little boy was ill and like to die of pneumonia. Mike never said much. He just went about looking after the waste baskets. But when you asked him how the little boy was getting along, then you knew another side of Mike.

Sometimes I think that the kid who has Mike for a parent is a mighty lucky kid.

2 April 1925, Thursday:

YESTERDAY'S Beacon Journal carried the picture of a round, pleasant faced, bespectacled gentleman, who at first glance looked to be either the president of a prosperous chain of grocery stores or possibly the principal speaker at the Rotary club's annual banquet.

But the picture turned out to be that of Dr. Frederick H. Baetjer, learned student of the Roentgen Ray who has just undergone his 71st operation as a result of his experiments. With, I believe, something like two fingers left, Dr. Baetjer declares his intention of carrying on his work.

Now to me it was a pleasant surprise to find that a round plump spectacled little man with his hair parted in the middle could be capable of heroism. But suppose that a similar drama were being enacted on the stage. Then do you suppose that the leading role would be given to a plump little man with his hair parted in the middle? Ah no. In that event the leading role would be given to a gentleman with long thin fingers and a Van Dyke beard. The round little man with his hair parted in the middle would be given the role of butler, he would be allowed to go on and off with trays and to gossip with the parlor maid in the first act.

"When you and Jerry take your sight-seeing trip around Akron, there are several things which Jerry hasn't listed that must not be overlooked," writes Jake Falstaff.

"You must see the glistening sidewalk at Main and Exchange sts., which hurts the eyes when the sun strikes it at a narrow angle.

"You must stand in respectful admiration before the ancient, weather-beaten sign is front of a S. Howard st. hotel which says, 'This hotel under new management.'

"You must look at the empty niche at the top of the Y.M.C.A. building, and figure out what it was meant to contain.

"There is a tower in the Rubler & Beck bldg.. (which houses the Akron Furniture Co.) and the proper thing to do will be to look at that for a while, and talk about what a lovely place it would be for a studio. (It really wouldn't, of course. It would be too hot in summer and too cold in winter, and the windows would be so distracting that you would never get anything done. But it would be all right to talk about it.)

"Then walk across the new State st. viaduct. If you will stand at the west end, you will see two fine futuristic views which will give you a kindler feeling toward Herman Rosan and the other modernistic street-scene artists. One of these sights is the curving strings of box-cars, which make wonderful lines. The other is the jet-black fire escape at the back of the Bond hotel, which stands against the light brick background in lines that would make a cubist sick with joy.

"By the way, you will see, if you stand here any length of time, a regular ancession [sic] of junk wagons. Why they all cross the State st. viaduct I do not know, and I have no idea where they are going. Some day I hope somebody will get a whole page of pictures of junk men's horses. They are wonderful.

"Another sight for the futurist will be the leaning piles of lumber down in the canal flats there at the viaduct. And maybe somebody in the crowd will be able to tell why lumber is always stacked in leaning piles. It is one of the things one hears and forgets.

"Don't slight the alleys. There are fine things to be seen on Main lane and Wheeler lane.

"And out in that general locality you may find the store where they have the most exciting pieces of Chinese carving that have ever been seen in this town. I could tell you the exact location, but I shall be selfish. I have been dreading the purchase of one or another of the treasurers in that store for two years, and next Christmas I mean to buy myself a few of them. You see my position.

"The black and white artist could find something to sketch in the tower of the Union depot. And the writer of human interest stuff could pick up plenty of it if he went to the depot viaduct at dusk of a summer evening, and mingled with the hill-billies that are there from sheer loneliness, watching the trains pull in and out and listening to the whistles.

"The post office is worthy of scrutinizing. On the west side is a fine balcony, and on this balcony is a hat rack. In the west entrance is a mosaic of a man on horseback. It is the best public piece of art in Akron."

---

3 April 1925, Friday:

"NATURE is a wonderful study and you would be surprised how much real enjoyment you can get out of this world of ours just by the study of birds," writes H. B. Campbell.

"My advice is to get a good bird book and a pair of field glasses. Then some fine day when the sun is shining, take a good long walk in the woods and fields. The first bird you see, follow it and listen for it to sing, get the color of it even to its eyes and beak. Then if you cannot place the bird, be guided by your book. Once you start this study you will sit for hours and watch the birds sing, play and build their nests.

"Here are some of my experiences while observing the robin family. Many years ago a robin built its nest in a pine tree near my home. To my mind it was a very poor place for when the wind blew it would move the whole nest. I made up my mind to watch it.

"The nest was complete and the first egg was laid, and then the havoc started. Every day the nest was tipped over by the action of the wind and at last when the four little blue eggs were laid it was tipped at an angle of about 45 degrees. It seemed that any day it might tip over and out would go the eggs.

"About four or five feet away, right in the middle of the tree, was a large fork that would have held the nest very nicely. Most persons right then, rather than see the nest fall, would have moved it over to the fork. But I knew that that was useless, as the birds would leave this nest the minute it was moved. Instead I took a long chance and left it alone until the four eggs were hatched, and the young robins were in the nest.

"Then one nice day when both the father and mother birds were there I moved the whole thing over to the fork in the middle of the tree. To be sure they scolded and flew around me, but that was just what I wanted them to do so they would be sure it was their nest and their young.

"It worked out fine as they took up the nest in the new location the same as though they had built it there and raised their young out of it. It had been funny to see that old mother bird sitting on that lopsided nest. She finally got it done, but not say too soon, as I think in about two days it would have fallen out of the tree, and she would have had all her trouble for nothing.

"The old man robin does not as a rule do much work, but if it is necessary he will help all he can. I remember one instance where a robin built her nest and for some unknown reason it was destroyed just as she was ready to lay her eggs. This was a very serious case and something had to be done at once, if she was to raise her young. So she went and got her mate and I suppose explained it all to him, for together they built another nest in one day, and she laid the first egg that same day.

"Now you may think that there is nothing very great about that until you realize that it generally takes from three to four days to build the nest and that then the mother bird waits a couple of days longer for the mud in it to dry before she lays the first egg.

"Ordinarily the male bird will not help to build the nest at all, except in such a case as I have explained. Some birds will feed their mate while she is sitting on the nest if the day requires it. I mean by that, that if it rains all day or gets so cold that she does not dare to leave the nest for fear the eggs will get chilled, he will bring food to her.

"It is not often that he does this, however. What she will do is this: he will sit on the eggs himself, while she is gone away for food."

I am always envious of people like this, people who get on such intimate terms with old lady nature that they can tell a song sparrow from the gutter kind and can call the dragon-tongued whortleberry by its first name.

My own excursions into nature have been so fruitless. They have been confined almost entirely in rescuing the baby birds which the cat brought in and then lamming the cat severely. And my only reward has been that the baby birds died away and that the cat, instead of crawling into my lap and purring as he does with other members of my family, always skulks past me as quickly as possible and glares at me balefully, out of one eye.

Once, however, I did have an experience that was rather nice. A father robin was sitting up on our neighbor's chimney teaching his young son how to sing.

"Twitter up, twitter up," said the father robin and then the young one very faintly and far away, would say, "Twit up, twit up."

Until I shall have something else to add to it, it remains my one precious recollection.

---

6 April 1925, Monday:

"THERE'S nothing like a barber shop for getting the inside dope on things," writes C.H.S. "They were talking about the centennial in one the other day. A customer desiring to shut off a discussion on the prohibition laws asked the question, 'If 100 years anniversary is called a centennial, what is 200 years anniversary called.' That got 'em.

"Right away seven voices in seven chairs commenced. The loudest got this one over. 'That's easy. I can give it to you up to 400 years. Use for one, duo for two, trio for three and quarto for four.'

"'Yes bo,' said one of the barbers, 'the only thing you got right in that lingo is a quarto for four. I was saying a minute ago that the stuff you get nowadays is so diluted that a quart will hardly go around to four.'

"'I used to know the nicknames of all the states,' opined a man having his shoes shined, 'but I never could get these wedding celebrations straightened out in my mind. When you get beyond the wooden, tin, silver, golden and diamond weddings, the rest is all Greek to me. But why stop at 200 years. If these gland operations come out the way they say they do why some of these dudes will live longer than Methuselah[24].'

"'If you are talking about the 240th anniversary of the wedding of two people I'd call that a miracle,' piped in a bachelor who comes in every Saturday to have the hair cut out of his ears.

"'It's a simple question and deserves a simple answer,' observed a fat man just getting out of a chair. 'After the first centennial comes the second centennial, the third centennial, the fourth centennial and so on.'

"'This ain't no crossword puzzle is it?' asked an old man who had been reading a paper. 'If we are all going to guess on this thing how many letters does it have? Must is end in 'nial?'

"'Now you are getting down to brass tacks Pop,' said the owner of the shop. 'We know that the centipede is a bug with 1000 legs and when we get the name of one with only 200, that'll be the answer.'

"Much more of this same discussion would have gone on as under the guise of the bantering men sometimes seek light and truth and it was readily apparent that no one present knew the correct answer to the question, 'What is a 200 years anniversary called?'

---

[24] Methuselah is mentioned in the Hebrew bible, Genesis 5:21-27, who lived to be 969 years

But an Akron U. student happened in, in the midst of the argument, and now the barbers have the information written on a card back of the cash register.

100 years is a centennial.
200 years is a dercentennary.
300 years is a tercentenary.
400 years is a quadcentennary.
500 years is a quincentennary.

"And underneath is written 'After 500 years we don't care what they call it as we won't be here in this shop.'"

<hr />

7 April 1925, Tuesday:

I'M wondering though if conversation really flourishes in the barber shops as much as the men like to make out.

I went into a barber shop the other day to have a haircut and all that I heard during the entire period was the steady clup-clup of razors and the occasional slapping of hot towels.

The barbers were far from being conversational. In fact, all of them seemed to be downright morose. My barber seemed to be particularly heavy hearted.

"I don't know any funny stories," he said sadly, "I never can remember 'em."

"Well, then," I said brightly, "how are you getting on with your wife?"

"I ain't got any wife, lady," he said. "I ain't married."

Five minutes passed.

"I suppose," I said, "that I really ought to have a good tonic."

"No lady," he said, "Your hair is all right."

"Do you think a singe would do it any good?" I queried.

"I wouldn't advise it, lady," he said, "singes have gone out."

He brought me the mirror then and after observing that one side was cut shorter than the other, as usual, I told him it was a wonderful haircut and went out.

It's been that way everywhere I've gone. I can sit up conversations with traffic cops, motormen, delicatessen keepers, waiters and dog catchers. But when it comes to barbers, I'm all out of luck. Sometimes when I go by on the outside of a barber shop I peek in and slow up for a minute to see if I can't detect shouts of merriment. But it's all very solemn and quiet.

I don't know that it is really much better at the beauty parlors. You would think, you know, that a beauty parlor would be the ideal place for the exchange of those little matters which make life so interesting. But you never can tell who is on the other side of the wooden partition.

I shall never forget the day I was telling my girl Guinevere about the ridiculous way Hattie Sturgeon has of always wanting to run everything.

"Really, it is too amusing," I was saying. "She wants to be president of everything she belongs to. And she hasn't the slightest bit of talent. She was so dumb in school they had to send her away to one of those finishing affairs in the east. I shall never forget the day she was trying to introduce dear Professor Gulp to the study club, 'The speaker whom we have with us this afternoon,' she said, 'needs no introduction. I am sure that we all know Professor – Professor –' and then she had to look down at her slip to see what his name was. 'Professor Gulp,' she went on, 'will speak to us on the subject – the subject of – and then she had to look down at the slip again to see what he was going to speak on. She can't remember anything two minutes. And whenever a speaker is through, she always says the same thing. 'I'm sure we have all enjoyed this talk very much and we will now sing "My Country 'Tis of Thee." Really I don't see how she gets ahead and yet they keep electing her year after year."

Just at that minute somebody flounced out of the next booth laughing shrilly.

"Who was that?" I said to Guinevere feeling a sort of ominous foreboding.

"That," said Guinevere, "was Hattie Sturgeon. I kept signaling to you to keep quiet but you wouldn't pay any attention."

Really, now I'm beginning to see why they have all those signs, "Quiet Please" in the beauty parlors.

8 April 1925, Wednesday:

“ **H**ERE’S what’s on my chest,” writes Gus No. 2. “I want to protest against the trying in court of such cases as are going on. The only benefit, so far as I can see, is to provide copy for the papers and goodness knows they can get it anyway without the court actions.

“I want to see these court cases cut out – entirely. Cases, that is, of road scandals, murders and such like.

“First: They never get anywhere. Nobody is hurt. Everybody gets a lot of free advertising which we poor business men usually have to pay for. On the other hand most people who get the thrill out of these little incidents in our midst, as they read of them in the papers are madly jealous of the free publicity which they crave. They would do likewise, if they dared, if only for the moment in the limelight which it gives them.

“Second: They all cost us poor taxpayers so much money. Here I have the Beacon Journal sympathy I know.

“Please beg the government, court or whoever is responsible to cut it out and let all these cases go. I’m not joking even if tying cases is.”

If this is true, that even wrong doers are crazy for the limelight, then the backbone of newspaperdom [sic] is broken. Here for years and years now we’ve gone along on the theory that by holding the 60-watt candle up to wrong doing we were making sin so odious that a lot of people would stay good just for fear of being found out if they weren’t.

This reasoning of course did not apply to chorus girls nor to movie actresses suing for breach of promise.

If it should be found now that even butter manufacturers, cement mixers and county commissioners profit now and then by a little scandal – well, I just don’t know what to think.

There is one person I know who is not crazy to have her name in the paper and that is the woman who has been giving a little affair for 15 friends and who doesn't want it written up in the society columns for fear that the 32 others will read about it and get made [sic] because they weren't invited.

Years ago when I was trying to be a society editor my pillow was nightly wet with tears because of the various women who hung up the telephone receiver in my ear and the various others who swore up and down they weren't having parties when I knew perfectly well that they were.

The lip of some of these women will stay by me in my sadder moments to my dying day.

———————

So far as the average court case is concerned I think it could easily be dismissed in a few paragraphs to the great relief of the general public.

It is hard to conceive of a dollar [sic] case than the McShaffrey trial I doubt that one per cent of the readers of newspapers read the columns and columns of testimony which were reproduced.

The Chapman case was greatly over played. Reporters and cartoonists, driven by the importunities of city editors and the necessity for filling up space, created at last an esthetic bandit in whose fate the public will never feel more than cold concern.

Column after column was devoted recently to the reopening of the Stokes divorce case. It got so that after a while you didn't even rad [sic] the head lines. Yesterday I read that the Stillman case was to be reopened and I groaned.

All in all I would say that the public interest in a trial lasts just about as long as the reporter's does. And the reporter's interest invariably goes dead the second day.

———————

All along, though, I had consoled myself with the thought that publicity was a deterrent to crime. I have thought of how time after time in my own case I would have walked out with a handful of rubber washers from the ten cent store except for the fear of being caught and written up in the papers.

If it should appear now that the actual result would be merely to get me a better job —

I can not, of course, lay claim to being a local taxpayer as Gus No. 2 does. But I've been paying an income tax to the government for the past several years now and I know just how he feels.

⁓⟡⟡⟡◆⟡⟡⟡⁓

9 April 1925, Thursday:

BOOK Review: I let the dishes wait last night while I finished "The Constant Nymph[25]." I think if the Prince of Wales had been around I would have let him wait too.

There are, I think, two ways of reading a book. One way is to read it by the kitchen table with a coffee pot close at hand. The other way is to take it to bed with you along with a couple of apples and a box of saltines. The objection to the latter course is that the crumbs from the saltines will get in the bed and give you a rather bad night of it. The objection to the former course is that you will drink too much coffee and that will give you a bad night of it.

In any event "The Constant Nymph" will probably give you a bad night of it anyway. It is taken up largely with music and musicians, for one thing, and that is so unusual and delightful that you want to lie awake and think about it for a long time.

William J. Locke, a long time ago I remember, wrote a book called "The Beloved Vagabond[26]" in which music was properly treated. And a few years ago "Mary Wollaston[27]" came out and that was capital. Ever after that my ideal of a man to marry was Mary Wollaston's piano tuner.

But music in the average novel is treated rather carelessly. I remember one where the heroine, besought by the hero to play something soothing, sat down at the piano and tossed off the Ninth symphony. Another author always has his pianists playing Wagner. In a short story which I read one time a supposedly world renowned impresario makes

---

[25] "The Constant Nymph," a book by Margaret Kennedy, 1925.

[26] "The Beloved Vagabond," a book by William J. Locke, 1907.

[27] "Mary Wollaston," a book by Henry Kitchell Webster, 1922.

---

a speech in which he refers to Sullivan's "[28]Lost Chord" as being one of the greatest compositions ever written.

Of the other disturbing factors in "The Constant Nymph" the chiefest is that it seems to be a well nigh perfect piece of work.

I shiver when I think of what the movies will do to it.

A serious injustice which the movies are doing to us these days is that by their titles they are continually keeping us away from shows which we would like very much to see. They took "The Interpreter's House[29]" and called it "I Want My Man." They took "Aren't We All[30]" and called it "A Kiss in the Dark." They took "The Czarina[31]" and called it "Forbidden Paradise." A few years ago they took the much discussed "The Admirable Chrichton[32]" and called it "Male and Female." It seems to me that there is poor business sense in this as all of these had received extensive and expensive advertising under their old names. The new names give no hint, no clue.

Last week, with a couple of hours to spend, I found myself obliged to choose between some such titles as "Passionate Flappers," "Are Wives to Blame?" "A Vampire's Heart" and Through the Key Hole."

Exercising my usual uncanny judgment in such matters I chose the worst of the lot. Some of my friends who had the good luck to stumble into a couple of the others said that they weren't half bad.

"Have you," writes Fireside Reveler, "ever been on a job when two of the help stayed out sick and you had to work overtime, and were too tired event [sic] to read 'Demi Tasse and Mrs. Grundy' several nights and then you open your paper and find a guy in

---

[28] Arthur Sullivan's "Lost Chord" musical composition.

[29] "The Interpreter's House," a book by Maxwell Struthers Burt, 1924.

[30] "Aren't We All?" by Frederick Lonsdale, a 1920's drawing room comedy play, 1925.

[31] "Confessions of the Czarina," a book written by Paul Vasili, 1918.

[32] "The Admirable Crichton," a stage play written by J.M. Barrie in 1902.

Jo's chair who thinks Crusoe's man Friday belonged in "Treasure Island[33]!" and you throw your paper down and then you come home not quite so tired and you get the B.J[34]. and from the force of habit turn to that page and in a new chair your old pal smiles back at you and you look scornfully at the new guy and say, "Did you think you could put your stuff across with us?" and then you notice what a genial looking fellow he is and you read his column and you say to the wife, "Well, the Beacon sure knows its business, they've added a dandy column to their paper," if you ever have, Jo, say ain't it a grand and glorious feeling"?

I'll say.

———⁓⁓⁓◆⁓⁓⁓———

10 April 1925, Friday:

A LL of us, I dare say, get a wild notion from time to time that, hereafter, whenever we see anybody going along the street that we think we'd like to know we're going to step right up and speak to them.

There's a man like that who's been worrying me for a couple of weeks now. Every day I see him on High st. and every day he has a two-days' growth of beard. I'm dying to stop him and ask him how he never lets it get ahead of him.

There's another man whom I've noticed for years. He wears a soft grey hat with a wide brim and he lets his hair grow long. I always had an idea he was a gentle post of something until one day I overheard him having an argument with a woman companion.

————

It is this element of disappointment which makes it advisable, I think, never to strike up an acquaintance with persons who look at all out of the ordinary.

I once went to a contributor's banquet given by a well known columnist. Practically the first thing I did was to mistake one of the contributors for the head waiter. Shortly afterwards there appeared upon the scene a man who knocked me cold. He was a sort

---

[33] "Treasure Island," by Robert Louis Stevenson, 1906.

[34] The Akron "Beacon Journal"

---

of John Barrymore and Sir Johnson Forbes-Robertson rolled into one. Thin and esthetic looking, you know. I prayed that before the evening was over I might come to know him.

As luck would have it he sat opposite us at the table. He never said a word all evening but he ate steadily. And when he had cleaned up everything on his side of the table he reached over and took our bread.

Later I found that the most brilliant contributor present was the one whom I had mistaken for the head waiter.

A couple of years ago I lived in an apartment alongside of a prominent illustrator. Every day or so we noticed a terribly impressive man coming to call upon him. We were sure he must be a banker. He had the Wall street air. One day we happened to bump into a billboard and had the surprise of our lives. The man whom we had admired so much was indubitably the model who poses as the middle-aged society man enjoying a popular brand of cigarets.

My friend, Paul Davis, used to tell of seeing an old fellow in the subway whom he took to be a Shakespearean actor. The old gentleman had a leonine head, a shock of white hair and long slender fingers. He was continually muttering to himself. There was a quiet, gentle, old lady sitting always beside him and the old gentleman seized every opportunity to treat her with scorn.

One night Paul came upon him up in the Bronx. He was carrying a sandwich board outside one of the girly shows.

I think it may safely be asserted that whenever a man affects the unusual in pose, collars, hats or haircuts, he is sure in the end to turn out to be a bore.

Only right away I am struck with contradictions. Of Paderwski who wears his hair long. Of David Bellasco who wears his collar turned round. Of Oscar Wilde carrying the medieval lily in his hand.

And so I don't know.

Bill Haynes came up in the office today wearing a red bow tie. He had had considerable trouble in getting it tied. I tried to straighten it out for him, getting behind and tying it from the rear as I had seen them do in the movies, but it wasn't any use. The Jake Falstaff was summoned. Jake made a really beautiful job of it.

Bill just got back from Miami yesterday. He says he saw hardly anybody down there that he knew. It seems that the town has grown so fast that all the old timers have been swallowed up.

---

11 April 1925, Saturday:

THERE is considerable comfort in the report emanating from Washington that Mr. and Mrs. Coolidge[35] are not doing any flossing up, for Easter.

Easter, as any woman knows, in far from being the right time to be bursting forth in new bibs and speckled tuckers. That time is back in February when the old fur coat is molting, when the little afternoon model is refusing to yield its secrets up to energine anymore and when the soot above the radiators on the wallpaper is enough to drive anyone mad.

New clothes late in February are a spiritual necessity. New clothes in the middle of April are a nuisance and an extravagance.

Of course I know the talk. Easter, say the story books, marks the time when the whole earth is bursting into life. The blue jays go daffy and start stopping up the drain pipes with chicken feathers, old hair, brushes and such small pieces of laundry as they can extract from the week's washing without being seen. The cranberries burst into bloom. All through the spring nights the neighborhood tomcats assemble upon rear fences and

---

[35] U.S. President John Calvin Coolidge (1872-1933) served as U.S. President 1923-1929.

hold sisteddfod[36] to the moon. What more appropriate than that human beings should burst out in a little life and color too? And what better time than Easter morning?

But I don't know. When I was a kid I always had the idea that my challie dress with the pink roses in it, my patent leather slippers and my leghorn hat with the ribbon were just about the last word in splendor. But as I grow older a subtle change crept over my spirits. Now as I step out on Easter morning with my new blue serge, my five-dollar straw and my black silk stockings with only a small darn in the heel I have a feeling that all the gally dressed promenaders about me are turning and thinking, "Well, is THAT the best you could do?"

A solution of the difficulty I think would be to set out on Easter morning in clothes that are palpably old. Clothes so old that nobody would ever get the impression that you had tried to fix up but had found the means at hand hopelessly inadequate.

Thus by deliberately flaunting the whole Easter convention one could not only keep one's self-respect but one ought also to derive considerable satisfaction from sniffing at others who still follow the absurd notion of dressing up.

The Coolidge's of course have one tremendous advantage and that is that everybody knows how much Mr. Coolidge makes. Being perfectly able to afford a certain amount of style the Coolidge's can go on wearing their old clothes year after year and everybody says, "My, how perfectly lovely of them to economize when they don't have to."

With the rest of us it is slightly different. Nobody, with the exception of everybody in the office, the folks at home, the relatives in four states, the grocer, the ice man and the income tax collector, knows how much we make and consequently we are continually obliged to put on a let of dog in order to swell the impression.

There is one ideal condition and I earnestly hope that someday all those whom I love may attain to it. That is to have so much money that you can turn up at an exclusive dinner party clad in a middy blouse and golf stockings and everybody will say, "Yes, but you know she has always been so democratic, Money hasn't changed her a bit."

---

[36] A misspelling of the word Eisteddfod, a Welsh festival of competitions in music, poetry and drama

As it is you get an invitation from the J.K. Bow-Wows whom you're crazy to get on better terms with. You look over the wardrobe and you find that the little thought which you got in Paris in 1922 is still in excellent condition. All that ails it is that the waist line is way up under the arms, the skirt is two feet too long and the whole thing is embroidered in a cobweb design executed heavily in cracked ice. Your other choice is a little afternoon model with horrible sleeves and two strawberry frappes down the front. In the end you call up the Bow-Wows and tell them that you're terribly sorry but you've just had a telegram from your rapidly expiring aunt in Buffalo.

---

23 April 1925, Thursday:

"I have read your column long and eagerly," writes Ancient Admirer, "almost fatuously (what DOES that word mean anyway) I understand you have worked on a great city daily. You're working on a newspaper now. So because you're accustomed to reading the hearts and minds of people I write to ask you this question – What do you consider the more important – the kiss or the squeeze?"

The latter undoubtedly. In all my long and varied experience I have never known the former to vary by more than a half second but there are subtle nuances to the squeeze that make it one of the most delightful expressions of human regard.

Suppose you are in a crowded street car with someone whom you admire tremendously. Suddenly you feel an overwhelming burst of affection coming on. A kiss at such times is out of the question. But by waiting until the car gives a convenient lurch you can throw your arms around the admired one and demonstrate, without the other passengers being in the least aware of it, your esteem. A feeling of rapport is at once established.

Or suppose you and John Henry are out with a third girl whom John Henry doesn't like at all but whom he just has to be nice to on account of her being the daughter of his mother's old school friend. Naturally you and John Henry can't talk about the usual things. You've got to be entertaining to the other girl. But you can quietly press John Henry's foot under the table and when you are in the taxi cab John Henry can squeeze your hand. Of course if you look carefully you may find him squeezing the other girl's hand, too. But those things are disturbing. It is better not to look.

And then there are the squeezes that come in an art museum when you see something that you both particularly like and the squeezes that come when you are being helped into your coat.

As someone has so aptly said, there's nothing like being all alone when you're in the midst of a crowd.

"Isn't there a lot of bunk in the poetry of the sunrise?" continues Ancient Admirer in the same gushy epistle. "I got up at 5 a.m. once to see this phenomenon. Did I feel elevated, thrilled, wade over? I did not. I felt cold and hungry and silly. I doubt if there is as much inspiration in the sunrise as the legends say. In proof of this statement I note that no milkman ever wrote a great poem."

———

I don't know. I never saw but one sunrise and that was pretty much of a fizzle. An indigent newspaper reporter with whom I was for a time having dates once told me that he was going over to Central Park to see the sunrise. I gladly volunteered to go along.

We sat on a dewy bench beside a murky pond and waited. The taxicabs were just going home from the night clubs and their lights in the greyness seemed a little peculiar. After a while the park lights went out and we knew it was time for the sun to rise. Six o'clock came and seven. Still Phoebus dallied. A policeman came by, looked us over, shook his head and went on his way. I think we must have slumbered.

But along about 10 o'clock we happened to look up and there was the sun just emerging overhead. The mist had hid him until then.

We ate at the automat. The coffee was terrible.

———

"One the other hand," continues Ancient Admirer, "I wonder if Herman knows how brave he is. I can hardly wait until the descendants of old Hiram Perkins and the grandchildren of John Brown come in and bawl him out for giving more space to somebody else's grandfather than he did to theirs. Won't petty jealousy and neighborhood rivalry of the worst form await Herman's every misstep? If he survives this ordeal and still has faith in and love for Akron, then Heaven will be too good a place for him."

I think, though, that it would be better to have it that way than for them to get made because they were included.

———

Washington Irving, I understand, when he wrote his Knickerbocker History[37] had quite a time of it. All the Van[38] This, That and The Others got made because they strongly suspected that Irving was poking fun at them.

Today any families who were included in that history go about simply bursting with pride and their noses, instead of being the long Dutch variety, have gradually assumed an upturned half moon shape.

All of which doesn't help Mr. Irving in the least. I hope Herman's lot is happier.

———❦———

24 April 1925, Friday:

IT TAKES a good many years to achieve a canonization, I understand, but in centuries to come if newspaper reporters ever should require a patron saint I rather have an idea they would pick on Chauncey Depew.

Mr. Depew is the last of a generation of men whom I seem dimly to understand, although in my own time I have never met more than three or four of them. They were politer, for one thing, and they did things less hurriedly than our present industrial masters. They had more respect for government and more for religion and they were better read. What their private villainies were I am not proposed to say, but I have an idea that they were considerably exaggerated by a jealous populace.

Chauncey Depew never had reporters thrown out on their ear by eager menials, never lied about being in conference, never adopted a pompous, bully ragging attitude. Instead he employed one secretary, Charles Sundell, slightly younger than himself, and when a reporter, a little low on copy, wandered into the office Mr. Depew did not keep him waiting long.

Just how much this meant no reporter realized until he endeavored to call on Chauncey Depew in his home. Then he appreciated the difference. Mrs. Depew was in power there and she wasn't going to have Chauncey bothered.

---

[37] "Knickerbocker's history of New York," by Washington Irving, c. 1848.

[38] Referring to the Dutch surname, naming of Van, as in Van De Grift.

Yesterday was Chauncey Depew's 31st birthday. A couple of birthdays ago, I went to see him. He told me a story about a cub reporter who had also come to get a birthday story. "So this is your birthday, Mr. Depew?" the reporter said. "Yes," answered Mr. Depew. "Shakespeare, St. George and myself were all born on the 14th of April." The reporter wrote busily for a moment. Then he looked up. "Were you all born in the same year, Mr. Depew?" he queried.

Mr. Depew laughed heartily at the anecdote.

"And do you know," writes A Reader, "I had got an in the habit of sagging into a chair at the fag[39] end of every day and letting my weak mind drink up the stuff you write that when that day came, when this Jake Falstaff with his Pippins and Cheese[40] sat in your place, why, dear, oh dear, I just gulped for a minute. I sure thought you had gone to ironing shirts.

"After I had feverishly turned the paper over, however, your prop far weak minds came into vision. Oh, what relief! Then too, Pippins and Cheese adds to, rather than detracts from, my mental pleasure which I derive daily for the paltry expenditure of two cents.

"And now that I have got around to it is my usual slow fashion, permit me to say, different paragraphs written by your easy flowing pen have yielded me a harvest of laughs, quiet laughs to myself. The one, for instance, about gelatines, another about bread puddings – they coincide nicely with the way my family think.

"Then that one about the institution for old maids to take care of cast off babies was particularly convulsing to me. In my mind I tried to picture any of all the old maids I have known – capable business women, some of whom owned homes and a tidy business of their own; others who earned comfortable salaries; others still who earned small salaries and helped support the folks; others still, and these were in the minority, who were parasites living off their relatives and giving nothing in return. And not one would I think of who ever hankered to take care of a baby. No, I fear the institution would have far more babies than old maids.

---

[39] Referencing the burnt end of a cigarette, slang termed as a 'fag' in the 1920's

[40] Herman Fetzer, better known as "Jake Falstaff" to his readers, in 1920 began his column "Pippins and Cheese," taking its title and his pen name from Shakespeare's Merry Wives of Windsor (reference from Case Western Reserve University Encyclopedia of Cleveland History)

"Your paragraphs about different kinds of hell filled me with glee. Listening to a good woman talk about herself forever. My word, one would almost think you had at one time attached yourself to a talkative mother-in-law, one of the kind like the babbling brook which goes on forever.

"By the way, why are so many used cars for sale? A woman buys a sewing machine for life, but a man buys a machine and in a short time it isn't good enough for him, and still he thinks some other man would just love to have it. Or is it like what the drunken fellow said, "Roll on, you mortgagee""

"I have been a persistent and consistent reader of 'Demi Tasse and Mrs. Grundy,' writes L. I. M., "and I have had many a satisfied chuckle in consequence. But I let out a shout and a couple of unlady-like whoops when reading last night. 'Bromida, Daughter of Jazz.'

"It is the timeliest and most refreshing hit of sarcasm to be found in a month of Sundays. Years before I realized the basic difference between a lady and a flapper, I instinctively avoided, as I would small pox, the woman who loudly proclaimed herself a lady.

"Isn't it rather significant that the modern flapper requires so much defending and vindicating? Shakespeare said a mouthful when he declared, 'The lady doth protest too much.'"

Yesterday, though warm, was a very pleasant day.

There is a brief hiatus in written stories as Josephine marries William Rigby during this time. Her article written about her honeymoon in Niagara Falls, Ontario follows:

---

19 May 1925, Tuesday (after her Honeymoon):

I WAS disappointed in Niagara Falls. I can readily see how the old chap who first discovered it must have gotten quite a thrill out of the occasion. Then there were forests and possibly, not so far away from the pounding of the water, an occasional forget-me-not.

But today Niagara Falls is flanked on either side by dinky factories making wallpaper and shredded wheat biscuits and the vegetation, when there is any at all, is brown and unpromising.

My mother, when she came back from Niagara Falls brought with her a little ivory umbrella about as long as half a lead pencil. The handle of the umbrella was for holding needles and then in the very tip of it there was a bit of glass which you looked through. The bit of glass showed a view of the Falls but nothing more. Thus looked at it was magnificent. I wish now that I had never looked further than the little ivory umbrella.

Of course our real reason for going to Niagara Falls was the desire to get over into Canada, where English ale was to be had. We picked out the most promising place – a hotel with a chap out in front of it all dressed up to look like the Prince of Wales. The dining room afforded an excellent view of the Falls, the bus boy wore an exceedingly large ring on the fore-finger of his right hand and the head waiter, when he appeared, was most attentive. The ale, he regretted to say, would not be in until the 21st, but they had some lovely fresh buttered asparagus.

We took the asparagus along with some other things and the check, when it arrived, would nicely have taken care of a couple of Belgian orphans for the rest of their natural lives.

Across the way from the hotel was a little curio shop and the window of that, too, afforded an excellent view of the Falls, but the curios were disappointing. Indian moccasins made in Brockton, Mass., bread plates decorated with lions rampant and the coat of arms of the Windsors, souvenir spoons curiously frail at the handle and too ornate for oatmeal anyway.

And cut along with walks there were no rapturous newly married couples, no brides with corsages of lilies of the valley pinned to their coasts. The season, I guess, was a little early. At any rate, we counted in all but six persons. An old captain sunning himself on the bench outside the curio shop, a lame fellow pushing a lawn mower, a mother dragging a half grown boy beside her, a fellow in knickers hurrying along with a camera along over his shoulder, and, out in front of the hotel, that young fellow dolled up in his uniform staring patiently, onswervingly [sic] at the steady plunge of water.

Some day, I suppose, when that young fellow is old and bent, someone will come along and say, "I say, did you ever *see* Niagara Falls?"

All in all, I don't think I should care to be a tourist. The beauties of nature which appear so enchanting when viewed along the way from Erie to Buffalo become surprisingly monotonous when viewed on the way back from Buffalo to Erie. Also the cheerful optimism of the farms seems to be derived from something more than a steady contemplation of sunsets.

All along the road, I noticed there was a succession of bright new coops, somewhat taller than a henhouse, which advertised that a tourist might sleep there for $1.50 a night. Occasionally a door would be open, and it was revealed that the furnishings within consisted of a folding cot. The tourist, I gather, brings his own bedding.

Then in front of the farmhouses there were signs advertising that meals were to be had. Judging by the rate for a night's lodging I would gather that a farm cooked meal ought to come to two dollars at least. At that rate a week's touring ought to come pretty high. To say nothing of the blowouts, the leaking carburetors, the broken shafts, the mounting cost of hot dogs, the mosquitoes, the lack of hot water, the wakefulness that comes from sleeping in strange beds, the peculiar people one is thrown among, and the excellent telephone connections with the larger towns by which the farmers establish the price of strawberries, fresh eggs and the like.

And all for the questionable satisfaction of getting from one place to another as rapidly as possible.

In the face of such difficulties, my personal fascination is in stay home as long as possible and should the death of a rich relative ever make it imperative for me to travel then I shall go via Pullmen and stay at hotels where they have steam heat and running ice water.

<hr>

16 June 1925, Tuesday:

"IN naming city streets," writes Bill Haynes, "the wish of the city planners is that allotment men do not duplicate names. Much confusion arose from the names of Park place, Park street and Parkwood avenue and much time was lost by people who went to the wrong place is [sic] consequence.

"Now it seemed to me that the allotment men had just about run out of names and so I'm naming my new allotment after flowers beginning with A and running through the entire alphabet. By doing this I'm hoping to get away from common names as the principle that all the world hates a piker.

"For instance the first street was Arutus and the second is Buttercup, C was a sticker for a minute as the only name I could think of was Chrysanthemum. Now it is a terrible thing to handicap a child with a name that will be a sour one and a joke but now much more terrible to mis-name a street and think of a street going through the centuries carrying a name like Chrysanthemum. No I asked Howie Valesques, my next door neighbor, about it. Howie knows more about flowers than anybody else in the world and he promptly suggested Cosmos. Later I remember that Carnation was available but it was then too late as the name was already on the plate in the blackest of ink.

"D was easy, for who couldn't think of Daisy? But E was more difficult. After considerable thought I put down Elderberry. It is the name of a blossom which is very popular at this time of year. Its treatment depends as whether you like a dry wine or a sweet wine. If you prefer a sweet wine you put in more sugar and then you get a product something like what Chauvillian was in the old days.

"Let's see where as I – Oh yes. F was quite a sticker. I thought of Phlox using the phonetic spelling but then I remember that Helen Fisher or some of these crack spellers might see it and think I didn't know any better. Forget-Me-Not was chosen with Four O'Clock running a close second.

"G was easy and H was no harder. I produced Iris, and J, Jasmine and L resulted in Lotus.

"K was a sticker, though Krysanthemum, spelled along popular lines was considered but finally, with the aid of a flower catalogue, I came upon Kochia and Kochia accordingly was adopted although some local wag is sure to come along and change it to Kosher street.

"M and N were easy, and O supplied Oleander. Now maybe you think I was stuck with Q. Not a bit of it. All quinces have blossoms first. In fact all the letters are to be used except the letter U which I can't find anything for at present.

"The fact that the oldest allotter in town came near this system and perhaps had it in mind is evidenced by the fact that the oldest streets near the center of downtown Akron were named for trees.

"There is Ash street, Beech street and Cherry street and if the idea had been carried further and the streets laid out consecutively it would have shown that there's nothing new 'under the sun.'"

Weather note: Yesterday was certainly a bright, sunshiny day.

Social note: Carl Stubig is back from a tour of the far west. He reports he slept under blankets.

Literary note: Marjorie McClure's new book is entitled "A Bush That Burned[41]."

Editorial note: If winter would only come.

---

[41] "A Bush That Burned," a book by Marjorie Barkley McClure, 1925.

6 July 1925, Monday:

THIS column acknowledges with pleasure the receipt of a nice amber glare shield from Mr. T. J. McKenzie of Barberion. It seems that no sooner had Mr. McKenzie read our plaint the other night about our sufferings from glaring headlights then he immediately bethought himself of his new glare shield on which he has a patent pending.

"The very thing," said Mr. McKenzie, and indeed it is the very thing, and just as soon as our car, which we have not thought up a suitable name for yet on account of not knowing just how long we could keep up the payments, drives up, we're going to try it out.

This is the first present that this column has ever received, and it has made us so happy that we are thinking soon of writing an article about Steinway Grand pianos.

"'A.Y.L. writes you as follows,' writes Gus Kasch, 'It would be of interest to know what Gus Kasch stands for, we all know what he is against.' It is clear that A.Y.L. only reads your column and C.L.'s editorials else he would know that ex-Mayor Ryholt (might just as well being now) told all about it at his Ryholt-for-Mayor-club meeting. The ex said that he 'had not gathered together a lot of haphazard planks out of which to build a platform,' and the political reporter said that this was a 'dig' at Gus Kasch for his 5,000 word platform enumerating the things he stood for.

"Several weeks ago the city ed put a head on my platform (My politician as the late great T.H. called his'n) saying it looked like a cross word puzzle. It sure did and does puzzle some to know how I expect to overcome the opposition of the rubber barons in the effort to put a million a year tax on their 10 million a year profits in order to bring about the things 'Gus Kasch stands for' – more human happiness and less auto killings.

"It also makes some of the R.B.'s cross to think that it is coming. Suggest to A.Y.L. that he read the news columns of the B.J. It's a real newspaper except during campaign times.

"Anyway there'll be a hot time in the old town this fall."

Well, personally speaking, I've never been able to make much of anything out of anybody's platform, particularly when it happened to be a man's platform as it generally is. They all come out and say they're against corruption among public officials and for lower taxes and for a strict interpretation of the constitution and a few things like that which is just about as illuminating as to say green is a real restful color and the ten commandments are pretty good stuff.

Now if I were running for mayor of this town – as I was saying, if I were running for mayor of this town I'd come out with a few concrete planks that everybody could understand.

For one thing I don't like the way the garbage wagons have of all getting into a procession and then going past this office's windows at half past eleven every morning. Eleven-thirty is just the time when my fancy is turning in the direction of lunch. My idea for the collection of garbage is this: That the city buy all the garbage cans so that they will be of uniform size. Then the garbage man starts out in the morning with a collection of nice bright cans all cleaned with sal soda. When he comes to your house he takes up the old can, which is all filled with Sunday's watermelon rinds and things like that and leaves in its place the nice clean can. He doesn't even have to take the lid off. All the cans fit in their proper grooves in the wagon and the procession when it gets down to the Beacon Journal will be ever so much pleasanter than it is now.

Another thing that I don't like about this town is the paint that some people put on their houses. I understand that over in Italy, which is really a very colorful country, the green, the pale blue and the magenta houses all look awfully dear. But you can't go past a pale blue house in Akron without feeling just utterly crushed. If I were mayor of this town I'd get after Ed Rose and the rest of the councilmen with chocolate sundaes, date muffins and anything else I could bribe them with and get them to pass an ordinance that all the houses had to be painted white with green shutters. There's really no other color for a house.

Those who don't like it should build brick or stone houses.

And the next ordinance I would get passed would be to the effect that anybody who comes around to a newly married person and says, "Well, how do you like married life?" would get his taxes quadrupled for the next 10 years.

<hr>

7 July 1925, Tuesday:

ONE OF the fallacies that has caused women a great deal of suffering, and I dare say men too, is the idea that the greatest thing in the world is love. A book with a title to this effect was written some years ago by a gentleman with great drooping whiskers named Henry Drummond and while it was a well written book and all in all as fine a sermon as you would want to find anywhere, still it seems to me that Mr. Drummond erred in one respect; he should have made work the greatest thing to the world and given love a secondary place.

When I was young, say 20 years, I believed that work was just a make shift and that Love was All. When I was 25 and had had a few disappointments I still believed that Love was All but I had found that if you couldn't have love, work made a remarkably satisfactory substitute. Now that I am 30 I think that the ideal life is one in which both work and love have a part. I think I would place the proportions at two-thirds work and one-third love.

And if I could not have both work and love – I am not sure about this, I can't be sure until I am 60 – then I think I would let love go and stick to my job.

———

By love of course I do not mean entirely the romantic attachment which exists between men and women. I mean rather just the common back yard affection which human beings have for one another regardless of sex.

We have felt for so long that we couldn't be happy unless we had some great affection in our lives. I know a girl now, unusually attractive, unusually intelligent, who has a talent which, if she would cultivate it, would undoubtedly bring her a fair degree of fame in a few years. She doesn't cultivate it though. She mopes. She mopes because she is thrown among people whom she doesn't care about. She mopes because the one or two individuals whom she has set her heart on do not respond to her.

She doesn't realize that this golden talent which she is neglecting is the very sesame which would open for her all the hearts, the circles, the foreign lands which she so longs for. Instead she day dreams and yearns.

I have thought about this girl a great deal lately because we are all more or less like that. We have been taught for so long that love is all that we let the lack of it embitter our whole lives. And we turn our whole energies to longing for it thereby wasting our very means of attaining it.

We are like the spider which I tried to fish out of the bath tub this morning. All night long I dare say he had been crawling up the slippery sides and falling back – climbing up and falling back. Finally I got a piece of paper and tried to coax him to crawl on that so I could life him out. But the spider did not trust the paper. It moved. It was unfamiliar.

Neither his father nor his mother nor any other s [sic] spider had taught him that a piece of paper on occasion could be helpful. And so he kept trying to crawl up the slippery enamel until I rescued him by main force.

It may be of course that some of us have found human relationships which have proved entirely satisfactory. I do not know. But I think that it has been the experience of most of us that whenever we put too much store on the affection of another human being we ended by being disappointed. Parents, children, friends fail us when we need them most. Those men and women whom we so longed to know from afar turned out on close acquaintance to be incredibly selfish and stupid. Most people of course are that way on occasion anyway. The only difference is that if we hadn't cared so much we wouldn't have been hurt so much.

Work, it seems to me, never treats us that way. It gives us back jot for jot and tittle for tittle whatever we put into it. It makes us big instead of little. Instead of shutting us within four walls it brings the whole world to our feet. Moreover work well performed does the very thing which we in our lonely moments so longed for – it brings us the friendship of certain men and women who would never have known we were on earth. If we had just sat in our little dark corners and pitied ourselves and wept.

8 July 1925, Wednesday:

SOMEHOW I can't take much comfort from the statement issued from Paris that plump figures are going to be the rage again. It was only about a week ago that we learned that the muslin manufacturers were complaining because the women weren't wearing as much underpinning as they used to. "If this thing keeps up," they complained bitterly, "we'll have to give up our place in Switzerland and reduce ourselves to two town cars."

The statement about the plump figures smacks too much of an effort to boost the cloth manufacturing industry.

Or perhaps it's the candy manufacturers. I understand that the girls aren't going in for chocolate creams anywhere like the way they used to and that the caramel industry is facing one of the most critical periods in years.

Not that I don't wish it were true – that about the plump figures. So far as I have been able to discover those times when plump figures were fashionable were very pleasant times. I have seen pictures depicting them in a number of the million dollar movie houses. I don't mean the pictures on the screen. I mean the ones out in the $500,000 lobbies. And in practically all of them the women were lolling about on green terraces while men in long cloaks and guitars were sending them perfectly killing glances.

That is the way life should be – the women lolling, the men serenading them in deep rich baritones and everybody very cool and relaxed in the shade of forest trees.

But I'm afraid that those of us who were born behind the times will just have to continue to suffer while bobbed hair and the boyish form continue to be the ideal.

After all it is very satisfactory, or at any rate I imagine it must be very satisfactory, to carry about practically no weight at all, to be able to run up and down stairs without a peculiar heaving about the heart, to play golf in the morning, tennis in the afternoon, dance all night, sleep four hours and be at it again the next day just as bright and fresh as ever, to be able to pick up a yard and a half remnant and make a perfectly stunning frock out of it, to lunch on a 15-cent salad and a glass of iced tea, to be able to sit in an outdoor swing without feeling the branches creaking alarmingly over you, and to be followed by the admiring glances of all your friends.

These things we plumper ones never know. I will not say that we are openly jeered at but an astonishing number of people seem to take an astonishing amount of interest in our condition.

We are receiving an alarming number of pamphlets from corsetiers, the manufacturers of stylish stouts and people with reducing apparatus.

When we sit down to our lunch of soup, hash, French fried potatoes, a salad, rye bread, iced coffee and apricot pie a la mode it is with the certain foreknowledge that practically everybody in the tea room is going to turn around and send us doubtful looks.

These looks go so ominous that at one time in my life I determined to lunch only upon a bowl of bread and milk and a small pudding. At 2 o'clock my sufferings began and at 5 o'clock I had consumed 25 cents worth of pretzels.

Our troubles getting clothed are only too well known. There are never any remnants to fit us. The best you can do is to get two remnants and then you look like a trick sofa pillow. We see advertised an after the Fourth sale of lovely ten dollar frocks and when we get down town we find that the only things that fit us are in the $40 section.

How they got by in the old days I don't know. It may be, as some saver, that women weren't really plumper then. That they merely added to their curves such artifices as they found useful and in keeping with the fashion of the times.

But that I can not wholly believe. At any rate the picture that I see in the motion picture lobbies, and it is from these that I have gained the major part of my artistic education, would indicate that it was not entirely a matter of clothes.

<hr />

9 July 1925, Thursday:

IT seems there are a number of roads leading to Cuyahoga Falls. Bill, he who drives our car, brings home the groceries and laughs gaily when the toast is burned, doesn't like the paved road. He likes to get out on the little side roads where you can wander up and down hill, watch the growing corn and get close to nature.

So Tuesday night when we were starting out for Cuyahoga Falls, Bill said, "Let's not go the regular way. There're bound to be a lot of people on it. Let's go this way." "All right," I said in my usual docile fashion and I suppose if it hadn't been for the fact that there had just been a heavy downpour and our brakes weren't working everything would have been all right.

<hr />

This is where Mr. A. Herbruck of Route 7 comes in. Mr. Herbruck is one of those persons who restores your faith in human nature just when it is at lowest ebb. It was Mr. Herbruck and his able helpers who lifted us out of the ditch.

The way we came to be in the ditch is this way: we had been going along, just like a couple of kids you know, skidding from one side of the road to the other and only occasionally getting knocked through the roof. What the name of this road is I don't know except that it runs off to the left from Portage Path and so far as I have been able to make out runs diametrically in the opposite direction from Cuyahoga Falls. It is about four feet wide and winds sometimes to the right and left and sometimes up and down depending on where it can find the most boulders and mud holes.

Anyway we were on this road and along about the seventh mile, still being reasonably intact and with the hand brake at least working, we drew to one side to let another fellow pass. This is where the ditch was and our car promptly turned over in it. We fully expected that after we had done this much to let the other fellow past he would return and courteously inquire as to what he could do for us. He did not, however. For a number of minutes we could hear his car retreating in the distance. I listened carefully for a time hoping he would blow up or something but it is my certain belief that nothing happened.

It was really quite a pleasant spot that we had elected to stop in. A short distance away there was a little stream trickling and making really delightful music and down beside the river bed someone had carelessly tossed a leather sofa which at one time had evidently been quite good. After Bill had tried in various ways to get the car out of the ditch, we considered the possibility of sitting there on the sofa for the rest of the night and listening to the water music.

It was at this point that Mr. Herbruck and his friends came by.

After that everything may be said to have gone along reasonably well. "Are you sure this is the road to Cuyahoga Falls?" I queried of Bill.

"Uh-huh," he answered in his usual polite fashion and after that except for an occasional, Oh Gracious, Oh Gracious, Oh Gracious, or something similar. I clung to the edge of the window and kept silent.

The road to Cuyahoga Falls kept getting narrower and narrower. Eventually it became a sort of cow path overgrown with grass and with trees hanging over it.

"Are you SURE this is the road to Cuyahoga Falls?" I said sort of careless like in a manner to indicate that I really didn't care much one way or the other.

"Well," said Bill gently, "If it ain't we can't turn around now anyhow."

Three minutes later we drew up in a space about as big as the top of a bass drum. To the left was a ravine with a good lusty brook in it, to the right, so that you could put out your hand and touch it was a sharp incline covered with bushes and immediately in front of us was a cow pasture and a four foot fence.

Three dogs came out and barked at us. After they had barked for 15 minutes I thought I heard help arriving. But it was only a horse splashing across the brook.

This time no Mr. Herbruck and his friends came along to help us. After this fact had thoroughly penetrated, Bill decided to turn the car around.

He did it really very dexterously. We came out in Bath.

A beautiful little place, Bath.

10 July 1925, Friday:

I DON'T KNOW whether anybody will remember it, but two or three years ago an epidemic of marathon dancing struck the country.

I happened to be around when the epidemic started. A young man somewhere had danced for hours and a young woman employed as a dancing instructor in the upper reaches of New York city said she could do better. I was around for a part of the time, while she was establishing her record. I don't remember anymore how many hours she danced. It seems to me it was a couple of days and a night. Anyway, she wore out several pairs of stockings, several dance partners and subsisted mainly on tomato soup which was handed her in a cup from time to time by interested watchers.

After it was over, she seemed to be none the worse for her experience. Her endurance, I believe, she subscribed to reliance on a vegetarian diet and to the circumstance that she always carried a small Bible close to her heart.

In a week or so somebody was establishing a better record elsewhere, and the young woman was forgotten. Possibly now it may cause her a little thrill in retrospect to think that for two or three days she held the attention of the nation. I never heard though whether she was a particularly capable dancing instructor.

Just now we seem to be suffering from an epidemic of marathon Bible reading. A church congregation meets and determines to read the whole Bible through without stopping. The first time it happened I was rather interested. After all, it is fairly interesting to know just how long it does take to read the Bible through aloud. If they take it at the clip at which they generally take the Lord's Prayer they ought to get through nicely before supper time. And the statistics are no more foolish than the statistics we have on a multitude of other subjects.

Now, however, that a couple of dozen churches in as many cities have tried the same feat. I am beginning to wonder if the thing is a sort of friendly intercity sport, on a par with pole vaulting, long-distance dancing and endurance piano playing.

Not that I am opposed to the reading of the Bible. I occasionally take a little dip into it myself. My idea, though, would be not to take it in tote. I would prefer, rather, to read the story of Ruth three times and allow that as an excuse to skip the begats and the bloodier of the battles.

Miss Mary MacSwiney who will speak in Akron Sunday on behalf of the Irish republic has some interesting things to relate on the pangs of starvation. It was Miss MacSwiney's brother who aroused at once the amazement and the sympathies of the world by going without food for 74 days before finally succumbing to the ordeal. Miss MacSwiney herself when arrested by English authorities went on two hunger strikes, one of 26 days, one of 31 days. When you consider that the average person who goes on a hunger strike is not expected to live more than a month you can appreciate the terrible zeal with which the Irish patriot is inspired.

"The first week," said Miss MacSwiney, "you are still more or less active and you feel great pain and discomfort. But after that you are so weak you take to your bed and thereafter you are aware of very little except that you are growing weaker and weaker. There is too a great pain in the pit of your stomach. I do not know how to describe it. It is not such a pain as neuralgia, but it is still very real, nevertheless."

From both of her fasts she recovered with no apparent injury to her health.

It has long been a coarse of wonderment to me that those who go on a voluntary fast seem to fare so very well and indeed seem to improve their health while those whose misfortune brings to starvation seem to collapse in very short order.

The mind here, I imagine, has considerable to do with it. When we do without food willingly, we bear up very well. But let our pockets be empty and let us be put on the streets with no plate to turn and let four or five meal times go by and we become helpless and blubbering and very ill indeed.

---

11 July 1925, Saturday:

I DON'T know just how I shall dispose of all my money when I die but I should like to leave a little of it to the Travelers' Aid.

Of course it may be that when it comes time to die I shall have ha [sic] to seek out other welfare agencies – it may be that by then I shall have been fed by the Salvation Army on a cold night or been found congenial employment by the Y.W.C.A. But up to date the Travelers' Aid is the only agency I have every had actual contact with and while it was nothing spectacular still it always gives me a warm glow whenever I think of it.

The first time was when I had been sent down to Philadelphia to try to get a signed interview from a woman who had murdered her husband. You know how those things are done. The reporter does the actual writing but in all intents and purposes it is done by the other woman and the other woman's name goes over it. The thing took longer than I had expected and I was obliged to stay in Philadelphia over night. It was an exceedingly rainy night, I had tramped through a great deal of mud. I was without an umbrella and the prospect of a bath, and clean sheets appealed to me tremendously.

I went to the Hotel Adelphia and stated by plight to the clerk – that I was a reporter, that I was stranded in Philadelphia for the night and couldn't the matron fix one up with a tooth brush and a couple of necessities? I had heard of hotels which were as thoughtful as all that.

The clerk looked me over scathingly. "Well," he said after a three-minute survey, "we'll take a chance on you but the cheapest thing we got is $7.50."

I don't know why it is that people always treat me like that. Whenever I want to buy a pair of silk stockings the clerk says, "Yes, but the cheapest we got is three dollars," or if its spectacles I'm buying then they say, "Yes, but the cheapest we got is 75 cents."

Anyways, I was furious. Not only did I have two weeks' salary with me, but the office I was with, whatever the shortcomings, was always generous in the matter of expense money.

I told the clerk a few things, not nearly enough as I decided later, and then I went over to the railway station where I told my troubles to the woman at the Travelers' Aid desk. She immediately called up a hotel – it was one of those that I love most, an old one with tremendous rooms, tremendous beds, carpets four inches thick and creamy colored woodwork and there had the most blissful sleep in years.

And the clerk had grand manners.

The other time when I had to seek out the Travelers' Aid was when I was working on a story where I was supposed to be a girl from the middle west who had come to New York to get on the stage[42].

---

[42] Referencing her time as "Huldah Benson," which is another chapter in this book.

I walked into the Grand Central station one morning carrying a traveling bag and went over to the Travelers' Aid desk and told the two women there in charge of my ambitions. Of course I wasn't telling them the truth and as I found out later they strongly suspected that I wasn't but the thing that matters is that, truth or no truth, they took me in charge and looked after me. They told me where I might eat cheaply. They helped me find a room that was both clean and inexpensive. And they gave me a list of theatrical agencies that would be most likely to help me.

And they did it with as much concern as though they didn't have hundreds of other persons all waiting to be helped out of some sort of plight.

After they found out that I was only working on a news story I do not think they liked it very well but anyway I shall always be grateful to them.

Because things might have been so different.

<hr />

13 July 1925, Monday:

A FRIEND came in and showed me a letter a while ago which he had received from a woman living in the west. I do not know the woman's name and I did not see all of the letter, but the portion which I read interested me because while it expressed a sentiment, which one comes upon occasionally in the modern novel, this was the first time I had ever met it in real life.

"I have decided that if I can't get married before I'm too old to have children," the woman had written, "I'm going to have one anyway. You know my belief is that man made laws should not govern such things. Just because I can't find the man I want to live with all my life, is that any reason why I should give up that which I want most – a child? No, that's my business and God's."

<hr />

It seems to me that there is a very obvious solution to a problem of this sort. It lies in the orphan asylum. A woman is lonely and she would like to have a child. Tucked away in the orphan asylum are hundreds of children who are aching for a little exclusive attention all their own. I don't know much about it myself but I have been told by workers with children that there isn't a youngster who wouldn't rather have the poorest of homes for his very own than to be brought up in an institution, no matter if the latter place is endowed with millions, if he has trained nurses to wait on him and eats only scientifically prepared food. He wants his own home and his own mother.

Isn't making a youngster of that sort happy a better thing all the way around than bringing a new youngster into the world?

For even the child who is born of devoted parents and a happy home is bound to encounter a certain amount of unhappiness. How much more so the child whose birth, even in these enlightened times, must be a matter for covert criticism if not sneers and who, for a number of years at least, could ever have an honest explanation as to why he had just a mother and not a father as other children have.

"But," I can fancy the woman saying, "I could never love an adopted child as I would my own."

That, I imagine, is just a little bit bunk. At any rate I have known quite a number of mothers who unblushingly confessed that they cared very little for their children when they were first born. It was not until the baby began manifesting a personality of his own, not until he began showing that he recognized his mother and needed her that there began burning that very fierce affection which was to last through life.

And you have only to go through the hospital ward of the children's hospital or the children's home to learn that the most pleading hands in the world are those of a little abandoned baby.

The next objection is that adopted children don't turn out well. This objection has been so widespread that whole bureaus of investigators have been turned loose to get at the truth of the matter. What they found was this: that the adopted child has just as much chance of turning out well as your very own flesh and blood. You yourself may have known instances of children who had ideal parents but who stubbornly persisted in manifesting either Aunt Hattie's temper or Uncle Henry's inability to get along in school. You just smiled indulgently then. But if the child had been an adopted child – dear, DEAR!

The thing lying at the root of the matter I imagine is as unconscious selfishness which has grown up during the past few years. It has been hoisted on us by the Freudians who have made us believe that the unmarried woman with no chick or child to call her own would eventually become "peculiar." There are, I dare say, a number of women so constituted that they need drastic measures of some sort. But they're so rare. You only have to look about you to know that there isn't any healthier person in the world than a happy, jolly old maid who's resigned to her fate and who refuses to clutter up her mind with a lot of erotic notions.

The married women envy her, the men adore her and everybody's crazy to have her run out to the house for dinner. And if her heart's getting so full it insists on running over and if the boss keeps on increasing her salary so fast she doesn't know what to do with it, then let her get into her little Ford coupe and go out to the children's home and pick out a little big-eyed kid and bring it home with her.

It solves an old problem without creating a bigger one.

❧

14 July 1925, Tuesday:

ACCORDING to an editorial in the Akron Sunday Times the art of spelling, while a desirable thing to have, is still far from being necessary and the average human being can get by very nicely without it.

The idea, if I get it correctly, is that while Calvin Coolidge is doubtless able to spell, still if he weren't the world would never be the wiser. One's secretary can look after those things so nicely.

It's sort of hard, though, on those of us who don't have secretaries. And it's worse yet if even the secretaries can't spell.

We were talking a day or so ago with a well known author who is anxious to find a young man to whom he can give dictation. The opening would be a splendid one in many ways for not only would the young man have the opportunity of travel and of a leisurely time in the open but he would also have the advantage of contact with an alert mind which might prove invaluable to him in later years in a business way.

"But I can't find such a young man," grieved the author. "They know shorthand and they can use the typewriter but they can't spell. I get up in the morning keen for work and we settle down to business. Pretty soon I use the word 'Jocoalty.' 'How do you spell it?' says the young man. I stop and spell it for him. My train of thought is broken. A half dozen experiences like that in the course of the morning and I'm out of sorts for the day."

Cartoonists can't spell, sign painters can't spell but where in the world the writer in the Sunday Times gets the idea that it doesn't matter I don't know. Would he say that it was also immaterial if composers of music didn't know what key they were writing in? to be sure Irving Berlin gets by, by picking all of his pieces out on the key of F-sharp, but suppose there weren't anybody in the world who could transpose it for him? Not only would Irving's music get pretty monotonous but there would be precious few people to buy it. Saying it in music with six sharps is not the average person's idea of a pleasant musical half hour.

I have forgotten now whether the idea was original or whether it was something he had seen is a magazine but anyway somebody was suggesting the other day that we ought to find [sic] our fat men.

"For the fat man," he said, "Is out greatest criminal. He takes up more room in the street car than he pays for. He eats food which he doesn't need and which starving people ought to have. He is invariably a liability – life insurance companies refuse to insure him. And he offends propriety by dropping jelly on his necktie.

"I suggest that fat men be hauled into court and fined for each pound overweight. If a man is 10 pounds overweight let him be fined 10 pounds. That is, let him be put on bread and water until he is back to normal."

Somebody then remarked that a great deal more harm came from over-eating than from over-drinking and that reminded somebody else that he had talked with a doctor recently who said that he had never known anyone who was actually ruined by the use of drugs.

From then on it was practically no time until they got around to the subject of matrimony which is the cadence on which every well conducted discussion ought to close.

"The trouble with matrimony," said the man who had said that fat men ought to be fine [sic] (he's quite slender himself) "is that during courtship people aren't honest with one another. They pretend to a lot of virtues that they haven't got. 'Oh dear,' says the girl, 'I'd just love to go to a dance.' 'All right,' says the man, 'let's go.' All through the courtship he pretends he just loves to dance. After they're married she can't get him out from behind his newspaper.

"Or the girl discovers that the man she's endeavoring to charm is fond of the outdoors. She gets herself a suit of knickers and goes hiking and canoeing from morning till night. After they're married she puts on some high heeled slippers and a frilly dress and sits on the front porch all day long."

But dear, dear, if she didn't do it, somebody else would.

◆

15 July 1925, Wednesday:

BUDDIES
Or
Roommates I Have Known

PEARL

Pearl was pure. She would not go to a movie on Sunday and she thought damn was a very wicked word. She would not go with a fellow who smoked and she sang hymns every night after supper. One night Pearl eloped. The fellow she eloped with was my Albert whom I'd been having dates with every Wednesday and Sunday for the past three years. Incidentally Pearl took along with her my ivory hair brush, my green negligee, my suede purse and the three dollars I'd been saving up for a facial.

GLADYS

Gladys loved company. The company would start coming at 10 in the morning before Gladys had had her breakfast and would continue coming until two the next morning. It included a nurse temporarily out of employment, a movie actress temporarily out of employment, a divorcee, another divorcee, two college girls and a woman who had rejected a proposal of marriage in early youth. The company almost always brought along a couple of ukuleles and Gladys would make fudge which they would then eat sitting on the bed. Sometimes the bed seemed very crumby. However, you did not mind that much as you rarely got to bed. Gladys was a great lover of life.

STELLA

It had been in the contract that Stella was to wash the dishes. Stella's method of washing the dishes was to pile them in the bath tub and then go to the movies with whatever young man happened to be calling. When you came to your bath in the morning it was very trying. Sometimes it seemed as though the butter didn't get off the edge of the bath tub from one end of the week to the next.

DOROTHY

Dorothy was very neat. She was always getting up early to clean the house and nothing distressed her more than to find orange peels in the wash bowl. When you came home from work you would frequently find that Dorothy had taken all the beds apart to air and had sent all your old clothes to the cleaners. Whenever anybody set a glass of ginger ale down on the piano Dorothy controlled herself with difficulty and she was once positively rude to a young man who dropped a dish of creamed potatoes on the carpet.

LUELLA

Luella was beautiful and she knew how to dress. The way Luella kept up her chic was never to do anything around the house and never by any chance to pay her half of the bills. Whenever the rent came due Luella was always overwhelmed with remorse to find that that very morning she had been extravagant and bought a new little dinner frock. And never by any chance did it occur to Luella that there were such things as telephone, gas, electric light, laundry and grocery bills.

It wasn't entirely on this account however that Luella was obliged to leave. She had entirely too winning ways with the men. Introduce your steady to Luella and you could go to the movies alone for the rest of the winter.

BESSIE

Bessie was perfect. She rubbed you with alcohol when you were tired. She shampooed your hair. She got sleepy at night and woke up in the morning at the same time you did. Her old clothes fit you perfectly. Her opinions were just enough different to make an argument interesting. She knew how to cook and she did and she washed the dishes without grumbling when her turn came. She paid her half of the bills promptly and she never waited more than a week to return the dollar she borrowed. She had no religion, was a crack hand at pinochle and traded jokes with the ash man.

Bessie got married and went west to live, and her husband broke her heart.

---

16 July 1925, Thursday:

THE centennial celebration should teach us at least one thing: not to be so high hat about things of the past. Over at the art institute for instance they have collected together some old pieces of furniture, the beauty of which puts to shame the expensive overstuffed three-piece "suits" with which we persist in choking up our modern apartments.

And along with the collection has come an encyclopedia[43] loaned by Will Voris which although it bears the date 1831, is not nearly so funny as you might at first suppose.

The book, of course, has its moments. As for instance when Charles Goodrich, editor of it, gives his rules for bathing, Mr. Goodrich recommends a cold bath taken every morning either in the sea or in a clear river. If neither a sea or a clear river is at hand, then Mr. Goodrich permits a shower.

This, however, is far from being all. "One ought to bathe once a week the whole year through," he says, "in tepid water and it will be of considerable service to add to it some soap."

"It is a vulgar error," he says, "that it is safer to enter the water when the body is cool and that person heated by exercise and beginning to perspire should wait until they are perfectly cooled. Thus, by plunging into it in this state, an alarming and dangerous chillness frequently seizes them and the injury sustained is generally ascribed to their going into it too warm; while it doubtless arises from the contrary practice."

———————

Mr. Goodrich likewise feels very strongly on the matter of night air, particularly in bedrooms. "A practice equally imprudent with that of occupying a heated bed chamber during cold weather," he says, "is the one very commonly pursued of attempting to reduce the temperature of this apartment in summer by leaving the windows open at night. Many persons have experienced serious and irreparable injury to their health by being subjected in this manner, whilst asleep, to a current of cold air from without."

He deplores also the popular passion for feather beds and the tendency on the part of housewives to shove the children's bed under the larger bed in the day time. Mr. Goodrich, it appears, had no objection to fresh air. He merely wished it properly administered. And one can't help but admire him for his revolutionary stand on the matter of baby clothes. "The clothing of children," he maintains, "cannot be too short."

———————

A great many persons would doubtless be interested in chapter III which is headed "Drinks." After considering that water, which was formerly supposed to be one of the

---

[43] "A New Family Encyclopedia; or, Compendium of Universal Knowledge: Comprehending a plain and practical view of those subjects most interesting to persons in the ordinary professions of life," by Charles A. Goodrich, 1832.

elements, is now found to consists of two gases, hydrogen and oxygen. Mr. Goodrich passes to a consideration of other liquids and includes in the process a summary of the best apples for making cider and a recipe for making currant wine.

He explains also the source of the world alcohol. "This is said to be an Arabian word," he says, "which signflies antimony. It is so called form the usage of eastern ladies to paint their eye brows with antimony, reduced to a most subtle powder; whence at last it came to signify anything exalted to its highest perfection."

In the text the words "highest perfection" are rendered in Italics.

The book contains many other things ranging from recipes for the cure of whooping cough to the population of the American colonies in 1701, but I think I shall always esteem Mr. Goodrich particularly for his remarks on housebuilding.

"The first thing done in the new parts of the country, when a spot is determined on for a house," he says, "is to cut down all the trees within many rods of it. And then, year by year, the work of destruction goes on as if the very sight of a forest tree were odious. The house stands alone in the clearing, its inmates and particularly its children, roasting and browned under the hot summer sun. by and by the nakedness and dreariness of the situation is felt and then are planted some Lombardy poplars 'all in a row.'

"Now the trees which we cut down with such an unsparing hand are the very kind which English gardeners cultivate with the most persevering diligence. And we too, shall cultivate them before long and shall think with the most bitter regret of the sad destruction which we and our ancestors have made.

"When about to build in a new country we should have, near our house, an acre or two of the forest and should guard it with the most watchful care. Morning, noon and evening it would be an agreeable retreat; its shade would be refreshing in our scorching heats; its noble form would gratify our taste; it would raise our thought to Him who is 'a shadow from the heat, a strength to the needy in his distress.' Let us then spare our noble forest trees. Many political considerations might be adduced to show the imprudence of our rude havoc among them, bur for these we have not room."

17 July 1925, Friday:

SOMEHOW or other I have always had a passion for waiters although why this should be I do not know. I think it is rather due to the circumstance that if you are alone in a strange city the waiter is frequently your only contact with human kind.

And if the opposite should be the case, if you should not be alone in a strange city; if, on the contrary you should live in a place where you are completely surrounded by relatives and friends, then the waiter is frequently a blessed means of escape.

He will pass you the potatoes without your having to ask for them three times, if you don't find anything before you that you want to eat he will go out and find something that you do want, he makes no comments on the attire in which you come in the table, and if you care to express an opinion on anything he will listen respectfully until you have finished and then agree that your views are entirely correct.

And all this may be had for a quarter.

———

It is ridiculous, this idea that waiters shouldn't be tipped. Where also can you get so much for so little? I have known days where I have been sworn at by bus drivers, hawled out by traffic cops, deserted by the men who vowed to love me and informed by the landlord that the rent would be ten dollars a month more beginning on the first. And I have gone downtown stopping in convenient doorways from time to time to mop up the tears and have finally edged into my favorite restaurant.

And what did I find? The head waiter hunting me up a place by the electric fan and remarking respectfully that it is a nice evening, the bus boy rushing up with a fresh table cloth, the waiter proper arriving on the scene and requesting to know whether I will have clam broth or melon.

I tell you there are moments when your whole outlook on life can be changed by the circumstance that one human being, no matter how humble, is interested for the time being in whether you will have clam broth or melon.

———

I remembered just now Mr. Petrini. Mr. Petrini waited on me those mornings when I could be extravagant and have a 75-cent breakfast – fruit, oatmeal with scads of cream, hot muffins, boiled eggs and coffee. Mr. Petrini had come from Switzerland and he was longing to go back. He loved the mountains and the little flowers that grow in the snow.

He recalled some of the old taverns where celebrities used to come, Kreisler[44], Mengelberg[45] and once the crown prince. Mr. Petrini thought of them regretfully, his hands crossed above the white apron over his round belly. But he would never be going back. There was little money to be found in Switzerland and since coming to America Mr. Petrini had acquired responsibilities. There was a wife and a baby and rents were high.

The names of most of them, though, I never learned. There was a girl whom I particularly loved. On those times when I was late and the rush was over she would stop and tell me about her mother. The old lady had raised a large family, most of whom had gone away and forgotten her. The old man hadn't been any too good to her either. There were just two girls left to her now and both were waiting table. This winter they had heard of jobs to be had at a new hotel in Florida and they were going to take them so that Ma would have a trip south. The preparations for that trip were beautiful. For one thing Ma whose proportions were expensive, got new $12 corsets, the first at such a price that she had ever had in all her life. And Ma had new silk dresses and underthings with ribbons on them. One morning my girl didn't show up and I knew that the hegira[46] had taken place. I often used to wonder about Ma – whether she used to spread the underthings out on the bed so that she could take in their glories all at once and whether she was comfortable in her new corsets.

As for the girls I knew there had been no $12 corsets for them. I guess when one's spirits are holstered up with love one doesn't need such trifles.

---

18 July 1925, Saturday:

---

[44] Fritz Kreisler (1875-1962) Austrian violinist and composer.

[45] Willem Mengelberg (1871-1951) Dutch conductor.

[46] Hegira, a journey escaping from a dangerous or undesirable situation: exodus; a reference of Muhammad's departure from Mecca to Medina in ad 622

I T WAS only last night that Mr. Perley was contemplating suicide. Mr. Perley felt that he had sufficient cause for suicide. For one thing he had been informed that the office in which he was employed was undergoing reorganization, and that after the first of the month his services would be dispensed with. And for another thing, the young woman upon whom Mr. Perley was lavishing his middle-aged affections had broken a date to go to the stock company, only to be discovered later by Mr. Perley wantonly riding down Main st. with a handsome stranger in a newly painted coupe.

As Mr. Perley reflected on these things, he decided that he had had about enough. Life, he told himself, was an imposter, a bit of grass held before the nose of a donkey. In his present state of mind, Mr. Perley had no difficulty in identifying himself with the donkey. "You slave all your life for a heartless concern," he said bitterly, "and when they get ready to kick you out they kick you out. You lay all the affection of a vigorous manhood at the feet of a silly empty headed woman, and she tramples on it."

And so Mr. Perley set upon the preparations for his suicide. He would have no difficulty in the matter, as he had some pills at home in the little box on top of the dresser which were particularly bad for a weak heart. Mr. Perley had been informed that his heart was very bad. He would take the pills and stretch himself on the bed and in the morning, the landlady would discover him stiff and cold, and there would be a great hue and cry and possibly a writeup in the paper.

And when a certain young woman read about it she would suddenly realize with a great shock how great had been her loss, and thereafter those who looked at her would marvel at the sad expression in her eyes.

The trouble was that Mr. Perley couldn't find the pills. They weren't in the little box on the dresser and they weren't in the pocket of his dressing gown and they weren't in the bottom of the trunk.

"Oh well," said Mr. Perley, "tomorrow night will do just as well. I'll get some more pills tomorrow."

This being his last night on earth Mr. Perley decided that he would get into bed and that he would then lie awake and think about death.

Mr. Perley did lie awake and think about death for full five minutes, during which time a tear trickled from beneath his eyelids and glistened on his cheek.

At the end of this time, he went to sleep and snored loudly.

This morning was a bright, sparkling morning and as Mr. Perley rose to greet it he forgot temporarily that this was the day appointed for his death. When he finally did remember, he dismissed the thought very quickly and selected one of his brightest ties – a tan striped with red. Then he sprinkled a little toilet water on his hair.

As Mr. Perley walked downtown, he couldn't remember a time when he had felt so absolutely on his toes. The morning continued to sparkle. The grass and the trees were, if anything, a darker green than usual. Overhanging the sidewalk was a bush with white berries. Mr. Perley picked a cluster of the berries and stuck them in his coat. Two little boys stopped at the curb to stare at him, and Mr. Perley could hardly resist the impulse to pat them on the head. Pretty girls, all dressed in bright colors, kept coming out of the side streets and joining the main stream on its way to work. Downtown the banners and the flags strung up for the Centennial celebration fluttered and danced in the breeze.

"How beautiful," said Mr. Perley, "how absolutely beautiful. Just think of it, if I had done – had done what I was going to do last night, I wouldn't be here to enjoy all this."

It was at this point that the young woman who had treated Mr. Perley's devotion so badly, started crossing the street. She spied Mr. Perley, and on her face there was an expression of mingled regret and affection. She stretched out her hands.

"Howard," she cried, "Howard!"

But Mr. Perley who at that moment had his eyes glued on a pair of lavender clad ankles failed to hear.

20 July 1925, Monday:

I DARE say the average person considers it a great privilege to ride in a parade on a float but it seems that even this dignity is sometimes fraught with discomfort.

There is the case of Rocco Cascioli, Akron contractor, who, when the via-duct was opened, was invited to ride in the parade representing Christopher Columbus.

As Christopher Columbus, Mr. Cascioli was obliged to wear a pair of red tights. The float was gotten up to represent the Santa Maria and Mr. Cascioli was to be lashed to the mast and given a spy glass with the instructions that he was to hold it up to his eye from time to time and make out to be looking for land.

Mr. Cascioli donned the red tights and all who saw him were bound to admit that he looked remarkably well in them. Blushing uncomfortably from their praise, Mr. Cascioli mounted a ladder and was accordingly lashed to the mast.

The tights were thin, however, and the day was cold. The time, as you may remember, was October and there was more than a hint of chill winter in the air.

As soon as the novelty of his situation had worn off sufficiently for him to resume his composure, Mr. Cascioli took stock of himself and discovered he was cold. He grew increasingly cold as the minutes lengthened into hours. It was a long parade. Statistics say that it took ever so long to pass a given point and that there were ever so many people in it.

Remembering that he had a role to play Mr. Cascioli endeavored to look like Columbus seeking for land. This was not so difficult as might be imagined as there was nothing at those moments which Mr. Cascioli would have liked better than to get on a little solid earth himself. Whenever he put the spy glass up to his eye however, his hand shook as with ague. And whenever he endeavored to smile down at the little children gazing up at him his teeth chattered like so many castanets and the expression on his face resolved itself into one of prolonged discomfort. The mast to which he was attached swayed about in the upper air uncertainly and on those occasions when the wagon was passing over a bump, Mr. Cascioli merely closed his eyes and waited.

―――――――

The parade came to an end at last, up by the Union station. Mr. Cascioli's Italian friends who had been having the roles of sailors on the lower deck promptly deserted the Santa Maria and bolted for a nearby Italian club where they could get warm refreshment.

They forgot all about Mr. Cascioli lashed to the mast. So did everybody else.

"Hey," called Mr. Cascioli, "Hey," but all those who had been in the parade were scurrying for places to get warm.

Mr. Cascioli looked about him forlornly. From his vantage place he could see into second story windows where men and women were grouped about tables and chatting with one another agreeably. They were eating and Mr. Cascioli could see the rich warm steam from the coffee. In one place a grate fire was glowing. Mr. Cascioli felt as though his heart would break.

"Hey," he called out, "Hey," and this time, as luck would have it, a small boy heard him.

"Please – if you would – a ladder," said Mr. Cascioli.

The small boy said that he would see what he could do and 15 minutes later he came back with a man. Mr. Cascioli explained his situation to the man and the man disappeared and 15 minutes later reappeared with a ladder.

Mr. Cascioli came down the ladder very, very carefully. Just as he reached the sidewalk a very pretty young woman passed by. She turned and regarded Mr. Cascioli in his red tights. Mr. Cascioli promptly became the same color as the tights and the warm glow which suffused him was the first he had felt in four hours.

The taxi driver, when he came, offered Mr. Cascioli a coat which Mr. Cascioli accepted gratefully.

"Now," said Mr. Cascioli, "now I know that nothing can kill me; not after I have lived through that."

---

21 July 1925, Tuesday:

THERE are two things which I like to do more than anything I know of," writes Jerry. "One of them is to walk the street of a large city in the dead of night, when all is still and most folks are in bed. Peering into the faces of the few people I meet at this time I can see written the stories of their lives. During the day people are on guard and keep their true selves hidden, but night seems to set very much as a subtle liquor, washing away the shell and leaving exposed the thoughts they try so hard to keep covered during the day.

"The other thing I like to do is to see that city while the holiday spirit rules its heart. It is almost as though we revert a few hundred years to the time before we achieved our so-called higher civilization. It is very easy at such times to imagine what the French revolution was like. The air is charged with a devil-may-care attitude, eyes sparkle, girls flirt recklessly and young men flirt back and make remarks which bring hearty guffaws from their cronies, the sort of the remarks that would be barred from drawing room but are considered quite all right at this time.

"And the characters. Here is the man, born with misshapen hands. Cover them with red paint and you'll have an example of justice as handed out by Robespierre. Here is this life he is demonstrating and selling tire patches and seems quite content with things as they are.

"Women, who look as though they had stepped out of their native Hungary. Parading down the street in all the finery of their country, they are proud of it, and they should be. Their's [sic] is an heritage we do not possess. They have the faculty of enjoying themselves. When they play all thought of work is cast to the background. They worked yesterday, they'll work again tomorrow, but today, ah, this is holiday, work is very dim and there is no hardship until tomorrow and tomorrow will take care of itself.

"There's a man with the long hair, face and hands browned by exposure to the elements, clothes ragged and unkempt, looks more like a desert rat than any man I've seen in years. And a man, running a cat stand. He might have been transplanted from the Levant. Ingratiating and polite enough until you show your disinterest in his wares, then his sneers and mild abuse. Flash a badge on him and he'd give a perfect impersonation of a monkey in a cage picking fleas obvious to the surrounding crowd.

"And the girls, selling Centennial emblems and paraphernalia. How different they are from one another. Their manner of approach and sailing methods. Here's one who spots you a block away and meets you with a smile. I don't see how anyone can resist her.

"There are others who wait until you are just ready to pass and then spring out and take you by surprise. Before you know it you have a badge and your purse in a few cents poorer. And the girl who meets you at the corner and follows you to the next, giving all kinds of reasons why you should have a ribbon. I suppose it was very much the same with the little rosettes of the revolution, someone had to make some money and nothing would be more natural than to have pretty girls call them.

"Here's a youngster with a billfold, throwing cards and memoranda right and left. He pauses in his throwing and looking over his shoulder I see that he has found a picture of a girl. The girl is pretty but the pose is naughty. The picture is deposited with loving care in a grimy pocket and the throwing of cards continues. I wonder if he was clever enough to snitch it or whether he found it.

"Soon darkness will envelop the city and with it will come the mardi gras, with all its vivid color and bodacious brilliancy. There will be clowns, more than enough to satisfy any kid's heart. There will be Columbines and harlequins, kings, queens and princesses. There will be love and laughter, youth will come and revel. Old age will come and live again the days when it was young, too. It will be a night of hilarity, then – tomorrow will come, but tomorrow, is capable of taking care of itself, I guess."

22 July 1925, Wednesday:

IT IS always pleasant to know how people came to be married, although too often, I'm afraid the recital (illegible-savors?) of the commonplace. They met at a dance. She liked the masterful way he had guiding her about. For his part, he had decided that he had about enough money in the bank to get married. And she thrilled him in exactly the same way that some half dozen other girls had thrilled him when he didn't have any money in the bank.

And so they were married.

"And we fell terribly in love," they say.

Today, however, I heard a story about an Akron couple which is a little different. She was going some place or other and was obliged to change trains at New Philadelphia. The night was cold. She placed her bags on the little station platform and started walking up and down. A few seconds later a man came along, set his baggage down beside hers and started walking up and down.

Then the train came. They both made a rush for their suit cases and in bending over they rapped their heads so smartly together that both the girl and the man sat down abruptly in the snow.

"I do hope you're not hurt," he said politely.

"Not at all," she answered, "I do hope YOU'RE not hurt."

It appeared that he wasn't either, and so they scrambled up out of the snow and boarded the train.

After that there was nothing for him to do to show how sorry he was except to take her out in the dining car to supper, and when they got down to the caramel pudding with maple syrup, always a delicacy on dining cars, he asked if he might write.

She indicated that he might.

And so they were married.

I was thinking the other day of a man who came into the office three or four years ago with the story of his life written out in lead pencil on these five-cent tablets that the children use.

Every year there are generally one or two persons who come along with their life histories written out and contrary to what you might imagine these histories. [sic] If the writer has been at all honest, are extremely interesting. The object in coming to a newspaper office is, of course, to find someone who will correct the spelling and the punctuation and cast the thing into some sort of literacy shape.

Such a task, however, is well nigh hopeless and anyone is foolish to undertake it. For the writers of the histories, anxious as they are to have their lives cast into book form and sold eventually for a couple of million to the movies, are extremely unwilling to part with any of their pet notions. Suggest that certain events be eliminated and certain others be re-arranged in order to add to the dramatic interest, and they will fight as though you had suggested that a beloved child be handed over to the executioner.

This man to whom I referred earlier had written out his life in such detail that the stack of pencil tablets had become extremely high and the contents when cast into print would make at least two exceedingly stout volumes. His idea for an introduction to the whole was that four men should be sitting in a club and that one of the men should then begin telling his story to the three others. I pointed out that to tell such a story in a single evening would be impossible – that it would take at least a week to tell it and that no one could expect four men to be sitting in a club that long.

My friend, however, was obdurate and so we parted.

His loves and marriages, I still think, would make extremely diverting reading. He first married a childhood sweetheart, who was killed on her wedding day by a runaway horse. For years he brooded on how he might best honor her memory. He finally decided that he would do it by marrying a street walker and making her respectable. After interviewing some half dozen street walkers, he finally found one who seemed to desire to be made an honest woman of, and married her. The experiment, however, was not a success. Years later, while sitting in church, he was attracted by a lovely voice in the church choir. He found that the voice belonged to a young woman who was extremely anxious to continue her musical education. He sent her away to school. She came back a mature young woman.

And so they were married.

And this time, the experiment was a success.

━━❧❦◆❦❧━━

24 July 1925, Friday:

"IN case you're interested," writes Jerry, "Here are some of the Akron Girls I Might Have Married and didn't.

―――――――

"Her name was Lulu, and she was. I don't remember where or how I met her, but somehow or other she appealed to me. The reason I think was because she showed such an interest in me, in what I was doing and what I was going to do. She went out of her way at times to teach me refinement.

"My interest to Lulu died an easy death the first night. I took her to dinner. She quaffed her coffee. I'm willing to admit that it's all right to quaff coffee, but one should stop quaffing when one has reached the bottom of the cup.

―――――――

"Jane was Lulu's antithesis. She didn't care a hang what I was or what became of me so long as I was agreeable to her wishes. Very seldom could Jane and I agree on anything. If I was for anything Jane was against it, and vice versa. Our interest in each other vanished the night we both agreed the show we had seen was rotten.

―――――――

"Betty Ann was an old fashioned girl. At least I thought she was. Betty Ann and I were in the habit of spending night after night out on the lake. In a canoe, she reclining gracefully in one end, with one hand dragging languidly through the water while I sat in the other end softly strumming a uke and singing sweet songs of love. She interrupted me one night while I was singing 'O Sole Mio,' to ask me if I didn't think Rudolph Valentino danced divinely. That was that.

"May lived her life by epigrams. For everything she did she had a suitable epigram. If she couldn't think up an original one she borrowed one from Ben Franklin.

"She thought it would be such fun to play a little game of epigrams; first she'd think up one then it would be my turn. I sneaked in a book of them one night and we stayed up until 6 o'clock next morning epigraming [sic]. That book was a godsend. She ran out and I still had five more in the book to spring on her.

"I really liked Anna more than any girl I know at that time. At first I called only on Saturday evenings. Then Wednesdays was added. Then she thought it would be nice if I were to come on Mondays also. At that point I left town. The following week I got a letter from her telling me to come over Friday night. When I got there Friday night her mother met me at the door with a vicious look in her eye. She asked me what I thought I was doing. Boarding there?

"Another girl I wanted to marry and didn't was a school teacher I had in the second grade. She had hopes of making an artist of me. I remember I thought so much of her that when the time came that I was promoted to the next higher grade I refused to leave but sat in my seat and blubbered. She came and sat down beside me and put her arm around me. While wiping my tears away she talked to me and fixed everything quite alright.

"Another girl was one whom I have seen but three times. The first time I saw her on Main street, about a week before I went away with the army. The next time was after I came back. I was riding in from West Market street on the street car. She boarded the car at Merriman rd. She came downtown as far as High street where she got off. I followed her as far as the Y.W.C.A.

"The next time I saw her she was waiting for a street car at the corner of Main and Market. Someone tapped me on the shoulder and I turned to speak to him. When I turned back again she was gone. I have never seen her since, and probably never will meet her, but manlike I often wonder who she is and if she noticed me. She had the most entrancing smile I have ever seen."

❦

25 July 1925, Saturday:

IT is really astonishing the force which a newspaper wields in a community. Today for instance we have a letter from the secretary of the Non-Flapper club.

"Quite a number of girls in our office," she writes, "wish to express their appreciation to you for the idea in your column Wednesday nite [sic]. We feel that this is a worthy cause and would be glad to assist in working out the idea. Our share in the Centennial celebration has been very small owing to our non-flapper tendencies.

"We feel sure that you will appreciate this fact and understand our willingness to be of some service. We feel that this may encourage other girls who feel as we do.

"If the parade is to be held please call Portage 1179-J and give full particulars."

Unfortunately the parade has been called off, at least so far as Centennial week is concerned, by the fact that Joe O'Neill has had so much to do that he just didn't know which way to turn. First Carrie sprained her ankle then Genevieve, the girl who comes in to wash the dishes, eloped. Then all the children took down with the measles and the plaster came off the bathroom ceiling.

And if that wasn't enough, says Joe, didn't the laundry go and lose his canary shirt, the one with the chrysanthemums on it, that he'd planned to wear in the procession.

Otherwise the parade would certainly have taken place as Joe doesn't know anything which has created so much discussion. Hardly had the announcement gotten around than Joe's telephone started ringing. It rang enough to drive a body crazy. Most of the time it was women who wanted to march in the parade. But one time it was a woman who had a suggestion. Her suggestion was that there should be a third division made up of women over 30, no, under 30, no, over 30, well anyway, of women either over or under 30 who had always worn corsets.

If there is anything I should like to see it is a parade of the women who have always worn corsets. I hope that the line of march is a long one and that they hold it on a hot day in August.

If there's one thing on earth I've suffered from it's these women who have always worn corsets and who won't rest contented until they have every other woman trussed up the same way.

"My, my," they say, poking at me with their thumbs as though I were a tomato that they were a little dubious about. "160 pounds you say! My dear, you ought to wear a corset. Now I have one that's a perfect love - $3.50 from Claw and Hammer's. It's the most comfortable thing – I never know I have it on – and just look at the room I've got!"

There is one woman, she has four teeth out in front where everybody can see them, who is particularly annoying.

"If you don't get a corset pretty soon," she says to me, "you won't be able to get through a door. Believe me. I don't think it's refined."

"Caroline," I have said to her time and again, "Caroline, if you would just forget about my shape and go and get your teeth fixed you would be doing a great deal more for the civic beauty of Akron."

But I say it under my breath. If I were to say it out loud she would think she had been irreparably insulted.

———————

And the men are just as bad only in a different way. I have a relative – I will not mention any names, but he is very fond of eating – who went downtown one day to get a suit and the haberdasher wished on him a girdle to be worn about the bread basket. This girdle was a trifle light as air weighing approximately half an ounce and not having a single whale bone in it. My relative wore it for two days and then put it away in the box which held his seal skin cap and his ear muffs.

One day he was indulging in mild reproaches.

"If you don't get a corset," he said, etc., etc., etc.,

"All right," I said, "I'll make a proposition to you. You get out your girdle and wear it and I'll wear a corset."

He hasn't said a word since.

L EOPOLD SCHEPP, aged millionaire, invites the public to tell him how to dispose of his fortune and of the 2,500 letters received the first day one is from a woman who wants $4,000 to get married on and another is from a man who wants help to finance his invention for enabling one armed men to play the saxophone.

It is queer, considering how earnestly most of us long for money, how sincere our intentions are of doing good with it once we get it, that we should be so helpless once the opportunity presents itself. The grand plan which shall alleviate human suffering and make the world a happier place to live in never comes. Instead our minds continue to revolve around and around the little things, a trousseaux, a house, a garden and a cow, a patent for one armed men.

I know that if some one were to walk into the office right now and offer me a million dollars the only immediate thing I could think of buying would be a wash board.

A newspaper which has been giving certain of its readers the privilege of spending a day and night in New York exactly as they please has found that the most any man or woman could spend in a day was $50. Liquor of course was excluded and I dare say there were some restrictions on the matter of purchasing clothing. Likewise there was to be no wholesale giving to chorus girls or poor relations. Otherwise the happy vacationist might indulge himself as he pleased.

In almost every case the program was the same: a room at a big hotel, breakfast in bed, luncheon at the Ritz, a matinee, dinner at the Astor, the theater, a cabaret and supper.

I have no quarrel with such a program. It is, with the exception of breakfast in bed which is more of a discomfort than a luxury, exactly what I should do myself.

The illuminating thing is that it all should cost but $50 – a sum within the reach of every stenographer and wash woman in Akron.

Just how one might go about spending a day of luxury in Akron I don't know. My own idea would be to take a box of crackers and a couple of apples and go to bed and stay there. I wouldn't even read.

Another idea would be to go out and sit under a tree on the Portage Country club gold links and go to sleep.

Another idea would be to sit in the last row of a movie house and go to sleep.

Certain things I know I would not do. I would not go bumping around in any automobiles. I would not go fishing. I would not go on any picnics. I would not go any place where there was singing or dancing or chorus girls or radios. I would not go where anybody was talking about evolution and I would not go to any circuses or carnivals or freak side shows.

Using the New York example, however, it might be interesting to figure out just how much a day of so-called luxury might cost in Akron. A room and bath down at one of the hotels, I dare say might cost $5 – a suite considerably more. Breakfast in one's room might come to $3. The ensuing walk down Main st. and back across the viaduct would cost nothing, neither would the ride around the lakes as on mature consideration one would decide not to take it. Luncheon, through the connivance of a friend, might be had at the City club, and that again I dare say would cost around $3. In the afternoon one might go to the Colonial (35~cents) and in the evening one might take a taxi ($2) to one of the lake inns for dinner ($2.50). Following this one could come back to the city ($3) and go to a movie (50 cents) and thus be all nicely tucked away in bed by 10 o'clock with nothing to listen to but the West Hill cars, the Arlington cars, the Cuyahoga Falls cars, the taxi cabs, the motor horns, those dear little whistles that the children are still blowing from the Centennial, the traveling man moving trunks around upstairs and the delegate from Parsons, Kan., having an argument with the assistant manager out in the hall.

---

29 July 1925, Wednesday:

"WELL here I am in dear old Indianapolis," writes Mollie.

"A committee of two, in censoring the reading matter of the two million people of the state, has included 45 magazines in their banned list, and though they have no official connections, and the law is agin' them, they are causing no end of trouble. They have written all the libraries in the state asking if they have obscene books in their libraries and enclosing a list of so called objectionable books containing such volumes as "So Big" and "A Lost Lady." The librarians are wild, and have no redress but cunning and they are all too ladylike to cues.

"Of course the publishers will see a steam roller, but meanwhile I am working amiably to change the point of view of one member of the committee – a woman who thinks Edgar Guest is our leading American Poet, that the soldiers' monument here is the last word in aft?, and that Amy Lowell's poem in the July Atlantic is sufficient evidence to prosecute the lady even though she be in her grave.

"Was in Chicago last week and loved it. My most God-fearing friend has turned her phonograph case into a cellarette."

We had our first pie last week. And while the rust [sic] was a little thick and there might, as Bill tactfully suggested, have been a little more sugar on the apples, still it seems to me it might have been a great deal worse.

The secret, I have found, is to use twice as much shortening as the recipe calls for and half as much ice water. It seems that it is also necessary to poke holes in the crust. I had known about this but forgotten it again and the cook book did nothing to set me wise.

It was when Bill came home and I showed him the dark gooey mass collecting in the bottom of the oven and sending up a peculiar burning smell that I remembered.

"Did you ventilate it?" he inquired in that quick way that men have of knowing all about everything.

"No," I said, "I forgot."

So I took a fork and ventilated the pie and after that everything was really very nice. I thought at first that part of it might be due to the fact that the pie was served hot, but the next morning when, unable to hear the suspense, I got out of bed early and ate the remaining piece cold I found that the crust was still malleable and the apples had miraculously sweetened up.

The lemon pie was not such a success. I had intending putting the lemon pie into the extra crust which, like the remainders I used to have in my arithmetic problems, had somehow been left over when everything should have come out even.

But of the lemon pie recipes in the cook book three called for milk and all five demanded that the lemon be grated on a grater. At that particular moment I was without both milk and a grater. Also there was a great deal of insistence upon something called Meringue II. I was at least a half hour discovering that Meringue II came about 30 pages later in the book. And at so time at all did I discover whether you put the meringue on the pie and then slipped the whole under the broiler flame as I was sure I had seen somebody do or whether you lit up the whole oven and let it get brown that way.

The outcome of the whole matter was that we had ice cream for dessert.

I don't know just what to think about cook books anyway. There was the night we were having fillet of sole. I had bought the fillet of sole at the fish market and it had cost 25 cents. Then I looked up the way to cook it in the cook book.

"Put the fillet of sole in a baking dish," it said, "and cover it with a cup of white wine and some bay leaves and some other things. Then take a small lobster, split the claws and cut up fine and take six small clams and make a broth and do a number of things to that for hours and hours, then pour over the fillet of sole and garnish with truffles."

That to me who has never seen a truffle in my life!

I dipped the fillet of sole in egg and cracker crumbs and fried it and aside from the fact that Bill was late and the has [sic] brown potatoes were cold and burnt everything was really quite fair.

But what do you do when imagination fails you?

---

30 July 1925, Thursday:

SOMEHOW there is keen tragedy in the day's news that Rudolph Valentino is losing his hair. A man may, and Valentino did, breast/breach law suits, marital entanglements, calumny and even degrading employment (remember Valentino's beauty mad tour) and still come out on top of the wave.

But when a man's hair starts coming out the situation is well nigh hopeless. When the man happens to be a movie actor it becomes heart breaking.

It is useless to talk toupees, or, as Valentino is reported doing, to resort to painting over the chilly potions of the scalp. Us women detect the imposition and be loyal as we may to these males to whom we are already attached we may as well be real frank about it and admit that it is very, very hard to love a bald-headed man.

Just why it should be males who run preponderantly to baldness nobody ever seems to have found out. The thing seems to run back to antiquity. Even Elisha who had such astonishing ways with the bears couldn't command one little spear of hair to grow on his pate. The best he could do about it was to get mad.

The only persons who have ever been able to maintain any composure about it have been the cartoonists and the author of an old, old encyclopedia which I picked up recently. The encyclopedia included among other things a short chapter on sex. "One way by which the sexes may be distinguished," it observed, "is that the males frequently become bald."

One explanation is that men go about wearing close fitting head gear. This would seem to be borne out by the fact that Parker Lowell who seldom wears any hat at all has a really very fine head of hair.

But if close fitting hats do the damage what are we to say for the women of Brittany and other foreign countries whose hair fur thickness and length is not to be equaled anywhere and yet who wear close fitting caps almost from the minute they are born?

My own explanation is that men are bald simply because they are peculiar.

A man will complain bitterly if a frying pan goes unwashed for a couple of days but he will leave old razor blades all over the wash bowl and say, "Well, that's your hard luck" if you happen to cut yourself on them.

He will make all kinds of nasty remarks about how fat you're getting and then go down and look at himself in one of the chewing gum slot machines as though he thought he had Apollo Belvidere backed off the map himself.

He will raise Cain if you keep him waiting 10 minutes but the bacon can burn up while you wait for him an hour and then he'll say "Yes, but in my case it's different."

He can bring home a terrible bore for supper and expect you to be nice to him just because the bore happens to be an old schoolmate, but let you bring home one of YOUR schoolmates and he says, "The next time that idiot is coming here let me know and I'll eat downtown."

He inquires plaintively as to why it is that so many women have a hard time getting up and getting breakfast in the morning when it's such a simple thing to do but you ask him nine times to empty the ice pan and then you can do it yourself anyway.

He can't understand why a woman doesn't do all her own housework, play the piano, raise a family and read all the bst [sic] books besides but let him go downtown and open up an office and he has to have a stenographer and an office boy and a scrub woman and a janitor and then he comes home at 5 o'clock at night and says how tired he is.

All in all when you consider how little there is there to nourish it, it's no wonder men get bald.

1 August 1925, Saturday:

"IT grieves me to think that I have been wasting time writing sonnets for Ted Robinson and epitaphs for Jake Falstaff, when all the while you needed help with the cooking, poor child," writes Kent. "to begin with the hashed browned potatoes, which you probably didn't begin with at all, the secret is a heavy iron frying pan and a slow fire. And don't bother a hungry man with fillets of sole. Get a pound of halibut steak, pat it dry in a tea towel, salt it evenly on both sides, dip in a mixture half flour and half yellow cornmeal with a little salt added and fry in bacon fat to a nice brown.

"And the best lemon pie filling I know of isn't made with milk at all. Here it is:

¼ c. cornstarch
1 c. sugar
1 ¼ c. water
2 egg yolks
1 lemon, juice and grated rind
1 t. butter

And the meringue calls for:
2 egg whites
5 t. sugar

"Have the crust baking in the oven while you make the filling in a double boiler and don't think you can read 'Talk of the Town' while the meringue is browning under the broiler, because you have to watch it every minute.

"As for the apple pie, you're right about the shortening, and I hope you don't forget to salt the crust. Sprinkle the lower crust thickly with flour, add apples, sugar, a little cinnamon, if liked, and more flour around the edge. Dot with butter and use one tablespoonful of water, for a small pie, or two for a large one, so there will be steam to cook the apples. Then comes the top crust, and for heaven's sake, Josephine, don't just ventilate it. Take a case knife and draw a little fern in a dotted circle, thus: (illegible) and while you're doing that, you can think about Thoreau, who loved his Dicksonia [sic], and hadn't anybody to put one on his pie crust.

"And if, in spite of all this, the pie's a mess, just say to yourself, 'Well, what's a pie, anyhow?'"

"In my eight years of pie baking experience," writes E.G.H.. "I have found the enclosed recipe the best for lemon meringue. We like it better without the grated rind and it is almost sure to burn unless cooked in a double broiler.

"One time when I was about 15 years old, we lived in the country and our church had the privilege of serving a lunch at a public sale in the neighborhood. My mother volunteered to make some pies and before the sale day came she was called away on account of sickness. One of the women told me that we could furnish something else, but I was determined to make pies.

"I had never baked one before in my life and after studying the cook books decided if a little was good, more would be better. When they were done they were about the consistency of an ice cream soda and the meringue ran one way and the filling another. After hauling them over a bumpy road in a basket there wasn't much left but the crust. My family never got tired of telling that story, especially if I had a new beau to dinner. Therefore, when I got married I resolved to make such good pie they would be ashamed to tell it, and I believe I did, as I haven't heard the story for several years. I can also make a perfectly delicious butterscotch pie. Would you like the recipe for it?"

WOULD!!

3 August 1925, Monday:

I T SEEMS that Mrs. Lars Hansen was a recent visitor in this city, whereupon she wrote to her friend Lee Aldrich of Newell, Iowa, in part as follows:

"I will tell you about our trip to Akron. West through Marshalltown to Clinton, over the Mississippi river to Illinois. A fine graveled road, nice country, fine big houses. I didn't see many corn fields, just small ones. Went through woods and river country, through a big Indian camp where they had cute little huts. They have a big Indian school and the little kids go fishing. Went through Indiana and found it a poor country with everything dried up. They have had no rain for three months. We stopped at a farm house for water. I asked him what he fed his cattle in the winter and he said they either had to sell them or let them starve. Poor farm houses. The soil is sandy and clay. They have fine paved roads. Arrived at South Bend, Ind., and stopped there, and arrived in Ohio the next day. The country here is sandy, too, and hills. Got to Akron which is surely some city. Tommy and I went downtown to see the rubber plant, which covers blocks. The Firestone is a large one. You can smell the rubber before you get there. I can't see how people can stand it in there. At just 2 o'clock people come out and a new shift goes in. You see thousands of people going and coming. You cannot pass a car from 2 to 4. Street cars are all loaded. Just two blocks from where I stay a toy balloon factory blew up the other day. One man went through the floor but no one got hurt. Got a fine park here which costs lots of money. Would like to have you Newell people see that park. It is all cemented and everything you can think of. The band plays every night and a big radio program every night. The papers said there were 37,000 people there on July 4.

"We are going over to Cleveland Sunday to see Lake Erie. I like Iowa best to live in, where we raise the things to eat. Eggs are 50 cents a dozen and butter 58 cents per pound. Everything is high here.

"They have better lifeguards here than in Iowa. When you get to a bad crossing they have a red light. When the train is coming the light goes from one side to the other of the post. You cannot help but see it. At every curve is a lookout sign. Every cross road has a sign 'Look Out.' I have an Ohio paper and I never read about trains killing people like they do in Iowa. That's what they need in Iowa, better safeguards. I wouldn't trade Iowa for any state."

One can well picture the state of mind of Dr. and Mrs. Arthur I. Piper, who returned from 12 years of missionary work in the Belgian Congo the other day only to be "shocked and mortified" at the immodesty of the girls and women here.

Mrs. Piper, it seems, returned to these shores wearing a frock modeled very much along the lines of the one she had on when she left. It had a high neck, a long skirt and long sleeves. Thus attired she had sallied into the Congo and herself setting the example she had preached more and longer clothing until at last, after 12 years of effort, the natives were at least consenting to wrap a piece of cloth about their middles.

The question now confronting Mrs. Piper, one fancies, is whether it were better to return to the landable if somewhat slow process of swathing otherwise happy natives or to remain in America and preach the same gospel to Americans who, is it plain to be seen, are themselves rapidly hurtling into savagery.

There are, of course, a couple of solutions to this problem. One is that Mrs. Piper take the vote and see whether Americans or the natives of the Congo are most eager for her message. The other is that she take a tuck in her skirt, snip a few inches off her sleeves, spend the afternoon at the movies, bring home some delicatessen baked beans for supper and say, "Well, well, life is short, let's all be as happy as we can."

There are a great many persons, I imagine, who will always regret what the missionaries did to Hawaii. I have never been to Hawaii, to be sure, but I once supered in a play called "The Bird of Paradise[47]." The younger and prettier members of the company were dancing girls, and they were the native costume. It consisted of a grass skirt and some beads and the girls wore hibiscus in their hair.

Us supers were supposed to be natives converted by the missionaries and we were dressed accordingly. Our costumes consisted of mother hubbards hiked up in front and too long in the back. The whole was finished off with brown 50-cent bedroom slippers and we wore no hibiscus in our hair.

After the show was over you couldn't help noticing how it was the dancing girls who got the heavy dates. Us supers paid for our own ice cream sodas down at the corner drug store and then we went home alone.

---

[47] Referring to Josephine's time as Huldah Benson and "getting on the stage in New York"

4 August 1925, Tuesday:

THERE are times when it is a holiday and the others have gone away and left one, or when they have merely elected to stay downtown and go to the movies or when one has decided to stay home from work for a day.

At such times one eats along and while eating alone, if pursued indefinitely, is bound to result in a gloomy outlook on life and indigestion within; still, if indulged in occasionally it cannot help but induce a remarkable peace and contentment with the world.

For one thing it is possible, when eating alone, to sprawl the elbows on the kitchen table without fear of censure. Also to dip the toast in coffee. Also to eat a slice of bread whole. Also to lick the molasses off the spout of the molasses pitcher. Also to tilt back the chair. Also to sing at table. Also to experiment with how much one can cram into one's mouth at any one time.

Then, too, eating alone admits of a wonderful opportunity to clean up the past week's accumulations in the icebox. A cup full of left-over soup, a small section of cold halibut, a small tomato slightly deteriorated, a half of a muskmelon, also somewhat the worse for age, two pieces of celery, a small bit of cheese adhering to a rind, a cold boiled potato and four hardened dates are not matters which one could set before a critical family with any degree of composure. But re-arrange them slightly and set them before the solitary eater and immediately they become a highly satisfactory repast consisting of aperitif, soup, fish with potato balls and a salad.

This of course with the addition of coffee. It is the coffee, I think, which has brought on the opprobrium which so often attaches to solitary dining. Either from laziness or more probably from notions of economy the person who eats alone very frequently contents himself with the coffee left over from breakfast. This is a great mistake as coffee, contrary to other liquids, becomes cloudier the longer it stands. The coffee should be fresh.

It is especially urgent that the coffee should be fresh because it is a great pot of coffee together with an accumulation of reading matter completely surrounding the plate and extending down to the floor and up to the window sill which makes eating alone the pleasant rite it is.

As to the kind of reading matter which one should have at such a time it seems to me that most any kind will do except that it should not be too exciting. "The Red Lamp," by Mary Roberts Rinehart,[48] I think would not do at all as what with its murders in every other chapter and its mysterious lights moving over the marsh and its circles and triangles one would forget all about food and let the coffee go cold.

Essays are always good as are also those novels in which the author stops every third paragraph to digress.

My own particular taste at such times is for old Sunday newspapers. Just why it is that I cannot read a Sunday newspaper when it is new I do not know. I think it is because I am overwhelmed with the size of it. But after a Sunday newspaper has had a chance to grow old, after the funny paper has been disposed of, the sporting sections utilized for emptying the carpet sweeper in, the society section utilized to wrap used melon rinds in and the real estate ads spread out neatly over the wash tubs, then I find that I can get considerable enjoyment out of what is left.

I read every word of the four-weeks-old scandal of how Lady Marjorie Umpty-Umph was locked out of her town house by her irate husband, a prominent mutton chopped m. p. I gloat over the predictions of the latest distinguished scientist who sees the North Pole shifted down to the equator and humanity going about toothless and baldheaded. I suffer with the chorus girl who relates in detail the events which lead her to shoot her husband and sign a $50,000 contract with the movies. And I yearn to give advice to Broken Hearted Seventeen who writes to inquire whether she should run away with her married boss.

— ‽ᴇℯᴄꜱᴇℯ◆ꜱ℩ᴄᴇⳍ℩ —

5 August 1925, Wednesday:

IT SEEMS that there is something new now called numerology. I had known about numerology for quite a long while, but I had always thought that it was something abstract — something that you had to go and pay somebody five dollars for just to get the merest kind of reading.

But thanks to one of the Sunday papers, I have now been able to make my own reading. This paper furnishes a table showing what number all the letters in the alphabet vibrate to and all you have to do is to set down your name, follow each letter up with the

---

48 "The Red Lamp," a book by Mary Roberts Rinehart, 1925.

corresponding number and then add up the whole and look in the table to see what the result means.

It is so easy that it's just laughable – that is, until you see how your name comes out. For my own part, I've been feeling pretty disheartened ever since Sunday.

"First," said this article in the Sunday paper, "you want to add up the vowels and find out what they mean, for the vowels are the index to your inner character."

So I added up the vowels and they came out poverty, defeat, discouragement.

"Then," said this article, "you want to add up the consonants, for they show what outer influences are at work on your life."

So I added up the consonants and it came out something about love of change.

"Then," said this article, "you want to add them both together, thus showing what the net result will be."

So I added them both together, and it came out a nine, which means charm, talent, and things like that. It seems that folks like Kathleen Norris and Edna Ferber have had lots of 9's in their names.

I was feeling pretty cocky just then, but all at once it occurred to me to figure out my birth date. So I did, and it came out poverty, defeat and discouragement again. It seems it's a game you can't beat. To be sure, the numerologists recommend changing your name, but what good is a new name with a birth date that persists in coming out poverty, defeat, discouragement?

———

To be sure I have heard of some persons who did profit by changing their names. Neysa McMein[49], the well known illustrator, is one of them and there are some others whose names I don't recall just now.

---

[49] Neysa McMein (1888-1949) born as Marjorie Frances McMein, an American illustrator and portrait painter – known for her portrait of Dorothy Parker, and part of the Algonquin Round Table. She had an open marriage to John G. Baragwanath, during which she had affairs with Charlie Chaplin and George Abbott. She was elected into the Hall of Fame, Society of Illustrators in 1984.

Chorus girls, I suppose, are the best illustrations, although their names seem to have been gotten together more from a desire for euphony than a regard for numerical vibrations.

Somehow, though, I wish I hadn't taken up numerology. Because until then I had thought I was getting along so well.

We were wondering today, or at any rate Wilbur Peat was, why people never put pictures in their kitchens.

"Here it is," said Wilbur, "the most important room in the house and yet generally the ugliest. Instead of having the pots and pans hanging around the walls, people put them out of sight in cupboards. And instead of having nice strings of garlic and red peppers hanging up they put them away in the cellar. And instead of hanging pictures on the walls, they put up an almanac and think they've done their duty."

It was my turn then to inquire what pictures would be appropriate for kitchen use, and Bill, who is always so practical suggested that a nice dead fish would look well.

It is hard though to decide just what pictures would look well in a kitchen. Some of those gaudy still life flowers which one always likes but invariably hesitates to buy I think would go well. Also I once saw a sun's head which I would like to own and put there. She was an old, old sun and her face was like a dried and wrinkled potato which has gone through the winter and come again into spring. The artist who painted her had put her on thin strip of board, and the man who owned her had found her in a forgotten corner of somebody's attic. He kept her now on a dark landing of the stairway because, and this was curious, although she was all done in browns, she still gave a curious effect of light breaking through.

Yes, I think I would rather have her in my kitchen than any other picture. And then, when the time came to string the beans, I would sit and look.

---

6 August 1925, Thursday:

I RODE in the Wild West parade yesterday. I did not ride all the way, and I rode inside a stage coach instead of upon an elephant, a camel or a band wagon which would have been more picturesque.

Still the experience such as it was, was sufficient to cure me of any suppressed hankerings I might have had to follow the life of the circus.

The lady elephant trainer rode beside me and opposite us was the "banner" man – he who takes down the banners and things as the show is packing up to leave town – and another man, the lady elephant trainer's husband, I think, whose profession I was not able to find out.

The lady elephant trainer had had a sad night of it. "You know," she said, "the engineers on these trains are all freight engineers and they regard us all as so much baggage. They don't care how they jerk us around."

She wouldn't have ridden in the parade at all, it seemed, only that Babe, the elephant, was out of loaf sugar.

"I give her a piece when I get on her back," said the lady elephant trainer, "and then another piece when the act is over, and you just should have seen the look on her face in Youngstown yesterday when I didn't have any for her. I made up my mind that the first thing I was going to do when I struck this town was to hunt up a grocery store and get Babe her sugar."

It was along about this time that a grocery store with an imposing front hove into view and the lady elephant trainer climbed down out of the stage coach and waved farewell. She was a nice companionable person, and I was sorry to see her go.

The banner man said that there had been four marriages among the show people in the last couple of weeks. One of the cow girls (he called her a cowboy girl) had married a Mexican tumbler and then another girl had married the sword swallower and there had also been a couple of others the details of which he hadn't bothered about.

It was a perilous thing, he said, to be married to a sword swallower, because, contrary to what most people believe, a sword swallower actually does swallow swords.

"You can take one and push it down for yourself and see," said the banner man, "and lots of times a sword swallower actually does hurt himself."

The fire eater, he said, prepared himself for the ordeal by first taking into his mouth some sort of chemical which protected him from burns.

For the most part though the parade was monotonous. The stage coach was hard and it bumped about unevenly and there were frequent long pauses in the procession.

The only relief from the tedium came when some pretty girl would smile in on us, whereupon the banner man and the lady elephant trainer's husband would rise to the occasion and respond with a wave of the hand and a few appropriate remarks.

As we bumped along Main st., with the calliope wheezing a few feet behind us I looked up to the second story windows where the people were hanging out over the sills watching he parade go by.

Surfeited as I was with two hours of circus experiences it seemed to me that up there in those second story windows was where life was really going on and I longed more ardently to know what was happening up in those hot stuffy little rooms than I ever had to get at the (illegible – super?) philosophy of Jo-Jo, the dog-faced boy.

A girl with bobbed hair and a youth were looking down out of a window. Then they looked at each other and smiled. They were so obviously happy that your breathing came hard for a moment.

A little further on a man was holding a little boy on the window ledge. He was twining the child's hand about his finger. They had pulled an iron cot up to the window so the sick women on it could look down and see the parade. She regarded the cow girls, the Indian squaws and the (illegible – Cossacks?) for a while. Then she turned and resumed her monotonous staring at the ceiling.

Two girls were sitting on a fire escape. A dapper young man was coming along with a package under his arm. The two girls regarded the dapper young man with interest. He rewarded their interest by climbing the fire escape to address them whereupon it developed that the package under his arm was a bundle of magazines and that the young man was taking subscriptions.

The two girls promptly lost interest.

"Blaaaa!," they said, "blaaaa!"

---

7 August 1925, Friday:

I HAVE been realizing just the past few days how starved one can get for music.

And I am wondering about those people who a few years ago voted that certain money from the community chest shouldn't go to support a community orchestra because such things were "luxuries."

Just how I think I would gladly forego dessert for a week or the movies for 10 years if by so doing I might hear a string quartet for half an hour.

There is certainly a penalty which we must pay, I guess, for living where everyone has the vote, for then everything, our schools, our colleges, our religion, our art, must all be brought around to conform to the mentality of the voters which, so the psychologists tell us, is never too high at best.

We have miles and miles of improved streets, but a pitiful little art museum. We have thousands of cheap motor cars, but no music. We have occasionally at any rate, a new sewer. But the public library must struggle along as best it can with hopelessly inadequate funds.

If I, with the mentality of a 14-year-old, must writhe and squirm because I can't go to Cleveland or New York or Chicago where music is to be heard, what must be the feelings of the 18-year-old mentalities and the 21-year-old mentalities who are tied here year after year and who, when they ask for a little beauty, are met with the proud assertion that Akron has just put in five miles of new gas mains?

But, my dear, say the voters, you are forgetting the radio.

No, I'm not forgetting the radio. I've been thinking of it all along. That is what makes the situation so dreadful. There are thousands of people in this town who actually like the hear "By the Waters of Minnetonka" rendered on the corner with variations. They like to hear it come squeaking and scratching in, interrupted by screaming static and preluded by silly speeches by a silly announcer.

The phonograph is credited with achieving remarkable things in the musical advancement of the people. The radio has undone all this. It has even gone further. It has taught the people not only to tolerate racket but to demand it.

"They're advertising an electric typewriter now," writes Ancient Admirer. "You don't have to punch the keys any more. All you do is touch the keys and the motor does the rest. Just like an adding machine, you know. The question is, will this make writing so easy that the variest moron can qualify? Or will it free our writers from the physical effort of typing and thus release more brain energy for thinking?

"Also, why do soft drinks have to be colored pink or green or yellow to get us to down them? Are we all kids that have to be coaxed with gaudy colors or is the red color a sign that the manufacturer's conscience hurts him for selling just sugar and water and so he puts in a dash of color to make up the nickel's worth?"

<hr />

8 August 1925, Saturday:

"I see now," writes E.L.G., "that a New York orchestra leader named Ernie or Sammie or Bennie or something like that has interested six pastors in installing red-hot jazz orchestras within the chance to play the good old hymns with a modern slant.

"I suppose this will cause a great deal of horror in many vicinities, where hymns are revered and jazz is profane.

"But to me it is astonishing that nobody thought of it before. Of course, somebody did. The Salvation Army and its kindred organizations has been refusing for a long time to 'let the devil have all the good tunes.' In a southern tourist city, four or five years ago, I heard through the soft air of the evening, confused with minor sounds, the strains of 'Yanka Mala Hicks Dule.'

"I went to investigate. It was a band of religious street singers, and the air was the same but the words were vastly different. It made a right good hymn.

"There will be people who regard the jazz revisions of the old hymns with shock.

"'It is a shame,' they will say, 'to spoil that good music with this nasty jazz.'

"The answer to that is that at the time the hymn tunes were written, their style of music corresponded on the jazz of today, and was looked upon by authentic musicians with as much pain and grief as the highbrows today award the merest mention of the only new thing that is beneath the sun – jazz.

"Let us not take jazz too lightly. Somewhere in the United States – perhaps in our own city – some genius in writing the first great opera that has come into the world for many years and is writing it in jazz.

"The only thing wrong with jazz is that it is practiced by so many amateurs and – because of its novelty – is getting by popularly on that basis.

"When jazz is written – as it certainly will be in its time – by men qualified to compose music, it will be as great as any other musical medium that has been found.

"It is a contribution which this period will leave to posterity – and such contributions from any age are few indeed. It behooves us to think well before condemning it."

"I am totally unsophisticated," writes Dearie Me, "and something puzzles me terribly.

"About these channel-swimmers for instance. What is there in it for them? Suppose they do swim the channel. Is there a Nobel prize or something for it?

"I have never seen them in vaudeville. I have never heard about their writing books on how it feels to swim the channel. Now do they get any compensation for such a strenuous effort? Is there anything that makes so much exertion worth while?

"And then I am puzzled about coast-to-coast walkers. Why do they do it? And how do they live while they do it? Are they people fairly well off and possessed of annuities so they can afford to fritter away their patrimony on such expeditions? Or is there some way, unknown to me, whereby a person can make a living out of just walking?

"Certainly mayors don't pay them for carrying messages to the mayors of other cities."

Well, it is hard to say just what there is in it for a channel-swimmer. Glory, of course. And that, to so many people, is worth more than money. And it gets them jobs. I suppose expert swimmers are in demand for jobs in some places. Well, supposing you were an employment manager, and the president said to you, "Look here, we need an expert swimmer down in Department 44B," and you put an ad in the papers, and in response a young woman came in, and you asked her, "What have you done to qualify you for this position," and she said, "Well, once I swam the English channel."

Would she get the job?

About coast-to-coast walkers, some of them are newsboys and sell papers in each town they visit. They get good corners, and make enough to carry them on the next place.

Or they sell shoe-strings, or music (which they illustrate by singing it publicly), or other sorts of things.

And some of them are walking on bets. But I have never figured out who it is that bets people $5,000 that they can't walk from New York to San Francisco in 180 days. They must be terribly sporty persons.

<hr/>

10 August 1925, Monday:

I WONDER why it is that the stage exercises such a glamor for us when we are young and why, when we grow older, the glamour so perceptibly vanishes. It is because the burning admiration which we feel for the actor gives place in course of time to a sort of pity or is it merely that life itself gets so interesting that the goings on on the stage roust of mediocrity become tawdry and common place by contrast?

I can remember the time when the biggest event in my life was to be given a dime to go to the stock company matinee on Saturday. I worked pretty hard for that dime. I dusted and I practiced my (illegible) and I washed dishes.

The stock company I recall was Cook's stock company and it played over Link's drug store in Sandusky, O. The hall had formerly been a small skating rink. But the stock company took over the skating rink and put in a couple of hundred kitchen chairs and then it became a theater. Mr. Cook could generally be found at the door taking tickets. He almost always wore a checked suit. At one time in his life I believe he had sold medicine.

The first man whom I ever truly loved was the leading man in this stock company. His name was Arthur Molyneaux and his hair fell elegantly over the rear of his collar.

<hr/>

The stock company was generally just through with its morning rehearsals as I was coming home from school at noon. I was nine and I played with paper dolls but nevertheless my heart could beat passionately. If there was no sign of the stock company going down the street to lunch I would lag fearfully. If it was going down the street to lunch I would run so that I might get past within a few feet of it.

I used to make up scenes with my loved one. It would be dusk, about 4 o'clock, and my mother would have sent me to Link's drug store for two ounces of camphor. As I would be passing down the street, I would carelessly drop my handkerchief. Suddenly out of the darkness would come a deep, throaty, well modulated masculine voice.

"Pardon me but I believe you have dropped your handkerchief."

"Why yes, it is my handkerchief," I would say, "thank you so much. Oh Mr. Molyneaux if only I might tell you how I have enjoyed your acting."

"It is a mere nothing," he would answer, "although I may tell you that the true artist does appreciate appreciation." And then we would walk along in the dusk and he would tell me of his hopes and aspirations.

There was another member of the stock company whom I valued only slightly less. His name was Harry Gay, and he roomed with a woman who knew my mother. She used to come over and tell me all about him – how he was in reality a member of the French nobility and terrible time his ancestors had getting out of the country during the revolution – tales I suspect in which truth got rather theatrically tangled up with the stage script.

Unfortunately I never met either of these gentlemen in person. The stock company broke up and went away and the next time I heard of it it was playing in a text somewhere in a piece called "The Devil's Kitchen."

It was in vain that I pleaded with my parents to be taken. They were bound for church or something and refused to be altered in their course. The best I could do was to drag along and make up new scenes with myself and Mr. Molyneaux during the silent prayer.

And who will ever forget the glories of Horn's stock company here in Akron? Of the heart disturbing W. O. McWalters and the spirited Alice Clements? There was a chap named Arthur Sims I remember in the company who was very frequently the villain. He would be shot or hanged or poisoned one week only to bob up again the next. And then there was a comedian – Swift I think his name was – who married a local girl and lived for a time next door to us. We never saw him – actors don't keep civilized hours – but there was a terrible thrill just in knowing he was there. And there was Henry Hicks who's here now with the new company. Do you remember how you throbbed and thrilled when he was Adam Ladd in Rebecca of Sunnybrook Farm[50]? He was just the kind of Adam Ladd that you would have picked.

Nowadays when the curtain goes up at the stock company you're only mildly interested. You merely hope that the show won't be too much of a bore and that the fat lady in the rear of the house will quit her whispering.

But back in the old days when the curtain went up – Ah, that was a joy so great that it hurt.

❧ ✦ ❧

11 August 1925, Tuesday:

WE LISTENED to a lecture on art the other night. It was a purely informal lecture, the sort of thing that comes up you know when a half dozen persons are sitting about talking about nothing in particular and putting an occasional collar on their near beer. But it settled something I have long wondered about – namely, what constitutes the best sellers in art. Our informant was an ex-newspaperman who had lost a couple of jobs on account of writing socialistic editorials on the side and who had now gone into the business of selling pictures.

It seems that the way in which the ex-newspaperman had happened to think about the matter at all was this: His wife had been scheduled to speak before a women's club and at the last minute was unable to go on account of illness. So the ex-newspaperman took her notes and went in her stead.

Once on the platform, however, he was unable to make head or tail of the notes and this was queer, for his wife writes an unsually [sic] plain hand.

The ex-newspaperman looked down into the sea of faces before him and saw that it was plainly expected of him to say something. And so he opened his mouth and started talking. Once started he found he couldn't stop. What gradually took shape was this lecture on the six best sellers in art.

---

[50] "Rebecca of Sunnybrook Farm," a children's novel by Kate Douglas Wiggin, 1903.

It seems that your baby's picture is a swivel frame is the first best seller.

The second best seller is your sweetie's picture in a swivel frame.

The third best seller is your own picture in a swivel frame.

The fourth best seller is entitled "Spring Song."

I may be wrong about the name of this last but at any rate you will recognize it. It represents a child in a green dress sitting on a wooden bench gazing at a wooden robin sitting on a green twig.[51]

The ex-newspaperman said that five million copies of this picture have been sold in the last two years and that inasmuch as there are only about five million homes in the United States and inasmuch as some homes cannot afford one of these pictures there is only one conclusion to be drawn, namely, that certain of the more prosperous home [sic] have two copies of "Spring Song."

The fifth best seller is "Day Break" or "Dawn" or something like that by Maxfield Parrish. It has those nice rootbeer blues in it and is really the very thing to hang over the mantel or over the davenport which you got with the three-piece over-stuffed suite.

The sixth best seller – now what in the world. I don't seem to remember what the sixth best seller was, but probably you can fill it in yourself.

The ex-newspaperman said that at first he intended the lecture to be quite harmless but once he got started he got reckless and didn't care what he said. He got sort of drunk with honesty. He waded right in and told those women what awful dubs most of us were in art and what fearful things we were in the habit of hanging on our walls and what an awful mistake it was to put a large white mat around a picture that ought to be framed close and how much better it was to have a good print or two than to put $23 in a mother of pearl lighthouse and how finally, quivering and exhausted, he tattered down

---

[51] Referring to "Spring Song" by the German artist, Simon Glucklich (spelling variation: Gluecklich). Prints of Spring Song were popular in the United States in the 1920's. Two versions were created, using Simon's blind daughter as the model. The original shows her eyes closed, and later were retouched to show them open.

from the platform hoping to find a backdoor out of the hall before he should be mobbed and hanged, drawn and quartered.

But it was too late. The women had him. They swarmed about him, practically cutting off circulation. They said they didn't know when they'd heard such a sweet lecture and where could they get copies of that dear little picture – the one about the child and the robin.

***

12 August 1925, Wednesday:

I T SEEMS that this column got a little tangled up in its matinee idols. At any rate –

"How could you, how could you!" exclamation points Bee. "Why are you so terribly forgetful! Of course we know you are very busy (sic) and that little things are likely to slip your mind! But what we cannot understand is how you ever mistook our girlhood matinee idol to be a plain Arthur! Of all things, Arthur Sims! Didn't we spend many a wakeful night musing and bewailing the frightful downfall of our hero-villain of the old stock days? How you could call him Arthur when it was Alvah-Alvah Sims is more than my poor imagination can fathom. Alvah was mystical, impenetrable, romantic, but Arthur – well, all I can say is don't ever let it happen again!"

I am naturally of a kindly disposition but one of those things which I refuse to do is to hunt a job for anybody.

There was Clarence for instance. Dear, dear, the time I spent hunting jobs for Clarence.

Hunting jobs for Clarence was not a particularly easy matter. Clarence was just out of high school, he knew neither shorthand nor typewriting, he couldn't drive a car and his eyesight was poor. Also Clarence didn't have exactly what you would call a selling personality. Clarence despised trade. His secret dream was to inherit a great deal of money and be a gentleman.

However Clarence's mother – a widow – was making out none too well in a local abstractor's office and so we all set about hunting a job for Clarence.

Clarence found it impossible to remain in the offices of Hale and Wellmet, attorneys. Mr. Wellmet, it seems, was too conceited for words.

Then, after a half day's experience, Clarence resigned his position with Pattycake and Pattycake, dealers in hay, grain and feed. The dust of the place, it would appear, made Clarence cough. Also Pattycake and Pattycake frequently got in a shipment of chickens for the Saturday trade and Clarence never did care for poultry.

Clarence stayed a week with Brown and Sepia, art dealers, and all his friends were jubilant. Even his mother chinked up a bit and got herself a new hat. But Clarence had to give it up. Brown and Sepia, it developed, had disgusting notions about getting down to work at 9 o'clock mornings.

It was at this point that Clarence's friends gave up too. They said it was just no use trying. Clarence loafed around for a couple of months and then he fell in with an elderly millionaire and his wife bound for Europe. The elderly millionaire and his wife fell hard for Clarence, they liked his refined ways. Now they insists that Clarence must never leave them. And Clarence's weekly letter to his mother contains a nice pink check.

And then there was Ruthie. Ruthie was always hunting a job.

"Do you know where I can get a job?" she would ask mournfully.

"Why yes," you would answer, "Goldblum's have got an ad in the paper today for 50 new salesladies. I'm sure you could get a job there."

So Ruthie would go down to Goldblum's and stand in line. She would be careful to be the very last person in the line. Then she would come home and tell how she had stood in line for hours and how closing time came before they could interview all the applicants.

Or else you would call Ruthie over the telephone.

"I just hear of a swell job down at Lieder and Tafel's," you would say. "No dictation, short hours and $200 a month. But you'll have to hurry because there'll be a mob of girls after it."

"Oh all right," Ruthie would say, "but I simply can't go tomorrow. We're getting up a beach party in the afternoon and in the evening the Lightfoot girls are giving a dance and it'll take all morning to make over my green model. Besides aren't Lieder and Tafel those fellows that have that office in that awfully dark building? But if you hear of anything else I do wish you'd let me know because Ma'll positively kick me out if I don't get something to do pretty soon."

It's been three years since Ruthie started looking for a job and she's never landed one yet. She's getting married next week though to a real estate salesman from Miami and they say her solitaire cost $400 if it cost a cent.

⸺ ✦ ⸺

13 August 1925, Thursday:

I SUPPOSE we'll have to get a trap for Scrabble although I hate to do it. For really he has been a very well behaved rat, eating next to nothing, you might say and only attesting in very small ways as to his presence at all.

The first time that I knew he was there at all was a few sights ago when he endeavored to tear the paper wrappings off the new ironing board. It may as well be admitted that the ironing board had been standing there quite a few days without anybody paying any attention to it and it may well be that Scrabble reasoned that it was high time somebody unwrapped the ironing board and put it where it belonged.

Really he got quite a bit of the paper off which he distributed in accusing bite all over the kitchen floor. He had less luck with the wash boiler which is of copper and not exactly what you would call resilient.

The next night when I woke up Scrabble was sitting on the window still gazing mournfully in the direction of the Country club.

Reasoning that he might have lived there at some time and was anxious to get back we endeavored to make the way easy for him by putting up the screen. But that Scrabble prefers to remain with us is attested by the neat pile of shavings which we find every morning now just outside the door of the closet – the smaller one – where Bill keeps his clothes – the other ones.

And here again Scrabble has shown his consideration. He might have gone into the kitchen and eaten some of the potatoes or he might have slipped into the ice box and eaten up that cheese that we're going to have with the spaghetti some night in a few weeks when we eat at home. Or he might even have eaten the yard stick which Katie uses to stir the clothes with on wash day.

But no. He chose to tackle the closet door which has never closed yet on account of being swelled up with the dampness. He is chewing at it carefully so that in a few more nights I think he will have it all planed off so that it will not only go shut with ease but will also probably have an inch or two to spare.

The trouble is that I've never been able to feel quite at ease with a rat about. I always have a feeling that if I put my foot outside of the bed he will stand up on his hind feet and bite it.

Also the Saturday Evening Post had a perfectly terrible article about rats in it a couple of weeks ago. It seems that rats are fearfully intelligent and that when one of them gets caught in a trap the old mother rats will bring their young ones onto the scene and then they'll all stand around in a circle pointing out the moral.

Also rats just love mice and will frequently corral them up and fatten them until they're all pink and tender to eat on Sundays and holidays.

Also when they want something that's been put away out of their reach they'll frequently form Zouave combinations to get it that would put the local Tadmors out of countenance for a week.

And so I suppose it will be either us or Scrabble who will have to go. And while Scrabble is still numerically outnumbered two to one I think it would be a wise time to strike. You never can tell how soon he might take a motion to bring on his relatives and if, after they'd attended to all the closet doors they should suddenly determine to tackle Bill's shoes, well, we'd just have to wait another year for the phonograph, the grand piano and the trip to Europe.

I don't think I'll get the trap until tomorrow though and meantime tonight I'll put out the cheese in a convenient corner and, it may be, a little bacon.

14 August 1925, Friday:

WE were speaking this noon of the peculiar ways that husbands have of washing dishes.

The bride had observed her husband washing dishes for the first time last night and it had disturbed her almost as much as that Sunday afternoon when she had happened to look over and observed him sleeping with his mouth open.

"He just would do the dishes," she said, "he said he was the crack dishwasher of Cuyahoga Falls. I tried to make it easy for him by fixing up a nice suds in the dishpan and then what did he do but let the hot water run all the time and ruin it all.

"He would hold a plate up under the hot water and slosh it around for a while and then he'd put some soap on the dish cloth and wash the plate holding it up in the air all the time.

"He held the pans up in the air that same way and scrubbed them. I thought he'd never get through. He did wear an apron though, I'll say that for him. If he hadn't his clothes would have been ruined.

"I just said to him, 'If you had to do dishes every day you'd soon get over a lot of these notions.'"

The society editor who has been married a little longer said that she had her husband pretty well trained by now except that when he wipes the dishes he spreads them out all over the table. "He seems to think," she said, "that each plate has to be aired."

It came my turn to recall the dish-washing performances of my Uncle William. If there was one thing that Uncle William loved it was to get out in the kitchen and do up the dishes while the women folks were away at a missionary meeting or something.

Just why it was that Uncle William was never able to find any soap but the toilet soap on each occasions nor any towels but the hand embroidered guest towels I was never able to make out. Certain it is however that each of Uncle William's dish-washing exploits was sure to end in grief with Uncle William retiring hurt and unappreciated to the back yard and the women folks demanding what in the world was the use of a man trying to help around the house when he did more damage than good.

The next man whose dish washing tactics I had occasion to observe was what you might call thorough. He would polish each plate and cup and saucer until the pattern was practically obscured from it. He would attack the spoons until they bent under the strain. And after it was all over he would spend an entire half hour arranging the silver in precise piles which would immediately fall into disarray the moment you juggled the drawer.

The next man whose dis-washing tactics I had occasion to observe – and he is undergoing surveillance at present – is really quite perfect except that he likes to wad the dish cloth up in a tight little ball when he is through and then hide it. Sometimes you find it with the scrubbing brush and sometimes up the clothes hamper and sometimes back of the sugar bowl.

It may be true of course, the bride's contention that if a man had to do dishes three times a day he'd get over his little tricks. But I doubt it. Men, I have observed, are singularly averse to change, particularly when they suspect that you are trying to reform them.

The conclusion to Mary Roberts Rinehart's "The Red Lamp" is out and as usual it is disappointing, as mystery stories always are. I am beginning to think that it would be far better never to publish the completion to a mystery story but just to let you keep on guessing.

Perhaps, though, it is merely the length of the thing which is at fault. There is probably no mystery which deserves to be dragged out the length of a full novel. Certainly one never feels a let down when it is a short mystery story and the author happens to be Edgar Allen Poe.

━◦⌒◦⌒◦◆◦⌒◦⌒◦━

19 August 1925, Wednesday:

IS IT possible for a woman to be handsome? We've just been having a serious time about it here at the office. I had always thought that when a woman was too – too – well you know, too everything to be called beautiful, that you called her handsome. That meant that she was not only beautiful in a way, but big and brainy and gorgeous and everything else to boot.

But the city editor, as exasperating a man as ever lived, says that only men are handsome, while Webster has it that handsome is something that comes half way between pretty and beautiful.

————

"Reading the story in your column the other day about going to Florida to make money," writes Mary W., "I am wondering just how many people ever sit down and figure up what the interest on a little money amounts to in a few years.

"For instance we just celebrated a centennial. Now suppose we start with just $1. If someone had put a dollar to work 100 years ago drawing 4 per cent interest and added the interest annually to the principal why today that dollar would be worth just $340.

"Again if $1 was put to work drawing eight per cent interest and the interest collected annually and added to the principal, it would in 100 years amount to $2, 263.

"The same dollar handled in the same way drawing 10 per cent interest would in 100 years bring$13,803.

"To carry the illustration a little further even at the expense of one's imagination with regard to usurious interest. Take $1 loaned out at 12 per cent interest, and the interest annually to the principal and in ten years we have $88,075.

"And if that doesn't convey the power of a little interest working night and day for 100 years let us suppose $1 is drawing 18 per cent interest under the above terms and we get the fabulous sum of $15,145,600.

"All of the above proves that great oaks from little acorns grow. It is true that many will say who wants to wait 100 years, and where can you get 18 per cent interest. To them the lesson is lost.

"The point of all this is that if just the expenses of a trip to Florida were put into real estate most anywhere in Akron it will double and treble [sic] in five years.

"I am not in the real estate business nor the banking business nor am I speaking for investments of any kind. I recently took a little auto trip around Akron and noted with great interest the growth of the city is the outlying districts in all directions.

"I found people who had figured out for themselves that Akron would continue to expand and grow and they took a few hundred and invested it in a little property. Some had taken a small profit and reinvested.

"One can learn many profitable lessons from these small home owners scattered along the highways. The mass of people who scoot by their places is their automobiles never stop. It might pay some of them if they did. It is not difficult to establish confidence with them and their observations on values and opportunities are often illuminating.

"It is the old hoax that distant fields look greenest. And we overlook the things that are prospering and developing right under our noses.

"One man with scarcely any capital has started on the outskirts a number of concrete block garages and he has enough of them already to insure him $5,000 a year one income.

"I suggest you make a tour of the outlying sections some day and ask a few questions of the men and women who have established little places along the highways and who to all intents and purposes are getting something out of life without risking too much.

"East money is hard to get and it invariably has its price and not everyone is able to pay this price.

"Anyways, one can learn heaps by seeing Akron first and getting firsthand information of the pioneers who are boosting and building without much publicity out along the arteries of traffic where the small homes and stores and garages and oil stations mark the steady growth of a substantial industrial center."

———⁓◦◦⁓◆⁓◦◦⁓———

21 August 1925, Friday:

"YOU know I have been coming here for about eight years," writes Ellen, vacationing, "so really I know my way about the village quite well. It takes some years to acquire a thorough knowledge of a city of 200 souls, let me tell you.

"The library is my immediate Mecca although if it happens not to be Saturday after 2 p.m. it is not so immediate. They only open once a week and one pays five cents a week for the new books. As it happened however I arrived on Friday so I hadn't long to wait for my pilgrimage.

"I found the library hoard in the throes of a baked goods sale. Cookies, pie, cakes, etc., all over the place. You see a few of the townswomen started the library out of the goodness of their hearts and with nothing more material to give the prospect impetus. They have about 100 books, I believe, but are in sad need of some new ones. In fact some of them are so old they barely hang together and were the popular novels of my girlhood. So there, picture their antiquity!

"The woman must needs (illegible) every mile to decoy a few dollars into the treasury (illegible) as lawn (illegible), baked goods sales, etc. I was almost moved to tears at the thought of all those delicious looking cookies and pies being sold on the auction block to Harold Bell Wright and Zane Grey. And to observe those seriously be-aproned and be-spectacled matrons anxiously shooing flies off the sacrifice will the food and tender expression of a mother adjusting the veil of the bride.

"It was quite exciting here over Sunday with motors coming and going, depositing pretty ladies and husbands on a leash but everything is as quiet as the grave this morning. The dining room at breakfast was like a cemetery with nothing but the champing of toast and bacon to break the stillness.

250

"There was one exception. Maggie, one of the old retainers did create a welcome diversion by dropping a tray of poached eggs and oat meal. Poor Maggie, I'll have to tell you about her. If I could only describe her adequately. She is tall and extremely thing [sic], has a long thin pinched face, big dull black eyes, a long nose that turns up at the end, a mouth like a fish's and such a ghastly blue grey color.

"You will wonder that anyone has an appetite for food after gazing at this paragon but Maggie excites only sympathy. She is a paregoric fiend[52]. It seems her mother was one before her and taught Maggie the trick. She is allowed only a two ounce bottle at a time and she goes to the town seven miles away three times a day to get it. If she hasn't the price of a car ride she walks. Every cent she makes goes for it. Can you imagine anything more tragic?

"She was once a revered and honored bookkeeper, even as I, but is steadily growing worse until she is so weak she is dropping trays which will mean her dismissal here and a journey to the county house a mile away.

"Heavens, what an example for me. Do you think I shall ever arrive at the place where I will crawl on my hands and knees to the drug store at Merriman and Market to get my Lucky Strikes?[53]"

---

22 August 1925, Saturday:

I SEE by yesterday's paper where Herman Fetzer denies that the average person's life story would make a great novel. Or, to quote him exactly, "the great majority of them have the same story with only a dissimilarity of detail."

And doesn't Herman know that almost every story in the world is the same story "with only a dissimilarity of detail?"

---

[52] Paregoric is a camphorated tincture of opium, similar to Morphine

[53] A brand of cigarettes

There is a woman in this town whose husband is unfaithful to her. There are 5,000 women in this town whose husbands are unfaithful to let us say, whose husbands are unfaithful to them.

Of course I'm only one of those amateur writers whom Herman takes issue with, but it seems to me that someone who knew how to handle the details could make 5,000 good stories out of the lives of these women who are trying to work out of this one tawdry, commonplace little situation.

Of course we can't look into these women's hearts and know exactly what they are thinking but we can look into our own hearts and hearts, after all, are pretty much alike.

We might make one story about a woman who pretended that she didn't care. She went ahead and worked out her destiny along her own lines but always with a secret ache in her heart. Years later her husband discovered he was quite made about her, always had been. They made it up. And then the woman had the bitterest ache of all. She discovered that she couldn't care any more.

Or we might make a story about the woman who endeavored to win her husband back by love. She flattened herself out on the domestic altar, cooked his favorite foods, sat up night after night with croupy children, smiled wanly at his boorishness and said "Yes Henry, Yes Henry" to everything he chose to put upon her. And she died finally without anything ever happening.

Or we might make a story about the woman who didn't care a rap one way or the other but who had too much pride to let herself go down in defeat. With clothes, allurement, other men and anything else she could employ upon his susceptibilities she won him back to her and when she had him thoroughly bruised/trussed up she threw him down hard and eloped with a second violinist.

Or we might make a story about the woman who dies the messy thing, who cries, storms, begs, pleads and finally drags the whole thing to divorce court where she has the doubtful satisfaction of seeing the other girl's name played in large type and the girl branded forever as a breaker of homes.

Or we might make a story about the woman who did nothing at all because she had found out long ago that nothing really matters.

Or we might build our story not about the woman but about the other girl. It would go something like this: Once there was a girl who loved her boss. Sometimes the boss's wife would come down to the office and talk to the girl in a friendly fashion and then the girl would feel strangely disquieted. But then she would say, "Why should I care. He doesn't love his wife. Why should I care about another woman."

Suddenly the boss's wife died and almost before she knew it the girl found herself married to the boss.

One day the girl – now the wife – came down to the office and there was a new girl there.

And the girl went out of the office and walked and walked but she knew that never again would she be happy.

Sometimes I think that every story ever written is a crucifixion story. There is a little Jesus in our hearts made up of ideals and faith and love. And one by one the darts and the (illegible) come until finally the little Jesus is quite dead. Afterwards, some people say, there is a resurrection. But there are others, who say this is all bosh.

---

24 August 1925, Monday:

THE Old Settlers held a scandalous session Saturday noon during which one ideal was cracked, two reputations were critically gone over and 11 anecdotes were related. All in all as enjoyable a time as we have had in a long while.

The ideal which was cracked, I may as well say, was my own. My ideals are always getting that way. It concerned a well known actress who, I had always firmly believed, was a member of the S.P.C.A. and who wore only artificial furs.

Time after time I have seen interviews, with this actress to the effect that she wouldn't think of bringing suffering to dumb animals and urging the reader to send in his contribution to the society which has, I believe, its headquarters in Boston.

I suppose I would have gone on believing that until the end of time and retaining my childish hopeful expression had it not been that one of the Old Settlers remarked:

"She's a member of the S.P.C.A., isn't she?"

"What!" exclaimed another Old Settler, who knew perfectly well what she was talking about. "Why her home is filled with stuffed animals, and she wears every kind of fur you can think of – tippets and everything."

I was so bruised by this revelation that I drank three cups of coffee in absolute silence.

We all had a try at the Eleanora Duse[54] anecdote. The way is finally emerged was this: that at their last meeting D'Annucio said, "You will never know how much I have loved you," and Duse replied, "You will never know how thoroughly I have forgotten you."

I'm not sure yet, however, that that was the way it went. I mean to look it up as I always like an anecdote where the woman has the last crushing word.

Then someone thought to inquire what had become of Dorothy[55], the daughter of Lillian Russell[56], and it developed that she was in retirement somewhere fighting a losing battle with illness and adversity but that she still retained something of her old beauty.

Somehow, no matter where you go or whom you meet, you hear nothing but love expressed for Lillian Russell. I wonder whether she was aware of it or whether her

---

[54] Eleonora Duse (1858-1924) was an Italian actress known simply as Duse.

[55] Dorothy Lillian Russell (1884-?) daughter of actress Lillian Russell and Edward Solomon. She later married and became Dorothy Calbit.

[56] Lillian Russell (born Helen Louise Leonard) (1860-1922) was an American actress and singer. Marilyn Monroe once posed as Russell in the magazine *Life*.

repeated domestic misadventures gave her a feeling after a while that there was no one in the world who cared.

After that we had discussions concerning Joseph Schildkraut and his dressing gowns. Irene Fenwick and how this she was getting, whether Katherine Cornell was a better actress than Pauline Lord, Jeritas and her artistic vagaries, Richard Bennett and his artistic vagaries, whether real people ever have artistic vagaries. New York parties and why the people who live in New York always think there's no liquor to be had any place outside of New York, the bust of Caruso in the Metropolitan[57] and whether it is better to eat a small fish with small bones or a large fish with no bones at all.

Speaking of liquor, I wonder why people praise it so inordinately. I would rather have a 20 cent bottle of near beer than wash tubs of champagne. But the minute you go to a friend's house he starts rummaging around in the cellar from which he emerges presently with a bottle and the pleased expression of a child.

Fearing to do anything to the expression you drink some of the liquor, remark that it's wonderful, simply wonderful and promptly become sick unto death.

I was thinking awhile ago of a New York press agent for whom I agreed to do some work on the side. I was to write some short paragraphs about certain celebrities for which I was to receive a dollar a paragraph.

I sent in 15 or so paragraphs as a starter and then sat down hopefully to reflect what I would do with the money. I would buy shoes or a new hat or help pay the rent or buy an electric fan or I could throw a party for a couple of the girls.

My press agent was prompt. He came bustling in a few days later. But not with the $15. "I've got something you'll like ever so much better, sister," he whispered, and he produced a shining quart bottle.

"Cost me $22," he confided, "but it's worth it. Real pre-war. Now run along and throw a party for your friends."

---

[57] A bronze bust dedicated to Enrico Caruso, a tenor, in the Metropolitan Opera House

I took the bottle with a sinking heart.

My editor was leaving for Seattle just then and I gave it to him for a going away present.

He liked it.

⁓⌇⌇⌇✦⌇⌇⌇⁓

25 August 1925, Tuesday:

WE DIDN'T get the Essex.

Not that I expected to get it, but Bill did. His trustfulness was just pitiful especially this last week when something went wrong with the old Chevvy's ignition and it cost $14.50 to get it fixed up.

"Never you mind," said Bill, "the Essex won't need any fixing for a year. Won't it be grand to have it all paid for! No more payments. And we can sell the old boat and have maybe a couple of hundred dollars clear and we can buy," and so on and so on.

I confess even I got so warmed up to the idea that whenever I passed the Essex out here on Market st., I'd stop and figure how many people could ride in it and where we'd put the groceries on the back seat.

In the back of the brain, though, I knew it couldn't be. I never win a prize at a bridge game, never find any money, never win a fat woman's race or a pie eating contest, never hit the darkie[58] with the ball.

Over in an office where I used to work the gang always played rhummy on Friday afternoons after the pay envelope had been passed out. Sometimes the fellows used to ask me to come over and stand by them and hold their hand. To bring them luck, they called it. After a while, though, they didn't ask me any more.

---

[58] A rather negative way of entertainment involving a person of color, otherwise known as the Jolly Darkie Target Game with a cardboard mouth bullseye and a wooden ball.

Not that Bill is much better off, I think it was only a couple of years ago that they were raffling off some kind of car at the armory. But had a couple of books of tickets. Next to him stood Leo Ferbstein with just one ticket. Leo got the car.

The thing that hurts is that it is generally somebody who doesn't need the car who gets it. It's just like life and that saying is the Bible, "To him that hath –"

I'd just like to know who did get the Essex. I'll wager anything it was somebody with four cars in the garage and diamond tiaras and an electric washer and tickets bought for Europe.

It is things like this which leads me sometimes to wonder if there may not be something in this astrology business. A person is born under certain influences and all through life you can see them at work.

I know a girl whom people just love to give things to. She goes to Paris and the manager of the French steamship line considers it a tremendous privilege to give her her passage across. She goes out to tea with a woman whom she hasn't seen in years, and the woman casually steps into a jewelry store and presents her with a little wrist watch. A friend of hers in Cleveland got lonesome to see her one day last fall and sent her railway fare to come from New York for the weekend. A friend of hers – an actress – gets engaged to a millionaire and sells her her [sic] entire wardrobe worth several thousand dollars for a hundred dollars and throws in a fur coat besides. She goes out to dinner with a club man and he tips her off to something good on the stock market. She goes out to lunch with an importer and he sends her three sports frocks afterwards just because he knows she'll look so cute in these.

There are other persons – not mentioning any names – whose luck is just the reverse. They give a dinner party with somebody else and the other fellow forgets to pay up. They get new shoes and they burst out on the side, they buy a new jersey, and it shrinks, they bet on a horse, and it comes in fifteenth. They pick out a movie to go to, and it turns out to be the worst in town. They buy magazine subscriptions from college boys and the magazines never come. They go down to the market to buy nice pink peaches and when they open up the sack the peaches come out preserves. They buy a melon for breakfast and it turns out squash. They give money to blind beggars who the next day are arrested as impostors. They buy wrist watches which refuse to run and automobiles which collapse at every third mile. When they go to Europe, they pay their own passage across and when their rich aunt dies she leaves all her money to the natives of the Canary Isles.

There's something in the starts [sic]. There's no other way to explain it.

❧

L AURA JEAN LIBBEY'S estate, I see by the papers, is valued at $37,027, of which the sum of $595 is bequeathed to her husband.

I always wanted to know Laura Jean Libbey and on two of three occasions I tried hard to see her. But after I had made my way to her brown stone front in Brooklyn and had hammered tremendously on the front door my only reward was to be sent away again by a plump elderly woman, Miss Libbey's sister, probably, or her secretary who affirmed solemnly that Miss Libbey was either out of town or indisposed or engaged in the most engrossing kind of work.

———

And then Laura Libbey died. I found the other day a sketch of her in a book of republished newspaper articles put out by students of the Columbia School of Journalism.

Irene M. Evans is the author of the article.

"In a house in the residential section of Brooklyn," she writes, she (Laura Jean Libbey's presided where the settings were as lavish as say she bestowed on her (illegible) and where she ruled with as gracious a (illegible) as might Gwyndelynne or (illegible – Vetta?) Even in the late nineties when American homes groaned with heavy draperies and every fashionable mantelpiece flaunted porcelain shepherdesses, her residence, with its chandeliers, its plush hangings and its lambrequins, was a marvel to visitors. Their feet sank in the soft depths of red and green carpets whose thickness (illegible) a 'solsolces tread,' one requisite of true culture. Such a frame suited her. It lent added luster to the numerous receptions which had won for her the proud title of 'Madame de Staed of Pempect Heights.'

"One hundred feet of shelves her paper covered volumes, placed side by side, occupied. Here, in this room, on the completion of her 89th play in 1895, she assembled her coterie and clad in a sapphire blue gown trimmed with all over Valenciennes lace, she read for them, 'If the Heart is Truly Mated.'

"Her 'pink room,' she would inform the seeker after information, was where she conceived the plots of her stories. In the more austere studio she was went to unfold the narrative to her secretary.

"Laura Jean Libbey, however, placed little value on book reviews so far as her own novels were concerned. She never sent a book to a newspaper for criticism because it was difficult enough, with her public demand, to secure copies for herself. In substantiation of that there is her own word for the statement that her books reached a circulation of four millions, a figure paralleled only by the Bible and Shakespeare.

"About her method of writing she was more lucid than authors usually are. 'You must know,' she declared 'that when one sits down to write one must have at least some notion of a plot. Often I begin by writing some kind of conversation, then somebody answers back something, and then I say more and fill it all in. That's the way a novel is written – I have no technical training for dramatic writing, but some things just come natural.'

"She indulged in some publicity work which savored very much of present methods. As a climax to her activities she sought the stage. For a compensation of $2,500 a week she appeared at the American Roof Garden, clad in white, and sang, recited, skipped and lectured. She even had a play all in readiness written by herself, in which she was prepared to take a stellar role if sufficiently persuaded. She confided her ambitions in Daniel Frohman who after witnessing 6 performances, advised her to abandon the stage in favor of writing. Whether his suggestion proved crushing, scribes do not record, but at least Laura Jean Libbey decided to abide by it.

"That was the last blaze of publicity she enjoyed before her death. From 1910 to 1924 she lived on without a magazine making any reference to her and without newspapers seeking the annual interview they had formerly featured. The 1919 Year Book of American Literature does not contain her name. But undeterred she continued. At the time of her death Laura Jean Libbey left two new novels to add to her library's already swollen shelves."

The newspapers state further that two months before her death Laura Jean Libbey sold all dramatic and moving picture rights in her novels for $7,500.

I wonder.

29 August 1925, Saturday:

THURSDAY soon we went out to Mogadore where the women of the Church of Christ serve luncheon for 35 cents. I say luncheon because I believe that is what they call it. In reality it more nearly approached the proportions of a dinner with pork, mashed potatoes and gravy, string beans, tomatoes, bread and butter, jelly and pickles, coffee and apple or lemon pie. There may have been other things, but I can't recall them just now because my attention was partially distracted by Ward Van Orman who seemed to be earnestly engaged down at the other end of the table.

What I started out to say though was that the meal was nearly ruined for me because I early started wondering what they were going to do with the left-over mashed potatoes. There were mountains of them apparently and I couldn't possibly conceive them all being made over into potato cakes.

I have that trouble every time we go out to one of these nearby resorts where for $2 you get chicken and goodness knows what else besides. We were out at such a place the other night. I knew where the corn fritters went. Bill ate them. But all those stacks of chicken and potatoes and noodles and hot biscuits that nobody could possibly dispose of!

Does the help eat them or do they give them to the Salvation Army or do they have chicken salad and cold noodles the next day for lunch? And if the help does eat the leftovers every day don't they go wild some days just yearning for bacon and hominy?

If somebody can explain to me the economy of such places I shall be very, very grateful.

In Mogadore I found that I had done considerable worrying to no purpose. For when I attempted to buy some of the food to take home for supper that night I was informed that aside from two pieces of apple pie they expected to use up every smidgen of it. How they fare on other Thursdays when Ward Van Orman isn't there, of course, I couldn't possibly say.

Edna Ferber saw the romance in these eating places once. I don't remember the name of the story anymore nor even the plot but I can remember being struck with wonderment that nobody had ever thought of it before. The woman who loved pretty things but could do nothing in the world but cook. Of her offices along that line for an unappreciative husband. Of the unappreciative husband's departure at last for parts and places unknown. Of the woman turning her home into an eating place. Of the people who came from cities for miles around to sample her fried chicken. Of how she bought at last the grand piano and the oriental rugs she had always longed for and sent her daughter to college and – Oh – you know the rest.

The women at Mogadore are cooking, not for the sake of grand pianos but to pay off the indebtedness on their new church. Personally I think the little white frame structure which they are leaving is prettier than the new red brick structure back of it but that, I dare say, is a very impractical notion.

At any rate there is to be a regular dining hall in the new place and new dishes and new silver and built-in cupboards.

The assurance is given, however, that the quality of the apple pie is to remain unchanged.

Coming back we encountered a series of tracks across the road where a freight train was doing considerable sashaying back and forth. I think the engineer would have let us by at the end of 10 minutes had it not been that Wilbur made the technical error of honking the horn at him. That made the engineer mad, and for 10 minutes more he drove his freight train back and forth, without, so far as we could discover, accomplishing anything much in the way of switching her.

However, we didn't mind. We had lots of time and if a little thing like that would make the engineer happy for the rest of the day, why, we wanted him to have it.

---

31 August 1925, Monday:

THAT she can be as happy in Akron as in New York is, I gather, the theme of the play "Tinsel," written by Grace Brown and Catherine Fields which is to have its presentation at the Playhouse Tuesday and Wednesday nights.

Coming at this time of year, nothing could be more appropriate. All of one's friends, it seems, are going either to New York or to Europe, from where they will return a year or so hence with the remark, "Well, I see the old town is as dirty as ever." They will be bursting with recitals and encounters with the great. They will have had tea with Lady Mountbatten and have danced with a prince at Monaco. They will know all the latest scandal about critics, actresses, magazine illustrators, authors and rubber brokers. They will have seen all the latest plays and will give you the outlines of a number of books which the authors have not yet completed. They will have new clothes and they will have discovered a number of ducky eating places which you must look up when YOU go east, my dear. A number of them will have launched definitely upon careers paying thousands of dollars yearly and will have returned home for a couple of weeks merely to say hello to the folks and gather up a few lead pencils and things.

And those of us who have had to stay at home all year, whose entertainment has been limited to mime sex movies and a perusal of the Ladies' Home Journal, who have met no notables save the president of a visiting delegation of drug clerks and who have heard no scandal save a couple of local stories, 10 years old, will be sick at heart, wondering what life can possibly hold for us.

Of course, in just what manner "Tinsel" seeks to (illegible – reconell?) as to Akron I can't know until Tuesday night, but I can think of a number of reasons for being contented.

For one thing Akron smells better than New York. There is something dry and chokey about a city where all the earth for miles and miles is covered with pavement, where there is scarcely ever a tree and where the vegetation is confined almost entirely to window boxes. The minute you come back from there you notice something. And then you discover it is the smell of earth.

It is possible to get as much to drink in Akron as in New York. I am saying this not on my personal authority as we have always lived in very modest coca cola circumstances, but I have it on the word of friends whose veracity I do not question that you can have just as wild parties here as anywhere, and that the people will behave just as stupidly. It was only a few weeks ago – but we will let that pass.

It is harder to find good food in Akron than it is in New York, but on the other hand when you do find a good eating place your joy is proportionately greater. I heard last night of a place in East Akron where you can have a chicken dinner for 50 cents, and Herman Fetzer discovered last week a Greek restaurant on N. Howard st., which I mean to try out. I don't know whether to try it out right away or to postpone the experience and let my hope grow.

It is easier to save money in Akron than in New York. One of the reasons for this is that in New York one is liable to spend a great deal of money by going to the theater. In Akron one buys a copy of Life for 10 cents and reads the reviews. By reading a review one can frequently work up a great deal of enthusiasm for a piece whereas if one actually goes to a theater one is not only out of the price of one's ticket but one frequently leaves the place later with a feeling of the greatest chagrin.

One doesn't meet a celebrity very often in Akron, but on the other hand, a celebrity almost always turns out to be a bore if you have to be around him very long. You take the average human being whom you meet and after you have let him tell you the story of his life he will generally subside and let you tell yours. He doesn't want to hear yours any more than you wanted to hear his, but, at any rate, he appreciates the fact that one has to have a little delicacy in such matters. A celebrity never does. He insists on doing all the talking. And if you try to get a word in edgewise he'll leave you flat and start reciting his line all over again to someone who will listen.

And finally one can get just as weary of Broadway and 42nd st. as of Howard and West Market. Believe it or not there can come a time when there's no thrill left in looking at the Washington arch. Most New Yorkers I have found are only waiting until they can get enough money to push on to Paris and once in Paris, I dare say, they feel they'll never rest till they get to Pekin.

⸎

2 September 1925, Wednesday:

BEING one of those who are frankly bored by sports of any kind it would be foolish to essay an opinion on the latest troubles of Babe Ruth[59].

It does seem to me though that almost every summer as far back as I can remember reading headlines there has been some sort of scandal in baseball circles.

Every winter or so you hear a group of men talking excitedly and you gather that something not exactly creditable has been pulled in football. You hear a group of high school boys talking and you discover that some amateur team has done the gallant thing by tucking in a few professionals where nobody would notice them.

---

[59] George Herman "Babe" Ruth (1895-1948) American professional baseball player

Nurmi comes over here and, I gather, behaves as ethically as is humanly possible. Stories of his accepting vast sums of money are promptly spread about him.

Americans go abroad to attend the Olympic games and the reports which trickle back are to the effect that some of them are not exactly good sports when it happens to be a European who establishes a record.

Dempsey refuses to fight Walls and various interpretations are put upon it.

Battling Siki behaves so badly that he has to be sent out of the country.

And yet talk to the average high school boy, football coach or sports writer and he will tell you that sports are valuable mainly for their high moral effect. They teach a man to accept odds gamely, to be a good loser, to reason quickly, to think cleanly, to eat moderately, to drink not at all and to go to bed at 10 o'clock at night.

They are also supposed to have some high educational value although just what this is I have never been able to find out.

The newspapers have a great fancy for running articles written by the starts of the sports world and it is not impossible to find columns of copy turned out by Siki, Firpo and Nurmi although none of these gentlemen is equipped with more than a dozen words of English.

But even were these men to turn out their own copy it could scarcely be less intelligible than the average sports article turned out by the hard working reporter under the name of some American luminary. The American luminary has neither the time nor the patience nor the ability to write his own views. He will, however, if given sufficient money and prodded sufficiently by the sports writer give expression in a word or two which the sports writer promptly expands into half a column approximating the luminary's language as closely as possible.

The result is baffling.

"Oh," but you say, "you admit you don't know anything about sports. If you did understand them then you could understand the articles."

Well, I don't know anything about steam heaters or radios or thermostats or submarines or the vicissitudes of the milk weed but if I encounter an article written about any of these things I can generally understand at least a third of what the author is talking about.

I have never yet been able to unscramble an idea from the average sports article.

I never was sent to interview Babe Ruth but Ruth Roure who used to work on the Akron Press attempted it one time and the effort to get the Babe to utter one intelligible sentence left her limp and exhausted.

I have had similar exhausting experiences with other sport luminaries from Charlie Paddock up and down the line.

After a while you discover that the outstanding characteristic of the men in the sports world is inarticulateness.

Now I have no quarrel with inarticulateness and I can get inordinately fond of anyone whose intentions are free from guile.

But the recurring scandals in the baseball world seem to make even the defense impossible.

Moreover I think it was Harvard college which a few weeks ago made the discouraging discovery that students who took part in athletics were doing none too well in their studies.

Henceforth if the ideal of male America is to be square shoulders surmounted by square hands why all right but let's not delude the high school youngsters with all this talk about clean thinking.

❧⸜⸝❧

7 September 1925, Monday:

THE Old Settlers held a large and enthusiastic gathering, but it was practically impossible to know what anybody was talking about, owing to the fact that two person would get together and start talking in an undertone and between keeping up a conversation on your right and keeping your ear open for anything that might fall from the group on the left, you really did not find out anything worth while at all.

All you learned was that "The Green Hat" was or was not a good book, that the play made from it was or was not a good play, that a great many people seemed to be having hay fever, that baked apple dumpling were better than the steamed kind, that it was a shame that the movie of "A Beggar On Horseback" had to be taken off after two days because of lack of patronage, that when you got down to counting them there probably weren't eight intelligent people in Akron, that it was awfully hard to find an apartment for fifty dollars and that marriage was bunk.

There was also some discussion of the wood cut of Beethoven which is on exhibit at present at the art institute, Orlando saying that it looked as though the old gentleman had been in the tomb for a good long while, but the rest of us, including Wilbur Pest, holding not that it was art and wasn't it wonderful that you could get it for only seven dollars.

I must confess that I learned something from this part of the discussion. I had definitely decided that the Beethoven was to be mine anticipating the time when I could hang it near the grand piano, as yet unpurchased. All I thought you had to do was to hand a five dollar and two one dollar bills to the attendant and then you took the Beethoven home and hung it up. But no. It seems you have to leave the Beethoven hanging where it is and write away to the artist and ask him to make another print of it for you. And the artist is in Paris.

We were having one of our community breakfasts Sunday morning and it was Jake who got to wondering whether the members of a string quartet didn't become extraordinarily devoted to one another.

This was something new to me as I had always thought of musicians as being primarily scrappy. And I yet don't know whether they stay together because they like one another or because they love music so much that all personal differences vanish.

Certainly the members of the Flonzaley quartet have stayed together for a good many years now and I know of no better example of how four individuals, by exercising a nice subordination of self can achieve a common beauty.

It may be that there is something about a quartet that lifts man out of his baser nature. Whenever a number of individuals gather about a board where the spirits are excellent and the flow is discreet there always arrives a time when they feel an overwhelming desire to burst into a four part rendition of Sweet Adeline. And though no particular forethought has been exercised in getting together these individuals still it will always be found that in some miraculous fashion a first tenor, a second tenor, a baritone and a base are on hand.

The same is true when a group of youths are on their way home from, say, the second shift. They speak for a time a love. Then they find themselves passing the home of Mamie, the beautiful cashier. Simultaneously they burst into song.

Somebody should look into the matter of quartets. It may be that there is something about this number four that calls out all that is mellow and unselfish in our natures.

8 September 1925, Tuesday:

AFTER all, the potato is probably our noblest salad. It was known and esteemed while tomatoes were still regarded as mantel ornaments and it was loved while Hawaii was yet unexplored and the combination of pineapple and cheese was undreamed.

The older generations had a way of fixing up a sort of impromptu potato salad. You took a large boiled potato and mashed it on your plate with appropriate quantities of butter and pepper and salt. Over this you cut an onion. Over the whole you sprinkled a few drops of vinegar.

Then there was a mashed potato salad which I haven't encountered for a good many years now. You mashed the potatoes and to them you added vinegar and salt and pepper and mustard and an egg and a little onion. The whole was beaten like everything and when it was all fluffy, it was borne in triumph to the table.

We have long had at our house a recipe which was known as "Ahna's." "Ahna's" method was to make a white sauce in a frying pan and to this she added vinegar, celery salt, a little onion and the like. Then, diced potatoes and cucumbers were added and the whole was served still reasonably hot.

My favorite potato salad, and I dare say it is the favorite with the majority of persons is the German kind where you start out by frying innumerable bits of bacon. The other kind, the kind made with mayonnaise, is good too, except that in public eating places it is ruined by the omission of the onion. Restauranteurs, it seems, are afraid of putting in the onion for fear of offending the taste of their more refined patrons. But when you consider that the number of refined persons in the world is comparatively small it would seem to be much better business to cater to the other kind.

I have been thinking about this woman who left her brain recently in a certain university that it might be measured and examined. Her contention was that a woman's brain is just as powerful as a man's.

Granting that the quality of a person's brain has a great deal to do with the size, which I doubt, I wonder why women feel this continual urge to show that whatever a man does they can do just as well if not a little bit better.

A woman's essential organ, I imagine, is the heart and not the brain and yet she lets that poor organ wither away while she starves herself into boyish form, gets herself a boyish bob, learns to swear like a trooper and goes in for law and heavy gin parties.

Now I haven't any objection to these things and I'd love to have a boyish form but if a woman really wants to attain distinction I doubt that she can do it by competing in the same fields with me. Sappho was remarkable for her poetry and St. Theresa for her wisdom. Catherine of Russia was a great ruler. Cleopatra was a great lover and in our own day Mme. Curie is a great scientist. But these have been isolated women separated by centuries. We have in all the history of the world no single great woman composer, no great woman dramatist.

It may be of course that an era is opening up wherein women will sufficiently suppress their dish washing instincts to become as great as their masculine predecessors have been. But sometimes I think women would do better by walking in exactly the opposite direction from the one that men have taken. Just what this is I don't know yet but I do know that it has very little to do with the brain. Instead it has something to do with affection and loyalty and things like that.

"But," you say, "then the world will never hear of you."

Well there was a woman 16 centuries or so ago whom they crushed with chains and then threw into the Tiber. I suppose in her bitter agony she thought that no one would know or care either. But they brought her bones to America a few weeks ago and I understand they're going to build a church over her.

⸺ ❧✦❧ ⸺

9 September 1925, Wednesday:

THERE is lying on my desk at present a picture of a scene from the modernized version of Hamlet which some company is putting on over in London. The queen has on one of those up and down no-waistline models with a sort of train falling from the shoulders. Polonius has on a regular butler's get-up while the king is looking very soup and fish[60] with knife pleats in his trousers and diamond studs in his shirt front.

---

[60] "Soup and Fish" means formal evening dress for men.

The scene, I take it, is that one where Polonius is offering to utilize Ophelia for purposes of royal intrigue.

They say that the idea has taken London by storm and that the man who thought it out is making barrels of money. It is a great pity that they didn't include a picture of Hamlet too in this clipping that I have on that individual is supposed to appear in the grave scene wearing knickerbockers[61]. I should love to see Hamlet in knickerbockers with a sport shirt tossed carelessly open at the throat and golf stockings turned correctly at the knee. But, no, Hamlet went about with his stockings ungartered didn't he? Just like any of the dear, modern university lads.

———

Whether they have also modernized the language of Hamlet the few paragraphs subtended to the picture fail to say. They do state, however, that when the modernized version is presented on this side of the water it will be touched up with a few "Americanisms," Cigarets and hip flasks will be in evidence and Ophelia will be found to be suffering from an atrocious libido.

The wonder of all this is, of course, that nobody thought of it sooner. They've been working over the Bible for a good many years now. How in the world do you suppose they ever slipped up on Shakespeare?

———

And after all there's nothing particularly sacrilegious about it. Those painters who flourished a few centuries ago and who loved to adorn the walls, the altars and the ceilings of the cathedrals were in the habit, I believe, of substituting the visages of certain notorious court personages for the somewhat pained expressions of the saints while more than one frolicsome lady, after due persuasion, assumed an other-world demeaner and allowed herself to be draped in habiliments appropriate to the Madonna.

As a result of this we have Flemish madonnas and Dutch madonnas and English madonnas and French, Italian and Spanish madonnas, but never, to my knowledge, a Madonna who looked even remotely Jewish.

———

[61] Knickerbockers or knickers, are baggy-kneed trousers for men popular in the early 20th century.

There are a lot of male actors however, I imagine, who will object strongly to the idea of playing Hamlet in tweeds and golf stockings. One of the strongest attractions of the role, it has always seems to me, was the black velvet. You take the average male and you'll find he's practically starved for black velvet. If he has nice legs the thing gets to be an obsession and if he hasn't nice legs he'll wear black velvet anyway and pad out the calves.

He loves the lines of the place all right, but it's those lines that start out with the gold neck chain, flow gracefully down the arm and wrist and terminate at a dainty silk clad ankle. After the audience has steeped itself in the melancholy beauty of this, then there is time to go on with "To be or not to be –"

I don't know why I haven't had my hay fever this year. Sometimes I think it's because I've been a better girl than usual and sometimes I think it's because Providence has figured that what with the ice pan running over and all I've had troubles enough.

Bothersome as it was I was always sort of proud of my hay fever. It seemed to go on forever like that Shaw play, "Back to Methuselah." It started in June when it was known as rose cold and it lasted through June and July. Then in August it was hay fever and it lasted through August and September. In October it was something you got from the smelling the dust on the leaves and that lasted through November. In December it was something you got from getting snow in your shoes and that lasted until April, after which it merged into just one of those bad colds that come from sitting on the ground when it's thawing. That took me up until June at which time I started in all over again.

Other girls were always dashing into a drug store after a chocolate nut sundae but whenever a drug clerk saw me coming, he started reaching under the counter for those large sized men's handkerchieves [sic] that come two for a quarter.

Not having it this year has been quite a saving, and I'm seriously thinking of taking up powdering my nose again.

---

10 September 1925, Thursday:

WE WERE speaking a while ago of the comparatively trivial things which one remembers out of one's childhood.

"There are two things which I remember most clearly," said Tueya. "One is of a woman who came to call on us and she had some chocolate candy done up in silver paper. We thought she was awfully stuck up because she wouldn't eat it. The other is about how we went to call on a doctor's wife and she showed us some six-dollar velvet pumps that the dog had chewed up.

"Oh – and I remember that my sister fractured her arm, but the only thing that impressed me was the funny way it stuck out at the elbow."

For my own part, I can remember how I hurt my arm one time and there was some talk of an amputation. All this did not horrify me, however. Instead I was delighted with the impression I could make on the other kids of the neighborhood.

Out of my first birthday party I can remember two things; that the refreshments cost six dollars and that we had bananas. I don't think I would have remembered about the refreshments costing six dollars had it not been that my aunt, who had given the party mentioned the fact frequently and with asperly. I think she felt that the other relatives should have done something about it. But the part about the bananas was my own and the memory lingers while the details of weddings and funerals and things which happened about the same time have completely vanished.

Out of the whooping cough I can remember riding on the street cars with my head swathed in a white veil and peeping out of the corner of it to observe a huge Negro woman sitting next to me.

And out of the measles all I remember is how the clock ticked, like a little boy riding a broom stick up and down the frost sidewalk.

We ordinarily think of children as being merely little men and women, but sometimes I wonder if the opposite contention isn't correct: that they are complete individuals until they are about 14 and that after that they become something else again.

Daisy Ashford wrote her prodigious novels while she was eight or nine and then she put away her note books never to take them up again. Over in Czecho-Slovakia the artist Cisek demonstrated that left to themselves children were capable of producing perfectly serious art. He did not regard this art as the forerunner of something mature. To him it was complete in itself and he almost invariably lost interest in the child as soon as it became 14 or 15. Very few of these children continued to be artists when they grew up.

Mozart wrote music at the age of five and you can if you wish consider that the later Mozart was another musician entirely.

The bad boy in school grows up to build bridges and span continents and the good boy in school grows up to live off his wife's folks.

I forget now how old Willie Sidis was when he entered Harvard, but it seems to me he was delivering lectures on the fourth dimension at the age of 12. They found him working in an office a couple of years ago. He was running an adding machine for $25 a week.

And just now, while I am sitting here musing over the trivial things which influence children, the voice of Lisle Croy, our energetic police court reporter, breaks upon the air.

"Here's a guy," he says, "who don't like the kind of bottles his wife is putting up ketchup in, and so he takes poison."

"Did it kill him?" asks Russ Henderson.

"Naw," says Croy, "he'll get better."

---

11 September 1925, Friday:

THE Terwilligers used to live on W. Market st., but the street cars were so noisy they sort of got on Mrs. Terwilliger's nerves and so the Terwilligers moved over into the suburbs, five minutes walk to the bus line, plenty of trees and nice neighbors, the kind that raise their own garden vegetables.

"My, my," said Mrs. Terwilliger the first day they were there, "It certainly does seem good to get away from all that racket. And have you noticed the birds? Really it almost seems as though one were right out in the country."

The next morning the Terwilligers were awakened by the sound of a shotgun. It seemed, as Mrs. Terwilliger informed herself later, just the Jessups who lived next door on the left hand side, had no love at all for birds and were exceedingly put out by their chattering. Mr. Jessup worked over in one of the rubber offices and in order to punch the time clock promptly at 7:30 it was necessary for the Jessups to get up at 6 o'clock.

Mr. Jessup's first act upon arising in the morning was always to go out and fire off his shotgun at the birds. Not only did this scare the daylights out of the birds but it gave Mr. Jessup a chance to drink in a few whiffs of fresh morning air, so necessary when one expects to spend the rest of the day in a rubber office.

Meantime Mrs. Jessup would be getting breakfast. The Jessup's ice box was on the back porch and Mrs. Jessup kept practically everything she needed for breakfast in the ice box. The Jessup's screen door had no rubber silencers on it.

First Mrs. Jessup would go out and get the butter. She would open the screen door and let that slam and then she would open the ice box door and slam that. Then she would go back into the kitchen and slam the screen door again.

Then Mrs. Jessup would remember that she had remembered the night before to put the musk melon on ice. So Mrs. Jessup would go after the musk melon and first she would slam the screen door and then she would slam the ice box door and then she would slam the screen door again.

The Mrs. Jessup would remember that the cream for Mr. Jessup's coffee was also on the ice. So Mrs. Jessup would go after the cream and first she would slam the screen door and then she would slam the ice box door and then she would slam the screen door again.

Mrs. Jessup would do the same with the eggs and also with the imitation maple syrup which Mr. Jessup always demanded for his oatmeal.

Then Mr. Jessup would leave for the office. Mr. Jessup was in the habit of filvvering to the office and in order to get the engine to running smoothly he would always start her about 20 minutes ahead of time. There was always a great deal of interest when Mr. Jessup finally got backed out of the yard.

Afterwards little Helen Marie Jessup, whom a phrenologist had pronounced a musical genius just from seeing the child's picture on the mantel, would practice her piano lesson for two hours.

Little Helen Marie was only 11 and she had already been learning Liszt's Second Hungarian rhapsody for the past two years. Sometimes the neighbors felt almost as though they could sit down and play it themselves.

On the other side of the Terwilligers Mrs. Terwilliger found that the Littledoves lived. The Littledoves were a newly married couple just trying to get along. Mrs. Littledove always slept until noon so she would always be nice and fresh to throw a party for some of the bunch in the evening.

The Littledoves' parties were always the gayest things imaginable. They never began until 3 o'clock and there was always the phonograph and the player piano and the radio to keep everybody happy. Mrs. Littledove knew a couple of the university fellows – had in fact been rushed by a whole fraternity before she married Mr. Littledove and they were always dropping in with their saxophones and banjos so there was really no reason on earth why everybody shouldn't have a good time.

The Littledoves' parties generally broke up about 2 o'clock in the morning with any number of cute things being said back and forth between the curb and the front porch after which the bunch would drive off and Mr. and Mrs. Littledove would retire upstairs to settle any little arguments which had developed during the evening.

Sometimes as many as two windows, a looking glass and four ginger ale bottles would be broken during these discussions after which Mrs. Littledove would turn in and Mr. Littledove would go downstairs to spend what remained of the night at a hotel.

Mr. Littledove was also something of a mechanic and he took great pride in the fact that he was building his own garage. Mr. Littledove just worked on the garage on Sundays. He would get up at 5 o'clock in the morning in order to get a good day's work in.

Mrs. Terwilliger says that sometimes she just gets lonesome for the sound of the street cars. She says she never noticed before how musical a street car could be.

---

12 September 1925, Saturday:

ONE of the redeeming things about having company, it always seemed to me, was that when company came, the house got cleaned. Let Aunt Anastasia write that she and Junior and Junior's Sunday school teacher would be down for the weekend and right away the curtains got washed, the wedding silver got polished, the best china was taken down from the top kitchen shelf, the shelf got scrubbed, a new soap dish was put up in the bathroom, a fresh patch of wall paper was put over that place in the parlor where the davenport rubbed and new fringe was put on the hall rug, the one that got tangled up in the vacuum cleaner.

At other times the house languished.

———

Such conduct is of course reprehensible. A house, as Aunt Margaret used to say over and over again, should be immaculate at all times.

Bearing all this in mind and knowing it perfectly well, it is remarkable how a house, even when it consists of one room, one bath and one kitchenette, can get away from one.

"Oh well," I said to myself consolingly, "some day we'll have company and then I'll clean it up."

It is now 5 o'clock and the company is due to arrive in three hours. If I remember correctly two razor blades are still rusting in the wash bowl, three towels are drying on the edge of the bath tub, the breakfast cups are languishing on the draining board, the curtains aren't hanging at all the way they should, there is dust on the book cases, cigaret ashes are in the apple dish, the sandwiches aren't made and a spider has set up housekeeping beside the fireplace.

Whenever I used to go visiting I never minded these things. In fact, I always felt that a little dust on the piano showed you were a welcome guest.

I can only hope that others will be as charitable.

———

Back at 135 West 65th st. we used to have a visitor who drove us to desperation. Bill says that whenever he meets anyone who's slightly deranged he always says to himself, "There must be one of Jo's friends."

Mrs. Aum was one of them. It was impossible to see from the second floor who was ringing the bell downstairs, and so before we were aware of it, Mrs. Aum would be upon us.

She had generally just met up with a man who knew a man who was an importer and this man had just gotten in something that was remarkably fine and she could see to it that we got all we wanted at $7.50 a quart.

Aside from the fact that neither Eleanor nor myself cared about such matters, we never had the $7.50.

We would carefully and tactfully explain this each time to Mrs. Aum, after which she would invite us to accompany her to Coney Island.

Mrs. Aum had the best times at Coney Island. On one occasion, Mrs. Aum went there with a gentleman friend, and the two of them stopped into a little restaurant and asked the man to fix them up a special little dinner. The man said it would take about an hour. So Mrs. Aum and her gentleman friend went for a little walk and would you believe it? When they started back they couldn't find that restaurant, although they sought high and low and had only a pint bottle between them. Mrs. Aum said that this was really the mercy of Providence, as she found out later that the man who kept the restaurant was a desperate character and frequently robbed his patrons.

On another occasion, Mrs. Aum was having a little argument with her gentleman friend and the latter fired off a pistol at her. But Mrs. Aum held the correct thought and the bullet swerved around one corner of the room and lodged in a chair leg.

You can see from this that Mrs. Aum was psychic and that Providence was indeed looking after her. Sometimes she had remarkable luck telling fortunes with cards and she could, by concentrating, cause pictures to appear on the wall.

One evening, just as we were settling down for a nice quiet time by ourselves, Mrs. Aum ran in. She had just a vision and she thought it would make such a sweet idea for a story. In her vision she saw a mother and child afloat on a raft. They had been floating for days. They had lost all track of time. "Oh, if we only knew what day it was," cried the mother despairingly.

"Never mind, mama," said the child, "I will pray!"

And so the child prayed and as she looked up she saw a procession of fishes across the sky.

"Oh mama," she cried, "see all the fishes. I know what day it is. It is Friday."

I thanked Mrs. Aum and told her I thought it would make a remarkable story.

But even that didn't keep her from staying until half past eleven.

---

15 September 1925, Tuesday:

"ARE you proud of Akron? Would you have your loyalty tested?" writes Ancient Admirer. "Then drive to Cleveland and try any one of the Akron methods of driving on any traffic cop you meet.

"You'll be lucky if you come home without a court summons. At least your ears will burn. For Cleveland cops care little for Akron's ways of making a left turn, or passing on the near side of a cop instead of around him.

"Canton's traffic guardians will be equally outspoken if you attempt to turn your car in the middle of a block. You will be cautioned, in Canton, also not to pass a car at an intersection. Quite a wise rule, but one which Akronites never bother with.

"Wouldn't it be well if Akron, Cleveland and Canton could all get together and agree one some system, and then standardize on it?

"Isn't there a need right now for some way of instructing incoming motorists as to Akron's ways of getting through downtown traffic? If we had a billboard on each of the four or five main roads entering Akron – East Market st., West Market, Copley rd., Wooster av., North Main st. – it would save delays, embarrassment and possibly accidents. It might be well to print these warnings, not only in English, Yiddish and the other foreign tongues, but also in colored man's talk. The number of dark-skinned drivers on the road lately is enough to cause apprehension, since most of them are reckless drivers.

―――――――

"When you come down to ways of preventing automobile accidents, you might as well start with stricter rules. ANYBODY can drive a car in Ohio, no matter how intelligent or clear-eyes or skillful he may be. Down in New York and Massachusetts you pass a road examination. We'll have to kill off a few hundred more people and then Ohio will come to that, too.

"Second-hand cars might well be inspected more rigidly, too. If the man in front of you is driving a wreck and a wheel drops off, you'll hit the ditch just as surely as if it were your own fault. Keep the cars bolted tight together and you'll avoid many a smash.

"New rules regarding left turns will save many a crumpled fender. Also roadside stands, barbecues, hot dog places and filling stations should be forced to provide parking place off the main road.

"We'd feel a little safer in making a trip between towns if Ohio had some system of state police such as Pennsylvania has. Remember the Akron man who drove off the road in the rain? The coroner reported that he had lived for hours with the weight of the car on his crushed body. They found him 15 hours later. Probably a system of motorcycle cops patrolling the roads would report accidents like this in time to save a life.

"Funerals are a traffic menace, too. Here are 20 or 30 cars in parade formation, completely blocking the road and forcing the driver to follow along at a snail's pace or to attempt the impossible in crowding past before some oncoming car blocks him. If the driver KNEW that this was a funeral, he might realize that his chance of getting by was limited and might drop into second gear until the cemetery had been reached. But he doesn't find that out until he has tried to pass and found that the close formation prevents him.

"A motorcycle cop at front and back of a funeral procession might save accidents. Of a banner on the rear car, announcing that this is a funeral would help. But we'll have a few more wrecks before Ohio is forced to pass such a rule.

"Meanwhile, Rhode Island will arrest you if you drive slower than 30 or 35 miles on an open road, experience having shown that the SLOW driver is the man who makes people frantic so that they take long chances and drive wild.

"New England won't let a minor or a drunk or a past offender drive a car, and Pennsylvania checks you up if you drive at night without proper lights.

"But Ohio bumps along, with few laws and lax enforcement. We have more cars than any state except California and New York; we have dangerous hills and slippery turns. How many more deaths will occur before we come to rigid control of motorists?

"Also it's too bad that the death of Stetinius[62] passed unnoticed in Ohio, where he was born and where he once headed the match industry. Barberton has never since produced a man as big, as fair-minded and as national in his vision. And they let him be buried, without even an editorial in the papers, or if there was one it was so small I didn't see it. But folks down Barberton way will tell you he was a gentleman, a wise and just executive and a good neighbor. May the hills of Ohio bring forth others like him."

---

[62] Edward R. Stettinius (1865-1925) American executive and President of the Diamond match company in Barberton, Ohio.

The traveling library we know today was begun in 1893 in the State of New York under the leadership of the great librarian, Melvin Dewey.

It cost 20 times as much to recruit the 2,400,000 men who fought on the Union side during the Civil war as it did to recruit the 4,800,000 raised by the United States in the late World war.

---

16 September 1925, Wednesday:

I HADN'T realized until the other day how thoroughly up against it the average school teacher must be when the fall term opens and she must look about for a room.

It seems that lists of available rooms are furnished [sic] the school teachers, but since there is no way of checking up on these the only way is to begin wearily at the top and start traveling down the line irrespective of how many others have done the same thing.

Jane Barnhardt, director of the art classes up at the university, was telling a group of us the other night how she had set out with another teacher to help her find a room. Mrs. Barnhardt before her marriage was Jane Sargent and her father had charge of Glendale cemetery.

The two of them started out bravely enough, but late in the afternoon their spirits lagged. It was remarkable the number of things that could stand in the way of getting a room. Any number of landladies wanted only men roomers. One landlady looked them over critically. "Why yes," she said doubtfully, "I have got a room, but I wanted somebody that would be company for my brother." Another landlady showed them all over the house only to inform them after the expedition was over that the rooms were already taken.

Late in the afternoon, a slight diversion presented itself. As the landlady opened the door a smile of recognition illumined her face.

"Didn't you use to be Jane Sargent?" she queried.

"Yes," said Mrs. Barnhardt, "I did."

"Well," said the landlady, "you don't look a bit different than you did in the cemetery."

The mystified school teacher had matters explained to her.

But they still were without room.

———

They tell of a little boy who started off on his first day in school in high glee last week only to run away home in extreme disgruntlement. "Why, what was the matter, don't you like school?" queried his mother.

"Aw," he answered, "they've got a lot of kids over there. They don't need me."

———

I didn't see "The Ten Commandments," but even if I had I don't suppose I would have noticed the distinction which a local minister was drawing last night.

"Now we know from the Bible," he was saying, "that Miriam was Moses' older sister and yet in the picture Moses was an old, old man, while Miriam was a young and beautiful girl."

Neither, I suppose, would I have had the discernment of the woman who was watching them film the early scenes of the picture.

"Why," she exclaimed suddenly, "you've got Moses wearing eye-glasses."

And it was true. They had gotten Theodore Roberts to put on whiskers and throw away his long black cigar, but they had altogether forgotten about his spectacles.

———

I used to work in a office where a nephew of Theodore Roberts was employed as cartoonist, and he told me considerable of the family history most of which, I find, I have forgotten.

As I recall it, though, the father of Theodore Roberts was a sea-going man and his later years he acquired an extensive line of vessels. Theodore Roberts inherited this hankering for the sea and it was taken for granted that he would inherit the ships and carry on the tradition. When the old man died and his estate was settled, however, it was found that a brother had inherited the business – a brother who cared nothing at all about the sea.

The ships rotted, the brother went into other ventures and Theodore Roberts and his black cigar drifted into the movies.

That of course could hardly be called a tragedy, seeing that Theodore Roberts has given delight to, I dare say, millions.

There is an element of tragedy, however, in the man who was born to toil not, neither to spin nor to perform any sort of practical labor but is compelled to do all of these out of sordid necessity.

You all know at least one of him. He is delightful. He has discrimination in food, music and pictures. He can talk charmingly of books, gold fish and landscape gardening. Given the opportunity, he would make life a matter of perennial satisfaction to his friends.

But he never has any money nor any prospect of inheriting money. Being intelligent he is moderately successful, but he must go every day to the office and the hours which should be spent in conversation or playing solos on the 'cello must be devoted instead to gathering statistics on the salmon industry or mailing brochures on fallen women to the uplift club.

No, he never inherits any money. Inherited wealth, I always find, descends to gentlemen with puffy eyelids who straightway go about spending it on diamond bracelets for chorus girls.

The saxophone was invented by Adolphe Sax about 1840 and officially introduced into the French army bands July 31, 1845.

<hr/>

19 September 1925, Saturday:

HOW pleasantly the lunch hour eats into the day's activities! For as anybody knows, it is frequently impossible to be of any good in the morning because one is so very hungry and then afterwards it is frequently impossible to be of any good in the afternoon because one has eaten too much apple pie.

There are some poor driven souls who have only a half hour for lunch. These grab a sandwich and a glass of milk, and this leaves them 7 minutes to shop for a fall coat, a black satin dress with buttons down the back, a yard of elastic and a jar of cold cream.

The Rotarians, the Lions, the Kiwanians, the Civitans and so on have longer. They have an hour, but even this hardly seems sufficient for the number of things they have to transact.

I went to one of these luncheons one time. The waiter brought in a plate on which there was some roast lamb, I think it was, and some mashed potatoes and some peas and a hot roll and a number of other things. Just as I was starting in on the roll, a man – a prominent member of the chamber of commerce, whose name you would recognize in a minute if I told you – spied me. "Well, well," he said, coming over and shaking hands with me. YOU here."

"Yes," I said, and we talked for about 10 minutes.

I was just starting on my roll again when another man, a fellow from the Goodyear[63], came up. "If this ain't a surprise," he said. "I suppose you're one of the speakers."

"No," I said. "I'm just visitin'," and so we talked for about 10 minutes.

He went away and I was just taking up my roll again when I saw Harry Chalmers. I winked at Harry and Harry winked at me, after which he came over and asked me why I wasn't taking harp lessons. I told him I was postponing harp lessons while I brushed up on the dishpan and rolling pin, and then just as Harry was going away, the president rapped for order and said, "We are very pleased to have with us today---"

Well I had made up my mind that manners or no manners I was going to finish that roll and find out whether the peas were fresh or canned. But after the first mouthful I saw it wouldn't do. The speaker was telling a dandy story about a Scotchman, an Irishman and a Jew but nobody was paying any attention to him. They were all looking at me and

---

[63] The Goodyear Theatre, part of the original Goodyear Hall which was built in 1919.

thinking, "Doesn't that girl know that luncheon clubs have nothing to do with luncheon?"

Miserably, I let fall my knife and set down my coffee cup with trembling hands. "Anyway," I thought, "they're going to have music. Maybe I can get a little of the pineapple while the soprano is singing."

But just as the soprano started in on "Star of Me" the president leaned over. "You can hear her better," he said, "if you turn this way."

So I turned my back on all that food and I never saw any of it again.

———————

No, three hours is the least that one can do a luncheon in and do it adequately, even if it is only of the 50-cent variety. For one thing, there are friends who have to be greeted and it is always terribly annoying to a friend to have you ask how the twins are, with one eye glued on the salad section of the menu card. Then there is the lengthy period which must be given over to deciding whether one will have soup or not and whether it will be chicken noodle or cream of tomato. After that, there is the long struggle to get the saccharin tablets to dissolve in the iced tea and to get the eye of the waiter to inform him that the last square of butter went on the floor. And finally there is the wait for familiar faces.

There is one couple whom I always wait for. He is a man of slight foreign build and he wears a Van Dyke beard. He might be a doctor or a bond salesman, but is probably neither. There comes with him a pretty girl. They talk a great deal and finally at the close of the meal, warmed by tea and companionship they get a little reckless. She takes up bits of bread and throws them and he catches them in his mouth. At least some of them. The others go on his tie or within his collar, giving him, I imagine, an occasional uncomfortable afternoon.

They are the only couple who are different. If anything should happen to them, I should miss them very much indeed.

———————

21 September 1925, Monday:

AN APARTMENT HOUSE ANTHOLOGY, SUITE 1

The Nathan's are getting ready to go to California. They are not going for about a year yet, for it will take that long for the estate to get settled. The estate belonged to Ernest Nathan's mother. It will be only a few thousand, and so that Nathans are going to do the sensible thing with it. They are going to spend it all.

"You know," explains Mary Nathan, "it came over me all of a sudden one morning. I was doing the dishes, and Ernest was in the front room playing Mozart. 'Why,' I said to myself, 'should I always be doing dishes, and why should Ernest always be playing Mozart?'

"It was then that we heard about Ernest's mother. Ernest was real pleased about it. He said that now he could lay off entirely for a year and devote himself to the opera. But I put my foot down on it. 'No,' I said, 'for once we're going to do what I want to do. I'm tired of doing dishes and selling magazine subscriptions and making over my old clothes. I've always wanted to go to California and now we're going. And I'm not going to do a lick of work for a year, do you understand? Not a lick. And I'm going to play the piano and have some new hats. And when the money's all gone you can worry as to how we're going to get more.'"

SUITE 2

Mrs. Riddle is a widow who works in a ladies' ready-to-wear store. She has a daughter, Maybelle, who is awfully popular with the boys. One of Maybelle's fellows, the one on the football team, gave Maybelle a German police puppy named Near Beer. All day long Near Beer howls because he is lonesome for Mrs. Riddle, and all night long Near Beer howls because he is lonesome for Maybelle.

SUITE 3

The Goslings haven't been married very long. Mr. Gosling is tall and thin and generally in need of a hair cut. He doesn't look very healthy. At night, when he comes home from the office he writes poetry on a typewriter which makes a lot of racket, but on account of the Goslings being so newly married the neighbors hate to say anything about it.

Mrs. Gosling is plump and pretty. She used to teach physical culture in Chicago.

In the morning, when Mr. Gosling leaves for work, Mrs. Gosling walks out into the courtyard with him. And first they look at the sky and then they look at each other. And then Mr. Gosling kisses the curl on the back of Mrs. Gosling's neck and the tips of each of her ten fingers. And then Mrs. Gosling for no reason at all turns suddenly and runs into the house.

SUITE 4

Mrs. Cateau lives all alone. She has bobbed hair which is very white, and her cheeks are very pink. Sometimes you will not see or hear anything of Mrs. Cateau for days, but if you look through her window at night, you will see her sitting all alone by a table. All around her will be a great many bottles and glasses. Sometimes on a summer night, when the windows on the court are open you will hear Mrs. Cateau telephoning. She will telephone all night long. "Hello," she will say, "Is Barley there? You know, Barley." But Mrs. Cateau always seems to get the wrong number.

Sometimes Mrs. Cateau gets quite hysterical and then somebody drives up in a taxi cab and takes her away.

They say that before Mrs. Cateau went away to France to do war work, her hair was yellow instead of white and that she was very pretty.

SUITE 5

The Bunnys are great people for parties. Mr. Bunny used to run a hotel in Jamaica and he knows how to mi the most wonderful things. Mrs. Bunny has a remarkable collection of negligees which she slips out of about 7 p. m., after which the Bunnys call up a couple of friends and run out to one of the roadhouses for dinner. Along about 10 o'clock, having run into a number of other friends, the Bunnys return home. Somebody starts the player piano, three of the men go down into the locker room in the cellar and Mrs. Bunny starts a discussion of the latest moral problem propounded by Jim Jam Jems.

Mrs. Bunny had a little girl once, but the little girl died. Mrs. Bunny says that if she didn't believe that people were reunited after death she'd go crazy.

THE BASEMENT

Bertha Winebrenner and Dot Hurley live in the basement. By splitting up the rent between them they really get along better than if each roomed out. Bertha is the head of the glove department at a local dry goods store, and Dot takes dictation from a couple of lawyers. Bertha was married once, but her husband left her a great many years ago, and now, as she sometimes confides to Dot, it seems as though it never happened. Dot had been in love once, but it was with a married man. Eventually she found out that he made love to a great many other girls, too, and after she had cried about it a little she was surprised to discover that she hadn't cared so much.

22 September 1925, Tuesday:

BUSINESS, it seems isn't so hard boiled after all. When John Richardson, of Robinson's book store, found his stock seriously damaged by fire, the other morning, every competitor he had in town called up to offer assistance. Although, as one of these informed him, "As soon as you get going again, I'm going to fight you as hard as ever."

I wonder sometimes about the cleaning women – these women who issue forth from their humble homes in the morning and spread to all parts of the city.

They descend upon the week's hamper of soiled clothes – the table cloths with the coffee stains, the bath room curtains, the shirts with the dreadful wristbands and the jelly down the front, the guest towels that have been used to polish up the bath room floor, and the handkerchieves that have been used to dust the mantel. They whisk the lot into fresh boiling soap suds and make a few magic passes over it with an iron.

And at night, when the cleaning woman goes home again she leaves behind her smooth piles of neatly stacked linen, handkerchiefs with the embroidery pressed out at the edges, shirts from the dinginess and the jelly stains have miraculously disappeared.

She has even done more. She has removed the ring from the bath tub, polished the soap dishes, mopped up the kitchen and washed and put away the breakfast dishes. She has in short done what Jehovah is said to have done for the world once. She has looked about her and observed where disorder and chaos lay and out of a seemingly hopeless proposition she has brought order and cleanliness and sparkle.

––––––

After the cleaning woman has done what would leave most of us exhausted and bedraggled for a week, she goes home and tends to her own housework. She cooks, she cleans, she sews, she mends. Sometimes she is a widow. If she is not a widow, then her husband is an invalid and there are doctor bills to think of. Her little girl must have a new coat to wear to school and her little boy must have plenty of milk and meat so he will grow strong and well.

It seems to me that there is something very wonderful about the cleaning woman, and I would like to find it out. But she will not talk. Yes, she came from the old country at such and such a time. Yes, she has some children. Three. Yes, she has a husband. No, he does not work. He is sick. No. It is his back. Yes, she likes chops. Yes, she likes potatoes. Yes, she goes to church on Sunday.

And then the cleaning woman goes back to the laundry moving swiftly so she may get as much done as possible before 4:30 comes.

We were talking the other noon about the short stories which we remembered most clearly and these, I found, were the ones I remembered best: "Lazarus[64]," by one of the Russians, I can never remember which is which, "Boule de Suif,[65]" by de Maupassant, and "Bliss[66]" by Katherine Mansfield.

Bill and Jake Falstaff always get me furious on the subject of Katherine Mansfield. I think she has written the best short stories I ever read. They consider her merely a rather clever imitator of the Russians in Class B.

"Could she," demands Bill, "have written such a story as 'Rothschild's Fiddle.[67]'"

And I feel that my stand is altogether justifiable for if "Rothschild's Fiddle" were such a good story, I am sure I would remember what it is about. Which I don't.

---

23 September 1925, Wednesday:

WE WENT to see Harold Lloyd[68] at the Orpheum last night. We went early – before supper time – so we would be able to get a seat and when we came out, about half past seven, the lobby was already thronged with people patiently waiting as far outside the front side walk.

---

[64] "Lazarus" a short story by Leonid Andreyev, 1898.

[65] "Boule de Suif" (loosely translated means dumpling or butterball, ball of fat or lard) is a story by Guy de Maupassant, 1870.

[66] "Bliss," a short story by Katherine Mansfield, 1918.

[67] "Rothschild's Violin" translated as Rothschild's Fiddle, a book by Anton Chekhov, 1894.

[68] Harold Clayton Lloyd Sr. (1893-1971) American actor and comedian.

Over across the street in front of the E. Z. sandwich shop the Salvation Army was holding a meeting. The audience consisted of a small boy lounging a little to one side of the bees drum, a woman standing in the door way of the sandwich shop and three men patiently holding up the front of the United Cigar store building.

Now the Salvation Army man was talking about eternal salvation and over at the motion picture house Harold Lloyd was doing nothing more original than to lose his trousers in the middle of a crowded dance floor. That trick, with variations, has been tried in a good many places for a good many years now.

And yet on one side of the circus hundred of people were rocking with mirth and hundreds of others were waiting for a chance to rock, while on the other side of the street three men, a woman and a little boy were listening rather boredly to a dissertation on their immortal souls.

We went into the sandwich shop and while I ate my waffle and poured as much cream as possible into my coffee I wondered if perhaps the greatest doctors, preachers, lawyers and solacers among us these days are not movie comedians.

We, who ordinarily run from a movie, bad gone without our supper because of a fair assurance that here we might get a laugh or two and forget bills for at least a little while. And out in the lobby people suffering from corns, bunions, fallen arches, callouses, nerves and spots before the eyes were nevertheless standing in line without a murmur, hoping that by exercising an hour of patience they might purchase thereby five minutes or so of mirth.

Charlie Chaplin[69], Harold Lloyd and Buster Keaton[70] – they are probably the best loved men in the world today. If there should be such a thing as an auction I doubt whether the entire wardrobe of the Prince of Wales would bring so much as one of Charlie Chaplin's pathetic shoes. It should be comforting to a certain part of the population, moreover, to know that here is a field which will remain forever unchallenged by women.

Neither on the stage nor in the movies nor in literature do women seem to be fitted for comedy. The male comedian may be cross-eyed or fat or his feet may turn out. He will

---

[69] Sir Charles Spencer Chaplin KBE (1889-1977) English comic actor.

[70] Joseph Frank Keaton (known as Buster Keaton professionally) (1895-1966) American actor, comedian, director, producer and stunt performer.

still be loved. But the woman comedian must first of all be pretty and sweet and alluring. How funny she is, is purely a tenth rate consideration.

I have been trying for several minutes to think of the woman who played with John Bunny[71]. I think her name was Laura Finch but I am not sure. After John Bunny died she was forgotten. She did have a small role in a play on Broadway a couple of years ago and the audience gave her an ovation. But that was all and so far as I know it put precious little oats in the nose bag[72].

Marie Dressler[73] perhaps came the closest to slap stick but her tumblings about I rather gather were offensive to most people.

On the stage we have had an occasional Charlotte Greenwood[74] who could walk about on all fours and still retain the respectful admiration of her public but Miss Greenwood is not one to whom might be applied the adjective great and besides she always ended up in the third act looking quite ravishing in a marcel wave and a peacock fan.

I don't remember any more whether Mabel Normand[75] was funny or not. Somebody did tell me a story once, however, which I shall always cherish.

It seems that Mabel, who was dining with friends at a hotel, lit a cigaret.

"Pardon me, Madame," said the water stepping up, "but ladies are not allowed to smoke here."

---

[71] John Bunny (1863-1915) American actor. The actress he did many domestic comedies was comedian Flora Finch (not Laura Finch as the article noted).

[72] A reference to a horse's oat bag which is suspended about the horses neck while it eats. Also known as a feedbag.

[73] Marie Dressler (born Leila Marie Koerber) (1868-1934) a Canadian-American actress, comedian and early silent film star of the Depression-era. She starred opposite Charlie Chaplin and Mabel Normand in *Tillie's Punctured Romance*.

[74] Frances Charlotte Greenwood (1890-1977) American actress and dancer who was close to six foot tall and best known for her long legs.

[75] Amabel Ethelreid "Mabel" Normand (1892-1930) American silent-film actress.

"Who the devil," retorted Mable, "told you I was a lady?"

❧❧❧◆❧❧❧

26 September 1925, Saturday:

THE leaves across the way haven't turned to brown and red yet, but when the wind blows through them, they give out a dry crackling sound so that we may know that autumn is upon us.

Contrary to what most persons, particularly poets would have us believe, autumn rather than spring which is the time for love. That is because there is both in autumn and in love a trace of sadness. When one is 30 and in love, this sadness can generally be traced to very definite things – the loved one is growing bald, or he smokes too many cigars or he loses money at poker or his relations are impossible.

When one is 17 and in love, there is really no excuse for sadness, and yet it is there just the same. One goes on long walks alone. One talks to one's self. One gazes into the sky with mute unframed questions. One sits upon a damp stone and composes two lines of a sonnet. One thinks a great deal about death and life and destiny and the fate of unborn infants and the meaning of the universe. With such a mood autumn fits in perfectly.

Naturally autumn is the time for weddings. The sky is bluer then, the colors are gayer, the air is crisper and always there is the suggestion of tears, like those bright drops that hover on the eyelids of her married friends when the bride starts her measured tread to the altar.

The bridesmaids look ever so much more attractive done up in the yellows, the oranges and the crimsons of autumn than they do in the pastels of spring; chrysanthemums are a great deal more impressive than sweet peas; the bride's going-away costume is invariably better looking when it is a new fall model touched up with fur and the dancing at the country club afterwards is always pleasanter when there is a touch of crispness in the air without.

Naturally, no wedding is entirely perfect. For a long time I've been wondering what ailed our weddings but I'm still pretty much muddled. Certainly this ought to be true: that after you've said the momentous words about "I do" and "I will," and the ring has been slipped on and the final pronouncement has been made you ought to feel like an entirely different human being. And yet it seems to be quite the usual human experience that you don't feel different in the least.

For a long time, I thought it was because our weddings were too large. "When you make a show out of it," I argued, "the bride's mind is so taken up with externals that she doesn't realize the solemnity of what's happening."

The sceptic, however, whose judgment in most matters is simply phenomenal, still holds out for large weddings. "You got so many more presents that way," he argues.

At least there is this to be said about it: the ceremony itself is so short that were you to strip it of "Oh Promise Me" and "Lohengrin," of the bridesmaids, the ushers and the cousins, of the kisses afterward and the chicken salad, there really would be precious little left to convince a girl that a tremendous epoch in her life had began.

It may be, of course, that getting married is a much longer process than we imagine. That it begins with the minute that we first set eyes on the loved one and continue through countless misunderstandings and making up again until – who knows – perhaps the end of time.

In that case, it seems to me that the best thing to do would be to have merely a rather boisterous party. For music I would have the Norwegian Bridal Procession and the Wedding Day at Troldhaugen instead of Lohengrin and Midsummer Night's Dream; the guests would wear anything they chose and instead of chicken salad and peas and ice cream frozen into rose buds we would have a great deal of liverwurst and beer.

But the whole, of course, would take place in the autumn, preferably October.

---

28 September 1925, Monday:

D EAR Josephine (writes Adrienne):

"I rise to protest.

"These modern biographers are diabolically busy white-washing all the passion flowers of history. It is not to be borne! Unhappy Sapphos! Betrayed Cleopatra! Unmasked Temptresses, all! How ye must turn in your perfumed biers at this snooping impertinence! Cleopatra is to become a virtuous housewife. Lady Hamilton is victimized by circumstance and a heartless lover. Fanny Brawne is become tender and true, and once I read an unpardonable vindication of George Sands.

"Now this annoys me very much. I like my villains and my sires to stay put. What is to become of romance with the characters constantly changing their roles? The villains slipping into the role of hero and the temptress becoming an ingenue! It's all wrong. Something must be done about it. Even Mike Arlen in his once famous novel, 'The Green Hat[76]' fell down on his job. He first presented us with a picture of fascinating ruthlessness – a woman who, he declared, was a creature from some hardier realm, (the perfection of our imperfections.) We licked our lips. At last a real old-fashioned Lorelei. What luck! But not a bit of it. He couldn't do it. At the end he had to paint her wistful colors as the little hurt child with a stiff upper lip. Outrageous! Are there no real vampires? No simon-pure black-guards?

"And that, dear Josephine, is the damnable part. There are none. We're all cut from the same pattern. Quite the same. Extraneous forces alone determine our reselions [sic] and our degree of virtue. The village maiden is surrounded by simple monotonous forces until she meets the debonair salesman. And perhaps the debonair salesman was a thoroughly virtuous man until he found himself among a crowd of roisterers, etcetera, etcetera. The greatest she-devil in history undoubtedly had her enthusiastic philanthropy. And the stingiest mortgage holder may be a devoted son."

And therein, it seems to me, Adrienne has answered her own plaint. It is better that we should know our people of history as a little bit good, a little bit bad. Not only do they become more human that way, but it gives us a better opinion of the integrity of the biographer. I like to know that Napoleon not only was a great man but that he was also a snooper at keyholes. The first and practically only spark of affection I ever had for George Washington grew out of the information that he had bad teeth and was obliged to stuff out his lips with cotton when he had his portrait painted. And I think Benjamin Franklin and his insufferable maxims wouldn't have seemed so much of a dud if our teachers had let slip a little hint that he had a weakness for ankles and petticoats.

I picked up a biography of Josephine the other day, wherein she was pictured as a woman just fairly bright, just fairly good. It had the ring of truth and I was anxious to finish it. But unfortunately I laid it down for a moment, whereupon someone thoughtlessly bought it from right under my nose. I read long enough, however, to learn that Josephine's exquisite tact for which she was noted was not a talent she was born with

---

[76] Michael Arlen (1895-1956), born Dikran Kouyoumdjian was a British short story writer and novelist. He drove around London in a bright yellow Rolls Royce and was referred to as a 'dandy' in the 1920s. His book "The Green Hat" was published in 1924.

and that if she was careful to bestow her charms where they would bring the greatest financial returns, still she was very devoted while the affair lasted.

That is the way I like my people – a little bit bad, a little bit good. And if sometimes the biographer seems to carry the whitewashing process a little too far we certainly ought not to cavil at it, seeing that the gossips of the period probably went to the other extreme and made matters a great deal worse.

————

The thing that interested me most in this Josephine book, though, had nothing to do with Josephine at all. It seems that when the directoire gowns came into fashion, the ladies didn't wear anything under them, not a smidgen.

Any flapper who can derive comfort from this information is perfectly welcome to it.

29 September 1925, Tuesday:

SOMETIMES when I see the postman going down the street, I think of the tragedy and the comedy, the romance and the pathos that must lie boxed up in his brown pack. The love letters, the reconciliations, that mean as much to us when we are young, the gas bills, the Ladies' Home Journal that mean so much to us when we are old.

This morning, the postman carried an unusually cheering load, including in his pack the following:

"Dear Miss Van De Grift:

"As I am leaving Akron, Oct. 1, for Chicago, Ill., where I got a wonderful position in the largest Hebrew school in the middlewest, and where I intend to attend the university, allow me to express to you my appreciation for the interest you took in my graduation from West High.

"On the same occasion I ask you to publish the following lines in the Beacon Journal, in any form or section, and with any changes you please.

"On the eve of my golden and most interesting period of my life so far, at the close of my most energetic and serious five years' period of hard but successful work on the field of learning and teaching in Akron, Ohio, I extend my thanks and appreciation, and send my blessings and best wishes to my countless friends in this city; especially to my fellow-teachers, pupils and their parents, as well as to the officers of the Akron Talmud-Torahs; and last but not least to West High: - I wish the best to West.

"JOSEPH LIEBENSON,

"Principal, Akron Talmud-Torahs."

"Dear Jo: As I always read your column, and everyone else reads it too – I am going to confide in you a grievance which I think common enough to the feminine population of Akron.

"I am not going to say, I am one of the unfortunates who has to do my daily traveling by bus, but rather I think I am fortunate that I have a nice bus in which I can ride to and from my work. I love it too – the lovely Glendale. I like everything about the busses but the way the men sit!

"They do not sit, they sprawl. The minute they land on a seat they forget there is another person in the world but themselves and spread out like a full blown fan. If the other person happens to be a man he bumps the intruding legs away, but if a lady she files into the aisle at every turn, clutches the seat in front or shrinks into her corner until there is no corner left.

"There are two men on the West Exchange bus line who have annoyed me twice in the same manner in the past week. I know both by sight now – and thought of reporting them to the manager of the company. I thought he might suggest to them that if they cared to occupy four-fifths of a seat they should provide their own transportation, but I have a better method. There would be too many to report!

"It isn't fair! I have no objection to the men hurrying in to get their seats before the women have a chance, and often stand back so that they may get there, but if I happen to get one too I want to half of it. A man could be taught to sit with his legs parallel just as well as I have been taught. The coal heaver who crowded me into the front seat last night and almost forced me on the floor is going to get his lesson if he ever sits by me again.

"you know you cannot use a gun in Akron, or at least it isn't done by the crowd I run around with, so I shan't try that. You are a girl of much genius in thinking out solutions, so I am telling you mine. If all the girls who ride the street cars and busses would put a safety pin in either garter – face out – they could, by the twist of the hand, open the pin and it would be unseen through the average dress but would be a very effective weapon for those prowling 'fans.' There would be but two things for the man to do – get to his own side of the seat or get up, for the pin would be very sharp, and it would have a solid backing. Also, it might be wise for those who are careless of posture in busses and cars to carry about with them iodine, for if no one else uses the method suggested I surely am going to try it.

"I am not trying to be funny. I am giving you the result of several indignation meetings which I have had with myself. Policemen tag cars that park too long, and I think men should be tagged who park their legs too far removed from their side of the seat. I cannot publicly put a sticker ON them, but I can, privately, put a sticker IN them! What do you think?

"BUSINESS GIRL."

━━━⟞୧୧୨⟜✦⟞୧ᡖ୨⟜━━━

30 September 1925, Wednesday:

T HE longer I live the more I become convinced that there are no depths to which even the best intentioned of us will not sink. I have developed lately a passion for listening in on the telephone.

It developed innocently enough. I took the receiver off the hook with the intention of calling the dry cleaner and Mrs. X (I hope some day to know her real name) was interviewing a prospective maid. It seemed that Mrs. X paid twelve dollars a week, that the apartment was not at all large and that she was particularly anxious to get someone who would be nice to the baby. Mrs. X said that he was a very well behaved baby and hardly cried a bit.

The voice on the other end of the line said she would think it over and call later but you couldn't help having the feeling that in reality she intended doing nothing of the kind and that children made her nervous.

Thereafter whenever I took the receiver off the hook it invariably seemed that Mrs. X was interviewing another maid. It got so after a while that I got just as anxious about the matter as Mrs. X must have been. I would listen carefully for any intonation on the other end of the wire which would give one an inkling as to whether the prospect was in reality fond of children, whether she could make good Boston baked beans, whether she was in the habit of scorching the luncheon cloths and whether she was likely to have many admirers.

Unfortunately those voices which were of the sweet fresh kind indicating that they just loved little children were so very sweet and fresh that you couldn't help picturing the owners going off and getting married just about the time you impressed them that the Mister's blood pressure was all wrong and he couldn't have sugar in his apple sauce. While the other kind, the ones where voices sounded as though they would be sure to bake the beans long enough and have the pork browned just right on the top of the bean pot and never, never leave the iron standing in the middle of the cluny [sic] centerpiece somehow gave out the vibration that they also would think nothing at all of giving the children a whole lot of soothing syrup to make them go to sleep quickly.

The one that called up this morning had an exceptionally nice voice though and she was anxious to promise anything as though she might have been out of work for a long time. I sort of liked her voice and I think Mrs. X did too. I hope she gets the job.

———————

It is too bad of course that ours is only a two-party line because otherwise one could doubtless pick up a good many things during the course of a rainy day. It is too bad, too, that there is no warning tinkle, such as there need to be on the old lines, to let you know that conversation is under way.

As it is I just have to depend on chance and if central unexpectedly says "Number please" I have either to think up a number quickly or else click up the receiver which, I understand, always makes central mad.

I hope that when Mrs. X finally gets the servant problem all settled nicely that she will take to calling up some of her friends again. I'm awfully anxious to know just which of her friends she favors most, what doctor she has for little x when he gets croupy, whether Mr. X ever gets out of patience about things, what Mrs. X serves when she entertains her bridge club and which dry cleaner, in her opinion, does the best work for the least money.

In return she is perfectly welcome to listen in on any of our conversations. Adrienne almost always has some interesting literary gossip to relate, the Romantick, who is working in a drug store now, has absolutely first hand information on what soaps are best for the skin while hardly a day passes that Mrs. Socrates hasn't hit upon a new way for using Campbell's tomato soup.

———⌘———

1 October 1925, Thursday:

S O FAR as I have been able to discover every woman in the world has a suppressed desire to start a tea room. Sometimes it's because she knows how to make toasted olive sandwiches that her friends are wild about, and it seems such a pity not to let the rest of the world know about it. Sometimes it's because she has an old house and a lot of china that she doesn't know what to do with. Sometimes it's because she's disgusted with all the other tea rooms in town and has just clipped a couple of Goodrich coupons that she doesn't know what to do with. And sometimes it's for no reason at all except that something in the back of her head keeps nagging and nagging at her until in desperation she goes downtown, buys up several bots of cretonne, paints up a couple of tables in orange and black, sets out some single stem vases and hangs out in front of her establishment, "The Bashful Cow" Dainty Salads, Exquisite Sandwiches, Luncheon, 50 Cents."

If there is any woman baffling with such an urge at present and likely to go down under it, here is a suggestion which, I hope, will make her wealthy. Don't start your tea room in Akron. Start it in Hudson or Cuyahoga Falls or Kent.

Harry Page[77], he who now teaches music in Akron, used years ago to have a little tea room in Hudson. It was a nice little place with a fireplace and a piano. But Harry deserted creamed chicken in pattie shells for Wagner and Higher Things, and now when we go through Hudson we are quite desolate for a place to eat.

I was in Cuyahoga Falls around noon today and that, too, had nothing to offer save these white topped affairs with tables for ladies and gents, where you are given your choice of fried ham or breaded veal cutlets with tomato sauce. I wish I had saved some of that tomato sauce to paint our little rusty electric stove with. It was a much prettier red than the paint I paid 45 cents a can for.

Adrienne and I went out to a certain little by the road place Monday afternoon for tea, only to be informed that they didn't serve tea on Monday afternoon. Adrienne sort of hoped that maybe they had a little cold chicken lying around and would make an exception in our case. But the woman didn't seem disposed to alter a rule of years and so we went on to Kent getting hungrier all the time.

Just as we decided that the situation was hopeless we came to a snug little hotel, one that I had learned to love years ago. We went in and addressed the youth at the desk.

---

[77] Akron resident, Harry Wallington Page (1888-?) Music teacher

"Can we get tea here?" inquired Adrienne.

The youth turned to another youth standing beside him. "I don't know," he said, "can they get tea in the coffee shop?"

"Sure," said the other youth, "tea, coffee, chocolate, anything you want."

And so we went in and had tea.

As we were saying only this noon, the trouble with the two or three places in Akron is that when the food is good and the location convenient the place is sure to be overcrowded and then you have to sit with someone whom you don't wish to sit with at all.

Lucretia was particularly mad about it. "I had just found a table over in a corner," she said, "and was getting settled with my book when the person in charge came over and asked if I wouldn't sit at a table where there were a lot of girls and let three men have my table. Over at this table where the girls were sitting was Hattie Bindlebinder whom I haven't spoken to in years – ever since that time she made that mean remark. Well, my impulse was to walk straight out the door and leave the tea room flat. But then it occurred to me that Hattie and everybody else would think I was being put out on account of not paying my bill or something. And so there wasn't anything to do but go over there and sit. I tried as best I could to ignore Hattie, and Hattie ignored me. But my luncheon was just utterely [sic] ruined.

"I eat here every day now. The food is terrible, but at least you can have a little privacy."

---

3 October 1925, Saturday:

T HE most interesting thing that came out of the Altrusa meeting last night was the information that Elise Houriet[78] weighed four pounds when she was born. If you know Elise and in all probability you do you will not believe this.

---

[78] Akron resident, Catherine Elise "Elsie" Houriet (1883-1959)

The next most interesting thing was that Elise promised that before the winter snows came she would get up another steak dinner for us out in the open providing it wasn't held near any water.

The last time Elise got up a steak dinner for us the place was near the water, the far side of Silver lake to be exact. You had to take a row boat to get over there. Practically everybody who came took a row boat and got over very nicely but when Ada Lee Collins came she said she wouldn't think of going on the water but would drive around the lake instead. Four others of us didn't want Ada Lee to go alone and so we rode around with her.

It was quite a long ride around the lake and then after a while the road stopped utterly and you got out and walked through a woods where there were trees and briars and brambles and vines and fallen logs and musky places and a great many mosquitoes. We walked and walked and I got three runners in my new $1.95 chiffon hose and the darkness began falling like everything and Ada Lee Collins and Dr. Marian Stevenson who was with her completely disappeared.

After a while Dr. Pauline Halbert[79] and Dr. Carrie Herring[80] and I – we were the ones who were left – decided that probably it would be just as well if we went back the way we came and left Ada Lee[81] and Marion Stevenson to their respective fates. And so we went back and climbed over the same logs and got scratched by the same briars and I tore a few more runners in my stockings and got bitten by quite a few more mosquitoes and finally we came to the road where the cars were. The cars belonged to Ada Lee and Dr. Stevenson and one of us knew how to drive them and so we decided we'd just walk back around the lake the way we came.

We walked and walked and walked and talked about operations and things and finally we came to where the boats were and there were Jane Barnhardt and Fanny Slabaugh[82] waiting with worried expressions to row us across. And when we finally did get to the other side there were Ada Lee and Marian Stevenson sitting by the fire eating steak sandwiches six inches thick.

---

[79] Akron resident, Pauline Mcdonald Helbert (????-????)

[80] Akron resident, Carrie Alice Herring (1891-????), residing in 1940 census at 297 S. College

[81] Akron resident, Ada L. Lee (1876-????), residing in 1940 census on Fernwood street

[82] Akron resident, Fanny Mae Slabaugh (1886-1961), living in Troy, Geauga Co. in 1940 census.

"Why, where in the world have you been?" they wanted to know. But we didn't say anything. We just took up a couple of steak sandwiches ourselves and some watermelon and potato salad and coffee and lemonade and chocolate cake and we didn't say a word to anybody for quite a long while.

Clara Brouse[83] told last night of some of her experiences in organizing training classes for nurses but I still couldn't get an answer to something that's worried me for a long whilst why do girls want to be nurses? It seems there isn't any explanation really. Either you want to be a nurse or you don't.

It seems that a girl who takes up the nursing profession has a better chance to get married than almost anybody else. Elisabeth Yost[84] said she thought it was because men have the feeling, you know, of wanting somebody around who'll do things for them and that probably every nurse in the world has scads of offers from her various patients.

Clara Brouse said she wasn't sure about the scads of offers but one thing was certain; it was just discouraging the way the nurses went off and get married. Here you'd spend three years training a girl and you'd be so proud of her because she knew how to fix the barley water and tie the splints and cherish the lumbago sufferers just right and then before you knew it she'd go and settle down with some healthy young fellow who probably never had so much as a toothache.

After that we had a discussion as to what people we'd most like to know if we got the chance and Ada Lee said she'd rather know O.O. McIntyre than anybody else in the world. Fanny Slabaugh was all for knowing Walter Hines Page if that were possible and I was all for Sherwood Anderson. But last night when I got home I tried to finish "Dark Laughter" and got so bored with it I couldn't, so now I think I'd rather know Charlie Chaplin.

---

[83] Akron resident, Clara Florine Brouse (1885-????)

[84] Akron resident, Elisabeth J. Yost (c.1887-????), Akron nurse, living at 134 N. Highland ave on 1940 census

6 October 1925, Tuesday:

IT seems that there is a girl named Mira Nirska who is making quite a success in London just now. She plays the part of the Indian squaw in the London production of "Rose Marie" and incidentally she does some difficult dancing.

Some of the English critics have declared that Mira Nirska's dancing to one of the most beautiful things about an unusually beautiful play while the press agents, sending the things which would doubtless appeal to English audiences have spread the story far and wide that Mira Nirska is a half breed Indian of the middle west, that she has any number of Indian superstitions, that she wouldn't think of dancing without a certain turquoise necklace, that she has painted her skin with some sort of permanent pigment and any number of other interesting things.

Time was when Mira Nirska was just plain little Grace Roth of Akron, O. You perhaps went to school with her. I can remember the first time I saw her. I can remember the first time I saw her. She was pounding a typewriter in the office of an interior decorating establishment in which my father was interested.

I had gone over after school to get some money to pay the gas bill with and there behind the typewriter on the desk was a slight dark haired young person almost completely obscured behind stacks of movie magazines. "She's terribly interested in the movies," my father whispered under cover of the racket, "and she wants to act on the screen."

The young person stopped her pounding. "Hello," she said, and I said, "Hello," during which we sized each other up. I was in high school then and studying Grey's "Elegy in a Country Church Yard" and "Washington's Farewell Address" and any number of other high brow things and I must confess I felt slightly superior to a young person who obviously read nothing but movie magazines.

Francis X. Bushman was in his hey day then and one day I learned that Grace Roth in some miraculous fashion had obtained an interview with him to see whether she might not do for screen material. She was to meet him in Chicago or some such place. What course the interview took I do not know. The Beverly Baynes and the Mary Miles Minters were the darlings of the fans just then and certainly Grace Roth had nothing of their smug doll baby prettiness. You liked to look at her but you didn't know just why.

Anyway Grace Roth returned from her interview with Mr. Bushman and proceeded with her typewriting.

The next you heard was that Grace Roth had gone to New York to study dancing and then for two years you heard nothing at all. The young woman had obviously done a very foolish thing. To be a success as a dancer, you know, you have to begin while you are still a child and the bones are pliable. Then, too, dancing lessons are expensive and the course is long and in New York there is the added problem of living expenses. Then, too, thousands of other young women, young women with rich fathers and dating relatives and influential theatrical friends, were also striving to be dancers. What chance could an unknown young woman from Akron, Ohio, possibly have? It would have been far better if Grace Roth had stayed at home and gone on with her typing and then maybe some day she could get a nice secretary's job with a rich rubber magnate.

In two years Grace Roth came back to show the folks at home what she could do. She decided to put on a performance at Music Hall. There was scenery to secure, musicians to hire, programs to have printed, tickets to sell. On the day of the performance Grace Roth was taken ill. All that morning and all that afternoon she fought off her illness, rehearsing over and over her dances in the cold clammy air back stage.

And that night Grace Roth danced just as she had said she would and the folks she had known in the old days went home a little puzzled saying, "I didn't know she had it in her."

Grace Roth went back to New York and first you heard that she had danced for the opening of the Capital theater there and then you heard that she had married a song writer named Ben Schwartz and then you heard that she had danced in various capacities in some of the big revues and then you heard that she was to have the big role in the London production of Rose Marie. And then you heard that not only did she have the role and not only was she dancing it but that day after day stolid Londoners were standing patiently in line in front of the ticket office just in the hope of seeing her do it.

They call her Mira Nirska now and they say she has strange exotic blood in her and that she wouldn't think of dancing without her Indian necklace. It really brings her marvelous luck and soon she is to have her own show for which Ben Schwartz will write the music.

But sometimes I think that maybe her real amulet is something else again – something that you wouldn't notice unless you happened to be standing in the wings and should see a queer heaving just under the turquoise necklace when she has come off the stage and is feeling particularly tired.

---

7 October 1925, Wednesday:

EVERY week or so the same heartbreaking wall goes up. Some youngster has set off for the university with high hopes and for the first few weeks everything goes well. Then suddenly she discovers that her life is blasted, her hopes ruined, her future darkened, her ambitions laid low because she hasn't been asked to join a sorority. Sometimes it is something very definite, like religion or nationality, which keeps her out and sometimes it is something not so definite. At any rate the girl's heart is broken, her sense of justice receives a sad wrench and, in the case of sensitive natures, I suppose the damage is sometimes irreparable.

When I went up to the university nobody asked me to join a sorority and I can't remember that it saddened me particularly but because I know that a great many girls, and a good many boys too, are saddened by just such things and that it sometimes embitters the memory of their whole college experience. I should like to reprint parts of a letter which I came across the other day. It is called "A Father to His Freshman Son" and was written by Edward Sanford Martin.

"I hear a good deal about clubs and societies," he writes. "How is it that if a youth shall gain the whole a scholarship and all athletics and not 'make' the proper club he shall still fall something short of success in college. Parents I meet who are more concerned about clubs than about either scholarship or deportment.

"There is a democratic ideal of a great college without any clubs where the lion and the lamb shall escort one another about with tails entwined and every student shall be like every other student. This ideal is a good deal discussed and a good deal applauded in the public press. Whether it will ever come true I can't tell, but there has been some form or other of clubs in our older colleges, I suppose, for one or two centuries, and they are there now and will at least outlast your time; (page torn) may be you will have to take thought about them in due time.

"You see, clubs seem to be a sort of natural provision just as tails were, maybe, before humanity outgrew them. The propensity works to include the like and incidentally but necessarily, to exclude the unlike. Whether it is the Knights of the Round Table or the Knights of the Grater, or the Phi Beta Kappa you see these principles working. The measure of success in a club to its ability to make people want to join it and that seems to be best demonstrated by keeping most of them out.

"Now the advantages of the clubs are considerable. The drawback to the clubs is their essential selfishness, and their disposition to take you out of a large family and limit you to a small one, and one that is not yours by birth or entirely by choice but is selected for you largely by other persons.

"In any club you yield a certain amount of freedom and individuality, the amount being determined by the degree in which the club absorbs you. Don't yield too much; don't take the mould of any club! A college is always bigger than its clubs and the biggest thing in a college is always a man. Some men take their club shape, such as it is, and find a sufficient satisfaction in it. Others react on their clubs, take what they have to give, add to it what is to be had elsewhere and turn out rather more valuable people than if they had had no club experience.

"At all events don't take this matter of the clubs to hard. For those youths, comparatively few, who by lack and circumstances find themselves eligible to them, they are an interesting form of discipline or indulgence and I will not say they are unimportant. The trick is to get the kernel and eliminate the shuck.

"A large proportion of people do the opposite. If you can manage that way with the clubs – provided you ever get the chance – you will be amused to observe in due time how large a proportion of your brethren value these organizations for their except to persons justify doubtful of that. For the shuck, as I see it, is exclusiveness which is not valuable except to persons justly doubtful of their own merits. Whereas the kernel is the fellowship of like minds which has always been valued by the wise."

---

8 October 1925, Thursday:

I LOVE the milk man. When you have been lying awake all night and have watched the sky change from black to grey and are listening to the first faint twittering of the birds and are feeling a little sad, you don't just know why, the milk man comes clattering up to the back door. He puts down the bottle of fresh cream and takes up the empty bottle which you washed carefully and put out the night before and you know that while others have been sleeping the milk man has been out in the cold and dark. He brings milk to the kids and cream for the breakfast oatmeal and buttermilk for the dyspeptic and schmear base to make a Dutch pie. I love the milk man.

I LOVE the shoeshine boy. He tucks the laces of your shoes out of the way to keep them close. He puts on six kinds of polish. He polishes your shoes with a rag and a brush and a buffer. He wears a funny little cap on his head and a dirty apron. If there are no other customers he will tell you about his home in Greece. The shoeshine boy sleeps on a little cot in a curtained off place in back of the store. He makes three dollar a week. Some day he will own a restaurant with a great many mirrors.

I LOVE little girls. They eat their food daintily. They keep their frocks clean. They learn to play the piano and to dance upon their toes. They love new hats and to look at themselves in the looking glass. Then they grow up they will cause a great deal of trouble.

I LOVE little boys. They are always dirty. They like to hammer things. They build boats and pester you to read the funny papers to them. They gobble their food. They ask embarrassing questions. They tear their trousers and wear out their shoes. They make faces. They listen to everything you talk about and repeat it to the neighbors. They always want a nickel. When they grow up they will cause a great deal of trouble.

I LOVE music. It takes away all the bitterness. It makes you want to do noble and unselfish things. It tells you that you can do noble and unselfish things. There are a great many people who say they love music. "Oh play for us Mr. Pentatone," they plead for hours and hours. And finally Mr. Pentatone does play and everybody sees how loud they can talk.

I LOVE the wastebasket. Its arms are always open for cigarette stubs, empty candy boxes, old chewing gum, banana peels, apple cores, unpaid bills, old garters, lead pencils, safety pins, magazines, typewriter ribbons, last week's flowers, theater programs, silk stockings with runners in them, old rouge boxes, neckties, dill pickles, bedroom slippers and a great many other things. I love the wastebasket.

---

12 October 1925, Monday:

I'VE been wondering lately how it is that the grocery boy, the laundry man, the toot and awning man and the plumber always know just when it is that you are taking your bath.

You can take your bath at 8 o'clock one morning and at 11 o'clock the next. It won't make any difference. All the people whom you are to have any dealings that day will wait until you are nicely settled in the tub with a cake of soap, a Turkish towel and the morning newspaper. Then they will come and knock at the door.

If they would only come in a bunch it wouldn't be so bad. But they are very careful to space their calls three minutes apart. There is a knock at the door. "Who is it?" you yell. "Wait a minute." And the knocking keeps right on. You mop up hastily, scramble into a bath robe and some slippers and make for the door. It is the laundry man. You had feared it would be the laundry man. You had hoped he wouldn't come until next week because you didn't have the money to pay him with.

"Will you take a check?" you query hopefully. Oh yes, he'll take a check. So you give him the check that Grace Brown had given you to buy that etching of Beethoven with. The check has to be endorsed. The laundryman can't find his pencil. You hunt all over the house for a pencil. Finally you find the stub of one in the coal scuttle. You sharpen it with the bread knife and the laundry man takes the check and gives you $1.40 in change and goes away.

You return to the tub to find that the Turkish towel has fallen in and is floating on top of the water. You wring it out and hang it on the radiator and get out a fresh towel. Just as you get settled there is an other knocking. This time it is the grocery boy. You tend to him and when you get back you find that the second towel has fallen into the water. You wring it out and hang it on the radiator and then there is another knocking at the door.

It keeps up that way all morning until you are dressed and have your nose powdered. Then nobody pays any attention to you for the rest of the day.

It is too bad on the whole that more hasn't been written on the subject of bath rooms. It seems to me that there is room for a choice debate as to whether the tub is to be preferred to the shower. I met a woman the other day who voted unreservedly for the shower because that way you didn't have a ring to clean out. But when you use the shower you have to wring the curtain out so I don't know that you really gain much.

Of course there are some people who don't care anyway. They would just let the rings go on accumulating indefinitely and unfortunately these are frequently the very persons to whom you have given your tenderest love. They will even do more. In order to demonstrate how they can chin themselves from the curtain rod they will step into the tub with their nasty, muddy shoes on in spite of the fact that they've spent hours and hours that morning cleaning up.

Another queer thing about men is that once they get in the bathroom they have a peculiar notion that nobody else has any right there. You can talk yourself hoarse trying to get them to shave and after they've held out long enough to demonstrate who's boss they'll go in and shut the bathroom door with a loud bang. Then you just dare to come in after the cold cream or anything. You just dare.

"It's a funny thing," they'll bark. "You've got all day long to tend to your rat killin' but the minute I come in here you've got to tag along too. It's too bad a man can't have 10 minutes to himself. Now clear out of here, "etc., etc., etc.

Really if a man hated to shave as much as some of them seem to indicate you'd think he'd be glad to have somebody come in and take his mind off the agony.

Another peculiar thing about man and his bathroom behavior is his attitude toward soap. In order to save soap he will just let the water run over his hands and then wipe on your best linen towel. But if he sees a soap dish all full of water he will drop a nice new cake of soap into that so that by morning it will have completely disappeared. If the soap dish isn't full of water he will drop the soap in the bottom of the tub where the water will drip on it and it can melt that way.

Also you can have the bathroom just full of soap for a week and a man will never touch it. But take the soap out into the kitchen for some reason or other and immediately he'll start sputtering.

But you know how men are. If their shirts are a day late in coming back from the laundry you'll never hear the last of it. But if they've got 12 clean shirts in the drawer they'll wear the same one four days and even then you'll have to sneak it late the laundry bag when they aren't looking.

---

14 October 1925, Wednesday:

I GUESS that date I had with John McCarthy will have to wait for a while now.

It was only a couple of weeks ago that I saw John down on High st. "Now you mustn't think I'm neglecting you," he said. "We're going to have lunch together very soon."

"Sure, John," I said, "any old time."

And now today, just as though it might have been anybody else, I read in the paper that John McCarthy was dead.

––––––––––

I loved John McCarthy and that love stretched back over a good many years. I was trying to write a play with a medicine man in it[85], and I was in doubt as to how a medicine man would talk. I found a cheery individual down on the corner of Main and Market sts., who was willing to help me out. It seems he had been a follower of side shows for years. On the top of an old packing box he dictated to me a couple of medicine man songs and the "spiel" that went with them. That the songs were authentic I haven't the slightest doubt, but they were almost too authentic for the fairly refined purpose which I had in mind.

Then Jim Dunlevy told me about John McCarthy. "He'll help you out," he said.

And John McCarthy did. Just how good or how bad a play it was I'll never know. But everybody had at least one thing to say about it. "We liked the medicine man part," they said.

––––––––––

I think all of you must have come to know him even if you didn't know his name was John McCarthy. Most often you would see him standing down by the Buchtel hotel corner. His big thick glasses and the blue eyes peering through, the diamond ring through which his tie was looped, his coat cut in a little at the waist as actors love to have it, his shoes which had been tan once, but which he had carefully blackened.

Somehow my heart always ached for John McCarthy, although I never knew why it should. He was always happy, always contented, always overflowing with some prospect that was to bring in big money.

One of his dreams was to revive some of the Irish plays to which Dion Boucicault had starred. "I suppose you would do characters," I said. But no, John was for doing the

––––––––––––––––––––––––

[85] Referencing her play "The Lonely Road" which earned her a spot in Dr. Baker's Harvard 47 Workshop

juvenile leads and he danced a little and sang a bit just to show that although nearing 50, he was in as fine fettle as he had been back in the old days at Tony Pastor's[86].

The last time he came up to the office I gave him an old program from Tony Pastor's which I saved for him. John and Nellie McCarthy were billed among the performers. He had lost all of his other old programs or else given them away and he was tickled with it.

At other times he came up to the office he would tell how happy he and Nellie had been – "just like a couple of kids. Sometimes we had money, and sometimes things looked pretty bad, but always we were happy, because we had each other." And you, fresh from a reading of the latest problem novel, from Sunday news supplement discussions of philandering husbands and faithless wives, wished somehow that someday the idyl of John and Nellie McCarthy[87] might be written.

I loved John McCarthy and I think that everyone who knew him loved him. I loved him for his gentleness and courtesy, his never speaking ill of anyone and his brave heart that served to keep him warm when the wind blew more bleakly than usual.

And for his sake I hope there is a heaven where he and Nellie can play together on the big time and where there will be no gas jets to sputter fitfully under a pan – a very tiny one – of frying sausages.

15 October 1925, Thursday:

---

[86] A theatre built in 1868, namesake of Tony Pastor located at 143 E. 14th st. in New York, known for vaudeville shows and home of actors John and Nellie McCarthy. Later became called the Olympic Theatre in 1908 at the time of Tony Pastor's death.

[87] John and Nellie McCarthy, "The Broken Brokers" high class vaudeville artists, according to a Vaudeville book by Gus Williams, 1900.

"YOU know I read the papers, Jo," writes Ancient Admirer. "I read pages 1, 4 and 8 of the Akron Beacon Journal to get the weather report, Jake Falstaff and your Demitasse column every night. Sometimes I read them in the reverse order — 8, 4, 1, just for variety's sake. Maybe those are the nights that I think my name will be mentioned in your column. Or maybe it's the night that my wife has already started reading page 1 and I have to be satisfied with the middle section of the paper.

"I read other papers too — Time, the International Book Review, System, and occasionally a copy of Life of Judge that nobody leaves in the dentist's office or the barber's chair.

"So I know all about the play called 'The Beggar on Horseback[88],' and the unusual and clever movie it has been made into. I decided to see that movie when it came to town.

"But has it been to town? Has it played the Strand or the Orpheum? If so, I missed it.

"Last week, 'The Beggar on Horseback' was playing a movie theater on the corner of Manchester road and West Thornton street. I was tempted to call you up, Jo, and see if you'd go over there and see it with me. Properly chaperoned, of course.

"But I held back, partly because it's such a long ride over there and back, and also because I still hope it will appear in some other Akron theater.

"See what your influence can do in this direction."

As I understand it, "A Beggar on Horseback" did come to Akron and was at the Orpheum for a couple of days. Some of my friends saw it and were crazy about it, and just as I was all set to go, having rushed through with the housework and decided on an omelette for supper, I discovered "A Beggar on Horseback" had been taken off.

Some said it was on account of poor business. They said that in the most delicious parts, the audience just sat there and acted bored. And then some others said that when they were there, there was a good house and the audience seemed to be having a great time. So I don't know. I'll ask Mr. Kadlowec about it.

---

[88] "The Beggar on Horseback," a play by George S. Kaufman and Marc Connelly, 1924.

I'm sorry, though, that Ancient Admirer didn't let me know it was playing somewhere else, because I should have loved to go, and I know we would have had a swell time.

Anyway, there's comfort in this. Charlie Chaplin's coming. Tonya and Eunice and I went down to see a pre-view of it at half past eight this morning at the Strand. Previous to this, we went down to Leatherman's and had wheat cakes and sausages and coffee and speculated on how many men were eating there, because their wives wouldn't get their breakfasts. They didn't any of them look especially discontented, though, and there was one fellow with a wave in his hair who had on a tie with swell red dots in it.

Then we went to see Charlie Chaplin. An early morning showing of a film is always a curious thing. The house is quiet and dark and smells of O'Cedar polish. The scrub woman is just finishing up, there is no music and the rows and rows of empty chairs look stark and funereal. We went upstairs and sat in the first row of the balcony, with our feet over the railing, and then the film began and there was Charlie going along a mountain pass and a bear ambling patiently behind him.

After a while, the bear turned aside, without Charlie ever seeing him, and that is one of the reasons why a Charlie Chaplin film is always better than other peoples.

There is precious little slap stick in the present film and a great deal of pathos, and I suppose that that will furnish argument for a great many persons who prefer the Charlie of the old custard slinging days.

Personally, I prefer the pathos and when Charlie, starving in Alaska, was compelled to boil one of his shoes for dinner, I thought regretfully of the pancake which only an hour before I had left untasted and swimming in syrup on my plate.

---

16 October 1925, Friday:

"**D**EAR Josephine (writes Anonymous):

"I wonder if you answer questions. For instance, if a person is puzzled in knowing how to spell proper names. I went through common school and was considered a good speller but now either spelling has been changed or I was taught wrong.

"Which is right – Grace or Grayce, Fay or Faye, Lily or Lillie, Mary, Marye, May or Mae, Catherine, Katherine or Kathryn, Edith or Edythe, Ethel or Ethyl, Jane or Jayne, Eleanor or Elinor? Did you ever hear the name Myrrh? What does it mean? Also Hortense?

"What is your opinion about naming girls Betty Jane, Betty Ann, Betty Lou, Sallie Ann, Sallie Jane, etc. Don't you think that when a girl becomes 10 years and over that those names will sound ridiculous. Seems to me they will be laughed at.

"I love such names as Mary Josephine, Mary Elizabeth, Mary Belle, Mary Katherine, Mary Louise, Mary Ann and Mary Jane and no matter how old they are they still sound well to my way of thinking.

"Are cousins allowed to marry in Ohio?

"Josephine, what church do you attend? From your articles in the paper I am in doubt.

"Hope these questions will not tire you. Will not sign this letter as I am uncertain about the spelling of my own name.

Well as to the naming of infants, either kind, I have always held that it is best to give them a good substantial name like Mary, Sarah or John. Then if the child grows up to be ravishingly beautiful the name, possibly by contrast, will sound all the better. And if the child shouldn't grow up to be beautiful there will be no incongruity.

One of the most distressing cases I ever knew was of a very homely girl named Desdemona. And I once knew a blond weighing 250 pounds who was named Birdie.

That names in the long run do have considerable to do with one's character I have no doubt. Marjorie Barkley McClure has emphasized this in one of the scenes in her new book when she has Aunt Lizzie tell the little girl Harmony that she has been given this name in the hope that it will help her overcome her family tendency to had temper. As for myself I think that if I ever got down to the writing of books I would name all the pleasant women either Mary of Catherine and I would name all the disagreeable ones Hattie.

The back of most any dictionary is always a useful place to find what names mean but as for their spelling I believe one is allowed to spell them anyway one pleases. And perhaps it is just as well. We have so little to say about our names. And if a girl has been named Grace and she doesn't like it and it gives her some small comfort to spell it Grayce I for one am all for letting her have it.

First cousins aren't allowed to marry in Ohio, I believe, due to the theory that close intermarriage is bad for the race. Those who uphold the theory point to the number of imbeciles among the reigning families of Europe where intermarriage has long been practiced. Those who don't hold in the theory point to the royal families of Egypt where it was customary for the ruler to marry his sister. Cleopatra I believe was early betrothed to her own brother.

Experiments with white rats and guinea pigs it seems have confirmed both theories so that you can take your choice.

As to my religion, I haven't any and I don't go to any church.

Someone was telling me something about Walt Whitman the other day which it seems is not generally found in the biographies. You know how Whitman was always singing of brawny men with axes on their shoulders and hair on their chest. After a while you got the impression that Whitman must have been just that way himself. But they say that on the contrary his voice was thin and high pitched, that he put up a valiant struggle to make his frame sturdy and strong and that the flowing beard which he affected and the collar open at the throat were merely a part of his attempt to make himself over into the thing he admired.

17 October 1925, Saturday:

WE WERE sitting around the little red stove last night, talking of one thing and another and after we had covered fruit salads, how much a honeymoon ought to cost, overstuffed furniture, the new winter coats, cock roaches and men we got around to the blessings of poverty.

Ordinarily there is no subject which makes me madder than the blessings of poverty, but it occurred to me while we were talking that some of the most fascinating people I have known were poor.

There were Ridley and Louella. Ridley and Louella lived in the basement below us with their seventh-hand piano, which they had gotten for $40, their wedding silver and their two or three pieces of battered wicker furniture. Ridley was writing a book. It was about a man with a weak chin who married a girl he didn't love just to show the world that he could. The book was called "Face Value" and eventually it was sent off to the publisher.

While waiting to hear from the publisher, Ridley would occasionally sell an article to a Sunday newspaper. On such an occasion, Follie and I would go down and eat with Ridley and Louella. Then on another day, Follie would sell a fashion article, and Ridley and Louella would come up and eat with us. Between times we languished and dined on boiled potatoes and onions.

There was a quiet man who used to come to see Ridley and Louella. His name was Maxwell Anderson and he was some day to become rather famous as one of the authors of "What Price Glory." But I didn't know that then and besides, as I said, he was rather quiet and so I didn't pay any attention to him.

Meantime Ridley and Louella's bank account kept getting lower and lower and to complicate matters, Li'l Ridley was expected to put in an appearance in a month or so and the doctor said that what with the high cost of things in general no really healthy baby could expect to get a start in the world for less than $400.

On the day that Ridley and Louella's bank account got down to $7, a letter came from the publisher saying that Ridley's book had been accepted and that a check would go into the mail in a very few days.

Ridley was jubilant. He was so jubilant that he went out and engaged lovely hospital accommodations for Louella, and he bought a Ford coupe and a new typewriter, and then he heard of a newspaper that was on sale on Long Island, and he went over and bought that and he leased a house at $50 a month for two years. Then the whole gang tore down to Broad's and had a thick steak and dill pickles and French fried onions.

The only trouble was that Ridley's check didn't come. There was a week of anxious waiting and then another week. Somebody else wanted to buy the newspaper if Ridley didn't want it. The people who had sold Ridley the typewriter kept coming around and knocking at the door, but when they saw Louella, so pretty and sweet, they mumbled something about it being a nice day and went away again.

Eventually the check did come, it had been lost in the mail or something, and eventually Li'l Ridley did come, and he was a girl, and eventually Ridley and Louella and Li'l Louella and Nina, the dog and, the wedding silver all loaded up in the Ford coupe and started west where, so far as I know, they may be living happily and carelessly to this very day.

But I always love to think of the things Ridley bought that day on the strength of $7 in the bank.

And then there was the Princess Golitzine, who was none of your flappers, but tall and blond and magnificent. She had been a wealthy American girl, and she had married Prince Dimitri Golitzine whose father, if you happened to notice it in the papers, was executed some time ago by the soviets.

The prince and the princess fled from Russia and eventually the princess made her way to England where she endeavored to recoup her fortune by establishing racing stables and raising blooded dogs. The money to do this was sent to her by her mother in America. The venture failed and the princess salvaged from it just enough money to pay her passage to America.

And then a very pitiful thing came to light. The princess found that in order to keep her in funds her mother had sold all of her fine furniture, had given up her cars, had lived huddled up in one cold little room of her apartment and had existed on canned milk and crackers. A few days before friends had come and had taken her away to a sanitarium, nobody seemed to know just where.

Penniless the princess dashed over to the Plaza where she had visited in splendor a few years before and demanded a car and a chauffeur. Just what magnificent proportions the bill amounted to I have no idea, but anyway, she rode and rode until she found her mother.

Having found her, and still penniless, she established her in suitable quarters and surrounded her with wine and food and flowers and a nurse. Then she went out to hunt work.

Just how she paid all those bills I'll never know, but I had a note from her later, saying she was going to play in a movie which had to do with the Russian revolution.

<hr>

19 October 1925, Monday:

"DEAR Josephine," (writes U.M.E.): "Perhaps you, as a news writer, can tell me why it is that newspapers so often fail to follow up stories with the sequel we are waiting for. Why is it that they serve to us a corking good piece of news about a waiter who was thrown out of a nine story window by a quartet of drunks and then fail to tell us in subsequent editions if the waiter lived or died and did he leave a family of 10 or a million dollars.

"A man is knocked off a speeding car and killed. The car continues on to the hospital with a woman about to be confined. What happened to the woman? Did the shock affect her? And was the child a girl or boy and was he or she christened Aloysius or Genevieve?"

Frankly I don't know why they don't follow them up. For days I was wild to know what happened to the waiter but the newspapers were absolutely dumb about him. I suppose some day the trial will come up and then we will know but it seems a long time to wait.

And then there was a story several months ago about a tramp who was walking along a railway track and discovered a rail out of place or something. He succeeded in stopping a fast passenger train and averted what might have been a disastrous wreck. But you never knew whether the president of the company sent for him and made him a handsome present or whether one of the passengers on the train was an old sweetheart of the tramp's who was now a widow with a golden haired child or whether the tramp just slipped off down the rails and disappeared into the night and was never heard of again. If newspapers would look into these matters properly they would save their readers a great deal of mental distress.

Of course there are times when a city editor, with a lazy afternoon on his hands and nobody to play red dog with, lies back in his chair with his thumbs together and begins thinking, "Say now, I wonder what became of So-and-So." This occasionally results in a good story.

There was the story of Willie Sidis, the Harvard prodigy, who disappeared from view several years ago. He was discovered not so long ago running an adding machine for $25 a week. The story, I think, was one of the best I ever read.

And then there was the story of Henry Sigel, of Sigel and Cooper fame, who established stores in New York, Boston and Chicago and then endeavored to establish a bank. The bank failed and Sigel was fined and given a federal prison sentence. I do not know whether he ever served his prison sentence or not but at any rate a couple of years ago when some inquiring reporter thought to look him up he discovered Henry Sigel running a little haberdashery store in, I believe, Hackensack, N.J. Sigel had the assistance of one clerk. He was a bright eyed little man and I think one of the pleasantest afternoons I had was sitting in the back of that little store listening to him tell the tale of his former splendors, his houses, his servants, his carriages and his three marriages and of how, as an immigrant boy, he had taken his sweetheart walking and bought her apples.

For years the papers have been full of the doings of Evelyn Thaw but Bob Dorman; a news photographer with whom I used to go on assignments, bethought himself one day to look up Pom Pom, Evelyn Thaw's son. He found Pom Pom to be a handsome youngster of about 12 with ambitions to be a physician. It made a good story.

Some of the follow up stories I wouldn't mind looking into are what Patty Arbuckle has been doing in the last few years, whether Mrs. Hall is still employing private detectives to solve the mystery of the Hall-Mills murder, and whether Mrs. Charles Garland is finding that it is a rocky road she has to follow in conforming to her husband's somewhat difficult ideals.

---

29 October 1925, Thursday:

ONE of the most fascinating problems in geometry I used to think in school was when you could take a little segment of a circle and from it reconstruct the whole circle. Likewise in later years I used to marvel when I went through a museum and saw how patient little bald-headed men with big spectacles could pick up a stray tooth or a jaw bone or a piece of tail and from it reconstruct a whole dinosaurus.

Something of this principle holds true in books I think. If you open a book at random and the first sentence pleases you, you can generally depend upon it that the whole book is interesting. It will pay you to get about the business of reading the whole thing.

I picked up a biography of Duse the other day written by a woman named Jeanne Bordeaux, if I recall correctly. I opened it in the middle, and the first sentence I saw was a silly rhapsody of some kind. Nevertheless, I started in at the beginning, determined to read the thing through. But it was useless. The whole thing was as dead and futile as that first sentence I saw in the middle.

Yesterday, though, I picked up a biography of Catherine the Great, written by Katharine Anthony. And the first sentence I encountered, somewhere toward the back, was to the effect that Catherine got up every morning at 6 o'clock to be about her writing and that she always drank five cups of strong coffee for breakfast.

"Here," I thought, "is something I like." And so I started in at the beginning to read about Catherine the Great, and I kept right on. The bed wasn't made and the dishes kept getting drier and drier in the sink and the wind whistled, and women with butter cakes to sell came and knocked at the back door. But I kept right on. And when, at half past four in the afternoon, they finally got Catherine buried, I couldn't remember when I had put in such a profitable day.

It's funny how you can live what is presumably your life and still be so ignorant. I always thought that Catherine the Great was that same Catherine, ignorant and easy going, who had been a camp follower and who married Peter the Great. And when I found that instead of being a camp follower she was a quite well educated German princess I was pretty much put out about it. The story would have been a lot more fascinating the other way.

But even as it was, it was a mighty good story. It seems that instead of having 200 lovers, Catherine, had only 12, if you include her husband. And to some of them she was faithful for as long as 10 and 12 years at a time. Considering the prevalence of modern divorce that is really a better record than some American women could show.

Catherine loved uniforms and tall, handsome figures and she didn't care much whether her lovers had brains or not. She merely wanted them to be docile and to know how to make pretty compliments. I guess the poor things had a hard enough time of it. Every night at 10 o'clock they had to escort Catherine to her rooms and every morning at 10 they had to call on her. All day long they had to be in readiness to take her to her carriage or lend their arm at a court function and between times they had to watch their step. Some of them held out under this regime for as long as two years and then they find a way to war or anything that offered.

As to her children Catherine never seemed to know much what became of them except the first couple, and after that she lost track of them. She gave her real love to her grandson Alexander, whom she intended to be a great military leader, and fearing that the little boy might grow up afraid of guns, she took him out to where the firing was with the result that made him permanently deaf.

———

I think I forgot to relate a couple of months ago that Jerry, the house painter, has started for Florida.

"We had no trouble in getting work," he writes. "There's lots of it here, but it's all union. Rooms are very high. Five dollars per week in with about five other fellows. My bro-in-law and I pitched a tent and so far haven't paid anything but for eats, which run us about 50 cents each a day. Milk is 27 cents a quart, eggs 90 cents a dozen. A chicken dinner costs 90 cents and up. Butter is high. Everything else seems to be about normal. So far we haven't found any starving people and no bread lines of 20 thousand. And as for starving myself, I've gained five pounds since I came. The fellow we came down with is building a house, and when it is finished, the three of us are going to latch in if on the community plan."

30 October 1925, Friday:

“ “YOU’RE being married now,” writes Good Housekeeper, “and interested in finger bowls and other household impediments. DO tell us a nice strategical way of doing away with old Geographics[89].

“I use that word strategical advisedly, for no open, honest, aboveboard manner will do. If you approach them in your best nine a.m. house cleaning spirit one of the darn things will fall open at ‘A Journey in Liberia’ and what with Harvey Firestone buying the country and the Smith’s talking of living there, you cannot resist parking the pile on your knees and reading a bit. Then it’s eleven o’clock and no lunch planned. You put ‘em back for a few more days to finish that article and next spring you do it all over – only the article this time will be about Italy and you’ll remember the clever things Dr. Douglas said when he returned.

“And the pile grows!”

Yes, I know, I know, and not only that but the Geographics are done up in such grand paper and the colored pictures in them are contrived at such obvious expense that it seems not only foolish but downright wanton to throw them away.

To be sure, we haven’t any Geographics here, but we had years of them over at the other house, and first they overflowed the bookcases, and then they overflowed the tables, and then some of the chairs had to be moved out on the front porch, and then there was some talk of selling the piano. And every month there’s another one to add to the pile. Not that the current issue, once it is read, is ever looked at again. But there is always the thought that maybe some day you might want to look into one of them, or perhaps your cousin Stella might come to visit with two restless little boys and the restless little boys might just love to look at the pictures.

I suppose the best attitude to approach them would be an attitude of Doing Good. You could do them up in bundles and ask your husband to take them over to one of the hospitals and after three or four months he might possibly do so. Or you might give

----

[89] National Geographic magazines

them to the Salvation Army. Or you might sell them to the rubbish man and add the 12 cents which he gives you to your contribution to the community chest. Or you could do them up in a box and send them to the penitentiary at Columbus, the expense of shipping being only slightly in excess of what a two years' subscription to the magazine would cost.

As for myself, I've never had any trouble about throwing away anything except books. I have perhaps six books which are valuable. The rest I'll never look into again, and if I should happen to want one of them in a hurry, I could pick it up very easily at a library. In spite of which I've shipped and expressed and freighted and parcel posted my books cross country and back again, down south and up to the north. Books are heavy things, and I am sure I could have two very nice new fur coats this winter with the money which I spent toting them around. And yet if I had to move tomorrow, the first thing I'd begin packing would be books.

The fierceness with which human beings cling to certain possessions, old furniture, old china, old silver, old clothes, has in it, I think something more than just foolishness. It is part of a very natural longing to belong to something. We underestimate, I think, the hold which inanimate things have upon us. We speak feelingly of the sorrow which comes when children are torn from their parents, lovers from their sweethearts. But what about the old man who sees his favorite chair taken and given to the junk man, the old woman who sees the old kitchen clock put on the dump pile?

I read a story once about a couple of theatrical troupers who had to be always on the jump. But wherever they went, the woman carried with her two china tea cups. When the trunks were opened and the china tea cups set out it was home.

And I knew once an old bachelor who lived in rather musty quarters, completely surrounded by old newspaper clippings which he had spent years in collecting. He fell ill one time and well meaning relatives threw all his newspaper clippings away. It broke his heart and I think I can see, in a dim sort of way, why it should.

---

31 October 1925, Saturday:

THERE is something about a snow fall which seems to make people a little giddy. I was looking out of the window a while ago and a woman was going by. She had grey hair and she was quite staid looking and I have no doubt but that when her study club meets she is given to seconding the motion in a distinct and authoritative voice. But now she was certainly acting queer. She was kicking at the snow and making little running jumps and then all at once she bent down and made a snowball and threw it. The street was quite deserted and I have an idea it never occurred to her that anybody might be watching out of the window. If she had seen me she probably would have been terribly embarrassed. But my only feeling in the matter was an immense comfort that other people could get a little crazy sometimes too.

The thing generally happens in the out-of-doors. Indoor, I have noticed, there are but two things that will bring it on: music or a new hat. If the housewife is alone and happens to start the phonograph or the player-piano to going she will leave the dust mop and the scrub pail and start doing the most fantastic things. She will wave her arms gracefully as she has seen the esthetic dancers do in the veil dance. She will take short running steps bringing the knees high as she has seen Mordkin or Ted Shawn do in the spear dance. If she can't think of anything else to do she will just whirl. Afterwards, tired, happy and exhausted, she will return to the scrub pail.

If it is a new hat she will go in for dramatics. She will put it on at a becoming angle, wrap a scarf about her throat and make for the hall mirror which is the one she always looks best in and where the light isn't too strong. "Oh to be in England, now that April's there." And she will conjure up an imaginary lover from whom she must part because her duty is to her husband and little innocent children. "I'm sorry, Ormond," she breathes. "I'm sorry more than I can tell you, but it can never, never be."

That over with she goes back to the dust mop and if she happens to notice her choppy fingernails and the freckles on her arms and the wisp of grey hair across her cheek and her funny old shoes, I suppose she must laugh at herself a little.

I haven't the slightest doubt but that men are the same way. At least we've all known the man with the day's growth of beard who loves to boast that he's of the "he" variety. But just come upon him some day quietly when he's looking at himself in the looking glass. You don't need anything else to convince you.

For those who are given in their solitary moments to mumbling to themselves, that boardwalk that juts around the outside of the new Keith theatre is an excellent place for betrayal. It has so many sharp turns you know. You can be going along thinking that the street is quite deserted and talking to yourself when suddenly you will turn a corner and bump into a whole crowd of people just coming from lunch at the Y.W.C.A. It's too late then to close your mouth. You just have to assume a stern expression and pass on.

It seems to me I've met any number of men talking to themselves as they came from the Elks club. I think in most instances they had just made a speech with which they were mightily pleased and they were going over a few of the high spots again. In the other instances they were composing bright comebacks which they wished they had said but which they hadn't thought of in time.

Those chaps who keep the blockhouse down by the Union station say that it is remarkable how people going over the bridge talk to themselves. The iron wall is high, you know, and they think they are alone.

Being alone, of course, is always a prime requisite. It is for that reason that every person, if he can't go out on solitary walks, should have a room where he can go in and shut the door and turn the key. Then an hour or so later he can issue forth and the world will never know but that at all times he is a sane, normal human being. Just like the rest of us.

---

6 November 1925, Friday:

"THE saddest business in the world, I'm a-thinking," writes Ancient Admirer, "is that of bringing in automobile wrecks, (illegible sentence), because there's something inevitable about dying and being buried. Sadly (illegible sentence) hospital and ambulance work, because no matter how painful it may be the work of healing and curing is the best that can be done under the circumstances. And sick people sometimes get better.

"But automobile wrecks are so sudden, so merciless, so blind in selecting their victims. If the fool drivers who race along at high speed with faulty brakes would only crack their own necks, no one would need worry. But they don't. They crowd some careful, conservative driver off the road and topple him over in the ditch. They kill the woman passengers and the driver escapes. How often you read that 'the driver escaped with injuries, while the rest of the party were dead when found.'

"No the man who chases a wrecker out into the dark on a sudden call meets a situation which a moment ago was joy and now is grief. Happy, care free motorists, just as ordinary as you or I, are suddenly cast into a tragic melee and are surrounded by blood and death. As expensive car is more or less junk. People are in tears. Maybe next week there'll be another white cross here to mark this event, but tonight we are thinking not of next week, but of the end of the world.

"I'd hate to be an ambulance chaser or an auto wrecker, yes-siren! The very thought of accidents on every hand is enough to make me limit my Sunday driving to the barest essentials."

Maybe so. But the saddest wrecks I think are the old man going home at night from the shops. Somehow I had sorta forgotten these men for a while because whenever we wanted to go any place we had Rosinante[90] to go about in. But Rosie's carburetor froze during the cold snap and then while we were waiting for her to thaw out the gasoline leaked out of her, and ever since she's been standing forlorn and dejected out in the back alley.

Meantime, I've been going about on the street cars, and that made me think of the old man again. Whenever I look at one of them then I think of Grandfather. When Grandfather was 14 years old he invented some sort of improvement on a plow and his father, who was a hard headed Dutch farmer, sold it for $400 and a brace of ponies.

Grandfather grew up to be a blacksmith, but on the side he was always inventing things. Some of the inventions brought in a little money, one of them brought in a great deal of money. But Grandfather had no head for business. When I knew him he was a stooped old man going away with a dinner pail on dark winter mornings to work in the factory which he once had owned.

I didn't think much of Grandfather's tragedy in those days but I think of it now whenever I see the stooped old men with gnarled hands and dim grey eyes. There has been no suddenness about their fate – no sudden flares of light, no clanging of ambulances, no head lines in the newspapers. But year by year their backs have best a little more, their eyes have grown a little dimmer, rheumatism has twisted their hands into tighter knots of pain.

The shops have done this to them. Perhaps if they worked in the fields it would be the same. I don't know. I only know that it isn't fair.

Sometimes I get tearfully angry at men. It seems to me that they're a dreadful, profane, selfish, tobacco smelling lot. And then sometimes on the other hand I wonder at the

---

[90] reference to Rocinante, Don Quixote's horse

nobility of them. They marry some girl who has been moping around after them and they bring up a brood of not particularly lovable children.

They go to work every morning, they come home every night. On Saturdays they turn over the pay envelope to their missus. They listen to a recital of the day's woes, they spank the children, read the paper and go to bed. It is this way, year after year. A chew of tobacco, a neck tie at Christmas, that is about all that life brings them. They grow old and the children go away and forget them. Afterwards you see them going down Howard st. in shabby overcoats peering wistfully into the windows.

I wonder why they do it.

———⌇⌇⌇◆⌇⌇⌇———

7 November 1925, Saturday:

GLADYS

Gladys was one of those sweet and proper children. She never scuffed her shoes. She never wipes her nose on her sleeve. She kept the front of her dress clean. She played her waltz on the piano when company came. She had naturally curly hair. She was pretty. She was one of those children of which the relatives said, "Oh dear, why CAN'T you be like Gladys." I never was what you might call real fond of Gladys.

STELLA

Stella was the family drudge. Stella was a step-child. Stella's father was poor. After Stella came a whole flock of little dirty nosed step-brothers. Stella dressed the brothers in the morning and put them to bed again at night. Occasionally she washed them. She washed the dishes and ironed the clothes and scrubbed the front porch and helped with the family mending. Between times she went to school. Occasionally she came out to play for a half hour. But there was always the youngest brother to be dragged along. When Stella was 14 she ran off and married a young fellow who worked in the paper mill. She still drudges.

CORNELIA

Cornelia was a professor's child. She was brought up on all the approved theories. She wore glasses and had bad teeth. Cornelia liked to play improving games like authors. She thought postoffice was terrible although she needn't have because nobody ever sent her a letter. When Cornelia was 11 years old she was ready to go to high school. When she was 17 the local paper ran a story about her to the effect that here was a girl who had never been to a movie or seen a funny paper. Cornelia had a beaux once, a nice brown-eyed fellow with ideals. After they had gone together for six months he asked Cornelia for a kiss. Cornelia felt she had been insulted and told him that she wished never to see him again. She thought he would come back. But he never did.

LORETTA

Loretta was boy crazy from the moment she opened her eyes and gazed at the handsome young doctor who was thumping her on the back. When she was six she deserted the little guests at her birthday party to sit on the stair steps and hold hands with Lavander Nealy and when she was nine she was definitely engaged with a blue china bracelet to Willie Knox who had bought the bracelet at the ten-cent store. Loretta never cared much whom she spooned with and she always had more bids than she knew what to do with to the high school dances. This made the other girls mad. "Never mind," they said, "she'll come to no good end. The fellows may play around with her but when it comes to getting married they'll pick out a sensible girl who always gets 90 in Latin." Loretta was graduated by the skin of her teeth and six months later she married a wealthy fur dealer from Detroit. She has a limousine, four servants and six children and they say that when the cook leaves unexpectedly Loretta goes out and gets up a seven course dinner with her own hands.

LUCY

Lucy always loved those fairy stories where a knight with a tall white plume comes riding down the highway. When the other children were roller skating or trying out swimming exercises on the sidewalk Lucy would curl up in the hammock and read and keep her ginghams clean. Lucy was pretty and shy and sweet and a great many youths came to love her but somehow they never seemed to talk like the knights in the story books and because they couldn't talk prettily Lucy doubted whether their plumes were as white and flaunting as she would like to have them. One time Lucy went away to a big city for a visit and there she met a man who told her that her eyes were like twin starts and her hair was fairy gold. And Lucy gave him her heart which he very promptly threw away.

---

11 November 1925, Wednesday:

SOME CHAP writing in the Sunday papers has made the discovery that it takes three college women to produce one child while one homely, unintelligent woman may be producing two or three..

"The lesson to be drawn from this," he says, "is irrefutable. Homely, unintelligent women ought to be encouraged to go to college while any woman who measures 120 or over in an intelligence test ought to be rigorously excluded."

This, he thinks, would give us a race of perfectly lovely children and improve things generally.

What I can't see is why the gentleman, he is, to be precise, an editorial writer on the New York times, should link intelligence with a college education or a college education with beauty. I have a dreadful time remembering figures but it does seem to me that of all the participants in this year's beauty contest at Atlantic City only a couple of the girls had been to college.

However, as luck would have it, I have some figures here from an essay by Havelock Ellis which Donald Grey sent me a couple of weeks ago.

"How little all that we understand by opportunity... counts for in the development of genius in woman," he writes, "is shown by the remarkable fact brought out by Dr. Castle that in the most recent historical period eminence has been attained by a proportionately smaller number of women than was the case in the eighteenth century. This is so as regards England, France and Germany as well as America. Italy is, in a small degree, an exception; but on the other hand, Italy in the fifteenth, sixteenth and seventeenth centuries was more prolific in eminent women than in either the eighteenth or the nineteenth. Even within the ordinary range of ability it would appear that opportunity, as tested by that college training which is usually held to mean so much to men, plays but a very small part. A few years ago Amanda Northrop investigated the 977 successful women of America on the basis of Who's Who in America and found that only 15.5 per cent of them had received a college training. More-over, the college played a decreasing part and the percentage of successful American woman who had been college bred was less for those born between 1860 and 1870 than for any preceding period."

Leaving the matter of children out of it, however, the whole idea is beautiful. Colleges, owing to the great number of persons who attend them and also to a number of other things, aren't made for geniuses or for people who tend to be original. They are designed to suit the average intelligence. A girl who is a little brighter than the average but who has any timidity in her makeup is absolutely flattened out by college. On the other hand you and I know any number of dumb Doras who blossomed out miraculously when they went to college. College didn't make them intelligent but it exposed them to a number of ideas which goodness knows they would never have picked up if they had had to hunt them out themselves. They have met various kinds of people, they have been compelled to listen to lectures part of which they understood and they have learned what views they must hold in order to get by with the greatest number of people. The result is that they get by very nicely in most walks of life and if they are kind-hearted to boot everybody will love them. Their lives will be far happier than their sisters who measure 120 in the intelligence tests and are therefore sent out into the world to find out what life is all about and what they are going to do about it.

◦◦◦◦◦◆◦◦◦◦◦

16 November 1925, Monday:

I LOVE the dish pan. It is very useful. You can pile the dishes in it and pour some water on them and it will wait and wait for you to come to do them – just as patient as anything. If somebody else is using the laundry tube you can do your washing in the dish pan. If somebody has gone off with the scrub pail you can use the dish pan to scrub the kitchen floor with. The dish pan will hold the potatoes and cabbage that you are getting ready for dinner and you can also use it to carry coal in. And if you cousin's dear little boy comes to visit you and insists on driving nails through the carpet you can generally distract his attention by giving him the dish pan and letting him play circus parade on it with the cake spoon.

I LOVE the old silk log cabin quilt. It is made up of bits from the dresses that our sisters used to wear. Ellen, the pretty one, used to hang over the log cabin quilt for hours. "Now this," she would say, "Is a piece of that old tea gown that Rose had when she was married. She always looked so sweet in it. And this is a piece of the silk dress I wore that night that Oscar Wetztraub took me to the minstrel show at Crump's theater. He said it was the prettiest dress I ever had. And this is a piece of that striped dress that we gave Ma one Christmas. She never would wear it. She said it was too gay for a woman of her years. You wouldn't believe it but when she was young Ma had more beaux than any other girl in town. And this is a piece of that dress that Alta never got to wear. She wanted to live so she could wear it. She said it was the prettiest dress she ever had. Ma put it away in the bottom bureau drawer and every once in a while we'd catch her going in there and crying over it. And this is a piece of the dress I wore to the Sunday school picnic the time Charlie Teasle got drowned. Poor Charlie, the girls were all crazy about him. And this is a piece of the dress Mag got for the World's Fair. She got lemonade all over the front of it."

Ellen and all of them except Mag are gone away now, and the old log cabin quilt is showing signs of wear.

I LOVE the paper boy. He is polite, he is very business like, he has big brown eyes and he knocks on the door very, very loudly.

I LOVE the typewrxxer. It gott all the d%ost. It is never brushd. There are choc&%te creams on its keysXXXXXX. It is a steppedon and sat on anditgtushrpvedunderthecouch anyyetitstillpwriterxep nicewordslipethese. I am?goings to buy it a newpribbon for Christmas. [sic – this is exactly as Jo wrote it in the paper]

I LOVE the chaize with the blue flowers on it. You would never think we got it for half price which was $37.50. You can go to sleep in the blue chair or darn socks in it or read. It will also hold laundry, galoshes, bed clothes, wet umbrellas, babies, hat boxes, cedar chests, fresh fruit and coffee percolators. When you take the cushion off the blue chair to dust it you will find in the corners of it four hair pins, a box of matches, three ends of cigarets, an apple core and a nail file.

I LOVE the people who pass our house. They all look in our windows and they say, "Dear, dear, I wish I could know those people. They must be very interesting. And they have washed their windows."

I LOVE the book reviews that Howard Wolf writes in the Beacon Journal. They are grand. He is a smart fellow.

※

18 November 1925, Wednesday:

"MAN or Woman. Which Makes the Better Automobile Driver? Woman, Say the Scientists. However Traffic Cops Testifies for More Male. And Then There Is the Story of Mrs. Marian R. Shaw, the 'Mile a Minute Blonde' of Long Island."

"Not long after they were gone a tousled head was thrust up from behind the head gate. It looked carefully around a moment. Then Joe Frederick drew himself out of the water." This thrilling narrative of western life will be continued next week.

———————

"Learn about Women from Tax Collector" Urges Girl Reporter. "No, I really don't think either sex has it on the other in regard to honesty," says F. L. Foley, chief of the audit section of New York's second district. 'I believe a majority of the women state their incomes truthfully. A good many of the difficulties arise when they try to figure up their exemptions." In other words, says the girl reporter, a large number of women seem to believe that a kindly government allows them to write off their doctors' and dentists' bills. They see no reason why they should pay taxes on an appendix which is floating around uselessly in preserve jar or a tooth that was chipped by a filbert shell in Aunt Lottie's birthday cake."

———————

"Catalysis – The Miracle of Chemistry." Through it are manufactured shotgun shells, newspapers, cigaret holders, radio parts, fertilizers, vegetable lard, soap, automobile tires, dyes, artificial ice.

———————

"November's Children Are Angels or Devils," says noted astrologist. Among the persons born under this sign are Mabel Normand and Thomas A. Edison.

———————

"My name is Harold Dunn. I am a high school student but I want to be an inventor. I am working on an invention now and I want to know if the letters in my name are good for this sort of thing." Yes, Harold.

———————

"Dolly Sisters Quit Moulin Rouge. 'We were riven [sic] five tiny parts,' they say 'which would have kept us on the stage barely a quarter of an hour.' 'An, no,' retorts the manager of the Moulin Rouge, 'the roles of the Dolly Sisters would have kept them on the stage at least a half hour.'"

———————

"Rich American Woman is Her Rival," says Lady Georgina Douglas who last May married the seventh son of Abdul Hamid. "I don't want anything more to do with him."

"Girl Gamblers Gain in Britain. Thousands of Children Encouraged To Play Horses, Say Reformers."

"Wronged Wife Faces Charge of Killing Rival." When Mary Lee Scott, 27 years old, sought balm for her wounded heart a few months after the courts severed her matrimonial ties she summoned Dr. James Felton Farmer, 20, who had been introduced as a "welder of broken romance."

"Mongol' Man's Birth Place," says Roy C. Andrews. "Conditions were favorable for his appearance there 500,000 to 1,000,000 years ago."

"'Dinty' Moore's Daughter, Known as 'Miracle Woman,' Weds. 'Miss Mary Moore who suffered a broken back and fractured skull four years ago, was married yesterday. She received treatment from Dr. Adolf Lorenz, famous Austrian surgeon, and her recovery amazed surgeons."

"My Favorite Poet is Longfellow," says Nathalia Crane, child genius of Brooklyn.

"Pastor Sees Spiritual Ills in New York."

"Kidnappers, About To Bury Woman Alive, Scared Off."

"Miss Helen Kaznoski proves herself to be champ by spelling correctly 100 words a day for 30 days. Her father, Lewis Kaznoski came to this country from Polan'."

"Valentino To Go Through Life Alone. 'To generalize on women is dangerous,' he declares, 'to specialize is infinitely worse.'"

19 November 1925, Thursday:

HAZEL WENDELL – she who writes those nice ads for Polsky's – was up the other night and we got to talking about hope chests.

Now the only hope chest I ever had was one I started 11 years ago with a Cluny luncheon set and two bath towels. Somebody who wanted to give a party borrowed the Cluny luncheon set and I forgot just what happened to it after that. And as for the bath towel we sort of fell late the habit of getting one of them out when the family supply ran short so that after a while the blue in them got pretty much faded and it really wasn't worth while thinking of putting crocheted edges on them any more.

I always felt that my life had been a sort of dismal failure because I didn't have a hope chest but Hazel gave me a new slant on the matter.

"Wouldn't you," she said, "like to see the hope chest of a girl who's been engaged about four times?"

I certainly would, particularly if she was a girl who was born about 1890 and who began assembling things when she was about 15. I dimly seem to recall the things my relatives were wearing in those days. There were the corset covers for instance. These corset covers were made of stiff muslin and they were gored so that they dipped in prettily at the waist. Around the top was an edging of hand made lace which scratched and then just below this would be a nicely executed design of holly hocks or a basket of pansies embroidered in colors. Sometimes the corset covers were padded out in front to give them a rich fullness and then to help along at the hips they had an extra poplum or something.

The petticoats which went along with these were gored too and they always had a foot or so of ruffled embroidery at the bottom and then there was always a somewhat plainer ruffle to go along with this and give it body. In other matters the umbrella style prevailed.

I think it was after this that the passion started for crocheted corset cover tops and boudoir caps. If a girl was going to be married and her friends gave her a shower you could depend on it that at least nine of them would come bearing boudoir caps all nicely crocheted in pink or lavender with corset cover tops to match. The idea was that if you wanted to be real modish you wore one of those peek-a-boo waists that the ministers took so much to heart and then under it you wore one of those corset covers and the design and the color showed through too alluring for anything.

Just how much the boudoir caps were worn in the boudoir I don't know as a lot of women got careless after they were married and didn't care whether their husbands saw them in curl papers or not. But they felt differently about the grocery boy and if you were to go to most any grocery store about 10 o'clock in the morning you could see the most charming and festive array of intimate headgear imaginable.

All the household effects seemed to step right along with the lingerie. The pillow slips had embroidery on them which left full and complete designs on your ear and there were crocheted edgings on the sheets which got caught in the washing machine every Monday. There were dollies and pin cushions and things and embroidered photograph frames.

By just what degrees we came to our present state I don't know. But downtown in the windows they're showing something called teeny-weenies. These consists of a band of something or other to which is attached a quarter of a yard of the same thing and you put them on and then you step into your little sports frock and two stockings and two shoes and you're all ready for the day. The present day hope chest simply must have at least half a dozen of them. However, as Hazel says, the minute you send back the ring you'd better begin wearing out the things in your hope chest. Otherwise you're going to find yourself encumbered with a lot of things which are going to look awfully peculiar a couple of years from now when hope sings again in your breast and you get engaged to that dandy young medical student from Dayton.

CONTRARY to current opinion it has always seemed to me that the things which come easiest are always most worth while. The things which one has to work hard for generally turn out to be not worth the effort. I spent hours and hours the other afternoon digging out items from Sunday newspapers. Then I put a heading over them "Sunday Newspapers." The printers who set the items in type forgot to put the heading over them so that, so far as I know, nobody knew what any of it was about. And the items, as I read them in Wednesday's B. J. didn't seem to be particularly snappy.

It's the same way with a lot of other things. Scramble into an old sweater, let your nose go unpowdered and start out for a walk and four people will tell you you look just wonderful. Order a new dress from the dressmaker, spend two weeks trying it on, put on beauty mud, cold cream, freckle remover and wrinkle vanisher, get a marcel and a manicure and go to a dance and not a soul will give you an appreciative word.

Or take meals. You can bake and stew and fuss all day and the gentleman whom you did it all for will take about three bites of the roast, decide to go without pie and tell you the coffee is terrible. But throw a lot of left-overs out on the table and he'll eat them all and tell you he doesn't know when he's enjoyed anything so much.

———————

Richardson Wright in his book "Truly Rural" which has to do with country houses and gardens and things has some pleasant things to say about kitchens. For one thing, when he gets his ideal kitchen, he is going to hang on the walls fine old French prints which have to do with the art of cooking. I think something of that sort must have been in my mind once. A retired banker named Woodward, a man who has since become rather famous as the author of "Busk" and "Lottery" and a more recent book called "Bread and Circuses" gave me a menu card which he had picked up in some funny old French restaurant. It was about a foot by a foot and three, I should say, and surrounding the "poulet avec pomme frite" and the "jambon avec pinard" and some eight or so wines were pictures of red faced gentlemen in flowered waistcoats and ladies in tight waists and trains and remarkable millinery. I bore it home in triumph, intending to have it framed as soon as I had taken the butter prints off it, but the young women with whom I was living and who had gone in lately for Holbein couldn't see anything in it. It was always in the way on dusting day and she sniffed at it so repeatedly that I finally lost heart and let it be carried away with the Sunday papers. I am not a person of strong character.

I wish that I had that menu card now to frame and hang on the kitchen wall. There are at least four places where it would look well.

———————

Then Mr. Wright would have a shelf of books to put in the kitchen. Most of them are French books which I never heard of and whose names I could never possibly pronounce but which apparently have to do with the delights of eating. He would also include Fannie Farmer's "The Boston Cooking School Book" and Mrs. Rorer and Ellwanger on "The Pleasures of the Table."

For my part, my kitchen library would have thus far but two books, "The Boston Cooking School Book" and "half Hours in the Kitchenette." Mrs. Rorer I don't think I would care to have as she is always telling you to take a pint of cream or a quart of wine when such a procedure is obviously out of the question. Oh yes, and there would be the cook book that I had in Central High school. I didn't think so much of it in those days but now when I have only one egg and a tablespoon full of butter to do with I turn to it hopefully and it never fails me.

It is encouraging, I think to find that the kitchen is being treated with greater and greater respect. Back in the old days, I understand, when nights were cold and steam radiators unheard of, the kitchen stove was the center of the household. Then there came a time when kitchens were despised, the pots were neglected and people sat in the parlor. Nowadays kitchens are not regarded as social centers either, but they are painted white and made very, very sanitary. With that as a starter it ought to be easy, with the addition of some book shelves and pictures and curtains trimmed with rickrack and pots of flowers on the window sill to restore the kitchen to its old supremacy.

For lack of space we eat in the kitchen these days and there are times, especially when it has just been scrubbed, that in spite of the wash boiler where we have to keep the potatoes and the apples, and the clothes hamper and the carpet sweeper and the broom, I fall so much in love with it that I hope we'll never be rich enough to eat elsewhere.

23 November 1925, Monday:

ONE of the most dreadful persons on earth is a woman who insists on talking about her family when you want to talk about your family. Mrs. Pommefrit is one of these. Mrs. Pommefrit has just left. I don't know when I've felt so exhausted.

"My dear," she said, bustling in, "I meant to get over to see you sooner, but you know how it is – a house full of company. Homer motored over Thursday from New York with a crowd of young people and never sent me a word – not a word. I always say to the children that I'm perfectly glad to turn over the house to them any time, but here was I with all the sheets in the wash and the two extra cots both down in the cellar and —"

"I know, I know," I said, "but a person of your temperament doesn't mind little things like that. Now, my great aunt Sophia made it so miserable when company came that —"

"No, no, no," said Mrs. Pommefrit, "now don't misunderstand me. I'm always glad to have the house full of young people. You may remember that when my sister Ellen's youngest daughter was married, I —"

"My DEAR," I said, "I must tell you about a young uncle I had who ran away and got married once. He met this girl on Friday and on Saturday he put his tooth brush in his pocket, and they ran away to Indianapolis and —"

"I gave her a wedding that cost me pretty nearly three hundred dollars," said Mrs. Pommefrit determinedly, "and that in spite of the fact that Ellen and I never did get along. She never was like any of the rest of us. And CLOSE: She never put more than one egg in a cake in her life, and as for clothes —"

"My dear," I said, "If you think you have queer relatives you should listen to mine. In all the 20 years that Aunt Henrietta and Uncle John were married she never had a nickel to call her own. He wanted her to have charge accounts so he could snoop over the bills and see if she paid too much for things. Time and again I've heard her ask for five cents for an ice cream soda. And then there was Cousin Minnie —"

"Ellen found a blue serge one time," said Mrs. Pommefrit, "that the ragman would have rejected and didn't she —"

"Cousin Minnie," I said, "was the biggest troublemaker I ever knew. She would descend on the family when everything was going peaceful and within 24 hours she'd have everybody tearing each other's hair, P'er system —"

"Ellen took this blue serge," said Mrs. Pommefrit, "and decided she'd make it over for her first girl, Grace Marie. It was so short, and so she pieced it out with some green flannel on the bottom. It was a fright, but nobody dared say anything, and she made Grace Marie —"

"The way Cousin Minnie did it," I said, "was to come up to you and get your sympathy and then get something that she could tattle to somebody else. Then she'd get them to say something and tattle it back to you. She was big and rawboned and —"

"She made Grace Marie wear it in school," said Mrs. Pommefrit, "and the next day the poor child came to me in tears. The other children had been making fun of her clothes. I went right down and bought her a Peter Thompson with my own money and –"

"Well, Minnie, really," I said, "was downright ugly, but she had this idea that every man was fascinated with her. I'll never forget the time –"

"do you think Ellen would let her wear it?" said Mrs. Pommefrit. "No, She put it in the closet and Grace Marie had to go on wearing that fright of a serge. That's the reason when she got married I said she was going to have a nice wedding. For my own part, I don't believe she would have married so young if –"

"Cousin Minnie was married," I said, "but her husband was the meekest, most browbeaten thing in Martin's Perry. Everybody said that –"

"Now Ellen's other children," said Mrs. Pommefrit –"

"Cousin Minnie never had any children," I said, "and it's a good –"

"My brother Henry," said Mrs. Pommefrit, "was married twice, and he had eleven – nine girls and –"

"My dear," I said, "would you believe it, my Uncle Ishmael was married three times and every one of the 17 children was a girl. He said –"

"Really," said Mrs. Pommefrit, "I must be going."

She seemed a little cross.

---

24 November 1925, Tuesday:

EVERY three or four weeks there comes a time when you simply must rearrange the clothes closets. The number of these, if you happen to be living in a two rooms and bath, is two.

The smaller of these, the one located in the entrance hall, is not difficult to rearrange. It is the male clothes closet. Its entire contents consists of 22 tin coat hangers sent back from various laundries, a clothes brush and a pair of No. 11 shoes with mud on them and two holes in the right sole. To set this closet to rights you run your finger over the shelf to see how much dust has accumulated there since the last time and turn the clothes brush over on its bristles. Then you pick up the shoes by their laces and shake them gingerly to see whether any of the mud comes off. It doesn't. Then you shut the door.

The other clothes closet is quite a problem. On the shelf, a slab of board which measures possibly a foot and two inches across, there are four summer hats, three winter hats, a flat box which holds collar and cuff sets, a hat box which holds the switch you had made that time you had your hair bobbed, an electric curling iron, four unused jars of massage cream, two high school pennants and the remnants from your green velvet evening dress and next to this there are two blankets, a bed spread and a pink comforter which keeps falling off.

As you regard this array a bright thought strikes you. You unstrap the trunk, throw everything out on the floor and discover that by denting in the crowns of the hats they all fit in very nicely. Then you throw everything back in the trunk and lock it. The shelf now becomes commodious enough to permit the pink comforter to stay put.

You now turn your attention to the clothes books. There is always one of these which slants so that the minute you put anything on it it immediately falls to the floor with a loud clatter. Seven garments now proceed to do this. You decide that you will move these to another book and hang negligees on the slanting book because they don't weigh so much. You hang the negligees on the slanting book, and they fall just the same.

It then occurs to you that there are a number of summer things which you won't be wearing for several months and you might as well put them in the trunk. You unstrap and unlock the trunk, the contents of which immediately burst out. To get everything in again with the addition of the summer things is quite a task, but eventually you do it and get the lid down again with the timely assistance of the janitor.

You now have one more book than you had before. On this you hang a button bag and your fur coat. Then you sink exhaustedly into the nearest chair.

Closets are queer things. If you have just one it is sure to be full and if you have seven they are all sure to be full, too. They demonstrate almost better than anything else how remarkably things will condense and expand.

When I was a child I was always excessively annoyed at the insistence which my feminine relatives put on clothes closets. We could go out to look at a house which was for sale (we didn't really have any money but of course, the agent couldn't know that until I took him confidentially aside and told him) and right away my feminine relatives would start saying, "It's a nice house, but only two clothes closets. We could never get along with only two clothes closets. What in the world do people mean by building the way they do these days."

This irritated me beyond words. To my mind you bought a house because it had a nice coat of paint on it or a fireplace or an apple tree in the back yard or a cellar door that was good for sliding on.

But now I know better. Some day I'm going to build a house with acres of clothes closets. And they'll be all lined with cedar and the shelves will be three feet wide and there'll be shelves for shoes and shelves for hat boxs [sic] and all the hooks will be a self-clamp kind that nothing could possibly slide off of.

26 November 1925, Thursday:

WHAT I like about Thanksgiving is that it is so frankly materialistic. On the Fourth of July we celebrate the birth of our Independence, a very elusive sort of thing, and on Christmas we celebrate the birth of one who urged upon us poverty and meekness and self denial.

Thanksgiving however urges us to be thankful for things which we can plainly see and touch and feel – for turkey and pumpkin pie, for coal in the cellar and enough money to pay the taxes with.

And this is as it should be. The things of the spirit are beautiful and necessary but I like a good healthy appreciation of things of the flesh too. It is good to wake up on Thanksgiving morning and know that there is sugar in the sugar box and cream waiting on the front door step, to know that next month's rent is fairly assured and to hear the cheerful sound of steam in the radiators. It is good to go over home and eat more than is good for you and to sit around afterward, stupid and placid and peaceful. Afterward there is time to think of self denial and the cleansing of the spirit and of the humble rejoicing which is Christmas.

There are of course a number of things which I would like to be thankful for if I could. I would be thankful if something would be done about the coal situation so our curtains wouldn't have to be laundered every three weeks.

I would be thankful if it were possible to get short vamp shoes in Akron.

I would be thankful if I never again had to listen to the phrase, "100 per cent American."

I would be thankful if all Sunday newspapers were abolished.

I would be thankful if newspaper headline writers wouldn't split their infinitives.

I would be thankful if electric stoves didn't run up the bills so high.

I would be thankful if Mrs. Rachmaninoff had never written his celebrated Prelude in C sharp minor.

I would be thankful if those who bring me candy would bring me flowers or stew pans instead.

I would be thankful if those who offer me likker[91] would offer me tea instead.

I would be thankful if somebody would invent silver that didn't tarnish.

I would be thankful if somebody would invent bath tubs that didn't get rings around them.

I would be thankful if there were more movies as good as Buster Keaton in "Go West."

I would be thankful if people didn't write anonymous letters.

I would be grateful if all telephone wires were put underground.

And a great many other things.

27 November 1925, Friday:

---

[91] A spelling of liquor

O NE of the most helpful things imaginable these days is to pick up a magazine and go through the sections marked "Useful Christmas Suggestions for HIM."

There is a new fountain pen desk set out according to one of the advertisements, which is designed to set a man capering with joy. It consists of two or three fountain pens in appropriate holders, and then there is a tray and some blotters and other things to go along with it. The only trouble is that the set is large and impressive and there would be considerable difficulty in finding a place for it on a desk which is holding in addition a typewriter, 11 selled collars, a box of thumb tacks, a filing cabinet, a pair of scissors, a hammer, a set of Robert Louis Stevenson, a last Christmas muffler, two empty coca cola bottles and a tube of shaving cream.

Another lovely Christmas suggestion for HIM is a complete shaving outfit, all done up in satin the way we women get our presents. There is shaving soap and cream and a special kind of talcum and shaving lotion and styptic pencil, and it all fits together in the darlingest box padded out with the color he loves best. The advertisement shows a great, strong, husky man with his face all full of lather. He is saying, "Well, Mary, you certainly picked out what I wanted that time."

A walking stick, according to certain of the other ads, is just what every man is secretly hankering for. So far as that is concerned I haven't the slightest doubt but that it is true. But I'd like to see any man walk down Main st., Akron, O, one of those days with a walking stick and not be out dead by every other man and woman in town. Dave Brown has a whole umbrella stand of walking sticks but he doesn't dare carry them. Fortunately the Goodyear sends him abroad ever so often and then Dave sneaks a couple of the best looking sticks into his luggage and just revels. However I don't think I will buy him a walking stick. He would merely break it neatly in two with a few disdainful words or else use it to balance the best salad plates on.

One of the things which sets a man entirely beside himself, according to another ad, is a clever leather traveling bag completely equipped with toilet articles. The picture shows the complete equipment. There are two military brushes and a clothes brush and a shoe brush and a comb and a holder for the tooth brush and a holder for the soap and a mirror and some manicure things and a place for a flask. It all folds up very compactly. So far as I can figure out you buy another suit case to put your shirts and collars in.

The other absolutely unique things which he wants for Christmas, according to the ads, are silk evening mufflers appropriate for the opera or dining at the Ritz, exclusively patterned ties from $7.50 up, silk handkerchiefs, silk socks, woolen socks with sweaters to match which will knock everybody absolutely cold on the golf course, dressing gowns at $175, pigskin belts and lavender striped suspenders. So different from last year that hardly anybody need have the slightest trouble.

Unfortunately the person whom I have in mind doesn't wear suspenders and his belt shows signs of holding together for another year yet. His silk dressing gown was purchased some time ago at a sale at O'Neil's, he refuses to smoke although it's my private opinion that there's nothing like a pipe to make a place home like and when he travels he always leaves the manicure scissors at home so there'll be plenty of room to put the box of candy in on the way back. However as to the socks and things, they have to be purchased immediately, Christmas or no Christmas.

Of course, one might say, "Now this is my Christmas present to you only I'm giving it to you now because that shirt you've been wearing is a fright" but somehow it isn't the same. On Christmas morning there ought to be innumerable bundles all done up with tissue paper and red ribbon and holly. If there aren't a whole lot of them there is always disappointment and it does little good at such a time to say, "Well, I know, but you remember I gave you your things on Thanksgiving."

And so in spite of all the helpful ads, ads which probably cost thousands of dollars, I still don't know what to do about it.

---

28 November 1925, Saturday:

OWING to the efforts of Ethel Boleyn Myers, woman's page editor of the Beacon Journal, a convention slightly different from that which usually favors the city will come to Akron next October.

This will be the convention of Ohio newspaper women and those who happen to meet the women will, I imagine, go away with prolly the same feelings which I had once after I had viewed a troupe of Russian dancers leaving the railway station.

I had seen the dancers give a performance the night before when, what with their spangles, their red-heeled boots and their gorgeous head dresses, they looked indescribably beautiful. The next morning at the railway station, however, there was some of this. The men looked languid and insufferable and not altogether clean, while the women were dowdy and tired and run down at the heel. It was a bitter disillusionment.

In some such fashion there exists a popular stage picture of the newspaper women. Whenever you see her on the stage she is always smartly clad in attire which inclines slightly to the mannish: she is dreadfully good looking, she carries a notebook and pencil, and she is very, very brilliant.

In my life I have known only one or two newspaper women who looked like that, and they were not so well known or so well paid so, well, as Marguerite Moors Marshall, for instance, who is decidedly plump and matronly, who wears peculiar hats sitting high on the top of her head, who carries her rubbers to work in a market basket and who is probably the cleverest interviewer in the United States.

However, after the first disillusionment is over with; I imagine there is no nicer lots of women to come amongst than a group of newspaper women. This is primarily because they are not so smart as they are supposed to be. Probably every one of them got into the newspaper business through an accident of some sort. She went to work as assistant editor at $12 or $15 a week; she was insulted by some of those matrons whose pictures look so lovely and sweet in the Sunday supplements; she made mistakes, she got her verbs all wrong, and she sent widows traveling to Europe with husbands who had been dead 20 years. And the city editor, after he had told her about it, would mop up her tears and tell her to be a good girl, and he wouldn't fire her for another week yet.

Later on she began to get other assignments. She interviewed murderers about to be sent to the electric chair, girl shoplifters, visiting millionaires, authors, and returned explorers. She was thrown out of peoples' houses, she posed as a chambermaid to get first hand evidence on current trials, she climbed smoke stacks for thrills and was threatened with law suits and annihilation by irate subscribers.

And out of it all there began finally to emerge a mellow young woman who wrote her stuff in short sentences of one syllabled words, who developed an uncanny knowledge of what was libel and what was not, who frequently left a good part of her week's pay behind when she was sent out to interview an abandoned mother with six wailing children to be applied to trite word "laterating" not because of inherent brilliance, but because of the things she had brushed up against.

Your newspaper woman is not always up on the world's great literature and she is frequently hazy in matters of geography, but she knows that the smug financier who gives his ten rules for success in the current popular magazine is the same chap who tried to get fresh with her once and she knows that the minister's wife who sings so loudly at the missionary meetings puts an insufferable amount of work upon her laundress.

She's come in contact with too much unhappiness to be cynical, but she's hard to fool. And when a lot of them get together for an experience meeting ---

---

It will be refreshing, I think, to have 150 or so of them descend on Akron next fall and then tell the rest of the world what they think of the town.

---

30 November 1925, Monday:

IT WOULD be fun to buy a lot and build a house on it but I think I would run as far as possible from that allotment which advertises itself as being "close to millionaires' row" and (illegible – mentlose) as one of its advantages the circumstance that it is close to a school which is "patronized by children of the rich."

It isn't that I have any objections to millionaires. The few that I have known have for the most part been as nice as could be. But it seems to me that there is just as much of an insult in wanting to be near a man because he has a lot of money as there is in trying to avoid some other man because he hasn't any money. And I think the millionaire must resent it as much as anybody.

Moreover I don't know that there is really a whole lot of advantage in wanting your kids to go to a school which is patronized solely by the children of the rich. The children of the rich are undoubtedly cleaner as to hands and ears than the children you would find in schools in some other parts of the city and their standard of intelligence may possibly be a tiny bit higher. But children are sensitive and it must be terribly hard on the kids of installment house parents to have to roll home from school with Ma in a second hand flivver[92] while their schoolmates are called for by chauffeurs in livery and first hand Rolls Royces.

And I don't know whether the children of the rich have as much fun. I have a friend who used to do summer playground work when we were paying more attention to playgrounds than we do at present. Every two weeks or so it came her turn to spend a day at one of these "children of the rich" schools. She always groaned when that day came. She tried her very best games out on them but it was no use. They were bored. They didn't want to play. "Honest," she said finally, "I didn't know what to do. It seemed to me there was nothing left but to serve pink tea.[93]"

---

[92] A flivver is an early twentieth-century slang for an automobile

[93] "pink tea" refers to a formal afternoon tea marked by a high degree of decorum; a decorous or namby-pamby affair or proceeding – (reference: Merriam-Webster)

———

A book came to the house the other day which was about home owning. Some parts of it, it seemed to me were pretty bad, but at least it had some sensible things to say about neighborhoods. And the sum and the substance of it was this: move into a neighborhood where you will find people like yourself.

It would be pretty lonesome, you know, to scrimp and save and eat a great deal of hash and forego the trip to California just so that eventually you could build in the neighborhood of the rich and then after you had moved in and had the curtains up, to find all your neighbors calling by without so much as a look in your direction. And there are other predicaments. I knew a woman a few years ago who had saved and worked hard for years just so that she and her husband might buy a house in the "nice" part of town. She was weeding the flower bed one afternoon and she had an old sue bonnet on her head and her face was red and her hands were full of loam when who should drive up but her most fashionable neighbor come to call.

The neighbor alighted and came up to the walk with her card case in her hand. "Is Mrs. Smith in?" she queried.

Now my friend, if she had not had foolish notions about the grandness of neighborhoods and the like, would have said, "Why I am Mrs. Smith" and she and her new found friend would have gone into the house and she would have washed her hands and made some tea and they would have talked about gardens and how much fun it was to grow things yourself and they would both have been very happy.

But no. My friend had slaved to move into this neighborhood and she still felt, in spite of the fact, that she had arrived there, that she was still somehow poor and inferior. And so she pretended that she was Mrs. Smith's maid. "No," she said, "Mrs. Smith is out but I will tell her that you called."

———

The pleasantest way to build a house I think would be to pick out a lot where the town was just beginning to be country. It would not be an expensive lot but it would have an apple tree on it and a couple of other trees and a nice view over the hills. And I would build a stone house that had few and as big rooms as possible and I would arrange them so that the apple tree came just by the back door step. And there wouldn't be any neighbors at first but gradually, as friends came to call, they would begin wondering why they never thought of living there themselves. And we, instead of going out after other people would bring people to us.

And there wouldn't be any worry as to whether the kids were in a fashionable school or not, for about all they could learn in any school would be the multiplication table and the rest they would get at home out of the books in the old secondhand bookcase.

⁓ ⟨ornament⟩ ⁓

5 December 1925, Saturday:

MY friend Mr. O. N. Potter, the well known advertising man, is in trouble. Mr. Potter, who is an apple cheeked bachelor, lives at the Y.M.C.A., and it seems that one of the maids over there during an energetic cleaning up of his room the other day threw out all of Mr. Potter's clippings.

Mr. Potter has been wandering the streets disconsolate ever since. "Why, some of those clippings were invaluable," he mourns. "I'd been collecting them for three years and more."

Fortunately Mr. Potter's personal collection of clippings, those which he carries about in his coat pockets, are still intact.

I think that possibly you may have noticed Mr. Potter and his clippings. First Mr. Potter wears a great suit and then over this he wears a sort of belted raincoat model. This coat is always thrown open and back and it sags rather heavily at the rear. That is because the pockets are full of clippings. They balance the pockets of Mr. Potter's grey suit which are also full of clippings.

———

Mr. Potter had these clippings weighed once and he found they weighed 13 pounds. Mr. Potter keeps adding to them and when his pockets won't hold any more he takes them down into the pressroom of whatever newspaper he happens to be visiting and has them rolled out. This permits him to add quite a few more clippings to the lot.

Mr. Potter's favorite newspaper writer is Dr. Frank Crane.

"Why," he says, "if that man's sentences were to be taken out and broken up into blank verse they'd sound just like Shakespeare." He also approves of the writings of Royal Copeland, Jake Falstaff and others. He cuts them all out and saves them and some day, three years from now, when he wants to prove something, he'll produce the necessary clippings and show you.

It was Mr. Potter who brought the Beacon Journal editorial room a great beautiful watermelon all the way from Iowa last summer, and the other day when I met him on the street he presented me with a handful of chestnuts. It seems he had brought the chestnuts back from the Amish country which he had just been looking over.

"It's a wonderful country," he said, "I'd like to live there some day. Why, the people are so honest that even the chestnuts haven't any worms in them."

And I guess it is true. They were very good chestnuts.

Mr. Potter, along with W. T. Sawyer, believes that the Y.W.C.A. is the best place in town to eat. "Do you know what they have over there?" he says. "Mush, old-fashioned mush. I get me a couple of bowls of that and some milk and I tell you it's good. I don't suppose there's any other place in town where you can get it."

Of course Mr. Potter eats other things besides mush. In fact the regular patrons of the Y.W.C.A. always try to get a table near Mr. Potter's just so they can watch him eat.

"But pshaw,'" says Mr. Potter, "I only eat one meal a day so I might as well make it a good one."

It may be this, the mush you know and the pie, together with his love of walking, he has been known to walk all the way to Medina, which has given Mr. Potter his innocent blue eyes and his fresh pink and white skin. This, and the fact that he won't tell how old he is.

I think it was Joaquin Miller who set Mr. Potter the example. "Joaquin Miller," says Mr. Potter, "never would tell how old he was. He said he didn't know because they had lost the family bible. And maybe he had forgotten. Anyway I don't believe in people telling their age – it ain't years that make people grow old, it's ideas."

Neither will Mr. Potter tell what the initial in his name stand for. And perhaps it is just as well. We all should have some mystery about us and Mr. Potter, the frankest, kindest soul who ever lived, has, I am sure, no other.

7 December 1925, Monday:

THERE wasn't much mending to do tonight – just a couple of buttons to sew on and a pair of socks to darn. The darning, I must admit, was something of a disappointment. That was because I tried to do the right thing and use a darning egg. I've never had any real use for a darning egg. That is because years ago when I was first learning to darn we lost the family darning egg. We sought for it high and we sought for it low and finally in desperation we scrubbed up a potato and used that to thrust into the toes and heels of the family hosiery.

The potato, I may as well say right now for the benefit of those who may be caught in a similar predicament served ever so much better than the original darning egg. It had a curve for every conceivable kind of hole – for the great big gaping vent made by a very masculine big toe, for the tiny little hole made by the tack which got out of place in a lady's shoe and made her ever so much torment, and for the yawning, jagged affairs which always managed to appear in my own heels even when the stockings had been guaranteed to wear for six months.

The potato fitted all of these. Once aware of its excellence we gave up the search for the missing darning egg and never under any circumstance would we buy another one.

Tonight, when I tried to do the right thing and use a darning egg, things happened just as I knew they would. The needle, if it went in right on one side, absolutely refused to come out on the other. It got rasped on the hard shiny surface, the darning egg, being black, made it difficult to see the black threads, the sock, being pulled into all sorts of unnatural shapes, curse out full of curves and bumps and the darn itself looked as though it had been made by an impatient bachelor.

Hereafter, I shall put the sock over my hand, just as I have been meant to do in the past. I don't think I shall use a potato. They cost 70 cents a peck.

I don't know whether anyone has ever remarked the sedative effect which darning has on the nerves. To a woman it brings, I imagine, the same calm which a man achieves when he goes fishing. The needle pokes its way in and out. Your eye follows its point and eventually a part of your mind goes to sleep. You hang sort of suspended in contentment. You decide that there is nothing pleasanter than to sit in a warm house and smell the apples in the Chinese dish over on the table. The plot of a romance comes into your head, but you will not sell it to the Liberty magazine. You will not even try to write it. You will keep it all to yourself, for after all, the real things of life are – and the needle comes unthreaded and you stick your thumb, and the button basket falls on the floor, and you remember that you forgot to tell the milk man to leave extra cream in the morning.

A darn is a funny thing, for it always has to be done on the right side. Hems and things should be done on the wrong side, but a darn has to be done right side up so you can see just how it is going to look every step of the way.

One of the things I can't understand is why my darns look as funny after I am through with them. I weave the threads in and out as carefully and as lovingly as though I were making tapestry. And then, just as I am rolling up the sock, I take one last fond look at the darn it is so dreadfully queer looking that I doubt it is mine. There are too many threads here and not enough there, and the whole is bunchy and uneven like a map of Italy. My only consolation is that it isn't nearly so bad as the darning the laundries do.

<hr>

9 December 1925, Wednesday:

WE HAD an argument last night about a man whom I have never seen and whose name I do not know but whom, I am sure, I shall always be very fond of.

This man, it would appear, has never done anything useful all his life. He has never worked, never married, never gone to war, never bought rubber stock, never fixed a furnace, never played golf, never gone to church, never emptied the ice pan under the refrigerator. He has never worried about whether he had a clean collar or where his next meal was coming from or whether there was going to be enough money to bury him with. He lets his relatives do that and meantime he lives in a little room completely lined with books and the only time he ever ventures forth is to walk from this room to the public library and back again.

It was one of his young and animated relatives who was telling us about him. "Why," she said, "he's never lived. He's never done a single thing you could call useful. He's never had a single experience he could call his own. He gets all of his experiences second hand. Out of books."

It was that part about his never having done anything useful which made me know I should love the man. I don't know that I have ever known a person who was absolutely useless. All those I have ever known were filled with a purpose. They had either taken on a great deal of life insurance and were tolling to pay that off so they could retire at 50 and play golf or they had joined the Alexander Hamilton Institute or they were going to Chicago to study for grand opera or they were going to China to save souls.

If you didn't meet them personally you read about them in the magazines. John Jones early resolved that no matter what life did to him he would smile, smile, smile. He is now president of the Goodwill Stocking Factories, has a town house and a country house, a yacht, nine police dogs and a son in Harvard. Emory Emerick at the age of 12 decided that every dime he earned should go into a bank by itself. He is now president of three banks, lives in a house with electric refrigerators in it and goes to the Episcopal church (high), Mary Smith early resolved that she was just as good as any man going. She started in by laying bricks, is now a millionaire contractor to school where they can learn to do esthetic dancing and be directors of the Little Theater movement.

I admit it has infected me along with everybody else. Whenever I meet a child I say, "And now, my dear, what are you going to be when you grow up?"

The child invariably says he doesn't know and I am invariably horrified.

For our whole education has been to show us that the one thing necessary in this world is to be useful. When I was a little girl I used to like to read. "Put that book down and practice your music lessons," wailed the relatives. "Reading will never do you any good but when you grow up you can earn $25 a week maybe giving music lessons."

When the time came to go to high school I consulted with certain teachers about what course I should take. "You want to take Latin," they said, "because you have to have Latin to get into college and then with a college education you can get a teaching position and probably earn as fair a salary as you would at anything."

Nowadays when I talk to youngsters about what courses they are going to take they say, "Well, I'm certainly not going to take Latin or Greek because they're dead, they don't help you any in a job. I suppose I'll take English, that's a cinch course, and then I'll take commercial arithmetic and commercial geography and probably some Spanish because the United States is having a lot of trade with South America these days."

And when you talk with business men about what they would like to see the board of education do, they say, "Well, I'd like to see the girls learn how to cook and sew and run a typewriter so they can support themselves if they don't get married and I'd like to see the fellows turned into good carpenters and machinists. All this fol de rol[94] about dead languages and ancient history is nonsense. They don't help you any to get a job."

Sometimes I've wanted to shriek and ask, "Isn't there anything in the world but jobs, jobs? Do we study music only to become music teachers, do we go to college merely to get a better job? Isn't there anybody in the whole city of Akron who can love a poem or a book or a language for its own sake?

———————

And so it's pleasant to think of that old chap living uselessly among the books he loves. I wonder that the relatives, instead of worrying about his winter flannels, don't run in instead to talk with him every time they get a chance.

The librarian's heart at least must beat a little faster when she sees him coming.

———————

11 December 1925, Friday:

FOR supper the other night we had four broiled perch which had cost 45 cents. Two of the perch were eaten and two were left. The next day I looked in the cook book for the chapter entitled "What To Do with Leftovers: Fish." It said you could make very nice fish croquettes out of fish and hard boiled eggs and white sauce and egg and cracker crumbs and deep fat. So I took the two left over perch and with them I put 15 cents worth of eggs and several cents worth of the other things including butter which is 62 cents a pound and made the croquettes. There were four of these croquettes and two were eaten and two were left.

Now there is no chapter in my cook book on what to do with left over left overs and we have to eat. I myself could eat the croquettes to love them but that is obvious folly and a habit which I am fighting desperately to overcome. Once I made a move to throw the croquettes away. But there arose before my mind the (illegible) figures of that French

———————

[94] "Fol-de-Rol" or Folderol means useless or nonsense, sometimes in reference to an accessory or ornament, and has been used since 1820.

family which could grow fat and happy on what the American woman slips into the incinerator.

I am beginning to wish now that I had thrown the perch away in the first place. It was a lot of trouble cutting the bones out of them, the croquettes obviously cost more than the whole preposition was worth and then there is the mental strain of seeing them lying fat and complacent on a bread and butter plate every time I open the ice box.

Jake Falstaff says that the great trouble with Mrs. Falstaff is that she will throw away the left over breakfast oatmeal which he would like very much to have the next morning but she will save and save the left over Swiss steak which he doesn't care about at all, this is probably only partly true – you know how men exaggerate things. He probably gets the swiss steak the next evening in stuffed peppers only he doesn't know it. But it does seem to me that left overs are a terrible problem. There are about 20 prunes out on the kitchen shelf which are all dried up from long neglect. I thought I would stone for this long neglect by making them into a nice pudding. But the pudding had to have all kinds of egg in it and then there was a custard sauce to finish up with. The prunes didn't seem worth it. Probably we'll have to stew them for breakfast although I like orange juice ever so much better.

I wonder if the men in the rubber factories have such terrific economic problems.

I didn't get much out of "Faber" the newest Wasserman novel to be translated into English. Faber comes home from six years of war and discovers that something has happened to the idyllic love which formerly existed between himself and his wife. The situation I dare say is sufficiently distressing but being a psychological situation it needs careful treatment and Wasserman doesn't seem to have given it that. He has crammed into a slight book which may be read comfortably through in an evening enough material to make five novels. There is Anna Faber and her father's devastating influence upon the lives of her four children, there is the tragedy of Clara Faber, there is the tragedy of Faith, there is the story of the almost mythical Princess and her building of the Children's City, and finally there is the story of Faber and Martina and their love.

You can fancy two or three of these threads being interwoven to form a good heavy German novel well worth the digging out but Wasserman has thrown them together in haste and the net worth is that more of the characters nor their troubles seem to be particularly real. You lay the book down and sleep comfortably through the night and the next morning the only feeling you have is that you with you might have known more about the Princess – a creature who actually appears only a few pages before the book's ending.

12 December 1925, Saturday:

I T WAS sort of nice the other night to read that the old B.J.[95] was starting a campaign to help Akron's 100 neediest families. By this time I dare say the coupons are all in and a couple of the folks who sent them have cut down on their Christmas lists just for the joy of filling up a basket they hadn't anticipated and seeing some little tyke grow goggle-eyed with pleasure.

And when you come to think about it, wasn't it nice of the Beacon Journal to think about it in the first place? For there are newspapers and newspapers, you know.

There are newspapers whose owner lives away off and never looks at anything but the circulation figures and the amount of paid-up advertising. There are newspapers where everybody barks at everybody else and the faces of the help change almost from week to week. There are newspapers where the reporters practically have to punch a time clock and where, when they turn in an expense account, they have to explain why they paid $1.25 for a meal and couldn't get enough to eat for a dollar? There are newspapers so wrapped in conservation that their life blood froze back in '74[96] and they haven't a subscriber anymore under 50 years old. And there are newspapers thriving on sensationalism which lie and distort and intimidate so that they may hand out their daily biliousness to the weak minded.

That's why it is pleasant to work for the Beacon Journal or, if you can't work for it, to find it tucked up by the front door when you come home at night. Not that I think the Beacon Journal's perfect. I don't like the way it splits its infinitives and I think some of its advertising is ugly beyond words. But you know what makes a reporter swear by this paper. It's when you come back from an assignment and you say, "Now I've got all of the story here and I've got the girl's name and her picture. But if you run it it is going to break her heart and ruin her reputation." And the city editor looks it over again and you wait and wait and finally he says, "Well, I guess we'll not run it."

---

[95] Referring to the Beacon Journal

[96] Referring to the year 1874

Not a day passes I dare say when the Beacon Journal isn't doing something to justify its existence on that side which isn't the business side of the ledger. Sometimes, as in the present instance, it lets it be known that there are 100 needy families in Akron and trusts to the good ness of human nature to do the rest. Sometimes just for the fun of it, it gets up picnics for all the school kids in town and it does it merely in the hope that when these kids grow up they'll think back some time and remember that they had a good time. Time after time, where publicity isn't possible, it digs down into its own pockets to relieve the lonely and friendless. And every day of the year, no matter what news matters may be crying for attention, it throws upon its columns for the good of the blind, the crippled, the civic drive, the educational campaign, the little kid who wants to be adopted, the old couple seeking for their son.

Huh, I can hear you saying, all that may be true but you can see what's back of it all. It's just to make people like it better.

Well, bless your heart, isn't that the thing animating all of us?

---

15 December 1925, Tuesday:

D OWN in the VILLAGE there used to be a little restaurant, a little hole in the ground affair, where you knocked three times on the door and after the proprietor had let you in you were served to a very good dinner and a very fair sort of wine. If you behaved yourself and the proprietor liked you you were bowed out with smiles and urged to come again. If you didn't behave and the proprietor didn't like you you [sic]were also bowed out with smiles but this time he seized the occasion to whisper that hereafter when you came you were to knock five times instead of three. "The police, you know." This with a knowing wink.

A week or so later you would take some friends over to this place boasting all the while that "it" was the easiest thing in the world to get if you only know the tricks. And you would knock five times on the door and it would remain steadfastly closed. And you would knock five times again but the entire establishment apparently would be dark and deserted. No friendly door would open to let out the appetizing smell of garlic and spaghetti.

I have wished sometimes that there were a special kind of knock which one could have in common with one's friends and, say, the grocery boy and the laundry boy. Then when other people knocked at the door, you wouldn't have to open it. For even in an apartment house where unremitting vigilance is kept up, the agents still manage to slip in. And it takes such hours and hours of time explaining to this one that you can't buy her cakes because you want to make your own cakes, to another that you can't buy her candy because you simply have to cut out some sweets, to another that you can't subscribe to any more magazines because you never read those you have now, to another that you've just bought four gallons of furniture polish at O'Neil's.

I suppose all of us would like to be as fair as possible to agents – I am sure it must be the hardest business in the world – but if I listened to the please of all of them who come knocking at the door we'd have to turn Rosie back to her original owners, forego all Christmas presents, sell the wedding silver and eat pancakes without syrup for supper.

———————

I understand from my friends who live in houses rather than apartments that it is practically impossible to take a nap or to devote an uninterrupted hour to a book or an acquaintance because of the continual stream of agents at the front door and the back. You will be up in the attic looking for last year's Christmas ornaments and suddenly there will come a violent ring at the front door bell. You tear down the two flights of stairs, sure that it must be a telegram from Great-Uncle Matthew, saying he'll be here for the holidays.

Instead it is a thin faced, rather weary woman who tells you that she'd been sent expressly to call upon you by such and such an organization. You let her into the front room, and then it develops that she is selling a set of music books for children. She has the samples all nicely tucked away in her coast pockets. When they are all spread out you wonder how in in the world she managed to look so thin. She starts her sales talk and after you think you have been polite long enough to tell her that you have no children, that you have no piano, that you have no money, and that even if you did have 10 children, two grand pianos and a million dollars you still wouldn't buy that particular set of books. But it does no good. She is sure you could buy them as a Christmas present for your second cousin Alice's little niece Ishbell, that the cost is a mere trifle, only 27 cents a day, and that maybe some day you will have a piano, one of those nice ones you can buy on the installment plan. If that doesn't work she tells you how she's a poor widow working to bring up three little girls, and if that doesn't work she gets downright mad and tells you a few things.

The result is that your afternoon is ruined, you feel you've been a brute, you hate all widows, you have to postpone looking for the Christmas ornaments to another day, and you haven't time to make the rice custard for supper.

I've been told by those who know more about it than I do the rates an agent rarely pays. The agents tramp wearily from one house to the other and eventually they drop out and their places are taken by other weary ones. If this is true, I wish it could be thoroughly advertised. A world without agents would be a much happier place to live in.

— ⁓⁓ ✦ ⁓⁓ —

17 December 1925, Thursday:

ON a cosy grey morning like this with the wind whistling outside and no heat in the radiators there is really nothing pleasanter than to drop your typewriter on your knee and do your daily stint in bed. It gives you that grand careless feeling and if your elbows get too cold you can always stop a minute and put them under the covers . . . The only trouble is the typewriter seems to tip a little. I wonder if the cook book would help – then two cook books. I wonder if there's anything in either of them about mushrooms but I suppose you could just broil them with the steak and put butter on them. Isn't it nice, to write this way in bed – I bet a person could write a lot of novels . . . The Christmas tree will look nice over there by the fireplace – I wish they had had green holders instead of blue though. Maybe we can paint it. If we do I'll have to do it myself – Bill won't. Maybe we'd better put it over there by the window – it'll get more air that way – that one last year would have lasted a month . . . There's somebody at the door – wouldn't it be lovely if it was the janitor – then I could tell him – Oh yes, Yeager's – just put them there on the table – it's pretty cold out I guess isn't it? Yes, it's so cold in here I have to stay in bed to keep warm . . . Now I wonder if I should have told him that – why DO I have to be so confiding . . . Lights for the tree will cost two dollars and something and if we get three strands that'll be six something. I don't see why they should cost that much . . . I wonder what Eleonor Meherin gets for writing "Sandy?" I guess she gets a lot, I should think if a person got up like this and wrote in bed every morning they could soon write a serial – it's so easy to concentrate. I bet I could write one. It would have to be about a flapper and she would have to be very beautiful and you could make it just dangerous enough, you know, only everything would end happily and you could sell it for $25,000 to say nothing of the movie rights . . . I wonder what I'd do with $25,000. I could get a flower to put in the kitchen window and some new phonographs records and four strands of lights for the Christmas tree and . . . Oh I know what I'd do – I'd move into a place where the radiators weren't temperamental . . . I wonder how those people who used to live in cold attics got along. Maybe they wrote in bed. If I had my choice of going cold and hungry and eventually being famous or of keeping warm all my life and having enough to eat I wonder which I'd choose. Why couldn't a person be rich and famous both, I bed they could. I bet all this talk about poverty being conducive to greatness is just to make us contented with our lot . . . Of course it's nice to write in bed – you can concentrate so well – I wish the telephone wouldn't ring just when I'm getting started . . . That reminds me, I must call up Edith Sadler and tell her how glad I am she's elected president of the Business

Women's club. And I must order some holly – I guess I've got enough red ribbons – why is it that red always looks prettier at Christmas time than any other – I guess maybe it's because it's such a warm color. Wouldn't it be nice if the radiators were warm – hot – boiling . . . I wonder if that chap was serious who was going to put away ten dollars at interest for a thousand years and then give it to some university or other. I wonder where the universities will be a thousand years from now – and this country – and the banks. The interest on ten dollars for a thousand years ought to be a lot of money – maybe a million. I'd like to figure it up only I never could do those problems in school and anyway it would take a lot of paper. I wonder what I'd do with a million dollars. We could get a lot of Christmas tree lights and maybe have Katie come twice a week and – that's a funny creaky wagon going by outside – no it isn't – oh Gods periwinkles and lambkins, it is, it's the heat coming on in the radiators.

<hr>

18 December 1925, Friday:

EVERY once in a while you go visiting for the night or you meet with a crowd of high school youngsters whereupon somebody thrusts an autograph album at you with the request that you write something clever in it.

Now I take it that in the old days there were people who could do that sort of thing. They could toss off something, "to Julia" or "to Lucasia" or "to My Lady on Seeing the Dimple in Her Elbow" and it was really quite good.

But when anybody asks me to write anything clever in an album I can think of but two things. One is, "As sure as the vine grows round the stump you are my precious sugar lump" and the other is, "Roses are red, violets are blue, sugar is sweet and so are you."

There was a singer a couple of years ago who gave me her photograph and on the bottom of it she wrote in French, "To Josephine whom I know so little and yet love so much." She did it so readily that I couldn't get over the feeling that she had probably written that same sentiment to dozens of other people. For I just can't believe that there are people in the world who can think up appropriate things to say on the spur of the moment.

Somebody was saying last night that this was probably due to the decline of letter writing. And he cited the tremendous number of greeting cards covering all sorts of occasions which we find these days in the gift shops.

<hr>

Certain it is that there is a precious little need these days of thinking up your own message of condolence, cheer and congratulation. There are cards for the fellow to whom you would like to send a Christmas present but haven't the money, for the fellow whom you meant to buy a present for but forgot, for the old schoolmate whom you last saw 10 years ago and who is now in the hospital with lumbago, and for the man who has just become the happy father of twins.

Somebody else has thought up the sentiment appropriate to the occasion, somebody else has set it down in verse, somebody else has but it to just the proper dimensions and somebody else has made the cartoon to go with it. All you have to do is to put down a quarter and lick the stamp.

And yet I don't think that letter writing has really gone into a decline. It seems to me that I get a great many letters which are very worth while indeed and I dare say that others have the same experience.

To be sure the letters I like best are the kind which a good many persons are inclined to sniff at. They are the letters which come from somebody back home, they are fat and bulgy and sometimes they are written first in pencil and then traced over with ink. They state that the cat ate 32 cents worth of liver last week, that the living room curtains have just been washed and they look awful pretty now they're hung up, that Mrs. H. is poorly and they think it's a floating kidney, and that Mr. K's hens are laying fine, that the old man is thinking some of getting a radio, that they had pumpkin pie for dinner Sunday, that the Methodist church has a new preacher who has some terribly advanced views, and that Mary, the black washerwoman has some new false teeth. After going through 10 pages of details like that you feel as though you've been back to the home town and gossiped with everybody on the street.

One of the great troubles with the letters which come this way is that about two-thirds of them come accompanied with the adjuration, "Now for heaven's sake don't print this. It is just for you alone." And I always grieve considerably because I love to share things.

Ancient Admirer is about the only person who is considerate in this respect. He just sends his letters on and you can do what you please with them. Sometimes I have a feeling that he is really this column's sole contributor. Somebody was saying the other night that we ought to have a contributor's banquet but you know how dismal such an affair would be. Ancient Admirer and I sitting with a bottle of gingerale and a couple of macaroons at some lonely table somewhere – no new faces to look at, no new views to listen to, no nom de plumes to be unraveled.

No, I guess such an affair will never be.

If a starfish finds a tidbit too large for it to swallow, it extends its stomach out of its mouth and digests the morsel outside.

---

23 December 1925, Wednesday:

IT seems to me that it is pleasanter to open them as they come instead of waiting for Christmas. Christmas is such a short day. Some persons make their annual pilgrimage to church on that day and there are the family presents to be opened and the Christmas dinner to be eaten and the calls to make bearing gifts and the calls to receive from others bearing gifts. All in all it is too short a day considering all the preparations we make for it. The best we can do is to stretch it out a little by opening the presents as they come. I opened such a nice one a little while ago. Now I'll be able to smile about it all week.

I've taken to reading the London Mercury lately. It is very different from our American Mercury – so soothing, so restful. This month's issue contained the announcement that henceforth the London publication would contain a department devoted to the movies seeing that this industry was really arriving at considerable proportions, a poem called "Falstaff's Sister" which I loved, an announcement of a sale of some manuscript of Burns and others, two stories in neither of which I got the point and a corking good article on Edith Wharton. It seems it is the intention to discuss one American author each month and Edwin Arlington Robinson. Vachel Lindsay and Willa Cather are among those set down for future consideration.

After I had finished the London Mercury I had a delightful nap. I've been wondering since what it would seem like to live in a land where there was no Ku Klux, no prohibition and no vigilance committees and where one could step out into cities which were two thousand years old.

Sometimes it seems to me that the school histories and the returning missionaries have done us a great wrong. The school histories tell us from the time we are little tads that

America is the greatest country in the world, that her constitution is perfect, and her statesmen have been impeccable, that her wars have always been fought from the noblest motives. And when we read how the whole of Germany could be tucked away in a part of Texas we nearly burst with pride.

And then the missionaries come back from foreign countries and they tell of the dreadful goings on in India, of the terrible blood-thirsty Turk (really you know he ought to be the prohibitionists' ideal), of the backwardness of poor China.

I talked with such a missionary once. She had been down in India for 20 years. She pictured a people so full of sickness and despair that my heart bled. And then I found out that in all those 20 years she had never bothered to learn a line of Hindu dialect, had never read a line of Hindu philosophy. The poor wretches who came to her could talk to her in English or not at all and she had never been even faintly curious as to what might be going on in their heads.

There is a novel here in our bookcase called "The Stranger" written by a man named Arthur Bullard whom I never heard of. It is a very straight-forward piece of work done without my attempt at fine writing but after you have finished it you feel that you have a far more honest picture of the orient than you are liable to get from the average missionary tract. At least you feel that the poor oriental has two or possibly three virtues.

And yesterday I read a poem written by a Chinaman who lived something like 400 before Christ. In it he deprecated the tendency of the Chinese businessman to chase dollars to the peril of his soul.

Somehow when you consider the size of the world and the age of it and the tremendous variety of it you wonder at these nice Sunday school going young men who can conceive of no greater thrill in life than to go snooping around to find out what's in the bottle on their neighbor's medicine closet.

---

25 December 1925, Friday:

I HAVE been thinking that if any of us have a half hour to ourselves today, say sometime between four and six when the Christmas pudding has at last began to sit comfortably and some of the folks are upstairs taking naps and the children have gone to the neighbors, it might be a good thing to roach along the book shelf and take down Josephine Preston Peabody's drama of the Pied Piper of Hamelin.

Most persons of course will maintain that dickens, and Dickens only, is the ideal Christmas reading, but we have had old Scrooge and tiny Tim for so many years now. It really would pay to get better acquainted with the Piper. To be sure, nowhere in the drama does the word Christmas occur, but there is a great deal in it about children, whose very special holiday this is, and about the Lonely Man, who loved them and whose birthday we are celebrating, and finally there is the figure of the Piper himself, who did not care particularly for the winter-locked hearts of Hamelin.

I was reading now at the end of the play where the Piper is kneeling at a wayside shrine and pleading against taking the children back to Hamelin.

"I will not, no, I will not, Lonely Man!
I have them in my hand, I have them all -
All - all! And I have lived unto this day.
You understand ....
You know what men these are
And what have they to do with such as these?
Think of those old as death in body and heart,
Hugging their wretched hoardings, in cold fear
Of moth and rust? While these miraculous ones,
Like golden creatures made of sunset clouds,
Go out forever - every day, fade by
With music and wild stars! - Ah, but You know,
The hermit told me once, You loved them, too
But I know more than he how You must love them:
Their laughter, and their bubbling sky lark words
To cool Your heart. Oh, listen Lonely Man!
....

Oh, let me keep them! I will bring them to You,
Still nights, and breathless mornings; they shall touch
Your hands and feet with all their swarming hands,
Like showering petals warm on furrowed ground -
All sweetness! They will make Them whole again.
With love. Then wilt look up and smile on us!
....

Why not I know - the half - You will be saying.
You will be thinking of Your Mother. - Ah
She was different. She was not as they.
Here in some dawn of day for Hamelin - now!
'Tis hearts of men You want. No mumbled prayers;
Not greed and carven tombs, not misers' candles;
No offerings, more, from men that feed on men;
Eternal psalms and endless cruelties!...
Even from now, there may be hearts in Hamelin.
Once stabbed awake!

Look,	Lonely	Man!		You	shall	have	all	of	us
To	wander	the	world	over,		where	You		stand
At	all	the	cross	ways	and	on	lonely	hills	–
Outside	the	churches		where	the	lost	ones	go!	–
And	the	way	faring	men,	and	thieves	and		wolves
And	lonely	creatures,		and	the		ones	that	sing!
We	will	show	all	men	what	we	hear	and	see;
And	we	will	make	Thee	lift	Thy	head	and	smile."[97]

---

26 December 1925, Saturday:

"**D**EAR JO: (writes Lucia)

"Something should be done about this Christmas card business.

"Not only does it embarrass me financially but also mentally so great is the struggle to be different yet also in good taste. Each January during the painful ordeal of distributing small monetary portions among Christmas creditors, I make firm resolution to send no cards the following Yuletide. Then along about October comes a gift shop salesman. I look through the assortment and the salesman leaves with an order. Worse yet – the simple card with corresponding simple price which I had in mind appears commonplace under his suave demonstration and when I sign my name on the dotted line, I have ordered something different and also something expensive.

"I have passed through various stages in my quest of the distinctive. After successive seasons of wise men and old English coach scenes I tried the personal note. Snap shots of the entire family including Junior and the Pup.

"A cheerful though misleading touch to this particular card was a luxurious fireplace with huge burning logs prominently placed in the center. This feature produced the desired effect on one's long distant friends, but locally no doubt caused loud laughter from those persons acquainted with the gas logs in our simple dwelling. Moreover the informal snap-shots didn't seem to come out just right. I looked as if I were recovering

---

[97] The Pied Piper of Hamelin, a play in Four Acts, by Josephine Preston Peabody. Published by Houghton Mifflin, 1909-1911. The Original is held with the Library of Congress.

from a very long and severe illness, eternally bringing upon myself the 'hasn't she aged' remarks from the catty.

"After my cards have been sent and I am complacent in the thought of a duty well done, along come greetings from sources I have entirely overlooked. Then there is a last minute frantic search over leftovers which bear sentiments 'to Dad' or of such clownish nature as to be altogether impossible.

Well, I haven't sent any Christmas cards for a good many years now but it wasn't intrepidity. It was simply that I was appalled at the proportions the thing was assuming. After all there are perhaps a dozen persons to whom one needs to send a Christmas greeting. Six of these you can call on the telephone and the other six you can write personal notes to. The hundred or so others to whom you send your engraved greetings have open only one possible procedure. They open it, run their fingers over it to see whether it is really engraved, make a mental note to thank you for it when they see you and put it on the mantel over the fireplace. Sometime before New Year's the whole lot goes into the wastebasket.

We used to try to save them at our house. Most of them were so handsome it seemed a shame to throw them away. And we saved them in hat boxes and shoe boxes and bushel baskets from one year to the next and finally we saw the uselessness of it all.

Ordinarily my mind doesn't run in practical channels at all but when I see the stacks and stacks of cards adorning our gate log table, grateful as I am for the thoughtfulness behind it all, I can't help thinking of all the dollars there represented. And seeing that most of us are sort of strapped for funds at Christmas time anyway, wouldn't it be better to forego the engraved card notion and devote the ten or twenty or more dollars represented to some little kid who hasn't had much of a chance?

And afterwards let's take up the matter of Christmas candy.

---

29 December 1925, Tuesday:

ONE of the things for which the business woman always pities the stay at home woman is the circumstance that the latter never meets any interesting people. It must be dreadful, she reflects, to stay cooped up within four walls all day and never have anybody to talk to but the grocery boy or a chance brush peddler.

And then she swings around in her chair and starts pounding the typewriter and between times during the day talks with the following persons:

A doting father who has five sons all in the Boy Scouts. He gives a detailed account of just how far each one has progressed.

An elderly gentleman with a German Bible published in 1870. He is sure it must be worth a real deal of money.

A woman acquaintance who would like to convert her to a new religion.

Another woman acquaintance who has just been to the movies and still has another hour on her hands before it is time to go home and get supper.

Four men who have just heard a dandy new joke. It is a variation of the same one she heard at Chautauqua last summer.

A man taking subscriptions for a number of magazines which she doesn't want.

A woman selling a new kind of lingerie.

A man selling silk stockings three pairs for five dollars.

A boy selling corn crisp.

A woman selling homemade chocolate creams.

A Western Union messenger boy.

A fellow who met a swell girl at the Eagles[98] last night.

----

[98] The Eagles Temple, a prominent Fraternal Order of Eagles building in Akron high-styled in Art Deco architecture and home to thousands of members.

Now I don't know but it seems to me the conversations one has at home are just as pleasant. There is the morning conversation when one orders groceries. You don't k now who the young man is at the other end of the line but his voice, dear, dear!

"Good morning," you say, "I'd like a box of baking soda."

"The ten cent size or the five cent size?" he queries.

"Oh I don't know, the ten cent size I guess."

"The ten cent size is a pretty big box. It lasts a long time you know."

"Oh all right then, send me the five cent size. I don't do much baking.

"No, and besides one never used much soda anyway. How about some nice oranges this morning. We have some lovely ones at 60 cents a dozen."

"Well, all right. No I guess you'd better not. We have quite a few left over from Christmas yet. Oh I'll tell you, have you some nice apples this morning?"

"Yes we have some nice apples. How many would you want?"

"Are they all right for pies?"

"Yes they are nice Baldwins. You can use them for cooking or eating either one."

"Well then, send me three pounds, no four pounds, no, I guess three will be enough."

You can string it out that way for ages – and when there's that little touch of mystery of not knowing whom you're talking to. Really it gives a tremendous zest to housekeeping.

And after a while the laundry boy comes and you have a lengthy discussion with him on the merits of the valet system and whether it's going to be a cold winter and he tells you about his mother's cough and then the janitor drops in for a minute and tells you about his wife's rheumatism and then the grocery boy comes and he's forgotten the whipping cream and you have to call up the grocery and have one of those nice conversations all over again.

Really I can't see where staying at home is so dull.

30 December 1925, Wednesday:

A RED BIRD was fluttering around the kitchen window this morning. He was such a splendid fellow that ordinary bread crumbs somehow seemed inadequate. And so I gave him some of the Christmas fruit cake. He ate it uttering contented little chirps all the while and the sparrows, their feathers fluffed out to unnatural plumpness, sat about on the bushes and watched him. Afterwards they flew down and ate what was left.

Most persons I know have an intense dislike for the sparrow. There is one woman in particular whose annoyance at them is so great as to amount to mental distress. No matter where she goes to live, and she has moved about a good deal from place to place, there is sure to appear, about the third day, a male sparrow who takes his place somewhere along the neighbor's eaves and starts to chirp. Other members of the family, so far as I know, are never aware of it. But my friend becomes sleepless from the annoyance, she grows wan and pale and nervous and nothing will do but that her husband must buy a shotgun and dispatch the disturber.

This, eventually, he does and there is peace for a week or two until a sparrow appears on some other eave and starts to chirp.

In the winter, possibly because the sparrows are unusually quiet then, my friend seeks to atone for everything by feeding them generously from the bread box and bewailing the fact that undoubtedly next summer they will repay her by waking her up at 4 o'clock every morning.

But I like the sparrows somehow. For one thing they are smart enough never to be caught by the cat. And they subsist, goodness only knows how, through the very coldest of winters while other birds make for the enervations and soft dalliances of the south. It happens perhaps once in a year that I can look out of my window on a cold day such as this is and see a cardinal. But the sparrows are always there, fluffed out on the bushes, their tails perky as ever, their little feet shifting from twig to twig as the cold gets too much for them.

Moreover for those of us who must spend our lives close to city streets the sparrows are almost the only birds we come to know. There are certain colored books gotten out which tell you all about the lettuce bird and the tanager and the oriole, their habits and size and the length of their tails. But these are futile, as descriptions always are. For my own part I'd like to see a book all about the sparrow. Then I could say, "Why yes, I've noticed that myself."

Mary and Ellen and Carol and John came over to see the Christmas tree this afternoon. For a time the atmosphere was somewhat constrained. I think there had been some parting instructions before they left home about polite behavior. I was really a little worried about them. Mary and Ellen and Carol sat in a row with their dolls and John balanced himself on the edge of his chair only making occasional flourishes with his wooden sword.

Eventually, however, John came across the little cedar chest which had come from Panama with candy in it. John decided he would play pirate. Mary and Ellen and Carol promptly abandoned their dolls and decided they would play pirate too. The bathtub became the ship. The idea was that you stood on the edge of the tub band then jumped. This was called walking the plank.

After that everything was normal.

I find though that I really don't know much about children. I had counted on the ice cream creating a sensation. On the contrary it was a distinct flop. Ellen brought hers back first. "If anybody wants this," she said politely, "they can have it because I don't like it."

Then Mary and Carol brought theirs, "it's too much," they said. "We can't eat it."

Only John stood valiantly by. "It's really a shame," he said, "especially when you tired so hard to please us. Believe me I'm going to eat all of mine if I bust. However, if you ever should be having us over again you needn't bother about having ice cream because you know a lot of children don't like it."

They went home a little while ago. They said they had a very nice time.

---

31 December 1925, Thursday:

DOROTHY DIX had something to say about happiness the other night. She said it consisted in making up your mind what you wanted and then going after it.

That is one view. Another view, an oriental one, seems to be that happiness lies in not wanting anything at all. At any rate, I remember reading a fairy tale as a child called "The Shirt of Happiness." It seems that an eastern kind fell grievously ill and in attempting to prescribe for him a good many of the court physicians lost their heads. Finally some old crone who had been hanging about the bake ovens in their kitchen sticking her fingers in the roast when the cook wasn't looking announced that the kind would be cured when he should put on his back the shirt of an absolutely happy man.

Straightway an immense caravan set out with the intention of finding such a man and taking his shirt from him. They had a good many adventures. Eventually one of the number came upon a man singing by the road side. This fellow, it appeared, didn't have anything, never had had anything and didn't expect to have anything. The king's emissary was delighted. "At last," he exclaimed, "I have found an absolutely happy man. Would you be so kind as to give me your shirt?"

"Why," answered the happy fellow, "I'd be only too glad to, but you see I have no shirt."

Edwin Markham made a poem on this theme, but possibly because he thought a shirt wasn't refined enough he called his poem "The Shoes of Happiness." The idea, however, was the same.

There are a good many other admonitions which have to do with happiness, one being that it is better to love than to be loved and another being, that it is more blessed to give than to receive. Neither of these I suspect is wholly true. At any rate I love to receive.

But the greatest, most poignant happiness, I have fond, lies in doing something for somebody else and finding they appreciate it.

In that event someone in Akron should be made very, very happy by the following letter which came through the mails yesterday. It was written on Christmas evening by a woman who has had much to contend with. She did not say that I might not and so I am using her name, which is Mrs. Davis, 248 Tallmadge av., Cuyahoga Falls.

"I am one of the poor," she writes, "whose family of children has been made happy by the generous gifts of people belonging to different organizations in Akron and Cuyahoga Falls. I am poor because they heavy hand of affliction has been laid upon me through one of my children. There are four others to be provided for and everything that was given me this Christmas by all these kind hearted people is going to help us this winter more than any of them will realize.

"Everything was so nice and wrapped up so prettily and carefully that we are overwhelmed with gratitude. I wish I could thank each person who has worked so hard the busy days before Christmas to get things ready so that a child might be made happy.

I know where some of the present for other families have also brought more joy and happiness than ever, the donors had wished they would.

"But the best of all is for people such as we are to know that there is so much sweetness and generosity in a world where there is also hardship and affliction."

There were a lot of lovely things which came our way this Christmas but somehow I liked that letter best.

Chapter VIII.

Demi-Tasse & Mrs. Grundy in The year 1926

Demi – Tasse

- and -

Mrs. Grundy

- by -

Josephine Van de Grift

───────※───────

1 January 1926, Friday:

ONE of the mistakes which most of us make in our New Year's resolutions is that we generally resolve upon things which, if carried out, would of necessity, make us disagreeable to other people. We will go to church every Sunday, we will tell no more lies, we will arise at seven every morning and take a cold bath, we will cut out apple pie.

If we succeed in carrying any of these out we become boastful and if we fail to carry them out we become melancholy and in either event nobody will love us. And what, I ask you, is existence without love?

───────

To sleep as long as possible every morning.

To do as little work as possible every day.

To eat a great many chocolate eclairs.

To keep open house at all times.

At all times to have extra boiled potatoes in the ice box.

To be kinder to my friends.

To ignore absolutely my enemies.

To wear loud and flashy clothes.

To throw left-over spinach into the incinerator.

To open as many charge accounts as possible and keep them going.

To tell the truth only when it makes the other fellow happy.

To spend a lot of time talking over the telephone.

To make no effort to tell funny stories.

To make no effort to interrupt husband when he is telling a funny story.

To agree with women friends that Mae Murray is a grand actress.

To agree with men friends that war is necessary.

To agree with other men friends that coca cola and the latest importation from Furnace st. makes a grand combination.

To keep cigarets on hand for visiting women friends.

To have the guest towels laundered.

To read a risqué magazine every week.

To buy some jazz records for the Victrola.

To launder the living room curtains only at Easter and Thanksgiving.

To serve more canned beans.

1 February 1926, Monday:

W E USED to refer to him as Ambrose, And then when he came he was a girl. And so we have named her Mary in the hope that she will grow up to be mild and sweet and good like that other Mary.

It is queer though how the thought of Ambrose still persists, as though there had actually been such a little boy and he had gone away.

Of course his name wasn't really to be Ambrose. That was just a joke. His name was to be something very masculine sounding, like Bill or John.

But you know how it is with names of that sort. You give them in jest and after a while the jest vanishes and they seem to belong. And I think that if he had ever come actually to be born I would always have called him Ambrose in my heart. That is the way with notions persisted in too long.

Ambrose was really a very fine little chap although I can't recall that he was in any way remarkable. He used to have a bad habit of coming to the table with very dirty hands. "Ambrose," you would exclaim, "leave the table immediately and wash those hands. The very idea!" And Ambrose would go away and come back a minute later with palms a shade lighter but very shady knuckles. You groaned as you thought of the condition of the towel.

Sometimes Ambrose wasn't old enough to wash his own hands. Then you scrubbed him all up till he shone and dressed him up in his little brown coat with the beaver collar and you went for a walk along Portage Path. And the snow was very white and there were red berries on the bushes and you told him the name of those berries and how they seem to be there in the winter time and you told him how some birds fly south in the winter time but how there are others which prefer to stay with their friends in the north and you told him how the rabbit makes his tracks and how there are caterpillars which sleep all snug and tight in their beds through the long cold months. For you had been reading up on those things just so you could tell them to Ambrose.

And then suddenly Ambrose would become all of nine years old and he would be having a terrible time with his multiplication tables. "No, Ambrose," you would say sternly, "you can't go out to play until you've done the seven's." And while you did the dishes Ambrose would perch on a stool beside the sink and slowly and laboriously work out seven times eight.

And then sometimes Ambrose wouldn't be a little boy at all any more but he would be grown big and strong and would have gone away to college and you would be going to see him play on the football team. You didn't know anything about football but you yelled just the same because you were glad Ambrose was grown up big and strong. You remembered how afraid you used to be when he had to cross the street car tracks.

One thing you never were sure of was just what profession Ambrose was going to take up. You didn't want him to be a minister or a lawyer and you were quite, quite sure you didn't want him to be president of the United States. In a way you thought it would be splendid if he could be a surgeon. Yes, there was Ambrose, a grown man with twinkly eyes and hair a little grey about the temples. His hands were strong and very, very sure. And he worked in a big hospital where there were little children and his strong, sure hands took their little legs and backs and made them straight again.

Suddenly came the disturbing thought that Ambrose would probably insist on choosing his own profession. And Oh, horror of horrors, he would want to choose a wife!

———————

All this, however, as I said before, was obviated by the simple circumstance that when Ambrose came he was a girl.

And so we have named her Mary in the hope that she will grow up mild and sweet and good. About the mildness I don't know, though. Her voice is loud and piercing and when she wants anything she seems to get very red in the face about it.

5 February 1926, Friday:

H AZEL WENDELL and the Romantick came up last night and we got to talking about pullmans. Hazel had just come back from Toledo on the Capitol limited.

"If you ever want grandeur –" she said, spreading out her hands.

It seems the Capitol limited had a diner with little coops at each end where you could sit in with your gentleman friend and have a tete a tete[99]. And the waiters not only wore white coats. They wore white trousers and white shoes as well. And the vestibules were white and had rugs in them where you could shake the snow off your feet. And the chair car carried a manicurist and a barber and a stenographer. And in addition to this, each section of the chair car had great tall partitions so you could sit in what was practically your own little parlor and enjoy the utmost privacy.

―――――――

It was this last luxury that the Romantick and I took exception to. Who wants privacy, demanded the Romantick, when you're traveling? And indeed who does. Of course I suppose one of those rubber officials who has to commute to New York all the time must get pretty bored after a while and would just crave a chance to sink back of a partition and think over the next dividends. But for my own part when I have gone to all the trouble of saving enough money to ride on a pullman I want to see who the other passengers are and if possible get acquainted.

Not that I've ever had any luck. When I was younger I used to make up all sorts of romances every time I went traveling. I would buy my ticket and get on a train and then who of all persons should be my traveling companion but John Barrymore.

―――――――――――――――――――――

[99] A "Tête-à-tête" is a private conversation between two people, and comes from the French word Tête literally meaning 'head to head' conversation.

"Pardon me, Mr. Barrymore," I would say after a while, "but I just can't help speaking to you after your Hamlet. Really I think your acting is wonderful."

"Oh, it's nothing, nothing," he would retort modestly, "but really I don't know when I've met such an intelligent young woman. You know the women in New York are all such duds. May I take you out to supper?"

After that everything was beautiful.

But nothing like that ever really happened. I'll admit that my traveling companion was generally a man, but such men! Coming up from Miami it was a Jewish salesman for women's wear. He said if I ever lost my job on the newspaper I should come to Miami and he would give me a job as a model. He was really terribly agreeable. And then when we got to the Grand Central station he passed me in tow of a very corpulent woman. He looked at me kind of scared and didn't say a word.

Coming back to Akron there was a Greek candy merchant who got off at Youngstown. He wanted my telephone number but when I told him I was a newspaper reporter he sort of lost interest.

And coming down from Albany there were two physicians. It was a chair car this time and they didn't know I was in the chair. They started talking shop. I dare say it would not have embarrassed them if they had known I was there but at that time I wasn't sure. So I slunk back in my chair and they talked shop and still more shop and I suffered and suffered.

While traveling on a pullman I have never met anyone handsome, anyone interesting, anyone under fifty. But I don't want any high partitions put up I still haven't lost hope.

6 February 1926, Saturday:

OUR Rosie is getting pretty wheezy now and there are a couple of rents in her roof where the rain comes through. And so we went to the auto show the other night.

Howard Taylor was there telling folks what a grand car the Cadillac was and right beside him was Dave Towell handing out sales talk and never paying the slightest bit of attention to the pretty girls strolling by and we saw Enoch Jones and Bert Eckermann, although what possible detecting he could do at an auto show I don't know, and Harry Harriman and Henry Heeps and Dr. Bottsford who said he'd just come down to look at the Fords and Lisle Croy and Bee in a good looking hat and quite a number of other people.

Every once in a while we'd come across a six-cylinder sport model with a couple of girls sitting in it trying not to look self-conscious. Bill said he couldn't see what thrill they got out of a stunt like that. But I know. First they were hoping that a good looking fellow would come along and notice them and take them over to the Greeks for ice cream and maybe to the East Market gardens. And to the back of her head one of them was pretending she was a movie queen and this was her own car and she was making two thousand a week and in the back of her head the other one was pretending that she was engaged to a millionaire and he had just given her this car and she was waiting for him out in front of his brokerage office.

Of course when whole families travel from exhibit to exhibit and climb into all the care and bounce up and down on the upholstering I don't know what they pretend. Maybe they enjoy the bouncing and then maybe they like that way of putting in an evening.

It hurt me though to think of Rosie being exchanged for any of these shiny new upstarts with its wire wheels and its dabs of red and its nickel plating. Who knows how Rosie might be looking today if ever she'd had a chance?

What Rosie's past may have been I do not know but I do know that since she's been with us she's had no luxury. She's had a great deal of love but no luxury. All summer long she stood out on highways and in the back alley and the sun beat down on her and blistered her paint. And when winter came she still stood out in the back alley and her radiator froze and the snow piled up on her hood and her steps and all over her top. And yet, a little dusting with the broom, a kettle of hot water, a few tender words, and Rosie would start to wheeze and then to thump and then to purr and suddenly she would be off, up the hills and down again, past the filling stations and the garages and the hot dog stands, only coming to a stop whenever a cop hove abruptly into view.

Of course Rosie had to have repairs. Sometimes it was a question whether to have Rosie repaired or pay the rent. Eventually we would decide to pay the rent and then Rosie would have to be coaxed along with special tenderness. Coming out Merriman road she would frequently show an inclination to stop altogether. Then Bill would have to speak to her. "Here, here now," he would say "none o' that, none o' that," and Rosie would struggle and heave and start on her way again.

Going through the auto show I couldn't help wondering if Rosie had ever been bright and shining and chipper like these other models and what her ambitions had been in those days. I hope she has been happy with us. And I hope that whoever gets her will be good to her.

***

8 February 1926, Monday:

BILL was reading last night about some hospital which had adopted the slogan, "Some day you may need our help, help us when we need yours."

I don't know whether I know much about hospitals. A couple of times I've had to go over to the city hospital to interview Arden Hardgrave, the first time on "Why the nurses do bob their hair." And once, it must be four or five years ago now, they let me go into the nursery and see all the babies. I think it was feeding time and the babies were all wrapped in their blankets and laid out on their carts to be trundled down the hall. They looked like so many tight little loaves of bread. Aside from that I thought a hospital was a place where they dosed you with a great deal of medicine and the nurses were all stern and very, very ancient.

Now, having spent a couple of weeks in one, I know better. A hospital is like a nice hotel. They bring you ice water every little while. They bring very nice meals to you on trays. You get clean sheets every day. They put a brass reading lamp by your bed's head and a bell so you can ring if you want anything. You have to get awfully cantankerous and work up a fever over something before they'll give you any medicine. And the nurses –

Bill was always pretty enthusiastic about nurses. When he was in the Army of Occupation there were six of them in the village and he always says that war is a wonderful thing and he'd go right away if we ever had another one. Now I know why.

It was at the People's hospital where I spent my two weeks' vacation. Along about seven o'clock in the morning Miss Tryon would come in with the breakfast tray. I wish you could see Miss Tryon. She is young and pretty and sweet and if it weren't for her white uniform you would never believe that she was a graduate nurse and had gone through all kinds of heavy text books. Miss Tryon confessed that she liked to get out in the snow and hike and that she always washed her face in cold water and this, I haven't the slightest doubt, was responsible for her lovely complexion.

A little while later Miss Worden would come to give you your bath. Miss Worden came from Canada and while she smoothed the sheets she would tell you about the new little house her mother had just bought. Miss Worden liked to dance and she washed her face every night before she went to bed which, no doubt, was responsible for her lovely complexion.

Miss Worden would take the flowers out and put fresh water on them and then after her would come Miss Atwell bearing something all wrapped up in a pink blanket. "The baby gained two ounces yesterday," she would announce and then, if she had a minute to stay, she would tell you how she had her future life all planned. How she had come from Omaha and how soon she expected to go on to the east and take work in a children's hospital. For Miss Atwell loved children above all else and intended to give her whole life to them.

And then when night came Miss Ethels would bring you your hot malted milk and put up the window and give you an extra blanket and put out the light and shut the door and everything would be quiet. And hours would pass and out through the window you could see the lights on one of the downtown banks blinking and still sleep wouldn't come and finally in desperation you would put on your signal light and you would hear someone running up the steps and your door would open and a soft voice would say, "What did you want?"

This would be Miss Tarr. And Miss Tarr would get you the drink you wanted or put the window further up or put it down or turn off the heat or turn it on, anything to make you comfortable and let you go to sleep. Dear, dear Miss Tarr.

And so I hope the hospitals will be successful in their drive. Because some day you may have an ache or a pain or an accident and then you will first appreciate what it means to have someone gentle and capable to smooth the sheets and bring you a drink in the long night hours and put the window up and down.

9 February 1926, Tuesday:

JOYCE KILMER had a queer notion, according to a biography of him we were reading the other night. It was that food atoned for the loss of sleep. And he would tell of how a struggling young stenographer had supported a whole family of younger brothers and sisters by taking home extra work evenings and then sitting up all night and eating.

It is encouraging to find somewhere – anywhere – a kind word is favor of eating. Jake Falstaff maintains that eating is one of the major delights and I dare say that until 10 or 15 years ago practically everybody would have admitted that it was at least a minor delight. But nowadays, eating is regarded as a sort of grossness. It is a necessity, people grudgingly admit, but an unpleasant one and something to be gotten over with as quickly as possible.

"Let's run in here and have a tea," say my friends gaily when I meet them on Main st. And I "run" in and I order a shrimp salad and sandwiches and hot chocolate and bon bons and ice cream. My friend orders a cup of tea and some saltines. She doesn't put any sugar in the tea and I frequently reach over and finish her saltines.

Now that Dr. Lulu Hunt Peters is writing for the Beacon Journal I feel as though I were making a desperate stand by the last trench. For Dr. Peters has a sense of humor, and when a woman displays a sense of humor about anything the situation for the other fellow is well nigh hopeless.

Now tonight, providing the oven works, we're going to have mince pie and roast beef. I hope that Bill brings home somebody pleasant to supper, and that the table legs don't wobble. I hope that the pie holds together and that the beef is tender. I hope that the Victrola doesn't wheeze and that we sit around and drink coffee and read things out of books and talk for a long time afterwards. And if all these things come to pass then it seems to me that going on a diet and acquiring a slim shape and being able to wear the current fashions and living to an old, old, lean, old age could hardly be worth the candle.

I realize, however, that the tide is all against me. One of these days, they'll even start to legislate about it. Somebody – Mr. Volstead's grandson, maybe – will get congress to pass a bill making it unlawful to eat only so and so much. They will outlaw the potato, the caramel pudding and the pork chop absolutely. When I go over to the Acme, I'll have to carry along a little card entitling me to four carrots and so much spinach. When I want to give a dinner party, I'll have to pull down the shades and bribe the corner policeman with a pint of ice cream. And Monday's newspapers will carry doleful accounts of people who collapsed over the week-end from eating lemon cream pie. When

They do these things, they tell us, so that we can think higher thoughts, save our money, find things to fit us at the bargain sales and live to a ripe old age. But I don't know. Sometimes I wonder if it's going to be much fun living to a ripe old age.

12 February 1926, Friday:

THOMAS EDISON was 79 years old yesterday. But if I had been at the birthday dinner I think that instead of devoting my attention to Thomas I would have talked instead with Mrs. Edison[100]. And I would have asked her about the trials and tribulations of being an inventor's wife.

Thomas, say the newspapers, has been in the habit of spending 18 to 20 hours daily in his laboratory. Now you know what that means, No Thomas at all at breakfast and luncheon. An absent minded Thomas at dinner.

"Thomas," I am sure Mrs. Edison must have said hundreds of times, "something has gone wrong with the washing machine. I wish you would please fix it."

"Eh what, what was that?"

"I said something was wrong with the washing machine and wouldn't you please fix it."

"Why certainly, certainly, be glad to."

And Thursday would go by and Monday would come and then a whole procession of Mondays and still the washing machine wouldn't be fixed. Thomas would be too busy figuring up the electricity that was wasted every minute at Niagara Falls.

And I dare say when they were first married Mrs. Edison must have had a terrible time keeping her house in order. Just about the time she got the kitchen cupboards

---

[100] This would be Mina Miller, Thomas Edison's second wife he married in 1886, after he was widowed in 1884 by first wife, Mary Stilwell.

straightened up Thomas would be out there trying to make the front door bell ring with a teaspoonful of salt and a couple of aluminum pans.

"Dear, dear," she must have said to herself, "I'll certainly be glad when Thomas confines his experiments to his laboratory." And pretty soon Thomas did, 20 hours a day. No Thomas to go to the movies with, no Thomas to come home and spank the children, no Thomas to help entertain the evening callers, no Thomas to mow the front lawn, no Thomas to hang the sitting room curtains.

And it may be that the situation was even worse than that.

"Oh dear," Mrs. Edison might say, yawning, "I'm certainly sleepy."

"How much," Thomas might have inquired, "did you sleep last night?"

"Well," Mrs. Edison might have reflected, "I went to bed at 10 o'clock but those terrible Spivie's[101] next door kept up such a racket that I didn't get to sleep until 11. And then I had to get up early this morning to take the flowers over to Sunday school while they were still fresh. No, I don't suppose I slept more than seven hours and a half."

"Well," Thomas might have said, caustically, "I get along on considerably less than that and you don't hear me complaining."

———————

Somebody once pointed out that Thomas Edison didn't need much sleep himself o' nights and accordingly he invented the phonograph so nobody else could sleep either.

We are having troubles ourselves along that line although it really isn't Mr. Edison's fault. You see we have one of these new fangled phonographs which are supposed to be the last word on tone production. On ours something has gone wrong with the little thingamajig that gives you the sound. Right in the midst of Ave Maria or something soft like that it starts to rattle.

"If I could only take a whole evening to this thing," says Bill, "I know I could fix it."

———————————————

[101] British slang, "spiv" refers to an unemployed person who makes money by dubious schemes, and who lives by one's wits. Modern equivalent would be a slacker.

And so every night he refuses all invitations out, dashes home, swallows his supper, gets out the best kitchen paring knife and starts fixing it.

He fixes and fixes until midnight. He plays all the records through and then starts in at the beginning. And still the thing rattles. I'm beginning to get a little worried about the neighbors.

⸎ ❦ ⸎

13 February 1926, Saturday:

MR. DON KNOWLTON, writing in this month's American Mercury, discusses various Ohio cities. From the discussion one gains the impression that if there is anywhere an uglier, more dismal city than Akron, O., Mr. Knowlton would like to know about it. Mr. Knowlton does not care for the little uncovered stream which trickles somewhat malodorously out of our North valley. He dismisses our seven-million viaduct with a word. And he proclaims further that Akron is very, very dirty.

I had noticed this latter circumstance myself. In the morning when I go to put the windows down I find the sills all laden with huge chunks of soot. I take down the pickle dish to put the elderberry jelly in it and my thumb leaves marks all around the edge. I spend all of Monday scrubbing the kitchen shelves and the following Friday when visitors come to call they say, "Well, we always knew that girl couldn't keep house."

But just as the vaudeville performer down at the colonial gets a laugh every time he mentions Kenmore, so do present-day magazine writers get a laugh every time they mention Akron. They're making a joke out of the old home town and it makes me mad. And it makes me all the madder because most of it is true. We are dirty, we are ugly.

To be sure, Wilbur Peat of the art institute can go prowling around town and point out a smokestack which is beautiful or a pile of ash cans throwing long graceful shadows. And as Bill points out, instead of complaining about the soot we've got coal to burn. And as Grace Brown, just back from Europe, has pointed out, Akron has a lovely electric street cleaner.

In spite of which my heart goes right on yearning for parks and a Main street all full of tall white skyscrapers and municipal concerts and an art institute surrounded with flower beds and special patented smoke consumers.

However, if these things ever did come to pass I would want them to come as the result of Akron's own enterprise and not as gifts from somebody with money. Ordinarily it is quite the thing to say, "Well, look at So-and-So, he's a millionaire, why doesn't he do something for the town!" But sometimes I wonder just how much of this is good for a town.

Whenever you go to Philadelphia everybody talks about the things that Edward Bok has done, the concerts he has sponsored, the study he has encouraged, the prizes he has offered for this, that and the other.

And when you go to Rochester all you hear is the name of Eastman, Mr. Eastman built this theater, Mr. Eastman endowed that college.

There is excellent argument for all this – I can think of 10 or 12 arguments myself – but I think if I lived in such a town I would grow a little weary of hearing the same name over and over again. And I think I would rather live in a town a little less heavily endowed where the citizens occasionally roused and did something for themselves.

Such a town as, for instance, Akron.

15 February 1926, Monday:

"D EAR Jo:

This department is in receipt of the following letter:

I address you thus familiarly because I do not know you and because the subject I wish to discuss is familiar to us both, in fact it had to do with our earliest influences.

"In welcoming you to 'The Royal Order of Motherhood,' I wish to impress upon you several items which may or may not interest you. Thus:

"It is the oldest organization in the world.

"The constitution depends upon the health of mother and babe.

"The by-laws depend entirely on the mother's disposition.

"The passwords are three and will gain you entry into any group, providing you speak loud enough. They are, 'Now MY baby –'

"But the real point upon which I wished to touch is the emblem of this great order; we mothers all wear it plurally and frequently during the early months of our offspring, and yet it seems to me, while it is one of the familiar necessities of life upon which so many things depend, we do omit the praise which is its proper due.

"Never have I seen it expressed in ode or essay or in any way referred to other than in ridicule. And since I feel so keenly that at this point has been bluntly overlooked I call upon you to use the many adjectives in your possession to modify this error.

"I shall look forward with pleasure to seeing the column devoted to this interesting subject and being generous by nature will give you one or two suggestions as to its treatment.

"I know you will be amazed to learn that our emblem doubtless inspired the well known slogan, 'Safety First.' I have felt that the real prick of the effectiveness was lost by the omission of the little word 'pin' but doubtless the author felt that the whole point would be lost by its inclusion.

"And my last suggestion is one that I feel sure you will follow in these early days of your novitiate[102]; in lieu of the customary lost button which you will now have no time to replace on your husband's clothing, just bestow him smilingly one of your temporarily unattached emblems. But do not wait to note the effect. Just –

Letty Malone."

But I understand that they aren't using 'em as much as they used to. Now MY baby wears only four and you can even get along with three, depending on how you do them up. A lot of people still cling to the old-fashioned triangular style in which case you just use one for the top and one for each stocking.

Aunty Robin, however, started out our Mary with a sort of quadrilateral effect. You fold 'em square and then use two for the top and two for the bottom. In a way it's more complete and more reassuring.

---

[102] A period of training as a novice, typically in reference to a monastery or religious order

As for the skirts and bands and things, they tie with a great variety of tape bows. Sometimes, especially when you have been held up all day and the baby is 10 minutes late for her tiffin, you tie the shirt to itself only backwards, in which case everything has to be done all over again. It is all very interesting.

On the whole, though, it is a very satisfactory emblem to be wearing on the front of one's bungalow apron. And if, as has been pointed out above, there is no immediate use for it then one can always use it to fix up the hole in the living room curtains or do the week's mending.

I understand there is an Akron man who telegraphed his wife from Chicago the other day as follows:

"Wire safety pins immediately buttons all off pajamas."

---

17 February 1926, Wednesday:

LOLLY came up last night bringing with her doughnuts and cream puffs and cod liver oil and flowers and chocolate creams. Lolly brought a half pound of the chocolate creams and the flowers she brought are here in a black bowl by my typewriter. There are three strands of freesia, yellow and pink, and three stalks of pussy willow and three long green leaves of the freesias.

I have been thinking while I looked at them how much better Lolly's way is of doing things. If I had been going visiting I would have taken at least a pound of chocolate creams and if I hadn't had money enough for a dozen chrysanthemums I probably would have railed about it and taken nothing at all. As it is we had just the proper quantity of chocolate creams and this afternoon the freesias look delicate and spring time like in their black bowl. If they had been chrysanthemums or American beauties they would long ago have toppled out of their quart milk bottles. In my present mood I should like to organize a League of Delicate Givers.

All of us, I suppose, come to the point where we realize that our lives as things go are half lived. And if we have made a mistake out of the first half we vigorously resolve to do something better by the other half.

Now that I think about it I wish that I had been politer in my first half. It is a common notion among Americans I imagine that there is considerable virtue in being bluff and outspoken, in blurting out what we consider to be the truth without regard for the other person's feelings. We have met a few cultured Europeans, it may be, and realizing that a suave manner, an unbending etiquette, a soft voice can frequently hide cruelty and cunning we have endeavored to show our scorn by having no manners at all. I used to despise any woman who was tactful. I was sure that at heart she was deceitful. I based my philosophy largely on the conduct of two sisters. One was always sweet and pleasant, the other one sarcastic. I worshiped the sarcastic one. I was sure that time would tell. And time did. At heart they were exactly the same.

Sometimes though I meet a woman obviously as gentle within as she is without. And then when I am interrupting somebody else or talking at the top of my lungs or trying to be smart or eating my dessert when it isn't time I remember her and make my resolves all over again.

Kiki and Luce just dropped in and we got to talking about the Earl of Craven and the Countess of Cathcart. Kiki was furious. "If they're going to deport him," she stormed, "they might as well deport 99 per cent of the men in New York." She also got to thinking up the ladies who might go along with them but the list grew too long to set down here.

Luce also had ideas about the matter. "What I don't get," she drawled, "is why the government will take up time and money over a trivial thing like that when babies are starving and coal is going up and miners keep getting entombed and congress won't do a thing about prohibition."

For my own part I don't know what to think except that from her pictures I would judge that the Countess of Cathcart was a quite charming woman. I haven't met many sirens in my life but those that I have met I generally liked within 60 seconds. And it took just half that long to see why men ran away with them.

---

18 February 1926, Thursday:

MRS. C. C. MOORE, a prominent society woman of San Francisco, according to the public prints, has just issued invitations for a dinner which is to be eaten entirely with the fingers. The menu consists of caviar, eclairs, celery and things, cream of asparagus soup (you take this from the cup), stuffed crab legs, breast of baby chicken, artichoke hearts and something or other in cornucopias which I take to be dessert.

The affair is to be strictly formal.

Whether Mrs. Moore stated in her invitations that the dinner was to be eaten with the fingers I do not know but I have no doubt that the 50 guests to be, as soon as they read about it in the papers, promptly sent in acceptances. I know that Fred Barton and I would be tickled to death to go to a dinner where you didn't have to bother with the silver and where you had a good excuse for licking your fingers between courses.

So far as that is concerned we had a little breakfast modeled somewhat on the same order at our house this morning. It consisted of warmed over coffee and three doughnuts left over from night before last. I was not aware at the time, however, that I was doing anything fashionable. As a matter of fact I was a little embarrassed. I always have considerable trouble dipping doughnuts – I am liable to forget and hold one up in the air whereupon the coffee trickles slowly down to my elbow – and so I waited until Katie had gone back to her washing and then I pulled down the shades so that the procession of agents who keep a steady march to our backdoor wouldn't see me.

This news item has cheered me up considerably.

The advantages of giving a dinner without silver are of course obvious. For one thing you don't have the mad scramble to get it cleaned before the guests arrive. Afterwards there is not the bother of washing up, of counting it, of discovering a salad fork missing, of going through the list of guests to see who might have taken it and of subsequently discovering that it had been thrown out with the apple peelings.

What bothers me though is just how to manage with the coffee. I never take sugar in my coffee and consequently I would have no trouble at all. With Bill, however, who likes his coffee the consistency of soft fudge, it would be different. Possibly his solution would be to tip the sugar bowl into the coffee and then sip the syrup slowly from the top.

It would be a tremendous relief, however, to prepare for a dinner party secure in the knowledge that you wouldn't have to keep saying over and over to yourself, "olives with the fingers, peas with the fork." That young woman who absolutely ruined her husband's business future by her ignorance of proper trencher tactics would still be sailing prettily if she had dined at Mrs. Moore's.

The matter of menus of course would require considerable thought. My favorite dessert, caramel pudding with walnuts and whipped cream, would have to go by the board. One could have baked potatoes though just by breaking them in half with the skins on and dipping them in butter. We used to do them that way when we were kids and baked potatoes out of doors in the leaves and although one occasionally bit into a piece of gravel the net result was really very satisfactory.

Tonight, according to Mrs. Moore's excellent though in the matter, I have prepared the following menu:

Olives   Celery   Nuts

Hot Dogs

Buns

Milk

A new worry has been wished on women, who are being shown they cannot adopt men's styles without assuming the difficulties which attend them. The new straight skirts of the tailored suits are creased now just as are men's trousers. In order to preserve the knife edges it may even be necessary for some women to tuck their skirts under the mattress and sleep on them as men have done for generations.

⸺ ❧❦ ⸻

20 February 1926, Saturday:

THE telephone over here isn't nearly so interesting as it was in the other place. There is hardly ever anybody talking on it. Last night our bell tinkled and I went to the phone and I said hello and a man's voice said hello and I said hello and he said who did you want and I said our bell rang and he said so did ours. I waited then for him to say something more but he just hung up the receiver.

There is more music here though than there was in the other place. Across the hall there is a little girl, she is so good, who practices her music lessons every noon. In the other direction there is somebody who plays The Rustle of Spring and upstairs there is somebody who plays Paderewski[103]'s Minuet Antique. And my neighbor next door whistles to her baby when she cries. It is a very lovely whistle, all full of birds and spring time, and the baby seems to like it. There are some babies in this world who are not so fortunate as to have mothers who whistle. Some babies have mothers whose voices are dreadful and who don't know any songs anyway except for the first and last stanzas of My Country, 'Tis of Thee.

Another thing which we miss a lot is the pair of stone lions which were out in front of the other place. They really gave everything quite an air and whenever anybody wanted explicit directions for coming out you could always say to them, "Oh you know, the entrance there by the stone lions." You could pat the lions on the head as you went out in the afternoon and when you came back they would still be there, guarding the place like everything.

This place hasn't any stone lions. It used to have a sort of fountain effect in the middle of the court and Bill used to have a lot of fun stepping over it. He could just make it. Sometimes when he would be moody and melancholy he would go out and step back and forth over the fountain until he felt better. He's quite depressed since they took the fountain away and won't come in the front entrance at all any more.

On the other hand this place has a nice window box where you can put butter and things. We can't use the ice box on account of the kitchen table coming in front of it. And so we use the window box. It keeps things delightfully cool. You bring in the milk from it and the cream has swelled in a great white ice cap all over the top of the bottle. You bring in the celery and it is limp and cold. You bring in the lettuce and it is frosted over with icicles. You bring in the butter and you have to take a hammer and the screwdriver to get the lid off the dish.

The kitchen on the other hand is just as warm as anything. Leave things around in it for a while and the butter melts, the icicles thaw, the celery revives. And when you take the flat iron down from the shelf you could really go to ironing with it right away without going to all the bother of heating it up.

---

103 Ignacy Jan Paderewski (1860-1941) a Polish pianist and composer.

The grocery boy says doggone these hot apartments, they just keep him in perpetual fear of influenza going from the heat into the cold outside again. But I tell him he should just try living in a cold apartment for a while.

⁓⁓⁓◆⁓⁓⁓

23 February 1926, Tuesday:

D EAR JO: (writes John Earle Miller).

    "When I look at the calendar it says Feb. 16; but when I look across the street to where the kids are making tea-rings out of white sand, I think it is the Fourth of July. If it weren't that the skin of me is hot and sunburned, I'd certainly expect to wake up with the wind blowing the sheet off my head, and make through the snow for the 7:40 Spicer car.

"At first I hated Florida. As soon as the train passed the Mason Dixon line it began to show signs of spring fever. The further south we traveled the weaker that engine got until it moved no faster than Saturday traffic over Bowery st., And you know what that means.

"My first glimpse of this real estate, borrowing from the clever speech of a certain Akron friend, thrilled me with the desire to take the next train back to God's country. Of course, I'll admit that my mood and the environment had something to do with it. The room was cold, the porter had called us late, and I had to get my initial view between acts, so to speak. But I can assure you that I missed nothing while I washed the soapsuds out of my eyes, or while I crawled under the berth for my toothbrush. Acts there were many; but all set in the same scene. The view showed white sand and fir trees. Broad stretches of white sand and fir trees. Great areas of white sand and fir trees. The fog covered everything like a soggy meringue, small patches of ugly sky showed here and there, and a raw wind messed up the whole business. It was then 8:30 of a Saturday morning. And that was my first picture of the 'sunny south.'

"But by 10 o'clock Jacksonville looked like the night before instead of the morning after. It was positively radiant. The fog and cold wind had picked up their zippers and left. The sun poured down, drying the heavy dew on the fruitstands [sic]; and my overcoat proved to be excess luggage.

"In Jacksonville I had my first experience with a sightseeing bus. My place in the world's work is now very clear to me. I shall set myself up in the sightseeing profession, and profession it is. I had no idea before that folks should be interested in what most of us are fairly well accustomed to. We should be interested in seeing the public library, the best churches, postoffice [sic], waterworks, all school buildings, hospitals, bank corners, and other public places where the great unwashed scratches its matches. Also, you do not 'drive' down a street. You 'tour.' Fancy, 'touring' around our postoffice! You get a certain grade of humor too. Almost English. The guide tells you that Florida is so rich that every blade of grass has a green back, every bird carries a bill, and that every flower has a scent.

"Of course, we went to the famous ostrich farm. I failed to appreciate the fact that I was walking around the most widely known ostrich farm in the United States, the world for all I know. It isn't nearly as pretentious as it sounds. I don't see why they call it a farm. Pen in that little park out there where the Rose av. Car line comes to an end, tear out the trees, and led a gang of ostriches loose in it. You will then have a replica of the wonderful ostrich farm. The ostrich is a queer bird. He wallows in the sand; and is a dirty hoofed customer. He keeps his fine feathers hid under his wings and only shows them when he lifts up his arms, as it were, to air out his tips. There was only a hundred of them around the place. That doesn't sound so big, does it? The unusualness of the ostrich must be the cause of the interest the northerner takes in him. I wonder if the southerners would be that interested in our cattle farms. They should be. They should see what a high type, self-respecting cow looks like. The cows down here are so low down that most of the natives use condensed milk.

"The story circulated around Akron about the cost of food never was started in Jacksonville. The most I could eat at Morrisons, which is saying a good deal, only cost me 90 cents; and then I couldn't finish all of the whipped cream on my peach shortcake. And Morrisons is no greasy place, either. You do not eat alongside the marble slab where the Spanish mackerel lies looking up at the menu sign. A waiter carries your tray into a dining room, done in pea green and dull black, places your food on a table decorated with fresh flowers and rose-shaded lamp, and doesn't even hang around for the usual thin dime.

"And that for Jacksonville. I'll go down to the Spa now, and swim awhile. Do I like Florida by this time? Does a potato like the sunshine? Well rather!

"Yours for better weather."

※

24 February 1926, Wednesday:

MR. GROSJEAN, the hair bobber, came up the other morning and we got to talking about music.

"A man has to be born again to become a great singer," said Mr. Grosjean. "It's like religion. A man is born and he goes along not caring much about anything and then suddenly he gets the love of God in his heart and he is transformed. That's the way it has to be with a singer. He has to love what he's doing. If he doesn't love it all the music lessons in the world aren't going to make him great."

Mr. Grosjean recalled the days when he used to sing with the Tuesday Musical club chorus and the Liedertafel.

"Those were great days," he said. "I sang with the Tuesday club chorus when Evan Williams directed it. We went to Canton one time and took a prize. I think the Liedertafel on the whole sang the better music though. We used to have great saengerfests[104]. I remember when Rita Elandl was the prima donna for us. She had a beautiful voice."

I asked him why he wasn't singing now.

"Oh I don't know," he laughed, "I got too old I guess."

And he took out the clippers and began snipping at the back of my neck.

On the whole it is very pleasant to have a barber who can talk about music. Conversation with most barbers is so difficult. You tell him you would like your hair cut with a V in the back and then after you have discussed the weather and he has told you how he came to be acquainted with his wife there really isn't anything left to do. You can look at yourself in the mirror but that isn't always encouraging and if you turn around and stare at the men getting shaved and lathered your barber is liable to get cross and deliberately ruin your V.

Some barbers I understand have quite a stock of funny stories. There is one for instance about a fellow whose nose came way down on his chin and the barber complained that

---

[104] Saengerfest, or Sängerfest, also Sängerbund-Fest, Sängerfeste, which means "singer festival", is a competition of Sängerbunds, or singer groups in German singing societies and popular in Ohio in major towns such as Cleveland.

by the time he got his nose propped up so he could shave his lip he could hear his heart beat.

I know a fellow who has laughed about that story at least 15 times. But I don't know. I've never been able to see anything very funny about it.

Maybe though I'm not telling it right.

You know that high chair up in the attic that your little Henry Augustus used to sit in? Well, the Florence Crittenden home at 51 Cotter av. would just love to have it along with a couple more like it.

You see they have four youngsters over there whose mothers go to work every day. First they needed cribs for the youngsters and when the Beacon Journal told about it the four cribs promptly arrived, the gift of some thoughtful citizen. And he sent along mattresses too.

Now the home would like to have a couple of high chairs. And if you have any baby blankets or little sheets or little pillows or anything at all in fact, why, just send them along. The babies are all beautiful, all fat and all kicking their heels and they'll appreciate everything you do to make them more happy and comfortable.

4 March 1926, Thursday:

"**M**Y DEAR JO: (writes Fanchon)

I was reading through your column the other night about this special barber of yours and wondered and wondered why you did your hair that way instead of spending an afternoon in a barber salon when I recalled about the baby and realized what an additional sacrifice a mother has to make these days.

"Not getting out to the barber salon! Why, my dear, how can you keep up with what's going on? I realize that a radio gives some things and an afternoon at bridge now and then gives a great deal, but after one is used to the kink of all gossip fests, how can one forego the salon?

"You know when I first began to cut my hair, I had it done at the same place where I had my marcel[105]. But a friend of mine who wore hers straight and very short was certain a man barber could do a better job in a regular he-barber shop, for he would be used to a shingle. And even if he didn't know so much about it there were so many other barbers about he could just motion one over during a hot towel lapse and get helped out of a difficulty.

"Being los tin [sic] leisure one day I agreed to go with her to a cutting and say, I've never missed an opportunity since. You evidently don't know about his particular barber salon, but it goes like this: you go in all puffed and full of stage fright from having to pass among so many men, and then you turn a confident smile on Frank.

"Frank stands by the cash register and takes in all the women patients he can handle. About a table strewn with papers and ex-magazines are men in negligee. We women never go over to this table unless the men have their collars on, but from the front row back you can learn quite a lot.

"It used to be better, tough, before the boys realized they had had one more freedom snatched from them. One afternoon who should be sitting there, but Ethel Miley's husband. You know how she always talks him up as being so good looking. Well, Jo, he was so mussed up I wouldn't have known him from a Saturday night bath room in a family of small children. Maybe we didn't speak to her clearly the next time she guiled this handsome stuff.

"And then another time, Mabel Maxwell's little husband was just jumping off the bar when we came and before he saw us he went over in the porter to get his tie tied and Tom – that's our porter – asked when he was going to get a wife that could teach him to tie his own tie. We giggled and he saw us. But we didn't care. Tom was right. If Mabel would just back him up a bit –

"Lot of things like this happen while you're smiling at Frank, hoping all the time that he'll take you next. And when he does – well, you don't want to have a shampoo or anything that might fill your ears, while the chances of current education are so good. Just a little lead now and then and her and there suggested by different folks you see, either waiting or being done, and you can learn everything that's happened since you were there last and a good generous surmise on what will happen till you meet again.

"What a sacrifice mothers must make! But, Jo, you aren't alone. Why, I have another friend encumbered with such an extensive family that she had to let her hair grow for

---

[105] A marcel wave – a type of hairdo styling technique in the 1920's using hot curling tongs to create waves of curls.

the simple reason that she can't afford a day in the barber salon. However, there is sunshine behind all clouds. Just think, some day you can take the baby and be able to stay twice as long."

❧❦❧❦◆❦❧❦❧

5 March 1926, Friday:

BURLESQUE seems to be something which men consider very amusing and women something very horrible. And if the courts eventually should decide that the East Akron burlesque house is to be closed I have no doubt but that just thousands and thousands of women will heave tremendous sighs of relief. As for the men, however, I doubt that they will be correspondingly depressed. Burlesque, I have felt on each of the three occasions when I attended such a show, was just another of these delights which have been slightly overrated.

Last winter I went up to Cleveland and saw the Winter Garden show[106] or some such spectacle in which there were at least two scenes in which girls were shown either entirely nude or else shielded with the flimsiest of gauze. A delighted Ah! went through the audience. Some time later I went out to the Miles Royal and saw a number of young women in practically the same state, except that the lingerie they wore looked as though it had come from the 95-cent counter. Delighted guffaws went through the audience followed by vigorous hand-clapping. In this same show a comedian tumbled out of the wings and every time he bumped himself the audience went frantic with delight. Some time later still, I went to see a show called "Blossom Time,' and in this show another comedian went through practically the same antics to an audience that was similarly appreciative.

I am not saying this because I am wild about burlesque shows. Those that I have seen left me acutely miserable. But so did "Blossom Time."

---

[106] Minsky Brothers' National Winter Garden, American burlesque presented by the four sons of Louis and Ethel Minsky, and ran from 1912 to 1937 ending in New York City. Comedians such as Red Skelton and Abbott and Costello performed with Minsky's.

Leaving the statute books out of it, I wonder, and keep wondering, why we criticize the movies, books and the stage always from the standpoint of morals, never from the standpoint of taste.

If a stranger should come into an Akron home and persist in telling shady stories all evening, it is not likely that he would be invited to come back. But the plea would only be merely that he was rude, certainly not that the morals of the household were in danger of being corrupted. Likewise we would exclude a woman who responded to a dinner invitation clad only in negligee, or a youth who persisted in telling all his erotic experiences, or a boor who kept his hat on all evening and did parlor tricks with a vase and an umbrella. But we tolerate all these things on the stage, in the movies or in books so long as it can successfully be shown that nobody's morals are being hurt.

In reality, of course, morale and taste are the closes of affinities, but somehow the reformers never seem to think of it that way.

———————

Katie was all glowing this morning because Angela was home again. Angela is 10 years old and as pretty and sweet as anyone could wish. But a year or so ago, Angela developed a cough and she was listless and wouldn't eat. Katie was worried and then they took Angela to see a funny smiling chap who wore glasses and whose hair was getting a little thin on top and whose name was Dr. Hyde. Dr. Hyde tweaked Angela's ear and made her stick out her tongue and do all sort of remarkable things. Then they bore off to Sunshine cottage which, as everybody knows, is a part of Springfield Sanatorium.

Angela was there six months and Katie went to see her every Sunday. Two weeks ago, Angela came home.

"You should see her," said Katie this morning. "Her cheeks – my, so pink! And she eats everything I cook. And what you think. She wants to take dancing lessons."

6 March 1926, Saturday:

A TRAGEDY

ON the other hand, my dear young friend, could we but look into anothers' hearts, a great deal of unhappiness might be averted. You asked me for the butter but a moment ago and my hand trembled so that I could not pass it. Do you see the gentleman yonder who is being seated by the waiter? You did not observe it but as he passed us he gave me a look so searing, so bitter, that for the moment I was overcome. And yet, could he but know it, I am of all persons in the world his warmest friend, his dearest benefactor.

I see that you do not know him. Surely, however, you have heard of him, Dr. Arne Andersen, head of the Swedish Institute for the Attainment of Harmonious Proportions. All day long a procession of limousines hails before his door. In two short years he has grown from a nonentity into a person of distinction and affluence. An opera singer is said to have lost her voice with languishing over him. And yet he maintains always this sour and dismal expression, makes no friends and goes everywhere alone.

Ah yes, you already have suspected it. It was a woman. And such a woman. Eyes like corn flowers – a skin of snow – you will pardon me for a moment if I seem to give way to emotion –

She came to Dr. Andersen one day for treatment. He was merely an unknown masseur then. He fell madly in love. Her manner captivated him. Her beauty too, you say? No, not her beauty for at that time she was fat. She waddled. Her wrists and ankles had disappeared beneath rolls of flesh. Her cheeks were cream puffs. She heaved and rolled in her gait. Her breath came in short little puffs. But she was docile and placid and yes, I must say it, sweet. The unknown Swedish masseur was captivated beyond words.

But he was also collected, this Swede. He knew that at heart he was a poet, a Scandinavian of the utmost fastidiousness. He feared the day when his love would cool, when his heart would quail before this mountain of flesh which he had married.

And so he set out to make Helena thin. He prescribed early morning exercises. She overslept. He prayed with her to diet. She wept and said he was starving her.

In desperation one night he sat alone. Suddenly an inspiration struck him. It was the inspiration which has since caused Dr. Arne Anderson's Swedish Institute for the attainment of harmonious proportions to be incorporated for a million dollars.

The inspiration consisted of an apparatus for the ironing away of surplus flesh. Perhaps you are familiar with it, my young friend, but if you are not I will tell you. The patient stands upon a small round platform clad only in a sack. Then an electrically propelled coil is fastened about her and as it moves slowly up and down it gradually smooths away all surplus tissue.

In an ecstasy of joy and anticipation the doctor summoned his beloved. The treatment, since it involved neither discomfort nor loss of sleep nor the denial of food, appealed to her. She acquiesced. They embraced.

You may believe it or not, my young friend, but within three months Helena had emerged into a beauty. Her eyes were now completely visible. She was slender. She walked with grace. She no longer heaved. There was merely the suspicion of a dimple on her elbow. Dr. Arne Anderson was entranced.

But alas, my young friend, how frequently are our joys but the prelude to grief. Other men now found Helena attractive. One night, without so much as a farewell to her benefactor, she eloped with an Austrian whom her romantic fancy had somehow pictured as a nobleman in disguise. In reality he was but a collector for a small and unimportant furniture house.

As for Dr. Arne Andersen he was blind with rage and disappointment. He would have left the country. But they would not let him. They came in swarms. On foot and by limousine. Other fat women praying to be made beautiful.

He has everything now to make him happy, a fortune, adoring women, no encumbrances. In spite of which he will not smile and goes everywhere alone. And yet, could he but know it, he has even greater cause for happiness and there is no man who would sooner enlighten him than myself.

For I must tell you, my dear friend, that Helena has gone back to her old ways again. How she eats – and sleeps – she rolls in fat. She heaves. She puffs. Her eyes, her eyes of corn flower, are little by little disappearing beneath the flesh. Her house is neglected. Her husband groans each night at the thought of returning to it.

How do I know all this? Alas, my dear young friend, alas, I am that Austrian.

---

8 March 1926, Monday:

ONE of the pleasant things about conducting a column is that one's friends are always so helpful. We are sitting here by the fireplace (there is no fire in it), Fanchon is playing with the bellows. Evelyn is lying on the couch and Lolly is rocking. I am wiping the dust off the typewriter with my forefinger and wiping the same on my stocking. I am engrossed in thought.

"Why don't you write about Dr. Douglas' typewriter?" says Fachon, "did you ever see it?"

"No," I say, "I never did."

"Neither did I," says Fanchon. "It's electric."

"I suppose," I say, "that he talks into a dictaphone and then –"

"No," says Fanchon. "I don't know just how it goes, but you just have to touch the keys and then the electricity does the rest. He says though, that he doesn't dare to write anything on it that he intends to send out – it's just for her personal –"

"Why don't you write about how they manage to keep the same ice on Valley st. from year to year?" says Evelyn. "I slipped on the same piece of ice this afternoon that I did last year and cut my rubber in the same place."

"Why don't you write about spring," says Fanchon, "and how the little children all go out and play in the mud. Why, dear me, I could think of a lot of things to write about."

"Don't forget," says Lolly, "that there are some ----'s on the radiator."

"I wonder," I say, "if a person couldn't write a column about ----'s. Wouldn't that be all right?"

"You couldn't," says Fanchon, "they aren't considered polite. And besides, what would you say about them?"

"Why," I say, "I think they're very fascinating. For one thing there are three different ways of doing them and then everybody you meet always tells you something different about them."

Fanchon thinks it over. "No," she says finally, "of course you can do as you lease. It's your column, but I don't think you'd better."

———

"Do you know that down here they eat ALL THE TIME" writes A. T. Kingsbury encouragingly from Mexico City. "Carry their little charcoal stoves with them and sit right down on the pavement, steps of a church, public park or sidewalk cook their tortillas, cakes or chicken and eat, eat and then eat. We have seen at least one hundred of these cooking establishments going at one time and all in sight of each other. And for fear the passerby is hungry they offer to sell some of their victuals to him.

"All kinds of merchandise are sold on the street but eatables seem to have the call. Vendors of oranges, bananas, nuts of all kinds and sliced pineapple with pieces of coconut about one in every 10 feet along the street.

"And please tell the people that in spite of all this eating the Mexicans are not fat or flabby. They have all the pleasure of eating and have the whitest and hardenmost teeth I have ever seen."

H. M. didn't care much for John Earle's description of St. Augustine. I don't have her letter by me, but as I recall she maintains St. Augustine is a lovely old place with lots of moss and shuttered windows and such.

For my own part, however, I hope never to hear the name of Florida or any part of it again, until they do something about taking the seeds out of their oranges.

9 March 1926, Tuesday:

THIS department today is consumed with the question, "Should a Husband Tell?"

It seems that several months ago there was a chap who felt sort of peculiar and he went to see some doctors and they said he'd have to have an operation.

"How soon?" he queried.

"Right away," they said, "tomorrow morning."

"Aw," he pleaded, "let me have 24 hours anyway."

So they let him have 24 hours and he went home.

"Bernadine," he said that night to his wife, "Bernadine, of course this thing may not amount to anything at all but on the other hand they said it might prove serious and — and — Bernadine, there are some things I want to tell you."

And so he told her about his whole life, about the time he went to the high school party and stole the ice cream, and about how, three years after they were married, the firm had raised his salary and he hadn't told her anything about it and about how, two years ago, when he was on a convention to Cedar Point, he had danced seven times with the same blonde. And he wept and they both felt that in all their lives they had never been so much married.

———————

Now if this man had died I have no doubt but that Bernadine would have grown into a sweet old lady with a cap and ribbons and a sad, slow smile. She would be thinking always of those last perfect moments. Now that there was nothing more to fear it would cheer her, as it always cheers a woman, to know that in her heart she held the perfect knowledge of a very imperfect man.

The trouble is that he didn't die. And after he was well and the doctor bills were paid and he was able to go to conventions again Bernadine began to get a straight and deep furrow between the eyes. And occasionally she would remind him of a few things.

"I wish," he keeps lamenting to himself and now and then to a couple of understanding male friends, "I wish I'd never told her."

———————

Two Americans of acknowledged brilliance have laid down certain rules for conduct. Mr. Emerson said, "If you would be known not to do a thing, don't do it," and Mr. Clemens said, "Be good and you'll be lonesome." The corollary of this latter statement is, "Be bad and you'll regret it." But you won't regret it half so much if you don't tell.

———————

One of the compensating things for being bad is that it gives you such a kindly feeling toward all other people who are bad and inasmuch as the latter sort predominates in the world it really makes quite a sizable fraternity.

The composition for being good is, of course, that delightful feeling that you are superior to practically every other person who walks the earth.

———————

Whether men have the same experiences as women naturally it is impossible to tell. But every woman knows that there is nothing in the world more disastrous than to confide your secrets to an intimate friend. Next week you will have a fall out and your secrets will be all over town. And sometimes they'll be all over town even if you don't have a fall out.

More disastrous than this however must be the moment of weakness which moves a man to confide in a wife. A wife sits at home so much of the time. And four walls can get so close. And a woman's sense of humor is such a variable quantity.

⁕ ⁕ ⁕

10 March 1926, Wednesday:

JOSEF HOFFMAN[107] played over the radio Sunday night and we made considerable preparation to listen to him. First we hinted around and go ourselves invited over to a house where they had a radio. Then I fed the baby up tight so she'd be responsibly sure not to wake up too early and spoil things. Then we sat around and listened to some rather dismal Sunday evening hymns and to a soprano who, according to the announcer, had been a regular fairy godmother to the boys across the seas. Finally Josef Hoffman was announced and we drew up our chairs reverentially prepared to listen.

Out of five numbers played by Mr. Hoffman three were Chopin's Minute Waltz, Rachmaninoff's Prelude in C sharp minor and Rubinstein's Melody in F. The two others were a Chopin ballade and a Spanish fandango which I didn't catch because the baby waked up just then.

Somehow, seeing that we'd made up all those preparations, I couldn't help wishing that Mr. Hoffman had played some things a little less hackneyed. The plea of course is that the people – meaning the old couple up in the Canadian prairies and the telephone lineman out in the strawberry patches of Dakota – must have what they want. But sometimes I wonder if Bill and I and the folks we gang around with aren't the people too and why our wishes are never consulted. Rubinstein's Melody F is played at every high school graduation exercises from here to Parsons City, Kansas, and points west. And I know of at least one thousand people who hope they never have to listen to the Prelude in C sharp minor again. Between you and me and the gate post I'm ready to

---

[107] Referring to Josef Hofmann, a Polish American pianist and composer (1876-1957).

wager that even Mr. Rachmaninoff is weary of the Prelude in C sharp minor and tears his hair whenever he recalls the day he wrote it.

If there ever is a revolution in this country I think it will come from those people who don't always want happy endings to their stories, who don't care for the Waters of Minnetonka, who don't read the American Magazine, who don't care if they're never president of a rubber company, and who don't think it's funny when one Jewish comedian strikes another Jewish comedian across the rear with a curtain pole.

They are generally placid souls, these, chemists out at the rubber works, occasional stenographers and school teachers who have never been known to utter a harsh word in their lives. But some day they're going to become weary of continually being fed what the people want. And they're going to boil over and start slashing around and the carnage is going to be terrible.

I wonder sometimes at the existence of interior decorators. You would think that at best their lives would be uncertain and yet they seem to thrive and prosper and eventually put on lots of dog[108].

For my own part I am perfectly willing to wear ready-made clothes and I would just love to engage a gardener to take care of our garden if we had one but I don't think I would ever want to engage an interior decorator even if our curtains do hang funny and one of our three chairs is a sad, sad mistake.

For an interior decorator deprives you of all the fun of seeing a house grow. Fancy having no antique table in the hall for people to fall over, no brass coal scuttle to put cigaret ashes in, no bridge lamp that the shade's always falling off of.

They say that when an interior decorator strikes town you can always tell what houses he furnishes – they all look alike. I understand that some of them even buy books by the yard and put them in peoples' libraries.

But somehow the houses I like best are those where the shades are cracked, the chairs have deep sunken places in them, the springs of the couch have a hard time keeping concealed and the Victrola records have warps in them from being left on steam

---

[108] An idiom for "putting on the ritz" or adding something lavish or extravagant.

radiators. I always like to go to houses like that. I wonder if people will like to come to ours.

～⌒⌒⌒◆⌒⌒⌒～

11 March 1926, Thursday:

"A NICE one you are," writes Eleanor,[109] "why a two-months-old child – boy or girl, no one knows – and not a word to Aunt Dotty. Don't you know that one usually prepares cards omitting only the name and date of der tag and then the day after, Henry mails them to interested friends too far away to read it in the Beacon Journal or Plain Dealer. What sort of a friend are you anyway? Besides depriving your offspring of an appropriate gift, I almost feel like ignoring everything. A word as to something you would like which you HAVE NOT GOTTEN, Ruth[110] sent Martha Loomis a pair of brass candlesticks for a wedding present. Martha received 30 other pairs. Can you conceive it? And in this hey day of Edison.

"Gee, what a city,
    "Bituminous
        Has simply
            Ruined us.

"When I think what I used to say about Akron and its dirt! Instead of my usual apology for being late, I have changed to one for being dirty. It seems to collect on me – the human magnet for dirt. You try to be dignified and impressive when calling on prospective pupils' mothers and then after the interview you glance casually in the mirror going down on the elevator and see large splotches of soot splashed over the nose. At first I was sensitive about speaking of it to my friends when they got dirty, but now if they speak of it to me I can usually come back with "Well, dear, so have you, WHAT a coincidence."

---

[109] Note to self: This Eleanor is likely the American opera singer and actress Eleanor Painter Strong who lived near Cleveland. 1940 census shows her living at 10494 Lake Shore Blvd in Bratenahl, Cuyahoga, Ohio. She is on the 1920 census in Manhattan, NY with husband Louis Graveure.

[110] Note to self: Who is Ruth? How is she related to Martha Loomis? Who is Martha Loomis?

"For heaven's sake write and say something definite about the baby, I suppose it is never to hear any Chopin, will be fed on whole wheat bread and use men's handkerchiefs all its life. Well, write."

There were quite a few women in the audience of "What Price Glory,"[111] the other night, and I haven't any doubt but that a good many of them went home disappointed. Here for months we've been hearing about the terrific swearing the piece and at least 12 different persons have told us 12 different versions of the story about the old lady who went to the matinee and lost her space.

———

There was hardly one of us, I dare say, who didn't sally out to the Goodyear, Monday night, without the delightful feeling that she was about to be corrupted. And there was hardly one of us who didn't come home later in the evening and regard her husband with increased respect. For my part, I know that I heard all of the words in "What Price Glory" on each of the three occasions when Rosie got stuck in the mud.

I was talking about it to a friend of mine over the telephone just this morning. "Well," I said, "what did you think of 'What Price Glory?'" "Why," she answered, "I didn't think it was so terrible. You should just hear Harry[112] swear."

———

I believe it is in Finland that they haven't any swear words. Just why this should be I don't know, as it ought to be the easiest thing in the world to create a few. However, the Finns are peculiar as anyone can attest who has ever tried to eat finnan haddie[113].

---

[111] "What Price Glory" Broadway play debuted in 1924 and ran for 435 performances at the Plymouth Theatre (now called the Gerald Schoenfeld Theatre) in New York. In January 1926 the silent movie debuted and ran in theatres nationwide.

[112] Referencing the character of First Sargeant Harry Quirt in "What Price Glory" and though it is a silent film, the swearing between the characters of Quirt and Flagg had the film receive hundreds of complaint letters by angry lip-readers who read the words.

[113] A cold-smoked haddock fish, traditionally from a hamlet called Findon or Finnan in Aberdeen, Scotland.

But America, when you come to think of it, doesn't seem to be any too well equipped in this respect. You can't for the life of you think up more than 10 or 12 bad words. And after you're married a while you don't even notice those any more.

⁓ ⁓ ✦ ⁓ ⁓

13 March 1926, Saturday:

SOMETIMES I wonder just what goes on in the minds of charity workers. Most of them, when they go down to work in the charity organization society offices are girls just out of college. Does the daily contact with human frailty and disaster soften them or does it make them cynical? Do they take a burden of woe home with them each night and brood over it in the darkness or do they, like doctors and nurses, come to regard it after a while as just part of the day's business?

Probably the latter, else they couldn't survive for very long. All unknown to themselves, however, the charity works must be going through wonderfully broadening experiences.

A couple of them dropped in here today – socially not professionally – and they were telling of the successful completion of a family drama that began back in 1912.

The family was named Basila and it lived in East Akron and the children were Joe 16, Rosie 8, Angelica 6, Mike 2, and the baby. Hard times came and the Basila's came to the charity office for help. The charity offices gave food and clothing and went on to other matters.

Next year the Basila's needed help again. The father had been killed and they were in danger of losing the little home which they had started to buy. The charity office saw to it that the Basila's kept their home and that a settlement was made form the company for which the father had worked.

Trouble, it seems, became a habit with the Basila's. By 1915 one of the charity workers determined she was going to get the Basila's straightened out or perish. The children were undernourished, Angelica has a disturbing cough, Joe, who had been working off and on, didn't have a very good record. The charity worker got busy. Joe was returned to one of his old jobs and his employer promised to look after him. Angelica was taken away to the Springfield sanatorium. Rosie was taught to cook "American." Mrs. Basila was placed in line for a mother's pension and she further expressed a willingness to attend Americanization classes.

Today the Basila's are plump and radiant. Joe is married and paying for a little farm. He lets Mike help him in the summer time. Rosie is working out at one of the rubber offices and not using nearly so much rouge as she used to. Angelica, her cough all gone, is learning fine in high school and thinking she will become a school teacher. Mind Mrs. Basila has rented part of her house and that with her pension and a little help from the children, is taking excellent care of her. "Sure," she smiles, "I speak English good like Italian."

The other morning it seems a young couple showed up at the charity offices requesting the loan of a little gasoline. They had started out sometime before from a little town in southern Ohio, their assets being a Ford sedan, which the young man had unostentatiously borrowed from his father, and $30.

The young man was terribly attractive, slender and dark, with elegant long sideburns curling over his cheeks. The girl was somewhat more husky. She was hatless and it was evident that she hadn't been to the manicurist for sometime although this may have been due to the fact that after they had spent seven of the $30 she quite thoughtlessly lost the remaining $23.

Questioned by herself the girl said she was married to the sheik but they hadn't gotten along at all well with his folks and so they were coming up north looking for a job. The sheik told substantially the same story, that is, that they were married. His data on the subject, however, seemed strangely different from his companion's.

After the charity worker had listened to both stories she thoughtfully sent the girl back home to her father who was overjoyed at seeing her again and promised that hereafter she could have all the beaus she wanted and a new dress too if only she wouldn't go traipsing over the country with any dad-busted feller with sideburns.

As for the sheik he evidently secured the loan of a little gasoline elsewhere as he disappeared and was never heard from again.

I like stories like that, the kind that end happily. And it must be sort of nice to be a charity worker and realize that you had something to do with the happy ending.

15 March 1926, Monday:

OCCASIONALLY in the past women have done things better than men and it may be that in the future women will do a great many things better than men. It is to be hoped that when that day comes, however, women will know how to take their successes gracefully.

To me the fact that Jacob Nesbitt killed his wife doesn't seem nearly so dreadful as the trivial bickering which preceded it. Here were two young people of average intelligence who lived pretty much as you and I do. They were sweethearts for a good many years, they went to college, they were married. And then the wife went into business and discovered that she was better at it than her husband was.

Now I suspect that there are a good many women in business who are clever at it and know it. They may be making considerably more money at it than their husbands are. But these women are tactful. They don't crow about their superiority and such extra money as they bring in they stow away in a convenient sock so that some day they both may take a trip to Europe. They realize that some people are just born to be business like and some aren't. And they realize too that some husbands who are terribly impractical and failures in a business way can be awfully sweet and dear in other ways. And they tell him about his sweetness and his dearness and forget all about what a failure he is in practical things. And he keeps his self-respect and somehow, in spite of it all, a happy home emerges.

Mrs. Frances Drake Nesbitt, it would appear, couldn't quite see things that way. She was better than her husband and she told him so. Her folks, to her way of thinking, were smarter than his folks and she told him so. In fact she seems to have told him quite a number of things and occasionally, she was an athletic sort of girl, she even used her first to make it more emphatic. It is too bad of course that a tragedy had to result but those of us who have ever seen any of the Frances Drake Nesbitt's in action don't feel nearly so sorry as we might.

I have never seen any of these Kitchen Aids which the Nesbitt's quarreled about. Possibly they were some of these potato peeler-cork screw-measuring spoon affairs. At any rate anyone who looked at a Kitchen Aid would doubtless never guess that it could inspire smug complacency in a woman and blind rage in a man. Occasionally a married couple will quarrel over a third person and we can understand that. Occasionally married actors will become jealous of one another's success with the public and we can, in a measure, understand that. But that a man and woman should grow to hate each other over a household appliance, is altogether unthinkable. If a playwright should ever attempt to make drama out of such a subject we would hoot him.

There must be a good many Mr. and Mrs. Nesbitt's, I imagine, whose troubles never culminate and hence never reach the headlines. That is the reason we fail to realize, unless we are having some such troubles ourselves, how much downright nasty bickering is probably going on under the cozy roof tops of Akron.

Ordinarily I don't worry much about this state of affairs because I have always told myself that probably all the parties concerned enjoyed the bickering and if they didn't they could get out.

But occasionally I suppose there is a husband who is a timid soul, who is afraid to beat up his wife for fear of what the neighbors will think of him, who is afraid to give up his job for fear he will never get another, who is afraid to meet the rest of the world because he has learned it despises weakness, who is, in short, afraid of everything because he has been beaten at every turn.

If Jacob Nesbitt is such a man he will probably know his first happiness if they take him away and shut him up somewhere. Being surrounded by people who are slightly or entirely "off" certainly can't be any worse than having to face a nagging woman every night and morning. In all probability he will be superior to most of those whom he encounters. And there will never again be the fear of going out in the morning and coming back in the evening with a dismal confession that he has fallen down on the job.

---

16 March 1926, Tuesday:

THE Marion Tailey[114] controversy evidently is still raging.

"This town is divided into two," writes Eleanor, "those who do and those who do not like Marion Tailey. I have never known such a satisfactory conversational substitute for the weather. Now that she has sung over the radio there isn't a fireman or a gangster who doesn't entertain an opinion. The thing that's galled most of the professionals is her calmness. My dear, one Metropolitan singer just raved when she admitted how calm Marion Tailey was. I suppose that is one of the wonders of 1926 – a non nervous debut at the Metropolitan. A lot of anti's said she wasn't a musician but

---

[114] Marion Nevada Tailey (1906-1983) American opera coloratura singer. She was the youngest prima donna to debut at the Metropolitan Opera in New York in 1926.

when she stood up on the orchestra pit the other night and sang a score by Stravinsky they had to take it back.

"I'm going to the League of Composers tonight. Julian Carillo[115] is having his premiere of his sonata in quarter, eighth and sixteenth tones. It is to be played on an ensemble of new instruments especially constructed by his nibs. I know lots of singers and some violinists who could have sung and played his sonata without any trouble at all and yet everyone seems to thin [sic] it's going to be very exciting. 'I've never heard quarter tones!', and yet some have paid as high as $7.50 to hear Galli-Curci[116] render some at the Metropolitan."

———————

A scientist working for long year over in Lorain[117] has announced that he finally has been able to create life. This and that were mixed together and exposed to something else with the result that snails came into being and also some kinds of weeds.

A statement of that sort is a pretty serious thing to make and so I presume the scientist was not making a premature announcement but somehow, for the sake of the rest of us, I hope that he is proved wrong. If life at last is to prove nothing more than the accidental fusing of chemicals then most of us are going to be pretty miserable.

I don't know why it is but I do know that it is true that just as much as we need daily food so do we need something outside of ourselves to worship. When we are little we hear of a vague something called God. We don't think about it particularly, we worship our parents. Eventually we discover that even parents are not all knowing and we turn to other persons – a school teacher, a friend, a sweetheart, a child. These in their turn fail us and so we turn back to God again. A time of stress comes and knowing nowhere else to turn we pray and that prayer is apparently answered. A sort of mystery comes upon us and a happiness. We think anew of the old legends of the saints. We perceive that there is nothing in the world which can disturb us.

If this scientist working over in Lorain should now prove to be on the right track with his snails and his weeds it will doubly true that nothing can disturb us but the knowledge will come with a sort of despair. It will mean that all the prayers that were ever answered

———————

[115] Julián Carrillo Trujillo (1875-1965) Mexican composer, conductor and violinist

[116] Amelita Galli-Curci (1882-1963) Italian coloratura soprano.

[117] Lorain, Ohio

were accidents. It will mean that poor Joan, afraid of the flames, and the other martyrs more calm were all victims of a tremendous joke. It will mean that from raptures and visions and joy and humility we will have to turn to the sober contemplation of the action of the H2804 on certain vegetable matters.

I don't like the idea.

<hr>

19 March 1926, Friday:

A Story That Doesn't Mean a Thing

ONCE upon a time was a woman who was a Devoted Mother. Four times a day she put clean rompers on her little boy. She had his sand pile sifted four times. She took him to school every day and brought him home again, although the distance was exactly one block. She never let him cross the street alone. She did not let him play with other children for fear he would learn bad words. She did not let him have a dog for fear he would be scratched. She did not let him have roller skates for fear he would sprain his ankle. She did not let him have a bicycle for fear he would break his leg. She did not let him go bob-sledding for fear he would break his neck. She made him promise never to marry because that would break her heart. She boasted that for the first 13 years of his life he had never been out of her sign One Minute.

The neighbors all said What Beautiful Devotion.

This woman went to a fortune teller and asked her what the future held for her son. The fortune teller said, "Rest assured, your son will never do anything to make you unhappy."

And he never did. Nor anything else.

<hr>

On this same street there lived a woman who neglected her children Something Terrible.

There were four of these children and how they were born and the way they grew up was this way:

The first one was born in a cabbage that grew beside the garbage can. When he grew up he was always eating and when he had finished what was on his plate he would reach over and eat what was on his brother's and sisters' plates.

The second one was born in a white rabbit's burrow. Whenever she talked she wrinkled her funny little nose and whenever she was going any place she hopped.

The third one hopped out of a rose that grew beside the sitting room window. He was always putting his mother's perfume on him and trying to climb the roof of the house.

The fourth one was left on the front door step one morning by a prize fighter who said she was too tough for him. She could lick anybody up to the fifth grade and played catch on the Rattlesnake Nine.

The home life of these children was so terrible that the Monday Afternoon Stitch-in-Time club, the Tuesday Afternoon Croquet club and the Thursday Afternoon Bach Beethoven and Brahms circle got completely disorganized and at least six women intimated that they were going to say something to the pastor about it while three women privately resolved to write to this woman, only not signing their names of course.

For the Neglectful Mother sat down in the morning and read poetry while her children went to school with naked heels. When the truant officer came to complain that Number Four hadn't been seen for three days the Neglectful Mother retorted that it was spring and she didn't blame the poor kid. Sometimes she would bundle up the whole tribe and go visiting for a week. Then they would come home and do the washing on Sunday. It was commonly reported that there wasn't a dish in the house that didn't have a nick in it and that the soft boiled egg was never completely washed off the coffee cups. The whole lot of them was forever falling out of trees or getting lost or forgetting to eat. They wore each other's clothes indiscriminately so that when Number Two got run over by the milk wagon the neighbors came and wept and took up a collection and bought ice cream for Number three.

When these children grew up – what do you think? – not one of them amounted to a thing.

But they were very, very happy.

24 March 1926, Wednesday:

I HAVE a friend whose husband, when their daughter was born, brought her an electric coupe instead of a baby carriage. My friend would then put the baby in a market basket on the seat beside her and go sailing gaily over town. I thought that this was merely the happy arrangement which one family hit upon but it seems that others must be doing it too.

At least I was talking to the furniture man yesterday and he said the automobiles had put a dreadful crimp in the baby carriage business. Stores now buy perhaps just a dozen or so baby carriages and then they try to get rid of them in a couple of weeks if possible. And as for expensive carriages – well, nobody will look at them anymore. They merely want something that the little high school girl whom they rent by the hour can push up and down the sidewalk after school. For the rest of the time they load little Aloysius up into the family car and everybody goes gallivanting off together.

———

I have always felt that the baby carriage played a more or less important part in my life. I think I was to have been named Gretchen or something like that when an uncle appeared on the scene and said that if they would name me after himself and his wife he would buy the baby carriage. So they named me Helen Josephine (the uncle's name was Joseph[118]) and Helen Josephine it has remained. I have always felt that Gretchen would have been a far more suitable name for a young woman who eventually became quite fat.

———

However it is hard to feel quite sorry that the baby carriage is passing. They were never I imagine very comfortable things, either for the baby or for the person who stumbled over them in the hall. I can remember when they used to have an umbrella sort of arrangement over the top which flaunted considerable fringe around the edge. The umbrella could be moved up and down but no matter which way you put it it never seemed to be very effective about keeping the sun out.

Then at night the baby was not infrequently put to bed in them and the whole arrangement must have been rather hard and stuffy.

---

[118] This is referring to her mother Bess Gates' sister, Helen Wallace Gates who married Joseph Louis Geysie.

Today we have hardly done things any better. We have invented those hard little wooden carts which fold up when you get on the street car. Babies are put in these and dragged up and down Main st., the sun beating down on their little sagging heads. Sometimes I have wanted to go up to these mothers and make a few carefully selected remarks but I have always quailed. I am not combative and I always give way before an irate woman.

———————

Of course the baby carriage was always a great comfort when you went to the grocery. You could put a peck of potatoes in it and a leg of lamb and a dozen of canned goods on which the grocery was having a special and a half dozen grapefruit and some apples. And if the family poodle happened to have wandered along and was getting tired you could load him in too. Occasionally with all this the baby got crowded out and bumped his nose on the sidewalk but he could always be gathered up and put to rights again. I have never heard that the casualties from this source were very severe.

And then on Sundays Pa could load the baby up in his carriage and take him for an airing. It was Pa's excuse for not going to church. He could sneak the Sunday newspapers under the seat in some fashion or other and then walk down a shady street till he came to a convenient tree. They must have been wonderfully soothing, these Sunday morning sessions between Pa and the Sunday newspapers and Nature and the baby.

———— ❦ ————

26 March 1926, Friday:

"**D**EAR JO:" (writes John Earle Miller)[119].

"On the Sunday of our trip to St. Augustine I arose early and went to church.
So much had been told me about St. Augustine that I stood rather in holy awe of the earliest ___ of our civilization in United States. Having forgotten much of my history, I thought of St. Augustine sort of reverentially.

———————————

[119] Akron resident, John Earle Michael Miller (1893-1966) worked as a foreman at a rubber plant and resided at South Broading st.

"An hour later bacon and coffee in my stomach, and three dollars in the pocket of the guide, I started in a big "de luxe" bus for St. Augustine.

"As we approached the outskirts the guide reached for his megaphone and drawled, 'Ladies and gentlemen, We are now approaching the oldest city in the United States, Saint August-eene,' (To say it correctly you hang onto the last syllable). Immediately our eyes took on the tense look of eager, inexperienced tourists; and we were soon rewarded.

"What do you suppose was the first thing to which he called our attention? The graveyard.

"Nearly all of the tombstones were of the tablet type, and originally must have stood upright. Now they are bent over like weary soldiers marching home. They are green with age; and from the old tall trees above, the grey moss flutters down like mourning veils. No human soul was to be seen, no flower was there, and no Don Jose knelt grieving beside the grave of his Carmen. I could easily have been moved to honest tears by the plaintive desolation of the place if our guide had not yelled: 'The city gates of St. Augustine. Time for lunch.'

"The oldest house in the United States was at our disposal for 15 minutes. Imagine! Fifteen minutes to count the patches on the quilt that covers Maria Theresa's bed.

"A funny old man with sideburns, a rheumatic knee, and a red nose pointed out the items of interest on the lower, floor, such as the original deed to the property. Having gruffly delivered himself of his oration, he dismissed us with a flourish of his cane and told us to go upstairs and look at what we pleased.

"Some of the furniture is so old that they keep it roped in. That prevents fat ladies from sitting on frail chairs. There was one Chippendale highboy that I wanted for our dining room at home. Of course, I couldn't have got it in the back end of the bus; and furthermore, the place was quite thoroughly policed. All the same, I wanted that highboy.

"Well, all is all, I scampered so frantically from room to room that my neck was all corkscrewed by the time the smart Alec on the bus tooted his horn. I defied him long enough to make a wish at the wishing well. I wished he would fall in and drown.

"I sighed over the beauty of the famous Ponce de Leon hotel where the rates are $20 per day and up. Mostly up (per our swaggering guide). But I have been in better places since; and we only drove by the place at that. I could have spent the time taking pictures of the queer Spanish houses with the weather beaten balconies running across the front. On some of these balconies, beside bunches of drying garlic, wrinkled grannies sat sunning themselves and looking down on the tourists racing all over the town like mad March hares.

"On the way to the entrance of Fort Marian we glanced hurriedly at the remains of the old most where, in centuries gone past, blood flowed thicker'n cider. We were met at the gateway of the fort by a member of the St. Augustine Historical society who conducted a lecture and exploration that was a fight, both by word and foot. She gathered her flock together at each sign post, wound up her speech concerning that particular spot, let it run down, and scurried on to the next section of the relay, the flock panting behind her.

"They make a lot of old Chief Osceola. I am not quite clear as to just exactly who he was, but he had something to do with the claim to the land around St. Augustine. They showed us the dungeon where he died. More Spanish maneuvers. In another room was his wigwam with Seminole housekeeping paraphernalia scattered around it, an old Indian canoe, and dummy figures of the chief himself, his youngest daughter, and the wife.

"We saw the secret dungeon. Take it from me, Horatio Alger never thought up anything as ghastly as this really was. The Spaniards took their prisoners into an outer room, removed a secret stone from the wall, and shoved their victims into an inner chamber that was pitch dark and air tight. The opening was then closed, and the Spaniards went into the chapel next door to hear mass, while the prisoners smothered to death.

"The Fountain of Youth attracts many. Can't you just see Ponce de Leon staggering up there with a weary, bilious look in his eye and then skipping away like a playful young goat? It costs a quarter to walk down the steps to the spring where he actually drank his morning tonic. The water doesn't taste much different from Akron's city water. And I didn't see any old folks coming back with new teeth or kicking up their heels. It was a riot to see them climb down from the bus and hobble over to the round enclosure above the spring with an expectant look on their faces, and then limp back looking for all the world like wanting their quarter back.

"Good Bye."

27 March 1926, Saturday: OMITTED (article written by substitute writer from Akron U, Dorothy Shreve)

1 April 1926, Thursday:

ROSIE'S gone and a pert young thing has come to take her place. This successor to Rosie hasn't been named yet for as Bill pointed out on the road to Medina yesterday you can't name a car the way you name a baby. In the case of a baby you name it George Washington Jones or Julius Caesar Dalrymple and expect it to grow up manifesting those characteristics. But with a car it is just the other way around – you let it go without a name until it manifest some outstanding characteristic and then you christen it accordingly.

This new car is neat – you'll have to admit it. She is painted grey and she has tires and disc wheels and distinguished upholstering and a place in the back where you can put the oysters and things that you're bringing home for supper. And she is to have a garage to stay in the door of which is blown off but Mr. Limrin said he would put it back again Saturday.

And so, all in all, I suppose we should be quite proud and satisfied. And yet I can't help thinking of Rosie. I wonder if she is out in a backyard some place with people poking their fingers in her ribs and sniffing at the thin places in her tires. And I wonder if she understands that we really didn't want to get ride of her – that it was merely the expense of getting her repaired every week that was keeping us patched and starved looking.

At any rate she may be comforted with the knowledge that it will be a long, long time before we forget her. Yesterday, coming back from Medina, this new upstart balked at a hill and Bill had to throw her into second or first or whatever it is they do when they climb hills. "Rosie never would have grumbled at that," said Bill sadly and I looked out the window in the other direction and blew my nose.

———————

Last night we organized The Society for the Bringing of Happiness into Millionaires' Lives. You know how sad millionaires always are. Their wives are dreadful gadabouts and their children sass them and grow up to very bad ends while their friends are really not friends at all but just sycophants who stand about worshiping the money instead of the man. Read almost any modern author and you'll realize how terrible it must be to be a millionaire. Even Dorothy Dix, who is this column's favorite lady writer, was talking just the other night about the unhappy lives they lead. And O. O. McIntyre who is this department's favorite writer about things in New York, also has a great deal to say about the distress of the rich. He hardly knows a rich man who doesn't lead a lonely existence at his club while his wife squanders everything she can lay her hands on at Montmartre and Lido.

———————

My personal impression is that millionaires must be perfect wizards at covering up their real feelings. I saw a man whizzing out Medina road yesterday in his little high powered motor. I don't know just how much he has but it is reputed to be an awful lot. And sad though his heart might have been he certainly had one of the most contented expressions on his face that I ever saw in my life. And I knew a woman once who had a great deal of money and instead of envying me it seemed to me that she was, in a way, sort of patronizing me. And I knew another awfully rich man who, even though his heart was breaking, managed to laugh almost all day long and flirted with a great many girls and didn't seem to care if his wife never came back from Miami.

This new society that we've organized is going to get out after these millionaires and in case they don't know they're unhappy we're going to point it out to them. After they understand their true condition we're going to buy them little vines that they can plant by their backdoors and give them little books so that they can manage their expenses on the budget system. And in case they should go into a restaurant in January and order tomato salad we're going to point out to them how very, very much happier those persons are who don't order vegetables out of season.

---

2 April 1926, Friday:

THERE has been, quite a lot of traffic in the back door lately. Every morning at 10 o'clock a very talkative young fellow and a very silent one come with a basket of bread. The talkative young fellow has a remarkable lisp, and leans against the door bell while he delivers it. The silent one carries the basket and makes trips back to the wagon for rye bread or cinnamon rolls or whatever happens to be missing from the basket.

On Saturdays a young man comes with cottage cheese and candy. Just why he should have hit on this particular combination I do not know. Anyway he has memorized quite a piece about how the cottage cheese is made with cream, etc., and after he has left our door I hear him delivering the same speech, word for word, at all the other doors.

On Wednesday a dark eyed young man comes with doughnuts. They are very excellent doughnuts. The dark eyed young man said that undoubtedly next time I would take a dozen of them, and I think that next time I undoubtedly shall. He also said that hereafter he would have pies, "made by an excellent family of German extraction – under ideal sanitary conditions – any kind you want."

But somehow I still hanker to my own pies. Just as Bill hopes night after night that he'll win a game of solitaire, so I hope day after day that some time I'll turn out an apple pie that isn't peculiar.

I keep wondering just how much this small back door trade amounts to. In "Little Old New York[120]" there was an engaging character by the name of Delmonico who went about peddling sandwiches in a basket. Will these people who come to our back door eventually become discouraged and quit, or will they become bakers and restauranteurs and have huge electric signs in front of their places? Personally, I hope that the chap who makes the doughnuts remains in business. They are certainly excellent doughnuts. As for the young man with the lisp who leans against the door bell I have an idea he eventually with go into vaudeville.

It seems to me that the American Mercury is getting to pretty much of a bore. When it first came out I used to put a copy under my arm and go about hoping that someone would notice it and say, "Well, there goes an intellectual young woman."

But after a while you get weary of hearing the Methodists, the Ku Klux Klan and the Babbitts being panned all the time. You wish to goodness that Mr. Mencken would either find something else to pan or else be quiet. This current issue of his has a story which is supposed to be very brazen and which caused the magazine to be suppressed in certain parts of the country. And yet when I read it last night it seemed to be merely a juvenile sort of brazenness and I was sorry I hadn't gone on washing the dishes.

Sometimes I suspect Mr. Mencken and Mr. Nathan want the world to understand that they are in America, but not of it. They are like a couple of young men who are ashamed of their parents and of the living room furniture and of the golden oak buffet from Sears Roebuck and the butter dish with the lid on it. And they're so afraid that you won't notice how superior they are to these things that they keep sneering about them all the time. You wouldn't mind if they joked about a couple of the things and go down right mad about a couple of others, but after that you wish they'd go ahead and think of other matters and let the world find out for itself whether they're superior or not.

I've sort of fallen in love with women's magazines lately. Not with the stories, which always end the same way, nor with the editorials which are always wishy-washy, but with the advertisements. The advertisements tell you new stents in interior decorating and

---

[120] "Little Old New York," a play written by Rida Johnson Young and turned into a film in 1923.

fixing up the attic and making corn bread and all sorts of things. William McFee in some recent magazine article said that the most interesting literary work in America today was being done by way of the advertisements and it is easy to believe it.

<hr>

5 April 1926, Monday:

IT SEEMS that a certain Miss Mason who keeps a stylish school on the Hudson[121] discharged one of her teachers recently alleging that the lady had bad table manners.

"She is a failure in a private school," Miss Mason is quoted as having said, "but you might be able to get her a position in a public school."

And now the teacher, Miss Mary Cochrane Rogers by name, is suing Miss Mason for slander.

One wonders just what the breach in table department could have ben that it should cause a young woman to lose her job. Did Miss Rogers by some chance forget to take her salad from the left or did she handle the bouillon a little too zestfully, did she let appetite overcome discretion and eat everything that was on her plate or did she forget to break her muffins into sufficiently refined pieces? Certainly she could never have performed that crowning error – dipped her toast in the tea.

Personally, I hope that Miss Rogers gets the $15,000 which is the extent to which she feels her reputation has been damaged. Meanwhile I shall watch the papers carefully to find out the exact nature of her shortcomings.

On the other hand it was not exactly polite on Miss Mason's part to intimate that a teacher might be a rank failure in a private school and will succeed in a public school. One rather gets the impression that in Miss Mason's opinion a public school teacher is, well you know, the merest bit inferior. As a matter of fact, of course, she was probably entirely correct, in her statement. A teacher who forgot occasionally to use her salad

---

[121] Miss C.E. Mason's School for Girls, the Tarrytown on the Hudson River, Tarrytown, New York.

fork might still be a wonderful basketball coach and know her math, from equations to solids – qualities which are slightly more important in the public school curriculum.

Having never been in a private school I am in no position to comment on its shortcomings. I have gone to public school, however, and it has occasionally seemed to me that in the public school we might devote a little more attention to the niceties of conduct.

I know that when I was a freshman just entering high school there was something scheduled for Friday afternoons which was known as "society." This, I reasoned, must be an hour given over to instruction in proper behavior. However, when Friday afternoon came I found that "society" was a sort of club. You elected a president and rad papers and had minutes of the last meeting and learned a great deal about Roberts' rules of order[122].

In all the years since than there has never been one occasion when I needed Roberts' rules of order. But there were a good many occasions when a little firm grounding in Emily Post's[123] rules of conduct would have stood me in excellent stead.

It may be of course that manners, whether in public or private school, are something which must be absolved rather than taught. The most gracious young woman I ever knew came from the Elizabeth Duncan school in Potsdam and I can't remember that any of them ever mentioned having had a course in proper conduct. They read beautiful literature, listened to beautiful music, gazed on beautiful paintings. This may have had something to do with their daily conduct which was almost invariably pleasing in spite of the fact that a good many of them had in the beginning been waifs and fondlings.

---

[122] Roberts' Rules of Order was first published in 1876 by the U. S. Army officer Henry Martyn Robert

[123] Emily Post (1872-1960) American author famous for writing books about etiquette

7 April 1926, Wednesday:

BABIES, I have found, are a good deal like husbands. They have to have a cross spell just so often.

Whether you are dealing with a baby or a husband the course of events seems to be just about the same. They get a sort of ominous expression about them and nothing you do pleases them. You try and you try and they keep getting madder and madder. After a while you reach the limit of your patience and you get mad, too, after which the husband or the baby comes to terms almost immediately. The smiles and the affection and the nice behavior which they can manifest the minute they perceive your dander is up is just too marvelous for anything.

Of course the sensible thing to do would be to get made right away or what is even better, get mad first. Then one might be assured of an almost continuously happy home life. But dearie me, how few of us are practical in such matters.

The reason for all this is that today has been one of Mary's difficult days. She wasn't hungry and she wasn't thirsty and she wouldn't take her orange juice. She wasn't damp and there weren't any pins sticking her. In spite of all this she hollered. She didn't want to lie in her bed and she didn't want to lie on the couch and she didn't want you to hold her. She just hollered.

There was one thing she did want to do. She wanted to sit up. Just how these ambitions seize on babies I don't know. The books don't seem to say very much about it. They say that at six months a baby should be sitting up and that it will achieve this triumph all by itself. But there isn't a word about the preliminary months. It does seem that there ought to be some preliminary months. Even a grown person can't lie flat in bed and suddenly assume a sitting up position without considerable help from his elbows.

Anyway Mary wanted to sit up so I propped her up in the big chair and she sat there and smiled and smiled while he head wobbled around and she looked, if I do say it myself, just the slightest bit silly.

After a while her eyes dropped and I reasoned that if I took her up very quietly I could plop her into bed without her knowing anything about it. But such a child! Such intelligence! She woke up right away and started hollering again. The battle lasted most of the day. Now that peace is finally settled over the home it seems almost unearthly.

Of course it is reassuring to know that your child is possessed of ambition and spirit. What I can't understand is why they always elect to manifest it at such inopportune times. Saturday, as I recall, was a day in which I had little to do and Mary slept all day long. Today, when my head aches and the dishes are waiting and something has gone wrong with the electric lights and the groceries aren't ordered she decides she will perfect herself in the art of sitting up. What I should have done, naturally, was to have explained it all to her this morning and then left her to have it out with herself. But you know how we women are, we keep hoping that peace will come by pleasant channels.

And then too, Mary may be doing a little reasoning of her own. She may be saying in effect: "If you hadn't stayed up and played solitaire till 1 o'clock this morning your head wouldn't ache and the dishes would be done and the groceries would be ordered and you'd have plenty of time to help me sit up."

I hope not though. It is very disturbing to a parent to have a critical child.

10 April 1926, Saturday:

DEAR Parker:

Last night we went out for a little ride and coming back along the Canton road we couldn't help noticing the steady procession of Mr. Donahey's white crosses. Sometimes they were close to a railroad crossing where you would rather expect them to be and sometimes they were at other places where you wouldn't expect them at all.

Now after all the snow and rain and everything it was a fairly pleasant night Parker and quite a lot of other persons besides ourselves were out driving. Of all those who passed us I imagine there were about six who dimmed their lights. The 84 or so others let us have it good and plenty. Sometimes the fellow behind would have his lights on full and the fellow on front would have his on full and not only that but a spotlight, too, so we couldn't help being blinded and once we got way over on the side of the road and when the other cards had passed we saw we were mighty close to a mighty deep ditch.

This is something that I've talked about before, Parker, and it's something that a great many other persons are talking about but nobody seems to know exactly what to do about it. And I was just sitting here and wondering, now that you're editor of the Akron Motorist, if you couldn't start a campaign of some sort about these headlights – put up little cards maybe asking motorists to be polite about their headlights. Bill says that some day all important highways will be illuminated and we won't have to have headlights but of course I don't know just how soon that is going to be. Meantime those white crosses keep bobbing up more and more.

As ever,

JO.

There is a certain style of house which always fringes the edge of every town. It is a wooden box-like structure with a little porch running across the front. The yard about it is mud and there is not a tree in sight.

There seems to be neither sewer nor water nor gas for these houses. They are scorched by the sun in summer and in winter the wind blow upon them hard and the snow drifts through their cracks.

I don't know what this passion is which seizes on certain people and makes them move where they can enjoy neither the independence and the shade of the country nor the beneficence of sewer connections which the city has to offer. However it is by them that cities grow. They go just beyond the city limits and pitch their wooden structures and after awhile they dig a garden and maybe plant a tree. A little while later some other adventurous soul shoves up alongside and then another and another. Pretty soon there is a community clamoring to be taken into the city limits. Then the man who built the first house gets restless and looks about him. The neighbors are too close. His cabbages are big and of the tenderest green, his trees are just beginning to throw their shade but to him it is all gall. He can't breathe. After awhile he gathers up his family and moves on. A few miles out he comes upon a sea of mud. It is balm to his eyes. He stretches and looks about him. There is neither a tree nor a shrub nor a smokestack in any direction to close him in. Once more he breathes. He hoists his cigar box in the midst of the mud and his wife gets out the frying pan and the coffee pot.

There is an opposite of this man in the man who hugs the rubber factories all his life. Bill says that it is surprising but it costs practically as much to live close to a rubber factory as it does to live out where the air is a little less dense. The answer is laziness.

It is pleasant to sleep till 10 minutes before the whistle blows and get to work in three minutes. Consequently there is always considerable competition to live close to the factories. It is really dreadful when you think of it. The trouble is that in some form or other we all do it.

12 April 1926, Monday:

W E WENT up to Cleveland the other night to see George Arliss[124] in "Old English[125]." Guy Wortley and E. L. Marting were there too and a few other persons who looked familiar.

Between acts the usual number of men got up, fumbled around in their pockets for cigarets, tramped out over the feet of their women companions and the feet of other men's women companions and returned two minutes after the curtain of the next act was up.

"When I was a girl," plaintively remarked the elderly woman sitting next to me, "I always said that a man who did a trick like that needn't bother about taking me to the theater a second time but the girls nowadays don't seem to mind. But then lots of things have changed. We used to be ashamed to let a man know we need powder. Now look at them." And she waved her hand over the audience where about a third of the women were making up for the next act.

We got to talking about opera then and I remarked that I didn't believe I had ever seen a strictly modern opera.

"Why," said my friend, "didn't you ever see 'Marguerite'?"

"No," I said, "I never did."

"That's funny," she said, "I thought every girl had been to see Marguerite."

---

[124] George Arliss (1868-1946) Englsh actor, author and playwright, and the first British actor to win an Academy Award.

[125] "Old English" is a Broadway play by John Galsworthy (1867-1933).

It occurred to me later that she was probably thinking of "Faust[126]" but of course that didn't help the situation much. And anyway the curtain went up and a minute or so later the men came tramping back again.

———————

A good many articles have been written from time to time on various professions open to women but so far as I recall not much has been said about the profession of baby tending.

I had never though much about the profession of baby tending until recently and then I discovered that you have to engage a baby tender days and days ahead so great is the demand for her services. Sometimes she is an elderly woman of independent income who finds baby tending a sueful way of occuying otherwise lonely hours. Sometimes she is a woman who, by devoting al lher time to it, derives a very fair income. Sometimes she is a school girl who finds that she can study and tend babies at the same time and have extra pocket money besides. The very capable young woman who came to take care of Mary the other night said she had earned all her college spending money in just that fashion. The most popular baby tender in Akron is the woman who insists on doing the family mending for you while the baby sleeps. My personal feelings in this matter are that such a woman should have a very nice monument erected to her by grateful citizens.

I have decided now, since making these investigations, that in years to come I too will become a professional baby tender. I really can get on quite well with a baby now. I know when to pat it on the back, when to cluck-cluck at it and when to put it to bed. I already know how to darn. In addition to these qualifications I intend to take up story telling so that if there are older children in the family we can have a story hour. I might also, although I'm not sure, take a course in taffy pulling. Anyway it seems to me that it is a profession which has almost unlimited possiblities and in years to come when my ample form takes its way down the street I can just hear the children running out and crying, "Oh goody, goody, here comes Aunt Jo."

———————✦———————

14 April 1926, Wednesday:

————————————————

[126] A grand opera based on "Faust et Marguerite" by Michel Carré and Jules Barbier, and premiered in Paris in 1859.

T HE argument that Bill and I had last night was about whether the married woman or the single woman meets more interesting people.

"The married woman does of course," said Bill, "she can pick the people she wants to meet."

And right away I had a picture of what Bill was thinking. He was thinking that after a woman was married she joined an uplift club and then the club invited a celebrity to come and speak to it. The celebrity came and after his speech the women all clustered around and shook his hand and said, "Oh Mr. Barbecue, I've enjoyed your talk SO much. I've read all your poems and I've been wanting to ask you what you meant in the third line of--"

And Mr. Barbecue would shake their hands limply and answer as politely as he could and refuse all invitations to stay over and run to catch a train and say as he sank down in the Pullman, "Well, thank God that's over."

Meanwhile 50 women would be telling husbands what a clever remark that dear Mr. Barbecue made and at night they would like awake and wonder in the darkness if that hadn't been a peculiarly meaning look Mr. Barbecue had given them and they would sign and wish they had been married to a celebrity instead of to a wholesale meat dealer.

A year or so ago I heard an account of how Amy Lowell came to address a woman's club. I forgot just all of the things she did but I do recall that she reproved the entertainment committee bitterly because they had provided only salad and sandwiches when they surely must have known that she always had a heavy dinner in the evening.

Like all the other nice things in life interesting people are entirely accidents. Sometimes celebrities are interesting and sometimes they aren't but even if they are interesting there's no fun in standing in line with 300 other women just to meet one.

It is the little intimate meetings with interesting persons which count and this is where the business woman gets her innings. She, like the married woman can join a club and be lectured at and stand in line. But on the other hand she stands just as great a chance of running into the celebrity accidentally or in the course of the day's business. She may have to see him about a contract and get invited out to lunch. She may have business at his home, get a view of him in his shirt sleeves, gossip with his wife, listen to him air his views on the short-comings of kitchen sinks. If it is a woman celebrity they can get business matters out of the way and then have a heart to heart talk on waist lines.

My own personal view of the matter is that interesting people are liable to bob up anywhere. A married woman who meets and talks with one person a day has one-tenth the chance of the business woman who meets 10 persons a day. Aside from that an interesting person is liable to bob up most anywhere – he may be a printer or a dry cleaner or a house painter. The trouble is that a lot of us are lost in a sort of glamour so that we can't tell an interesting person when we see one. I read several weeks ago about a rubberworker who was trying to write novels. When asked where he got his ideas he answered, "Oh, just out of the air." Meantime all about him other rubberworkers were living and dying and getting married but that sort of interest was something he couldn't see.

I suppose it is because painters, actors, musicians and the like are far off that we set our hearts on knowing them. One of the reasons I wanted to be a newspaper reporter was the hope that some day I might meet Jascha Heifetz[127]. Well I did and it was dreadful. The only good thing that came out of it was that it started the cure.

---

15 April 1926, Thursday:

I HEARD last night of the death of an old lady whom I had known when I was a child. She and her husband had come from Germany when they were quite young and in due course of time they had set up in the brewery business. I don't know how many years the struggle lasted, but eventually the brewery prospered, they built themselves a fine brick house, their daughter married well. When I knew this old lady the daughter had to dress her hair for her because her hands trembled so she could not get them to her head. They said it was because she had worked so hard when she was young.

After the old lady was dressed and her hair combed and she had given orders to the cook and had run her handkerchief over the top edge of the pictures to see if everything had been dusted she would sit down and unravel old socks and stockings. After she had them all unraveled she would knit them up again into new socks and stockings. She did not have much regard for color and the results were generally pretty much pied. Neither, so far as was discoverable, did anybody wear the socks and stockings which the old lady so earnestly put together. However she kept at it and seemed to derive considerable satisfaction from it. It was a habit of her youth which she wasn't quite able to overcome.

---

[127] Jascha Heifetz (1901-1987) a Russian-American violinist.

I know another old lady, otherwise quite modern in her ideas, who still clings to two-piece union suits[128], hour glass corsets, high laced shoes and woolen petticoats. The Christmas shopping for this old lady is always quite difficult because the shops don't offer much variety in the things she wears.

Considering the oddities of this generation which is rapidly passing one wonders what our peculiarities will be when we are old. In our family we have always been great hands to treasure bacon drippings, a habit which is already looked upon more or less coldly by certain of our friends. I remember when I was living with Florence I carefully collected a whole half cup full which she callously threw away when it came her turn to wash the dishes. "Don't be such an old granny," she said heartlessly, "use butter."

Some day I suppose thirty years from now I will stand by with smouldering wrath and see Mary pour bacon drippings down the sink.

In a way though it is difficult to see just what the next generation is going to have to complain about. What with our step-ins and our chiffon hose they certainly can't scold us for bundling up. Such money as we've had we've thrown around carelessly and we've bobbed our hair and sat up till three in the morning.

It is quite conceivable of course that the next generation will right about face and become terribly conservative. It is generally argued that young people are always wild and free but this is something that I very much doubt. At any rate I don't know of any worse lot of prudes than my particular gang was when I went to high school. We decided not to speak to one girl because we thought she looked coarse. One girl wept bitterly because she thought a certain boy was looking at her too much. We held indignation meetings when it was discovered that a girl whom we knew indulged in petting[129]. We discussed the horrible end to which she undoubtedly would come. We prayed a good deal. I think I was 22 years old when I heard my first doubtful story.

This not altogether pleasant idealism is I imagine very necessary part of youth which can be held in abeyance but not entirely overcome. Personally it wouldn't surprise me a bit

---

[128] Simple cotton or wool flannel long underwear worn under other garments, and earns its name by uniting the upper and lower pieces into one garment in "union."

[129] Amorously embracing, kissing, and caressing one's partner.

if the next generation would have dreadful reactions and go about saying, "For goodness sake, grandma, leave off the cocktails and go to bed."

—⁙⁙⁙✦⁙⁙⁙—

13 April 1926, Tuesday:

YESTERDAY at dinner we were speaking of wet and dry matters, and one member of the party said he thought the prohibition amendment would be repealed and another said he didn't think so. The drys[130], he said, would go ahead demanding, "Do you want the saloon back?" and even the very wettest would go to the polls and vote No. In case it were repealed, however, he wondered if it wouldn't be a profitable matter to get into the saloon business. Somebody else said yes, profitable, but not respectable for long. Then everybody fell to and ate their pudding which had an unusually interesting sauce on it and you could tell they were all thinking hard.

The saloon as I understand it was an institution peculiar to America. At any rate there seems always to have been considerable opprobrium attaching to it. In Germany it would appear there were beer gardens and the like where whole families went, drank their schnaaps, talked and laughed and had an altogether agreeable time.

But in America, except in the case of very wretched women, only men went to saloons. As a child I always regarded them with considerable awe. Their windows were always shielded in some fashion or other, their doors were made out of old shutters. There was saw dust on the door sill, and when the doors swung back and forth they gave out a not especially pleasant smell of stale beer. I was always sure that the men who came out of them went home to beat their families.

It was not until three or four years ago that I managed to get inside one such place, I suppose there were quite a few of them which in one fashion and another managed to

---

[130] The "drys" consisted of many groups of people that wanted to prohibit alcohol and were anti-saloon. In contrast, the "wets" believed prohibition led to more illegal activity and that prohibition had no bearing on its prevention.

survive. This one was on the edge of the Harlem black belt[131]. Two evangelists, a white woman and a black man, were conducting religious services up there in some sort of huge ramshackle wooden structure with a tin roof and a number of reporters were dispatched thither to see what might happen. It was a boiling hot day. At 4 o'clock in the afternoon a corner policeman, advised us that the only place to secure refreshments was at Al's place in the middle of the next block.

Al had on a dirty apron and he wiped off the marble with an exceedingly dirty rag. The stuff which he served us was exceedingly cool and good. Aside from that the place, swinging door and all, seemed decidedly commonplace.

It is to be hoped that if the saloons do come back the years through which we have just passed will have taught us how to make them pleasanter places. This is plainly one of the professions which women should go into the business of saloon keeping they would doubles trim the place up with cretonne and pile up the counters with lettuce sandwiches and buttered Swedish wafers. On the other hand the men, when they had their day, weren't entirely successful. My idea would be to have a man and his wife run the place jointly.

The ideal saloon immediately becomes apparent. In one of the windows it should have a considerable array of bottles. The saloon keeper who has any love for his trade must of necessity come upon any number of odd bottles and in time he should have quite a collection with their history. If he wished he could put only filled bottles in the windows and then he could keep the odd ones inside in a glass case. Saw dust is apt to be messy and I think I would eliminate that but I would keep the old square tables and chairs. The free lunches which soaped up the counter in the old days seem from all reports to have been quite remarkable and I'm sure I would retain those but I would eliminate the mirrors almost entirely. They make a man self-conscious in his drinking. Instead I would accumulate by degrees some vigorous German prints.

It would probably be wise to keep a radio far, far away from the place as one of the chief benefits of drinking is that it loosens the flow of ideals, an effect which would be almost exactly counter balanced by the radio. The occasional appearance of a German band would be all right and there would be no objection to a customer occasionally singing providing his voice was good.

---

[131] Harlem is a predominantly African-Amercian neighborhood located in Manhattan, New York, with a rich history. The Harlem Renaissance during the 1920's brought about a great influence to literary and artistic culture, and great contribution to the rise of jazz.

As to the refreshment beer and Swedish punch are the only articles I am familiar with so I would have to leave the choice of that to some one else. I heard once though of a waiter who could hold five, or maybe it was seven, steins of beer and fill them all at once. If he is still anywhere around I would like to hire him.

⸻ ❧⬥❧ ⸻

19 April 1926, Monday:

IF YOU are a woman and have a husband who gads nights or, on the other hand, if you are a man and have a wife who gads nights.

I know of no better way to put something all over them than to stay quietly at home and read Ring Lardner's[132] most recent volume of short stories, "The Love Nest." The task can be finished nicely by bed time.

"Hair Cut" is the best story I have read in a long time and immediately after it, I would place "Who Dealt?" The half dozen or so other stories in the volume are just average and should be read merely for entertainment. The two I have singled out, however, should be read for your soul's good.

In both of these stories, Lardner's method of procedure is the same. Both are monologues. In "Hair Cut" a garrulus[133] barber dilates on certain of the town's characters, one of whom, in the barber's estimation, is a wonderful cut up. The tragedy which he reveals is all the more bitter because the barber is too obtuse to see it. In "Who Dealt?" four persons are seated about a bridge table and one of them, a bride of three months, is jabbering. And as in the case of the barber she, too, reveals a tragedy of which she herself is altogether unaware.

Up to date, my favorite Lardner short story has been "Some Like 'Em Cold." I now add "Hair Cut" and "Who Dealt?" And although I don't know enough about literature to pose as a critic I doubt whether there is anything in American short stories which is finer than these.

---

[132] Ringgold Wilmer "Ring" Lardner (1885-1933) American sports columnist and short-story writer

[133] A word that is named after the bird species of jays, and means "talkative" or "fond of chatter."

I had to interview Lardner one time, but all I can remember about it is that Lardner is that Lardner was inexpressibly bored and made repeated attempts to get away. The place was the Polo Grounds[134], where the world series was being played. Underneath a section of the grand stand a dining room had been set up where free lunches were served reporters by one of the athletic clubs. I was talking to one of the waiters and he was telling me how much his feet hurt when all at once I spied my quarry. He was drinking something at one of the tables.

I had been instructed to interview him on "The Sober Side of Humor" and during the 10 minutes or so that I had him button holed I don't recall that he smiled once. Neither did he give me any information that I wanted. Every once in a while some woman would spy him and call out, "Yoo-hoo, there's Mr. Lardner, hello, Mr. Lardner." and Mr. Lardner would incline his head slightly and continue to look bored. After a while he said:

"I tell you, I can't think of any of the things you want just now. Suppose you give me your address and I'll write out some of this stuff and send it to you." So I trustingly gave him my address and he went away with it and I never saw nor heard from him again.

—

20 April 1926, Tuesday:

DEAR Josephine: (writes Lotty Malone),

"You see I call you other than the familiar 'Jo' with which I first addressed you because we have been introduced. Should I be privileged to know you intimately I shall doubtless address you by your full and proper name. This will prove the truth of Jake's recent proverb, 'Familiarity breeds respect.'

"At any rate I'd like to talk with you about the servant problem. The other night in the wee sma' hours our clock, usually so reliable, went on strike and dropped the tray. Nothing seemed broken excepting the silence and I soon discovered that the thread of my beautiful insomniac revery was also completely severed. Naturally I was irritated,

---

[134] The Polo Grounds was one of three stadiums in Upper Manhattan, New York City, used for professional baseball and football, and originally built for the sport of polo in 1876.

but what do you think! When I raised my head to cast a withering glance at the offender there the poor thing stood with both hands before its white face.

"Then I fell to reflecting on this servant so common in all our homes. True, it is always too fast or too slow, but so are we all of us and who am I to condemn that am called in mine own household, 'The family poke.'?

"Then consider the maintenance of the family clock. A shelf and a key are all it needs for overhead and upkeep. Take our flivver in comparison (only I'd rather you took the one next door.) After the initial cost comes oil, gas, tires, a garage, a garage bill, spark plugs, alcohol and eventually paint to say nothing of the crocheted filet fringe for the rear curtain. Does a clock need any of these? No. Does a clock serve us as faithfully? Yes.

"Another thing: clocks are especially interesting to children even if the results are sometimes disastrous. A friend of mine who has a small son with an alarming curiosity told me that her nicest clock simply went to pieces over the knees of her boys. I confess I would have liked to know whether, like the house that Jack built, the small son also went to pieces over the knees of his parent. But I never heard, for I've discovered that in matters concerning other folks' discipline as with those pertaining to clocks one does far, far better not to be too inquisitive."

I don't know as I had ever thought of a clock in just that way. I know that our clock is not a servant. It is a master. I have named it Moses because of its perpetual adjurations, "Tick tock, tick tock," it says, "every second is bringing you nearer to eternity. You haven't mended Bill's shirt, you haven't sewed the button on his coat. The kitchen floor has butter on it. The bedroom windows ought to be washed. You haven't written your novel, you haven't written your short story, you haven't written your column, you haven't put cold cream on your face, you haven't washed your hair. Every second is bringing you nearer eternity. Some day you will die and you won't have done any of the things you ought.

A watch is a useful thing relieving the tedium of married life. You can turn it an hour ahead when your husband isn't looking and he will be awfully surprised when he gets down town next morning. The other night Bill threw cold water on me, or maybe he hit me with a book, I don't remember just which, anyway I was mad and so after he had put his watch under the pillow I slipped it out and turned it ahead. The next morning I had compunctions and was going to turn it back but I couldn't get it.

After a while Bill woke up and looked at his watch. "It's funny," he snorted, "that you couldn't tell a person what time it is."

"Why," I said, "I don't know what time it is."

"You just looked at the watch."

"I didn't."

"You did too."

"I didn't."

"All right then, you didn't."

"Well what time is it?"

"It's half past eight."

So Bill piled into his clothes and banged out of the house and I went to sleep again with a happy feeling knowing he'd be too pleased for anything when he got down to St. Vincent's church and found it was only half past seven.

A wife who can think up little things like that will always have an interesting home life and time and again her husband will look at her and say under his breath, "Well, well, what WILL she think of next?"

———— ⚬⚬◇⚬ ————

21 April 1926, Wednesday:

SUNDAY morning at breakfast H. was telling me about a dream he had had. "I thought I was in a delicatessen," he said, "buying some meat. I smelled something that was wonderfully savory and I turned around and saw it was cheese. 'I've certainly got to have some of that cheese,' I said to myself and I told the girl to wrap me up some. While she was wrapping it up I was wakened by the landlord rapping on my door and brining in my breakfast. I have been wishing since that I could have seen the surprised look on that girl's face when she turned around and found I wasn't there."

————————

I like little dreams like that one of H's and I like people who, like H, can give a clever twist to the telling of them. Otherwise dreams are liable to become long drawn out and tiresome, particularly if it is some one else who is telling them.

I have always been a little suspicious of dreams as they are treated in literature. All night long the heroine dreams of thunder storms and the next morning she learns that her lover has been killed. Or else she dreams of reunion with him and the next morning he comes riding in over the hills. These auguries and presentiments which authors delight in have never been my lot. I can dream of thunder storms all night and the next morning I will get a check for $2.50 in the mail. Or I can dream of nothing at all and the next day will learn that the mortgage is to be foreclosed.

I have friends who say they can go to sleep and finish a dream after they have once waked up but that too is something that I know nothing of. The nearest I can come to it is that sometimes in the midst of a dream I keep assuring myself that it is not real.

There are two sorts of dreams. I imagine, which come to practically every one. They are the dream of thwarted purpose and the dream of being improperly clothed.

Last night I dreamed of going down the street with very little on. "Never mind," I said to myself, consolingly, "this is a strange town and nobody will know you." There is a Freudian explanation for such dreams as this, but since everybody has them I don't know that they are anything to be embarrassed about.

A dream of thwarted purpose, I imagine is just as common. You are trying to catch a train and you can't make it; you are trying to get dressed and you can't find anything; you are trying to catch up with somebody and he is always a little ahead. The explanation for this is, I understand, that in your waking moments you are consumed with an ambition which you are unable to fulfill. You carry the struggle on into your dreams and you wake up limp and exhausted.

There is one dream which children seem always to have after they have lost someone whom they loved. They dream that the loved one has come back. "Why," says the child, "I thought you were dead." "Oh, no," says the loved one, "I've just been away on a visit."

I dare say everyone who reads "Peter Ibbetson" tries for a while afterword to "dream true." You like down and you cross your feet and you place your hands beneath your head and you think of such and such a person very hard. But nothing ever happens.

Dreams I have found rarely concern themselves with persons and events about which one has thought a great deal. Instead they are of trivial matters – a kitten in a tree, a rag man who stops at the back door.

Sometimes I dream of rarely beautiful music, but I have a suspicion that if I could examine it in my waking hours perhaps it wouldn't be so beautiful after all.

— ✦ —

22 April 1926, Thursday:

MARY and I had a pleasant two hours together yesterday. Heretofore when she has been taken out in her carriage she has complained bitterly all the way and fought and chewed her wrappings. Yesterday however she became resigned and even smiled upon passersby who stopped to greet her.

First we went down Wya drive and called on Mrs. Betzler and Alma who weren't at home and then we went on down to Merrimas rd. to Market st. and called on the Deneke's, Elizabeth and Esther and Hermine, where Mary was entered as a prospective music student, and then we bought the groceries and talked with John Stickle for a moment and then we came home altogether a very satisfactory afternoon.

It makes for greater harmony, I have noticed, if the upstairs curtains are all alike.

There was one house which had a silver tea pot in the front window. I think it was probably an heirloom and they were very proud of it.

A gardener was working out on somebody's front lawn with a red wheel barrow. There should be a law compelling all gardeners to use red wheel barrows.

There was house cleaning on in a great mansion. The furniture on the front porch however was ugly and uncomfortable looking. Housecleaning lets the passerby in on a great many secrets.

In front of Temple Israel a little boy came along on roller skates. "Hello," he said. "Hello," I said. "Look at Nellie," he said, "she's laughing at you." Nellie was the little boy's dog.

About a block before you get to Market st. there is a house perched high over a garage. Of all the houses I looked at I think I would most like to live in that one. You could fix it up funny. There would surely have to be a studio over the garage.

Further back was the duplex where the Jake Falstaffs used to live. The Falstaffs moved eleven times in three years. The Falstaffs love to move. Just about the time Tonya gets the last curtains bought and Jake gets the kitchen stove to sitting level they feel the moving fever coming on.

There was a boy coming along the street who looked oddly familiar and then I knew it was Philip Schwan. "Hello," I said. "Hello," he said but he looked a little perplexed.

Mr. Ritter was out in front of his grocery store inspecting the window. It must be fun to own a grocery store and fix the tomatoes and the cauliflower and the asparagus so they look artistic.

Two women were parting. "Now come over soon," said one, "and stay all day and we'll just have a good time."

On Market st. Mr. Bilan's new red and white street cars were going up and down. They look ever so much better than the orange ones. I wonder if the effect will be the same next August. And why did they change to red. Will people ride sooner on a red and white street car than on an orange one?

A lot of youngsters were out driving their father's cars. It must be dreadful for spring to come along and to be young and not have a car to take your girl out in. Maybe – but I doubt it – there are some girls who would just as lief[135] walk.

⁂

23 April 1926, Friday:

D EAR JO (Writes a Woman Who Minds Her Own Business)

"I wonder if you will let me have a place in your column for an old story by a new person. I always read your column and I hope the fellow that I want to talk

---

[135] An Old English word implying gladly or willingly.

about does too. If he does he will I hope, try to imagine how near he came to getting poked in the ribs with my umbrella.

"Last night we (hubby and me) went to the Grotto's Frolic at the Armory. Everybody will remember it had rained some and was still suspicious looking. We took a seat in the first row behind the reserved. Mine the second seat from the aisle. All went merry as a wedding bell until the seats in that particular row were filled except the one next to me, and it was finally taken by a tall man. Tall is all that I can say by way of description, for I didn't look at him close enough.

"I am in the habit of minding my own business whether I go alone or with anyone else to a movie or anything else. We couldn't hear everything very well and if I missed something my husband would whisper it to me and I did the same. This fellow had not been there very long until he began bumping my arm with his elbow. At first I thought it an accident and remained calm enough but after about seven more accidents, I boiled inside but sat trying to conceive what would be the best thing to do about it. I didn't say anything to my husband for he has a habit of doing things before he thinks and I could just see that fellow with his head 'chawed' to pieces and the whole show spoiled. I kept moving closer to him after each nudge and I am not so large that I can not sit on one of those chairs which were rather roomy and have a bit left on the side but still I received three more nudges in succession. At that I fairly ached to slap his face and I looked around to the left of me for one of the ushers with his black hat and tassel but the only one I could see was way across from me and I didn't want to cross in front of all those other people to go to him so sat planning what I was going to do the very next time he nudged me. If it made a scene and caused the whole show to stop, I was going to have him put out, but just then that usher came from across the way telling everybody that sat behind the reserved seats that they could move up now as there was plenty of reserved seats vacant.

"Now I'm wondering who had to put up with the pest the rest of the performance. I am sure he would choose his seat next to a woman. And I wish some one would inform me of a way to treat a death courting male who doesn't know any better than to practice on a wife whose husband sits besides her and he can't fail to know it. He will get beside the wrong person some time I hope and I want to know how to handle the next one that sits beside me."

But honest I don't know what to do in a case like that. In the old days there was the hat pin[136] but anybody should try to find a hatpin this this day and age.

Two or three years ago I knew a woman who recommended jiu-jitsu[137]. All you had to do, she said, was to learn two or three simple tricks and after that you needed never to be afraid of mashers. Even jiu-jitsu however would be a dead loss in a situation where you were trying to prevent a scene. Possibly you could complain to your husband that you had a dreadful headache and then on the way out you could tell the usher about it and he could have the pest removed.

The colossal conceit of the male is something that I've never been able to understand. It seems to be something he's born with. A woman who is moderately plain will go through life saying to herself, "Oh my goodness, nobody could ever possibly care for me," and when somebody does she is tremendously grateful.

A man however can be poor as Job's[138] turkey, he can be cross eyed, knock kneed and toothless and he still fancies that he is irresistible. If a woman pities him he immediately concludes she has been smitten. If she repulses him he concludes it is but to lead him on.

One Christmas eve a couple of years ago I was going home on the subway. The only other person on the rear platform was a man with a kiddie kar[139] in his arms. There was plenty of room for him to stand but instead of that he had to come over and lean on me. No matter which way I moved he had to lean on me. And yet he was a respectable looking man and the kiddie kar made it obvious that he was thoughtful of his family.

---

[136] Hatpins became popular in the 1880's when bonnets gave way to hats, and became used as a weapon in self-defence for women at the turn of the century. They were decorative and functional to hold the hat to the head, and typically 6-8 inches in length.

[137] A Japanese martial art method of close combat defense

[138] Biblical figure who's wealth, children, and physical health are taken away

[139] A vintage 1920's wooden tricycle by H. C. White Mfg. Children's toys

One time at a flower show I stopped to ask an elderly gardener about some prize gladioli[140] he had been raising and he took my address saying he would send me some data on the flowers. A week later he came to call. When I made it plain I was in no mood to be called on he reproached me bitterly for having led him on.

Just what kink this is in the masculine make up I don't know. I was talking about it one morning to my boss and he said that women were just as bad.

"Why," he said, "coming down to work this morning a girl kept pinching my knee."

So I don't know.

⁓•⁓

26 April 1926, Monday:

B ILL was reading a long article in the paper the other night by some chap who maintained that music couldn't express anything definite in the way of ideas. Although he didn't say it in quite that way the idea was that somebody hearing Mendelssohn[141]'s wedding march for the first time and not knowing the name of it would probably never think of it as being a wedding march at all. Later, after he had been to about 20 weddings, he would never hear those triumphant chords of course without being faintly aware of the scent of orange blossoms. But that would be entirely a matter of association.

I suppose this is true to a certain extent. "Humoresque[142]," I have been told, was intended by the composer to represent the uncertain course of a young man who had more to drink than was good for him. And yet most of us think of "Humoresque" as being essentially sad – I think the picture it calls up to most people is of a sad-eyed clown with tears streaming down his grease paint.

---

[140] Another spelling for gladiolus flowers

[141] Felix Mendelssohn 91809-1847) German romantic composer

[142] Piano music consisting of 8 cycles or pieces written in 1894 "Humoresques" by Czech composer Antonín Dvořák (1841-1904) and published by Friedrich or Fritz Simrock (1837-1901)

It is rather far fetched, however, to assert that music can express no ideas at all. One would not have to be particularly acute to know that "Ase's Tod[143]" is the funeral music of a peasant, just as Chopin's funeral march is the death music of an emperor. One would know, without being told, I think, that ladies and gentlemen were moving about in the Strauss waltzes and that a very different sort of people were performing in the Irish dances which Percy Grainger[144] has arranged. In the Pastoral symphony of Beethoven there is a thunderstorm which one would know was a thunderstorm, whether there was any descriptive matter accompanying it or not, and it seems to me that the rush of water is very apparent in Mendelsohn's "Fingal's Cave."

I realize of course that in these instances which I have cited the music is descriptive of various sights and sounds and that not all music can come under such a category. Certainly the music of César Franck[145] could never be so classified and, to mention a very familiar composition, "The Afternoon of a Faun[146]," would probably mean just as much, just as little to its hearers if it bore no name at all.

————

Music, it seems to me, bears a close relation to pantomime. The mime has certain set gestures by which he expresses love, hate, despair. Music has certain set rhythmic forms which are as easily recognized, the waltz, the march, the jig. The closer he adheres to these forms the easier it is to know what it is all about. There is something being played and you know it is a waltz. Very well then, it must be either a gay or a sad waltz and that is all there is too it.

When music departs from these set forms and enters upon strange rhythms then imagination and mood enter in and after that music may express either as much or as little as the bearer wishes.

---

[143] "Aces' or 'Ases Tod" by Edvard Grieg (1843-1907) Norwegian composer

[144] George Percy Aldridge Grainger (1882-1961) Australian-American composer

[145] César-Auguste Franck (1822-1890) Belgian-French romantic composer

[146] Claude Debussy's music "Prélude à l'après-midi d'un faune" based on the poem by Stéphane Mallarmé

The weakness of any argument of course lies in the demand that music at any time should express anything concrete. It is a childish state of mind which requires that Beethoven should have played his moonlight sonata to a blind girl, that Chopin should have written a waltz about a puppy dog's tail.

But perhaps those who are arguing about the matter do not mean quite that. Perhaps what they mean is that music can never express a philosophical idea, as for instance, that sorrow is greater than joy, or that faith, hope and charity will always triumph in the end.

Even that, however, I doubt. If Schopenhauer[147] had been writing music I am quite sure he would have written always in the minor scale and that he would have ended each composition with the fifth tone of the scale which is a tone of violent inquiry. Whereas, if Emerson[148] had been writing music, I think he would have jogged along in the major mode and ended each composition with the third tone of the scale which is a floating tone of serenity and calm.

---

28 April 1926, Wednesday:

ALTHOUGH I wasn't there to see for myself I understand that dinner coats were worn Monday night for the opening of the new Keith-Albee theater. In some fashion or other word got around that evening dress was to be absolutely the thing and consequently all Monday afternoon business was left to struggle along as it could while every fellow who could raise four dollars made for the nearest haberdashery.

This leads me to suspect that men are not so averse to prettying up as legend would have us believe. Just give them a legitimate excuse and they're off. Or even half a legitimate excuse.

---

[147] Arthur Schopenhauer (1788-1860) German philosopher

[148] Ralph Waldo Emerson (1803-1882) American essayist and philosopher

My heart aches to think that I couldn't be there to see the Mayor maybe and Jim Hemphill[149] and Ed Brouse and Roy Reifsnider[150] and the rest all slick and shining with lavender water on their ears. I'll wager the performers on the stage would have got precious little attention.

It is perhaps a pity that the majority of us don't dress up more. Getting into better clothes of an evening gives us a better opinion of ourselves and it stimulates conversation.

However it is easy to see why a good many of us don't. The business girl who has been in blue sere all day longs to come home and get into gingham which is clean and cool and doesn't scratch. The man who has been polite and conversationally brilliant all day doesn't want to carry it through the evening. He wants to come home, get into his house slippers, rolls up his shirt sleeves and slouch.

Years ago when I had notions I resolved that if I had a home of my own everybody would dress for dinner of an evening or bust. I have since found that you can't hold a baby with one hand, broil a steak with the other, answer the telephone, set the table and still dress for dinner. Also, considering how apartments are built these days, there might be some incongruity in getting into evening clothes to eat boiled potatoes and fish cakes off a drop table in a kitchenette. In some families it is even worse. They have to eat off the top of stationary tubs.

And so such evening clothes as I have had are slowly mouldering. The blue one got too tight ages ago. The yellow one has terrible beads on it. The green velvet is collecting dust while it waits to be steamed and made over.

This is a part of the maddening inconsistency of life. If you are a millionaire or if you are terribly famous you can wear old clothes till the crack of doom and people will say, "How democratic, how delightful!" I know of one man, quite a well known writer, who wanders into the most impressive functions in golf knickers or an old sweater or whatever he happens to have laid his hands on that morning. People are perfectly frantic

---

[149] Akron resident, James R. Hemphill (1861-1948) working as President of an insulator Co. and lived at 962 Herford dr.

[150] Akron resident, Roy Elsworth Reifsnider (1889-1929) or Lee Roy Reifsnider (1885-1974)

to have him come to their houses. And I heard the other day about a girl who has millions and she went abroad and wandered about the north of France in a single little light weight frock. On cold days she wore her bathing suit under it.

But people like us who heave a sigh of relief every week when we get the grocery bill paid can't go to a social gathering and feel very frolicsome in our old clothes. We know that the people who notice us will not think, "How democratic, how delightful." Instead they will think, "Poor dear, she had that four years before she was married."

Also our rich relatives, if we have any, aren't much help. "Now Mary," they say in effect, "is just a poor girl and she can't have any use for finery." And so they send Mary a half dozen nice black Hein stockings.

All this as I intimated before, might be obviated if we dressed up more. Then our evening clothes wouldn't moulder and get too tight and we wouldn't be embarrassed when unexpected invitations arrived.

Anyway Monday evening's performance showed that a lot of people are glad and eager to fix up if they only get a chance. It wouldn't be at all surprising in the next few days to see a cane and spats[151] going down Main st.

<hr>

29 April 1926, Thursday:

ONE of the reforms which I should like to see inaugurated pertains to chocolate creams. Every week, Bill brings home a box of candy and I have yet to open one where about a third of the chocolates weren't filled with strawberry. I despise strawberry fillings. Everybody I know despises strawberry fillings, and yet the manufacturers go right on making them.

On account of strawberry fillings more than one tragedy has resulted. I read just a few weeks ago about a very dreadful one. It seems there was a woman who loved candy and her husband brought it to her all the time. Well, she'd open the box and be polite and pass it around and everybody would take a piece. Then they'd bit into it and discover it was strawberry. Then they'd put the other half back in the box. By the time this

---

[151] Victorian men's accessories: gloves, shoe spats, walking canes, watches, suspenders, etc. A spat was an accessory, typically white or grey, that attached to cover the shoe to protect it from mud and soil. Worn over highly polished black shoes.

woman's family had found pieces of candy that satisfied them, there'd be nothing but strawberry half pieces left for her to eat. She went completely out of her mind one day and slaughtered them all.

On the other hand, there is hardly anybody who doesn't just love caramels. The minute you open a box of candy everybody starts poking around in it to locate a caramel. If they're lucky they may find one caramel in the top layer and one in the bottom layer. The meanest man I know is the fellow who made a lot of chocolate squares to look like caramels and then filled them with strawberry.

Another reform pertains to sauce pans. Every woman knows, and would be perfectly willing to tell any man who asked, that when you take a sauce pan off the fire you hold it in the left hand and scrape out the contents with a spoon held in the right hand. This means that the little lip on the sauce pan should be on the right side provided you hold the handle of the pan toward you. And yet every man who makes sauce pans puts the lip on the left side. I have one sauce pan where the man did the sensible thing and put a lip on both sides, but it's the only thing of its kind I ever saw.

Alfred Kreymborg's autobiography, "Troubadour," has been lying around here for I don't know how many months. I carefully avoided reading it because I was sure, possibly because of the figure on the cover, that it was another of these soul searching confessions where the man just simply insisted on telling ALL. However, I picked it up the other day and then I discovered how much delight I had been denying myself. For "Troubadour" is a "nice" book and a charming book, adjectives which couldn't apply very well to most of the biographies which have come along in the past few years.

One of these days I imagine that those men and women who have rushed so gladly into print with the intention of telling everything, will be slightly embarrassed. For one thing, they will discover that erotic experience isn't "everything," and for another thing, they will discover that they have made themselves a little cheap. I keep wondering how Alfred Kreymborg avoided the pit fall.

There is a couplet which he quotes from Heine which is worth thinking about:

"Aus meinem graten Schmerzen Mach' ich die kleinen Lieder."

My German is very limited, and I have never yet found out the English equivalent for schmerzen. I suppose, however, it might be freely rendered, "Out of my great heart-ache I make little songs."

Out of his heart-aches Alfred Kreymborg has made little songs which put together, make a sensitive and memorable biography. Possibly it is out of other heart-aches that all worthwhile things come.

30 April 1926, Friday:

I HAVE been thinking that perhaps the reason Akron hasn't had more civic consciousness in the past has been because it hasn't had enough things to be proud of. You know you can go to visit in some towns and the minute the supper dishes have been stacked out in the sink they'll load you up in the flivver and say, "Now while daylight lasts I want you to see our million dollar library" or our fifty acre park, or our de luxe highway or whatever it happens to be.

And then you can go to some other towns and your host will cough apologetically and say, "Yes, I know it's a dirty, ugly hole but it's where I earn my living and that's good enough for me."

Heretofore Akron has been pretty much in this second class. Whenever you would be riding down Main st. with your guests you would try to distract their attention by telling them that men in the rubber factories were making twelve dollars a day. After you had taken them out and shown them how rubber tires were made and had told them how many men were employed and how many billions of dollars were involved in the business you had nothing left to boast about.

I suppose the viaduct[152] was the first thing we had to boast about. Even with its poor cracked and crumbling sides it really is an achievement and I dare say every person who looks at it from down around Old Portage thrills at the beauty of its arches.

And then, although it wasn't a strictly local matter Sunshine cottage came into being out at Springfield sanatorium[153] and that was something to be proud of.

---

[152] The North Hill Viaduct in Akron, Ohio was built in 1922 and closed in 1977 due to deterioration, and in its place the "All-American Bridge," was built, and carries Ohio State Route 261 over the Little Cuyahoga River.

[153] Sunshine cottage was run by Dr. Clarence L. Hyde at the Springfield Lake Sanatorium, of which Dr. Hyde served as superintendent from 1920 to 1945. In 1934 it was renamed the Edwin Shaw Hospital named after Edwin C. Shaw, a Board of Trustee member.

The other night a million dollar theater opened its doors and some time in the next few months a new children's hospital will come into being.

Some of the things which might happen in the next few years could easily be these:

A new post office might be built at Prospect and E. Market sts. And the old post office could be turned into an art museum. This was one of the things that the late Mrs. Henry Robinson used to dream about.

The folks who run the Erie railroad[154] could get together and erect a new Union station.

A hotel could be built above that distressing hole at Prospect and E. Market sts. In every hotel I've stayed in there were always a lot of freight trains switching under the window all night. This one would be different.

All second hand cars now weathering storms in peoples' front yards might be put in handsome show rooms with expensive plate glass windows.

The council and the school board might take a lively interest in preserving trees.

The library might get a handsome annuity.

All one story wooden shacks might be torn down.

We might have a symphony orchestra.

It occurs to me that I have forgotten the new city building which has, I understand, some very handsome furniture in it. And I might also add that Portage Path is being dug up again and that Portage drive, just around the corner from us, shows signs of being paved.

---

[154] Erie railroad skirted Lake Erie with many stops connecting New York to Pennsylvania, and later to Cleveland, Ohio.

1 May 1926, Saturday:

THE interest in spelling contests which sprang up for no particular reason a year or so ago and is continuing with unabated zest ought to do much in years to come for the well being of the United States Fancy stenographers who can spell Schenectady, sign painters who can spell shoe repairing, grocery clerks who will snap the grocery windows neatly and put only one "l" in watermelon.

Years and years ago spelling contests were quite the thing so the old folks tell us and I suppose that is the reason that is the editor's mail those letters which come in a trembling and faltering hand almost invariably abound in long words which are spelled correctly while those letters which come from the younger generation frequently cause considerable puzzlement. The explanation is, I believe, that the movies and the Charleston have come to take the place of the spelling bee. So far as the movies are concerned I would say that a spelling bee is a great deal more exciting.

———————

Certain of our friends have taken up lately a game called Pig which in more refined circles than ours is known, I understand, as Ghost. Somebody thought of playing Pig at a very opportune moment the other night as we had just settled certain matters pertaining to religion and had run out of arguments concerning divorce. It would be very difficult to tell someone who wasn't initiated how to play Pig. It suffices to say that it concerns words and their spelling.

I think when we first started to play it we felt rather childish. After a while we were amazed to find that so simple a game should be so fascinating.

———————

Occurrence, I think, was a word that bothered me more than any. The C's and the r's had a bad way of piling up and after you'd looked at the word a while it was sure to look wrong, no matter which way you spelled it. And then there were embarrass and harass. If you got too giddy you were almost sure to put two r's in the latter word. Phthisic, one of the trick words in our old spelling book, wasn't hard at all because you knew it was a trick word and were all primed for it. The word which is most persistently mis-spelled today seems to be is obbligato.

Somehow or other, although it probably would have made matters easier for foreigners, I never could feel any sympathy for Mr. Roosevelt's reformed spelling fad. Language has its own slow method of change and that is all right but those arbitrary changes are an affront. We might as well pass a law that all babies' ears should be snipped. It is even irritating to pick up a newspaper where tho't and bro't are the rule.

If I had my way we would even cling to such English spelling as favour, savour, colour and the like. There is a certain sweetness to such a word which is perceptible not only to the eye but to the ear as well when the word is spoken. I wouldn't be surprised if this had something to do with the beauty of English voices.

At any rate we have succumbed to nervous desire to shorten words, take out every unnecessary letter as though it might be an offending appendix, without in any way, so far as I can discover, lessening the anguish of the school child or making him a better speller. Our spelling is dreadful, our speech slipshod, our voices rasping. It would be pleasant in the midst of this to discover that spelling contests are having not only an immediate and practical value but that they are restoring in us some respect for English speech.

---

4 May 1926, Tuesday:

A NOTHER thing that is hard to understand is why a grown up cat should cost more than a kitten.

I was talking to a friend the other day about her black angora. "I paid five dollars for him," she said, "but I suppose he ought to be worth about twenty-five now."

"Why?" I asked.

"He's grown up now," she said.

I don't know how long a cat lives, but I suppose eight years would be a good guess. If you buy a two-year-old cat you've already lost a quarter of him. Personally I wouldn't give more than $2.75 for a two year old five dollar cat.

Besides you've lost his kitten-hood, which is the nicest part about a cat. There isn't anything cuter than a fluffy kitten with blue eyes and a flag staff tail and whose diet consists entirely of milk. There isn't anything more distressing than a grown up tom cat which gads around all night and yowls on back fences and eats only liver and young robins.

There are two of this latter variety which prowl up and down outside our windows all night. It is hard to fancy that they were ever innocent little kittens. And the notion that they could possibly be increasing in value with age is simply preposterous.

Carl Van Vechten once wrote a book about cats called "The Tiger in the House," which was not only unique but excellent reading. I meant to read it all but after a while I came to a chapter which told how cats and witches were put into cages and roasted alive, and I could go no further. Somehow I seemed to feel sorrier for the cats than I did for the witches, possibly because the witches had at least an inkling as to why they were being persecuted. I think, perhaps, I should have skipped the painful parts and gone on, but I know I shan't because the horror will always cling to the volume.

I would by no means recommend so dreadful an end for these cats which prowl outside our windows, I can't help wishing sometimes though that they would have a peaceful decease.

It is difficult to see why women so persistently have been compared to cats. Cats are independent, proud and selfish. Women are none of these things. Cats toy with their victims, accept their daily rations without gratitude, run after mice. Women do none of these things. Cats dislike dogs. Women adore them. Cats purr after they have been fed. Women before. Cats love the dark. Women are afraid of it. You never know what a cat is going to do next. You always know what a woman will do next.

Or at any rate that is what Bill says.

Practically all of these foregoing attributes of the cat however will be found to apply equally well to men. It is for that reason I suppose that spinsters are popularly supposed to be very fond of cats.

Classifying people generally however it will be found that the world is divided into two sorts; those who like ripe olives, Dickens[155] and cats; those who like green olives, Thackeray[156] and dogs.

As a child I was always bringing forlorn cats into the house and sneaking milk to them out of the ice box. Just as regularly I was spanked and the cats were put out on the high

---

[155] Charles John Huffam Dickens (1812-1870) British writer and social critic

[156] William Makepeace Thackeray (1811-1863) British novelist and author

road. For this reason I resolved that some day when I had a house of my own I would fill it up with cats. Now however I find my interest has waned. I think these two tom cats which prowl outside our windows night have had something to do with it.

※ ~~~~ ❖ ~~~~ ※

WE went down town for breakfast Sunday morning, and after a while we got to talking about snobs. Phyllis said she was sure everybody in the world was snobbish about something and after he had thought it over awhile Harry said he guessed he was snobbish about being European. Phyllis didn't say what she was snobbish about, but she told of a friend of hers who had gone to Labrador with the Grenfell expedition. It seems that the party had to stay for a time in a little fishing village of about a dozen huts. Phyllis's friend accordingly sought out one of the women and put up at her hut for the night. The next morning one of the other women approached and told her that she had put up with entirely the wrong people, if she expected to maintain her social prestige in that village she would better board at one of the other huts.

"You see," exclaimed Phyllis, "wherever you go you are bound to find snobbery of some sort."

Bill couldn't think of anything he was snobbish about and although I know I don't think I'll tell.

As for myself, although I'd never thought about it before I discovered I had always been snobbish about brains.

———————

I have always felt that children and young people were particularly snobbish. When I was in the second grade in school there was a very ragged child who used to come by the name of Sophy. Sophy insisted on walking home with me one afternoon and I burned with shame and hoped that no one would see me. A few years later there was a girl in school whom I was very fond of but I would never go to her house to play because she lived on the edge of the Negro district. These things are particularly hard to understand because our family lived exactly the same as did thousands of other families. In high school one morning my particular set was stunned by the information that a certain girl had a personal maid to dress her hair every morning. We pretended to turn up our noses at such effeteness but inside we were burning with envy.

Occasionally I have visited orphanages and consulted the children on the sort of homes they would like to be adopted into. Almost invariably their highest ambition was to live with a family which had an automobile.

I don't think this is anything to grieve about particularly. It is merely part of the human yearning to be different. In the case of children it is easy to understand why externals should count so much.

As we grow older the woman with the childish mind continues to be pleased by externals. I dare say, she gloats over her fine car, her frocks, her jewels, her town house, her husband's membership in such fine clubs. If she smiles at us when she passes we say, "My, how democratic." If she cuts us we say, "My, what a snob."

Meanwhile we go on nursing our own pet little snobberies. Although we don't have it so much in the middle west pride of family is a little matter which upsets the equilibrium of a good many people. A few years ago the woman whose husband drove an Overland was terrifically superior to the woman whose husband drove a Ford. A woman who lives in an apartment where rents are known to be high will always give her address to the store keeper with considerable satisfaction. I heard the other day of a girl who divided all persons into two classes; those who said dressing table and those who said bureau. A couple of years ago a young woman coming to a strange town decided to join such and such a church because the pastor's name happened to be in Who's Who[157].

As I said before I have just discovered that my pet snobbery was brains or what passed for brains. If people read Zane Grey and like Carrie Jacobs Bon's music I was kind but patronizing. If they read Dreizer and liked Cesar Franck and Brahms I respected them tremendously. Even these distrinctions however are beginning to fail me. It gives one a very lost feeling.

---

6 May 1926, Thursday:

---

[157] A biographical reference book of notable citizens, published annually.

I HAVE been wondering why the cigaret ads never show women smoking. Any one can tell by looking at the bill boards that they're hard up for an idea. That this particular idea shouldn't have occurred to them is unthinkable. Therefore it must be some question of ethics.

But it is hard to figure out just what the ethics might be. At firest I thought maybe it was because they were afraid the women's clubs might boycott them. But the women in women's clubs don't buy cigarets. Then I thought of a number of other things but none of them seem to fit.

It seems to me that if they'd only give women an active part in the picture some dandy ads could be figured out:

> "I knew you were my kind of man, George, because you smoke my kind of cigaret."
> "After a hard game of bridge, when the coffee and the sandwitches have been served, And the gossip has commenced
>
>   – Have a Camel!"
> "My dear, have you met that new Mrs. Dogberry?"
> "No, but I know I'm going to like her because I saw her in the drug store yesterday and she was buying Camel cigarets."
> "Ask Mother, she knows!"

Doran Dill,[158] the nice young fellow who runs the Acme over our way, brought the groceries in yesterday and after I'd looked at him a while I discovered that the thing which made him look so queer was a brand new mustache.

"My wife doesn't like it," he said, "and that's why I'm wearing it. After she gets used to it I'm going to take it off."

"That's right," I said, "You gotta show 'em who's boss," and Doran said "eh?"

I don't know what it is that gets into a man every once in a while and makes him want to raise whiskers. I suppose he gets tired of looking at the same face in the mirror every morning and the monotony drives him desperate. He knows he doesn't dare to part his hair in the middle and so he decides to raise a mustache or something. Even Merle

---

[158] Akron resident, Doran K. Dill (1901-1978)

Constiner[159] who doesn't need anything beyond his own natural willowyness to distinguish him is raising chin whiskers.

Back in the 1850's I understand this sort of thing was considered quite correct. A man wasn't virile if he hadn't raised yards and yards of beard. You pick up a story where a handsome youth of 21 is paying court to a beautiful southern belle and the author casually mentions that the hero's vest buttons were completely obscured by his luxuriant Van Dyke[160]. Kipling, who was writing stories about that time, made one of his heroines say that a kiss without a waxed mustache was like an egg without salt.

Women have changed a lot since those days, so much so that there's nothing which makes them madder than to have some one whom they're rather fond of start raising whiskers. So far as I know only one man to date has shaved off his mustache when a woman protested and it is my private opinion he was ready to take it off anyway. Other men simply smile exasperatingly and go right on raising them.

<hr/>

8 May 1926, Saturday:

I think it was the American magazine which first told of Sinclair Lewis' early strivings to become an author. It seems was in the habit of rising early and doing his writing on the kitchen sink before starting out to work. Later Mr. Lewis' "Main Street" became popular and he was able to devote all his time to authorship instead of just a couple of hours before breakfast.

To me this was always a tremendously interesting story and Mr. Lewis was one of my heroes. The idea of anybody getting up early in the morning to become an author was a challenge to the imagination. For hours mornings I used to lie in bed and marvel at it.

Now it seems to me Mr. Lewis has done two incredibly silly things. He has stood up in a church pulpit and defied God to strike him dead. And he has refused the Pulitzer prize awarded to his "Arrowsmith."

<hr/>

[159] Akron resident, Merle Constiner (1902-1979) a Writer, residing at 26 Alfaretta av. in 1930 and then on Main st. in 1940.

[160] A style of beard named after Flemish painter Anthony van Dyck, and consists of growth of a moustache and goatee with cheeks shaven.

The notion of defying God to strike him dead implies the notion that God must be tremendously interested in Mr. Lewis and his affairs. This of course may be true. One afternoon when I was out with Mary a woman stopped me and said, "God has been very good to me. Whenever I say this to any of my friends they say, 'Oh, what does God know about you!' But I say what is the use of having a God if he doesn't care about each one of us and our troubles."

And so it may be that God knows all about Mr. Lewis. If that is the case God has ignored Mr. Lewis sublimely.

Having in a manner of speaking thumbed his nose at the Almighty, Mr. Lewis then turned his attention to other matters and told the committee which awards the Pulitzer prize a thing or two. He resented "the inquisition of earnest literary ladies." He felt that such agencies as awarded the Pulitzer prizes would make American literature "safe, polite, obedient and sterile." Apparently Mr. Lewis had always regarded "Arrowsmith" as a pretty good book. The decision of the Pulitzer committee must have thrown dreadful doubts into his heart.

One wonders just what harm could have come if Mr. Lewis had graciously accepted the Pulitzer prize. If he did not care to accept the money himself possibly some member of his family would have been pleased to buy a couple of bonnets with it. The very circumstance that the Pulitzer committee elected to confer its prize on "Arrowsmith" would indicate that it is far from being as old womanish as Mr. Lewis would have us believe. And if Mr. Lewis actually fears that American literature is to become "safe, polite, obedient and sterile" then certainly there could be no more politic course than to make friends with the earnest literary ladies and gone on writing more Babbitts and Main Streets.

To one person at least Mr. Lewis will henceforth remain an ideal that is shattered. These things happen so often that one wonders sometimes whether it would be better never to have an ideal at all. In Mr. Lewis' case, however, there was a warning at the very beginning. What else could one expect of a man who got up to write at four o'clock in the morning?

IT SEEMS to me that it would be far better if all cosmetics came unscented. There was a girl who got on yesterday morning and prepared to go away for the day. Her bath salts, dusting powder and lavender water all smelled of lavender and that was all right. Then she put on some theatrical cold cream which smelled of lemon. Then she put on some rouge which smelled of something else. Then she put on some face powder which smelled of something else. Then she applied a lip stick which smelled of something else. The she touched her ear lobes with some perfume which her gentleman friend had paid eight dollars an ounce for at Christmas, and it smelled of something else. Then she went down and got on a street car.

It may be that there are some women who can get the exact cosmetics they prefer in the exact scent they prefer, but I doubt it. Suppose you go in for lavender which is a very nice scent to go in for. This month you can get a lavender scented rouge which suits you exactly. Two months later you won't be able to find that shade of rouge anywhere in town. A new shade has come in and if you still want to smell like lavender you'll have to wear orange rouge which makes you look a fright. Several months ago a firm sent me some new face powder which they were manufacturing. It was done up in the most attractive silk bag imaginable and the powder was almost unbelievable smooth. It made you look gorgeous. But the scent was paralyzing. It would have overpowered anyone to whom you were talking. Cold creams are just as hard to secure. By the time you find a cold cream the texture of which suits you you will find at the same time that it is scented with a mixture of carnations and tube roses.

That is why it would be far better if all cosmetics came unscented. Then you could carry your own particular kind of perfume and scent them yourself.

We were talking about various things yesterday, among them, why hospitals are almost always built on street car lines, why hotels are almost always built above railway switch yards and why banks are almost always built on street corners.

It felt peculiarly bad about this latter circumstance. "A bank doesn't need any advantage from location," he maintained. "If a man is putting his money in a certain bank he will go there no matter where it is located. Banks ought to take the middle of the blocks and leave the corners to other concerns which need the advantage.

I don't want to be a negative mother, and so yesterday I bought Mary a teething ring, a lavender one with pink stripes. My argument went something like this, "Now, it isn't fair to ask Mary to take her thumb out of her mouth unless I have something better to substitute." So now whenever Mary puts her thumb in her mouth I take it out and give her the teething ring. Thus far it has worked handsomely, for she doesn't try to eat the teething ring. It is fastened to her wrist with a nice pink cord and whenever her hand starts wandering toward her mouth she encounters the teething ring and stops to play with it. I hope that this experiment will be of some use to other perplexed mothers.

---

12 May 1926, Wednesday:

THE longer I live the more convinced I become that there isn't any such thing as justice.

Yesterday Phyllis came to take Mary and me out in her flivver[161] and we were ambling along Medina road enjoying the scenery when another car came along, knocked us into the ditch and scooted off. I was making lightning calculations as to how I could protect Mary but the flivver loyally refused to upset. It skidded along in the mud, righted itself and climbed back on the road. Then Phyllis stepped on the accelerator and we tore after the other car.

Now if this were any sort of a proper world that other car would have run out of gas so that we could have come up behind and casually taken its number. As a matter of fact though it was our car which ran out of gas. Or at any rate something went wrong. The flivver faltered, lurched, stared on, coughed, trembled and then came to a complete standstill! The car ahead gaily disappeared from view.

There was a woman sitting beside the driver though and Phyllis says not if she lives to be a thousand will she forget the woman's hat. So we still have hopes.

It has occurred to me since though that that man is probably his own worst punishment. A fellow who would endanger the life of a nice little girl like Mary and then rush off without even saying he was sorry is probably suffering this minute from gall stones. I am sure that nobody loves him, not even the woman with the awful hat.

This leads one to a consideration of sin and its punishment. I have noticed, particularly in the last few years, that every sin I have committed, from the little ones to the big ones, has been neatly and effectively punished. The punishment generally hasn't come along

---

[161] Early twentieth-century slang for an automobile, and was the nickname for the Ford Model T, the first mass produced automobile.

for a long time and when it did come it was almost always from other individuals than those whom I had hurt but it was punishment just the same and I flatter myself that I recognized it when it came. I never could understand just why it was that the punishment was always twice as bad as the crime but perhaps it has to be that way in order to impress us.

———————

I think that those of us who have this experience worry less and less, as we grow older, about retaliation. Someone does us an injury and we don't know whether to be Christian and pretend we're oblivious to it or to be human and get mad. After a while though we see that it is better not to get upset at all. Circumstances take care of things far more effectively than we could.

Just what will happen to this man who knocked us into the ditch of course I can't say. I'm afraid that in his case even if he were knocked into two ditches he still would fail to recall the two women and the baby who were poking along in the middle of the road that May afternoon.

———————

The personal tax assessor was here this morning. He said they didn't tax phonographs because they had no resale value and weren't we lucky that we didn't have a radio to be taxed? I said yes and that wasn't all. Then he wanted to know about the furniture and I told him which things we had got at sales and which were wedding presents. He said it was a great mistake to value furniture at what you paid for it. The correct thing to do was to value it at what you could sell it for. That cheered me up and we parted on the best of terms. I never knew that tax assessors could be so nice.

Fred Kelly, he who does card tricks and writes Little Ride Lights on Life in the Beacon Journal, says that the sensible thing to do is always to buy old furniture. He says that at one time he bought a bed spring for $20 and never used it. A year later when he tried to sell it he got 20 cents for it. Now he just buys old chairs and things for anywhere from ten cents up to a quarter and then when he doesn't need them any longer he sells them for antiques.

———————

13 May 1926, Thursday:

A Young man whom I had known for a good many years called me up the other day. He said he was tired of working in an office and would like to get into newspaper work and did I know of any openings. I said I didn't know of any openings but one could never tell what would happen and the best thing for him to do would be to go down and interview a couple of managing editors.

"If I should get job," he said, "what salary do you think I ought to ask to start on?"

"I don't know," I said. "I started in at fifteen dollars a week but of course that was a good while ago.

The voice at the other end of the line waited a while and then said, "Oh!"

This morning I called up the young man to ask him how he was getting along. "Why," he said, "after I talked with you I got an idea that maybe I could write advertising copy. So went to see the president of a concern here and he said he was getting out a little book with a lot of figures in it and if I wanted to fix the figures up so they wouldn't sound so bald, why all right. So I fixed the book up with an introduction and a conclusion and took it back to him and he said it was fine and how much did I want and I said fifty dollars and he said all right."

A couple of years ago when I was out of a job I went to see a great big advertising concern in which I had a friend, a nice round faced courteous Dutchman. He took me to the president and the president gave me a lecture. He said that the writing of advertising copy had nothing to do with literature. He said that the writer of good advertising copy was first of all a salesman. He said that a clerk from a cross roads store out in Arkansas who knew how to sell shoe strings over the counter would write ten times better advertising copy than a newspaper man who had been on Park Row 20 years. I went from his presence humbled and chastened and still jobless.

Just how much of this is true I don't know. Sherwood Anderson I am told wrote excellent advertising copy in Chicago before he broke away to become an author and I doubt that there is anything of the salesman in Sherwood Anderson. William McFee a couple of months ago explained in a magazine article how the literature of the future would consist of advertisements and although he was being mildly cynical the arguments sounded convincing. The remark of the chap who said he read the Saturday Evening Post for the ads has been heard so often that it has become a bromide. Bill brought me home three women's magazines the other night. The editorials were banal, the stories saccharine. The advertisements were the only things that didn't drive you frantic.

It is fairly easy to understand why, in the case of the average American magazine, the advertisements should be more interesting than the stories which envelop them. The theme of every advertisement is "Our Product Is Best." The theme of every story is "The Fellow Gets the Girl." The writer of the advertisement tells his story in one paragraph. The writer of the story tells his story in 10,000 words. One can't be blamed for getting a little groggy.

In the case of the young man whom I talked to this morning, I have an idea that whether he follows literature or whether he follows advertising or whether he combines the two he will be a success. Perhaps some day he will go back and write advertisements for that very office he was so weary of. He has the salesman instinct which is, first of all, respect for your product. It occurs to me now that perhaps respect for one's product is also the thing which makes enduring literature.

---

15 May 1926, Saturday:

"**D**EAR JOSEPHINE: (writes Ancient Admirer)

We was all surprised by our house (if that grammar is poor blame it on a careful reading of Nice Baby) as I say, we was surprised to find that your husband Bill has gone to New York for a vacation. Not that I care personally, but it sort of looks like he's doubting Herman's judgment. You see, Herman went to New York, looked the town all over from Trinity church to 42nd street, and said he liked Akron much better. In fact, Herman quite disapproved of the town in every way. And still Bill goes there. How do you account for that?

"Is it really true that Bill has gone and left you for two weeks? This would be a grand time for all of your former sweeties (don't know whether I qualify under that head or not) to come to your support with long and ardent contributions. This would give you more time (a) to write fond letters to friend Bill, (b) to re-read Dickens during the two weeks' quiet or (c) to try to drown your loneliness in buttermilk.

"Unfortunately, I have a baby lawn to play nurse to and so will be unable to write much for your column until snow comes again. But no doubt the above suggestion might help.

"Your friend Fred C. Kelly[162] has finally decided not to buy a new car. He says, "I looked them all over, but the old Packard is only seven years old and it runs so fine that I hated to give it up." He also admitted that a certain car, which looked so well in the show-window that he went inside and climbed in the driver's seat for a demonstration, was so short that it pushed his knees up under his chin. "It evidently never occurred to the car builders that people come in assorted lengths," he laughed down from his lengthy six feet."

As I understand it however this trip to New York wasn't a vacation. It was business with attendance upon the Four Marx brothers[163] tucked along the side. I am quite sure that I have this correct for when I mentioned to Bill that I might take my vacation at the same time he said, "Why not wait until later and maybe we can fix up something together?" It is altogether impossible that he could be contemplating two vacations in one summer. Anyway he'll be home Tuesday and won't he be surprised when he sees the nice new paint on the kitchen chairs.

I suppose this would be as apt a time as any to discuss whether husbands and wives should take their vacations together or separately. That husbands and wives need a respite from each other's peculiarities occasionally nobody will deny. I have found however that the course of the days when they are separated goes something like this: First day terrific loneliness; second day, loneliness; third day, callousness; fourth day, faults; fifth day, recapitulation of the other party's virtues; sixth day, disgruntlement with everybody except spouse; seventh day, ardent letters urging immediate reunion. If a person had gone away for a two weeks' vacation the other week would be a total loss.

My plan would be this, sad so far as I know is absolutely original. First the wife would go away for two weeks, then the husband would go away for two weeks. Then they would go away together for two weeks. There isn't the slightest doubt but that they would be so overjoyed at seeing each other again that they would have a perfectly lovely time.

---

[162] A former Ohio newspaperman, and close friend of Orville and Wilbur Wright, brothers who flew the first "Flyer" plane and were aviation pioneers, and Kelly is also author of "The Wright Brothers" a biographical book published in 1943.

[163] A vaudeville comedy group performing from 1905 to 1949 of five brothers using the stage names of Chico, Harpo, Groucho, Gummo, and Zeppo.

This would take care of the vexing problem as to where to go for one's vacation. During her two weeks the wife could go to Cedar Point[164]. During his two weeks the husband could go fishing in Canada. Then for the two weeks they have together they could compromise and both go to Atlantic City.

—⚬⚬⚬◆⚬⚬⚬—

18 May 1926, Tuesday:

"I SIMPLY had to write and tell you," writes R. F., "how your article on winter underwear touched a cord in my heart. Years ago, (I am now 32) I was obliged to wear heavy underwear of the real old fashioned two piece variety and Oh how I hated it. Being somewhat overgrown and inclined to be fat I resembled a feather bed tied in the middle when I was rigged out. And mind you I always had a cold in three days. I am thankful that we have the sensible bloomers and comfortable one piece union suits so that our children may go forth to meet the wintry winds comfortably as well as warmly clad.

"Last Friday being so warm I asked my two boys, seven and four, how they would like to put on their summer union suits. They were not long in getting out of bed and dressing I can tell you. Later in the day I saw my four year old displaying his summer underwear to one of his play mates and when his dad came home for lunch he was greeted with the cry, 'We have on our Baby Dees.' And they didn't catch cold either."

Now you see it did do some good.

The New Yorker came this morning with a nice story about Grace Coolidge. It seems she was in the habit of going to a lot of concerts and Calvin didn't like it. "I don't see why you want to go to so many concerts," he said fretfully, "when we have five pianos in the house."

---

[164] Cedar Point, Sandusky, Ohio – a peninsula that stretches into Lake Erie with Canada just across the way.

A little while ago I was talking with a friend over the telephone. "I wish you could see this house next door to us," she said. "There was such a nice family lived in there and the children were so happy. Now they have moved away and the house looks so lonesome. Every day people come to look at it and then they go away again. The windows of the house are all here and the dust keeps drifting across the porch and they're going to cut down the trees in front. The house doesn't take much interest in the people who come to see it. I think it must have a heart ache somewhere."

Bill is back and he says New York is terrible. It seems that the first thing that happened was that he went into a barber shop to get a shave and it took all his strength to fight off the boot blacks coat dusters, manicurists, etc. Then he and Paul went to a vaudeville show and it was awful and after that they went to the Vanities and that was terrible. He says it wasn't that the Vanities was indecent or anything. It was just cheap. He says the best place he ate was at a French restaurant around Fifth avenue and 12th st., and the next best place was at the Village Moon, where you had to have a card to get in. He says that one of the book shops in the Village[165] which used to be pretty nice now has a proprietor who clanks around in boots, spurs and a sombrero and that next door is the Pirates Den or something similarly named, which has three pirates sitting out in front with knives in their teeth. After that he wanted to know if I didn't want to go to New York for a week or two, and I said no, I guessed not.

I know that in these parts it is quite the thing to sit around and roast Akron and say Oh, if I could only get to New York. But I know from experience that it is just as possible to get fed up on New York as it is to weary of the continual sights of South Main st. Moreover most of the people I knew in New York were simply bursting to get to Paris, and I wouldn't be at all surprised to find that those who had got to Paris were simply bursting to move on to Constantinople.

19 May 1926, Wednesday:

---

[165] In this instance, the "village" may refer to Greenwich Village based on his above comment of location of 5th avenue and 12th.

I have a friend whose work in life is to listen to peoples' troubles, give them advice, find them jobs and help them generally. Lack of self control, she told me the other day was one of the big factors in creating human unhappiness. Religion, she thought, might be one of the things to offset it. "I have often wished," she said, "that all the different sects might agree upon certain simple religious truths which might be taught in the schools."

"Well," I said, "it ought to be easy to teach that to do right brings happiness, that to do wrong brings unhappiness."

"Yes," she said, "but wouldn't that be morality instead of religion?"

And I was stumped.

However as Mary grows older and goes to school I can think of certain things I would like for her to be taught whether they might be classed under religion or morality or literature.

I would like for her to know the stories of the Bible and if the teacher cared to ask her what she learned from those stories I wouldn't have the slightest objection.

I would be very happy if every morning of her life her teacher would read to her some of the lovely poetry of the bible. I would stipulate however that as much of the poetry be covered as possible that the teacher shouldn't limit herself to the 23rd psalm.

I would like to have her know that in China there once lived a great man by the name of Confucius and he taught that politeness and respect for one's elders and for the laws of one's country were very necessary ingredients of happiness.

I would like to have her know that there was once a mule driver named Mahomet who became a great leader of his people and that among other things he taught them to refrain from intoxicating drinks but even that did not make them altogether kind and happy.

I would like for her to know that in India there was a great prince named Guatama who gave up all that he owned, even his wife and little son, that he might learn what was truth and that among other things he taught that evil was its own punishment, that good was its own reward and that it was a very good thing never to become unduly excited or unduly depressed about anything.

And I would like for her to know that while, in Christian countries, most dreadful cruelties have been practiced in the name of the gentle Jesus, that in the same name these same cruelties have been endured.

I think that instead of worrying her as to the exact manner in which the world was created and the exact date of it I would instead show her some of the wonders of it as it is now. I would not want her bothered with doctrines of infant baptism but I would want her to know some of the principles of getting along with her playmates.

I can't help but think that out of this there ought to come a fair measure of self control. Being familiar with various creeds and beliefs she could cling to her own and yet still be tolerant of the other person's. Knowing something of the beauty of the world she certainly would not need to be taught to respect the creator of it. Being familiar with the troubles of the saints her own aches and pains could not seem so momentous. And she certainly could not fail to observe how all of the great leaders found considerable virtue in some sort of self denial.

---

20 May 1926, Thursday:

I RATHER gather that somebody up at the Business Women's club is worried about Bill's meals. They have sent word that a special business man's lunch will be served on Thursday and Friday of this week those being oddly enough, the days of the club's annual bazar[166]. The idea I suspect is to gather the men in, fill them up with corned beef and cabbage and apple pie a la mode and then turn them loose in the bazar they being in such a beatific frame of mind that they will carry home all sorts of aprons, boudoir caps and ice bags. In Bill's case the idea goes even further. I can see plainly an element of pity in it. However the truth may as well be told now as any time. Bill's favorite food is beans, out of the can. His favorite dessert is ice cream. Any woman who think to please him by rising at dawn and baking, brewing, boiling, basting and pot roasting all day long had best desist at once.

Everybody I meet these days is writing his or her confessions so as to win one of the big prizes offered by True Story magazine. H. is writing about a dress model who got into the Follies and was met everywhere she turned by vultures in human clothing. G. is writing about a girl whose parents scrimped and saved to send her to a fashionable boarding school. She determined to marry a man with money and dear, dear, the price she paid. J. is writing about a woman who almost ran away with a married man and had a change of heart in the nick of time. For my own part I think I shall write about a man

---

[166] A variant on the spelling of the word "bazaar" and references a market of shops.

who fell in love with his stenographer and who wasn't reconciled with his wife until their little girl fell ill of a fever.

The details of the contest though make me a little suspicious. Seeing that each story is your very own confession no names are to be signed. Just how a person could check up on who got the prizes is a little baffling. Even at that though it is probably worth while to go ahead and write a confession. The process seems to be fairly simple. You write in the first person. If you are a girl you write the confession of a man. If you are a man you write the confession of a girl. They're always so much more imaginative that way. You start out by saying that not for the world would you tell this story, if it weren't for the hope of bringing some other erring human back to the straight and narrow. Then you go ahead and write it being sure to put in a lot of seductions and having virtue triumph in the end.

True Story, I understand, is Bernarr MacFadden's most thriving publication with a circulation of 2,500,000 every month.

I was up in his offices on a couple of occasions. The last time was when he had moved over on Broadway. It was at that hour in the afternoon when the office help was supposed to take its exercise. All the stenographers and bookkeepers had to stand up in town and make their arms go this way and that way while a man down in front said "one two, one two." They kept this up for 15 minutes.

Back in one of the little cushy holes a perspiring middle aged man was grinding out confessions. He had just finished one about a chorus girl and was starting another about a stenographer.

Bill says there's a pool room here in town where a lot of fellows hang out who write a confession from time to time and pick up a little pie money. If this is true I'd like to meet one of them sometime and hear what he has to say about it.

---

21 May 1926, Friday:

I DON'T recall just how many years the Civic Drama association has been in existence. I think it is about four. During this time it has excellently staged and presented a number of well known plays, brought a certain amount of unsuspected acting ability to the fore and sustained a deficit of $1,500. To wipe out this deficit a benefit performance is to be given at Goodyear theater on the evening of June 8.

There is hardly any doubt that the necessary amount of money will be raised. The question confronting its well wishers on June 9, however, my well be whether the Civic Drama association is not immediately going to tumble into debt again. I realize keenly that I am the last person in the world who has any call to tell any other person or any organization how to keep out of debt. I realize, too, that some of the conclusions I have drawn during the past four years may be entirely wrong. And because there is no one in Akron who wishes for a successful little theater more than myself I would like to say a few things.

It is generally agreed, I think, that the object of a little theater is an experimental one. It is generally known, I think, that those little theaters which have been successful have started on a modest scale. The Akron little theater has neither been the one nor done the other. It started out brilliantly and overwhelmingly with a masque which had never been presented before, an out-of-door Shakespearean production and a street carnival. Each of these in its turn was successful. The public was tremendously interested. From then on the interest has been dwindling.

The chief reason for this dwindling interest is, I think, that the Civic Drama association has chosen to produce Broadway successes rather than original plays. I would base this conclusion upon the interest aroused by a single play, "Tinsel," written in collaboration by two Akron women. Everybody we knew, and a good many we didn't know, broke engagements, canceled trips to Cleveland, broke up dinner parties, in order to see "Tinsel." The reason is fairly obvious. They wanted to see "Tinsel" and decide for themselves whether it was any better than the three-act comedy they had tucked away in the trunk back home. For the first time in its history, the theater was filled.

It matters not that "Ice Bound," "Lilies of the Field," "Arms and the Man," "The Rivals," plays which the Civic Drama association excellently produced, were undoubtedly better in content and construction than most of the plays moldering her in Akron. The fact will always remain that they are old stories. There isn't one of us who wouldn't rather see a new play a'borning.

Another thing which happened when the Civic Drama association was being organized was that the society lists were eagerly scanned for those who should take part. Now it not infrequently happens that a young woman who is prominent in social affairs is at the same time a most excellent actress. I think, however, that if I were engaging her for a part I would make it plain that it was on account of her histrionic ability and not because of her social standing. It is largely a matter of attitude. When I tried to explain this to someone she told me that it would be impossible for the Civic association to succeed without the aid of society. That this idea was not wholly correct I think has now to a considerable extent been proved.

It seems to me that it is not necessary for Akron's Civic Drama association to maintain its present theater if even that tiny hold is too expensive. It seems to me that it is not necessary to have endowments nor long lists of important sounding names. What it does need, I think, is that the 12 or 15 people who honestly love the theater, should get together, produce original plays, consent to take part in them, whether all the roles are leading ones or not, stage them in a store room if necessary and be content if 15 or 20 people came.

If I recall correctly Eugene O'Neill's early plays were first produced on somebody's back porch.

22 May 1926, Saturday:

I THINK it would be sort of nice if newspapers wouldn't print articles about hay fever and things. The other night I was reading an article about hay fever and the new cures for it and all at once I remembered I hadn't had a cold for ages. Then I wondered if there was any chance of my getting a cold. The next morning I woke up with one – a dandy. My eyes are red, my nose is red, my throat is scratchy, the tears keep coming in spite of all I can do. I thought I could sleep it off last night but somebody's puppy had been left alone and he barked all night long. I wish I'd never seen that article about hay fever.

"Did you see about Hazel Wendell's[167] party?" I said to Bill. "No," said Bill. "Well," I said, "she's going to give a riding party Sunday morning and then they're all going over to Old Portage and have breakfast." "If it's a riding party," said Bill, "she'd better serve a buffet lunch."

I wish I could remember the name of the groom who used to take me riding on Sunday mornings. He drank fearfully but was kind and indulgent. He taught me how to mount

---

[167] Akron resident, Hazel B. Wendell or Hazel Pearl Reighard Wendell (1907-1992)

the horse, how to hold the reins, how to sit backward when we were going down a hill, how to sit forward when we were going up. Or maybe it was the other way around. Anyways I was just getting to the point where the horse was allowed to trot when my man had an overdose of something and disappeared altogether. I couldn't bear the thought of learning from anybody else and so gave up the pastime.

Books brought home by Bill during the week including "Lonesome Road," a group of one-act Negro plays by Paul Green[168], "As I Look at Life," some rather silly articles reprinted from the Cosmopolitan magazine, and the Cross Word Puzzle book, fifth series.

One of the plays in the "Lonesome Road" is about a negro camp meeting which I understand no one has ever thought of doing on the stage before. It reminded me of an idea I entertained a long time ago of trying to build a play with a revival meeting as the big scene. A lot of us must recall the revival meetings which Aimee Semple McPherson[169] conducted in Canton a few years ago. It has always seemed to me that there was tremendous drama in them. Reverting to "Lonesome Road," it seems to me that these plays reveal more about the problems of the Negro than is likely to be found in larger and thicker books.

"As I Look at Life" contains such chapter headings as "It's Great to Be Sober Again," "I Planned to Murder My Husband," "I Was That Sort of Woman." According to the foreword it is dedicated to "those readers whose intelligent interest and faithful support makes possible the continued high quality of Cosmopolitan with which is combined Hearst's International.[170]"

The Cross Word Puzzle book is just as fascinating as ever. It has the answers in the back but that doesn't seem to be much of a temptation. Sometime it might be interesting to gather statistics on the Cross Word Puzzle books how many wandering husbands

---

[168] Paul Green (1894-1981) Author who wrote numerous plays about the lives of poor people, including Abraham's Bosom which won a Pulitzer Prize in 1927.

[169] Aimee Semple McPherson (1890-1944) also known as Sister Aimee, was a Canadian-American Pentecostal evangelist in the 1920's and 1930's famous for founding the Foursquare Church.

[170] Cosmopolitan magazine, first published in 1886 as a U. S. family literary magazine, and in 1925 was combined with Hearst International, and in 1965 became a woman's magazine which continues in circulation today.

they have kept at home nights, how many fond hearts they have united, how many millionaires they have created through the sale of spectacles and lead pencils.

※ ~~~~◆~~~~ ※

25 May 1926, Tuesday:

OUR janitor, Mr. Myers, rung our back door bell vigorously this morning. "What do you think, Josephine," he said, "my daughter's got a ten pound boy."

That's one of the nice things about living in an apartment. You may not know your neighbors very well but you certainly get on dandy with the janitors. Mr. Myers was too excited to remember the baby's name but anyway we had a long talk, about doctors and hospitals and nurses and how much babies ought to weigh and symptoms. Then Mr. Myers went away and I gave Mary her bath and asked her if she remembered the day she and I first got acquainted and she said "guh."

In stylish apartments it is the thing to refer to janitors as superintendents or caretakers or something equally toney but somehow I like the word janitor, which is perfectly respectable and means keeper of the doors.

For a janitor is not merely a person who stokes the furnace and sweeps down the back steps. He has the peace and comfort of a good many human beings in his keeping. He keeps you warm and snug in the winter time and in summer he puts in the screens. He cleans out the drain pipe and cuts the grass and hunts up the ice card when the wind blows it down. He keeps an eye on the baby when you have to run out for a minute and he loans you a loaf of bread if you happen to have missed the man in the morning. And if, after he has done all sorts of friendly things for you, you happen to press a new necktie on him, he says, "Oh, pshaw, now what did you go and do that for?"

That's the kind of janitor our Mr. Myers is. It seems he used to be janitor of a high school and then in odd hours and in the summer time he did paper hanging and house painting. Sometimes over at the high school he'd have an hour or so to spare and then he'd put it in reading some of the books in the library. He got so you couldn't trip him up anywhere when it came to United States history. Then his eyes failed and he had to give up reading and painting both.

Now Mr. Myers has a radio and at night, when Bill and Mary and I are coming home from a ride, we can see him down stairs with the phones fastened tight to his ears and the happiest expression imaginable on his face.

They say that children take after their grandparents and so I think that that little 10-pound chap who came to town this morning ought to be pretty nice. Of course when a baby is born you can't help feeling a little sad. You know that when he grows up he is bound to have heartaches and nothing you can do can keep him from them. But on the other hand you know that wonderful things are in store for him too. You know that there will be beautiful days, like the day he was born on, when he will be so happy he will almost burst. You know there will be rainy days when he will snuggle down in a corner to the delight of Robinson Crusoe. You know that friendship and love are in store for him and that if some of these are disappointing there will be others splendid almost beyond belief.

I hope he comes home soon. There are any number of things I want to discuss with his mother. I want to see him grow and on these pleasant summer days, when the wind is right, I want to hear him squeal.

26 May 1926, Wednesday:

IT HAS always seemed to me that one of the best preparations a girl can have for marriage is to live around with a lot of room mates. The analogy isn't perfect but it will do. Most of us never have more than one husband in our lives. It is quite natural at times to object to the way he parts his hair and to wish for a different husband. At such times there is nothing more useful than to sit down and consider one's past room mates.

I always read Dorothy Dix[171] and her advice to husbands and wives and I can't help noticing how she emphasizes prettying up and not nagging and things like that as the ingredients of happy marriages. My personal reaction to this however is that if two people like each other they'll put up with most anything. If they don't like each other

---

[171] Dorothy Dix was the pen name for Elizabeth Meriwether Gilmer (1861-1951) American journalist and columnist.

all the prettying up in the world isn't going to help things. I have based this conclusion upon my room mates with three of whom I got along.

I think I would even have gotten along with Pearl if I had been older. Pearl had been married and had run away from her husband. Before that she had been a nurse. Pearl knew all about life and she had an extensive stock of hospital stories. I was shocked beyond words. I have since thought that after she found out how shocked I was she went about doing it on purpose. She also borrowed my electric curling iron and rented it out to other girls at five cents an hour. I was very glad when her husband came and got her.

———————

Esther came next and I can't draw any conclusions from her because Esther was just right. She had just the right degree of intelligence, talent, kindliness, and humor. I think she is the only girl I ever knew whom I could describe without putting in any "buts."

———————

However one could draw conclusions from Eleanor. Eleanor's long suit was to tell you all your faults. She came from a family of brothers and sisters where you did that sort of thing as a matter of course. Whenever we would come home from a party she would occupy the hours till dawn telling me all the things I had done that were wrong. Every third night Eleanor would demand a truth party. "All right," I would say, "You start." "Well then," Eleanor would say, "First of all I will tell you your virtues. You are very kind to dumb animals and I think you are intelligent. Now as to your faults –" The recital would last for hours.

Eleanor also took away my fellows. But I adored her and we were happy.

———————

Kathleen was never worried by untidiness. When she had a date she would doll up and drive everybody completely out of their senses. The rest of the time she sat around in flannelette pajamas with a brown sweater tied around her shoulders. Newspapers and old magazines and breakfast remnants and lingerie which had neglected to go to the laundry accumulated in Kathleen's room until you had to fight your way through. She slept till noon and never came completely to until dinner time. And yet it was more pleasure to be with Kathleen than almost anybody I have ever known. She had lived in Freeport with the vaudeville set. She had traveled over Europe. She had read everything going. She was clever. She was fairly kind. There was nothing I loved more than to hear her talk. I think I would be content to be with Kathleen if she sat around in flannelette pajamas till the end of time.

And that is the reason, more or less, that I think if married people like each other there isn't anything else that can actually matter.

—ꙩꙩ꙲ꙩ◆ꙩꙩꙩ꙲—

28 May 1926, Friday:

A FRIEND of ours sent out the April issue of the Atlantic Monthly some time ago, recommending that we read the leading article in it. The article was a lengthy one and for some reason or other I kept getting sidetracked in my reading of it. I finished it just a little while ago and now I am wishing that some old-timer of the town might have read it with me and explained it as we went along.

For the article seems to deal with things close to home. It is called "Olympians in Homespun" and it deals with the musical strivings of a little town called Woolwick. Woolwick is close to another town called Verona (Ravanna) and occasionally the people of Woolwick journey to another town 11 miles away, where they hear Theodore Thomas' orchestra at the Academy of Music. Being anxious to have an orchestra of their own they engage a German professor of music, Herr Gustav Seidl, to train them in various instruments.

Now I am told that this Herr Gustav Seidl is none other than our own Professor Sigel whom, for a good many years, I used to watch daily going past our house on Crosby st. I had ambitions to be a musician myself, then, and I used to hope that one time he would stop and talk with me, but they told me that he had become discouraged with the lack of appreciation accorded musicians and urged all young people including his own children to take up other lines of endeavor.

I am wondering now if Professor Sigel has seen the Atlantic Monthly article, and if so, whether he is not a little cheered. For if these things are true then he had a large part in shaping the lives of a community whose single passion seems to have been music.

The writer of the article, Lucien Price, makes it a happy community which dared to take up culture only after aday of hard toil, which had its taffy pullings and its busking bees but which also produced Shakespeare, sang Handel and played Beethoven.

I had a letter from Paul yesterday: "I'm not press-agenting at this writing," he says. "Have been with Arthur Hopkins[172] for two seasons – but this one brought nothing but duds, so I was cast out on the streets some weeks ago. My fertile brain evolved nothing better than the idea of promoting a couple of plays that have, I think, money in them as well as two of my own which have been considered but not accepted as yet. If you are not too finicky sexy you might write a little fantasy on seduction. The managers believe that anything sexy will go – and apparently they are right. There is a piece of Daly's[173] (a reconstructed church at 62nd st., off Central park) doing upward of $10,000 a week on its little 'Sex[174]' plus blatant vulgarity."

The mall man also brought the very first entries in the contests which will be a part of the Ohio Newspaper Women's convention her in October. They were a book review and a column from nice Pauline Smith of the Columbus Citizen.

29 May 1926, Saturday:

WE were speaking the other evening about the bringing up of children. Two of us were married and the other was a school teacher, so you see we really had a right to.

The school teacher said something which surprised me. She said she was firmly convinced that all children took things which didn't belong to them and told things which weren't true. And she told about a little girl who, whenever she was dining out, quietly extracted the tips which the older persons left for the waiter. When New Year's came around this little girl announced that among other things she had resolved not to steal any more. Her parents were dreadfully pained and shocked. They hadn't been aware at all that anything like that was going on.

---

[172] Broadway theatre producer and director known for co-writing "Burlesque" in 1927.

[173] Daly's 63rd Street Theatre and Hall was a Broadway theatre active from 1921 to 1941. It was built in 1914 and demolished in 1957.

[174] Mae West's "Sex" premiered at this theatre in February 1926. It was written by and starred her, using the pen name of "Jane Mast."

The school teacher was of the opinion that parents didn't need to be shocked at all at such things because all children did them and they almost invariably reformed naturally when they reached their 'teens.

I confess that the school teacher's words took a considerable load off my mind. All these years I had been grieving inwardly at the memory of how bad I had been and how good other children undoubtedly were. I am setting this down now in the hope that if anyone else has been grieved similarly he or she will see it and be comforted.

After we had talked awhile I broached my pet theory which is that while children are sublimely unaware of what we call morality they have an abnormally keen sense of justice. It then developed that we all had had practically the same experience. When we were young we were given a weekly allowance of ten cents which we were encouraged to place in an iron bank on the cupboard shelf.

After a couple of dollars had accumulated something like this went on: "Henrietta darling, Mama hasn't enough money to pay the grocery bill. Will you let her have the money in your bank? She'll pay it back next week."

Henrietta pridefully hands the two dollars, delighted to be of some use to the family. A week goes by and nobody says anything. Another week goes by and still nobody says anything. Then Henrietta gently broaches the matter, "Mother, may I please have the two dollars you borrowed?" "Why, Henrietta Jones you ungrateful child. Didn't Papa and I take you to Cedar Point last summer? Didn't I just get you a new pair of shoes? What in the world do you expect?"

After that I think a child is to be absolved if occasionally she extracts a dime from the family purse.

One of the things I don't think I would worry about though is the Santa Claus myth. I dimly recall the terrific agitation which the Ladies Home Journal set up about it. "Tell your child there is a Santa Claus," they stormed, "and when he finds out the truth he will never trust your word again."

It seems to me, however, that the Santa Claus illusion lifts so gradually that there is no element of shock in it. It takes a good many Christmases before a child is entirely sure of the matter, and by that time his principal reaction is a prideful one that now he's a big boy who can guard the secret very carefully from the younger ones.

Reverting to pocketbooks N. related something which happened the other day. "I was expecting a check which hadn't come," she said, "and I was afraid I couldn't do the shopping I had planned. 'What are you worrying about?' said my oldest. 'You know my purse is in the top dresser drawer.' 'But I don't want to do that,' I said. Then she came over and put her arm across my shoulder. 'Why, Mother,' she said, 'don't you remember how when we were young we could always go to your purse any time we wished?'"

31 May 1926, Monday:

BATHTUB BARTIES

ACCORDING to newspaper reports Miss Joyce Hawley was told by Earl Carroll that she might pose in the nude in one of his shows for $30 a week and Miss Hawley expressed satisfaction with the contract. Then, after Miss Hawley had gone away, Mr. Carroll entered her name in his card index with the following peculiar notation: A1-OK-DD?

The significance of these letters was not revealed until almost the last day of Mr. Carroll's trial. It seems that the A1 meant that Miss Hawley had a good figure. The OK meant that she would be placed in a New York show instead of in a road show. The DD meant that she was a Dumb Dora. The question mark meant that Mr. Carroll wasn't sure but that Miss Hawley might develop intelligence later on.

Miss Hawley's mother, Mrs. Tony Daugeles, did not comment on her daughter's intelligence but she did express the opinion that her daughter was lazy. This may be the reason that Miss Hawley was willing to work in the nude for $30 a week. It may be too that Miss Hawley found herself in the midst of such keen competition that she was willing to work for a sum of money which is ordinarily paid a moderately good stenographer. And then again she might have been an ambitious girl and reasoned that this was merely a beginning step which by perseverance and keeping everlastingly at it might lead to better contracts. Even Mr. Carroll conceded by a question mark that Joyce might not be as dumb as she looked.

I was reading the other night the story of a woman who told how she had left her husband and lived six months with another man. The woman's name was Elizabeth Something-Or-Other and her picture accompanied the article. "That must be a fake name and a fake picture," I said to Bill. "No woman would tell things like that."

"Oh I don't know," said Bill. "Some people will do anything for notoriety."

This may be another reason why young women are willing to take part in artistic tableaux for $30 a week. Somehow though the figure depresses me. I was sure it was higher.

Mr. Carroll apparently is also among those souls who are willing to do anything for publicity. Some few months ago he went to jail rather than pay a fine for displaying artistic undraped figures in his lobby. Then he bought the Countess of Cathcart's play. Then he gave a bath tub party. Mr. Carroll's taste in parties is probably one explanation as to why his shows are so bad. One can't help wondering if it wouldn't be just as well if Mr. Carroll spent as much energy brushing his shoes as he does to getting into newspaper head lines.

It seems to me that if I were a young woman contemplating a career in the chorus, I would hesitate a moment and consider whether, after all, it might not be better to take up stenography. Statistics show rather dismally that chorus girls don't marry millionaires nearly so often as the Sunday supplements would have us believe. Ginger ale baths can hardly be considered the best thing for the complexion and the crop of butter and egg men is variable at best. Meantime there is the problem of getting along on $30 a week a sum, I understand, which is thoughtfully reduced when one goes on the road.

---

2 June 1926, Wednesday:

OUR janitor, Mr. Miles, (I've been calling him Mr. Myers for months and he was too modest to tell me about it, "Aw gee what difference does a name make" he says), our janitor, Mr. Miles came up the steps Decoration day with a wholle lot of cigars in his hand. "Say Josephine," he said, "does you husband smoke?" "No," I said, "and he doesn't drink either or play cards. He's an awful moral man Mr. Miles. Oh I know what you are bringing up cigars for. It's on account of your new grandson. "Yes," said Mr. Miles, "that's it. I guess I'll hunt up something else for you folks."

I watched him knock at the apartment next door and then the most dreadful thing happened. The blood rushed to my head and I broke out in perspiration. Not until that moment had it occurred to me that when our Mary came we didn't give a single cigar or chocolate cream to anybody. At least I never thought of it being too excited and happy and I'm sure Bill didn't or he'd have said something about it.

Of course I suppose we had a good excuse this being our first experience but you know how some people are. "That," I can just hear them saying, "is something that everybody ought to know whether they've ever had any experience or not." I'm so embarrassed I don't know what to do and I know it's going to take us years to live it down.

It seems there's been a nice elderly chap around town exploiting a new international language called Ro. His method is to go up to prospect and say, "Well, I can see you're an intelligent man." After that there's practically nothing to do but accept the dollar and mail him the magazine.

Ro[175] is different from Esperanto and other international languages in that it starts right in on the ground floor and makes up its own words. Here is a sample which I borrow form the little book which tells all about it: *Giya tagnah, Raday Jones. Ab no relef so is ap gibts. Ac wefa ol ducaf?* This means, Good evening Mr. Jones. I have not seen you for a long time. Have you been out of town? Here is another one: *Birah el at bira cim gol at biss. Ag kecab oc at biss in waqaq birado tafs*, the meaning of which is, Mercury is the planet nearest the sun. It travels around the sun in terrestrial days.

Just how necessary an international language is of course I have no means of knowing. There must be some need for it or people would not work at it so hard. I had an elderly friend who taught Esperanto in a fashionable girls' school and he was dreadful serious about it. After a great deal of coaxing he finally translated "Yes we have no bananas" into Esperanto for me but I think he felt all along he was performing a desecration.

For the past half hour I have been trying to put "Thanks for the Buggy Ride" into Ro but the task I am frank to confess is beyond me. The word for horse is *musal*, the word for horsepower is *gepaf*, the word for gasoline is *bakrag* and the word for pilgrimage is

---

[175] Ro is a priori 'philosophical' constructed language using the Latin alphabet constructed in 1904 by Reverend Edward Powell Foster (1853-1937), who may be the "elderly chap" Josephine refers to but we do not know if it was him promoting his own ideas.

---

kecap. However I can find absolutely nothing for the simple expression "walk back." If such a simple task as this is beyond one how in the world would we ever accomplish such expressions as Red Hot Mama, Jazz Baby and So's Your Old Man!

The Ro dictionary has in it a word for butler but absolutely nothing for electric washing machine. It has a word for dinner and one for restaurant and one for cabbage but nothing for onion soup au gratin. It may be of course that the idea is to start with a few simple world and then add to them as we go along. In that event Ro, in a few years, would have lost some of its harshness and probably have acquired some words of four and five syllables. Who knows, perhaps after several hundred people have tinkered with it it would be just as funny and complicated and hard to understand as any of the languages we have with us this minute.

---

3 June 1926, Thursday:

IT'S funny how things happen. Yesterday Kiki and Mary and I were going through town and down at the corner of Main and Market sts. we saw a man having trouble with a traffic cop. It seems the man wanted to go across the street and the cop wanted him to stay on the sidewalk. "Well," I said to myself, "I'm glad somebody in this town has trouble with traffic cops beside Bill." Then the cop brought the man back to the sidewalk and I saw it was Bill. They stood there sassing each other and then the cop put out his hand and pulled a sort of lever that was in a box and my heart absolutely stopped beating. He was calling the patrol!

Hastily I handed the baby over to Kiki and scrambled out, my speech to that cop all prepared. It mattered not, I would tell him, that Bill and I had had our differences of opinion. It mattered not that he brought more magazines home than we could ever possibly read. It mattered not that he bought phonograph records when he needed socks, this man was my lawful wedded husband and if he went to jail in the patrol wagon I was going along too.

As I approached the cop a crowd collected, sympathetic women pressed forward to be of what assistance they could and ugly men leered. Bill however refused to let me deliver my oration to the cop. Showing absolutely no surprise that I should have appeared on the scene so opportunely he spoke out two words. "Beat it," he said hoarsely, "beat it." Being perfectly trained and knowing how masterful Bill could be on occasion there was nothing to do but make my way back through the crowd and climb in again with Kiki. Then we drove disconsolately around the block.

"We'd better go up to the City building," I said finally, "and watch them bring him in."

So we went up to the city building and there was Harry Welch standing on the front steps and sniffing the nice spring air. I signaled to him frantically.

"What do you think," I said. "They've arrested my husband for jay walking."

"I don't see how they could have," said Harry. "Here's the patrol wagon right here by the curb and the other one's got a flat tire."

"I'm sure they did though," I said. "The cop was awful mad."

"There hasn't been any call for the patrol," said Harry, "but if you want to you can come in and look the place over."

"No," I said, "they wouldn't have time to get here yet. I'll just stay here and wait."

"I suppose you think they'll walk him up," said Harry. "Look here, what makes you think they arrested him?"

"Why," I said, "I saw the cop pull a lever."

"What kind of a lever?" said Harry.

"Oh," I said, "a little lever that was in a sort of pole or box or something."

"Oh," said Harry. "Well I think he was just changing the signal light so the traffic could go on."

I felt tremendously relieved at that. "Well anyway," I said, "if they should bring him in will you please let him out in time for supper?"

"Sure," said Harry.

So I went home and put the potatoes on and after a while Bill came in only 45 minutes late.

"It's funny," I said, "how I always happen in on your most embarrassing situations."

"I didn't look half as silly as you did," Harry[176] said.

⸺⸺◆⸺⸺

4 June 1926, Friday:

I SUPPOSE there are other persons besides those eight University of Chicago students who are endeavoring to live according to Christ's principles. A case in point is that of Charles M. Sheldon[177] of whose experience I was reading some time ago.

Mr. Sheldon, it seems, is the author of a well known book called "In His Steps," which relates the experiences of certain persons who had tried to live as Christ would have them. Mr. Sheldon has maintained that he himself was trying to follow those same Christian principles set forth in his book and he added that he had not encountered any insuperable obstacles and that he had been happy. Although his book ran into 22 million copies he accepted none of the profits from it. Although calls came from wealthy churches elsewhere, he persisted in preaching to his own little flock for $2,200 a year. Believing that the Christian was of necessity a pacifist, he, during the war, preached the doctrine of "love your enemies," although federal agents were on the point of arresting him and many of his parishioners walked from the church.

I imagine that a good many persons have tried Mr. Sheldon's experiment without, however, arriving at Mr. Sheldon's happy conclusions. They have tried to live honestly according to Christian precepts and after a week or two weeks or a year they have had this experience; they have had fixed the right cheek smitten and then the left; having walked two miles with their brother they have been beaten up and robbed; having shown charity and forgiveness to the evil doer they have heard themselves help up as nit wits. "It won't go," they have said to themselves bitterly, "the world despises a man who tries to be a Christian."

---

[176] *(I think she meant to say Bill here).*

[177] Charles Monroe Sheldon (1857-1946) American congregationalist minister and leader of the Social Gospel movement.

A. Maude Royden[178], the English woman preacher, has written an article dealing with this identical problem. The trouble with a good many of us, she says, is that we try to practice the Christian virtues of humility and self-sacrifice and love and peace before we have acquired the pagan virtues of courage and honesty and honor. Looking into her own life she found that a lot of times when she had thought she was being self-sacrificing and humble, she, in reality, didn't have the moral courage to be anything else. She was plain scared. And she speaks of the women who, loving to hear it, said, "What an unselfish wife!" "What an unselfish mother!" make door mats of themselves while their families become more selfish and thoughtless every year.

I suppose it is all a variation of the old riddle, "Out of strength cometh sweetness." We admire the strong man who is gentle. We despise the weakling who can be nothing else. There is a man in this town who was rather nasty to me once. I called him up about something or other, a perfectly polite request, and he banged the receiver in my ear. Ordinarily I would put him down as an old crab and forget about him. But I happen to know that one day he chased miles after a motorist who had run down a dog and gave the man as sound a berating as he had ever had in his life. And so I shall always like this man knowing that he puts his kindness where it counts.

I'm afraid that most of us aren't like that. We are patient and sweet and long suffering and kind because the other fellow has us frightened. And then we wonder why he goes on mistreating us and why people don't respect us.

I think there is some explanation in this, too, for the popular notion that a wife loves a husband who beats her up. That, of course, is not true. But I do think that women give their very best devotion to the men who could beat them up and don't.

---

5 June 1926, Saturday:

WE WENT to the stock company last night, and it was almost like old home week. First there was Mr. Cool out in the outer office and he told us about the new car he'd just bought and then inside the theater the orchestra was playing and

---

[178] Agnes Maude Royden (1876-1956) British preacher, lecturer, author and suffragist for women's rights. Later became known as Maude Royden-Shaw.

the curtain was going up, and there was Ed Lilley and Henry Hicks on the stage and after a while Pauline with a new hair cut and some marvelous clothes.

The last time I saw Pauline was in New York. She was just opening in a new show and I was feeling pretty cocky. Probably down in our hearts we were wondering if we'd ever see dear old Akron again. The next day I got fired. Pauline's luck was somewhat better. I have an idea, though, that destiny intends that certain persons shall stay close to Akron, or at least come back to it at regular intervals.

A stock company is a funny thing. At first you go because you're bored and want to see a show. After a few times you forget all about the show and go because you want to see the players. After a few times you forget all about the show and go because you want to see the players[179] [sic]. You get a sort of lively affection for them that never dies. Our bread man, for instance, has a voice just like Henry Hicks'. Whenever he comes down the back walk mornings calling out "Bre-a-e-e-e-d-man" in a sort of descending fifth I get lonesome for Henry Hicks, although I've never said a word to him in my life. I remember how ages and ages ago he played Adam Ladd in Rebecca of Sunnybrook Farm[180], and how we used to look at him and hope that someday we could be married to somebody just as grand.

Bill has always maintained that Pauline was a peach and I suppose the reason may as well be told right now. It seems one afternoon they had run into a little side street restaurant for a sandwich and – No, I guess I won't tell after all. Anyway it's by little things that you come to know and like people.

It was Aunt Robin, from whom, by the way, I got a postcard this morning, who told me that department stores maintained such things as telephone shoppers. It seems you call up the telephone shopper and tell her whether you're blond or brunette and then she

---

[179] (yes, this sentence was published twice)

[180] 'Rebecca of Sunnybrook Farm' is a 1903 American children's novel by Kate Douglas Wiggin. It was dramatized for theater in 1909 and produced on Broadway by Marc Klaw and A. L. Erlanger. In 1917 became a silent film and in 1938 it would become a "talkie" movie starring Shirley Temple.

goes and buys what you want and sends it out C.O.D[181]. or charge as the case may be. The telephone shopper I always call is named Jane Adams and I found by experience that she saves me money. I go downtown intending to buy two white petticoats for five dollars and I come home with one orange colored one for $7.50. I go downtown intending to buy one of those house-dresses which look so wonderful in the ads for $3.98 and I come home with a pair of cherry colored Japanese pajamas three sizes too small.

The telephone chopper is removed from these temptations. You tell her how much money you have to pay and what you want and she goes and gets it. Almost invariably she saves you money because she knows her stock. She is really one of the nicest institutions I know of.

<hr/>

7 June 1926, Monday:

I WENT over to the Old Trail school Friday to see some of the closing exercises. First the French class put on a dramatization of Little Red Riding Hood and then some of the older children, the sixth and seventh grades I think, put on a dramatization of a story about brownies.

I was all prepared to shudder at the fate of Little Red Riding Hood. The version that Grandmother read to me years ago was before people knew anything about child psychology. At any rate nobody had tampered with it to give it a happy ending. In it Little Red Riding Hood[182] was crunched up thoroughly by the wolf who then went to bed, pulled the covers over his nose and settled down for a good long nap. It was my favorite bed time story. Grandmother always objected to reading it. She said it gave her bad dreams. I can't recall, however, that I was at all saddened by Little Red Riding Hood's fate. And I was thoroughly disgusted with a version of the story which came along later – a version in which some wood choppers appeared on the scene and ripped open the wolf with a scissors whereupon Little Red Riding Hood stepped out, fell in love with the wood chopper who had rescued her and lived happily ever after.

<hr/>

[181] Cash-on-delivery

[182] The version she refers to is by Charles Perrault, the first version published in 1697, included in a collection of stories with morals. The version with the woodcutter is from the Brothers Grimm and appears in 1857.

I was glad that the French class in their dramatization put no such strain on the credulity. To be sure a handsome wood chopper did appear on the scene but it was in answer to Little Red Riding Hood's screams and he dispatched the beast, clad by the way in last winter's fur coat, before any actual damage had been done.

"Robin Goodfellow Plays a Trick[183]" was the name of the play about brownies which the older children wrote and staged. It seems that years ago, in none other than merrie England, there lived a dame, a pink cheeked plump little dame with blue eyes and a peculiarly youthful treble, who thought that all this talk about brownies was the greatest nonsense. With a good many Would'st thou's and Dost thou not's she refused to let her little daughter put a bowl of cream outside for Robin Goodfellow. Then the two of them went to bed. After a while, just at midnight I believe, Robin Goodfellow, clad in something which looked suspiciously like a brown union suit, came skipping in and when he found there was no bowl of cream outside the door he fell into a dreadful rage. He brushed his feet into the seat on the hearth and then jumped on the table and left footmarks all over the nice clean breakfast cloth. You can imagine how the good dame and her daughter felt next morning. So that night they did put a bowl of cream outside the door and later, when Robin Goodfellow came and drank, he was so delighted that he set the table and straightened up the kitchen and swept it clean in good flourishing dust raising strokes. After that there was nothing to do but for the good dame to admit that brownies were stern realities and could, with a little thoughtfulness in the matter of cream bowls, be converted into the best of household helps.

It is sad to think how things have changed. Some time, during the dark hours of every night, a brownie comes to our house but he leaves cream he doesn't take it. I say cream by courtesy. In reality it is a thin substance bearing a faint resemblance to top milk. We pour it into our coffee and if we pour a very great deal we can tell that it is there.

Once a month the brownie leaves a little ticket with the cream telling us that our bill the past month has been so and so much. Eventually we put a check in the cream bottle and the brownie takes it.

That is all that we know of him, all that he knows of us. Whether he is tall and big with red hair or whether is little and slight with dreamy eyes we don't know. We don't know

---

[183] Robin Goodfellow is the name of Puck, from William Shakespeare's "A Midsummer Night's Dream" and denotes a fairy or a prankster. He is introduced in Act 2 Scene 1 when one of Titania's fairies encounters Puck and calls him by his name of Robin Goodfellow.

what he does with our check, whether he has dear little children to feed or whether he is saving up to have a dairy of his own some day.

As for us he doesn't know whether we pay for the cream by going to an office every day or by staying at home and giving music lessons. He doesn't know whether we have one child or four nor how long we cook our oatmeal. I think, however, that he must have figured out one thing about us and that is, considering the attenuation of the cream, that we are very very patient and we are not at all robust.

---

8 June 1926, Tuesday:

I TOOK out the Sunday newspapers awhile ago. There was quite an armful of them and I couldn't help thinking of all the tons and tons of paper that go into the newspapers every week. Why it must take whole forests to keep them going.

And then I thought of all twaddle that goes into Sunday newspapers. Last night I read and read until I was almost blind, vainly hunting for an idea of some sort. And nary an idea could I get. There were automobile advertisements and pictures of bathing girls and advice to the love lorn but it was all trite and old. A woman with two children and a drunken husband who beat her and starved her and was unfaithful to her and she wanted to know what she should do about it. The answer was that she should just keep on being sweet to him and maybe everything would come out all right.

A girl newspapers reporter got a job for a couple of days in a musical comedy. You would think that in that length of time she might have dug up a little tragedy or human interest or something. But she didn't. All she had to report was a rather uninteresting conversation which two chorus girls had about clothes.

Members of the Federation of Women's clubs gathered in convention somewhere held a discussion as to the qualities of the ideal club husband. The thing in itself made a fair news item but I couldn't see the conclusion the women reached. They decided the ideal club husband was a man who encouraged his wife to join clubs, who went with her to conventions and ran errands for her while there. Now I think women ought to join clubs all right but it seems to me a husband like that one pictured above must be sort of sickly. My ideal club husband is one who barks every time you go to a meeting, who gives imitations at the supper table of the secretary reading the minutes of the last gathering, who hands over the money so you can be a delegate to the convention but who piously thanks heaven that he doesn't have to go along.

Then somebody with a lot of time on his or her hands sent out a questionnaire to several hundred college students asking them what sort of wife they wanted. Anybody would know what came back. These seniors in Cornell and Harvard and Kansas and California wanted wives who were religious but not fanatic, who kept the house immaculate but who never said a word if you tramped in mud on the kitchen floor, who looked ravishingly pretty on nothing a year, who petted, but only with them, who were intelligent, but no more intelligent than their husbands, (preferably a little less so) who neither drank nor smoked nor gadded, who gave up careers to settle down in the home, who read good books and magazines but never uttered an opinion at the wrong time, who washed, ironed, cooked, sewed, fished, skated, rowed a boat, danced, swam, rode horseback, played tennis, played golf, raised a family, taught a Sunday school class, sang ravishingly, played the piano, loved to have the husband's friends and relatives in to dinner, never had any trouble with the hired help, made their own hats, got the house cleaning out of the way quickly – but why go on! You sometimes wonder, seeing that the college senior knows so perfectly what he wants, why he so frequently doesn't marry her.

Then there was a note about the newest thing in luncheons. It seems you send out a little questionnaire to your expected guests asking them if they're dieting and if so just what their diet consists of. You also ask them who their beauty doctor is and just what brand of facial pack, wrinkle cream and skin nourisher they are using. Then the guests come and are placed at tables where their own particular kinds of vegetables and desserts are served. Afterwards they repair to a fixed up beauty salon where they put up their facial packs, lean back and relax and watch a fashion parade go by.

The idea seems to be that a party like this undoes a good deal of the damage which has been done at previous parties and as such it seems to be a pretty good idea. It was the most sensible thing I could find in the Sunday papers.

9 June 1926, Wednesday:

I LEARNED just a little while ago that Dr. Ganyard,[184] the well known dentist, is to be our new landlord. You can fancy how pleased I was for Dr. Ganyard and I, whether he knows it or not, belong to the same organization – the Akron Actors' club. Doctor Ganyard is a member of it on account of having been a real actor at some time or other, and I am an honorary member of it on account of being such a nice person. Dr. Ganyard was never at any of the meetings I attended, but now that we are in the position of landlord-tenant I feel as though we know each other awfully well anyway.

I have been wondering for the last couple of hours what I could ask Dr. Ganyard, [sic] for now that he is our new landlord, but for the life of me I can't think of anything except a little cupboard in the corner of the kitchen to keep the furniture and silver polish in.

Sometime when the doctor comes around to collect the rent I want to ask him if he's sorry he isn't any actor any more. And I'm terribly afraid that he'll say it was a hard life and an uncertain one and that he would much rather, now that he's looking at things sensibly, be a dentist and a landlord.

The other night, after the show was over, I walked across the stage at the Colonial and looked out over the empty chairs. If I had been younger I would have pretended I was a great actress and that those chairs out there were full of tumultuous applauding admirers of my art. But now I could only wonder what had become of all the glamour.

---

[184] Akron resident, Frank William Ganyard (1886-1969) Dentist, residing at 322 W. Market st. in 1920 and 8 Jefferson av. in 1930

I remembered how Ethel Barrymore[185] had played at the Colonial in "Alice Sit By the Fire"[186] and "The Twelve Pound Look"[187] and how, in the latter piece, she had curved her hands before her in a caricature of fat Sir Harry[188] and his fat friends.

I remembered how in later years the Horn stock company had played there and how one of our schoolmates had been allowed to play policeman and butler in the productions from week to week. We viewed him with a mixture of delight and envy — delight that we had gone to school with someone who would now indubitably become a great actor, envy that he should be circling about among the leading man and the leading lady and the comedian on equal terms, should know how they ate and talked and who was really married to whom.

Whenever we read how an actress of 40 is just essaying Juliet or how a young man who is making beautiful love in some current production is in reality a grandfather we marvel at how the people of the stage keep their youth. Sometimes I think, though, that it must be the other way round. There are certain persons born who are perennially young and these take to the stage. How else could they go about among the flimsy stage trappings, look out over the rows of empty seats and no succumb to a wild desire to go into catering or dressmaking?

Bill says that this is all bosh. He says the actor's favorite music is "The Palma" and that as long as this keeps up loudly and strenuously the actor is happy.

And so I don't know. I mean to ask Dr. Ganyard about it when he comes for the rent.

---

[185] Born Ethel Mae Blythe and died as Ethel Barrymore Colt (1879-1959) American actress and member of the famous Barrymore family of actors.

[186] "Alice Sit By the Fire" was written in 1905 by Scottish novelist Sir James Matthew Barrie, known as J. M. Barrie (1860-1937), the same year he also wrote Peter Pan.

[187] "The Twelve Pound Look" is a 1920 British silent film directed by Jack Denton and written by J. M. Barrie (1860-1937).

[188] Referring to the character of Harry Sims in the aforementioned play.

12 June 1926, Saturday:

IT MAY be added that Akron has no slums. At least as far as I have been able to discover. There are, around the rubber factories, dark and gloomy boarding houses. Going out certain streets one comes across somewhat ramshackley negro quarters. There is occasionally a somewhat unsteady wooden structure on Furnace st. But even these have their garden plots, their geraniums in the front window.

Sometimes we grow sick at heart at the ugliness of our school buildings, with their hot blistering sides and their flat treeless play grounds, when we think we can't stand another minute these rows and rows of second-hand cars out East Market st., we can pause and reflect that if Akron isn't so very beautiful at any rate neither it is so very desolate.

———————

Speaking of schools, something nice and not a little touching happened at Portage Path the other day. Miss Myers, the principal there, who has spent years in building up the school, is to be transferred in the fall to a new building. And so the other day each child in the school brought a gift offering of two pennies clutched in a tight moist palm. I don't know just how the pennies were presented, but I dare say they were all put in a great bag which required at least two fourth graders to lift.

It may be, of course, that they didn't give the pennies that way. They may have converted them into a fat round gold piece[189] before presenting them. I think, though, that if it were myself I would rather have the pennies. And I would put them on a shelf in the kitchen cupboard and then in years to come when I was feeling a little low I would go get the bag and lift it down and see for myself just how much a whole school full of love weighs.

———————

I am beginning to worry about Mary's reading. Already she has attained to the dignity of a high chair, and she can ba-ba and ma-ma. I also thought for a day or two that she was saying da-da, but it turned out that it was the child next door instead. It stand to reason, however, that Mary will be demanding literature soon, and I don't know whether to lay out a prescribed course of reading for her or just turn her loose. Bill says that at

———————

[189] A gold one-dollar piece is a gold coin that was regular issue in the U.S. from 1849 to 1889. It was composed of 90% gold and 10% copper.

———————

491

the age of seven, he was reading "The Scarlet Letter"[190] and the Henty books and that now, when he thinks of them, he gets the plots curiously mixed. At the age of eight I dimly recall reading "The House of Seven Gables," the Nick Carter weeklies[191] and "The Young Ladies' Repository."[192]

Recalling these delights, I hesitate to lay down a prescribed course of reading for Mary, "Mother Goose" at three, animal tales at five, Norse myths at seven. For, book agents to the contrary, I don't want Mary to read the identical things that thousands of other children are reading. I don't want her to have just a chaste and proper excerpt from Ivanhoe.[193] I want her to grow breathless over the whole thing. I don't want her to wait until she is 15, to read "Lorna Doone,"[194] and then, when I have duly presented it to her, decide that such a heavy book involves entirely too much labor.

Evan at the risk of any number of calamities I am inclined to think that as soon as she is able to spell out her letters, Mary will have to choose her own reading. That course settled upon, I dare say some day I shall come upon her reading "Madame Bovary,"[195] and I won't know what to do about it — whether to remain perfectly quiet or hide it under the dish towels.

---

[190] Written by Nathaniel Hawthorne (1804-1864) American author. Additionally he wrote "The House of Seven Gables"

[191] "The New Nick Carter weeklies" were part of what were known as "dime novels" made inexpensively and equate to modern "mass-market" paperbacks and comic books.

[192] A monthly periodical from Cincinnati, Ohio published from 1841-1876, and was devoted to literature, arts, poetry, and doctrines of Methodism.

[193] A historical novel first published in 1819 by Sir Walter Scott (1771-1832) Scottish novelist, playwright, poet and historian.

[194] "Lorna Doone: A Romance of Exmoor" published in 1869 by Richard Doddridge Blackmore (1825-1900) English novelist. He pioneered a Victorian romance movement in books that continued with Robert Louis Stevenson (1850-1894) and others.

[195] The debut novel published in 1856 of Gustave Flaubert (1821-1880) French author

Probably the better course would be to hide the ornery books under the dish towels – "Pilgrim's Progress"[196] and things like that. Then Mary can have the delights of surreptitious reading and become imbued with moral notions at the same time.

---

15 June 1926, Tuesday:

I do not like hot weather.

Every once in a while I'll meet a girl and she'll say to me, "Oh do you know, I just ADORE hot weather. All winter long I just FREEZE, just simply FREEZE. I wear my suit under my fur coat and a sweater under my suit. I just nearly die I get so cold. But when hot weather comes I just revel in it. Oh how I wish days like this would last FOREVER."

And I look at that girl sadly because I know that never can we be friends.

In hot weather the ice man comes. He brings in mud on his big boots. He leaves the mud on your nice clean kitchen floor. He chips little pieces off the ice and leaves those on the kitchen floor. He sets the milk bottles out and leaves those on the kitchen floor.

In hot weather you are gummy all the time. If you don't wear enough petticoats people make crude remarks about your silhouette. You cling damply in all the chairs. You powder your nose until you are frantic. You drink lemonade until you are bilious. You go out to the lakes and get bitten by mosquitoes. You stay at home and flies pounce on you.

In hot weather you can't get anything done. You wake up in the morning all full of ambition and a hot monsoon descends on the streets and seeps through the walls and leaves you groggy and helpless. The curl comes out of your hair, the starch out of your frills, the resistance out of your backbone.

---

[196] "The Pilgrim's Progress from This World, to That Which Is to Come" is a 1678 Christian allegory book by John Bunyan (1628-1688). It has been cited as the first novel written in English, is translated into 200 languages, and has never been out of print.

In hot weather people ask you to come and visit them. You get on a train all full of dust and red plush. You breathe cinders. You eat watery cantaloupe and medicated chicken a la king and peas out of a can. You read confessions magazine and get stuck up with chocolate bars and par boil all night in a sleeper. You arrive at your destination. In 30 minutes you have seen everybody you wanted to see and said everything you wanted to say. You wish you hadn't come. Your friends wish you hadn't come. You wear up all your clean clothes. You arrive home with a suitcase full of soiled ones. You swear you'll never go again.

In hot weather everybody has the windows up and you don't dare to talk over a few matters with your family without everybody knowing about it for a block in each direction. You don't dare to enumerate to your husband the couple of things that are wrong with him or play your favorite phonograph records or sing or gossip over the telephone or talk over the people in the third floor back.

In hot weather people come to visit you. They sleep in your best bed and think nothing of it. They expect you to drag them around to movies and chicken dinners. They can't see how you can get along without a radio. They put three spoonsfuls of sugar in their coffee. They wash out their stockings and let them fade on the dish towels. They stay a week longer than you asked them for.

In hot weather there are thunderstorms. The water comes through the front windows and the back windows, the front porch and the back porch. It flows down the water spout and overflows in the cellar. Then you have to use all the sheets, lace curtains and old petticoats in the house to mop it up.

In hot weather green onions grow and you don't care to eat them.

<hr />

16 June 1926, Wednesday:

IT BEGINS to look now as though Bill and I might be going to Chicago next week. At first we meant to drive over, and in case all hotel accommodations were taken, sleep on the park benches. But yesterday Bill heard of a dandy excursion train which was clearly designed for people like us. You get your fare both ways, reservation at a hotel, transportation for your luggage, breakfast every morning and trips on the sightseeing busses all for a very modest sum indeed.

I told Bill that so far as I was concerned I would just as life cut out the trips on the sightseeing busses but Bill said no, whenever he went to a town he always took a trip on a sightseeing bus and he hadn't any intention of changing the habit of a life time and besides it wasn't going to cost anything extra so I suppose we'll have to go.

As for the hotel I don't suppose it will be anything extraordinary but I never did like hotels that were too Ritzy. I like the old-fashioned kind with high ceilings and turkey red carpets and chamber maids who tell you all their troubles.

I think the first thing I will do when we get there will be to go down Michigan avenue and stand in front of the old Y. W. C. A. Of course it may not be standing there any more in which case one already overflowing heart will break. This Y. W. C. A. had been outlawed from the national organization for some reason or other when I knew it but it was still struggling along under the management of a board of directors which met every Thursday.

The board of directors wore awful hats but there was this to be said about the matter — we always had better lunches on Thursday.

I wish I could remember the names of some of the women there. There was the tall thin one with the red hair and the white dresses who presided over the dining room. When she wasn't looking we collected sugar and butter off the tables which we carried upstairs and converted into fudge in a chafing dish set over canned heat. The canned heat always gave out just before the fudge reached the soft ball stage and we ate the fudge with a spoon.

Then there was the little dried up one who presided over the library. She admitted only orthodox literature into her library. One day I asked her if she had H. G. Wells' "God the Invisible King." "No," she snapped, "and I don't intend to have it either."

Then there was the fat one who read Edith Wharton behind a little iron cage. She issued the laundry checks. Whenever you wanted to use the laundry you gave her a nickel and she issued you a check. It occasionally happened of course that at certain times when you wanted to use the laundry you either didn't have a nickel or else you wanted to use it for other things. so you went down to the laundry the back way. Then the fat one would flurry down and demand of every girl that she show her laundry check. She never demanded it of me. She said I had too honest a face. To this day I can think of her only with tenderness.

Then there was the elevator man. He was just terrible. He got conscripted for the war and we were all so tickled to see him so we took up a collection and bought him a wrist watch. The third day he was back. He'd been rejected for flat feet.

And finally there was Victoria, the little Polish girl who scrubbed. Victoria so sweet, so gentle, so gay, her hands all rough and red from scrubbing. Victoria cried when we went away. "Don't cry dear," we said, "we'll all be back in the fall." But we never went back.

Afterwards I think I shall walk up and down the avenue and examine whether the stones have softened any over which I used to tramp night after night skying over the parts of Bach Sarabandes[197] and gavotte and gigues. I wonder why in those days I thought life so difficult.

<hr />

17 June 1926, Thursday:

BILL is going to a stag party tonight. There are a lot of women who wouldn't want their husbands to go to a stag party but I'm always glad when Bill goes. It puts him in an angelic frame of mind for a week afterward. He comes home along about one in the morning reeking with tobacco, overflowing with a couple of good ones he hadn't heard before and full of complacency at a couple of wise cracks thought up all by himself on the spur of the moment.

Just what goes on at these stag parties Bill will never tell. He won't tell where the party's been held nor who went nor what they did nor what they had to eat. But I always ask anyway. He had such a lot better time when he thinks I'm dying of curiosity.

One night last summer Tonya and I found out where one of these stag parties was to be held and we went over later and stood outside the window and listened. Somebody was playing "I Hear You Calling Me" on the phonograph. After it was finished somebody said "Well that was real nice" and somebody else said "Say George I wonder if you've got that Swedish lullaby?"

<hr />

[197] A dance in triple metre, and referring to Johann Sebastian Bach. It was often paired with a jig or gigue.

After about a half hour of that sort of thing Tonya and I felt we'd simply have to do a little cutting up of our own so we went down to the drug store and ordered two chocolate nut sundaes.

———————

One of the pleasantest things about the season just approaching is that at last they're apparently going to do something about the mixed bathing proposition.

Alack and again alas[198] if they'd only done something about mixed bathing years ago full many a romance would have turned out differently. I need hardly say that I am referring to Elmer.

Elmer was one of the sweetest fellows who ever came sparking a girl on Sunday and Thursday nights. He sang, he danced, he kept his clothes pressed, he had a car, he always invited your parents to go along, he could talk about anything, he remembered your birthday, when the gang went out to Summit Beach he always paid for the lemonade and hot dogs, he made $35 a week.

Elmer and I had come to an understanding and were already saving up for the golden oak dining room suite when the most dreadful thing possible happened for the first time I saw Elmer in a bathing suit. I had never dreamed that anybody's knees could be so knobby.

It was all over in a few minutes.

I never told him why.

———————

There are times when I think I will never bake another pie. In spite of the fact that I mix every pie with prayer and crimp the edges with excerpts from Jeremiah, the fillings simply will not congeal. I put in flour, I put in the egg, I bake them fast, I bake them slow. Nothing does any good.

Tonight it was a rhubarb pie. When I took it out of the oven it looked beautiful. When I cut it the insides ran out like very thin jam. I was going to put it in deep dishes and

———————

[198] An expression meant to imply regret or sadness

———————

pretend it was rhubarb cobbler or something but luckily Bill knew I was trying to bake a pie and so he thoughtfully brought home some ice cream.

— ❧ ❦ ❧ ✦ ❧ ❦ ❧ —

19 June 1926, Saturday:

ANOTHER sort of back door traffic has set up now. Every hour or so a rosy cheeked boy comes with flowers to sell. Last night it was beautiful ragged white peonies with some sort of slender scarlet blossom to set them off. This morning it was old fashioned garden flowers. After that my two bowls, the green one, and the black one, were used up and I could buy no more.

I think that whether I analyzed it or not the same idea raced through my head as I bartered with the flower merchants. "You," I thought, "are the only son of a widowed mother who keeps you clean and clear eyed and rosy. You assist her by keeping up a paper route and, now that school is out, by selling flowers. She hasn't much to go on but she has a soul for beauty as is attested by the scarlet daisy flowers among the white peonies."

Of course that probably isn't the case. They undoubtedly have thick layers of strawberry conserve on their bread at every meal and the nickels and dimes I turn over to them may be going into a motorbike fund. Anyway the flowers are lovely. I am glad it is flowers they are peddling and not aluminum cooking utensils.

It occurs to me now that when I am old I may raise flowers for a living. There are a good many persons I fear who never give a though to picking out a suitable career for that time when the grinders shall have ceased to grind and the windows will be growing a little dark. It is obvious, however, that old age, like youth, has its suitable employments.

For a good while I had thought that about the only employment open to me would be scrubbing up the floors of the Second National building at night after the office workers had gone home. I was not unpleased at the prospect as the job of scrub woman opens up a good many vistas of jolly companionship. The principal hardship had reasoned would be upon my knees which had not been toughened by prayer. Later I would go to the infirmary and be as pleasant about it as possible.

The genuflexions of flower raising, however, are another thing again. In marble office buildings one kneels and scrubs and the muddy feet of the first passer by, are the only reward for one's toil. In a garden one kneels upon the springy sod. The seed is planted, a stem and leaves and buds appear. There is beauty in it for all the world to see.

I say this with hope rather than conviction. Actually I have never been able to make anything grow. I have probed about the roots of my plants. I have given them water and air and sunlight. I have dosed them with aspirin and castor oil and charcoal. Being told that flowers will grow only for those who love them, I have approached them from time to time and given them every assurance of my devotion. It has all been in vain. The ferns wither, the primroses droop, the carrot which I place on the kitchen window sill, refuses to put out leaves. The only things which flourish are the potato shoots.

With age, with more experience – I keep telling myself.

Not that I have given up the idea of baby tending in my old age. It stands to reason, however, that there will be ten or fifteen minutes occasionally when the children will be sleeping. At such times I will take my trowel and my sun bonnet and my canvas gloves and steal out.

Between the two one ought to be able to get along very nicely indeed.

22 June 1926, Tuesday:

CHICAGO, June 21 – We went on a terrific bus ride this afternoon. It lasted for four hours and we were nearly dead. The only redeeming feature was the bus conductor who delivered the travelog.

The first thing you noticed about him was that he got his rights and lefts all mixed up. It was confusing to say the least, to be told, "Now on your left folks, you see historic Lake Michigan," and then when you looked in that direction to see nothing but a blank wall advertising Mrs. Walker's complexion remedies. After awhile you learned to look right when he said left and vice versa and everything went off nicely indeed.

The other peculiarity of our bus conductor was his modesty of statement. "Now just ahead of you, folks," he would say, "is the new union station and this station is the most modern and up to date in the – in the – well anyway in Chicago." Now we're coming to Lincoln park. Lincoln park is the most beautiful park – the most beautiful park – Lincoln park is the most beautiful park in this place."

Only twice did he overstep the bounds to which he had set himself. Once was when he declared that the statue of a certain lady, left over from the World's fair, was made of "solid gold leaf." The other was when he declared there were more vehicles on Michigan boulevard than on any other street, boulevard or avenue in the world.

Mrs. Con Mulcahy and Mrs. J. M. Doras and Margaret Harvey who were also on the bus ride said that all things considered they had had a lovely time.

———

The people walking along Michigan avenue didn't look particularly chic. One thing I noticed however was that a lot of them had finally taken to short vamp shoes. It used to be that Chicago women wouldn't wear anything but long vamp shoes which came to terrific points in front. It was this more than anything I think which gave Chicago women the reputation of having the largest feet in the world.

———

This morning we saw an elderly man and woman stopping traffic while they held an argument in the middle of a street car track. It seems she wanted to go to one church to mass and he wanted to go to another. As I said to Bill I bet there have been a lot of family arguments in the last couple of days. Last night while we were waiting for the train in Cleveland a woman walked right out of the station flinging back to her husband over her should that she wouldn't move a step. He ran after her and they eventually made it up and came back to buy their tickets. I do hope these men who have nice amiable wives who make no fuss when they travel will some day learn to appreciate them.

———

Over on a little side street close to one of the churches a woman had set up "The Rose and Grey Tea Room." I am certain that until a day or two ago it had been nothing but an empty store room which her quick eye had appraised and rented for a week. She was doing a thriving business.

Aside from the parks which are beautiful I haven't within the past few hours been able to find anything in Chicago which is either exciting or noteworthy. The memory of those streets which are nice is almost completely obliterated by the memory of those streets which are so dreadfully dirty and ugly. And they crowd each other closely.

23 June 1926, Wednesday:

CHICAGO, June 22 – One of the Chicago State street shops is showing a window of purple hats labeled, "Eminence Purple." I have wondered who it is that buys purple hats. Every spring there are purples and purples and yet I rarely see a girl wearing one. Sometimes I have a dreadful suspicion that they keep using the same hats over again.

The Michigan avenue shops it seems to me are far lovelier than those on New York's Fifth or Madison avenues. One is used to see frightful creations in the New York exclusive shops. I asked a woman who knew all about it once why the dress designers should such dreadful things and she said they rarely lost money on them. She pointed out that because a woman had money meant by no means that her taste was impeccable. She would wear anything which the wily modiste declared was exclusive.

———

At 1 o'clock this afternoon Bill and I went over to the Chicago theater principally to hear the music until seven at night. So we went across the street where one of those combination movie and vaudeville programs was being put on and it was pretty awful. We saw two acts of vaudeville consisting principally of none too expert dancing and then a movie started and it was called "The Unfair Sex."[199] We stood it for five minutes and I will say we've stuck out some very banal movies.

Then I stopped in one of the stores to get some stockings and the girl told me they didn't carry pointex heels.[200] She said they tried to sell them last summer but nobody would buy them so they had a sale to get ride of them. Chicago sure is funny.

———

[199] A silent black and white 1926 film by director Henri Diamant-Berger and starring Hope Hampton and Holbrook Blinn. Released April 17, 1926.

[200] Onyx was a brand of stockings in the 1920's. Their popular "Onyx Pointex" sheer and "Sheresilk" stockings with mercerized lisle garter top and sole, featured heel reinforcement, coming to a point which "makes trim ankles look their best" according to a vintage department store magazine ad. Sold by Emery & Beers company in New York.

The cops are nice though. The traffic ones wear grey, cool looking uniforms with black bands.

––––––––––

Over on Michigan boulevard where the popcorn and lemonade stands have been set up the Coco Cola people have put up little automatic arrangements. You get a paper cup, put a dime in the slot, push a lever and out comes the Coco Cola. I asked Bill if Coco Cola didn't ordinarily cost a nickel and he said yes but it naturally would have to cost twice as much when you serve yourself.

Down by the curb an old black man was guarding a tiny negro baby lying asleep in his carriage. All the women who were crossing the street and a good many who hadn't planned to cross it arranged to start their crossing at the point so they could get a peep at the baby. The old man ignored them sublimely.

––––––––––

I don't know how conventions go usually but a good many humble people seem to have come to this one. You strongly suspect that more than one woman has made a serious sacrifice in order to come. Their shoes are worn, their gloves patched, their hats a little out of date. But they look supremely happy. I heard one woman this noon explaining something of the mass to her neighbor and I heard the words, "Our blessed Lord; the blessed weeping Mother."

When I was a little girl and indeed all my life I have always felt that there was something sacrilegious in mentioning the name of Jesus at all. It was something far off which was to be respected but had nothing to do with your daily life. These women as they sit in the hotel lobby and talk speak of Jesus as though He were their neighbor John. The purpose of this congress, so they tell us, is to attest vividly and concretely the belief of hundreds of thousands of people in the living presence of Christ. I think I am just beginning to see what they mean.

— ❦ —

24 June 1926, Thursday:

FOR some reason or other the elevateds in Chicago have a pleasanter roar than those in New York. In New York I lived two blocks away from an elevated and the noise drove me beside myself. Here there is one very close to our hotel window and we don't notice it at all.

I went to call on my one time music teacher, Julia Caruthers, this morning, but she was out of the city. Her secretary, Dorothy Parker, however was sitting at the same old desk. She wanted to know all about Hermine Deneke[201] and I told her Miss Deneke was getting along fine and about Walter Jones and about Mary and Bill and the phonograph and everything.

Dorothy said their scrub woman had come to work a little while ago. "Is there anything going on in town?" she queried, "I see so many flags around."

The buildings on the north boulevard including the Tribune building make a beautiful sky line. Making a great blotch across the whole however, is an electric sign advertising Sinclair Motor Oils. It seems to me that that must be one kind of advertising which doesn't pay. On the south boulevard a few years ago there used to be a particularly dreadful animated electric sign advertising Warner's Rust Proof corsets. So far as remembering the name of Warner I will always do so. But I would run a mile and then another one before wearing one of their celebrated corsets.

We saw some nice old dishes over in the art institute this morning. One of them was a great tureen shaped like a bunny. You lifted off the bunny's back evidently, piled in the mashed potatoes, put a square of butter and some white pepper on top and then put the bunny's back back on again.

The lavatory had a funny contraption in it for drying your hands.

You pressed a pedal with your foot and then a lot of hot air came rushing out of a tube and you held your hands there until they were dry. It sounded just like a vacuum cleaner.

According to the frocks in the show windows flowers are worn on the hip now instead of on the shoulder.

---

[201] Akron resident, Hermine Louise Deneke (1858/1869-1927)

Last night we saw some lovely poster pillows in a window for only $1.55. the shop was closed though and today when we went back to look for it we couldn't find it.

I guess what the girl told me about square heels in stockings was correct. I can't find a pointed heel anywhere.

Most of the stories written about the Eucharistic congress are excellent but some of them are mawkish in the extreme. One of the writers compared a sun whom he saw on Michigan av. In the early morning to "a lovely fawn out of its element." Other writers give you the impression that everybody in town is going about mumbling prayers and that a reverential hush is upon everything.

As a matter of fact everything is dignified and cheerful and pleasant, exactly as it should be. The priests go to the ball games in the afternoons and out to Riverview park. The nuns go about smiling a good deal and I think they must do a bit of gossiping. Everybody is happy. They are happy when they pray, happy when they sing. You can feel it in the air.

----

26 June 1926, Saturday:

IT was pleasant to come rolling home Friday morning. The streets were clean, the sidewalks shone, the trees were fresh and green, the breeze was cool. I wondered where I ever got the impression that Akron was ugly.

One of the things which ought to be worth looking into is how a man happens to take up the job of personally conducting. I am thinking of Mr. Storey – Mr. John M. Storey. Whenever Mr. Storey hears of a place where people ought to go he promptly organizes a tour in that direction.

Mr. Storey heard there was going to be a Eucharistic congress in Chicago and straightway he set about the business of assembling a party. I don't just know how many there were in the party but there seemed to be about 13 cars on the train and all of them were filled.

Mr. Storey made the train reservations, picked out the hotel for his people to stay at, arranged for their breakfasts, got up bus rides for them, helped them check their baggage, advised them on train connections, told them what to put in their picnic baskets, advised them what time they should be coming home from the expeditions and never lost the evenness of his disposition once.

If Mr. Storey said that the bus would be at the door at 1:35 the bus was there. If he said breakfast would be served at four, breakfast was served at four. Sometimes a bus would start out and you would wave goodbye to Mr. Storey standing on the sidewalk. Four miles out the bus would break down and there would be Mr. Storey calmly getting it started again.

If Mr. Storey said that your berth would be a lower six, why a lower six it was. If Mr. Storey said your baggage would turn up shortly in perfect condition, why turn up it did. Mr. Storey reassured the aged, calmed the excitable, assembled the wandering, cheered the homesick, called everybody by first name. I had hoped to be able to talk to Mr. Storey about his life work. I wanted to ask him how many people out of every party lost their coupons, how many got the wrong baggage, how many wanted their hotel rooms changed, how many missed the train, how many forgot what hotel they were staying at.

But I didn't get the chance. When Mr. Storey wasn't doing the things above mentioned he apparently was thinking up new tours.

One of the pleasant things about coming home is anticipating all the mail which has been piling up in your absence. There will be, you think, a couple of letters from warm friends, and a note from the editor of the Saturday Evening Post requesting an article which he will pay for in advance and a remittance from a chap who borrowed fifteen dollars from you seven years ago.

As a matter of fact all that we found when we came home this morning was a sample tube of tooth paste, an advertisement from a bank, a notice from a magazine that our subscription would run out in two weeks and a caustic note from a woman who, as is invariably the case, neglected to sign her name.

There was a pleasant side though. Mary had expanded at least an inch in each direction and Miss Mary Metzger who had taken care of her so beautifully had darned all the stockings and shined all the furniture and ordered fresh strawberries and cream.

30 June 1926, Wednesday:

ONE of the reforms which this department is hankering to take up has to do with the matter of dress manufacture. Years ago when you bought a ready made dress you found the hem sewed in good and tight and if you wanted to shorten the hem or lengthen it you had to hunt up an old razor blade and rip it out and steam out the places where the stitches had been and altogether it was pretty much of a nuisance.

They just baste in home nowadays and if they would only do the same with white collars and cuffs I'm sure millions of women would be made happier. If white collars and cuffs were only basted onto ready made dresses you could take them off when they became soiled and launder them and put them back and the whole frock would be fresh again.

If white collars and cuffs were only basted onto dresses you could take them off before you laundered the dresses and the greens and the yellows and the lavenders or what nots wouldn't run then and fade all over everything. I had a yellow dress which I loved. But the yellow ran and now the collar and the cuffs and the little flaps and the pockets are a bright lemon color.

A good many people doubtless wonder why a person wouldn't have ripped them off anyway. The trouble is that they're sewn in so tightly and thoroughly that when you rip them off the whole dress falls apart. And for a woman who doesn't know how to sew this is quite a tragedy.

––––––––

The greatest events of our lives I have found come to us quietly and unobtrusively. Last night Mary leaned over and bit my thumb. "Bill," I said, "Mary's got a tooth." Bill investigated. "She's got two teeth," he said.

––––––––

"You wrote about a dog and some rabbits the other day, which struck an aching chord in our hearts," writes Mrs. S. B. "It was on account of Rex, our dear Rex, whose life was snuffed out by a careless driver who without caring or stopping drove on. Our little son of four is grief stricken. We are not any too well off in this world, but if any one had offered us money for Rex we couldn't even have considered such a thing. You see we live on a big farm, but the roads being paved it is a mad rush all hours, day and night.

"Then to top it all a young man drove in the other day saying he was all out of gas and would we be good enough to lend him some. We did and we also gave him a pail to put it in and a funnel. He kept them all."

Why are some motorists so mean?

5 July 1926, Monday:

G ORDON DAVIES[202] was considering this noon the decline of the old-fashioned Sunday school picnic.

"We have so many other diversions these days," he said, "we don't consider a Sunday school picnic any fun any more."

It is hard to realize that we ever did consider a Sunday school picnic any fun. Your mother never let you wear the dress you'd set your heart on. She said it would rain and it always did. You got chiggers under your skin. You fell down and hurt your knee. The garnet ring from which you had unobtrusively borrowed from your elder sister fell into the water and was lost. The young gentleman upon whom you had set your affections took another girl rowing. I for my part am glad that we have become blasé about some things and Sunday school picnics are one of them.

———————

A pleasant way to spend the Fourth,[203] I think, would be to arise at 11, breakfast upon red raspberries and cream, put on something cool, stand at the window and watch it rain awhile, do a cross word puzzle, play a phonograph record, dine upon ice cream, go to bed.

In spite of this very sensible program, however, hundreds, say thousands, of people will get up before dawn, roll the family filvver out of its nice quiet garage and go tearing about over the country. They will drink highly watered lemonade, eat dubious looking hot dogs and unbuttered bread, they will get all dusty and red and freckled, and they will bump into other peoples' cars and come home with trailing fenders and sagging bumpers and shattered wind shields. Personally I shan't shed any tears when I look over the death toll Tuesday morning.

---

[202] Akron resident, Gordon Davies (1884-1939), Municipal Court Judge, at 104 Byers av. in 1920 and 41 Byers av. in 1930

[203] The 4th of July

And then going down High st., I bumped into Bill Smith who's running for sheriff, and Pat Hutchinson,[204] the kindest-hearted ex-sheriff that ever let a prisoner out of jail. "Hello, Pat," I said to him, and Pat says hello, but he looked kind of puzzled. After a while he came after me. "Say," he said, "I didn't know you. I thought you was one of the girls. How's the baby?"

So we talked the whole situation over, and I told him about Mary's tooth, and Pat told me about his boy, and the one who used to be an aviator, and how he's been married for a year and a half now, and they're so much in love they still go around holding hands.

And then I saw a lot of other folks, Esther Noonan[205] that was who was just leaving on a vacation, Elsie Gilbert who had just gotten back from one and her niece, Catherine Hoffman,[206] Mirlam Tipton that was who told me she had a beauty parlor of her very own now, Nelson Stone[207], all done up in a swallow tail,[208] Tommy Pitkin[209] in a new straw hat – a very satisfactory afternoon.

[204] Akron resident, Patrick J. Hutchinson (c.1877/1884-) Sheriff and private detective, residing at 212 South Railway st. in 1920, residing at 87 Belinden Way in 1940

[205] Akron resident, Esther M. Noonan (c.1892-1969) a Stenographer, residing at Kine av. in 1910, 824 Delaware av. in 1930

[206] Akron resident, Catherine Christine Hoffman (1910-1996) a Public School Teacher, residing at 800 Patterson av. in 1920-1940

[207] Akron resident, Nelson Clarke Stone (c.1853-aft1920) President of National Bank, residing at 144 Park st. in 1920

[208] 1920's men's fashion, a fancy fitted jacket with long tails in the back, a "swallow tail" usually in black or dark blue.

[209] Akron resident, Thomas Bendette Pitkin (c.1880) an Accountant, residing at 287 Wheeler in 1920 or Thomas Monroe Pitkin (1901-1988) a Historian

6 July 1926, Tuesday:

IT occurred to me the other day that probably the happiest man in the town is Bill Haynes.

Of course the chap that I saw going down the aisle at the vaudeville show may not have been Bill Haynes, out the ears and the cut of his hair were certainly like Bill's. He went and sat down in the second row a little to o ne side and then a lot of girls came on and danced and Bill got up and moved over to the center of the row.

"Wouldn't it be dreadful," I said to myself, "if one of them would step out and start kidding Bill," because you know how bashful he is. Why he'd probably outblush his red necktie.

What I started to say though was that there are few men in town who if they took a notion, could wander into a vaudeville show in the middle of the afternoon.

But Bill can.

If Bill wants to go fishing, he goes. If he wants to go to Florida and pick hybiscus, he goes. If he wants to go to Alaska and chase bears, he goes. If he wants to sit around and talk with Bill Sawyer all afternoon, he does.

Happy, happy Bill Haynes.

Bill Haynes never pays any attention to what the well dressed man is going to wear. He just goes on wearing the same suit and neck-tie and hat. Maybe he's got a car but whenever I see him he's either walking or riding on the street car. If Bill feels a funny sensation burning in him he immediately knows it's the call to sit down and write an article on duck hunting. And he sits down and writes it and the magazines snap it up before he's even put in all the commas. Bill Haynes eats what he pleases, goes where he pleases, wears what he pleases, makes friends where he pleases.

Happy, happy Bill Haynes.

So far as the vaudeville show was concerned it was pretty awful. Bill, my own particular Bill, went with me. First there was a movie and when it was over I said, "Well, thank heaven, that's over."

"The next act's going to be good," said Bill. "I saw it in Syracuse."

But it wasn't.

"Never mind," said Bill, "the next one is going to be better. I saw it last fall in Rochester."

It was terrible. "I'm going home," I said to Bill, "I'd rather take in washing and ironing."

"Ah come on and stay," said Bill, "I saw this fellow 20 years ago in Yonkers and he was a scream."

But 20 years ago Bill was young and not so particular.

And so in a way it may not be such a fine thing after all to be able to go to a show whenever you want to. Personally I hope the onerous duties of my job keep me from all of them for the rest of the summer. And it may be that Bill Haynes feels that way about it, too.

---

8 July 1926, Thursday:

IT was hard work getting across Market st. Tuesday when the rain came. I tried it for a couple of hours, retreating each time to the Y. W. C. A. where I fortified myself with a chocolate bar before starting out again. Up at Broadway a Lund laundry wagon was waiting to make the turn. "Could I go across the street with you?" I pleaded. The driver looked a little dubious. "do you just want to go across the street?" he queried. I assured him that that was all I wanted and so he let me sit up on the seat beside him and was very gracious about it.

I have wondered a good many times about the laundry wagon boy I drove around with several years ago. It seemed that several months before he had accidentally injured a school boy who had run out and hitched on the laundry wagon. The boy died and for months the chap on the laundry wagon grieved. Then one afternoon he saw a crowd collected along the bank of the Little Cuyahoga. A child had fallen in and was being rapidly borne away by the swollen current. The chap on the laundry wagon plunged in and rescued her.

The thought that he had saved a life to make up for that other life brought him the first peace he had known for nearly a year.

And I have thought a good many times of that girl who came to Akron from a little town away off somewhere to make her living and got a job in a laundry. And of how her poor hands which toiled so ceaselessly over the sheets and the skirts and the pillow cases were caught one day in the great mangle and crushed so that she died. "It was a merciful thing," I have told myself, "that she should have died." But again and again I think of her lying alone in the hospital with nobody much to care.

These seem to be things which are going on more or less all the time and yet the sheets which come home every week so smooth and white give very little hint of them.

I went up to the hospital this morning to see young John Peter Schweisgood.[210] He was small and quite scarlet and he gave unmistakable indications of being hungry. As I went away down the hall I couldn't forebear looking into some of the other rooms and in almost every one there was an ecstatic father. We keep reading articles in the magazines written by women wherein they tell how the arrival of little Patricia Jane made them a sister to all women. Sometime I'd like to get from some man an honest expression as to whether parenthood made him a brother to all men.

I know that shortly after Mary came Bill and a friend of his, also a father, sat down to have a good long talk and it was amazing to discover that their sufferings had been almost identical.

---

[210] Akron resident, John Peter Schweisgood (1926-1989), shown in at St. John's Hospital at 3409 Woodlin av. in Cleveland in 1930, along with his younger brother William, and would grow to be healthy and later became a Catholic Priest known as Fr. Peter J. Sweisgood O.S.B.

9 July 1926, Friday:

THE other night I put an advertisement in the paper for a woman to take care of Mary during those hours when I had to be away. The answers began coming immediately in great heaps, some of them sad, some of them amusing, some of them straight and to the point.

One of the things I kept thinking about as I opened them was that while most of these women were giving references, none of them was asking references of me.

I knew a few years ago a woman who couldn't afford to have help yet who had it all the time by the simple expedient of having it and not paying for it. She would engage a woman, put her of a week or two with promises of pay and maybe give her an old dress. When the woman's patience gave out she walked out and a new one was hired. This practice was kept up indefinitely and so far as I know the only inconvenience my friend suffered was that of breaking in a new woman from time to time.

I know a man who some time ago decided to rent an apartment. "What references can you give?" asked the agent. "What references can YOU give?" inquired my friend coldly.

And he was right. When you or I engage an apartment we promise to pay the rent with a fair degree of promptness and to dispose of our pet poodle and turn off the phonograph at a reasonable hour. But there is no reasonable assurance from our landlord in return that he will look after the plumbing, have the cellar steps scrubbed and keep us warm.

I mentioned this to a landlord once. "Why," he said, "If you shouldn't receive sufficient heat you can always go to law about it."

Fortunately most landlords are the sort you don't have to hale into court.

———

To revert to the matter of answers to my advertisements, I found myself inkling first of all to those which were correctly spelled and which did not start, "I seen your ad." – And yet I realized that that was really no way to judge. In years gone by I have had foreign women work for me who by no manner of reason could be expected to spell and yet they were the most faithful, conscientious souls that one could ask for.

However, with nothing but a letter to go by, I let spelling count and by that simple procedure eliminated nine-tenths of the letters. After that the winnowing was comparatively easy and the problem has now narrowed down to a choice between two.

These women with large establishments who have to hire a great many helpers in the home must have to make careful judgements.

There is for instance the problem whether to engage a woman who is very meticulous but cranky or one who is not so meticulous but is cheerful and obliging. Contrary to what a good many persons would expect I think I would hire the cranky one. The chances are that she would have a soft spot in her somewhere and after you found out what it was you could jelly her up. Meanwhile you would know she was doing her duty.

Then there would be the problem of whether to choose an elderly one or a young one. The older woman would go about her work with more assurance but on the other hand the younger one would be more willing to take orders. The older one might develop aches and pains but the younger one would undoubtedly decide to get married and leave you.

It is really quite a problem.

10 July 1926, Saturday:

GUS KASCH[211] was in the other afternoon and he got to telling Carl Stubig[212] about his Indian that marks the old Portage path.

---

[211] Akron resident, Gustav F. Kasch (1868-1946) President of Real Estate, Immigrated from Germany in 1872, residing at 122 Marvin av. in 1910-1930

[212] Akron resident, Carl Henry Stubig (1882-1930) Advertising Manager at Newspaper Co, Traveling Salesman at Rubber Factory; residing at 83 Dodge av. in 1920, 212 Herford dr. in 1930

It seems it all came from Gus's eagerness to get into an argument about something.

"You know," he said, "I kept telling the legislature that if they didn't put up a suitable marker to mark the old Portage trail, I, a private citizen, would do it myself.

"They called my bluff and so I started hunting around for an Indian. Out east I saw a cigar store Indian advertised for $25. I told this fellow I'd give him $15 for it and he said it was starting for Akron, express collect.

"Then I had it bronzed and set up.

"John Weber was humane agent then and he said the Indian ought to have a blanket for cold weather. I wrote to Senator Dick, who was then chairman of the committee of Indian affairs, about it and Dick wrote me a humorous letter in reply. But the Indian didn't get his blanket. Every once in a while I give him a new coat of bronze. I guess he's cost me more than $75."

Then Gus and Carl got to talking about matrimony and Carl said he thought it was a shame the way the people in the vaudeville and musical comedy houses keep poking fun at matrimony. He said it was no wonder people were losing their respect for the institution.

Gus said he supposed the newspapers had something to do with it because they were always playing up divorces. In reality, though, he added, this playing up of divorces was an excellent sign, for it was the practice of newspapers to play up the unusual and if divorces were really so awful common newspapers wouldn't consider them news.

Then Gus got to telling Carl about the Indians that used to be around here and I memorized the date 1804 but I forget now what it was about.

This morning, while I was eating my breakfast over at La Paix, Harold Tucker came in and sat down at the next place at the counter. I guess we both thought explanations were necessary so I explained to him that I was eating downtown because Bill was always in too much of a hurry to eat the nice buttered toast I fixed up for him at home and then he'd come downtown and eat and take 20 minutes to do it in and think everything was perfectly all right. And Harold told me that the reason he was eating downtown was because his wife had gone to Cincinnati. Then he ordered strawberries and shredded wheat and wouldn't put any cream on them. He said he never ate butter or milk or cream and I said to myself that wasn't it peculiar that every man had something odd about his appetite. Then Harold told me a funny story about Harvey Firestone and I told him a funny one about Clarence Dillon and we parted on excellent terms.

Then I saw Earl Cahoon[213] who said he was thinking of going out to Turkeyfoot to play his first nine holes of golf since he broke his leg and over on another street corner C. C. McNeil[214] was talking to E. C. Shaw[215] who looked cool and serene in a palm beach suit,[216] and going down Furnace st. whom should I see in a doorway but Lina, the beautiful if somewhat untidy Gypsy girl, who had told my fortune only a couple of weeks before.

"How many fortunes do you know?" I asked her. "Why," she said, "I know as many fortunes as I have hairs on my head."

The Romantick, who left for Detroit some time ago to take a position in a book store, has had considerable trouble finding a place to live. "It seems," she writes, "that the more respectable a place is the more people there are who are expected to use the same bathroom."

— ‿e꒰ᴄᴐ✦ᴄꙬᴐꙅᴐ —

12 July 1926, Monday:

---

[213] Akron resident, Earl Ester Cahoon (1876-1960) Proprietor and Druggist, Pharmacist at Drug Store; residing at W. Market in 1920, 79 Dodge av. in 1930

[214] Akron resident, Cecil C. McNeil (1889-1962) Real Estate Salesman; residing at 1059 West Exchange st. in 1930, Work dr. in 1940

[215] Akron resident, Elmer C. Shaw (c.1894-aft1920) Laborer at Rubber factory; residing at 177 Berry av. in 1920, OR Edwin C. Shaw (c.1863-aft1930) residing at 618 N. Portage Path in 1920-1930

[216] A "palm beach suit" is 1920's men's fashion featuring a double breasted suit, and an ad from the Literary Digest July 1920 book "Roaring 20s Fashions Jazz – Schiffer Book for "Collectors" by Susan Langley, show's a label "Tailored by Goodall, Palm Beach, Reg. U.S. Pat. Off, From the Genuine Cloth"

I'VE run across a couple of institutions lately which are almost unbelievably nice. One of them is Beard's pharmacy over on Merriman rd. The other day when we needed a couple of nursing bottles for Mary, didn't Mr. Beard send them right up. The bill was exactly 20 cents.

The other institutions is Fouche and Brittain's grocery store over here at Highland av. When you forget to tell them all the things you want they make a special trip out to your house anyway. And tonight, when I needed things for Mary, didn't their grocery boy go over to the drug store and get them for me and bring them out?

On a rainy day when the rain has just come in and flooded your living room and taken all the starch out of your curtains things like that can be wonderfully cheering.

I read a long time ago of a woman – a shut-in – who made quite a little income for herself by going in for contests. Whenever a magazine offered three dollars for a good cooking recipe, or a motion picture house stood ready to mail a thousand dollars to the person who suggested a name for it, this woman entered in and not infrequently she was successful.

John Funk was saying this noon that that sort of thing ought to be done on a large scale. A syndicate he thought, ought to be formed for the purpose of winning contests. There could be a scenario department, a novel department, a What's Wrong with this Picture department. People with minds who ran to that sort of thing could be employed and they could be equipped with dictionaries and set to work.

"Everybody, from filling station owners to silk manufacturers, is offering prizes these days," says John. "There's absolutely no reason why the rewards shouldn't be concentrated."

Sometime I wonder if there isn't drama woven round and about bobbed hair. The other day a woman gave in to the pleading of her 15-year-old daughter and had her hair bobbed.

Now every woman who has gone through the experience knows that when she has her hair bobbed some subtle alchemy takes place in her system. She becomes buoyant, joyous, different.

This woman of whom I speak had marvelous honey colored hair which she wore coiled in great braids about her head. The hair itself was beautiful, but the weight of it gave her a dragged down air. It was, if you chose to think about it that way, a symbol of her life.

Yesterday, when the barber's shears cut into it, she winced but she gritted her teeth.

He was an artist, that barber. A man other than he would have crimped this woman's hair until it stood out like electric sparks or else have marcelled it into hard, regular corrugations. As it was he shaped it to her head and left it absolutely straight. Twenty years slipped from the woman. She was a little girl. She looked at herself not a little frightened.

"Why, mother," said a soft voice away off somewhere, "you're beautiful!"

Somehow or other I have an idea that in a week or so that woman is going to tell her husband and her sister-in-law a few things.

⸺⸺⸺❖⸺⸺⸺

13 July 1926, Tuesday:

I had to call up Harry Benston the other day to ask him when his birthday was. "Aw," said Harry, "I don't feel as though I ought to tell you."

"You needn't feel the least bit embarrassed," I told him. "It's merely that either your birthday or Bill's is on the 10th of July or else the 20th and I can't remember which is which."

"Well in that case," said Harry, "It's my birthday which is on the 20th."

So, my mind at ease, I went down and bought Bill's new birthday present which was the new recording of the New World symphony[217] in five records and that night we played it and ate ice cream and cake and although there were only the two of us it was really a very nice party indeed.

---

[217] The Symphony No. 9 in E minor, "From the New World", popularly known as the *New World Symphony*, composed by Antonín Dvořák (1841-1904) in 1893. Astronaut Neil Armstrong took a tape recording of this symphony with him during the Apollo 11 mission, and the first moon landing in 1969.

Bill Haynes was a caller at this office this morning and left a pound box of candy. Come again, Bill.

Herman Kraft[218] is having trouble with his windshield.

Charlie Zimmerman[219] spent yesterday talking over old times with General Umberto Nobile.[220] It was Charlie who taught the General to speak English.

Major Peake is looking fine.

Jack Boettner[221] is looking fine too.

Also Herb Maxson.[222]

Bob Lee told a funny store this morning.

---

[218] Akron resident, Herman T. Kraft (1888-1960), Goodyear mechanical engineer figuring prominently in the design of dirigibles built for the U. S. Army and Navy. He worked with fellow engineer Ralph Upson, and together they have several patents for designing Goodyear blimps. He resided at 181 Buchtel av. in 1920, 267 Storer av. in 1930-1940.

[219] Akron resident, Charles H. Zimmerman (1893-1981), Aeronautical engineer; worked for Goodyear blimp company. He resided at 43 Ruth av. in 1920, 1089 Berwin st. in 1930, 1120 Avon in 1940.

[220] Umberto Nobile (1885-1978) Italian aeronautical engineer, aviator, and airship pilot of the airships Norge and Italia, and later became a General. He went to the U.S. in 1922 to be a consultant for Goodyear in Akron.

[221] Akron resident, Jack Boettner (????-????), Goodyear blimp pilot and manager of airship operations. On June 20, 1928 he landed the airship Pilgrim on the roof of the M. O'Neil Co.

[222] Akron resident, Herbert William Maxson (1901-1980), Vice President at Civil Steam school; resided at Crosby st. in 1910, 668 Peerless av. in 1930

Leslie L'Hollier[223] says it isn't true the women in Chicago are wearing short vamps.[224]

Clarence Hayward is back from his vacation. He is thinking some of going to New York in the fall.

Ethel Boleyn Myers[225] has had her hair bobbed.

Harry Vandegrift[226] is having a birthday today. This department congratulates him.

George Carson is feeling some better but is still limited to seven potatoes per meal.

Don Miller is back from his class reunion at Cambridge where he took part in a theatrical performance and helped carry in the bath tub. He says they didn't see any ginger ale.

Hugh Allen[227] is out of cigarets again.

Knoch Jones is out of sorts.

—————◦◦◦◦◦◦◦◦◦◦◦◦◦—————

15 July 1926, Thursday:

---

[223] Akron resident, Leslie Howard L'Hollier (????-????), working for the B. F. Goodrich Corp, and shoe inventor of several U.S. patents, for overshoes and methods for making and repairing shoes and shoe parts during 1928-1933.

[224] The "vamp" is the part of the shoe that covers the top front of the foot and is usually done in a strap, a T-strap, or a Mary Jane style shoe in the 1920's. Shorter shoes showed off more of the foot, which prior to this period was too scandalous to show and women wore boots.

[225] Akron resident, Ethel Boleyn Myers (c.1890-aft1930), Society Page editor; resided at 358 Spicer st. in 1910, 775 West Exchange in 1920, 183 Highland av. in 1930, who once lived at 124 Burton av, and was the Akron Beacon Journal's woman's page editor.

[226] Josephine's father, Harry Vandegrift, born in 1871.

[227] Akron resident, Hugh C. Allen (c.1883-aft1930), Newspaper Editor and Journalist; resided at 959 Wye dr. in 1920, 105 Ger st. in 1930

T HE disinclination to get out of bed mornings is ruining the careers of English working girls, according to the findings at a recent convention of head mistresses held in London.

It seems that the poor little hard-working British slavay [sic] just simply won't get down to her work by 9 in the morning and nobody seems to be able to do anything about it.

There is one person on this side of the Atlantic who hopes that she'll go right on being stubborn about it.

There is no personal grievance in this. I generally get down to work about 9 o'clock and I think that if I came in even at 10 minutes past 9 nobody would say a word. It is merely that I wish all others might be as happy.

I realize, of course, that there are some girls who actually love to walk into an office at 7:30 in the morning. If this were purely their own problem it would be all right. The trouble is that by their wholly incomprehensible zeal they make it hard for thousands of others who should never be getting out of bed before 8 o'clock at best. These latter souls, driven before their hour into a cold and cheerless dawn, go sleepily through the day, never experience the exaltation which comes from attacking one's work with zest, go wearily home at night, are dragged out to a movie, go to bed, just get into a sound sleep when it is time to get up and start the same dreary round all over again.

It seems to me that if these early risers realized the billions of dollars which are lost to industry through this sort of thing they would consent to sleep at least an hour longer in the morning.

Too much zeal of any sort seems to get people into trouble. I was reading this morning of a missionary in Korea who wrote the word "thief" with acid on each cheek of a little Korean boy who had stolen apples from his orchard.

The missionary hadn't thought that the acid would burn the boy permanently, but it did, and the boy was driven from school by the taunts of his playmates. I am sorry for the boy and I am sorry for the missionary whose upbringing was so gloomy that he couldn't laugh over the matter of a few sour, green apples.

Tiny Englebeck is looking real well.

Now that Mr. Kipling has revived the popular pastime of enumerating one's favorite great men I should like to pin a few laurels to:

The chap who invented safety pins.

The chap who invented cross word puzzles.

The fellow who put erasers on lead pencils.

Lord Something or Other who invented soap flakes.

Ring Lardner.

That Mr. Sullivan who made the rubber bands.

The man who invented indoor plumbing.

Lord Sandwich.

19 July 1926, Monday:

THE Altrusa club had a picnic over at Jane Barnhardt's[228] the other night where a new kind of picnic plate was in evidence. First there is a square sort of lacquer tray in black and gold which is quite inexpensive. On this you put your paper picnic plate which has divisions in it for potato salad and salted nuts and things. You get a fresh paper plate when the dessert course comes along and the whole arrangement is really very tidy.

---

[228] Akron resident, Jane L. Sargent Barnhardt (1878-1964) and wife of Harold A. Barnhardt, a professor of the Akron University Arts Department.

One of the things hard to understand is why a condemned criminal is given his choice of things to eat before taking up the march to the death house. For some reason or other it has always seemed to me that there was something gross about it. Certainly a man who is facing his last extremity can not be greatly interested in what is put upon his plate.

A friend of mine was telling me the other day how shut away she had been since her marriage. "All the women I know now," she said, "are housekeepers like myself and that's all they have to talk about. It gets so hum drum after a while. Nothing interesting ever happens."

And I got to wondering if that was a condition which really had to be.

For one thing most any woman can subscribe to magazines. In a case like this I don't think the ordinary woman's magazine with its banal editorials and its sweetish fiction is much good. There are, however, sprightly magazines in which some of the best minds of the country have put their wit, observations and experience. I think I would pick up one of these from time to time.

Then I think I would encourage my husband to bring his friends home to dinner. "But my husband's friends," I can hear some women wailing, "are mostly bootleggers.[229]"

Very well then, I think I would invite the bootleggers. It may be of course that the bootlegger will be a little shy at first about talking about his calling. The chances will be however that after a while he will blossom out and tell all sorts of interesting things. He will tell how he happened to leave street car conducting to take up bootlegging, how much more money he is making now and how much happier the wife and children are. He will have some interesting information as to who are good customers and who aren't and he may also have had some experiences with the law.

From what I know of women a good many of them deliberately shut themselves away from the interesting things of life by being, well you know, a little too particular. A new woman comes into the neighborhood and they decide they will have nothing to do with

---

[229] A 'bootlegger' in the 1920's refers to illegal production and traffic of liquor in violation of prohibition, and came into use in the 1880's denoting concealing a flask of illicit liquor in their boot tops when going to trade with the Indians.

her because she smokes cigarets something awful. If they'd only let themselves get friendly with this woman they'd discover she was a darb,[230] that she'd had a lot of trouble in her life and she could tell things that were more interesting than a Gloria Swanson[231] society thriller.

I realize of course that there are some women whom this program wouldn't suit at all. By nature they were meant to be exclusive. It is nice to be exclusive in a way but one shouldn't complain if at times things get a little dull.

⸙

20 July 1926, Tuesday:

THERE is also another way to save money. This morning I went into La Paix for my cup of coffee and there was my banker Louis Devore[232] sitting at the counter so I sat down beside him. After a while Louis went out and then I asked the waiter for my bill. "Why," he said, "I put it on that man's." So I have arranged with the waiter that whenever I come in and meet anybody I know he is to charge it on the other fellow's bill.

Louis said he'd never really realized until recently how many chores there were to do about the house. It seems his wife and the children are up at the lakes and so Louis feeds the rabbits and waters the chickens before he comes down mornings. This morning it took him two hours before he could even get out of the house.

I always thought I would like to live in Alaska and now I know I would after reading an article by a woman. I don't recall her name just now, who has lived up there for a number of years.

------

[230] A 'darb' is 1920's slang for someone or something very handsome, valuable, attractive or otherwise excellent.

[231] Gloria Swanson (1899-1983) American actress and producer, and sought after heavily in the 1920's as a top box office magnet for Hollywood.

[232] Akron resident, Louis Edward Devore (1886-1968), Accountant and Banker, residing at Harvard st. in 1910, 675 Roslyn st. in 1940

It seems that it does get hot in Alaska, 92 in the shade for instance, but that is during the three months of summer. The rest of the time it is delightfully cold.

During the summer months it is daylight all the time so the people do the sensible thing – sleep during the warm part of the day. The rest of the time they play tennis and go on picnics. They even have picnics at what would nominally be midnight. During the summer months everybody works very hard and the vegetables and flowers grow like everything. Then comes the lovely winter.

You know the disagreeable thing about our winters here is the slushing and the thawing and being splashed by laundry wagons. Up in Alaska you can predict when winter will come almost to the minute and when it does come it comes quietly and thoroughly – still, delightfully cold which forces things down to 40 below and still keeps going. The houses are snug and coal is cheap. What more could anyone ask?

––––––––

The thrifty housewife it seems bespeaks the hunter early in the season for a half of caribou, the quarter of sheep and such other meats as she may need. Then she puts them in a sort of winter kitchen affair and lets them freeze. Does she want a venison porterhouse for dinner? She goes out and cuts it and lets it thaw.

Does she want a dessert for dinner? She whips a can of tinned milk, adds a jar of strawberry conserve to it and sets it out to freeze. No bother with ice and salt, no turning of the crank.[233]

Some time in November the housewives it would appear hold a great pie baking. They bake the pies until the crust is at the cream colored stage. Then they set them out and let them freeze. As the pies are wanted they are brought in, put in the oven and the baking is finished.

––––––––

Along about March every year they have their spring scandal up there. From what I can make out the long period of darkness and the tenseness and the static get on peoples nerves about this time so that some man either runs off with his neighbor's wife or two men who have been partners for years start snapping at each other and one of them

––––––––––––––––––––

[233] Referring to a hand-crank ice cream maker, wherein rock salt is placed inside of an outer bucket and an inner bucket holds the milk-cream and flavourings. A hand crank is turned which churns it like butter and the rock salt cools the inside.

pulls a gun. The thing goes to court, then the sun comes up, spring arrives, the beds[234] start sprouting and everyone starts picnics all over again.

It must be wonderful to live in Alaska.

<hr/>

21 July 1926, Wednesday:

MY Friend Dorothea is in great distress. "Why," she demands, "do people have to have parties in hot weather? Everybody goes visiting in hot weather. Girls keep right on announcing their engagements in hot weather. Then everybody has to go ahead and have parties. Here I am with a party on my hands and I don't know how to decorate or what to serve and it's too hot to think about it."

I couldn't be of any help to Dorothea but Bee was – a little.

"I have a notion," she said, "to set up in business as a party suggester. People keep asking me what sort of parties they should have and what they could serve for refreshments and what games they could play. I don't know why I shouldn't go into the business and then charge a fee for it."

"Suppose you go in business right now then," said Dorothea, "and help me out."

"Well then," said Bee, "If I were you I'd have chicken salad and –"

<hr/>

I suppose it's being awfully disagreeable to say so but somehow I never could work up any interest in these parties where everything is in a certain color scheme and you work like everything all day long to get the refreshments to match.

My idea has always been to invite in a couple of people whom you like and if they want to make the coffee or bring the dessert with them why so much the better. Then you just sit around and talk. Occasionally my parties grow like snowballs – that is, you start out with a couple of people and then you meet a couple more on the street and invite them and then a couple of others drop in and you have to serve them coffee in a couple

<hr/>

[234] Gardens

of chipped lemonade glasses. Parties like that are always successes. The other kind – where you invite a lot of people two weeks ahead – are invariably flat failures on the chandeliers – well, my imagination just won't work that far.

It may possibly be true – what Dorothea was contending awhile ago – that the rocking chair is disappearing. Certainly a rocking chair is not included in the three piece "suites" which seem so popular at present and I seem to recall a good many homes, now that I think of it, where there is not more than one rocking chair at best. Mary, I have reflected on more than one occasion, is liable to grow into a young lady without ever knowing the sensation of being rocked.

In a way, if the rocking chair does go out utterly, life stands to lose a good deal of its poetry. There has been a good deal of its poetry. There has been a good deal said and written about the child who is rocked to sleep at twilight. There has been a good deal more said and written about the dear old lady in the lace cap who rocks in her chair and watches life go by on the front side walk.

It might be interesting some time to find out just when rocking chairs came into being.[235] It is hard to suppose that the Romans or Egyptians or Syrians ever used them. It seems as though by their very nature they had to belong to western Europe and to America. And it is hard too to understand why there should be so much romance clinging to a rocking chair and so little to the straight variety. I suppose perhaps the curves have had something to do with it.

---

23 July 1926, Friday:

"DEAR JOSIE:" (writes Eleanor)

---

[235] To answer her query, they first appeared in the early 18th century. Te first rocking chairs were of wicker and appeared in English gardens in 1725, but historians say American inventor Benjamin Franklin (1705-1790) had one as a child.

"As Dudley Digges[236] and Robert Simon[237] (the latter writer of lyrics for ye popular musical comedies) are sitting near and talking, talking there's no telling what this letter will be like.

"Here I am in Sconset.[238] The Intelligentsias from the 4 corners of the world come. We played some GAMES (as THEY called them) which left me wondering and with a cracking head. It's lots of fun but relaxation is done only in the privacy of one's own room.

"A musical comedy is being born here.[239] Lewis Senssler,[240] whose 'Queen High' is debuting over in Philadelphia, comes over from his cottage and about 1 a.m., he and Robert Simon are seized with music or lyrics and then creation begins at the piano. And such a piano! Perhaps I have handicaps before – I will admit that – but now by golly I'll feel like a Paderewski if ever I get seated at the old Steinway[241] again.

"Eras, a contemporary of Anita's, is here dancing and teaching. She is a protégé of Mr. Vanderlip's. Anita was married last winter without telling any one. She married a pianist which is good business for her who is, the pianist I mean, much younger than she is. They have gone to Europe and return in the fall.

"I simply can't write. There is a Russian here who simply overwhelms you with intelligence and repartee. The combination is so unusual as the man is really terrifically brainy. He is the life of the party and all the women are wild about him. He is working

---

236 Dudley Digges (1879-1947) Irish stage and film actor

237 Robert A. Simon (1897-1981) American composer, writer, librettist

238 'Sconset is a shortened colloquialism for Siasconset Beach on Nantucket Island, Massachusetts. Originally a fishing village settled in the 17th century, by the early 20th century it became a summer retreat place for an Actor's Colony of well-to-dos.

239 The musical comedy was "Ups-a Daisy," which debuted October 8, 1928 and was written by Robert A. Simon and Clifford Grey, with music by Lewis E. Gensler. He also worked with Gensler with another musical comedy called "The Gang's All Here" which debuted in 1931.

240 She has misspelled his name. Lewis E. Gensler (1896-1978) an American composer and songwriter. Queen High was also written and contributed to by Laurence Schwab, and Buddy G. DeSylva.

241 Steinway Grand pianos

his way through Princeton and having just completed a howling argument, he and I, my brain is in a whirl. Four days later, I guest I had better send this."

We were speaking a little while ago of the disappearance of the fan[242] – palm leaf, Japanese and otherwise. Time was when a nicely brought up child couldn't go to a party without a small paper fan suspended around her neck by a ribbon. And when the time came for her to graduate from anything! I grieve now whenever I think of the fans put away in my trunk. An ostrich one, too small to attract attention nowadays, a little dark one which might be made of some lacquered material, I'm not sure, and a lovely lacey one with painted gentlemen and ladies dancing minuets all over it. I am saving them for Mary to play with. It is too much to hope that they will ever be fashionable again.

And then there were fans, Chinese I think, which were made of silk stretched tightly to an ebony frame and either painted or embroidered. You hung these criss cross up on the wall because they were much too fine to be put to practical use.

"It's sort of funny, the only place where you will find palm leaf fans these days," says Gladys, "it's at the beauty parlors. You know when you get a permanent you have to sit perfectly still for six hours and you just about burn up so the attendant sits and fans you.

"It's about the only link left with the past."

---

26 July 1926, Monday:

I WAS interested to read an opinion the other day to the effect that Beethoven's Ninth symphony is not the greatest of that composer's creative achievements. The opinion was expressed by Samuel Chotzinoff,[243] pianist and critic for the New York World, and hopes it is of greater value than if it had been expressed by this humble scribe.

---

242 Handheld fans

243 Samuel "Shotzi" Chotzinoff (1889-1964) Russian pianist and critic for the New York World, a popular metropolitan daily paper, and later a music consultant for N.B.C.

Mr. Chotzinoff expressed some doubt as to the sincerity of those thousands and tens of thousands who had journeyed to the New York stadium on an oppressively warm night to listen to the celebrated symphony. He felt that a good many of them had gone, not because they honestly preferred this symphony to the Fifth, for instance, but because they thought it was the correct thing to do.

Mr. Chotzinoff's reflections cheered me to a considerable extent. For a good many years I have confessed to those who would listen that I hadn't cared much for the Ninth symphony. I had thought, though, that it was because something was wrong with my appreciation. "Some day," I told myself, "you will grow to understand the Ninth symphony and you will worship with the rest."

That Mr. Chotzinoff should now have the courage to pick flaws in the masterpiece has made me feel rather proud of my judgment. Unless, of course, it should turn out that something is wrong with Mr. Chotzinoff's appreciation, too.

It seems to me that the most useful thing which could happen to a woman would be to be compelled by some chance or other to spend a couple of weeks in the society department of a newspaper. She would learn things which would be good for her soul and come out of it a better woman. Incidentally, she might develop a sense of humor.

There is one woman in this town whom the society editors love. If they call her up to ask her about her bridge-tea this afternoon, she cheerfully tells them everything they want to know in the tone of voice which she uses for everyday conversation, and if she knows any gossip, she throws that in, too. So far as I know the society editors have never met this woman personally, but what they do know is that she is a real person and they would fight for her to the last trench.

Other women betray their real natures rather oddly – some by being snippy and hanging up the receiver, some by assuming an all too elegant manner of speech, some by being too anxious to keep things out of the paper which, to my mind, has always been as great a confession of egotism as if they were overwhelmingly anxious to have things in.

I think that if I were a young man and wanted to find out the real disposition of a certain woman I would consult with the society editor to whom she reports her luncheon-bridges.

I don't know just what is going to be the extent of the current discussion in the Editor's Mail, but if seems to me it would be very sad if we were compelled to do without saucers.

One of the consolations about breaking a cup is the consideration of all the things you can do with the saucer.

You can put the left-over chop in it and set it in the ice box.

You can put it on top of the prunes, so the juice won't spill.

You can feed the cat on it.

You can use it for a soap dish.

You can set the pot of geraniums on it.

You can put tacks in it when you are laying the stair carpet.

You can put water in it and set it under the table leg when you have red ants.

You can use it for a cigaret tray.

You can put it under the leak in the attic roof.

You can break it up and put it in the bottom of the flower box.

You can put lamp black on the bottom of it and play games with it at parties.

I honestly don't k now what a good many of us would do if the saucer were to go.

---

27 July 1926, Tuesday:

WHEN I was younger I used to pity the men whom I saw eating downtown in the mornings. "Poor fellows," I said, "indifferent wives – indigestion – etc.

Now, however, it seems to me that eating one's breakfast downtown has a good many advantages. There is, for instance, the matter of cream. Cream at our house costs 14 cents a half-pint and out of a half-pint you can get four cups of coffee. That's four cents a cup just for cream and you haven't counted in the coffee and sugar and the gas and the wear and tear on the percolator.

Downtown you get the cup of coffee and everything for a nickel and goodness I don't see how they do it.

––––––––––

Then there is the matter of monotony. If you have your breakfast at home the chances are that you'll have the same thing every morning, fruit, toast and coffee, fruit, toast and coffee. And always the same face on the other side of the percolator.

Downtown you get to look at a different face and the chances are that it will even smile at you. Even more. As you get better acquainted with the young woman behind the counter she will discuss with you last night's thunderstorm, the current movies, where her b.f. is going for his vacation and how much her mother paid for the imitation walnut dining room suite. Also she will lend fresh interest to any of the details of your life which you may wish to relate to her. Also she will bring you oatmeal if it is oatmeal you desire instead of prunes.

––––––––––

The wife at home is also benefitted. For one thing she can sleep longer in the mornings and for another thing she will probably go without breakfast altogether which will keep her tremendously in the matter of keeping fit.

––––––––––

"Dear Jo: (writes Alice)

"It's because you're such a good letter writer that I am writing to you instead of Mr. Blinn himself.

"You see it's this way. I've been going up to Akron university all summer where they have been teaching me to spell. I can't spell worth a cent, Jo, even when I sit tight on my dad's big dictionary.

"I start out early every week morning. I have to start early because Mr. Blinn's busses only take me half-way. I ride on the W. Exchange ones you know and then have a good 15 minutes walk between where I get off and the place where I take the Spicer car.

"Why Jo, I could get run over a dozen times before I get to the place where the Spicer cars turn up and they always turn up and GO when I see RED. By the time the GREEN turns on and everybody gets all around the corners of the car has gone.

"I hear some women fussing because Mr. Rybolt told Mr. Blinn he didn't like his big busses cluttering up Howard st., and the hill that runs down to Cherry and so Mr. Blinn had to send them through the slums and dark alleys.

"That's an awful alley, Jo. It's not safe for stray singles like myself coming home at night. And besides it's awful dirty.

"So please Jo tell Mr. Blinn to try it himself. Tell him to go down to the alley – especially when the wind is blowing – and to come past the cars that sneak around the busses, go up the hill, wait for the right, left and in-between turn cars, cross over the crossing and go south on Howard st. till he comes to Mill. There the turning will start all over again and he will struggle across Mill st. and go east. When he gets to Main he will wait some more and then he will have to cross two more times to get to the place where the lights change again and the cars run up the hill without him.

"Ask him, Jo, if he'd rather chase those Spicer cars than go unlearned? Ask him if he likes to be run over front, back and sides just to learn to spell as well as I can after six weeks. And ask him if he won't PLEASE start to move something – even if it has to be the University."

⸙

28 July 1926, Wednesday:

"THIS is just a reminder to write me a long and interesting letter," writes Eleanor.[244] "Mail is 7-8 of one's existence here, especially entertaining mails.

"The lecturers are beginning to arrive now. You can tell, them 50 feet away. All the first lectures are on psycho-analysis and other funny words beginning with psch. I'm sorry, I'd rather have almost anything else. Later we are covering art and world conditions.

---

[244] Eleanor Painter Strong (1891-1947) Broadway actress performing from 1914 through 1927 on Broadway, who died in Cleveland, Ohio. She married Wilfred Douthitt, aka Louis Graveure c.1916, and then Major Charles Henry Strong in 1931.

"Had a delightful conversation the other day with one of the guests. An ex-editor of McClure's[245] and The American Magazine. After he had left I found out he was David Grayson.[246] We talked about Mexico and cactus.

"Had a baseball game yesterday composed of Dudley Digges, Reggie Owen[247] (he was Algy in The Importance of Being Earnest[248] and has written some plays), Felix Salmond[249] and myself. My part was to get the balls that went over the fence.

"Reggie has just had a play returned and last night at dinner he insisted on reading the choice parts of the manuscript to us. One was between Mrs. Somebody and Vincent her son, who had bought several scores of pajamas.

"'Oh but Vincent,' wailed Mama, 'WHY so many pajamas!' 'Oh but Mother,' replied Vincent, 'there are SO many nights.' With his inflection it was screaming. The Salmonds saw him home.

This morning I went up to the Eagles' temple where the State Federation of Labor has been in convention and where Kate Richard O'Hare[250] was making an address.

Mrs. O'Hare represents the union of garment workers and manufacturers and incidentally holds the chair of psychology in a western college. During the war she spoke

---

[245] McClure's Magazine was an American illustrated monthly periodical from 1893-1929. In 1906 it formed The American Magazine and was re-styled as a women's magazine. After 1929, it was refashioned to The Smart Set.

[246] Ray Stannard Baker (1870-1946) American journalist, historian, and author. He used the pseudonym of 'David Grayson' to contribute articles to the American Magazine and others.

[247] Reginald "Reggie" Owen (1887-1972) English character actor

[248] This revival of "The Important of Being Earnest" by Oscar Wilde, debuted on Broadway at the Comedy Theatre on May 3, 1926 and ran for a total of 70 performances. Reginald Owen played the character Algernon "Algy" Moncrieff. It was directed by Dudley Digges.

[249] Felix Adrian Norman Salmond (1888-1952) English cellist and cello teacher

[250] Carrie Katherine "Kate" Richards O'Hare (1876-1948) American Socialist party activist, editor, and orator imprisoned during the first World War.

her mind on quite a few subjects and she was arrested and given a prison sentence of five years. After 14 months she was pardoned by Woodrow Wilson.[251]

Here are some of the things Mrs. O'Hare said this morning:

"On every day of the week, including Sunday, we are spending two and a half million dollars in a futile attempt to deal with crime.

"We spend more money every year to punish bad people than we do to educate good people.

"Over at Columbus your state penitentiary and your state university are just a block apart. In one you have science at its best. In the other you have conditions that are a survival of the dark ages.

"The reason for these conditions are that we ignore our prisons. We turn them over to any man who wants the job. Whenever a man is so shiftless and ornery that you can't make a dog catcher out of him you put him in prison and give him charge of the prisoners.

"I told the warden of the state penitentiary of Kansas that he was going to have a riot. I told him that when you buy food at 10 cents on the dollar and put the rest of the money in your pocket you're going to have hungry men on your hands, and when men are hungry, they strike."

If any woman is feeling a little bored with golf and bridge and the like she might take a little run up to the Eagles' temple and watch the faces and listen to the speeches. This department guarantees that it will give her something to think about.

29 July 1926, Thursday:

---

[251] Thomas Woodrow Wilson (1856-1924) American Democratic U.S. President from 1913 to 1921.

ELLEN is asleep and dreaming. Her rough hands are crossed upon her breast. Her features sag heavily in the moonlight. The thick braids of her hair lie darkly on the pillow.

In her dream Ellen is walking through the woods. It is autumn and the sun comes through the leaves in speckled flakes. There are dry leaves on the ground but Ellen's feet upon them make no sound.

There is a man walking ahead of Ellen, a young man with strong shoulders. Ellen tries to call out to him. Her lips form the words, "Hugo, Hugo." But no sounds comes. The young man is getting further and further away. If Ellen does not hurry he will disappear entirely. She tries to force herself to hasten but her feet are like lead. It is impossible to hurry.

Suddenly the young man has turned. He has seen her. He is coming toward her. His arms are outstretched. "Ellen," he cries, "Oh, my beloved!"

––––––––––––

The cat has jumped at the bird again. The clatter wakens Ellen from her dream. She sits bolt upright. There is no woods now but only moonlight and a shabby room. Beside her lies her husband, breathing audibly. There is a dark heap on the floor where he has thrown his clothes. From the kitchen beyond comes the chatter of the nickel alarm clock. "Perhaps the cat has got him this time," Ellen whispers to herself, "Perhaps I ought to go and look, But if I go back to sleep again –"

––––––––––––

"Oh, my beloved," says Hugo and Ellen, reaching up to touch his face with her hands, finds that his cheeks are wet.

"I thought," whispers Ellen, "that you loved someone else and you had gone away. I thought that I was married to Steve. Oh, Hugo, it has been so hard."

"You have been dreaming," laughs Hugo. "I have only been away on a little visit and now I am never going away again."

He draws Ellen close to him and she feels the heart beating under his coat. He presses his lips to her cheek.

"We will go away," he whispers, "and live in a little house."

"And at night," whispers Ellen, "we will lie and listen to the rain on the roof."

Hugo's hand is within her own two hands. She takes it and kisses each one of the fingers.

———

The cat, tired of his vigil, jumps down from the kitchen chair. And now there is no sound but the ticking of the nickel clock.

———————

3 August 1926, Tuesday:

DOES anybody know why they used to put covers on their bridges in the old days? Of all the people I've asked nobody seems to know. "Why," they say, "all the old bridges had covers on 'em." And that seems to be about all there is to it.

I suppose maybe it was because covered bridges came in an age when everything had covers, the butter dish and the soup tureen. The beds had tremendous canopies over them and the ladies carried parasols.

———

A covered bridge, of which I understand there are three or four in the vicinity of Akron, is picturesque enough in the daytime but it seems to me at night that it must be an abiding place of horrors.

When I was a child they used to tell grisly tales of covered bridges and I quake considerably at the memory yet.

One was about a man who had a grievance against another man and he took up a block of wood and waited for him in the covered bridge. Along about midnight the man came along, he had been to see his sweetheart, and he was whistling, possibly because he was happy but more probably to keep his spirits up.

The blow landed squarely and he died then and there. Unfortunately he turned out to be the wrong man.

Another one concerned a young farmer who was driven beside himself when he saw his young sweetheart taken buggy riding by a fellow from a neighboring township. It was spring and the river was swollen. Also the planks of the old covered bridge were loose and rattly.

The young farmer bided his time until the girls and his rival should be driving home. Then he went down to the covered bridge and tore up planks until there was a large gaping hole in the middle. The horse and the bright new buggy and its occupants crashed through and the swollen river bore them away.

Does anybody in this town want a laundress who does up shirts beautifully and has a nice disposition as well? Then this department would like to recommend Katie.

A long time ago Katie and her husband and little girl lived in Pittsburg and they were very happy. They had saved up something more than two thousand dollars and with this they meant to go back and visit in the old country. They sent the money over to a bank in Vienna and planned soon to follow. But just then the war came and everything was lost.

Now Katie's husband is ill and she has only her own earnings which must stretch to take care of the three of them.

This department thinks that it will cheer you just to see Katie coming in the door of a morning.

---

5 August 1926, Thursday:

NOTES OF AN AMATEUR PARENT

ONE of the things that worries me is whether Mary distinguishes between the person who gives her 10 o'clock bottle in the morning and the person who givers her her 10 o'clock bottle at night. Does she think both of them are her mother?
Or is it that she is interested in mothers not at all but only in getting her bottle promptly?

Certainly Mary seems altogether impartial in the bestowal of her approval. When I come home of an afternoon she crows and flaps her arms like a very young rooster and when I pick her up she clamps me tightly about the neck. But on the other hand she gives the same delighted greeting of a morning to Mrs. Harms who takes care of her when I am gone.

I have a suspicion that the parental urge isn't very strong in children. They give their devotion to whoever is good to them. And that perhaps is a good thing. It keeps us elders on the jump to win and keep a baby's approval.

A woman asked me the other day if, when Mary was older, I intended to spank her and I said I certainly would if I thought she needed it. I think, however, that I shall begin praying now. I shall pray that when the time for discipline arrives I shall spank Mary because she actually does need it and not because her mother is cross and nervous.

This matter of discipline it seems to me is a grievous problem. In years gone by I have known parents who started out with the laudable purpose of rearing their children entirely by love.

The children grew and kicked and screamed and interrupted their elders and were altogether very dreadful indeed. It seemed to me that for their own sakes if for no other reason a little corporal smarting where nature had provided the padding would have been useful and appropriate.

On the other hand I knew a woman who spanked her children generously but always saved up the spankings till the end of the day. She did this because she could be sure then that she was spanking them because they deserved it and not because her nerves were on edge. This is the method recommended in the educational books but somehow it always seemed a shame to me to spoil the last hour of the day with tears and smartings. The children by this time had undoubtedly forgotten what the trouble was all about and were prepared to be little cherubs. And as for their mother I am sure there must have been times when she took up the slipper with a heavy heart.

Of course as things look now Mary will probably never need any corrective measures. Aside from a fixed determination not to go to bed o'nights she really has the most remarkable disposition.

There is the matter of eating sieved peas. Mary does not like sieved peas. She shivers all over and makes dreadful faces whenever the matter of sieved peas is presented to her. But she eats them. She eats them like a little soldier reasoning doubtless that if she is brave in this she will be able to bear with the carrots and the spinach which comes later on.

And then there is the matter of musical appreciation. I have noticed that whenever we place a symphony or a string quartet on the phonograph Mary does not bang her rattle. Instead she holds it quietly and listens with serious attention.

I can tell from these things that when Mary grows up people will love to have her come and visit them. She may shiver slightly when cheese pie is presented her at table but she will eat it nevertheless.

And when she is taken to a concert she will listen with attention and decorousness and never, never think of tapping her foot or humming over some of the parts herself.

<hr/>

6 August 1926, Friday:

A MAN writing to Dorothy Dix the other day was wailing the dreadful way some women have of pulling their husbands down. This one was untidy, another extravagant, another a dreadful shrew and so on. He was just so discouraged, he said, that he had given up all intentions of getting married himself and purposed to die a bachelor.

I suppose maybe these things are true but let's not get too dismal over them. Let us consider for instance the extravagant woman. I think I know at least one extravagant woman who has made a success out of her husband. When she married him he was a store clerk making $25 a week. This woman instead of scrimping and saving and making over her old hats and doing her own washing and ironing went downtown and ran up a lot of bills. Her husband had to devise ways of paying them. The result was that he went into business for himself and built up a fortune. He looks a little gray now and his eyes are tired. But he probably isn't any greyer and tireder [sic] than if he were still a floor walker in a downtown department store. And his wife has had a glorious time.

<hr/>

I doubt that if a man really cares for his wife untidiness or bad cooking is going to change him. Certainly the opposite isn't true. You and I know of more than one tragedy where the wife was trim and neat, where her house was immaculate, where the preparation of every meal was a sort of a rite performed over the things her husband liked best. And yet the husband was a perfect snap dragon, perpetually grouching, perpetually making sheep's eyes at some other woman whose dresser drawers were a fright, who bathed with an atomizer but who knew how to flaunt the latest thing in hair cuts.

The most untidy woman I ever knew had a husband who adored her and after he died – well, all she had to do was to quirk her little finger. I am sure that of the many men who were pleading with her to marry them there was not one who wasn't perfectly aware that the piano keys were filthy, that the ice box hadn't been cleaned in months, that the dish towels were frights, that there were all sorts of odd accumulations about the handles of the tea cups. But did they care?

After a husband's fancy has gone wandering it is easy for him to assign all sorts of reasons for it – his wife's pie crust was tough or she wore a kimono to breakfast mornings. My personal conviction in that if she had done none of these things his fancy would have wandered just the same.

———————

It seems to me that the nagging wife has had more than her share of opprobrium. Is there any reason on earth why a man shouldn't call his wife to tell her he won't be home to dinner? If he were summarily to break dinner engagements with his friends he would be stamped as unpardonably rude and never be invited again. There is no reason on earth why the average male should think he has a right to reserve his bad manners for his wife.

The nagging wife must at some time or other have been an idealist else the cigaret ashes on the living room rug, the lawnmower left out in the rain wouldn't both her so. A nagging wife is of course almost impossible to live with but I would think that in at least 50 per cent of the cases she could be cured. The cure would consists of (a) mending one's ways so far as possible, (b) an old fashioned spanking followed with tears and hand holdings.

———————

16 August 1926, Monday:

AGES and ages ago when Bill and I went on our honeymoon we stopped in Rochester and bought a wooden spoon and salad fork. They were really a very attractive spoon and fork and I had an idea that shortly I would buy a Czecho – Slovakian bowl to go with them. It would be delightful on warm summer nights, I reasoned, to get together combination salads and use them for the principal part of our supper. The colors would be cool and inviting and I would learn to flourish the spoon and fork in one hand the way the waiters do in French restaurants.

The first disillusionment of my married life was that Bill didn't like combination salads – neither the cucumber nor the tomato nor the onion nor anything that went to make combination salads. The second disillusionment was that he despised that wooden knife and fork. Maybe it was the associations – I don't know. Anyway I had to learn to keep them out of sight with the result that the fork went into total decline and the spoon was used only for occasional cake mixings.

A week or so ago joy entered my bruised heart. It was discovered that Mary liked the wooden spoon.

———————

There are some parents I dare say who would feel a little grieved that their child should so obviously prefer a wooden spoon to a silver one. So far as I know no panegyrics have been sung to the child with a wooden spoon in her mouth.

And yet it is more than likely that the child with a wooden spoon is destined for greater happiness.

Her qualities, I take it, are the ordinary ones of kindliness and sincerity and wholesomeness.

When she goes to school her hand is not perpetually waving in the air in order that she may tell the teacher the right answer.

She never takes up toe dancing and she never plays pieces on the piano when company comes.

She picks just average people for her friends.

She thinks her father and her mother are a little bit of all right.

———————

If I thought it would do much good I would blazon abroad the announcement that some group or other out in Pasadena is offering prizes for one act and full length plays. The prize for the one act play is $100, the prize for the full length play is $200. The competition is open only to amateurs.

It so happens though that a couple of years ago John Golden or somebody similar was offering tremendous awards in order to uncover the Great American play. I told all about it, or as much as I had room for, and the only person who came up to see me about it was a young fellow who later conferred he wasn't writing a play at all but only wanted to have an excuse to come up and see what I looked like.

———————

In the present instance I don't even know whether the sums offered are sufficiently large to encourage anybody to write a play. However if you have one moldering in the trunk and don't know what to do with it you might get it out, furnish it up and send it off. The contest starts, if I recall correctly, in November and ends next March. The proceeds, if any, would at least buy a spring hat.

❧ ❧ ◆ ❧ ❧

17 August 1926, Tuesday:

"**Y**ES," said the little woman in the paisley shawl, "I haven't met any of the people in the other apartments yet but I feel as though I know all about them.

"The woman across the court lives all alone but she does a great deal of telephoning. I know that she uses a half pound of butter and a half dozen eggs a week and that she had one lamb chop for her supper last night. I know that she went to see 'Virtuous Husbands' at the Criterion Sunday afternoon and thought it was pretty good. I know that she has been feeling pretty bad with hay fever the last two weeks and that if her alimony had come as the lawyer promised she would go up to Canada for the rest of August.

"I know that the woman upstairs could take a job in one of the downtown offices at 60 dollars a month but that her husband doesn't want her to take it. She says she hasn't got enough to do all day long and besides she wants some new clothes. He says he isn't going to have all the men where he works thinking that he can't support a wife and hasn't he bought her all the clothes she needs? She says yes, he has. She hasn't had a dress that cost more than $6.95 in five years and if she ever got a ten-dollar hat on her head again she'd go completely out of her mind. He tells her that if she attempted to darn his socks once in a while she'd have something to keep her mind busy and she tells him what use is it for her to try to save money darning socks when he throws it away again playing billiards?

"The people downstairs have a year-old baby that cries all the time. The mother never says anything to it but 'shut up.' At night she and her husband lock up the house and go away and the baby cries itself to sleep.

"The people on the left have a phonograph which they play every night. They play 'Mother Machree,' 'I Hear You Calling Me,' 'Open the Gates of the Temple,' "M-O-T-H-E-R,' 'Ireland Must Be Heaven' and 'My Mother's Rosary.'

"The woman upstairs on the left has a bosom friend who lives in the house on the other side of the court. They get together almost every afternoon. I know that they both like a movie with a lot of style to it. I know that the woman upstairs thinks it's dreadful the way men eat and her friend thinks she'd rather have a man that ate than one that didn't. I know that they both wonder how the church can afford to serve a Wednesday night supper for 50 cents and that they think Mr. Whippet, the new Sunday school superintendent, has a great deal of class.

"And so, all in all, I can't say as I get lonesome. The only trouble with living in an apartment is that at night sometimes it's sort of hard to get to sleep."

18 August 1926, Wednesday:

ACCORDING to the dispatches the newest invention is one of these telephones you can see through. If the thing really works it will undoubtedly work a social revolution.

I don't know how it is in other houses but at our house the phone never rings except when you're in the bath tub. The procedure then is to catch up a bath towel, run dripping down the hall, take up the receiver and pretend you're just too cozy for anything. What will happen if they equip the telephone with these little seeing devices I don't know.

Another thing that happens almost every day is for somebody to call up and say "Guess who this is." Sometimes you can have five minutes of more fun guessing who it is. If you can see who it is the pastime is going to be utterly ruined.

Of course the principal advantage of a telephone has always been that it gave you a fair measure of protection. If you were calling up your husband you could pretend you were in tears when you weren't or if some friends were threatening to call you could tell them you were all dressed to go out when all you had on was a bungalow apron.

It will be dreadful to have every last avenue of possible fiction cut off.

The principal advantage to a seeing telephone I imagine would come when you were ordering groceries. If the grocer is trying to tell you how ripe the peaches are he won't have to think up comparisons. He can just hold them up and show you. And if it's a matter of lamp chops he can show you those too so you'll know how many to order. It also would be nice for him to have some device which would give you a flash at all the shelves so you could remember whether you wanted to order canned beans or not.

Another advantage would be when some friend of your cousin's in Bloomfield, Ill., came to town and called you up and wanted you to have dinner with him. You know how those things generally are. By seeing him first over the telephone you could hastily think up some other engagement.

Apparently there are no draw backs at all to another invention – an invention which has to do with furnaces. It seems that this device first crushes the coal and then feeds it to the furnace automatically. Although the article describing it didn't say so, I take it the device not only feeds the furnace automatically but also carries out the ashes and deposits them in the ash barrel or on the front steps as the case may be.

Should this device come into general use I dare say people wouldn't ever think of living in apartments any more. Whenever I say anything about wanting to get into a little house my friends all groan and say, "Yes but the furnace, the ashes, the lawn mower, the garden hose! Don't talk to me about houses!"

With an automatic furnace it seems to me a good deal of the distress would be done away with.

19 August 1926, Thursday:

A WOMAN called me on the phone this morning, "I couldn't sleep all night," she said, "for something that a friend of mine told me. She said she was coming out of O'Neil's yesterday and she found a crowd gathered on the sidewalk. She went over to see what it was and she found a woman beating up a little boy. She was so beside herself with passion that she couldn't control herself. She had given her purse and packages to a little girl to hold while she shook and slapped the boy. She kept screaming at him, 'Will you do it again. WILL you do it again' but the child was so frightened and full of sobs that she could not answer.

"None of the onlookers did anything. They just stood by and watched her mistreat the child. Don't you think that there ought to be something done to a woman like that? And if she'll treat a child like that on a public street in front of a whole lot of people how do you think she must treat him at home?"

Yes, I do think something ought to be done about it. The trouble with most of us is that when we see an animal being flogged or a child being mistreated we're so spineless and so afraid of getting our own hair pulled that we stand by and permit the weaker creature to endure goodness knows what torment. Not until something dreadful happens do we get into a righteous indignation.

I remember a few years ago a young step-mother who shook a little boy and broke his neck. The women of the city were so full of fury that they would have lynched the woman then and there. And yet her case was in many respects pitiable. She had a brood of tiny children to care for. They were poor. She was working desperately hard to keep the family together and make ends meet. She was tired and ill and nervous. Certain mothers whom I talked to told me that in the case of a small child it would be very easy to shake him in such a way that tragedy would result. It was this woman's misfortune that in this particular shaking tragedy did result.

The women of the town were fierce in their indignation. And yet I dare say there wasn't one of them who at some time or other hadn't meekly stood by and watched while some other child was yelled at and battered. "We haven't any right to interfere," we tell ourselves and under our very eyes we watch youngsters grow up with mauled bodies and bruised and aching hearts.

I think the thing which always comes to my mind whenever I see a woman who is a wife and mother behaving like a maniac is the jibes which from time to time are leveled at the old maids. There is a notion in a good many minds that for a woman just to become a mother immediately makes her sweet and gentle and lamb like. By inverse reasoning an old maid because she has never been a mother is bound to be cross and crabbed and interfering.

Somehow I can't help thanking God occasionally that there are old maids – old maids who go into the schools and give youngsters the tenderness that they never got at home, old maids who go into the nursing service and secure for youngsters the cleanliness and the fresh air and the food which their mothers are too indifferent to give them, old maids who every step of the way give something of the fullness of their own hearts to lonely youngsters who have never known anything but brawlings.

Last spring there was a little girl send home sick from the schools. Her mother slapped her and said she was only pretending. The little girl died. The school children sent flowers and the mother had several dozen photographs made of the casket.

That to my mind is a fair sample of some kinds of mother love.

21 August 1926, Saturday:

BILL was reading something from a book last night that had to do with the crinoline[252] age. You know, whenever you see crinoline girls on the stage they're always fixed up in lovely ruffly things and when they sway slightly you can see their darling pantalettes.

This chap who was writing the book, however, seems to have lived in the crinoline age and from what I could gather his idea was that we had prettied the mater out of all truth. It seems never to have occurred to anyone, he said, that women wore petticoats in those days. The petticoats, he went on to say, were of the red flannel variety in winter and a sort of ankle length muslin in summer. And their shoes weren't the baby doll things we see on the stage. They were real for sure shoes made of high black leather with elastic inserts at the sides.

It used to be the custom of bad little boys, he continued, to run down the streets and push against the women slightly so that the crinoline would bounce up. Then passersby could be treated to the spectacle of the petticoats. Apparently the pantalettes were plain and nothing to get excited about at all.

It is all very disillusioning.

Between times when Bill wasn't reading to me I managed to get through a dandy mystery story called "The Murder of Roger Ackroyd."[253] Mystery story writers must be hard put to it to get a new angle to a story. So far as I know the angle to this one was one nobody had thought about yet. I can't admit I was baffled to the very end – instinctively now I

---

[252] Crinoline is a stiffened or structured petticoat designed to hold a woman's skirt to create the illusion of fuller hips. The crinoline was originally made of stiff horsehair "crin" and cotton or linen.

[253] "The Murder of Roger Ackroyd" written by Agatha Christie in June 1926. Dame Agatha Mary Clarissa Christie, Lady Mallowan of the Most Excellent Order of the British Empire (1890-1976) English writer and known for her detective novels. She became Dame in 1971.

fasten the murder to the person who seems least auspicious – but, anyway, it was well worth reading. I started in after the dishes were done and finished by bed time.

Last night I got acquainted with Karl Butler's car whose name is Tillie the Toiler. I may have Tillie's history wrong – I wasn't thinking about statistics at the time – but as I recall Karl got Tillie second hand in 1917, and went all the way to the coast with her and back. Then he took her on a little jaunt to New York and parked her in front of the Plaza or the Ritz or wherever it is Karl stays when he goes to New York. Some men a little less loyal than Karl probably wouldn't have parked Tillie so conspicuously. A part of her interior is propped up with an oil can, some of her is held together with ropes and there's a considerable block of wood in one window where it rattles.

Karl didn't care though. He'd park Tillie in the most imposing spot he could find and if anybody presumed to make remarks Karl would jolly 'em along till they got to thinking Tillie was pretty nice too.

It seems that the door man at the Ritz or the Plaza asked Karl one day if it wasn't about time he was mounting Tillie and putting her in a plaster cast or something. "I don't see why I should," said Karl, "I got her from the Smithsonian Institute in the first place."

Karl says he's never going to sell Tillie. She's been too devoted. Some day when she gets too old to crash through pasture gates any more he's going to have her framed.

---

24 August 1926, Tuesday:

POSSIBLY the newspaper editor who had the ill humor and the poor taste to wish that Valentino[254] were off the face of the earth is feeling somewhat better now.

Of course I can't say that I would be awfully crazy about a man who wore slave bracelets myself. The propensity of every male to adorn himself however is a thing which every woman recognizes. The accepted method seems to be to put on a few

---

[254] Rodolfo Guglielmi, known as Rudolph Valentino (1895-1926) Italian actor who passed away on August 23, 1926, the day prior to this article date. He was known as "The Great Lover" of the Silver Screen.

plumes, take up a sword and march in a parade. Another method and one in high favor with traveling salesmen is to wear a very large diamond in the tie and one a little larger in a ring on the little finger. Still another method is to put on golf knickers and walk down Main st.

I suppose it was the unusualness of the Valentino adornment which irritated the newspaper editor. I can remember however a time when a man who wore a wrist watch immediately read himself out of masculine companionship. The war came and changed things considerably.

It was always a favorite gibe of those who did not like Valentino to refer to the fact that he had once been a gardener's boy and later a bus boy. And that, in America, is another thing hard to understand. We point with pride to the captain of industry who was once a newsboy. We prostrate ourselves before the novelist who was once a street car conductor. We relate with satisfaction how we knew Irving Berlin in the old days when he was a singing waiter. And yet in the case of Valentino it was always considered a smirch that at one time he had watered geraniums and that at another time he had carried trays to the kitchen. I have never known women to bring it up but I have heard men do it repeatedly. Just why they did this I was never able to figure out. One might almost suspect that the tolerance accorded the captain of industry, the novelist and the composer lay in the fact that as the captain of industry, the novelist and the composer rose in the world they did not turn into heart breakers. One might almost suspect it except for the fact that men are never catty.

Just what Valentino's real disposition was like I have no idea and probably no one else has aside from the two women who at various times were married to him. His first wife, Jean Acker, divorced him while he was still obscure and she was comparatively successful. Rumor had it that when their conditions were reversed and Valentino sky-rocketed into fame she repented her haste in rushing to the divorce court. It was she, so they say, who recently gave Valentino the slave bracelet[255] which resulted in the comment of the irate editor.

In any event I doubt that Valentino's life was ever happy. His cross country tour in the interests of a celebrated beauty mud which involved the looking over of thousands of love sick, screen mad flappers must have been galling. His conflicts with other members

[255] The famous platinum slave bracelet was designed and given to Valentino by his second wife, Natacha Rambova (1897-1966), a flamboyant art director and costume designer.

of the motion picture industry must have been galling. Here was a young man who could act and knew it. They put him to work in "The Sheik" and "The Young Rajah." Fighting free of them, enduring the long suffering in behalf of the campaign for the beauty mud, Valentino finally made "Monsieur Beaucaire" and "The Eagle." The public supported him half-heartedly. Plump marshmallow fed matrons and yearning high school girls were sighing for more like "The Sheik."

Valentino's last move was to give them "The Son of the Sheik." Just what sort of concession it was I don't know. Maybe he figured that the money from it would enable him to make a picture that he really liked. Maybe on the other hand he had decided that the game wasn't worth the candle. It is hard to tell.

Somehow though I can't help feeling sorry. Two women had promised to love him faithfully and well and yet when the time came to die neither was there.[256] He had instead thousands of phone calls including and from Mrs. "Peaches" Browning.[257]

He seems to have been a young man who all through the sorry tangle had clung to some sort of ideal. At the end when the ministers of his faith who had something to do with that ideal struggled to get to him they were pushed aside by hospital attendants.

The million dollars for which Valentino's life was insured will go to Joseph M. Schenck,[258] motion picture producer.

Poor, lonely Rudolph.

---

[256] It is now known he was engaged to Pola Negri (1897-1987) at the time of his death, and she attended his funeral on September 8, 1926.

[257] Frances Belle Heenan (1910-1956) known as Peaches Browning, an American actress who reveled in publicity and with the paparazzi, married a lavish husband she called "Daddy" who was Edward West Browning (1875-1934) and their marriage became spotlight for scandalous stories in newspapers of the era.

[258] Joseph M. Schenck (1876-1961) Russian-American movie producer

28 August 1926, Saturday:

ODYSSEY

Detroit to Akron[259]

JOHN A. KRONK FOR MAYOR
Last Chance To Buy Lots in Fordson.
Goodyear Means Good Wear
Slow
No Parking on Highway
Green for Governor
Walk to Left
Fresh Eggs
Long Pine Barbecue
Crinnin Homes $800 Down, $40 Month.
Thank You
Cross Road
Slow
Ed's Place
Light Refreshments and Auto Accessories
Sweet Corn 10¢ a doz.
Kelley's Place
Fresh Eggs
Slow
Chicken, Fish, Frog and Steak Dinners
Bar-B-Q
It Isn't Home Till It's Planted
Tourist Camp 50¢
Hot Fish
Eddie Gukert's Flying Field
8 mi. to Toledo
Gas 22c
Enter Wood Co. Leave Lucas Co.
Pups For Sale
Tourists' Camp
Try Green Seal
Mme. Frany Clairvoyant

---

[259] By today's rules of the road, this trip would be 192 miles and take about 3 hours to complete. If the highway rules of 1926 only allotted for a 35 mph speed limit, this trip would have taken her about 5 and a half. These are the road signs she saw along the way.

22 mi. to Fremont
Detour
Gas 23¢
You'll Come Back to Forest Park
Pickles for Sale
Detour 400 ft. ahead
Thank You
Enter Sandusky Co.
Ed's Place
Welcome to Fremont
Eat with the Kiwanis Club Thursday Noon
Speed Limit 35 mi. an hour
The Jollyville Inn
Thompsen's Honey Next House to the Left
Wanna Kum Bac Bar-B-Q
Welcome to Clyde
Speed Limit 35 mi. an hour Strictly Enforced
You'll Like Ben's Bar-B-Q
Suitame Cottage
Welcome to Bellevue Free Street Fair
Speed Limit 35 mi. an hour
Welcome to Norwalk
Speed Limit Strictly Enforced
Huron County Fair
Hotel Noggie
Detour
Danger This Curve Slopes the Wrong Way
Wet Water
Enter Lorain Co.
Detour Elyria
4 mi. to Elyria
Al's Place
Another Rybolt Furnace
Detour
God Is Love
Welcome to Medina
Cut Outs Prohibited
18 mi. to Akron
Are you saved?
"Everything 500 feet ahead."
You Break It We Fix It
4 mi. to Akron
National City Bank

2 September 1926, Thursday:

THE clothing stores, so they tell me, aren't doing the business that they used to. The automobile, I suspect, is responsible. For one thing, if you have $25 to spend, it is just as easy to go down and make the first payment on a second hand car with it as to buy a new dress. Having bought the car it takes all the money you can earn thereafter to keep it going. The other consideration is that when you're riding around in a car you don't need new clothes.

Sometimes I wonder if the automobile concerns aren't digging a great big abyss for themselves. Every year they get out a new model and encourage you to chuck the old one. You turn in the old one for the down payment and go right on with the installments. The fellow who gets your old car gets tired of it after a while and turns it in on a new one. He goes on paying in installments. Credit is boundless. Nobody expects a car to last more than a year. You run yours as hard as possible and then wish it onto the next fellow who's willing to be taken in by a fresh coat of paint.

I can't figure out just who it is but it seems to me that somebody is holding a large paper sack.

One of the things hard to understand is why anybody ever goes to the trouble of making children's toys. The other day being pay day I bought Mary one of these thingumajig wooden dolls and took it home to her. She glanced at it casually and went on tearing up the paper laundry bag she was interested in. The other day we went to Detroit and brought back for her a nice hand painted sanitary twistable rabbit. She didn't pay the slightest bit of attention to it but went on banging a tin pie pan with a wooden spoon.

I have come to the conclusion that these people who take a couple of wooden knobs and hand paint then and string them together to make a doll and sell it to you for anything from one dollar up to five are doing it just to please us elders.

I am sure that if Mary had anything to say in the matter she would come out with a plea for simpler things. Her happiest hour is on Friday when the laundry comes home and she can have all the brown paper wrappings to crackle up. Certainly her most perfect hour was that one of a week or so ago when I was trying to bake a cake and gave her the spoon and tin to keep her quiet. Christmas when we give her a drum to bang on I know she won't be nearly so pleased.

ONE of the things you notice about small towns when you're going about the country this time of the year is how pretty the streets are in contrast to the business sections. I was in a little town a day or so ago which was full of lovely green grass plots and old fashioned gardens and white colonial houses with green shutters. The few stores however were enough to drive anybody wild. The grocery store was smelly and dark and dirty. The dry goods store was housed in a lop-sided frame building, plastered with last year's circus posters. The combination oil station and garage was practically obscured by the loafers in front of it who had stained everything within reaching distance a dark and oleaginous brown.

It seemed to me as I looked over this little town that there was nothing plainer than the point where the hand of man had left off and the hand of woman had begun. The women had made their part of the town clean and orderly and beautiful. The men hadn't cared a rap how things looked so long as they could make enough money to live off.

One of the things hard to understand about a little town is why the cooking should be so consistently bad. The best cooks are commonly reputed to come from the country and most of the women in the small towns seem at one time to have been country girls. And yet the worst cooking in the world seems to be found I the small town restaurant. The coffee is beyond any words to describe. The bread advertises the fact that while it was still down at the general store it stood next to the kerosene can. The pies still bear the labels which were put on them in Chicago.

When Bill and I went on what for lack of a better word we refer to as our honeymoon we stopped in a little town for lunch. Now when you're just married you're a right to expect everything to be perfect. But it was a terrible lunch. There wasn't a redeeming feature about it. The quality of it exerted a depressing effect which lasted for weeks and gave a melancholy cast to the post cards which we mailed home. For the sake of honeymooners if for no one else I wish small towns would brush up on their cooking.

Aside from that it seems to me at the present moment that it would be awfully nice to live in a small town. Really the only advantage in living in a big city at any time was the fact that there you could go to the theaters and concert halls. But as things go nowadays you can't very well live right in a big city anyway. You have to move quite a distance out and then commute. There's no reason why you shouldn't move still further and add 10 minutes or a half hour to the time when you take a notion to run in to the theater.

Cities I find can prove awfully wearing in time. The racket and the dust and the smells wear out your endurance without your knowing it. The posters for burlesque shows and cheaper movies assail you on every side, the streets are being continually torn up, the churches are always having campaigns for something or other, the gas mains and the electric wires kill off the trees, street cars go screeching by on flat wheels.

It must be nice to get away from it all, to see whole streets of smooth lawns, to walk under whole groves of trees, to have no noise anywhere at all, no excitement save the quiet gossip of the Ladies' Aid.

4 September 1926, Saturday:

IT SEEMED to me that there was a good deal of justice raised in the cry of the Civil war widow the other day that Americans will raise a million dollars to build a memorial to a dead president but they will not allot a penny more than they are now giving for the aid and comfort of rapidly aging women.

Sometimes I get to wondering why we build memorials anyway. The Harding memorial is beautiful but useless. I am not in most things a practical person and wouldn't for the world argue that everything in the world ought to have some practical purpose to which it could be put. A memorial, however, is designed primarily with the thought of inspiring in the beholder a sense of veneration for the dead. I doubt very much that that is the thought which strikes the average beholder regarding the average memorial.

A couple of years ago I was walking down the main street of a little town. It was on the whole a pretty ugly street. The ugliness at one point, however, was broken by a memorial erected to a great man who had been born there. The memorial was beautiful in itself but I couldn't help wondering why all that marble and stone had to stand there so lifelessly. It would have made a very pretty little theater, or an amphitheater for band concerts in a park, or a hospital for children, or a library, or a small town museum. Or they could have taken the money and built a park and beautified the city streets.

Now they're talking of building a great memorial to Thomas Edison[260] over in Milan, O., where he was born. It seems to me that instead of piling a lot of marble into an imposing heap it would be far more gracious to take the money and build a model orphan asylum with it. Or establish a fund for indigent mothers-in-law. Or buy lots and lots of chewing tobacco for the old men in county infirmaries. Or buy silk stockings and slippers for the daughters of unsuccessful inventors. Or, most anything.

---

[260] Thomas Alva Edison (1847-1931) American inventor

Other useless things that people seem to be addicted to are diamonds, paper flowers and loving cups. The assistant society editor has a little finger ring act with a great synthetic ruby. I don't suppose the ring cost a great deal of money and yet it is far more beautiful than a diamond of the same size could ever hope to be. And yet people will buy diamonds and take them home to his wife. "They're just as good as money, Jo," he keeps telling me and yet I seriously doubt it. I never heard of a man selling a diamond for the price he put into it. The people who buy diamonds immediately have to rush downtown and put them in a safety deposit box where they lie and lie and lie. The very first time they take them out and wear them they get held up and robbed.

I don't know why it is that I like synthetic jewels but not synthetic flowers. I know a woman who makes beautiful paper flowers and yet they never thrill me. I would rather have one bedraggled daisy set in a milk bottle in the kitchen window than all the paper flowers in the world. And so I don't know. It is easy, however, to understand why loving cups are useless. It just goes to show what sheep we are that we should go on giving champion golfers loving cups when there's nothing to put in them anymore. Why not give a champion golfer a new niblick? Or a hundred dollars worth of balls or an electric percolator to take home to his wife or a new vacuum cleaner? Or to speak plainly, why not brush all pretense aside and just hand him a handsomely engraved check?

---

6 September 1926, Monday:

IT IS hard to understand why Tom Taggart of Indiana should resent the fact that Miss Ferber made him out a gambler in 'Show Boat." Presumably Miss Ferber had her facts in hand before she set about writing the offending paragraphs. Granting that Mr. Taggart was at one time a professional gambler why should he resent the circumstance being mentioned. A professional gambler, to the common run of us, is a tremendously interesting person, a person ever so much more fascinating than a politician, say. There are a good many of us, I dare say, who would far rather vote for Mr. Taggart, ex-gambler, occasionally calling the old days with delight, than for Mr. Taggart, moral politician.

I don't live in Indiana any more but I think if I did I'd fight shy of Mr. Taggart from now on.

This touchiness on the part of certain individuals regarding incidents of their past is hard to understand. A certain captain of industry whose biography was published recently, came to serious odds with his biographer because the latter had mentioned that the captain of industry had at one time been a horse trader. So far as I know, the business of horse dealing was a respectable and necessary one – just as respectable and necessary as the present-day business of selling automobiles. But the captain of industry somehow didn't like the notion of it being known. I'm afraid he thought it might detract from his dignity.

I don't know about men but women have an experience which happens very often. They keep hearing about some other woman who is brilliant and who seems to have everything. Although they wouldn't admit it for the world, down deep in their hearts they entertain a vague resentment against her. Then they meet the woman and they discover that she is fat, that her clothes don't fit her and that there are wrinkles in her neck and around her eyes. They look at their own trim figures and their resentment vanishes. They adore the woman from that day on. They have found, you see, that she really doesn't have everything.

For years and years there was a woman whom I didn't like. Although I didn't know it, I was jealous of her. I was jealous of her prettiness and her clothes and her home and her little flip ways. Then one day I found out that her husband beat her regularly and that she was a good little sport and never said anything about it. Immediately my resentment vanished. Some of it may have been pity and some of it may have been admiration at her ability to keep quiet but most of it was due to the fact that I had discovered that in one respect at least I was ever so much more fortunate than she was.

It pays, I think, to be frank about our poverty, our shortcomings, our lowly beginning or whatever happens to be our state. One of the most delightful persons I know is a man who will sit for an hour and tell you about his uncle who was a horse thief, his other uncle who was a bigamist and his aunts who took life with more zest than decorum.

He could, of course, tell me that he was descended from lords and earls, that he had a cousin who was presented at court and that his grandfather was worth millions. He could tell me those things but it wouldn't make me like him. It wouldn't make me like him at all.

---

7 September 1926, Tuesday:

ONE of the people I keep wondering about is Elizabeth Benson[261], the newest child prodigy, who is to enter Barnard college this fall, (I think it's Barnard) at the age of 12.

I saw a picture of Elizabeth the other day and she looked just as any other wholesome rather plumpish child would look in a Peter Thompson. I read the tail end of a newspaper article written by Elizabeth's mother wherein she stated that she didn't know exactly how Elizabeth came to be a prodigy. She had merely treated her pretty much as she would have treated any other normal human being and Elizabeth had done the rest. And I read a magazine article written by Elizabeth herself entitled, "Are Children People?"

Inasmuch as Elizabeth was allowed to develop normally instead of being subjected to somebody's theories of education the chances are that she will not suffer the slump which ordinarily comes to child prodigies. She may develop into a brilliant author – "Are Children People?" was infinitely better executed than the dozen or so other articles appearing in the same magazine – or she may marry or go into business.

Her case however has raised a lot of interesting questions. One of them is whether children really need a father. You know whenever a woman gets disgusted with the way her husband is doing things and makes up her mind that she's going to take the children and leave, the cry is always raised, "Oh, but you mustn't break up your home. When the children get older they'll need their father."

Elizabeth apparently got along very well without a father. Her mother was a widow and an invalid at that. Elizabeth had to get along not only without a father but with very little mother. She doesn't seem to have suffered from the circumstance at all.

Another thing that we've always maintained was that you really could not know about a thing unless you'd experienced it yourself. In writing "Are Children People?" Elizabeth went over a few of the things that parents do. She mentioned how they will casually take a child in their lap and extract confidence from him and then next day use these confidences against him. She mentioned how they will throw up all the things they have done for a child until they drive him frantic with rebellion. She mentioned how they will make promises to him and break them. She mentioned how they will scarify his soul in public. She mentioned all the silly questions they will ask a child when they are

---

[261] Elizabeth Benson was a child prodigy who at the age of 12 scored 214 on the Binet-Simon IQ test – at the time it was the highest recorded score in the United States. She wrote an essay published in *Vanity Fair* at age 13 and attended Barnard College at 12/13 (Vanity Fair, Sept. 1927, 68, 104).

attempting to strike up a conversation. "Dear, dear, and how old is the little man? And does he go to school? And does he like his teacher? Come here and kiss Aunty Brown. Aunty Brown just loves little boys. Do you know she's got two great big boys of her own! There now, what do you think of that!"

If Elizabeth Benson had never suffered from things like these, and she stoutly maintains that she never did, how in the world could she know so much about them?

Of course the prime question is whether one would like to have a child prodigy in the family and whether Elizabeth is really a prodigy. Maybe she isn't a prodigy at all. Maybe she is what every child should be and maybe the rest of us are sub-normal.

---

8 September 1926, Wednesday:

HAVE just read what you said in today's paper about the use women make of their first earnings," writes Myra S. Pitkin. "My grandmother, Miranda Fenn, taught a summer school in Milford, Conn., in 1814 when she was 16 years old. She earned five dollars – and spent four of them for a green silk parasol with an ivory handle. But she was one of those 61 women who organized that Female Mite society in Tallmadge in 1826 so she possibly outgrew her frivolity."

Among those, however, who spent their first money judiciously might be mentioned Miss Mabel Todd, director of music at Central high school. Miss Todd was still wearing her hair in curls when she hitched up the old family horse and went out to apply for a position in a country school. I think she found the president of the school board weeding potatoes. When he saw her slightness and her curls he tried to scare her out with tales of the big wild boys she'd have to deal with. Miss Todd however was confident – so confident that she asked for considerably more money than had ever been paid in those regions before.

---

9 September 1926, Thursday:

IT ALL came about on account of Tiny Englebeck walking into Bill's store this morning. Tiny was holding the lapels of his coat out in front of him.

"What do you think of that?" he said, "40 pounds since last June 15."

It developed then that, Tiny had bought a bathroom scales last June and along with it had come a free book about count your calories and get thin. On account of the book being a free offering from some life insurance company Tiny figured out that he could treat it and so he started in counting his calories.

Bread was the hardest thing he had to give up. It seems Tiny had been in the habit of taking a fresh loaf of whole wheat bread and a lot of butter and making right away with them. And then at night when the rest of the family was in bed Tiny would go out to the ice box and get a cold snack.

When Tiny started counting his calories he didn't know whether he'd have the courage to stick it out or not. But the next time he happened to think of stepping on his bathroom scales he found he had lost 18 pounds. He made up his mind to stick. The thought of Dr. Banker gave him courage.

"Now there's Dr. Banker," Tiny said to himself. "He's about as hard working a fellow as I know. And yet he hardly eats anything. He's rushing around all hours of the night and yet he doesn't eat. It must be that a fellow doesn't need as much food as he thinks."

Having made this decision Tiny went down and looked at the ice box. There was a half of a nice luscious apple Jonathan in the ice box left over from supper. Tiny thought of Dr. Banker and passed up the apple Jonathan.

"I'm going to lose five pounds more," said Tiny this morning, "and then I'm going to stop."

So then when we were going out to lunch Bill said, "If you'll take off 40 pounds like Tiny Englebeck I'll get you a piano."

"What kind of piano?" I said.

"One of those little apartment pianos," said Bill.

"I don't want an apartment piano," I said, "I'd rather have a grand piano. I'd rather have a second-hand grand piano than a brand new apartment piano."

"Where would you put it?" said Bill.

"We aren't always going to live where we are now," I said. So Bill said, all right, he'd get me a grand piano.

"There's another thing," I said. "If I were to take off 40 pounds like Tiny Englebeck I wouldn't look normal. I think 30 pounds would be a great plenty. What do you say now – 30 pounds – one grand piano."

"Oh, all right," said Bill, and we had lunch and I didn't eat any bread or beans or dessert or sugar or cream and I've been suffering all afternoon. If it wasn't for the thought of the piano – and of Dr. Banker.

It seems to me a great pity that upright pianos were ever invented. They are beyond all doubt the ugliest piece of furniture that people permit in their homes. The old-fashioned square pianos were wonderful. They didn't have ugly backs to them that had to be put up against a wall. They were low so that a tenor or – even better a baritone – could lean gracefully on one and gaze at the accompanist.

A photograph or a vase of flowers placed on one came within the easy range of vision. None of these things can be said for the upright piano.

I would think seeing that they are now making pianos small that it would be easy to create one which resembled the clavichord[262] or the spinet. These were graceful pieces of furniture. The present attempt to make a piano which shall resemble a match box as much as possible is to my mind a dreadful waste.

---

10 September 1926, Friday:

"SEVERAL days ago," writes M. S. S., "you made some comments on Miss Negri in which you mentioned that her mother died while insane, in the last few months – since she announced her engagement – I have read interviews supposed to have been given by her mother through an interpreter. Was it a 'medium' or do you have as much trouble keeping track of the stars as I do?"

Well, all I know is what I read in the magazines. It was Jim Tully who mentioned Pola's mother going insane and inasmuch as Mr. Tully had recently been in Los Angeles and

---

[262] Similar to a harpsichord, a clavichord is a stringed keyboard instrument that dates back to Medieval, Renaissance, Baroque and Classical times. The sometimes have beautiful paintings on the back of the inside of the cover when it is opened.

was writing for Vanity Fair, I took it he would be careful what he was saying. Not, I guess, that any of it really matters.

———————

I went over to see "Variety"[263] the other day and I'm still wondering why foreign male actors are so much better than the American variety. Take Emil Jannings,[264] who played the part of the cuckold husband. If an American had been playing the part he would have made the husband a hard-fisted, broad-chested, noble fellow who turned his glass upside down when the gin was passed and went out at evening to gaze at the sunset. Jannings had the courage to make the husband not only a hard drinker and a hard card player but he also did the more difficult thing – he made him a little silly at times. There wasn't a woman in the audience who didn't cringe a little, I think, when she saw Emil Jannings washing the dishes and later darning a hole in the stocking of Lya de Putti.[265] It didn't seem quite manly, somehow. Nor did it seem quite dignified for the two of them to come reeling home from the party. And yet, therein lay part of the explanation as to why "Variety" is a great picture.

The psychological truth is that a man who darns the stockings and washes the dishes so that his wife may lie in bed is bound to lose her in the end to some other fellow who uses women principally for door mats.

———————

The picture apparently was cut very considerably in order that it might not shock the sensibilities of Ohio audiences. What was left of it still made a fair story, the only irritation lying in the abruptness of the transitions.

One of the things I have long wondered about, however, is why movie directors object so much, in a manner of speaking, to using the asterisks which the novelists have found valuable.

Leaving the matter of censorship out of the discussion, I don't care, and I doubt that very many other people car, to be given the feeling that they are peeking into somebody else's bedroom window. And yet the movie directors feel that such scenes are essentially their prerogative and when anyone protest they are outraged. "Those things happen,"

———————————

[263] Variety was released in 1925 in Germany, and is based on Felix Hollaender's novel "The Oath of Stephen Huller." The American version was heavily cut (and replaced with title cards) so as not to show the characters in an adulterous love triangle, but rather as a married couple.

[264] Emil Jannings (1884-1950) Swiss actor

[265] Lya de Putti (1897-1931) Hungarian actress

they argue, "so why shouldn't we show them?" The time-worn argument might be brought in that people also actually take baths.

The other argument is that there are a good many things to art and in literature which are far more effective if they are merely suggested instead of being completely and entirely delineated. I recall a movie made by David Wark Griffith[266] called, if I remember correctly, "The White Flower."[267] At one point in the picture the scene stopped abruptly and you were shown the petals dropping from a rose. The thing made a vivid impression because you could read into it as much or as little as you chose. It possessed the added advantage of being beyond the reach of the censors.

If the censors stick by their guns it seems to me that in time the movies may develop a very definite and worth-while symbolism.

In "Variety," of course, the symbolism lay in the fact that at a certain point one of the characters drew a picture of the deceived husband showing him with horns.

It seems to me that touches of that sort are employed all too infrequently in the movies. Once directors do begin to use them the movies should increase tremendously in effectiveness.

<hr/>

14 September 1926, Tuesday:

ONE of the things which continually surprises me is how life persists in disarming us at every possible point. We decide that we do not like babies and somebody promptly leaves a very plump and attractive one on our door step. We criticize our neighbor for smoking cigarets and the next night we find ourselves, quite without premeditation, smoking them ourselves. We express in loud and certain terms our disapproval of a certain woman and a day or so later she does us inexplicable favors. We join a company where one of the number annoys us by stammering. A half hour

---

[266] David Wark Griffith (D.W. Griffith) (1875-1948) American film director

[267] "The White Rose" debuted in 1923. D.W. Griffith was credited as the director, and as the writer (as Irene Sinclair). The scene where the rose fades is roughly at the 40 minute mark, and signifies the moment when the characters succumb to their forbidden passions.

passes and we find that we are being looked upon coldly because we have suddenly taken to stammering ourselves.

All of which is by way of introducing the fact that Lolly brought me five gold fish yesterday. All my life I have vowed that no matter what came to pass I would never have gold fish in the home. And then Lolly brought these – five of them – in a little oyster pail.

Their names are Platyi and Guppyi, three Platyi and two Guppyi, or, it may be, the other way about, two Platyi and three Guppyi. They are each, at the wildest guess, a half inch long and when they are not swimming about you would swear they were not in the water at all.

Unfortunately, all that Lolly brought along to go forward furnishing the new home for Platyi and Guppyi was a small weed which requires to be planted in sand before it can really be of much use. In lieu of an aquarium for Platyi and Guppyi we took the apples and plums from the Chinese bowl and poured water into that. And in lieu of food we gave them this morning a bit – a very small bit – of Mary's 10 o'clock cereal.

The disturbing thing about it all is that now Platyi and Guppyi have arrived I have somehow acquired an ambition to see them thrive. I think Bill feels that way about it, too, as this morning he offered me a gold fish bowl which has been collecting dust in the back of his store for the past several months. Had it not been that my resources at the moment were down to 11 cents, I think I would have gone out immediately to purchase the sand, the pebbles, the newts and the water plants which go to make up a proper aquarium.

This winter, I dare say, when the cold nights come, I will be getting up at 2 o'clock in the morning to light an electric light bulb for Platyi and Guppyi so they will not feel the wintry blasts too keenly

.

———————

"Your discussion of the picture 'Variety' interested me very much," writes Thelma L., "and as I know a little more about the picture before the censors got out the shears I thought you might be interested in that part of the story.

"It was very evident that the picture had been cut up. In fact, the whole first part of the original picture was not shown as it probably was not in line with the American idea of a hero. This was the part in which Emil Jannings fell in love with Lya de Putti and ran away with her, even though she was married to another man. Of course, no hint of that was given out in the showing in Akron – they judged them to be man and wife. One judged him to be a foolish, too-much-in-love husband and that probably explains why he did the cooking and mending so meekly. I guess that part simply didn't jibe with the American film hero ideal so they just left that part out.

"And that makes the subsequent action, that is, Emil's killing 'what's his name,' the trapeze artist, seem rather queer and foolish, doesn't it, when all the time he had no more right to her than anyone else? No doubt he loved her but he was no better morally than the man he killed, so far as he was concerned.

"I liked the picture (what I saw of it) but knowing the rest of the story certainly puts a different light on the action."

15 September 1926, Wednesday:

WASH TUB ARISTOCRACY

A CHICAGO woman has revived the phrase, "wash tub aristocracy" and faces social isolation in consequence. Inasmuch as social isolation seems to be what the lady was striving for she surely can't feel very much put out.

But as for the wash tubs, they have behaved abominably in the matter. They have received the phrase as an insult and brooded over it accordingly. What they should have done was to accept the phrase as a tribute, wear it with dignity and smile complacently whenever it was mentioned.

I was reading the other night how St. Francis of Assisi came upon a beggar who was clad in a ragged brown shirt. St. Francis, who always chose the meanest things of life for his own, changed clothing with the beggar. Having put on the brown shirt he looked about for and finally came upon a piece of rope to hold it together. This he tied about his waist. It was a sorry enough get-up. But 10 years later 5,000 men were wearing this brown habit and a hundred years later they wrapped Dante[268] in it to lay him in his grave.

In some such fashion the wash tub deserves to be sublimated and elevated to the sphere where it rightfully belongs.

For the wash tub, properly considered, is an emblem of cleanliness and order and sweetness. The week's linen goes to it in a wretched state. It comes out fragrant and purified. There are excellent housewives who refuse to touch an iron to a bed about so

---

[268] Dante Alighieri (1265-1321) Italian poet

much do they love the feel of linen which has gone from the tub to the sunshine and thence, smoothed and folded, to the linen closet upstairs.

We pay extravagant homage to the preacher who purifies our souls. We buy expensive marble fonts into which he may dip us for baptisms. But what do we do about the equally necessary matter of purifying the week's wash? We hide away the laundry tubs in the cellar. We relegate the laundress to an inferior position and make her eat off the kitchen table. And when we want to be particularly unpleasant we refer to our social rivals as "wash tub aristocracy."

Of course I dare say there are social distinctions even among the wash tubs. I can fancy the old fashioned galvanized tub which we used to drag out in the back yard and set up on a wooden bench feeling decidedly inferior to a stationary wash tub which has both hot and cold running water in it and a rubber plug. Likewise, the stationary tub, with its wash board complement, must feel decidedly out of it sometimes when it regards the electric washing machine. And a laundress, I dare say, who works for a family where they have both electric washing machine and mangle and drier, must feel a sort of lofty pity for the laundress who works for a family where they have only stationary tubs and gas irons.

Even at that, though, it seems to me that the wash tub, any wash tub, deserves a respect which has been pretty generally denied it. Its function is purification, its glory something close akin to godliness. Granting that that which makes a man an aristocrat is something not immediately discerned by the world. I, [sic] know of nothing which gives a man more cause to hold his head up in the streets than the conscious knowledge that his shirt is clean.

16 September 1926, Thursday:

"IT IS A very remarkable feature of the editorial psychology of today," writes William McFee, "that they all worship O. Henry and lament his passing and reverence the O. Henry awards but the less like O. Henry you are the more they will love you. O. Henry was intolerably artificial and mushy. He had two gifts — slang and the snap ending. But his characters were pennygaff characters utterly divorced from real life and real literature.

"Of course you will perhaps grimace at some of my comments and say you don't want to do a sex story. Then for the love of God why do you both with fiction? There is no need to write fiction unless you wish to do sex stories. All the world is sex. I say sex —

not adultery. That's the trouble in America. If one says sex you all think one means adultery. Oh, no. There is plenty of sex in Jane Austen. There is the Perennial Bachelor in Katherine Mansfield's stories. But they are STORIES.

"When I look at my novel (page like this number 362 and much more to come) I wonder whether you realize that writing is work. I don't mean that it is hard unpleasant toil. It is grand. I got an idea one Saturday in July, worked on it at once, ie. As soon as I finished the piece I was doing. All Sunday I wrote and Monday, Tuesday I are in my diary 'Finished .... at five P. M. and sent it to Margaret. This is the stenog[269] in N. Y. I sold it to the Red book for $700.

"But what I was going to say was that I used episodes, memories and notes dating back a dozen years in that story. It had been in the back of my mind for months. When it finally came to a head the actual writing of 8,000 words was a pleasure. Three days' pleasure."

It seems I was wrong about Sapolio[270]. Today's mail brought a letter in which was enclosed a Sapolio and clipped from a woman's magazine.

This ad showed how Dutch women kept their stone floors polished in the 17th century – a very nice ad indeed.

I think however that a good many women shared my idea that Sapolio wasn't used any more. Adrienne was wailing the disappearance of it only last night. "I can't buy it anywhere," she mourned, "and it was always my favorite scouring cake."

Leaving the question of right and wrong out of the matter it should be evident by now that truth is a far more simple and a far less expensive method than falsehood.

Judging by the news reports Aimee Semple McPherson found herself in a situation which even to others is a minister of the gospel would have been embarrassing. She might had she so desired confessed her error, made professions of humility and returned with a fair measure of self-respect to her calling. "I am a sinner," she might have said

---

[269] Stenographer

[270] A brand of soap known for its advertising

just as she had said it countless times before and the world would have regarded her with mingled amazement and commendation.

Instead of which Mrs. McPherson seems to have done nothing save deny and cover up, deny and cover up. It is a very human way to act but, in the last analysis, impractical.

<hr/>

17 September 1926, Friday:

THINGS I DON'T LIKE

LEMON on honey dew melon
Red typewriter ribbons
Closed windows on street cars
Sugar in coffee
Wild west movies
Fishing
Radio
Windsor chairs
Circuses
Evangelists
Haldeman Julius
Diamonds
Rubbers
Baseball
Harry Snodgrass
Rubber plants
Cotton blankets
Hard lead pencils
Long finger nails
Fish glue
Having pictures taken
Mosquitoes
Adenoids
Wall paper
Calf brains
College pennants
Church entertainments
Fitted traveling bags
Telephone disguises
Fancy silverware
Dishes with gold bands

Fire sirens
Sunday afternoon sightseers
Roller coasters
Suspenders
Mae Murray
Edward S. Browning
Bell bottom trousers
Creamed codfish
Army officers
Cut glass
Green window shades
Chewing tobacco
Barber shop talcum powder
Embroidered stockings
Shoulder straps
Newspaper contests
Breach of promise suits
Cafeterias
Toothpicks

I went out to the country fair Thursday. I went with every expectation of having a good time. But the old flavor was gone. I suspect it was because the hootchy-kootchy dancers and the snake charmers and the strong men weren't there.

I hadn't realized before how much I liked that sort of thing. It wasn't that I ever went into the tent above but I liked the racket along the midway – the bally-hooers and the tom-toms and girls in soiled tights and imitation pearl stomachers who waved their arms about in what, I dare say, they took for the last word in sinuousness.

All this was gone Thursday. I couldn't even find a vendor of the old time ice cream candy. In the grandstand a band played lonesomely [sic]. Under a tent top the Ladies' Aid society of Mogadore was serving a dinner. "All you can eat for 50 cents." Mrs. Gates who was sitting at the entrance told me that out at the Mogadore M. E. church they were going to serve the same dinner every Wednesday only it would be "All you can eat for 35 cents." There were plenty of hot dog stands and an occasional shooting gallery of some sort.

But aside from things like these the old county fair was changed. Sometimes I wonder if some day it will go out of existence altogether.

18 September 1926, Saturday:

IN AKRON when an otherwise properly behaved young couple commits the pardonable mistake of getting married too early they are taken before Judge Howard Spicer who gives them a lecture and then sends them home to live happily forever after.

Out in the great and glorious west, or to be more exact, Kansas City, when a girl of 15 and a youth of 17 get married the judge sentences the girl to an industrial home for a year.

If the judge had sent the girl home to her mother we might have understood his action. If he had exacted from the young couple a promise that they would not see each other until the husband could support his wife we might also understand his action. But to send a 15-year-old girl to a reformatory simply because she had carried out what every other romantic 15-year-old girl dreams of carrying out is something that one woman at least is finding it hard to swallow.

There is at least one woman in town who is married at 15 and is glad of it. She is the deputy sheriff, Mrs. Greta Footman. Did Mrs. Footman have trials and troubles and tribulations? Of course she did, and so does every other woman, including those who married at 35, and those who never married at all.

It seems to me that there is a good deal to be said in favor of the early marriage in spite of all the things which have been said against it.

Young love may be foolish, but at the same time it is probably the most perfect love that comes into our lives. I doubt that the period of adjustment which follows it is any harder to go through than is that period which comes to the man and woman of 30, the woman having married because she was afraid she'd never have another chance, the man having married because he was tired of having his socks darned by the laundry.

Then the woman who married early has the satisfaction of knowing that when her children are grown she will still be young. A woman of 30 and her son of 14, it seems to me, can have a great deal more in common than a woman of 45 and a boy of 14.

They say a good deal about women who marry early and find themselves worn out with caring for a brood of young children. And yet a young woman has far more resiliency in such matters than has a woman who is rapidly nearing middle age. The older woman knows that by the time her brood is grown and ready to shift for itself she will be old and weary and possibly alone. The young woman knows that by the time her brood is grown she will still be young, she can rest and regain her vitality.

And finally the woman who married early can have a career, if she wants it, and the softer things of life in middle age when she is most ready for such things.

We have pretty hard things to say as a rule concerning the man who deliberately goes into another man's home and takes his wife from him. In this particular instance the offender is a judge and that I dare say, will excuse the action to some people. There are a good many others, however, who will see it in its true light – an example of our growing intolerance.

---

20 September 1926, Monday:

UNTIL last night I had seen what were to me two great motion pictures, "The Four Horsemen of the Apocalypse" and "Kismet." Last night I saw "The Last Laugh" and it seems to me that it is a picture as nearly perfect as a picture can be.

I had read the enthusiastic reviews which attended the first showing of "The Last Laugh," in this country. And I had read later how "The Last Laugh," for reasons inexplicable to those who liked it, had been a financial failure. There is little doubt but that "The Last Laugh," were it to be produced under ordinary conditions here would also be a financial failure in Akron. There are undoubtedly however a hundred, or two or three hundred, souls who would be as delighted with it as were the score or so persons who viewed it at a private showing at the Waldorf theater Friday night.

For the benefit of these, Ike Friedman, manager of the Waldorf, is go-to give a special showing of "The Last Laugh" at a time and place to be announced later. I would like personally, when the time and place are announced, to urge all those who like the exceptional in a picture to go to see it.

Sometimes Bill and I go away for a day or so and on such occasions Mary goes home with Mrs. Harms.

Then at night when Bill and I come home the whole place seems deserted and queer. It seemed deserted and queer last night. Everything was dark and quiet. The gold fish were snuggled down in the sad and you could barely make them out. Mary's carriage with her favorite rattle suspended from the side of it looked forlorn and dejected. Her bed was standing empty and quiet and I remembered how that very morning when I was fixing her bottle she had peeked at me over the side of it and laughed. And I remembered how the night before and a good many nights before that she had fought sleep as long as she could and had finally gone to sleep in it sitting up, a weary, determined baby.

And there was her cup and her high chair and her second best bonnet and her rompers with the sprigged flowers on them and her wooden cake spoon and her favorite talcum powder box and her woolen shirt drying in the window. I wondered if they missed her as much as I did.

———————

The last week or so I read "St. Francis of Assisi" by G. K. Chesterton, "Mary and Martha," by Anker Larsen, "Pipers and a Dancer," by Stella Benson and some essays by a book collector whose name I ought to remember and don't.

I have a friend who thinks that that passage in "St. Francis of Assisi" where Chesterton offers a paraphrase of "Consider the lilies of the field," is indescribably childish and futile but to me it is one of the loveliest conceits of the book.

"St. Francis" was mystical and so is a good deal of the philosophy underlying "Mary and Martha," the story of two Scandinavian peasant children who are separated and who flower and grow old and meet again. Mary coming at last to that wisdom which Martha had had instinctively.

As for "Pipers and a Dancer" it is not a book which one likes and yet I think I shall never forget those passages which have to do with Jacob's bridge party – to which nobody came.

———————◆———————

23 September 1926, Thursday:

ONE of the things I keep worrying about is what Mitzi does with her old clothes.

A fellow who works in our office is calling up a girl just now. I don't think he knows who the girl is and he's pretty sure the girl doesn't know who he is. This is the way the conversation goes:

"Hello.
"Well, how are you. Why didn't I see you down at the East Market gardens when it opened?
"Well, and I didn't see you at the Goodyear last Saturday night, either. Aren't you going there any more?

"Naw, that's just my cough. They send me back from Denver too soon.

"No, all I wanted to ask you was how was your husband. He's pretty well, is he?

"Well, I thought so. No chance.

"Say, you haven't got a date for tomorrow night, have you?

"Well, that's all right, because I've got a date myself. I just wanted to know. "Naw, I'm gonna listen in on the fight.

"Naw, you don't know who I am. You couldn't ever find out who I am.

"Naw, it's because I'm so handsome.

"Well, you ought to know. You're pretty good looking yourself.

"Well, I told you the last time that if you'd stand in front of the Second National at 11:30, you could see me go by on the other side.

"Oh, I'd know it was you all right.

"Well, I got some work to do myself.

"Sure, that's all right. Goodbye."

And he stands up and yawns.

I have been wondering what animated those 500 or 600 Ohio men that gathered in Medina that they should have taken up bee keeping. Certainly the profits from honey can not be too enticing. The explanation must lie in the fascination surrounding the bee itself.

The bee is commonly reputed to be very intelligent, but I doubt that the bee is intelligent so much as that it works from a highly specialized instinct of some sort. This is not meant in derogation of the bee. It is merely that intelligence, as we view it, makes one individual as different from another as possible, whereas in a beehive all the workers are pretty much alike. The individual doesn't seem to amount to anything at all. The bees apparently operate only according to one-half of the famous d'Artagnan motto[271]. This, however, may be a very excellent thing. It may be that the bees have gone a step farther than intelligence and have found that instinct serves us best after all.

Whatever it is that animates the bees, however, it is proving of sufficient interest to intrigue a growing number of men.

---

[271] "Unus pro omnibus, omnes pro uno" – "One for all, all for one" – made famous by its use in the novel by Alexandre Dumas, The Three Musketeers.

25 September 1926, Saturday:

I HADN'T realized until Thursday night how short a prize-fight really is. And the fact that 100,000 or so people journeyed clear to Philadelphia to see a bout that couldn't possibly have lasted more than 30 minutes and might very well have lasted only five or six is, to my mind, convincing proof that most of our entertainments last too long.

There isn't one of us who hasn't suffered at some time or other from a Wagnerian opera, a Shaw drama or a home talent vaudeville show gotten up by the ladies' auxiliary to the W. O. O. F.[272], which last practically until the next morning. The argument, at least in the case of the home talent show was that you couldn't charge folks a dollar admission and then not give them a run for their money. Prize-fights are convincing proof that the highest business acumen is to charge them heavy on the ticket and make the entertainment snappy.

—————————

On the whole it has been a most successful week. First, the assistant society editor gave me a pair of stockings which were too large for her, thus making sure of my gratitude for life, and then I made five dollars on Mr. Tooney, as his admirers seem to call him. To be sure the five dollars was already garnished even before I got it, but even at that it is the first money I ever won. I can't help feeling that a change has taken place in my fortunes and that even greater things are in store.

—————————

It was odd Thursday night, along about a half hour later everybody had settled in bed, to hear a newsboy going along Portage Path shouting, "Extry, extry. Tooney is the new champion."

Not that I had gotten the news over our own radio, which we haven't got. But Mrs. Burt and Eleanor upstairs have a very excellent one which they let me run up an listen to between getting a drink for Mary and arguing with her about the matter of going to sleep. And so I knew all along that "Tooney" was the champion and that my two dollars and a half was thereby doubled. It was old stuff that the newsboy was shouting going down Portage Path.

---

[272] W.O.O.F. – Women of Ohio? Federation?

They say that there was a good crowd down at the Beacon office but they tell me too that there is no doubt but that the radio has sort of spoiled the old time newspaper party. When I first came to work down here there wasn't the voting on a bond issue or the nomination of a dog catcher that wasn't made the excuse for party with all the help staying over time and the crowd hanging around till midnight at which time sandwiches and coffee were served. Along about 2 a. m. the Beacon sent us girls home in taxicabs and we felt that at last we were living life as it ought to be lived.

Nowadays people stay at home and listen in on the radio, they go to bed early and when the newsboys go along with the extra you don't hear a single window going up.

Now that the music season is about to open this department suggest that everybody start it off in proper style by reading or rereading "Jean Christophe."

1 October 1926, Friday:

BERT ECKERMANN[273] has taken off eight pounds. His vest is just practically hanging on him.

Harry Welch[274] has a new tie, grey with red polka dots.

Dan Gallagher was a visitor in this afternoon. He left a card showing all the newspapers he'd ever worked for – 25 of 'em. Dan said there might have been more than that but he couldn't remember exactly. He also said that all newspapers were great.

It can't be much fun to be a president's son. They won't let John Coolidge read his math notes.

When they fumigated Central high school the other day they unwittingly killed off all the things in the aquarium, all, that is except a lone mud turtle.

[273] Akron resident, William Egbert "Bert" Eckerman (1867-1943); Detective for the City Police Force; residing at 125 West Thornton st. in 1910-1920, 24 Casterton av. in 1930, 173 Hyde av. in 1940.

[274] Akron resident, Harry A. Welch (c.1871-aft1930); Detective for the City Police Force; residing at 1310 South High st. in 1900, 192 West Thornton st. in 1910-1930

It's warming up again.

A girl paid a two dollar down payment on a dress she didn't want the other day just to get away from a persistent clerk.

Ed Harter received Wednesday a very satisfying consignment of Virginia paw-paws[275].

And speaking of paw-paws, why doesn't somebody around Akron start raising them? When I was a child over in Indiana paw-paws were one of the things that made the coming of fall so satisfying. Everybody ate them. I wouldn't be surprised to find that it was this steady diet of paw-paws which made everybody in Indiana so literary. Certainly there is something about a paw-paw which induces a mellow contemplation in the eater.

Paw-paws have gotten as far as Columbus, O. Down there on market days you can pick up for a small sum whole baskets of them. It is reasonably certain that if they would grow around Columbus they would grow around Akron.

And yet people around here for the most part don't seem to know anything about them. It is a great pity.

---

2 October 1926, Saturday:

I LOVE little kittens. They are nice from the very beginning. Their tongues are pink. Their tails stick straight up. Their claws are like little pins. They are graceful. And soft. In their insides are little violin strings which hum and hum.

I love stubby umbrellas. You can put them in a trunk. They are beautiful in the rain. They do not poke people's eyes out. Nor stick in the cracks of the sidewalks. They blend with what you are wearing. They give color to dull days.

I love clean handkerchiefs. They make you feel refined. They are soft to the nose. They may also be used as shoe buffers, picnic napkins, hand towels, sponges, dust clothes, bandages, playthings for the baby, lamp shades, chest protectors, type-writer cleaners, spectacle polishers and saxophone mufflers.

---

[275] A North American fruit similar in taste to a papaya, but moreso a mango-banana

I love October. The leaves grow red and brown. The spiders spin great floating webs. The sky is that blue that Greeks speak of when they remember the Mediterranean.

I love the Union station. The trains come and people climb down from them. Then other people climb up the steps and the conductor picks up his little footstool. Up on the bridge young men and old men, married men and widowers, happy men and men reluctant to go home hang over the rail and watch the trains go by.

I love my desk. It holds old shoes, old handkerchiefs, old letters, chewing gum, safety pins, soap, a nail file, books that should go to the library, memoranda, tickets, membership cards, pamphlets, typewriter brushes, newspaper clippings, dust cloths, pencils, stationery, telephone numbers, rejection slips, paper weights, face powder, cold cream, copy paper, a dime bank and some keys. I go away from it at night and the next morning it is still there, not a paper moved, not a pencil out of place. I love my desk.

The exact date of the showing of "The Last Laugh," about which more persons are interested than I had at first thought possible, will be announced within a few days. Meanwhile it may be of interest to know that Akron has a "Film Guild." Since the Film Guild has just come into existence and since its membership extends more or less to any of those persons who are interested in films which are above the ordinary it is impossible to say at the present writing just what its program is to be. However it is encouraging to know that there are now banded together in Akron a number of persons who are prepared to give their support to films which may be artistic successes but which are commercial failures, such films, for instance, as "The Last Laugh."

Ike Friedman[276], manager of the Waldorf and other motion picture houses in Akron, has been a little reluctant about having it known that he was instrumental in organizing the Film Guild owing to the fact that Mr. Friedman's avowed business policy is to show in his theaters only pictures with a popular appeal. He is afraid apparently that some persons will get the notion that he has somehow turned highbrow.

The facts however are as stated above. A partial list of the newly organized guild contains the names of Mr. and Mrs. C. L. Knight, Carita McEbright, Wilbur Peat, Grace Z. Brown, Caroline Karnaghan, Ruth Karnaghan, Fred Barton, Marguerite Albrecht Barton, Mr. and Mrs. L. E. Judd, Marjorie Barkley McClure, V. D. Lidyard, Howard Wolf, Frank Eblen, William Rigby, E. H. Schwan, Luarine Wanamaker Schwan, Herman Fetzer, James Scott, Fred E. Ayer, Harry August, Jack Kelly, Mrs. M. E. Winter, James P. Dunlevy, Mrs. Philip Chaplin Jones, Malvyn Wachner, William T. Perry, Hugh Allen,

---

[276] Akron resident, Ike Friedman (1892-1938); Manager of Real Estate Co., residing at North Valley st. in 1910-1920

Ernst Lehman, Mr. and Mrs. Victor Rodzianko, Mrs. James H. Nesbitt, D. C. Rybolt, T. Ralph Ridley, Earle Poling, E. J. Samuel and Evan Williams, jr.

※ ❧ ❧ ◆ ❧ ❧ ※

5 October 1926, Tuesday:

I WAS reading in a woman's magazine last night – The Ladies' Home Journal I think it was – the first installment of the life history of the Queen of England. Katherine Woodward who wrote the story, told of the shyness of the queen, of her absolute inability to make small talk, of her reticence in discussing her personal affairs, of her devotion to her husband and family, of her long work day, of her pride in her distinguished lineage.

And I though as I read of another queen – a queen who is to visit our own shores shortly[277], a queen who feels no embarrassment when she sees her name affixed to an advertisement for a cold cream, a queen who writes, or who permits to have written under her signature, foolish blather for the newspapers, a queen who permits a newspaper woman to travel with her so that what she has for breakfast may promptly be reported in Tulsa and Dubuque and Burscough, a queen whom the movie people feel no embarrassment to approaching on the matter of little contracts, a queen who babbles and babbles and babbles about her democracy.

If Queen Marie of Romania should ultimately consent to appear as the Madonna in Mr. Max Reinhardt's next production of "The Miracle" there is no one in the world, I am sure, who would feel the slightest bit surprised about it.

My own personal taste in the matter of queens, however, runs to Mrs. Windsor of England. She may wear awful hats, but at any rate she wears them with dignity.

———

And while we're on the subject of royalty, I wonder if the Prince of Wales is as popular as he used to be. I saw a picture of him yesterday, which showed him laying in his great-grandmama Victoria's arms. He looked like an awfully nice baby. You can fancy that years ago when women looked at that picture they thought how the Prince of Wales

---

[277] Referencing Queen Marie of Romania (1875-1938) who arrived to visit the U.S. on October 18, 1926 with her son Prince Nicolas and daughter Princess Ileana. She first visited with President Calvin Coolidge in Washington D.C., then onto N.Y. and then traveled on a special train across the country to Seattle.

---

would grow into a fine upstanding young man, how he would go to school and become awfully smart, how he would travel and the people would adore him and how finally he would marry some nice girl and sit decorously on England's throne.

Instead of which the Prince of Wales has elected to cut capers like his royal grandfather, only with this difference – Edward VII, conversationally, seems to have been capable occasionally of a snappy come-back.

You probably noticed in Jake Falstaff's column, Monday, that "The Last Laugh" will be shown at the Waldorf theatre, Friday night at 11:10. Tickets will not be sold at the box office so that reservation will have to be by letter. And that is about all except that I still think "The Last Laugh" is the best picture I ever saw.

Following the discussion last night, which comes up shortly after the first of every month on "What Do We Do With All Our Money?" Bill asked me what I'd do if I had some money anyway, and I said I'd buy a lot of shoes with it and some hem-stitched sheets and a new kitchen table, and he said I had more hired girl's dreams than anybody he knew of. Then he asked me how I was getting along with my diet and I acted sort of embarrassed. Herman Fetzer says, however, that he thinks Tiny Englebeck[278] was better looking before he started to diet.

---

8 October 1926, Friday:

YESTERDAY I went up to the Masonic temple to have luncheon with Edith Clift who's been having the cooking school up there and who should arrive also but Sarah Stimmel[279] from Akron U. "Do you remember," she said, "how you called me up one day to ask if a girl who hadn't had home economics training couldn't be as good a housekeeper as one who had had? And then two days later you went and got married. Why didn't you tell me?"

---

[278] Akron resident, Amos Harmon "Tiny" Englebeck (1885-1952); Trial Lawyer and leader in the local Republican Party

[279] Akron resident, Sarah E. Stimmel (c.1871-aft1920) University Economics Teacher; residing at Corson av. in 1920

"Why," I said, "I don't remember that part of it but I'll tell you one thing – I wish I had had more home economics when I was in school and less trigonometry and I wish I had spent more time learning dressmaking and less time playing Chopin waltzes."

"That's just what a lot of the girls tell me after they've been out of school awhile," she said, "but when I tell the students that they won't believe me."

When ever I say things like that however I always feel a little conscience smitten. It sounds as though I thought life for a girl ought to be all dressmaking and cooking and that there oughtn't to be any mathematics and music in it at all. As a matter of fact, I don't believe that but I do believe that the proportions ought to be changed.

It seems to me for instance that children oughtn't to take music lessons with the sole idea of being able to play "The Joyous Farmer" when company comes. It seems to me that most children oughtn't to be allowed to perform musically in public under any circumstances. What I do think is that every child ought to know musical history, that he ought to be able to write his own little pieces and put them together with some regard for harmony and that he ought to know considerable about musical appreciation.

A program of this sort could be spread out over a good many years so that a young person could become musically cultured in course of time without all these dreadful hours and hours of practising. I think that a good many music teachers would be glad to give the youngsters who come to them that sort of training if the youngsters' mothers would allow it. But the greater number of them won't. Unless little Elizabeth Ann has a new piece every week which she can somehow muddle through to the infinite torture of the neighbors they won't believe that she is getting along.

Granting however that my notions did prevail an average of 30 minutes a day coupled with attendance at a good concert occasionally would result in considerable musical culture by the time a young woman was ready to be graduated from collage. The hours saved, could be devoted to the designing of her own clothes.

It is a pity I think that we can't design our own clothes. There must be something as satisfying about it as writing a sonnet or painting a picture, I feel this rather keenly because the best that I can do in the sewing line is a bit of occasional hemming and, once in a while, a fairly satisfactory darn on Bill's socks. There is nobody to blame for these short-comings. All my feminine relatives used to urge me to learn to sew. But I wouldn't believe them. "Some day," I reasoned, "I will write a successful novel and then I will pay other people to design my clothes." But it doesn't always work out that way. Nowadays when I see whole tables full of lovely remnants down at the stores it breaks my heart to think that I wouldn't have the slightest notion of how to put them together.

———❦———

12 October 1926, Tuesday:

IT hasn't seemed so long as that, but it was a year ago today that John McCarthy died.

Most of the time I forget that John McCarthy is gone. I see a little man going along the street, and I think, "There goes John," and then afterwards I remember.

I guess there are others who remember too. They tell me that every once in a while members of the Actors' club which John McCarthy founded go out to his grave and place flowers there. I keep wondering and wondering what it was that John McCarthy did which makes us care so much.

———

Some day I hope to have it explained to me by someone who understands such matters, why doctors are so sensitive. My great-grandfather was a doctor[280], but so far as I know, he wasn't sensitive. He just hitched up the old mare to the family buggy and went around through the countryside, doling out pills and calomel and checking the youngsters under the chin. He was married twice, and I think both of his wives were happy. I don't think they could have been, though, if he had been sensitive.

The first doctor who ever got mad at me was one who objected to my calling an osteopath a member of the medical profession. Of course I suppose that technically I was wrong – I've never had it made very clear to me – but to my mind a person who knew about nerves and ganglia and who had taken examinations and was in the business of making people well was a member of the medical profession. Granting that I was wrong I still can't see why the doctor in question couldn't have smiled at my ignorance instead of getting mad about it.

———

[280] She is referring to her great-grandfather, Dr. James M. Adams (1820-1894)

The next doctor to get mad at me was one who wrote me a lengthy letter containing a great many long words, among them a very long word very badly misspelled. My crime had been to set down in print the details of a simple operation as it had been told to me. So far as I knew I was being absolutely honest. The doctor didn't think so though. He accused me of perverting truth for the sake of sensationalism and his language was anything but pretty.

Now a third doctor is mad because he thinks that in setting down the details of the organization of a doctors' orchestra the other night, I was trying to be funny. An orchestra, particularly a doctors' orchestra, he maintains, is no joke. Well, I don't think so either. I was merely trying to be interesting. If anybody thinks that it's easy to be interesting day after day over births, deaths, lost kittens, suicides, bank forgers, family reunions, G. A. R. picnics, lion tamers, four generations, cross country hikers, child prodigies, cooking schools, one-legged men, runaway matches and doctors' orchestras, they should just try it.

Of course, I suppose doctors have lots of troubles. There have been a lot of ads in the papers lately urging people to pay their doctor bills and I suppose the whole medical association is so weighed down with ethics and dead beats and ailing humanity that it can't help going about after a while feeling heavy and portentous.

The nicest doctor I ever knew, though, didn't have a chip on his shoulder or, in fact, anywhere about him that I could discover. About all he ever did was laugh and occasionally try out the Charleston. And he seems to have been a real good doctor, too.

---

22 October 1926, Friday:

M R. ATCHLEY over at the N. O. P. Co., was telling me something this morning about herdics. A herdic it seems was one of those mule drawn busses which years ago need to travel out E. Market st. to Middlebury. I never had a very clear idea until now about Middlebury. (It was where Arlington st. runs into E. Market.) The herdics held eight persons apiece and they ran every half hour or so. The driver would go along the street and whenever anybody ran out and signaled him he would stop. It was also his duty to feed and carry the mules and put them up for the night, collect the nickels on the herdics, put straw on the floor to keep the passengers' feet warm, keep a fire going in the stove and promise to call out the stops for service passengers. In order to prevent catastrophes the speed limit was held down strictly to five miles an hour.

Then the herdics were succeeded by strap railways. A strap railway is one in which the rails are laid down on top the street. The city put down blocks of wood between the rails and in due course of time the blocks were worn out by the feet of the mules. Then the railway company was obliged to replace the blocks from its own pockets.

Ever since that time, according to Mr. Atchley, the street railway company has been obliged to pay for the paving between the rails. It certainly was an unlucky precedent.

As for the herdics they have gone but you know the habits that things have of swinging around in a sort of circle. We now have one man busses.

Mr. Atchley told me things about the conductors and motormen that I hadn't known. For instance each one gets one free suit a year. If he wants to get a new suit and have it charged he can and the company will guarantee the account. There is a clubroom for the men and the company insures them against accident and death.

Mr. Atchley says that he thinks the company has now the politest men it ever had in its history. The most neatly dressed ones, he says, are pretty nearly always the married ones.

It's a great pity that most of you aren't going to be able to see the lovely programs which the Ohio Newspaper Women's association is going to have for its dinner at the Woman's City club Oct. 20. Coburn Mueser[281] is giving the dinner. The Columbia Printing Co. made the programs. It printed them in a beautiful bronze which looks almost like engraving. Jane Barnhardt's[282] art class up at the university hand painted them with clusters of autumn flowers and now at the present moment a lot of people are here in the office tying them with bronze and orange and olive green ribbons. Carl Stubig is helping with the tying. For a long time he was handing in the queerest combinations. Whenever he was fixing up a bunch of grapes he'd tie it with scarlet ribbon which didn't look at all well. It then developed that Carl's idea was to get a color that was just the opposite of the one on the program. We gave him a long lecture on color combinations and now he's the most artistic tyer of them all.

---

[281] Akron resident, James Coburn Musser (1891-1965)

[282] Akron resident, Jane S. Barnhardt (1878-1964), Art teacher, residing at 142 Marvin avenue in 1940 census

Fred and Wilfred

FRED KELLY, the one who writes for the magazines, has a Chinese cook named Wilfred. Wilfred was born in Seattle but he has been back to the old country several times.

Fred and Wilfred, three Airedales, a cat and a Scotch terrier named Judy all live in Fred's farm house over in Peninsula. It is a snug little farm house all spick and span and new with ivory wood work and green doors and sprigged wall paper and it is all full of the antiques which Fred has been collecting. In the spring time there are apple blossoms boughs which throw shadows across the dining room windows.

There are four hundred or so acres around the farm house or maybe it is 2,000. Anyways Fred doesn't intend to do anything with his acres. He just wants them around so he can go out and take a deep breath occasionally.

You would think that a chap like Wilfred would get sort of lonesome out there with nothing to look at but acres and nothing to do but make chop suey for Fred and rag out of soup bone for the Airedales. But not so Wilfred. You see Fred knows a lot of parlor tricks. He can make a quarter go through a china saucer and he can tie his hands back of him with a lot of rope and then get out again as slick as anything. Whenever Fred sees a restless look coming into Wilfred's eye he immediately dispatches him for a couple of ropes and a saucer.

Wilfred is not a quiet Chinaman, neither is he taciturn. Fred's old pet Airedale is Badger who is 15-years old. Badger's eyesight is failing him and he is almost stone deaf. Whenever Fred speaks to him he has to shout. Accordingly Wilfred has inferred that in order to speak to any dog it is necessary to shout. His shoutings resound about the farm house all day long and they also resound through a good portion of the acres.

Another odd thing about Wilfred is that he has a sense of humor. The other day as an editor was about to enter the house Wilfred started talking Chinese very fast and Fred ostensibly started taking it down on the typewriter. "Now what was that again," said Fred. "Wait a minute I didn't quite get it." The editor stood mystified in the doorway for a minute and Wilfred nearly burst with satisfaction. He seemed to think it was almost better than the saucer trick.

We were out to Fred's for supper the other night and Wilfred made us wonderful chop suey and rice and delicious little cakes made of crab flakes mixed with egg and dropped into deep fat. Afterwards we thought we were going to get through the evening all right. But not. All at once, right in the midst of a discussion are women better letter writers than men, Fred jumped up exclaiming, "Say, did you ever see this one?" and he went and came back with two pieces of rope.

Well, we tied him up and then he remembered that he had to have a sheet and he went and got it and it was a new one with the label still on it and Fred said that was always the way at his house, he had to keep buying new sheets all the time because he kept forgetting to send the old ones to the laundry and then we tied him up again and put the sheet over him and the trick was a tremendous success and just at the very climax of it there was a sound out in the dining room and we looked and there was Wilfred sitting on a dining room chair watching Fred and all doubled up with laughter.

You know the way small boys look at Babe Ruth. Well, that was the way Wilfred was looking at Fred.

He got awfully embarrassed when he found out he was being observed of course. He went out and yelled at all of the Airedales and then pretty soon there was a sound as though the entire dishpan full of supper dishes had landed on the floor.

* * *

2 November 1926, Tuesday:

IN CASE you didn't see "The Last Laugh" at is previous showing this is to tell you that it will be shown again Thursday night at the Waldorf theater at 11:10. Be sure to go if you like exceptional pictures.

Last night I thought of a little boy whom I hadn't thought of for a long, long time. The newspaper women's convention was over and I was getting ready for bed. It had been a wonderful convention. We had talked about sex appeal and the newspaper and whether "Love Bound" had been a better serial than "The Flapper Wife," we had talked about urging editors not to re-write our stories, about whether crime should be played up or not, about the troubles of society editors, about the difficulties of writing humor, about the money that could be gotten from writing for trade journals, about Bud Stillman's sweetheart and whether he would marry her, about Flo Leeds and Queen

Marie and Herbert Swope and the New York Central and broiled chicken and fur costs and whether newspapers ought to pay for your expenses to conventions.

And then when I was getting ready for bed I kept thinking "The world is too much with us, late and soon, getting and spending---"

I couldn't remember how the rest of it went and so I got up and went to the book case and got an old school book, "Twelve Centuries of English Poetry and Prose," and looked up Wordsworth. Before I found Wordsworth however, I came upon a name half erased from the fly leaf. The name was Kenneth Lelansky[283].

It had been Kenneth's book and he had sold it to me second hand. He had tried to erase his name from it but the erasing, done I dare say with a school rubber, hadn't been successful.

And now he is gone and there was left of him only that shadowy name traced in a prim school boy hand and only family discernible in the dim light. Away off somewhere, somebody was playing a Mendelssohn Song Without Words.

Kenneth was shy and quiet and he had great dark eyes. There was a girl who sat on the other side of the room from him who reverently and silently loved him. She wore her hair in two great braids about her head.

I don't know whether Kenneth was aware of this adoration. I think that his mind was too full of Lancelot and Galahad to have any room for present day matters. And besides he was such a little boy. I suppose when he saw the girls hanging over the football heroes and the lads who made the track events, he thought that it must be pleasant to be so much admired and then forgot about the matter altogether.

The girl who loved him cried when they told us how sick he was. But when they told us he was dead she said nothing at all. Afterwards, when school was out, she went for a long walk all alone.

It is hard to count how many years have come and gone since then. The girl who loved him has gone far away. Her letters say that she is having all sorts of beautiful experiences.

---

[283] Akron resident, Kenneth H. Lelansky (1896-????)

I hope that they will always remain beautiful. But I think that some time she will envy Kenneth who went to sleep dreaming still of Galahad.

13 Nov 1926, Saturday:

HUGH WALPOLE, who was lecturing in Akron last night, thinks that women don't write as good novels as men. Not that Mr. Walpole intends to make any sex distinctions. His contention merely is that women, up to date, haven't written as good novels as men. Men novelists, he pointed out during the course of a conversation, had conceived and executed some very remarkable portraits of women but where would we find a woman novelist who had drawn an authentic portrait of a man? The portraits were invariably too sentimental, too romantic.

Mr. Walpole is of the opinion that the Hall-Mills murder is the most fascinating murder that ever was. Were he making a novel of it he would most certainly make Henry Stevens the culprit. It gave him a sort of odd sensation, he said, to come to America and find the papers so full of it. Four years ago when he was here the case was having its first run. Now he comes back and the papers are full of it again. He wondered at the calling car which was found in the rector's boot. "From the fingerprints," he said, "it would appear that every person in America had handled that card."

Mr. Walpole was sincerely grieved that America had no royalty. "You are such a romantic people," he said, "I would think that you could dress up Gene Tunney and Gloria Swanson and pay them a salary just to go about and be admired. It is evident that Mr. Coolidge would never do for such a role. The only advantage in sending Mr. Coolidge about would be that he would undoubtedly economize on the expense account."

It was far from a good thing, he thought, that everyone should be allowed to vote. The ratio of stupidity to intelligence was three, or so, to one and that allowed very dreadful things to come to pass in a country. Mr. Walpole would impose rigid intelligence tests on those who were to vote. What sort of intelligence tests, however, he didn't know, certainly examinations weren't the least bit of good.

The ratio of bad novels to good novels was even worse. If I recall correctly, it was something like four to one. Mr. Walpole would be only too glad if some system of censorship could be devised which should do away with vapid, neurotic novels. To show how sincere he was Mr. Walpole said he would even be content to be banned himself it it would do any good.

Mr. Walpole didn't think that he was at all dismal in the endings of his novels.

"We have gotten," he said, "beyond the age of thinking that for two people to get married constitutes a happy ending. We know too much. I try to bring my novels to a satisfactory spiritual and mental conclusion and that is far better than a happy ending in the material sense.

The Russians, he said, weren't really so pessimistic as we think. They just keep getting sadder and sadder over the misery of life until things touch bottom and then, knowing that matters can't possibly be any worse they cheer up remarkably.

And that is about all about Mr. Walpole. He looks like his pictures, his face is ruddy and he wears one ring on each hand. He thinks he has had a fearfully inadequate education and is enthusiastic over football. He prepares his lectures carefully and can deliver either one of them at call. He has mastered time tables. He is polite. He would be a very agreeable person to have about the house.

27 Nov 1926, Saturday:

THE revelations about the marriage of Consuelo Vanderbilt to the Duke of Marlborough are rather disconcerting. For a good many years now Mrs. O. H. P. Belmont, Consuelo's mother, had been one of my cherished figures. She had dared to get a divorce when divorces were far from fashionable and had brooked social displeasure in consequence. And when Bishop Manning had written her for funds to carry on the building of his church she had written him a highly caustic letter asking him if he had forgotten, in his zeal, that he was appealing for funds to a divorced woman.

"Now there," I said to myself, "is a woman with spirit."

And now the Consuelo-Marlborough affair has come along and spoil things. It seems that Mrs. Belmont even went so far as to have rather vulgar hysterics. She maintained that if Consuelo would not give up her admirer, a certain Mr. Rutherfurd, and marry the Duke, she, Consuelo's mother, would most assuredly kill Mr. Rutherfurd the next time she saw him and then Consuelo would be subjected to the anguish of seeing her mother strung up for murder. Just how personable a man Mr. Rutherfurd was I don't know. It is said he owns a great many East Side tenements. But any way it was a dreadful lot of bosh to tell a 17-year-old girl.

I'm afraid I shall never like Mrs. Belmont again. I suppose the safest procedure would be never to have any idols of any kind.

We were speaking a while ago of the disappearance of muff and hair ribbons. So far as the hair ribbons are concerned I can't say that I resent their passing very keenly. There were certain difficulties in getting them tied and in case you used one of those patent clasps it was almost certain to fasten to a very small strand of hair and then pull like everything.

Muffs though were something else again. To my mind one of those little barrel muffs was a highly satisfactory accessory to a street costume. If you didn't know what to do with your hands, and most persons don't, a muff made the solution to the problem.

It is easy of course to understand why the muff disappeared. Fur coats became common. So long as they had pockets in them, they were all right. You could go along on a cold day and be snug. But this year's fur coats don't seem to have pockets in them. I've hunted all through mine, the mush-rat one, and I can't find a sign of a pocket except for a little flummy [sic] diddle on the inside for my handkerchief. My hands just have to flop about aimlessly. Every once in awhile when the wind blows cold, I find myself yearning for a muff.

I don't see why cloth suits with muff accompaniments shouldn't come back in style. You can get lines from a cloth suit that you can never, never get from fur. And with a muff to keep your hands warm and a bit of fur to match about the neck of the suit, there would really be nothing else which could possibly be desired.

Chapter IX.

Demi-Tasse & Mrs. Grundy in The year 1927

Demi – Tasse

- and -

Mrs. Grundy

- by -

Josephine Van de Grift

———⟡———

1 January 1927, Saturday:

RESOLUTIONS, 1927

O laugh things off
⊤To get new hat
To get some phonograph albums
To answer letters immediately
To start a Christmas savings fund
To take a vacation
To get a grand piano
To get a chest of drawers
To move
To acquire dignity
To make a sponge cake with lemon filling
To read medieval history
To learn to drive a car
To write a sonnet
To read The Cloister and the Hearth

To get a hair cut
To go swimming
To pay cash
To get up in time for Bill to shave
To go without lunch
To play less solitaire
To get a new typewriter ribbon
To put more dimes in Mary's bank
To write to those folks up along the Hudson
To memorize people's names
To go to Cleveland some Sunday morning
To have a telephone in the new office next September
To buy some writing paper
To buy a pen
To buy brunet powder
To pay a professional visit to Pauline Heibert
To fix the pocket in the fur coat
To sent the spring coat to the cleaners
To get home earlier in the afternoons
To have more company
To have more baked chicken
To put less butter in the stuffing
To buy a new lamp shade
To have Bill's picture framed
To put new oiled paper in the bread box
To be nicer

---

5 January 1927, Wednesday:

BILL and I were coming down to work this morning in the chevvy just as usual when a traffic policeman stopped us. "Where's your 1927 license?" he barked.

I was waiting for Bill to sass him back because I've learned from long experience that Bill won't permit anybody, not anybody, to use a high tone with him. You can fancy how surprised I was then when Bill answered gently.

"I was just going down to get it."

"Get it?" snorted the traffic policeman. "Why haven't you got it already?"

"I haven't had time," said Bill plaintively.

"You've had since December 10," said the traffic policeman, "and then you say you haven't had time."

"Well I haven't had time," said Bill, "I was just going down to get it now."

"What I ought to do to you," said the traffic policeman, "Is to tag you. I've got orders to tag everybody that hasn't got their license."

"I'm going down to get it now," reiterated Bill patiently and the traffic policeman said "huh" and waved his hand sort of disgusted like and we started off down the street.

You never saw such a magical change then as came over Bill.

"Well, why didn't he tag me," he said belligerently, "instead of stopping me and taking up a lot of my time. There's a fellow that's got an old license and there's another and —"

He couldn't see any more just then and had to stop counting.

"I bet you could have told that cop a lot of things if you'd a wanted," I said admiringly.

"I guess I could have," said Bill and he went up and parked the chevvy on Summit st., just as usual.

I guess he didn't realize how upsetting it is to a family's morale for a wife to behold her husband's behavior before a traffic cop.

I was just reading an article, reprinted from Exceptional Film Plays, which tells me about "Polikushka[284]." I hadn't known that "Polikushka" was written by Tolstoi [sic] and I had had an idea all along that Polikushka was probably a girl. But it seems that Polikushka is a drunken, thieving, roving stableman about whom a humorous and pathetic tale has been woven. The part is played by Ivan Moskvin, whom a good many of us will recall as having done Tsar Fyodar and Luka, the pilgrim, in "The Lower Depths."

---

[284] Polikushka is written by Leo Tolstoy and there was a movie of the same title in 1922.

So now I want to see "Polikushka" more than ever. In case you haven't noticed any of the announcements yet it's being shown under the auspices of Akron Film guild, Friday night at the Waldorf theater at 8 and 10 o'clock.

<hr />

8 January 1927, Saturday:

"I MOST sincerely solicit your good wishes for my birthday," writes Anna Grabill, "which this year I see takes place at no other time than May 13 and Friday.

"Well, several years ago the same thing happened and the only unusual thing which took place was my first hearse ride. It was really the ride of a little patient of mine who passed away at 2 a.m. and the driver was good enough to see me safely to my home. Anyways, let's hope that all will be as well in 1927."

<hr />

Concerning this matter of birthdays I think that there are any number of women who are entirely too sensitive about mentioning them. A friend of mine was utterly crushed last year because nobody remembered her birthday. If she had started talking about it two weeks ahead of time the way I do there wouldn't be the slightest excuse for anybody forgetting. Although my birthday isn't entirely over yet, it even now (it is Friday afternoon when I write) has been unbelievably successful. There have been greetings and a flour sifter which I've been wanting ever since I was married and a bright new five dollar bill from a gentleman who was one of my very earliest acquaintances, and roses and things to eat. And Wilbur Peat has promised to go to the 10 cent store and buy me a tea cup and saucer.

Wilbur just came in with the cup and saucer. It is a lovely Czecho-Slovakian one with great gaudy flowers. I don't think he got it at the 10-cent store.

<hr />

And then Thursday night Mrs. Cleveland gave one of her famous dinners. There were 21 of us there. The board just groaned and groaned. After loads and loads of things had been served doughnuts and coffee were brought in and I thought my, what a nice dessert, only to find out that dessert was still to come. It was too, too, much.

A part of the time we talked about what we would do with a million dollars if we had it. I thought I would build me a house and then stay in it, but the others were all for buying a lot of clothes and traveling. All but one. Mrs. Cleveland said she would take her million and help all the poor people she knew.

I think that probably all of us, way down in our hearts, would be glad to spend a million on the poor if we thought it would do any good. But the minute you begin thinking about that sort of thing all the misery and wretchedness of the world loom up so great that you don't know where to start. And a million dollars doesn't begin to cover things.

Afterwards I walked home and looked in people's windows. It is a friendly thing which people do when they leave the window shades up at night. It permits those of us who are going by outside to peek in and share their firesides with them.

There was one house which I had always wondered about. It was always so neat and so proper outside that I wondered if perhaps the woman who kept it didn't keep newspapers on the floor of the front hall. But Thursday night when I looked in I saw a man sitting in his shirt sleeves by the fire and smoking so I knew that everything was all right.

Further on up the street there was a house in which two people were playing the piano and the violin. The windows were frosted so that I couldn't see clearly and at first I thought it was a woman at the piano and her husband playing the violin. But later it looked as though it were a brother and sister. The music sounded very happy.

And after that there was Harry Page's house, all full of lights and with the Christmas wreaths still in the windows and the Christmas festoons on the chandeliers.

It seemed as though, all along the way, everybody was happy.

---

31 January 1927, Monday:

WE WERE discussing last night whether Charlie Chaplin will find himself a ruined man after his divorce trial. Of course it is hard to predetermine such matters but it seems to me that the Peaches-Bunny Browning affair is going to be of considerable help to Charlie when his own time of stress occurs. A good many people are becoming rapidly disgusted with the gold diggers. They will see in Lita only another version of Peaches. Nobody can be found at this stage of the game who cares in the least what becomes of Peaches. I doubt whether they will care greatly what becomes of Lita. And they may remember, when it is all over, that there was a time when Charlie made them laugh.

The drawback of course that Charlie rarely made a club woman laugh and it is the club women who rule the country.

A Mill st., bakery is having a sale on fruit cake – cakes I dare say, which were left over from Christmas. Fruit cakes and violins and oriental rugs all seem to be alike in one respect – they improve with age. I've been wondering though just how old a fruit cake could get and still be edible. It seems to me I read a story some time ago of a piece of wedding fruit cake which was 50 years old or so.

I read something very disillusioning about Jack London last night. It seems that he had false teeth and he put them on the chair beside his bed every night.

Bill didn't seem to be interested at all in the information. "I suppose he put 'em there so he could watch 'em ache," he said and went on reading the New York Times.

Grandmother always liked to tell the story about the first time she wore her false teeth. She went up to the dentist and got them and then went down to order the groceries. She tried and tried to say "a loaf of bread and a pound of butter" but no sound would come. So then Grandmother took out her false teeth and was able to get along better.

The sweeper-up over at the Colonial one day found, among other things, a set of false teeth in his dust pan. Some time later a woman applied at the office.

"I lost my false teeth at the matinee here yesterday," she said, "and I was wondering if by any chance you found them."

"Why yes, I think we did," said the manager handing them to her and the woman immediately clapped them in to her mouth.

I HAVE often wondered about the state of mind of a burglar. Is he a timid soul driven by desperate by the wailings of seven hungry children, is he a hardened soul who discounts the fact that every family harbors at least one light sleeper, or is he just stupid?

Literature has invariably painted the burglar as a person either to be admired or to be feared or to be pitied or to be laughed at. People who hang around jails a lot however, turnkeys, deputy sheriffs, newspaper men and the like, never seem to feel much interest in him. I can't recall that I ever met an out and out burglar myself but I have met forgers, hold up men, Italian vendetta men and automobile thieves. Aside from explanations as to how the arresting officer made his regrettable mistake they all seemed singularly lacking in imagination.

There were sounds of prowling feet along the walk back of our apartment the other night and also at one time an ominous crash on the back porch so that I changed my original intention of going to bed and sat up and read instead. I kept assuring myself all along that it was all imagination but what was my surprise to be told today that the neighbor next door on that very night and at that very time had seen a man's face at the window. She had sat up all night in consequence and was worn and haggard the next day. If she had only had the courage to run over and tell me about it we could have screeched together and been a great deal of comfort to one another.

When I was younger and had better ideas about burglars I had always though that when the day came that I should actually discover one under the bed I would engage him in a discussion of philosophy or else invite him to play the piano and so gradually dissuade him from the idea of housebreaking and send him on his way a better man.

This was because I had seen a sweet play about a burglar. There was a girl and she was just trying on her wedding dress when the burglar broke into the room.

The girl was giving him a very uplifting talk and the burglar was practically dissolved in tears when the girl's father came into the room. It developed then that the girl's father and the burglar had met before and they were mortal enemies. While they were fighting back and forth you were able to piece out the plot which was that in the beginning the burglar had been as honest a fellow as ever lived until this other fellow had come along and stolen his wife. The burglar went straight to perdition then. As for the girl, "You think she is yours," screamed the burglar, "but she is mine – mine."

It all ended real nice with the girl and the burglar telling the other fellow what they thought of him and then deciding that they at least would live honestly and happily forever after.

I suppose it was from that play that I got my elevated ideas about burglars. It's only lately that I've begun to have suspicious.

⌒⌒⌒◆⌒⌒⌒

5 February 1927, Saturday:

THIS is not the column which was to have appeared in this space today. The column which was to have appeared concerned Baer's Agricultural almanac which John Richardson sent over to me a day or so ago. All yesterday afternoon I was going through that almanac, gleaning out choice bits of information – about eclipses and the grape crop and how to scrub a carpet on the floor. It made a dandy long column.

This morning I learned that Herman did exactly the same thing on Jan. 21. "If you'd just read the paper occasionally – "

Well, I do read the paper. First I read about the Bungles and the Gumps and Little Orphan Annie and then I read the Hollywood Girl and then I read the society column to see if anybody's engaged and then I look over the personals to see who's got new babies and then after that I read Herman's column. I save it for the last that way for the same reason that people keep their apple pie for the end of the meal. How I happened to miss the one about the almanac I don't know.

The deep and underlying thought back of all this is that a thing can look like plagiarism a lot of times when it isn't. To me it is the most natural thing in the world that a number of persons should start thinking about the same thing at about the same time. We grow up under pretty much the same conditions. We read the same newspapers and magazines. We are confronted with the same problems. Why shouldn't we start drawing the same conclusions?

The patent office at Washington says that applications for patents come in waves. One month they will all be for electric washing machines. The next month they will all be for glass door knobs.

Claude Bragdon, when he was writing his "Four Dimensional Vistas," was told by a friend that he had better hurry up and get it published because a man over in Russia was working out the same idea.

My ideas almost always turn out to be something that somebody else has thought about too. I suppose it's because I'm kinda pokey that the other fellow always gets his ideas published first.

––––––––––

"I was just noticing this morning," remarked the society editor a while ago, "the disappearance of the black umbrella. The only black umbrella I saw on the way down to work this morning was one belonging to a nice old lady and even that wasn't plain black. It had grey stripes around it. Isn't it a good thing, though, that we do have colored umbrellas. The day would be so dark and cheerless otherwise. The colored umbrellas bobbing around sort of make you think of spring flowers."

"I saw something this morning I hadn't seen for years," said the assistant society editor. "A two wheeled fish cart with a fish painted on the side of it and a fat man in the back blowing a whistle."

"Were you at the midnight movies of the Akron Film guild Thursday night?" writes Ancient Admirer. "Rather pleasant, wasn't it? Half a dozen leading characters and a million dollars' worth of wonderful scenery conspired to give us a delightful 80 minutes of travel and recreation.

"Best of all, there was no plot to harrow and worry us. We weren't asked to witness any bloodshed, or partake of any problems, or hold our breath while the hero performed a hair-raising feat.

"The boy was the best actor of all, I thought. But Moana rather grew more and more likeable as the film progressed. He had a handsome mahogany skin to start with, and then his sweetie rubbed him down with O'Cedar polish. And then the tattooing. It seems to be as painful to acquire a coat of tattoo as to have your appendix cut out, and takes the same three weeks; and strangely enough, they put most of the pretty tattooing where it doesn't show.

"Did you ever see a country with so few bugs? When they started to cook that meal over the open fire I remembered our last outdoor picnic, where we were visited by ants. But there don't seem to be any ants or bugs or worms that eat holes in leaves down there in Samoa. What a wonderful country to live in.

"We liked all the film except where the leading lady swallowed minnows alive. She was such a nice girl up to that point.

"I'd like to see the Beggar on Horseback."

---

7 February 1927, Monday:

THINGS I'M AWFUL WEARY OF

SOOT
Legs
Divorce cases
Il Trovatore
Newspaper articles on women who combine careers and marriage
Magazine articles on what's wrong with marriage
Soot
Goloshes
Bargain clothes
Stocking runners
Soot
Letters from Florida
Discussions of Charlie Chaplin
Pictures of battleships
Pictures of John D. Rockefeller
Anything about John D. Rockefeller
Soot
Dog pounds
Reminiscences of stage people
Reminiscences of anybody
Circuses
Animal acts
Bandits
Confessions of harem beauties
Health articles
Recipes
Legs
Golf cups
Soot
Soot
Soot

Why It Is Pleasant To Do Newspaper Work In Akron, O.

"YOU don't know me from a load of hay," writes Mac, "but nevertheless I religiously read your column each night and can honestly say I get more real enjoyment from it than from anything else in your sheet.

"The main object of this epistle: I don't believe I've ever read your opinion of the household time schedules printed in so many of our periodicals. Have you ever attempted to follow one? Neither have I. They're so funny sometimes. Do you suppose the person who writes them is blessed with a telephone, door bell or children?

"You know how it is to get in the midst of the 20 minutes allowed for clearing away and washing the luncheon dishes and have some dear friend call you on the phone and use up all that 20 minutes (and more) to tell you about what lovely new wallpaper she has in her bedroom and how she's decorating an old bedroom set. Now who'd want to wash dishes when there was something like that to listen to? And then Mrs. Brown comes and stays and stays and stays and several more 20 minutes have fugited [sic].

"Personally I'm not in favor of a stop watch system for the housewife as long as she's able to get things done efficiently and is sweet and smiling when her husband comes home for the evening meal. He'll never suspect it hasn't all been done by the clock and probably will care a great deal less."

Yes, I've noticed those schedules and I've never had any more luck with them than I've had with budgets.

Sundays, which are my days of rest, I've tried like everything to figure out a system whereby I could make the bed, wash the breakfast dishes, clean up the bathroom, straighten up the living room, get Mary bathed and fed and napped and get out of the kitchen by 2 o'clock in the afternoon. I can't do it. It's always 3 o'clock and sometimes worse.

A friend of mine puts the baby in the bath tub and then rushes around and does the housework while he plays. But Mary won't be left alone in the bath tub. She knows how to turn on the water and then when it comes rushing out she hollers. She won't sit quietly and play with her little celluloid ducks. Instead she dips the wash cloth full of water and then leans over the edge of the tub and wrings it out on the floor.

I couldn't for the life of me figure out what was the best time to clean the bathroom. There was no use to get up at 4 o'clock in the morning and clean it early because nobody had used it then. I couldn't clean it while Mary was sleeping because the running water woke her up. I think I solved it Sunday. It is to clean the bathroom while Mary is in the tub. Thus we have utility and companionship combined. But I don't know. I've figured out a lot of other things that I thought were going to be time savers and they weren't.

So far as these time schedules are concerned of course we know how people do it. A woman sits at her desk and figures out how long it ought to take her to make a bed. It doesn't occur to her that if you have two pairs of blankets on a bed it is going to take her at the very least two minutes more to shake out the extra one, put it back on and tuck it in. She doesn't consider that when you're doing the dusting you're going to discover that the window sills are all full of soot again, that your husband has upset all the bureau drawers looking for his flash light and that the rubber tires are off the baby's bed. They never think of any of those little things.

I don't think I'd want to live by a schedule however even if there was one that was practicable. You would get brain fever trying to keep track of it.

---

3 May 1927, Tuesday:

I MAY not have the details quite straight, but anyway, it went something like this: Two women up at the Woman's City club got into an argument about a bridge play. Not being able to settle it, they wrote to Milton Work, the bridge expert, and asked him his opinion. Mr. Work wrote back giving his opinion and enclosed a bill for $100. Horrified the women sought out a lawyer to ask him whether they had to pay it. The lawyer gave his advice and sent them a bill for $50.

Ethel's back from Texas and we've spent the day hearing all about it. In Austin they met Governor Dan Moody and his wife. Ethel says the governor in Texas makes only $3,500 a year and that Governor and Mrs. Moody have made up their minds to live within it. Mrs. Moody does her own marketing and a good part of her housework. Ethel says the governor's mansion is shabby looking and that the furniture is few and far between which seemed odd in view of the fact that the Texans were always boasting of what a rich state theirs was. She saw Ma Ferguson, too. She said Ma was living in state at one of the hotels and that she had very shrewd eyes.

Also Ethel saw a cowboy and almost fell over. She says he has red leather boots with high heels.

At one point their car had to be towed across a flood by a mule team. Ethel said the water was up to the mules' necks and it was the only time she got scared. At one point the water had receded from one of the roads and had left thousands of turtles behind. At another point a lot of frogs had decided to migrate from one stream to another. There were so many of them that they stopped traffic. People were shoveling them up into baskets and selling them.

Ethel liked the Ozark mountains best of anything in the whole trip. The Saturday night before Easter they got on a lonely road leading up into the mountains and it was so beautiful they just kept on going. After a long time they came to a little store and asked if they could get something to eat. The man in charge said his wife was away but he'd see what he could do. After a while he came in from the kitchen looking distressed and aske the girls if maybe they couldn't go out into the kitchen and make head and tail out of things themselves.

So the girls went out and there was a huge chocolate cake out there and some pies and a baked ham and some roast pork and goodness knows what all. They pitched in and made their own sandwiches and ate and ate. It cost them about 35 cents a piece.

Easter they thought they would go to the first church they came to but there didn't seem to be any, so they spent the morning in the woods and picked wild flowers for corsages.

You know I told you how Marion was disturbed about whether she should take one or two evening dresses along. She finally decided to take just one and when she tried it on in Austin it didn't fit. The girls pinned and pleated and hemmed it on her but it didn't do one bit of good, so then Marion decided she'd wear her dark blue silk. She'd been wearing that dark blue silk every day of the trip, to push automobiles in and climb fences and everything. Ethel says that every time they struck a hotel Marion would ring for a bell boy and give him the blue dress and tell him to have it washed and ironed and get it back by five in the morning. Marion ought to love that dress pretty tenderly, seeing how it stood by her.

6 May 1927, Friday:

LITTLE Mary Ellen Clark came to town Wednesday night much to the satisfaction and delight of Bill Clark, the Beacon Journal photographer. I don't know just how long Bill Bill [sic] has been with the Beacon Journal but anyway he was here when I came and that was eight years ago. Sometimes when we would be out on assignments together we used to talk about our possible children and Bill was always hoping that his family would consist exclusively of girls. If there were pictures to be taken Bill would go miles to take a picture of a little girl and would fuss with it until it was an artistic triumph. But little boys! Well you simply had to get down on your knees and pray with Bill to take a picture of a boy and maybe even then he wouldn't do it.

So we were kinda worried about Bill. "If it should be a boy – " we said and looked at each other dismally although down in our hearts we knew it really didn't matter because little kids, no matter what kind always turn out to be irresistible.

Anyway, Mary Ellen came and it's a good thing that Bill is taking his vacation just now. When he gets back a week from Monday I suppose he'll be just faintly normal. And won't Jimmy Schlemmer and I have the fine time, giving him advice from long, long experince [sic].

A Frenchman who has written a book called "Sardonic Tales[285]," or something like that (you can always make up your own titles for those French authors) tells a droll story about our American Indians.

He says that in certain tribes it was the custom to invite the old people to climb a tree. The tree was then vigorously shaken by the young bloods and the old folks who fell off were speedily dispatched with a tomahawk. Those who hung on were allowed to climb down and go about their duties for a while yet, it being reasoned that they were still some good for the fighting, the deer chasing and the what nots.

Although the French author doesn't say so this seems to be a logical origin for our expression, "Go climb a tree."

While I darned the stocking last night Bill read me Eugene O'Neill's new play, "Marco Millions." It is about Marco Polo and seems to be something of a satire on the go-getter. It makes an excellent play to read. Its principle merit on the stage, I imagine,

---

[285] Sardonic Tales by Villiers de L'Isle-Adam (1927) a collection of stories

would like in its pageantry and its music. For home talent production it would be ideal as it seems to have a hundred or more characters in it which would give all the members of the local dramatic clubs a chance. Those who have loved Donn Byrne's "Messer Marco Polo," however, will undoubtedly be taken aback considerably by this Marco. And as for the Tartar princess in the tale, you will never be able to weep over her as you did over Little Golden Bells.

The play has in it, however, one gem, so rare, so delicate, so obviously inspired by genius that, once you have read it, nothing else seems to matter. The is the poem which Marco Polo, at the age of 15, composes to the young woman who has inflamed his fancy and whom, along about act 3, scene 14, he marries.

This is the poem:

You are lovely as the gold in the sun
Your skin is like the silver in the moon
Your eyes are black pearls I have won.
I kiss your ruby lips and you swoon.
Smiling your thanks as I promise you
A large fortune if you will be true
While I am away earning gold
And silver so when we are old
I will have a million to my credit
And in the mean time can easily afford
A big wedding that will do us credit
And start having children, bless the Lord.

---

17 May 1927, Tuesday:

Why A Good Many People Don't Go To Church

SANDUSKY, O., May 16. (AP) –

Handcuffed and in prison stripes, George W. Wiles, Sandusky businessman, sang the "Prisoner's Song" in Old First church, Presbyterian, here in connection with its rededication.

Harry L. Cole, sheriff, of Erie county, led Wilson before the congregation. Original plans were for the sheriff to fire his gun, but it was decided the report might scare the many children present.

SORDID STORY

Once upon a time there was a woman who went to the grocery store and bought a pound of spinach. And she washed it and washed it and washed it and washed it and washed it and washed it and washed it and washed it and washed it and washed it and washed it and washed it and washed it and washed it and washed it and washed it and washed it and washed it.

JOKE

First woman (leaving the theater) "Who wrote this Caponsacchi anyway?"

Second woman. "Browning."

First woman. "Well no wonder Peaches left him."

HEALTH TALK

They say that 30 or so men out at the Goodyear are suffering from something called the squeaks[286]. They get it in their forearms and even though they are in the next room you can hear the squeak. It is said to be very painful and also contagious and the men have to be treated at the hospital.

SOCIETY NOTE

Fred Kelly is back from Washington, New York, Cleveland and points east and west. He says he's all loaded up with information and gossip and things. Bill and I are going out to see him tonight but not for supper.

CLINICAL NOTE

An Akron man was waiting outside a maternity ward the other day. After a while the doctor came out and said, "My dear man, you have a fine son." "That's splendid, doctor, splendid" said the man and he cut a few capers. "And in about a half hour," continued

---

[286] I'm unsure which contagious disease this refers to, but research points that it may be a type of gangrene or crepitus, which when the affected area is rubbed it releases distinct sounds in the wound that resemble a squeak or creak

the doctor, "you'll have another one." Whereupon the man ceased capering and started making figures on the back of an envelope.

NEIGHBORHOOD NEWS

Angelina came over Friday afternoon with a plate heaped high with strudel that her aunty had just baked. "Just think," said Angelina, "today was Friday the 13th and a girl in our room broke five pencils." The strudel was grand.

21 May 1927, Saturday:

THE nasturtiums are up.

I read a nice story last night about John Kendrick Bangs. It happened in New York in the days of hansom cabs.

It seems that Mr. Bangs was on his way home and he ordered himself an extremely handsome hansom to ride in. After they had gone a few blocks Mr. Bangs perceived a distressed and hungry looking alley cat sitting by the curb. Mr. Bangs had a kind disposition in regard to animals and so he ordered the driver to stop, got out and picked up the cat with the intention of taking it home with him. But the driver refused to allow Mr. Bangs to reenter the hansom with the cat. He had polished his cab with great care and it was nicely upholstered. He wasn't going to have it scratched up by any alley cats.

So. Mr. Bangs signaled another hansom which drove up just then and in this second hansom he installed the cat. The procession then resumed its ways toward Mr. Bangs' home.

A few blocks on they passed a delicatessen and it occurred to Mr. Bangs that his cat would probably like a herring so Mr. Bangs got out and purchased a herring. When he placed the herring in the hansom with the cat however the cat clawed at the paper so desperately that Mr. Bangs grew perplexed. He felt that in the interests of good manners, and also as a matter of discipline to the cat, the animal ought not to have its herring until it got home. He could not leave the package with the cat. He knew that, smelling as it did, he would never be allowed to ride with it in his own hansom. So, signaling a third hansom which was driving by just then, he stopped the driver and installed on the seat the herring. That done the procession of three hansom cabs, with man, cat and herring for passengers, resumed its course until it reached Mr. Bangs' house.

It is understood that the cat grew to a fat and sleek old age.

This story turns up early in a book that's been lying about the house a couple of weeks called "The Girl from Rector's." It's written by George Rector, son of the famous restaurateur, and you haven't any idea how fascinating it is, at least to any one who is interested in restaurants. George Rector tells of all the notables who used to eat at Rector's and of how Sarah Barnhardt ate and ate of their very special crab meat canape; of how he himself left Cornell law school to go to France where he spent a long apprenticeship learning how to make sauce Marguery; of how he and his father grew so weary of the elaborate preparations in their own restaurant that they frequently sneaked out the back door over to a white tile place to have a stack of wheat cakes.

Incidentally the book gives an infallible rule for distinguishing a mush room from a toad stool. If you've eaten it and you're still alive it was a mush room.

---

15 June 1927, Wednesday:

CONSIDERING all the joking that has been done about it you would think that store keepers would hesitate any more to put the largest and nicest products on the top of the box and the smallest and spoiled ones on the bottom. The strawberries I got down here at Five Points yesterday, however, were just that. There were just enough nice ones to make the top look pretty. The ones the rest of the way were beyond words. A boy behind the counter was working over the boxes. Somehow or other I could not see that it was good training for him. I am afraid that when he grows up he will get him a gold watch to wear across his vest and then feel that there is nothing else to be accomplished in life.

Later down at the corner grocery store some men were talking about how awfully extravagant some women were and how they threw more out the back door than their husbands could bring in at the front door.

"I guess," I said, "that you men pick out wives the way I do strawberries."

But at that all the men spoke up and said No, THEIR wives were wonderful. It would appear that it was just the other fellow who picked the wrong kind.

This morning Bill told Mary the story of the Three Bears. This is the way it went:

Once upon a time, Mary, there was a little girl named Goldilocks, and one day while she was out in the woods picking flowers she came to a little house. Now, this house was occupied by a family of Bears. There was a great big Papa bear and there was a medium sized Mama bear, and then there was a little Mary bear.

On this particular morning the Mama bear had made some nice soup for breakfast and set it out on the table, but when they sat down to eat it the Papa bear said, "OH MY, THIS SOUP IS TOO HOT," and the Mama bear said, "Oh, my soup is too hot," and the little Mary bear said, "Oh, my soup is too hot, too," so they left their soup to cool on the table and went for a walk in the woods.

While they were gone Goldilocks came to the cottage and walked right in through the door and when she saw the soup there on the table she started tasting it. And the Papa bear's soup was too hot and the little Mary bear's soup was too cold but the Mama bear's soup was just right and so Goldilocks ate it all up.

Then Goldilocks went into the living room and here there were three pianos. There was a large parlor grand and then a medium sized grand and then there was a little piano, just a small apartment piano. And when Goldilocks saw the large piano she –

But at this point Mary held the bed spread up in front of her face and said, "Peep boo" so the story of Goldilocks was discontinued.

You know the trouble we had with the morning glory seeds. Well, I dug them up and planted instead the ones that Pearl R. sent and Sunday when we got back from Washington weren't they all up as big as you please. It goes to show that if you have good seeds environment isn't going to matter much.

MY friend, Stella B., eats a good hearty breakfast. Her mother gets it for her. First Stella has fruit and then she has cereal and then she has bacon and eggs or waffles and eggs and toast and she always has at least two cups of coffee. If Stella doesn't have a good breakfast in the morning she gets so faint by 10 o'clock that she almost keels over. Stella likes a good lunch with one or two hot dishes and almost always pie and then at night she goes home for dinner which is bound to be ample you know because Stella has two brothers and, my goodness, if you coud [sic] see those boys eat! Stella is five feet and six inches tall and she weighs 119 pounds.

Lu S. has orange juice and a cup of black coffee for breakfast and for lunch she has a tomato sandwich and a glass of buttermilk. For supper she has a tablespoonful of minced lamb, a lettuce leaf with mineral oil dressing and some pineapple juice. She never touches candy, fresh bread or potatoes and not for years has she known the taste of sugar in her tea. Lu weighs 295 pounds and has given up all her clubs. She got tired of hearing her friends remark that she must surely be picking up a little roast beef or something on the side.

Harry S. never mentions food. The right of the way other people eat makes him ill. Whenever he is invited out he takes just a little of this and a little of that. He can't help it but his hostesses think it is because he doesn't like their cooking. They have given up asking him any more. Harry doesn't mind.

Myrtle and Clarence M. talk about food all the time. The best meal they ever had was in Rochester and the worst was in Catoosa, Okla. "Just give me a good, thick steak," says Clarence, "and some fried potatoes and some apple pie and, oh, boy." Myrtle likes steak, too, although she's never gotten over her fondness for chicken. She also likes all kinds of vegetables, fruits, salads, soups and hot breads. Between breakfast and luncheon Myrtle generally has a cup of coffee along with anything she can pick up and along about 11 o'clock at night she and Clarence almost always have a Dutch lunch. When Myrtle goes to church on Sunday the minister likes to look at her because she has an ethereal something about her that raises his thoughts to higher and better things. Clarence writes advertising copy for big concern, one of his most successful efforts being a little book entitled, "The Calories Will Get You If You Don't Watch Out."

Mr. Z. is vegetarian. He permits himself butter and eggs but no meat or broth soups and he never touches pie without first inquiring whether the crust is made with Crisco. Mr. Z. took up being a vegetarian for his spiritual good. He felt that lettuce and things like that would clear his thoughts and make it easier to resist the world. Mr. Z. loves to tell what vegetarianism has done for him. He tells it and tells it and tells it. Mr. Z. has two great sorrows. One is that his daughter, who left home three years ago, writes to him seldom. His other is that his wife is too materialistic. One time when Mr. Z. came upon her in a restaurant eating creamed chipped beef on toast, he shuddered and didn't go home until half past one the next morning.

❧

27 July 1927, Monday:

OUR young neighbor LaVerne was over the other day with a stiff neck. Of course, she said, "I'm not really sure it is stiff neck, I never had one before, but it sure hurts. I can't put my head up at all." After awhile she said, "I hope my stiff neck doesn't hurt tomorrow because I'm going down town with my mother and get some shoes. I hardly know what downtown looks like any more. I haven't been downtown since just after Christmas." After awhile she said, "Oh dear, but my neck hurts. It would be dreadful to have to wear it this way all the time. After my mother gets her work done she's going to bandage it up and put something on it."

The Frank, who had borrowed the lawn mower brought it home and, being still full of ambition, started to mow our back yard. LaVerne went out and helped him. It seemed to be a sort of Tom Sawyer White Washing The Fence affair, for Frank would say, "Here now, you let me push it," and then LaVerne would say, "Aw now, it's my turn. I'll just take it across once."

In the competition LaVerne forgot her stiff neck. By the time the back yard was completed her head was sitting almost normally on her shoulders.

I remarked that she must be feeling better. "Oh yes," she said, "but it still hurts a little. I wouldn't mind having a stiff neck if I was still in school."

Now I imagine that if LaVerne were requested to mow her own back yard she would do it sweetly and obligingly but hardly with the zest with which she tackled our back yard. I don't know why it is so much more fun to work for the neighbors when you are young. I know that in my own case I never cared about raking up our own leaves but I just loved to rake the neighbors' leaves. For the neighbors I would wash dishes, tend babies, run errands, anything. Even Mary experiences the fascination of distant pastures. She would rather travel up the next door back steps than her own.

Perhaps it is this feeling, carried on into later years, which makes us feel that the other person's lot is always happier.

Do you imagine that Dean Lucas will be as good a speller 20 years hence as he is now? Or will he be like the rest of us, slip back woeful, and write such things as, "She left her pale and mop on the back porch."

I don't think it is that we really forget how to spell. It is merely that we get into habits occasionally of letting our subconscious minds carry on and the subconscious mind, I have found, is something which you can't trust too far. So far as spelling is concerned it seems to work phonetically.

The thing that I liked best about Dean was his going into the contest a second time. Even if he hadn't won I'd have liked him just the same. He sort of make some old folks I could mention feel ashamed of themselves.

---

29 June 1927, Wednesday:

JUST when I was so happy about everything Ema Spencer, in the Newark O., Advocate comes out with this:

The Over-Zealous Morning Glory

Josephine Van de Grift of the Akron Beacon Journal has recently acquired a small garden, and in her first fine frenzy she planted among other things, morning glory seeds. At least that's what she thought, but when she complained that they didn't germinate we knew she must have been mistaken and that it was probably a couple of other seeds. Not content to let well enough alone, she pursued the matter with ardor, until now she reports a fine showing of husky seedlings. In her innocence she evidently does not know that each potential blossom, and there will be millions of them this season, will mean what would be equal to half a packet of seed, which will be broadcast with ebullient joy. Next summer Josephine will walk forth to find that every living thing in her garden has been strangled by a morning glory vine. They will even twine around little Mary, happily engaged with her sand pile. Bill, if he loiters at all on his blithesome way to the garage, will find each leg firmly lashed to the ground and will stand like a Pillar of Hercules unless rescued. Josephine has surely started something. But luckily she has only rented the property, so of course she can move.

Monday was clean up day around our neighborhood and when Mary and I took our morning walk Sunday we sized up what kind of rubbish the neighbors were throwing away. One family threw away a whole lot of paint cans and also quite a good looking wash boiler but for the most part we didn't see anything interesting. For one thing they hadn't put an awful lot of rubbish out Sunday and for another thing a good deal of it was all packed up tight in burlap bags so you couldn't see anything. It was surprising how neatly most of it was done up.

The thing we had most of was coat hangers. Honest, it's hard to see how the laundries get ahead considering the prodigality with which they dispense coat hangers. And they're the meanest things to have around. They're always getting caught among one another and when you're trying to get anything out of the closet without waking the baby then the whole lot of them falls down on the floor with a tremendous clatter.

Well, I took out a whole arm load of coat hangers and dumped them and also all our tin cans and a broom and a couple of mops and then the neighborhood children descended on the lot to see what they could find. So far as I know the only prizes this afternoon were a lead pencil and a pair of high heeled slippers which LaVerne was able to limp about in with the aid of some paper wadded in the heels.

And then Monday dawned bright and cool and beautiful and didn't the rubbish collectors go by and fail to turn our corner. So I called up Hez Russell and asked him if it was going to be necessary for me to drag all those tin cans back in the cellar and in the most soothing voice imaginable he said no, they'd be up right away and get them.

If there are ever any other housewives similarly distressed, remember the name, Hez Russell of the street cleaning department, and just call him up and tell him all about it.

---

1 July 1927, Friday:

THE ice man deposited his burden and wiped his face on his shirt sleeve. "It's gonna be another scorcher," he observed. Minnie, her hands in the dish water, felt too weary to turn around. "Yea," she responded, "I guess so." After he had gone she wished that she made some lemonade to give him. Then she remembered that they hadn't any lemons. She poured out the dish water and let the cold water from the faucet run over her wrists. Her head was heavy from the oppressive heat of the night before. Whenever she closed her eyes red dancing men kept spinning and spinning before her. She wished that she could be all day thus – with her eyes closed and the cool water running over her wrists. She thought of the kitchen stove with the grease splashed on it from last night's cooking, of the milk spilled and drying on the back porch, of last night's papers and collars and ashes strewn over the living room. "Oh I can't," she whispered, "I can't."

The baby screamed. He had fallen down the last few steps leading to the motion picture theater below. Minnie ran and picked him up. She carried him up stairs to the living room and sat down with him on a chair. He continued to scream. "Poor baby," she said and started stripping him of his small rompers and shoes. The baby kicked and still he screamed. Even the heat from his small body was torture to Minnie. Her clothes seemed burning into her flesh. The heat boiled up from the roofs outside and through the windows of the tiny apartment and glared down on the cheap furniture until the varnish sent up a fairly sickening odor.

Minnie carried the baby into the bathroom and filled the tub with cool water. Her back ached, her head ached, her feet had to be goaded into going through their accustomed motions. And still the baby screamed. Minnie sank down on the floor beside him. She buried her face in a towel and wept.

While she was cooking the hamburg and boiling the potatoes she thought of the supper she would really like to have. There would be tall stemmed glasses holding little balls of watermelon and cantaloupe. There would be a great big salad and little buttered rolls. There would be tall glasses of iced tea with spoons long enough to reach to the bottom and stir the sugar and the glasses would be set in little dishes so the moisture wouldn't run down and get the table cloth all wet.

The heat from the stove rose up and enveloped her. The heat from outside beat through the windows. When you looked out over the roofs you could see it rising in waves. Her neck smarted. The perspiration kept trickling down her back. The baby whimpered and tugged at her skirts. Oh, for great tall glasses with long spoons to reach to the bottom ...

The sheets were hot, the walls were hot, no breath of air seemed to come in through the windows. Outside automobiles were racing past, automobiles with happy people who knew how to get away from the torture. From the motion picture house below came the sound of the mechanical organ grinding out something or other for the last show. The baby stirred in his sleep. Minnie went to him and straightened the sheet. Then she went into the bath room, removed her cheap cotton night gown, wrung it out of water and put it on again. Then she crawled into bed again.

The clamminess for a moment was almost too cool for her skin. Then she began to feel comfortable. She closed her eyes. The little red whirling men took hold of one another's hands and danced away. She went to sleep.

———⚬⚬⚬⚬◆⚬⚬⚬———

4 July 1927, Monday:

A Letter Which Enables Us To Take
A Short And Much Appreciated
Vacation

"BEING a long-legged fellow who gets restless during long concerts," writes Ancient Admirer, "I have often thought I might enjoy grand opera if it could be fed to me in small doses, in an easy chair, with lots of leg-room in front and plenty of cool punch and tender sandwiches immediately following.

"Last Wednesday night quite a mob of us would-be music lovers gathered in the drawing room of Mrs. F. A. Seiberling's and heard just the kind of grand opera that men like.

"The opera produced was Thais. Just the juiciest bits were shown, and for the benefit of any guests from Kenmore and South Akron and Fairlawn who might not be familiar with the plot, the hostess had thoughtfully synopsized in it the program. This enabled the action to jump from one scene to the middle of the next, requiring the acting of only the two leading characters, which were portrayed by Mrs. Seiberling's niece and her husband. The niece, by the way, sings and acts with glorious enthusiasm, which is all the more amazing because six years ago she could hardly sing a note.

"Let's see who was there that you know. There was Carl and the Marjorie Mc-s [sic] and smiling Mary M- [sic] and her doctor husband, and Bob W- [sic] who has just received another promotion out at Goodyear, and several dozen others. Those of us who had put the old tuxedo away in moth balls wore white flannels, and that was all right too. That's one nice thing about Mrs. Seiberling's parties – whatever you want to wear will be all right, as long as the trousers are pressed.

"We had a lot more music too, as you can see by the program, Josephine. Mrs. Whiting Williams of Cleveland, whose husband has done all manner of interesting things such as working as a laborer in a coal mine, traveling around as a common workman both in Europe and America, played the violin with grace and abandon while her daughter Carol accompanied on the piano. When you see how much musical talent the Williams family has developed while pa has been digging coal, you can understand why Whiting has come back to Cleveland and opened an office there for good.

"Mrs. Welker played the organ. That's a commendable thing about Mrs. Seiberling. She seems to know the people who deserve public attention and encouragement, and routs them out of their niche and lets people hear and see how much talent there lies hidden in our home folks. We need more of that sort of local boosting. Let's pay more attention to the Dean Lucases who learn spelling out of our own books and bring home a prize, and the Mrs. Welkers who play the organ right here in Akron, and the nieces who develop a voice that artists love to hear.

"Along about midnight we had about $87 worth of sandwiches, with salad and ice cream and coffee and cigars that didn't make you cough and punch that was good without being alcoholic. Everybody chatted with folks they hadn't seen before for weeks and everybody had a charming and informal time.

"There was one thing I noticed, which maybe will interest you. The latest styles in women's dresses is a sack-like effect just as if someone had cut a hole in a burlap sack ad let the thing sag down around the shoulders. That's one style. The other is to make the dress look as if it were hung together with pins but of course the pins don't show. This style looks awfully sloppy to old-fashioned eyes, but the girls who wore that kind of dresses seemed to know what's what, so I imagine it's really ultra snappy and smart.

"There's only one thing I can't report to you, Josephine, and that's the meaning of a Latin inscription over the proscenium arch of the Seiberling's home theater. It's something about "Caesar in Egypt knocked the table over,' but that didn't make sense somehow. If you find out the real meaning, let me know. I spent three hours trying to decipher it without a dictionary, and I'm stuck for the right answer."

---

5 July 1927, Tuesday:

WHENEVER a wealthy young man proceeds to have five children, everyone says, "My, how lovely. That girl certainly isn't shirking her responsibilities." Whenever a poor young woman has five children everybody groans and says, "How terrible. That girl must be a perfect fool."

A street cleaner paused to rest awhile this morning on the stone wall that goes around Grace school. He had a kindly face, smooth shaven and all ruddy and sun-burned and he looked as though street cleaning was just a sideline with him and that farming was his real profession. When he saw us coming along from the grocery store he said to Mary, "Hullo there, what's that you've got!" and Mary told him it was a wow-wow and gave it to him to hold which, so far as I know, is a favor she has never bestowed on any other human being. Then we talked about the hot weather and our new friend made the only comforting observation I had heard yet. "Well," he said, "if we didn't have it we'd all starve this winter."

Dear, dear, when I think of how only last April we got up one morning and the furnace fire was out –

A friend of mine tells me that the Mayo clinic has taken up astrology in order to find out the proper diet combinations for folks.

Maybe it was just because I was in a frivolous mood but I enjoyed a couple of stories in the current Saturday Evening Post. One was called "Honeymoon Klats" and the other was called "Perfection-Limited." Did anybody else like 'em?

And speaking of magazines, wouldn't you imagine that there wouldn't be a single subscription left anywhere for these poor college boys to take! And yet they keep coming around. One would think the town had been exhausted ages ago.

Having purchased a new Colonial home some friends of mine, when O'Neil's had their sale, bought $35 worth of pine trees to set out in front of it. The man of the house worked one whole day putting them out. A couple of days later when they went over to have a look at the place the pine trees had completely disappeared. Well, after they had thought dismally of the things they would have bought. The detective looked the place over thoroughly and finally his face brightened. "I think I have a clue," he said.

The clue was the imprint of a wingfoot heel.

My friends have bought some bushes and things and are going to be content with that.

Speaking of one thing and another, is there any satisfaction which can equal that of striking out for a mosquito and getting him?

7 July 1927, Thursday:

"WON'T you please let Lolly know," writes Cuyahoga Falls housewife, "that she can purchase pie pans at the five and ten cent store which have rims around them and the juice from the pies never runs out in the oven. I discovered the pans one day and never have any more trouble with my pies running over."

———

When you come to checking up on them there are an enormous number of clubs and organized these days and a pretty large proportion of them are the sort which require speakers.

The usual procedure in such a club is for a committee to be appointed to secure a speaker for such and such a date and the committee naturally tires to get somebody good. If the speaker is from out of town his fee may be $25 or $50. If the speaker is a woman she is generally expected to take less. It not infrequently happens that an out of town speaker disappoints at the last minute and then the committee has to scurry around and look up somebody local to take his place. But do they pay the substitute the fee which the out of towner was to have had? Do they pay him anything at all? Not that anybody at the present writing has heard of.

———

My ire on the matter of clubs and their thoughtlessness rose recently after I had talked to a young woman of considerable and unusual talent. This young woman is an artist, she writes verses and she speaks entertainingly and well. The clubs have heard about her and they beseech her continually to come and entertain them. The young woman has gone. She has packed up her trappings in a couple of heavy suit cases and traveled hither and thither and yon at her own expense. The trouble is that the young woman is not wealthy. She does not have leisure. She has to earn her own living in the hardest kind of way. Her talent which should be developing and which should be used to bring her in an excellent income is being dissipated by clubs which tell her how much they have enjoyed her entertainment and then go away. These women would not thing of asking the grocer to donate them a loaf of bread. They pay their way every time they go to the movies. But they will go their club meetings and expect to be entertained for nothing and even feel a little bewildered if anybody mentions anything so materialistic as a fee, "Why," they say, "we gave her her lunch."

There is no personal plaint in this. For a couple of years I went around giving speeches. I've never pretended to be a speaker and how good or how bad they were I'll never tell you. I enjoyed meeting the folks and sometimes there were pleasant little after experiences. One club sent around a box of candy, two sent flowers and two, I think it was two, had the secretary write a little note of thanks. The rest failed to express themselves in any fashion. I didn't mind only sometimes I wondered if the thing had really been a complete flop.

Two experiences last year congealed my emotions on the matter of speeches. One was at a men's luncheon club where an imported speaker was the high light of the occasion. I am not sure but I think he got $30 for telling some ancient jokes and singing a few wheezy songs. A few weeks later I went to a women's club where another speaker was the drawing card. You or I, sister, at least could have kept the audience awake.

The remedy I would suggest for all this is for club members to make their own speeches. Most clubs are organized for self improvement and there's nothing quite so improving as making your own speeches. One club I belong to tried this program for a while and the things the members told were far more engrossing than the poems of some chap up in Elsinore, Wis., would have been. Then, if a club feels that it really must import a local speaker let it give him the same consideration that it would a man from out of town and talk money. It will mean fewer speeches but it probably will mean better ones. The little follow up thank you note also creates a nice feeling.

<hr>

8 July 1927, Friday:

THE HOME GAZETTE

Conclusion To A Realistic Story

I waited tensely in the darkness. While still my nerves were taut there came faintly at first and then with more insistence that music which I felt would soon drive me on to madness. It approached, receded, returned to beat about my head with its unearthly rhythm. Suddenly I struck. My fist encountered something soft and small and helpless. That which so recently had been filled with the joy of living now lay inert and still. A fierce and insane joy possessed me. I had killed my tormentor and pulling the sheet up about my ears I congratulated myself that the last mosquito for that night at least had been dispatched. I slept.

Weather Recollection
We have had some rain lately.

Garden Notes
The nasturtiums, those that Mary has neglected to sit on, are blooming nicely and are keeping the table bright with at least five blossoms a day.

Social Event
The editor of this department had callers on Thursday night.

Household Hint
Clothes pins may be used at the pegs on which to tie strings for the training of morning glories.

Exterior Decorating Note
A friend of ours has a house with a purple front door and she is also going to have purple shutters.

Advice to Busy Mothers
A child can be kept amused for a full five minutes if given a box of pancake flour and allowed to sprinkle it over the house.

Editorial
There ought to be a law that motorists who honk their horns for no reason at all should be given life terms down at Columbus.

Our Own Questionnaire
Why are garbage cans always too small?
Why does grass grow so fast?
Why do people never call you up except when you are taking a nap?

News Item
Our ice man's Ford broke down this morning.

Book Review
A book we have been reading called "Psychology – A Simplification" says that a new born child would probably never feel hungry if not encouraged to eat by outside stimulation. This is extremely difficult to believe.

Commercial Note
The ice house down at the other end of our block is doing a thriving business.

Thoughts From A Kitchen Window

The garage ought to be painted next year. There's something burning. I wonder if it's our peas. No. The sand pile looks kinda flat. The clothes pin box ought to be brought in. The back porch ought to be scrubbed. Maybe it will be. Wonder why the Chinese wool flowers never came up. Next spring we'd better dig the whole place up and fertilize it. The trees are waving nicely. So are the bushes. God bless all the people who refuse to cut down trees.

***

9 July 1927, Saturday:

"I HAVE a new baby brother," writes Sonya. "His name is Norman, and he is adorable. I was the first to see him and I am his Godmother. It seems that little Jewish girls are not supposed to have a Godmother or Godfather. Boys always do get the cream of everything. Norman is plump, he was 9 ½ pounds at birth. He has big blue eyes, and a pug nose. I like to bury my face in his neck. It smells of everything that is good and clean.

"Among the various things I learned during the last few weeks:

> To cook gefnelte fish.
> Dress and cook poultry.
> Bake a cheese kugel.
> Make coffee. (That is an art).
> Et cetera, et cetera.

"The only thing that I do not like about housekeeping, is to think of what to cook for dinner. Lunches are not so hard. The family never gives suggestions. When questioned as to what they would like for dinner, they shrug a shoulder, look obliging, and make the bright suggestion that I cook anything that I like. It's exasperating.

"Everything does not always go smoothly, but everyone ignores such trifles as burnt meat, or a pudding that has salt in it instead of sugar.

"I read Edna St. Vincent Millay's 'Recessional.' It makes one think and wonder.

"P. S.: What are 'Hounds of Spring'?"

Well, I don't know either but it seems to have something to do with poetry. I just looked it up in Crowell's Handbook for Readers and Writers but the hounds listed there are the Hound of Heaven and the Hound of the Baskervilles (see Sherlock Holmes). Somehow

I never can worry about little details like that. I can't remember yet the line that "Black Oxen" comes from. Anyway I suppose Sylvia Thompson must tell what "Hounds of Spring" comes from in the front of her book.

However, speaking of more important things, greetings to Norman. I hope he likes the world he has come to live in. I have just found out what the moon was made for. It was created as a very special jewel for babies.

My friend Mrs. Pericles says that it has a bad effect on her to iron. She thinks such mean thoughts when she irons – gets all filled up with self pity and things like that. Therefore she avoids ironing as much as possible – lets the table linens accumulate until she can send them off to a friend in Youngstown and get them mangled – and passes over the other things as rapidly as possible.

There are undoubtedly a few improvements which could be introduced into the matter of ironing and which might tend to life the melancholia which others than Mrs. Pericles suffer from. For one thing it would be nice to have the iron heated by radio so you wouldn't have to bother with a cord. These cords are always burning out when you're about three pieces from the end and they also get all tangled up in things.

Another thing which ought to be taken up is the matter of children's rompers. If there's anything harder to iron than some of the store bought children's rompers I'd like to know what it is. They put all kinds of complicated pockets on them. They put gathers in the sleeves where you never never [sic] can get them straightened out. They put on turn back cuffs and sew them down hard. And then they open them in all sorts of different places and put on as many buttons as possible. Zipper openings would be ideal for rompers. Then you could iron right along and you'd never, never have to bother with buttons.

---

11 July 1927, Monday:

ONE of the mysteries I can't solve is why that man down at Lamson's fish market always wears a straw hat.

I couldn't quite make it out but anyway the garbage man was complaining to his companion on the front seat. "That woman called up and wanted her garbage collected," he was saying, "and when I got out there, there wasn't anything to it but just flowers. That's all it was – just flowers."

An article in the current New Yorker has to do with the newspapers and Colonel Lindbergh. It reproduces a good deal of the hooey that was written about the young man at the time of his flight and it tells again the now ancient story of how he replied to one inquisitive reporter, "That's a damn fool question." The conclusion which the writer of the article arrives at is that Lindbergh grew steadily more weary and disgusted at the American or at least the New York press and that when a few other personages show the same attitude it will be a better thing for everybody concerned.

My friends LaVerne and Ruth called up the stairs Saturday to know if they might mow the lawn. "Why," I said, "I'd be delighted."

So LaVerne and Ruth mowed the lawn. When they had finished there seemed to be odd patches of long grass showing here and there but it was a warm afternoon and they had worked industriously.

Along toward evening they came into the kitchen. "What do you think Frank told us," they remarked, "He told us that one time he mowed the lawn for you and you gave him 50 cents."

"Yes," I said, "I did."

"Just think," they said, "for 50 cents you could go to the picture show five times. There's an awful good one down at the corner now. It's called 'Wedding Bells.'"

"You couldn't go to the picture show tonight anyway," I said.

"Why?" they wanted to know.

"Because," I said, "you told me a little while ago your father had gone away and you had to watch your little sister."

"Oh but he's back now," they protested whereupon I ceased arguing.

Along about half past nine they came around to the kitchen and pressed their faces against the screen.

"It was a swell show," they said happily, whereupon for some reason I felt enormously elated.

⁓⚬⛬⛬⚬

13 July 1927, Wednesday:

I HEARD the other day of a dentist who, when he is examining a prospective assistant, always looks first to her hands. If they are strong and muscular he engages her. The necessary mental qualifications, it seems, go right along with the hands and he maintains that his latest assistant whom he engaged solely on the strength of her hands has also proved the most satisfactory in other ways.

It was a small baby who got us to talking about hands. You know whenever a baby has long slim fingers they always say he has piano hands. As a matter of fact the best piano hands are those which are inclined to be muscular and stubby and which are capable of tremendous expansion through the middle. As to violinists I don't know but I imagine that it is far more important that a violinist have strong arm and back muscles than that he have fingers which taper exquisitely and delicately to a point.

A phrenologist told me once that if anything should happen to alter violently a person's mental characteristics, the bumps on his head would also change. How true this is I don't know but it is possible to a certain extent for a person's hands to change. A few years ago there came to this city an Hungarian with delicate and artistic sensibilities. His hands showed it. He was unable to make a living in his chosen profession, however, and went to work in the rubber pits. In a few years his hands had again become the most revealing part of him. They were weary, blunted, coarsened.

Sometimes hands will persists in revealing certain characteristics in spite of all that can be done for them. A woman whom I know is quite literary and has an excellent position as private secretary. She does no housework. And yet her hands always look as though she had just finished a hard week's washing. The fingers are puffy and red, the nails bristle. Her hands are the most engrossing part of her. They are telling something, but whether it is a prediction of the future or a revelation of the past I don't know.

Not that hands always tell the truth. I have a relative who has always done considerable housework and yet her hands emerge from the soap suds, white and soft and beautiful.

There are other women whose hands, the minute they get within six feet of a dishpan, being looking scarred and puffy and beyond the aid of any manicure.

Two things I have always abhorred – a woman who kisses other women when she greets them and a man with fat hands. There is probably some sinister explanation to all this, but inasmuch as I never read Freud it hasn't bothered me particularly. The most beautiful hands I think are those which do not taper too much but are inclined to be a little practical looking at the tips. And because one whom I loved very much had moons on her fingers I suppose I shall always like those, too.

Beautiful hands have always been fairly common, I think, but beautiful feet have been something else again. Chiropodists tell distressing tales of the women who come to them, but they do say that things, what with sensible shoes and all, are getting better.

The feet and hands of little children are so very perfect. It is hard to think what, for so many centuries, we have done to them.

14 July 1927, Thursday:

NOTES OF AN AMATEUR PARENT

WHEN Mary was a couple of months old she voluntarily dispensed with her 2 a. m. feeding. After she was put on three meals a day, she still had a bottle with her morning nap and one when she went to bed at night. We approved of this as it seemed an excellent way of introducing into her system the necessary quart of milk a day. Then I began to hear wild tales from other mothers. One had a little boy four years old, who wept and wailed if he couldn't have his bottle at night. The books said that by the time a child was two years old it should be getting along entirely without a bottle. I began to worry. Suppose Mary would refuse to give up her bottle?

I guess Mary sensed my worry. A couple of weeks ago she refused to take her morning bottle. That night she refused her night bottle. The next day the performance was repeated. So now Mary is entirely cured of the bottle habit, and she is only a year and a half old! I think it is very considerate of a child to abide by the rules in the book even if she'd never done more than look at them upside down.

The problem now is whether the child should be encouraged to call her father Bill. Mary pronounces it "Beel" and she likes the sound of it and says it over and over all day long. I remember being rather disagreeable once to a friend who wanted to know if I was going to encourage Mary to call me by my first name. She said she thought it was nice because "Mother" made a woman sound so old. But I have never grieved about growing old and I always thought "Mother" a very nice word indeed. And so, as I say, I was disagreeable about it, although I repented right away as I always do when I have been nasty.

Now that Mary has decided all by herself to call at least one of her parents by his first name. I don't know what to do about it. Somehow the thing doesn't sound so disastrous as I had thought it would. In fact it sounds decidedly pleasant to hear her from her bed this minute saying, "Beel, Beel, Beel."

The next most serious problem has to do with keeping clean. It is manifestly impossible to keep a child in the bathtub all day long. And yet if you don't, what in the world are you going to do? My friends come to call with children all spick and span and ruffled. Mary approaches from the back yard, her shoes full of sand, her knees black, the front of her rompers full of toast, apple and anything else she has been able to pick up, her face, nose and forehead waffle ironed from being pressed against the screen door and bearing in her hand anything from pinching bugs to ancient strawberries. And in such a state she is always more than eager to embrace somebody.

The washings bear witness that her clothing is changed. I wonder sometimes though if she wouldn't prefer a paradise where one suit lasted all summer and which was never, by any chance, invaded by a wash cloth.

15 July 1927, Friday:

Kidnapped

ONE Saturday when the little girl was being kept in with a cold her grandmother brought out an old scrap book. Grandmother leafed through the pages. After awhile she stopped and pointed to a newspaper item. "Look," she said, "that's about your school teacher."

The little girl spelled through the item slowly. It told how a man by the name of John Kennedy who was estranged from his wife had, on Wednesday last, driven up to the house where his little girl was living, had picked her up from the yard where she was playing and had driven off with her. Thereafter he had not been seen for two days but had finally been apprehended in a little town to the south and brought to justice. The child had been restored to her mother.

And now that child was grown up and had become the little girl's school teacher! The little girl spelled through the item again. She tried to think how many years ago all this had happened. She asked grandfather and grandmother said it had been 20 years, a very long time. Had the man ever tried to run off with the little girl again? No, he hadn't. But maybe she loved her father better than her mother and would have been glad to go with him? Grandmother didn't know.

All day Saturday and Sunday the little girl thought about her school teacher. The little girl liked her but she had never thought of her with any particular interest. She was a tall and rather large woman who wore shirtwaists and skirts. Her hips were large and she wore black shiny belts. Around her neck she wore a ribbon bow. Her hair was braided in a large mound at the back of her head.

The little girl decided that when she got back to school Monday she would look at her school teacher carefully. There must be something about the woman that she had missed. Here was a person to whom something wonderful and romantic had happened and it had been written about in the newspaper. The little girl, who had already spelled her way through two novels by Bertha M. Clay, could see it all clearly; the golden-haired child playing in the yard; the man with the shiny black whiskers driving up in the red wheeled phaeton; the abduction, the distracted mother and, finally, the child grown to beautiful and radiant womanhood and betrothed to an English earl.

The little girl wondered why her school teacher had never married. Certainly a person who at one time in her life had been kidnapped must have a great many suitors. Perhaps she had suitors but wasn't telling anybody and would be married in the spring with a great deal of éclat. The little girl wondered how her school teacher would look in a wedding dress. She decided that she had never looked at her school teacher rightly before. That golden-haired child who had been kidnapped could never have grown into this large woman with the stiff shirtwaists and the ribbon bows.

On Monday morning the little girl got to school early. Her teacher was marking things on the board. The little girl observed her only out of the corner of her eye. It was her intention not to look for a long time and then wheel suddenly and observe the transformation.

After a long, long time, five minutes perhaps, she wheeled. But the transformation did not come. It was all there just the same as it had been before – the shiny black belt and the hips and the braided mound of hair on the back of the head.

The little girl sat down heavily before her desk. For a long time she sat with her chin cupped in her hands. Then she got out her spelling book.

<hr>

16 July 1927, Saturday:

A NICE LETTER

DEAR JO:

Wednesday afternoon I went with Beth Hollis and Frank Hines out to the Rotary camp for crippled children at Rex Lake. While there Mrs. Kenneth Smith, you know her I think, for she and her nice husband stay out there each year with the kiddies during camp period, told me that they had to send four children home 'cause they were homesick. One little boy ran away the second day. She said they were nearly frightened to death until they located him at his home. Another little girl, Isabel, cried the first two nights and wanted to go home and come to find out she had a baby sisters and was used to putting her to bed. So they went to town and got her mother and baby and brought them to see her. They come often now and so everything is all right.

And by the way, Jo, I longed for you every minute I was there. You love of people would have found so much to work on. Each of the 129 crippled kiddies there was a story. There was Marcus, who was learning to swim in spite of his physical handicap and wanted more than anything else to go hunting turtles so that he could keep one in his bunk; Ruth, who couldn't walk a step but was able to keep her self afloat in the water and help some of the others along during the play hour in the roped in bathing place; Chester, who could dive like a veteran; PeeWee who was trying his best to do like the older boys; Red, freckle-faced and sunburned who was trying to stay under water for ten seconds without opening his mouth; Victoria, who gathered clam shells and loved their iridescent lining because they looked like the silk of Beth's lavender dress; Kasmene, who frankly told us she never saw us before when we called "hello" to her upon arriving, and oh so many others.

They were having such a good time it was hard to realize they weren't like other little folk. Lots of them were brought to the pool in coaster wagons and on crutches.

But they were not daunted by helpless legs and crooked backs. Hez Simmons and I sat in one of the wagons on the shore and watched them play. At first I was overwhelmed by the utter hopelessness of it all until he said in his great hearty way, "why when you have watched them for several years and actually seen improvement in most every case you forget all about that." And then I learned how the Rotary club keeps in touch with the children throughout the year; how their progress is watched and if none is evident, how ways and means are provided for their improvement if possible.

While we were talking other members of the club came. There was Dr. Smith, Howard Adams, Milo Sammons and any number of others, many of them with their wives and all joined in helping these little unfortunates have a good time every minute. Some of the children preferred the sliding board, sand pile, teeter-totter and swings instead of the water. Willing hands were ready on every hand to assist.

And all of the time under canvas awnings sat a group of convalescing patients from the Children's hospital that had been brought out for the day to enjoy the comradeship and fun.

Mary Bogrette was there from the hospital to see that each child kept well. She goes out each year it seems and you should see how those kiddies adore her.

She took us to see her improvised hospital, also the immaculate dining room, kitchen and sleeping quarters. Preparations were being made for supper when we left. I'll wager there was plenty of fun, for Mr. Hines left a big box full of rubber chickens that had feathers and stood up if you filled them full of air. All the way home I thought of the fine spirit of unselfishness back of things at that little camp. Thank God for an organization that is prompted by such a motive.

ETHEL.

Chapter X.

Calamity befalls Greatness

Calamity befalls greatness

—◦⚬◦⟨◦⟩◆⟨◦⟩◦⚬◦—

T was hidden from the public that Josephine suffered a stillborn child on July 19, 1927 at the Peoples Hospital[287] in Akron. A son was born. A son she likely would have called Ambrose, or even possibly John or Bill, as she spoke of when Mary was born. On his birth certificate though, he is only known as Stillborn Rigby. Sadness befalls the young Rigby family.

This childbirth caused major trauma and complications for Josephine, of which are not known other than those employed at the Peoples Hospital during her stay. She had been rushed to the hospital on July 18, 1927, the night prior for immediate surgery at 7 o'clock. The newspapers reported continually there was an intestinal disorder they were operating on that was critical condition.

Thus, for weeks following, Josephine would be at Peoples Hospital fighting for her own life. She received two blood transfusions including one from her own father, Harry Van de Grift, and another on Monday, August 8th, from a Beacon Journal proofreader whose blood she matched, known as Irene Britt. After five weeks of battling pain, and two weeks after her blood transfusions, she succumbed to her death on Sunday, August 21, 1927. Her official death certificate gives death as myocarditis. Age 32 years, 6 months, 24 days. Though sad to read, these news clippings are all that we have for the moments up to her passing.

—◦⚬◦⟨◦⟩◆⟨◦⟩◦⚬◦—

---

[287] Peoples hospital, founded in 1914, is now the Akron General Medical Center at 400 Wabash av., and the original building has been now replaced by additions and façades.

FEATURE WRITER SERIOUSLY ILL AT LOCAL HOSPITAL

Josephine Van De Grift, Beacon Journal Columnist, Undergoes Major Operation

HAS LARGE FOLLOWING

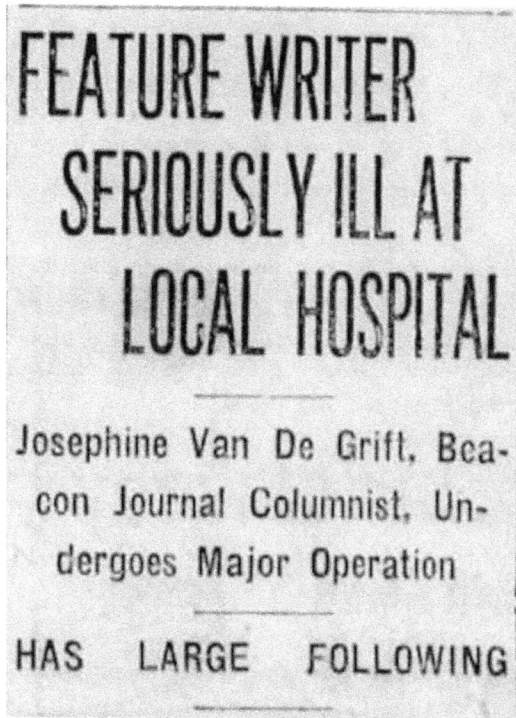

19 July 1927, Tuesday:

(image): **FEATURE WRITER SERIOUSLY ILL AT LOCAL HOSPITAL**

Josephine Van De Grift, Beacon Journal Columnist, Undergoes Major Operation

HAS LARGE FOLLOWING

MRS. William H. Rigby, 320 Fairy st., known to thousands of Beacon Journal readers as Josephine Van De Grift is in serious condition in Peoples hospital following an operation Monday night.

She was rushed to the hospital where an operation was performed at 7 o'clock. Hospital attendants reported her in serious condition Tuesday.

Seven Years On Staff

As a feature writer on the Beacon Journal for seven years, Miss Van De Grift has won thousands of friends through the human quality of the stories she writes. Her feature stories on Summit county people and Summit county happenings appeared daily.

Her column, "Demi-Tasse and Mrs. Grundy," on the magazine page of the Beacon Journal, is another daily feature which has increased her popularity with the reading public.

Central Graduate

Miss Van De Grift started her newspaper career in Akron as society editor on the Beacon Journal, after studying at old Buchtel college. She attended high school at Central.

While society editor she began writing feature stories and became well known through her brilliant articles. Her work attracted attention of eastern newspaper executives and she went to New York where she worked for a newspaper syndicate.

She returned to Akron several years ago and joined the staff of the Beacon Journal again, starting her column and writing features.

Has One Child

Miss Van De Grift was married several years ago to William H. Rigby, proprietor of the Rigby Book Store, 24 S. High st. They have one child, Mary.

She is a member of the Altrusa club and the Woman's City club, and has been an active figure in the Theater Guild activities.

Hundreds Of Telephone Calls From Friends Deluge Hospital Where Josephine Van De Grift, Writer, Is In Serious Condition

CONTACT between Josephine Van De Grift, Beacon Journal feature writer and columnist, and her hundreds of readers and admirers has not ceased while she is in Peoples hospital.

More than 500 telephone calls to the hospital were made Tuesday by anxious friends inquiring about her.

Many of those who called undoubtedly knew her only through her column, "Demi Tasse and Mrs. Grundy," and her feature writings.

Besides the telephone calls to the hospital, many were made at the Beacon Journal office, and at the homes of members of the staff last night and this morning.

Miss Van De Grift, who in private life is Mrs. William H. Rigby,

was taken to Peoples hospital Monday and underwent a major operation Monday night.

Her condition if still serious and has not changed since Tuesday, hospital attendants reported today.

The homely little happenings of life that Miss Van De Grift wrote about, and her interest in Akronites and their work, forged a bond of sympathy between her and her

readers that is being shown now that she is ill.

From the time the first word of her illness was given to her friends Tuesday morning the calls at the Peoples hospital began. They continued through the day and till late last night. Her closer friends, anxious for more than could be learned at the hospital call members of the Beacon Journal staff for word of her illness.

632

20 July 1927, Wednesday:

(image): **HUNDREDS OF TELEPHONE CALLS FROM FRIENDS DELUGE HOSPITAL WHERE JOSEPHINE VAN DE GRIFT, WRITER, IS IN SERIOUS CONDITION**

CONTACT between Josephine Van De Grift, Beacon Journal feature writer and columnist, and her hundreds of readers and admirers has not ceased while she is in Peoples hospital.

More than 500 telephone calls to the hospital were made Tuesday by anxious friends inquiring about her.

Many of those who called undoubtedly knew her only through her column, "Demi Tasse and Mrs. Grundy," and her feature writings.

Besides the telephone calls to the hospital, many were made at the Beacon Journal office, and at the homes of members of the staff last night and this morning.

Miss Van De Grift, who in private life is Mrs. William H. Rigby, was taken to Peoples hospital Monday and underwent a major operation Monday night.

Her condition is still serious and has not changed since Tuesday, hospital attendants reported today.

The homely little happenings of life that Miss Van De Grift wrote about, and her interest in Akronites and their work, forged a bond of sympathy between her and her readers that is being shown now that she is ill.

From the time the first word of her illness was given to her friends Tuesday morning the calls at the Peoples hospital began. They continued through the day and till late last night. Her closer friends, anxious for more than could be learned at the hospital call members of the Beacon Journal staff for word of her illness.

---

21 July 1927, Thursday: (to note, this is one month before her passing)

TRANSFUSION FOR WRITER POSTPONED

Rally By Josephine Van De Grift Causes Change In Physicians' Plans

READY at any time to perform a blood transfusion, attendants at Peoples hospital Thursday noon watched a slight gain in strength of Josephine Van De Grift, Beacon Journal writer, who is seriously ill there.

Blood transfusion was decided on by physicians Wednesday. Tests were made of several persons who volunteered to give blood.

Is Semi-Conscious

Rallying slightly Miss Van De Grift showed the first gain since she was taken to the hospital for a major operation Monday night. She was semi-conscious last night and showed enough improvement to warrant postponement of the blood transfusion.

Her condition still is critical, according to hospital attendants and transfusion may be resorted to later.

Telephone calls from readers of her column in the Beacon Journal continue at both the hospital and homes of her friends on the staff.

---

22 July 1927, Friday:

FEATURE WRITER IN CRITICAL CONDITION

Blood Transfusion Operation Will Be Performed In Case Of Relapse

CONDITION of Josephine Van De Grift, Beacon Journal feature writer and columnist, critically ill at Peoples hospital, following a major operation, was reported unchanged Friday.

She rested poorly during the night it was reported, but had gained complete consciousness.

Attending physicians described her condition as "holding her own and doing as well as might be expected under the circumstances."

Held In Reserve

Although a blood transfusion was proposed several days ago, it was postponed when she showed improvement. The transfusion will be held in reserve and will be made only in event of a relapse, it was declared.

While the writer's condition continued serious, hundreds of friends and readers were keeping in constant touch with the reports from the bedside, calling at both the hospital and Beacon Journal office.

---

23 July 1927, Saturday:

(image): **WRITER'S CONDITION STILL IS CRITICAL**

No Definite Change Reported By Physicians Attending Josephine Van De Grift

CONDITION of Josephine Van De Grift, Beacon Journal feature writer, continued very critical Saturday, physicians of Peoples hospital reported.

No definite change was noted during the night, attendants said. Physicians in charge of the case continued the close watch Saturday, prepared to perform a blood transfusion if her condition became worse.

She was taken to the hospital when a major operation became necessary to save her life.

WRITER'S CONDITION STILL IS CRITICAL

No Definite Change Reported By Physicians Attending Josephine Van De Grift

---

26 July 1927, Tuesday:

(image): **WRITER WILL GET WELL!**

**Hospital Authorities Say That Josephine Van De Grift Is On Road To Recovery
– News Means Much To Akron**

A week ago today Akron was shocked to read in its newspapers that Josephine Van De Grift lay at the point of death following a major operation which had been performed the night before.

Today for the first time the news from the hospital is definitely cheerful.

Since Saturday, she has shown improvement. Yesterday she was well enough to argue with her doctor. Last night she rested splendidly – the first deep sleep she has had since the operation. And today the conservative authorities at the Peoples hospital announced that – barring developments not now foreseen – Miss Van De Grift will get well.

How much this news means to the public in Akron will be seen from the fact that never, since the Peoples hospital was built, has any patient treated there been the subject of so many telephone calls of inquiry.

Not only the hospital was the object of these numerous requests for bulletins on Miss Van De Grift's condition.

The Beacon Journal office and all the employes of the Beacon Journal at their homes were repeatedly solicited for information during the days when it looked dark for Miss Van De Grift.

Hundreds of people who made inquiry knew Miss Van De Grift personally. During her service with the Beacon Journal she made many friends. There is no person in the city who has a larger speaking acquaintance.

Thousands of those who made inquiry had never, to their knowledge, seen her, yet they felt a personal interest because of their acquaintance with her column, "Demi-Tasse and Mrs. Grundy." In this column Miss Van De Grift made her readers intimate with her household affairs and with her husband – Bill – and her daughter – Mary.

Miss Van De Grift in her private life is Mrs. William H. Rigby. Her husband is proprietor of a bookshop at 24 S. High st.

---

28 July 1927, Thursday:

FEATURE WRITER REPORTED BETTER

Josephine Van De Grift Still Showing Steady Improvement In Condition

"SHE is much better."

That was the response Peoples hospital attendants made Thursday when friends of Josephine aVn [sic] De Grift, Beacon Journal feature writer, who has been critically ill at that institution following an operation nearly two weeks ago, inquired about her condition.

Steady improvement has been reported in her condition since Monday. She is said to be rapidly gaining strength. She slept well Wednesday night, attendants said.

---

2 August 1927, Tuesday:

WRITER TO UNDERGO ANOTHER OPERATION

Josephine Van De Grift's Condition Serious – Blood Transfusion Is Made

JOSEPHINE Van De Grift, Beacon Journal feature writer and columnist, was on the operating table at the People's hospital at noon Tuesday, undergoing, an intestinal operation. Her condition was reported as serious.

Earlier in the day she had undergone an operation for blood transfusion. Harry Van De Grift, her father, contributed the pint and one half of blood used in the operation.

Following the blood transfusion, her condition was believed fair enough to permit the intestinal operation, which was of urgent nature.

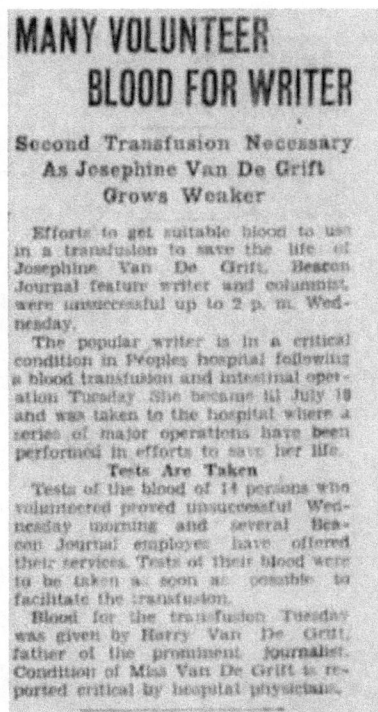

<hr/>

3 August 1927, Monday:

MANY VOLUNTEER BLOOD FOR WRITER

Second Transfusion Necessary As Josephine Van De Grift Grows Weaker

FFORTS to get suitable blood to use in a transfusion to save the life of Josephine Van De Grift, Beacon Journal feature writer and columnist, were unsuccessful up to 2 p.m. Wednesday.

The popular writer is in a critical condition in Peoples hospital following a blood transfusion and intestinal operation Tuesday. She became ill July 18 and was taken to the hospital where a series of major operations have been performed in efforts to save her life.

Tests Are Taken

Tests of the blood of 14 persons who volunteered proved unsuccessful Wednesday morning and several Beacon Journal employes have offered their services. Tests of their blood were to be taken as soon as possible to facilitate the transfusion.

Blood for the transfusion Tuesday was given by Harry Van De Grift, father of the prominent journalist. Condition of Miss Van De Grift is reported critical by hospital physicians.

---

4 August 1927, Thursday:

WRITER'S CONDITION SHOWS IMPROVEMENT

Unexpected Change For Better Noted In Josephine Van De Grift – Delay Transfusion

UNEXPECTED improvement in the condition of Josephine Van De Grift, Beacon Journal feature writer and columnist, has caused indefinite postponement of a blood transfusion that was to take place Thursday morning.

Physicians at Peoples hospital, where the Beacon Journal writer has been in serious condition since July 18, were surprised at the rally staged by Miss Van De Grift, and decided the blood transfusion would not be necessary.

Volunteers Blood

Blood for the transfusion was volunteered by Mrs. Irene Britt, 207 Beck av., employe of the Beacon Journal who was selected Wednesday after blood tests of 50 persons had been taken.

Up to Thursday morning, condition of the popular writer was so critical a blood transfusion was considered inevitable to save her life. She has undergone a series of major operations since her confinement to the hospital and was in a weakened condition.

New hope for her recovery has been inspired by the improvement in her condition.

5 August 1927, Friday:

(image): **FEATURE WRITER IS HOLDING STRENGTH**

Hospital Reports Show Josephine Van De Grift's Condition Slightly Improved

CONDITION of Josephine Van De Grift, Beacon Journal feature writer and columnist, remained unchanged Friday afternoon, according to report of Peoples hospital authorities.

Slight improvement in her condition Thursday caused postponement of a blood transfusion that had earlier been deemed advisable to save her life.

Undergoes Operation

Operation for an intestinal disorder and a blood transfusion Tuesday left the writer in a critical condition. Her strength was at low ebb Wednesday but staged a comeback Thursday.

Peoples hospital physicians were hopeful Friday that it would not be necessary to perform another blood transfusion.

———————————◆———————————

8 August 1927, Monday:

SECOND TRANSFUSION OF BLOOD IS MADE

Operation Performed in Effort to Save Life of Josephine Van De Grift

SECOND blood transfusion within a week was performed on Josephine Van De Grift, Beacon Journal feature writer and columnist, at noon Monday, in an effort to save her life.

She suffered a relapse in Peoples hospital Sunday, appeared to have regained strength early Monday and then had a turn for the worse that caused her doctors to order the second blood transfusion.

SECOND TRANSFUSION OF BLOOD IS MADE

Operation Performed In Effort To Save Life Of Josephine Van De Grift

Second blood transfusion within a week was performed on Josephine Van De Grift, Beacon Journal feature writer and columnist, at noon Monday, in an effort to save her life.

She suffered a relapse in Peoples hospital Sunday, appeared to have regained strength early Monday and then had a turn for the worse that caused her doctors to order the second blood transfusion.

"Extremely Weak"

Her condition was reported by hospital authorities as "extremely weak" and it was indicated that the second blood transfusion was looked upon as the only hope of saving her.

Blood for the transfusion was given by Mrs. Irene Britt, 207 Beck av., who also is employed by the Beacon Journal. She gave slightly over a pint of blood. Mrs. Britt was chosen last week when necessity of a transfusion seemed imminent, after 50 tests of other persons had proved unsuccessful.

"Extremely Weak"

Her condition was reported by hospital authorities as "extremely weak" and it was indicated that the second blood transfusion was looked upon as the only hope of saving her.

Blood for the transfusion was given by Mrs. Irene Britt, 207 Beck av., who also is employed by the Beacon Journal. She gave slightly over a pint of blood. Mrs. Britt was chosen last week when necessity of a transfusion seemed imminent, after 50 tests of other persons had proved unsuccessful.

9 August 1927, Tuesday:

STAFF WRITER SHOWS SLIGHT IMPROVEMENT

Josephine Van De Grift Has Restful Night At Peoples Hospital

JOSEPHINE Van De Grift, Beacon Journal feature writer and columnist spent a restful night Monday, following a blood transfusion. Slight improvement in her condition was reported by Peoples hospital authorities, Tuesday.

She slept several hours during the night and appeared refreshed this morning.

A pint of blood was injected into her system at noon Monday when her condition became dangerously weak. Blood for the transfusion was given by Mrs. Irene Britt, 207 Beck av., another Beacon Journal employe.

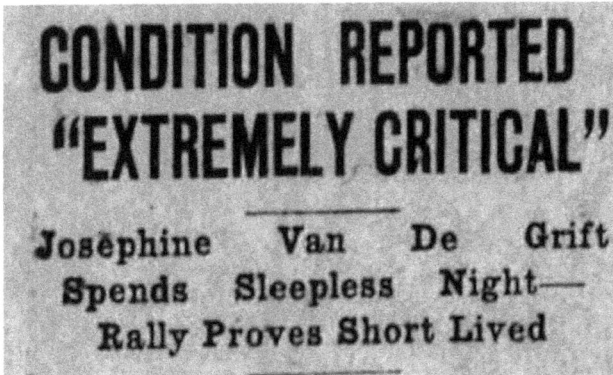

***

10 August 1927, Wednesday:

(image): **CONDITION REPORTED "EXTREMELY CRITICAL"**

Josephine Van De Grift Spends Sleepless Night – Rally Proves Short Lived

ONDITION of Josephine Van De Grift, Beacon Journal feature writer and columnist Cwas reported "extremely critical" by Peoples hospital authorities Wednesday.

A sleepless night Tuesday had serious results for the plucky writer and she was dangerously weak when morning came. Physicians today expressed grave doubts as to whether she could long continue her struggle for life unless improvement in her condition was noted soon.

The second blood transfusion within a week was performed Monday in an attempt to give Miss Van De Grift new strength and vitality. She rallied slightly a few hours after the operation, but the rally was short lived.

---

13 August 1927, Saturday:

RESTFUL NIGHT IS REPORTED FOR WRITER

JOSEPHINE Van De Grift, Beacon Journal feature writer and columnist spent a restful night Friday and her condition continued "the same," Peoples hospital authorities reported Saturday.

A blood transfusion undergone by the writer Tuesday apparently has given her renewed strength, although her condition was critical for several hours following the operation.

---

17 August 1927, Wednesday:

Restful Night Spent By Feature Writer

NO change was noted in the condition of Josephine Van De Grift, Beacon Journal feature writer and columnist, Wednesday, Peoples hospital authorities reported.

She slept well Tuesday night. Her (illegible) fighting chance for life although she still is in (the story cuts off here)

---

18 August 1927, Thursday:

WRITER'S CONDITION IS STILL UNCHANGED

CONDITION of Josephine Van De Grift, Beacon Journal feature writer and columnist continued unchanged, Thursday. Slight improvements in her condition were noted daily since a blood transfusion last week, until Tuesday. Since that time she has been holding her own but making no noticeable improvements, Peoples hospital authorities report.

---

20 August 1927, Thursday:

JOSEPHINE Van De Grift, Beacon Journal feature writer and columnist was reported in fair condition by Peoples hospital authorities, Saturday.

---

22 August 1927, Monday:

(image): "Mrs. William H. Rigby, 32, formerly Josephine Vandergrift, feature writer for the Akron Beacon Journal, died in Peoples hospital after an illness of two months, following several operations. Two blood transfusions failed to give her additional strength and she died of exhaustion, hospital attendants said."

The Woman That Volunteered To Save A Life

IRENE BRITT
Proofreader

This writer wishes to say Thank you, Ms. Irene Britt of Akron, O. Your kindness in donating blood to save my great-grandmother's life is honored and you will always be remembered.

Chapter XI.

The Mourning of a Great Writer

The mourning of a great writer

POPULAR WRITER DIES

Mrs. William H. Rigby, Better Known As Josephine Van De Grift, Popular Columnist, Succumbs In Peoples Hospital After Five Weeks' Illness

Josephine Van De Grift

AKRON FEATURE WRITER
LOSES FIGHT FOR LIFE

Mrs. William H. Rigby, Better Known As Josephine Van De Grift, Popular Columnist, Succumbs After Five Weeks' Illness In Peoples Hospital

A few words from author Kristin Carter-Groulx:

It is with great sadness, author Josephine Van De Grift, has passed on August 21, 1927. Leaving behind her a multitude of grieving readers and fans, a husband and a baby daughter just a little over a year old, Mary.

I shed tears reading over the announcements and tributes left in the papers from her readers and co-workers. Her sudden death left a hole in many hearts. Looking at the little photo to the left, and reflecting on my grandmother, who is Mary and unaware that her mother just passed.

A few short years ago, I underwent several surgeries of my own, fighting cancers and severe disease. I am thankful the new medical technologies exist. I too underwent multiple blood transfusions, just like Josephine would have, although thankful for all of the people who now donate blood to make saving lives like mine possible. I may never know your names, but I won't forget you. I have three children and think of them daily and the life had my fate been the same as Jo's. But I live on. I live to tell my own tale as well as those who came before me. I know in my heart Josephine would have wanted her story to be told and all of her many followers who missed her would welcome this book on their shelves.

August 23, 1927, Tuesday (image):

MARY AWAITS MOTHER

In Little Home On Fairy St. Josephine Van De Grift's Baby Watches And Wonders – Too Young To Know

JOURNAL

AUGUST 23, 1927 (THIRTY-TWO PAGES)

MARY AWAITS MOTHER

In Little Home On Fairy St. Josephine Van De Grift's Baby Watches And Wonders—Too Young To Know

"**L**ITTLE MARY RIGBY is in the house at 320 Fairy st., today wondering when her mother will come home.

Mary's happy year and a half in this world hasn't prepared her for the thing that happened Sunday. She is too young yet to know the meaning of death – death that came to her mother, Josephine Van De Grift Rigby, on a bed of pain at Peoples hospital.

She misses her mother though with a poignancy that will deepen with passing days. Through the writings of her mother, Mary is known to and loved by thousands of Akronites who have never seen her. This is her picture."

LITTLE MARY RIGBY is in the house at 320 Fairy st., today wondering when her mother will come home.

Mary's happy year and a half in this world hasn't prepared her for the thing that happened Sunday. She is too young yet to know the meaning of death—death that came to her mother, Josephine Van De Grift Rigby, on a bed of pain at Peoples hospital.

She misses her mother though with a poignancy that will deepen with passing days. Through the writings of her mother, Mary is known to and loved by thousands of Akronites who have never seen her. This is her picture.

Entire City Mourns Death Of Josephine Van De Grift, Writer

PAY FINAL TRIBUTES TO FEATURE WRITER

Hundreds Present As Solemn
High Mass Is Sung For
Josephine Van De Grift

(Continued From Page One)

Hundreds Present As Solemn High Mass Is Sung For Josephine Van De Grift

HER GENIUS IS PRAISED

Beacon Journal Officials, Employes Serve As Pallbearers—Burial At Holy Cross

(Pictures On Page 17)

To the genius of Josephine Van De Grift Rigby and to her humanity, Rev. John J. Scullen, pastor of St. Vincent's church, paid a tribute in the sermon which he preached at her funeral services this morning.

"The sorrowing ones and the weak ones knew her for their friend," he said. "They went to her as if by instinct, and laid their troubles before her. She did not ask who they were nor what they were, but gave them out of the fullness of her heart sympathy and understanding and encouragement.

"She gave these gifts also to many who had never seen her—whose contact with her had been only through the printed page. Not only in her written word did she uplift these unseen friends, but by her example also."

HUNDREDS ATTEND RITES FOR WRITER

---

24 August 1927, Wednesday (image):

FINAL TRIBUTES ARE PAID AKRON FEATURE WRITER

Hundreds Present As Solemn High Mass Is Sung For Josephine Van De Grift

HER GENIUS IS PRAISED

Beacon Journal Officials, Employes Serve As Pallbearers – Burial At Holy Cross

TO the genius of Josephine Van De Grift Rigby and to her humanity, Rev. John J. Scullen, pastor of St. Vincent's church, paid a tribute in the sermon which he preached at her funeral services this morning.

"The sorrowing ones and the weak ones knew her for their friends," he said. "They went to her as if by instinct, and laid their troubles before her. She did not ask who they were nor what they were, but gave them out of the fullness of her heart sympathy and understanding and encouragement.

"She gave these gifts also to many who had never seen her – whose contact with her had been only through the printed page. Not only in her written word did she uplift these unseen friends, but by her example also."

Tells Of Conversion

He told of her conversion to the Catholic faith while she lay on the hospital cot that was to be her death-bed.

"Her friends," he said, "and her own family may derive consolation from the fact that she died without panic – that she died in peace and confidence after her long suffering."

The sermon followed a solemn high mass which was sung by Rev. Patrick T. Burke.

When, at 9 o'clock, the retarded rhythm of the toiling bell began, there was seated in the church a great throng of people. There were close friends of hers from every walk of life – from the dignitaries of the city who had respected her for her excellence to the charwomen whom she had known and whose lives she had understood.

Outside, a premature autumn day was dazzling in its brilliance. Thick white clouds drifted across a sky intensely blue. These clouds, drifting between the sun and the earth, alternately darkened and lightened the interior of the church.

Altar Boys Appear

As the altar boys appeared behind the chancel, an organ lifted its gentile, compelling voice into the vaulted heights over the heads of those who sat, silently, in the pews. The altar boys, led by the symbol of the church, walked slowly down the aisle.

When they returned, the coffin followed them. Behind it walked the pall-bearers – friends of hers – colleagues in her life work.

ABOVE are scenes as the casket was carried from St. Vincent's church, Wednesday morning, following solemn high mass for Josephine Van De Grift, Beacon Journal writer.

The top photo shows a portion of the crowd standing on the steps of the church. Center shows pallbearers, Beacon Journal officials and co-workers, carrying the casket to the hearse, and below is another view of the pallbearers and casket.

They were followed by the mourners — the widower, her father and mother, and the friends who had been closest to her.

The ancient ceremonies of the faith were begun.

After the ritual at the church, the cortege moved slowly away to Holy Cross cemetery, where the last irrevocable service was done not what was mortal of Josephine Van De Grift Rigby.

The pallbearers were: J. H. Barry, business manager of the Beacon Journal; H. S. Seymour, circulation manager; Paul Bishop, assistant news editor; Howard Wolf, special writer; Carl Stubig, secretary to C. L. Knight, and Robert E. Powers, publicity man.

Cunninghams were in charge of the funeral.

Mrs. Rigby, for seven years a writer for the Beacon Journal, was known both locally and nationally as a columnist and feature writer. In May, 1925, she was married to William H. Rigby, a bookseller. Their home was at 320 Fairy st., in this city. One daughter, Mary, a year and a half old, is left motherless.

Mrs. Rigby was the daughter of Mr. and Mrs. Harry Van De Grift, 620 E. Buchtel av. She was a graduate of Central high school and a student at the University of Akron. She was a member of many local organizations of professional and business women.

Her death occurred Sunday afternoon following five weeks of illness, during the course of which two operations and two blood transfusions were resorted to in an effort to save her life.

A Loving Tribute:

VACANT CHAIR!

Josephine Van De Grift Occupied Unique Place In Affections Of Co-workers—Striking Tribute Written By Staff Member

On August 22, 1927, Herman Fetzer, well known to his readers as Jake Falstaff, wrote a tribute to his friend and fellow journalist, Josephine. A touching final tribute that comprised of nearly a full page reprinted on November 12, 1927. Thank you, Mr. Fetzer. You make my heart ache with your words that touch me deeply.

By Herman Fetzer

"

There will be no more columns under the title of "Demi-Tasse and Mrs. Grundy" and no more feature stories in the Beacon Journal signed "Josephine Van De Grift."

Josephine Van De Grift died yesterday at 3:45 p.m. at the Peoples hospital. One the hospital records she is listed as Mrs. William H. Rigby. That was her name in private life, but for every person who knew her by that name there were hundreds that knew her only by the other.

Her death closes a life in which the final audit must appear on the credit side.

Wins Place in Public Affection

She had achieved more than mere popularity. She had attained a public affection. Her excellence as a writer would have assured her of the former. Only her innate sympathy could have won her the latter.

To the people who were constant readers of her column – and they were legion – it is as if a blind were drawn over a window through which they often looked, and always with pleasure.

The little house at 320 Fairy st., becomes a private residence now. What goes on behind its walls will no longer be a part of the mental experience of a sympathetic public. The friendly figure which stood always at the doorstep, beckoning the world in for tea and talk, is inanimate now.

Mary is motherless. Bill is a widower.

After one day less than five weeks of pain, after operations and blood transfusions and the complicated attention of nurses and surgeons, Josephine crossed the narrow space that had lain between her and the shadows, and was alive no more.

Sympathy For Others

This pain which she endured hurt her less than the same pain in another person would have hurt her. The thought of another's misery was her greatest grief.

She could not sleep when Floyd Collins was held, crippled but alive, a prisoner in Sand Cave. A story about a man who had thrown a live guinea-pig into a furnace made her a changed person for a week.

This was linked with her generosity. No beggar who ever accosted her left without his piece of silver. It was oftener a quarter than a dime, and not infrequently it was a half dollar. After he had gone, she wished she had given him more.

She tipped waiters exorbitantly. When she was chided for this by her table companions, she said, "But their feet hurt them!"

Her desk at the Beacon Journal office was the mecca for Lord knows what queer fish. To every person who differed from the normal mass she freely gave her attention and her sympathy. This was, in part, because she knew that the world hurts every person who does not conform to its norms.

She had not conformed. She had been hurt. This recollection was not as important to her as the knowledge that the thing was still going on in the lives of other people. Her own experience merely opened a window into the secret histories of other human beings.

Splendid As Interviewer

As an interviewer, she was splendid. The person much used to talking with reporters was grateful to her because she dealt efficiently and tactfully with him. The person who was new to the experience she put at his ease, assuming the role of hostess to him, chatting with him about the questions she wanted to ask if it were a personal encounter rather than the greeting of a reporter and a person to be interviewed.

She was forever doing some small service for somebody. She wrote letters for people who did not feel at home with the written word; she transmitted telephone messages for printers who were prevented by their work from doing it themselves; she listened to the domestic troubles of many and gave each one what advice he needed – and what is more – the sympathy that he wanted.

Her speeches were always brief. She did not care greatly about speaking, but she hated to refuse. She was nervous in advance of her appearance and unsettled afterward. But she did not betray this in her delivery. Her speeches like her columns were intimate and friendly and confiding.

Won Friends Readily

People who attended them merely for the sake of saying that they had seen Josephine Van De Grift went away with the feeling that they knew her very well.

It was not her original intention to be a writer. She construed her talents to be musical – and there was no doubt that she had a sincere feeling and a definite gift in that direction. Her musical ambitions led her to Chicago for training. This was her first taste of life away from home.

It was through her music that she first wrote for a newspaper. She was asked to write an account of a musical event. The account so pleased the editor to whom it was given that she was offered a job. She took it. Thenceforth she was a newspaper woman.

For some time she conducted the society columns for the Beacon Journal, entering her connection with his paper seven years ago. Then she was given a try at feature writing. She was an immediate success at this. Her name over a feature story became a daily thing in the Beacon Journal.

Prize Winning Play

She entered a competition in playwriting. The prize was admission to the exclusive Harvard workshop for playwrights. Her entry ranked first. She did not follow up this opportunity to learn the technique of the drama, preferring to remain a newspaperwoman.

Five years ago this fall, a syndicate, attracted by the character of her feature stories, offered her a situation in New York.

She took the job. For a year and a half she lived in the metropolis, accumulating as miscellaneous a group of friends as she had in this city.

They ranged from millionaires to peanut vendors – from successful authors to the shadowy, impoverished denizens of The Village[288]. In The Village itself she lived a great deal of the time she spent in New York. She was fond of the queer people to whom one might speak on Washington Square; she loved the soft dreamy evenings of Chelsea.

She talked with Christopher Morley on the subway; William McFee wanted her to collaborate with him on a play.

Fragments of Life

There remains from her Greenwich Village experience a small sheaf of sketches – quiet little character studies which were not artificial enough for the magazines. Editors sent letters back with the manuscripts and said these were very excellent, but not the kind of material they wanted. Something commercial – something that followed the modern formula. But that wasn't what Josephine had found in the Village. She had found fragments of life.

After he return to Akron she started her "Demi-Tasse and Mrs. Grundy" column. The title was a combination of two she liked. From the first, it was immensely popular.

It was hard work. Some days it was done in a jiffy. On other days, the last paragraph would keep her chained to her typewriter until long after the night-side of printers had returned from their evening meal.

Now and then she touched upon a vein that was little short of greatness. She had a way of seeing into the hearts of lonely and timid people. When she dealt with them she was at her best.

Husband's First Customer

---

[288] Greenwich Village

At the time she returned from New York, Bill Rigby was opening his bookshop on High st. She was the first customer, and that encounter was her first meeting with the man who was to become her husband.

They were married in May, 1925.

Josephine continued her work at the Beacon Journal. And then Mary came, and a new personality entered "Demi-Tasse and Mrs. Grundy." Mary was known and loved as her mother was by thousands of persons who had never knowingly seen her.

The problems of the young mother entered into Josephine's writings, and the community which she had built up with all women was cemented by another bond.

She had become a local institution. Hundreds of people knew her well; other hundreds knew her by sight. But thousands knew her by her name and her writings and had never seen her.

When the word was printed, five weeks ago today, that she had undergone a major operation, and was in serious danger of death, it was a shock to the whole city.

Entire City Mourns

Her own friends had known that she was not well. But she had continued her column, and there was no hint of her condition in it. For many days the city with its multitudinous voices poured its queries into the ears of every agency that might give an intelligent answer: How was Josephine?

After a little more than a week the word was passed that she was better. Thousands were pleased by the news.

There was a turn for the worse. Another operation was necessary. To give her strength for it, a blood transfusion was needed. Her father, Harry Van De Grift, 620 E. Buchtel av., gave the blood that was required.

After the operation, gloomy reports came from the hospital. She was hovering between life and death. Another transfusion would have to be made. Literally scores of people offered their blood. It was difficult to find a person whose blood would do.

At length it was found that Mrs. Irene Britt, proofreader at the Beacon Journal, had the right type of blood. Mrs. Britt left a sick-bed to go to the hospital. She gave more than a pint of her life-fluid to the stricken writer.

No Efforts Spared

The slender fighting chances grew narrower and narrower. But no efforts were spared to bring her through the seemingly impregnable barrier between her and recuperation.

The efforts were in vain. Now and then it seemed that she was a little better. At one time, her condition was so serious that she was given oxygen. During the last two weeks she did little but hold her own.

Her decline became apparent during the week-end, and Sunday afternoon she died – a woman too young for death, but one who had done excellently well with what years were vouchsafed her.

The last human offices were performed for her at St. Vincent's church Wednesday morning at 9. Her body was interred in Holy Cross cemetery."

Herman Alfred Fetzer

Her longtime friend and co-worker at the Beacon Journal, Herman Fetzer, known as Jake Falstaff to his readers, shown here in November 1927 at a new office location. The desk, phone, and typewriter would be a similar set-up for Josephine when she worked there. Herman passed away a few years later in 1935. I enjoy seeing these old photos and can only imagine the conversations that transpired between two brilliant writers.

Chapter XII.

Along came

Mary

Along came Mary

December 31ˢᵗ, 1926, Friday (image):

Demi-Tasse and Mrs. Grundy

By JOSEPHINE VAN De GRIFT

MARY

Letter to a Little Girl On Her First Birthday

"MY DEAR:

Today is the day before New Year's and tonight when you are fast asleep whistles will blow and bells will ring and people will go to and fro in the streets, laughing and singing and throwing bright ribbons about one another.

They will do these things because they are glad that another year has been born. But they will do them too because they are glad that it is your birthday.

Can you fancy how sad it would be if there were no little children in the world? There would be no joy then in hanging colored lights on the Christmas tree nor, when the snow melts, in watching for the first anemones, nor, on summer nights, in listening to the music of little green

Can you fancy how sad it would be if there were no little children in the world? There would be no joy then in hanging colored lights on the Christmas tree nor, when the snow melts, in watching for the first anemones, nor, on summer nights, in listening to the music of little green frogs, nor, in frosty twilights, of turning those bright pages which tell of slender youths and sleeping princesses. All would grow cold and dark and the great earth would creak in its turning.

Someday, my dear, when you are taller and you shall have learned to spell in your book and to do your three times threes there may come an old grey beard with icicles under his cap and moss beneath his coat who will wag his wooden finger and tell you to be grateful to your elders.

Do not listen to him, my dear, or if you must be polite, listen only with your outer ear.

For it is your elders who are grateful to you. Until you came their happiness was only half happiness and in their sorrow there was not any gleam at all.

frogs, nor, in frosty twilights, of turning those bright pages which tell of slender youths and sleeping princesses. All would grow cold and dark and the great earth would creak in its turning.

Someday, my dear, when you are taller and you shall have learned to spell in your book and to do your three times threes there may come an old grey beard with icicles under his cap and moss beneath his coat who will wag his wooden finger and tell you to be grateful to your elders.

Do not listen to him, my dear, or if you must be polite, listen only with your outer ear.

For it is your elders who are grateful to you. Until you came their happiness was only half happiness and in their sorrow there was not any gleam at all.

Through you they put out their hands and touch and know the rest of the world. They know the humble joy of the charwoman and the pride of the man who is rich. They know what Mary felt and the mother of Iscariot, and the ewe who lies beside her little lamb in the field. And they know at last what beauty is and what love and what goodness.

These are the things which you brought with you on New Year's eve and these are the things which the people will be holding in their hearts tonight when the whistles blow and the bells ring and the many colored ribbons go cascading through the air.

"Why," they will say, "we are rejoicing because of a little child – the New Year."

Knowing all the while in their hearts that it is a little child which makes not only time but the whole world new.

And so this letter is written to thank you for your coming, to thank you for all the joy which you are yet to bring and to tell you how much you have meant to

ONE WHO LOVES YOU VERY MUCH."

Through you they put out their hands and touch and know the rest of the world. They know the humble joy of the charwoman and the pride of the man who is rich. They know what Mary felt and the mother of Iscariot, and the ewe who lies beside her little lamb in the field. And they know at last what beauty is and what love and what goodness.

These are the things which you brought with you on New Year's eve and these are the things which the people will be holding in their hearts tonight when the whistles blow and the bells ring and the many colored ribbons go cascading through the air.

"Why," they will say, "we are rejoicing because of a little child—the New Year."

Knowing all the while in their hearts that it is a little child which makes not only time but the whole world new.

And so this letter is written to thank you for your coming, to thank you for all the joy which you are yet to bring and to tell you how much you have meant to

ONE WHO LOVES YOU VERY MUCH.

A few words from author Kristin Carter-Groulx:

Childhood memories

I HAVE so many wonderful things to say about my grandmother, Mary. I only knew her for a short time, as she passed away unexpectedly at age 61 when I was about 15.

I was most surprised to read a story from May 12, 1926, where Josephine was run off the road with 6-month-old Mary in the front seat in a basket. It landed the vehicle in a ditch, but Mary was alright and was not injured.

My father told me of stories where Mary also wanted to become a writer and follow in the steps of her mother. There was a time also when she briefly wanted to become a pilot. She declared this at age 4! It made the local newspaper. In the eyes of Jo's readers, Mary was a shining star.

Mary Van de Grift Rigby Likes Stunt Flying Thrills

Daughter Of Late Beacon Journal Columnist, City's Youngest Air Enthusiast, Not Frightened In Climbs, Dives

THEY always knew Mary would be a wonderful child. Just a wee bit smarter than the ordinary run of children. For was she not the daughter of Josephine Van de Grift, their beloved newspaper columnist? And had they not followed her exploits from the very first, ever since she was a tiny baby?

Tired women in a hundred homes in Akron, settling down in their rocking chairs every night after the children were in bed and the supper dishes done, thumbed through the evening papers until they came to "Demi-Tasse and Mrs. Grundy."

"Listen to this," they would read— one to another—"Jo's baby, Mary, had her first tooth yesterday. Now isn't that cute! She beat my Freddie and he's three months older. She sure is a smart baby."

Or again, "Jo Van de Grift has bought a dog for her baby. D'you think we should get one for Jimmie?"

The day that Jo died they gathered up the paper mournfully. They hugged their youngsters a bit closer

—Photo by Gysin

Mary

February 1, 1930, Saturday (image):

665

Mary Van de Grift Rigby Likes Stunt Flying Thrills

Daughter Of Late Beacon Journal Columnist, City's Youngest Air Enthusiast, Not Frightened In Climbs, Dives

"THEY always knew Mary would be a wonderful child. Just a wee bit smarter than the ordinary run of children. For was she not the daughter of Josephine Van de Grift, their beloved newspaper columnist? And had they not followed her exploits from the very first, ever since she was a tiny baby?

Tired women in a hundred homes in Akron, settling down in their rocking chairs every night after the children were in bed and the supper dishes done, thumbed through the evening papers until they came to "Demi-Tasse and Mrs. Grundy."

"Listen to this," they would read – one to another – "Jo's baby, Mary, had her first tooth yesterday. Now isn't that cute! She beat my Freddie and he's three months older. She sure is a smart baby."

Or again, "Jo Van de Grift has bought a dog for her baby. D'you think we should get one for Jimmie?"

The day that Jo died they gathered up the paper mournfully. They hugged their youngsters a bit closer that night. "No more 'Demi-Tasse,' they said. "Poor little Mary."

Some of them even got out their best stationery and the pen and ink and wrote to the editor.

"Be sure to save her mother's clippings for Mary."

"Why nit [sic] publish the clippings in a book and get money for Mary?"

For Mary had suddenly become in a way the child of all Akron.

Remembered At Christmas

And when each Christmas time came around after that there were more than the usual customers at Rigby's little bookshop on High st. Time and again the door would open and a motherly faced woman with perhaps a youngster or two toddling along and a big package in her hand would step in. "For Mary," she would say half timidly putting it down in the fast growing pile of packages. And she would hurry out again.

Even after almost three years they have not forgotten Mary, you see.

And Mary is 4 now. Her little mind is unusually bright as every one predicted and she surprises with her mature questions and comments. She has inherited her mother's keen perceptions as well as her blonde hair and fair complexion.

And Mary is a flier.

Must Fly Frequently

"She teased and teased until about a year ago I took her on her first flight," her father, Bill Rigby, said. "I thought she would be frightened, but instead there was nothing to it. We have to fly winter or summer whenever the flying weather is good."

And so almost every Sunday at the airport one may see a golden-haired tiny child measuring her steps to match her tall father's stride as they hurry out to the "passenger entrance."

Last Sunday the pilot tried a few extra turns and banks. He zoomed low over the field at a 150-mile-an-hour clip, then pointed the nose sharply upward.

"Gee, there's a little girl aboard, too," said one of the spectators, "She'll be scared to death." But a few minutes later Mary stepped nonchalantly out of the plane, blue eyes sparkling. "I think I like the Fairchild best," she said gravely.

Plans Long Flights

Her longest flight thus far has been to Cleveland and back But her dad has longer trips planned for her in the future.

"It's what she wants to do most," he said.

And looking at the big scrap book of clippings which are being saved so carefully for Josephine's child, one cannot help thinking, "Mary, too, may be the inspiration for many a clipping in the next few years." "

Dreams of becoming a writer like her mother

A few more words from author Kristin Carter-Groulx:

Later, Mary did write several short stories and submitted them for approval and publishing. Upon receiving response letters that her stories would not be published at this time, although they were quite good, she tore them up. No original stories exist that we know of. Only the memories and dreams of being the daughter of an amazingly talented and adored writer and wanting to follow in her footsteps.

After her mother Josephine passed, Mary briefly lived with her father at 640 Sackett Street in Cuyahoga Falls, Summit, Ohio (as seen on the 1930 census). In 1940, she lived with her step-mother, Ora Ann (née Carl) Rigby, in Mount Vernon, Lawrence County, Missouri. The following news article was written about her when she was 9 years old and described her new life on the farm in Missouri.

January 16, 1935, Wednesday (image):

Mary, 9, Arouses Memories Of Josephine Van De Grift

Daughter's Resemblance To Columnist Grows As Years Pass

By ETHEL B. MYERS

"YES: She is Josephine's Mary. Many of you will have recognized the unmistakable likeness to her mother.

Those of you who have come to Akron in the last six or seven years will have heard of her, and hearing, wondered with so many others, just what had become of the baby Mary who belonged to all Akron through the many columns written about her by her mother, Josephine Van de Grift Rigby.

Everyone in and around Akron knew about Mary.

They knew when she first smiled and when she cut her first tooth.

They knew when she first said "Mummy." They knew when she took her first step.

Every mother who read the daily column, Demi Tasse and Mrs. Grundy, which appeared for several years in the Beacon Journal, had a person interest in Mary. They worried about her when she was ill just as they did about their own children. Then they stopped hearing. That was in 1927 when Josephine died.

DAUGHTER CLOSELY RESEMBLES MOTHER

Now Mary is 9 years old. From the first she resembled her mother. As the years pass – the likeness increases. Those of us who knew the parent see in Mary another Josephine. There is the same straight, blond bobbed hair, the broad brow and wide-set eyes, the same kindly mouth. And they say she has her mother's gentleness, her ceaseless quest of knowledge, her straightforwardness and her immeasurable love of people.

Mary now lives with another mother. They are on a farm in Missouri. There she has cows, horses and chickens. There she is growing up into a normal, healthy child.

Perhaps, sometime, this other mother will bring Mary back to Akron. We hope to have the opportunity of giving her the picture of herself – a smiling year-old baby with a chubby finger in her mouth – the gift of her own mother, her heart's greatest treasure.

We also would like to give Mary her mother's message to her on her first Christmas. That, too, many of you will remember from Josephine's column. It

ARY 16, 1935

Mary, 9, Arouses Memories Of Josephine Van De Grift

Daughter's Resemblance
To Columnist Grows
As Years Pass

By ETHEL B. MYERS

YES! She is Josephine's Mary. Many of you will have recognized the unmistakable likeness to her mother.

Those of you who have come to Akron in the last six or seven years will have heard of her, and hearing, wondered with so many others, just what had become of the baby Mary who belonged to all Akron through the many columns written about her by her mother, Josephine Van de Grift Rigby.

Everyone in and around Akron knew about Mary.

They knew when she first smiled and when she cut her first tooth.

They knew when she first said "Mummy." They knew when she took her first step.

Every mother who read the daily column, Demi Tasse and Mrs. Grundy, which appeared for several years in the Beacon Journal, had a personal interest in Mary. They worried about her when she was ill just as they did about their own children. Then they stopped hearing. That was in 1927 when Josephine died.

DAUGHTER CLOSELY RESEMBLES MOTHER

Now Mary is 9 years old. From the first she resembled her mother. As the years pass—the likeness increases. Those of us who knew the parent see in Mary another Josephine. There is the same straight, blond bobbed hair, the broad brow and wide-set eyes, the same kindly mouth. And they say she has her mother's gentleness, her ceaseless quest of knowledge, her straightforwardness and her immeasurable love of people.

Mary now lives with another mother. They are on a farm in Missouri. There she has cows, horses and chickens. There she is growing up into a normal, healthy child.

Perhaps, sometime, this other mother will bring Mary back to Akron. We hope to have the opportunity of giving her the picture of herself—a smiling year-old baby with a chubby finger in her mouth—the gift of her own mother, her heart's greatest treasure.

We also would like to give Mary her mother's message to her on her first Christmas. That, too, many of you will remember from Josephine's column. It was the outpouring of a heart brimming with love for the baby from whom she was so soon to part.

Josephine died when Mary was less than 2 years old. To her small daughter she left as a heritage the memory of a tremendously human person, one whose sympathies were honest; one whose heart was ever with the underdog; one whose understanding was never-failing.

MARY RIGBY

was the outpouring of a heart brimming with love for the baby from whom she was so soon to part.

Josephine died when Mary was less than 2 years old. To her small daughter she left as a heritage the memory of a tremendously human person, one whose sympathies were honest; one whose heart was ever with the underdog; one whose understanding was never-failing."

⸺ ⧟⸺⧟ ⸺

Sweet Sixteen and a secret marriage

A few more words from the author:

Mary's father, William Rigby, was drafted for the WWII in 1942. It was a transformative year for Mary.

She fell briefly in love with Melvin Brown (five years older) and was married in secret on summer solstice, June 21, 1942 at age 16. She falsified her true age on the marriage license and put her age as 18 (the legal age) and him as 21. The name on their marriage license was mistakenly entered as "Mary Rogsby" instead of "Mary Rigby."

When her parents found out, it was quickly annulled about two weeks later, as she was a minor.

August 20ᵗʰ, 1942, Thursday (image):

DO YOU KNOW?

"THERE WAS a columnist, for this paper, who, because of her great breadth of feeling and her ability to put that touch of genuinely human interest into writing, firmly entwined herself in the thoughts and memory of many Akron people ... and it is likely these people would be interested in one of her dearest possessions ... her daughter, Mary Rigby. That writer was the late Josephine Van de Grift.

Mary, now 16 years old, was here not long ago visiting a close friend of her mother's, Mrs. William A. Boesche, N. Portage Path. She is living with relatives, on a farm near Mt. Vernon, Mo. When she completes her last year of high school, Mary plans to follow in the footsteps of her mother and become a writer. She expects to enter the University of Missouri and major in journalism."

—— ⌾⌾⌾◆⌾⌾⌾ ——

Graduation and University

On April 23rd, 1943, she participated in her Senior class play, "The Pennington Case," a mystery in three acts written by Richard Hill Wilkinson, where she played Emily, a "colored" [sic] housekeeper. The action of the entirety of the play takes place in the living room of the Jonas Pennington home in Key West, Florida.

She graduated in May 1943 from Mount Vernon High School in Mount Vernon, Missouri. It is said she attended one and a half years of college in Kansas, as referenced in the notes below pertaining to her transcript. It is not believed she decided to go to University of Missouri to study Journalism as she had once intended to do.

Notes about Mary:

> "Mt Vernon High School: Admitted 28 Aug 1939 from MVJHS, Graduated 14 May 1943. Rank 24/87. Remarks: Splendid attitude; has a nice voice; Catholic in faith; gets along well with others; better than average ability. Transcript sent to St Mary's College in Xavier, KS on 8 Aug 1943. Mt Vernon, Lawrence Co., MO."

—— ⌾⌾⌾◆⌾⌾⌾ ——

Falling in love and a child of her own

She either met Ralph in Missouri or in Kansas. He was drafted into the U.S. Army in 1945 during World War II and went to boot camp in Ft. Leavenworth, Kansas.

She married Ralph Carter on April 27th, 1945 by an Army Chaplain, in Tyler, Smith County, Texas. Ralph was stationed for infantry training in Camp Fannin, Texas. He immediately was sent to Okinawa, Japan and returned home in December 1946 for the birth of my father, John.

Together they raised 14 children, with my father, John, being the oldest, born in 1946. Followed by Melinda Jo, Anne, Patricia, Robert, Daniel, Kathleen, Mark, Rachel, Todd, Gretchen, Flora, Jean and Erin. My aunt Erin is only three years older than me.

A note to the living family:

With respect to the family letter found in 2019 written by Mary as an adult just a few years prior to her passing, I have not included details in this book, as many family members mentioned are still living. It is a wish to come across one of her stories that perhaps was saved and be able to publish it. I'm certain she would love that. Just like her mom, Mary was a brilliant writer, sharing honest emotions and a genuine heart. There is no doubt she was an excellent storyteller.

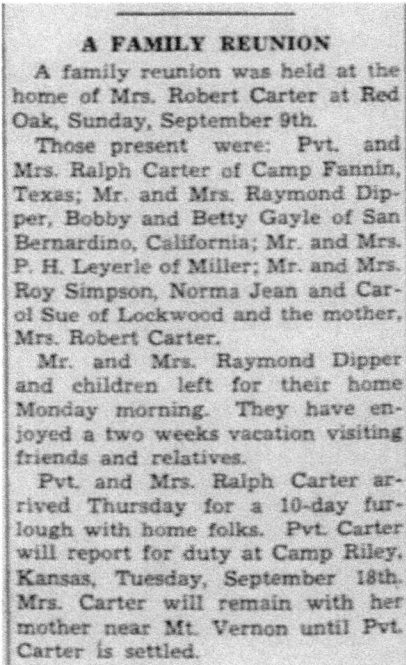

September 13, 1945 (image):

A FAMILY REUNION

A family reunion was held at the home of Mrs. Robert Carter at Red Oak, Sunday, September 9th.

Those present were: Pvt. And Mrs. Ralph Carter of Camp Fannin, Texas; Mr. and Mrs. Raymond Dipper, Bobby and Betty Gayle of San Bernardino, California; Mr. and Mrs. P. H. Leyerle of Miller; Mr. and Mrs. Roy Simpson, Norma Jean and Carol Sue of Lockwood and the mother, Mrs. Robert Carter.

Mr. and Mrs. Raymond Dipper and children left for their home Monday morning. They have enjoyed a two weeks vacation visiting friends and relatives.

Pvt. and Mrs. Ralph Carter arrived Thursday for a 10-day furlough with home folks. Pvt. Carter will report for duty at Camp Riley, Kansas, Tuesday, September 18th. Mrs. Carter will remain with her mother near Mt. Vernon until Pvt. Carter is settled.

Mary and Ralph, 1947

A few more words from the author:

For a few years after their marriage, they lived in San Bernardino, California from 1946 – 1950, where Ralph worked for the Santa Fe Railroad Company. They then returned to Missouri and settled in Lockwood, Dade County.

Worked in nursing after WWII

During or soon after the second world war, she attended nursing school and became a Licensed Practical Nurse. She remained in the occupation of nursing for over three decades.

Her second mother and the one who raised Mary was a nurse. Ora Ann Carl Rigby, a registered World War I nurse, served overseas and received a citation from President Woodrow Wilson on the White House steps in Washington D.C.. Ora Ann was widely known in Southwest Missouri, and helped to pioneer the public health nursing program in Missouri after World War I. During World War II, she was the Lawrence County nurse.

She later ran a nursing home known as "The Hedges" north of Mount Vernon, Missouri. She died in a fire which destroyed the home, after saving two people and returning to try to rescue two others. This was February 1, 1963. At the end of this chapter I have included those news stories.

In the early 1980's Mary, Ralph, and family moved to Evanston, Uinta County, Wyoming, where Mary continued to work in the profession of nursing, helping others, and saving lives – that helpful spirit reflected in both of the mothers that bore and raised her.

Mary's goodbye

She passed away in April 1987 and her remains scattered in a special sacred place atop the mountains in Summit, Utah where it is eternally Christmas.

Mary's half-siblings, David and Anne, passed away soon after in 1988 and 1993 respectively.

Mary's own children (all 14 of them), as well as David and Anne, have left many ancestors still alive in the world today. All of whom have a connection to these wonderful women, Josephine and Ora Ann. And also to William H. Rigby, whose parents came west to escape both the severe losses from the Irish potato famine and the harsh life of living in the coal and cotton-workshops in Salford, England.

I finished this book on November 1, 2019 – All Souls Day – and a day to remember our ancestors and their journeys before us.

Thank you.

Josephine's great-grand daughter & Mary's granddaughter,

Kristin

Three Elderly Persons Die In Flaming Home

MOUNT VERNON, Mo. (A) — The owner of a private nursing home and two of her patients died early today in a fire that destoryed the home north of Mount Vernon.

Mrs. Ora Ann Ribby, 69 owner of the Hedges Rest Home perished when she went back into flaming two-story, frame house for two elderly men patients. She had previously led an eldedly woman to safety and carried out her 14-months-old grandson, John Haley, and a 5-year-old paralytic girl patient, Tonya Orr of Aurora, Mo.

The men who died were Fred Garoutte, 74, of Mount Vernon, and Jim Lauderdale, 83, of Aurora.

Mrs. Mary Tunnell, the woman who was led to safety, said Mrs. Rigby left the children with her when she returned to the house. "The last thing I heard was Mrs. Rigby calling for Mr. Garoutte and Mr. Lauderdale," Mrs. Tunnell said.

There were only four patients at the home, a converted farm house three miles north of Mount Vernon on State Highway 39.

Three fire companies, two from Mount Vernon and one from Miller, fought the blaze. Cause of the fire was not immediately determined.

The alarm was turned in by Mrs. Rigby, who had operated the home since 1948.

Mrs. Rigby's husband, William H. Rigby, 73, said he was sleeping in a cottage some distance from the main house and awoke to find the building in flames.

February 1, 1963, Friday (image):

Three Elderly Persons Die In Flaming Home

MOUNT VERNON, MO (AP) –

"The owner of a private nursing home and two of her patients died early today in a fire that destoryed [sic] the home north of Mount Vernon.

Mrs. Ora Ann Ribby [sic], 69 owner of the Hedges Rest Home perished when she went back into flaming two-story, frame house for two elderly men patients. She had previously led an eldedly [sic] woman to safety and carried out her 14-months-old grandson, John Haley, and a 5-year-old paralytic girl patient, Tonya Orr of Aurora, Mo.

The men who died were Fred Garoutte, 74, of Mount Vernon, and Jim Lauderdale, 83, of Aurora.

Mrs. Mary Tunnell, the woman who was led to safety, said Mrs. Rigby left the children with her when she returned to the house.

"The last thing I heard was Mrs. Rigby calling for Mr. Garoutte and Mr. Lauderdale," Mrs. Tunnell said.

There were only four patients at the home, a converted farm house three miles north of Mount Vernon on State Highway 39.

Three fire companies, two from Mount Vernon and one from Miller, fought the blaze. Cause of the fire was not immediately determined.

The alarm was turned in by Mrs. Rigby, who had operated the home since 1948.

Mrs. Rigby's husband, William H. Rigby, 73, said he was sleeping in a cottage some distance from the main house and awoke to find the building in flames."

February 1, 1963, Friday (image):

Near Mt. Vernon

—Daily News Staff Photo

These five men are shown searching the smouldering ruins of a nursing home near Mt. Vernon for the body of the third victim of a fire which leveled the structure early Friday. The body was recovered yesterday afternoon.

Woman Tells Of Ordeal In Fatal Fire

BY LARRY KLINGER

"MT. VERNON – "I was in bed and woke up and saw the light and the first thing that struck me was that the house was on fire.

"I felt tremendous heat and looked into the other room and the ceiling was falling in."

Eighty-five-year-old Mrs. Mary Tunnell, one of three persons surviving the Hedges Nursing Home tragedy near here, made these comments at the home of relatives last night.

She told of her escape and related the heroism which cost Mrs. Ora Ann Rigby her life as she attempted to rescue two elderly patients from the burning building.

Mrs. Tunnell, of Mt. Vernon, continued:

"Then I started out of the door and went to the front steps of the house and met Mrs. Rigby. She hollered at me. 'Go on out to the cottage.'" Mrs. tunnel said that Mrs. Rigby then rushed back into the burning two-story home.

Mrs. Rigby, who had received a presidential citation for her work as a nurse in World War I, had already carried her 14-month-old grandson, John Hailey, and Tonya Orr, 4, a paralytic girl patient, to safety.

Jim Lauderdale, 83, and Fred Garoutte, 78, were still in the house. Mrs. Rigby's husband, William, was sleeping in the cottage to the rear of the 80-year-old home.

"Then she yelled to Lauderdale to go to the cottage too," Mrs. Tunnell said. "I heard her call to Lauderdale to get out of there. That's the last I heard of her."

"The other men hollered and screamed – then nothing," Mrs. Tunnell said.

• • •

Near Mt. Vernon

Woman Tells Of Ordeal In Fatal Fire

BY LARRY KLINGER
Daily News Staff Writer

MT. VERNON — "I was in bed and woke up and saw the light and the first thing that struck me was that the house was on fire.

"I felt tremendous heat a n d looked into the other room and the ceiling was falling in."

Eighty-five-year-old Mrs. Mary Tunnell, one of three persons surviving the Hedges Nursing Home tragedy near here, made t h e s e comments at the home of relatives last night.

She told of her escape and related the heroism which cost Mrs. Ora Ann Rigby her life as she attempted to rescue two elderly patients from the burning building.

Mrs. Tunnell, of Mt. Vernon, continued:

"Then I started out of the door and went to the front steps of the house and met Mrs. Rigby. She hollered at me. 'Go on out to the cottage.'" Mrs. Tunnell said that Mrs. Rigby then rushed back into the burning two-story home.

Mrs. Rigby, who had received a presidential citation for her work as a nurse in World War I, had already carried her 14-month-old grandson, John Hailey, and Tonya Orr, 4, a paralytic girl patient, to safety.

Friends here yesterday described Mrs. Rigby as "stern but very kind, loved by her patients." Mrs. Rigby, about five feet, five inches tall who weighed about 130 pounds was said to be "very intelligent and quick in her actions."

Mrs. Leila Fossett, Mt. Vernon, said "I asked her several times why she didn't take a job as a nurse somewhere else, where her work would have been much easier."

"She would tell me," Mrs. Fossett commented, "that she had reared her children and wanted to watch them ... and have them with her in the country rather than be a nurse in the city."

"The fire went so fast, it's unbelievable anyone got out," Lawrence County Sheriff Vernon Smith reported.

"Mrs. Rigby was quite a woman ... she proved that ..." another officer added."

Bibliography

&

Acknowledgements

☞

XIII

Bibliography & Acknowledgements

Every effort was made to ensure the integrity of the words remaining true to Josephine's column "Demi-Tasse & Mrs. Grundy." In the transcribed columns, if an error is presented, it is marked with a [sic] meaning 'thus' and the erroneous word is as it was in the newspaper when it was first published. Wherein news clipping images appear, I have included transcriptions of the text for ease of reading and accessibility.

In preparing this biography, the author relied largely on a considerable stack of clippings from the *Akron Beacon Journal* newspaper – which had been hand clipped and saved in a scrapbook by my aunt Patricia Carter Schrader (who has since passed). After researching and finding an article (in the chapter Along came Mary) from 1930, I've realized many of these clippings were clipped when Mary was still just a child. They were being saved for her and I'm happy they were! For where would we be without our daily cup of "Demi-Tasse & Mrs. Grundy."

Furthermore, I've included notes from my father's genealogical research, wherein he has framed a picture of young Josephine's life as she appeared on census returns and household indexes living with relatives. He also has visited Akron and found the maps and sources of her houses on Fairy st. and Buchtel av.

Additional sources are listed below.

Books

- Fetzer, Herman (as Jake Falstaff). *Pippins and Cheese*. (1960) Brookside Press.
- "George Pierce Baker." 2019. *Columbia Electronic Encyclopedia, 6th Edition*, May, 1.
- Kinne, Wisner Payne and reviewed by Theodore Hoffman. *George Pierce Baker and the American Theatre: 47 Workshop*. (1955) https://www.jstor.org/stable/4333576
- Morton, Thomas. *Speed the Plough*. (1798) http://www.gutenberg.org/ebooks/19407
- Roberts, Helen L., *The Cyclopedia of Social Usage*. (1913) Reference to Mrs. Grundy.

Newspapers and magazines:

- Chansky, Dorothy. 1998. "The 47 Workshop and the 48 States: George Pierce Baker and the American Theatre Audience." *Theatre History Studies*, p.135.
- Fetzer, Herman. "Pays tribute to Beacon Journal writer," *Akron Beacon Journal*, August 22, 1927.
- Fetzer, Herman (as Jake Falstaff). "Pippins and Cheese," *The Akron Beacon Journal*, July 8, 1925, p.4.
- Klinger, Larry. "Woman tells of ordeal in fatal fire," *Springfield News-Leader*, February 2, 1963.
- Martin, Judith. "Miss Manners: Mrs. Grundy," *The Akron Beacon Journal*, December 31, 1988, p.18.
- Myers, Ethel Boleyn "Mary, 9, arouses memories of Josephine Van de Grift," *The Akron Beacon Journal*, January 16, 1935.
- Reilly, Kara. 2013. "George Pierce Baker: A Century of Dramaturgs Teaching Playwriting." *Contemporary Theatre Review* 23 (2): 107–13.
- "A family reunion," *The Lockwood Luminary*, September 13, 1945.
- "A night under Garland's roof: close-up of millionaire philosopher," *The Californian*, October 24, 1922, p.4.
- "A night under Garland's roof: close-up of millionaire philosopher," *The Evening Journal*, November 4, 1922, p.13.
- "Akron's book store is now on Main street," *The Akron Beacon Journal*, September 26, 1928, p.5 (ad).
- "Allen theater: Mary Pickford in 'The Love Light'," *The Akron Beacon Journal*, January 18, 1921, p.10 (ad).
- "Blue Pencil Club Dinner," *The Chat (Brooklyn)*, March 3, 1923, p.5.
- "Buchtel orchestra plays for children," *The Akron Beacon Journal*, February 24, 1917, p.6.
- "Broadway beauty who weds for love, not money, blasts popular illusion," *The Berkshire Eagle*, January 11, 1924, p.4.
- "Can a 'greenhorn' girl succeed in N.Y. city? Girl reporter says yes," *New Castle Herald*, December 1, 1922, p.16.
- "Can an upstate girl succeed on stage?" *The Buffalo Times*, December 1, 1922, p.3.
- "Can up-state maiden succeed on stage?" *The Buffalo Times*, November 24, 1922, p.3.
- "Charles Chaplin in 'The Kid'," *The Akron Beacon Journal*, March 19, 1921, p.9 (ad).
- "Condition reported 'extremely critical': Josephine Van de Grift spends sleepless night – rally proves short lived," *The Akron Beacon Journal*, August 10, 1927, p.1 (cover).
- "Dialect is charm of the humor of Tom Daly's poetry," *The Pine Bluff Daily Graphic*, November 21, 1922, p.4.
- "Did you know that?" *The Akron Beacon Journal*, August 16, 1929.

- "Do you know?" *The Akron Beacon Journal,* August 20, 1942, p.16.
- "Dorothy Parker says it's not all fun to be funny," *The Salina Daily Union,* November 5, 1922, p.18.
- "Feature writer seriously ill at local hospital: Josephine Van de Grift, Beacon Journal columnist, undergoes major operation," *The Akron Beacon Journal,* July 19, 1927, p.1 (cover).
- "Final tributes are paid Akron feature writer: Hundreds present as solemn high mass in sung for Josephine Van de Grift," *The Akron Beacon Journal,* August 24, 1927, p.1 (cover).
- "Findley students edit school paper: Publication follows formation of Josephine Van de Grift writing club," *The Akron Beacon Journal,* December 17, 1930, p.17.
- "Getting on the stage: Girl reporter poses as 'Greenhorn' to try her hand at it," *The Austin American,* November 28, 1922, p.6.
- "Getting on the stage in New York as experienced by reporter," *The Richmond Item,* November 26, 1922, p.15.
- "Getting on the stage in New York: At last 'Huldah' gets real job," *The Evening Journal,* November 29, 1922, p.3.
- "'Greenhorn' girl tries for stage in New York: Young reporter poses as country maid from Akron and writes it up in series articles," *St. Joseph Gazette,* November 26, 1922, p.11.
- "'Huldah' in tour of booking agencies," *The Gettysburg Times,* December 12, 1922, p.4.
- "Huldah tries to land on one of Broadway's stages," *The Huntington Press,* November 26, 1922, p.9.
- "Humor doesn't come easy for the columnist," *Honolulu Star-Bulletin,* October 21, 1922, p.16.
- "Humor's sober side," *Bisbee Daily Review,* October 21, 1922, p.4.
- "Humor's sober side: Being an interview with Christopher Morley, another of a series on "how humorists get that way," *Bisbee Daily Review,* October 19, 1922, p.4.
- "Humor's sober side: Being an interview with Don Marquis, of a series on "how humorists get that way," *Bisbee Daily Review,* October 13, 1922, p.4.
- "Humor's sober side: Being an interview with Roy K. Moulton, another of a series on "how humorists get that way," *Bisbee Daily Review,* October 22, 1922, p.4.
- "Humor's sober side: Being an interview with Tom Daly, of a series on "how humorists get that way," *Bisbee Daily Review,* October 20, 1922, p.4.
- "Humor's sober side: Being an interview with Tom Sims, in a series on "how humorists get that way," *Fayetteville Observer,* October 17, 1922, p.5.
- "Humor's sober side: Being an interview with Will Rogers, another of a series on "how humorists get that way," *Bisbee Daily Review,* October 15, 1922, p.4.

- "Humor's sober side: Being the first of a series of interviews with humorists on "how humorists get that way," *The Central New Jersey Home News*, October 5, 1922, p.8.
- "Humor's sober side: Ring Lardner tells about it in interview of series on "how humorists get that way," *Bisbee Daily Review*, October 18, 1922, p.4.
- "Hundreds of telephone calls from friends deluge hospital where Josephine Van de Grift, writer, is in serious condition," *The Akron Beacon Journal*, July 20, 1927, p.1 (cover).
- "Husband's First Customer," *The Akron Beacon Journal*, August 22, 1927.
- "Is the 'real bookstore' becoming a thing of the past?" *The Akron Beacon Journal*, July 7, 1975.
- "Item writer spends week with Rockefeller on vacation," *The Richmond Item*, March 18, 1923, p.20.
- "January graduating class of Central High School," *The Akron Beacon Journal*, January 17, 1914, p.1 (cover).
- "Josephine Van de Grift column resumed today," *The Akron Beacon Journal*, February 1, 1926, p.1 (cover).
- "Josh Wise tells about it in interview of a series on "how humorists get that way," *Bisbee Daily Review*, October 17, 1922, p.4.
- "Man o' War's young brother regarded as a great colt," *The Pittsburgh Press*, April 15, 1923, p.28.
- "Mark Twain's self-written life story is here: Rigby's Book Shop," *The Akron Beacon Journal*, October 17, 1924, p.6 (ad).
- "Mary awaits mother: In little home on Fairy st. Josephine Van de Grift's baby watches and wonders – too young to know," *The Akron Beacon Journal*, August 23, 1927, p.17.
- "Mary Van de Grift Rigby likes stunt flying thrills: Daughter of late Beacon Journal columnist, city's youngest air enthusiast, not frightened in climbs, dives," *The Akron Beacon Journal*, February 1, 1930, p.12.
- "New Yale Theatre to be dedicated December 10: New edifice seats 700 and is first of type," *The Harvard Crimson*, November 19, 1926.
- "Oldest Prof. quite modern," *Honolulu Star-Bulletin*, November 10, 1923, p.31.
- "Philosophy of millionaire: Charles Garland gives his first authorized interview to woman writer," *Burlington Daily News*, October 25, 1922, p.7.
- "Popular writer dies: Mrs. William H. Rigby, better known as Josephine Van de Grift, popular columnist, succumbs in Peoples Hospital after five weeks' illness," *The Akron Beacon Journal*, August 22, 1927, p.1 (cover).
- "Radicals," *Time Magazine*, October 5, 1925.
- "Roosevelt honored by Findley pupils: Akron school paper issues edition dedicated to new President," *The Akron Beacon Journal*, April 5, 1933, p.17.
- "Scribblings of youth startling art world," *Honolulu Star-Bulletin*, December 29, 1923, p.24.

- "Society: Indianapolis has had many interesting visitors within the last fortnight," *The Indianapolis Sunday Star*, July 5, 1914, p.28.
- "Spirits reveal future of world in an interview," *The Salina Daily Union*, February 20, 1923, p.8.
- "St. Bernard makes pal of cat," *The Akron Beacon Journal*, July 23, 1924.
- "Staff writer shows slight improvement: Josephine Van de Grift has restful night at Peoples Hospital," *The Akron Beacon Journal*, August 9, 1927, p.1 (cover).
- "Van de Grift club's publication receive: Group named for late Beacon Journal writer 7edits school paper," *The Akron Beacon Journal*, May 14, 1932, p.15.
- "Well known feature writer admitted to famous workshop," *Akron Beacon Journal*, July 22, 1922, p.6.
- "What the future holds out for the world: Speaks of war and of peace," *Battle Creek Enquirer*, February 23, 1923, p.10.
- "Woman writer spends week with John D. Rockefeller spending vacation across street," *Battle Creek Enquirer*, February 25, 1923, p.8.
- "Writer will get well!: Hospital authorities say that Josephine Van de Grift is on road to recovery – news means much to Akron," *The Akron Beacon Journal*, July 26, 1927, p.19.
- "Writer's condition still is critical: No definite change reported by physicians attending Josephine Van de Grift," *The Akron Beacon Journal*, July 23, 1927, p.1 (cover).
- *The Akron Beacon Journal*.
- *The Springfield News-Leader*.

Online sources

- Ancestry
- FamilySearch.org
- Rootsmagic.com – genealogical database program
- Worldcat.org

Archives/Documentary fragments/other materials:

- AFI Catalog. "The Lonely Road," https://catalog.afi.com/Film/10352-THE-LONELYROAD
- Akron Public Library
- "Archives of the Blue Pencil Club of Brooklyn," https://tentaclii.wordpress.com/2013/08/29/archives-of-the-blue-pencil-club-of-brooklyn/
- Central High School, Akron

- Charles A. Garland: informal portrait, ca. 1922, http://credo.library.umass.edu/view/full/muph061-sl315-i001
- National Amateur Press Association: The First 100 Years: Flashbacks ... http://www.amateurpress.org/ajhist/apc.htm
- Rigby's Book Shop, Akron
- "The Lonely Road" 1923 film. http://www.silentera.com/PSFL/data/L/LonelyRoad1923.html

A special thank you to John Carter for the genealogical research on the Vandegrift and Rigby families, and for providing many of the historical photographs used in this biography.

—————⟨⟨⟨⟨◆⟩⟩⟩⟩—————

Additional Resources:

By Josephine Van de Grift NEA Service Staff Writer

Newspaper articles from 1919 – 1927 (including years 1922 – 1924 featuring Josephine's byline followed by "NEA Service Staff Writer") - which were *omitted* from this book (*otherwise it would be an extra long book!*) – many of these articles repeated in several newspapers nationwide U.S. and Canada. She covered a multitude of topics ranging from music and recitals, to sports and politics, to movie reviews and interviews, to the mundane and the offbeat. One thing is for certain, Josephine Van de Grift's byline was widely read by a diverse audience.

1919

- "250 children in rehearsal for children's crusade here," *The Akron Beacon Journal,* May 7, 1919, p.6.
- "Mrs. Seiberling and Harold Henry Heard in joint recital," *The Akron Beacon Journal,* December 13, 1919, p.6.
- "Musicians open big convention at Akron today: E. E. Workman welcomes music teachers at annual session," *The Akron Beacon Journal,* June 3, 1919, p.1 (cover).

- "Symphony concert winds up successful music convention," *The Akron Beacon Journal*, June 7, 1919, p.6.

1920

- "Akron couple, both past fourscore mark, celebrate 60ᵗʰ wedding anniversary," *The Akron Beacon Journal*, December 29, 1920, p.11.
- "Amid odor of sulphur and shoe blacking Charles has set up radical book shop," *The Akron Beacon Journal*, September 14, 1920, p.15.
- "Artists announced for coming season; 'Aida' pleases," *The Akron Beacon Journal*, March 27, 1920, p.6.
- "Charlotte Greenwood gives Akron Theater goers comedy treat of year," *The Akron Beacon Journal*, November 16, 1920, p.16.
- "Fairbank's latest film is replica of Los Angeles in the early days," *The Akron Beacon Journal*, December 24, 1920, p.3.
- "It costs one-third less to dress a wife now than it did just six months ago," *The Akron Beacon Journal*, December 11, 1920, p.1 (cover).
- "Little Dresden Doll ordered everything from potage to fromage when she was invited to have just 'bite to eat'," *The Akron Beacon Journal*, December 9, 1920, p.1 (cover).
- "Notably fine performance of 'Faust' achieved by Creatore Opera Co.," *The Akron Beacon Journal*, November 9, 1920, p.17.
- "Rock's revue de luxe gives Akron metropolitan thrills," *The Akron Beacon Journal*, October 5, 1920, p.16.
- "Santrey's famous jazz band will be added attraction at music hall next week," *The Akron Beacon Journal*, June 11, 1920, p.32.
- "Sophie Braslau scores real triumph in her concert here," *The Akron Beacon Journal*, January 17, 1920, p.6.
- "Styles in literature have changed with times, says Miss Edgerton," *The Akron Beacon Journal*, June 2, 1920, p.6.
- "The new woman is to be considered seriously in two Akron churches; will it be splay feet or lovely violet?" *The Akron Beacon Journal*, October 2, 1920, p.1 (cover).

1921

- "Art on Main street? Hungarian painter invades rubber province," *The Akron Beacon Journal*, December 23, 1921, p.6.
- "Bill Hart exchanges sombrero and chaps for policeman's billy," *The Akron Beacon Journal*, January 10, 1921, p.10.
- "Can always tell married man by his shoes, declares Akron dealer," *The Akron Beacon Journal*, February 2, 1921, p.1 (cover).

- "Characterizations are best thing in 'Dream Street' showing at Colonial," *The Akron Beacon Journal,* September 19, 1921, p.12.
- "Fairbanks departs from usual role in 'The Nut' coming to Allen," *The Akron Beacon Journal,* March 11, 1921, p.18.
- "Fakirs, pickpockets and card sharks shown in 'The Stealers," *The Akron Beacon Journal,* January 24, 1921, p.10.
- "Griffith's 'Way Down East' pleases at Colonial; Thrills in ice jam scene," *The Akron Beacon Journal,* August 29, 1921, p.9.
- "'He's a nice boy,' says Amelita Galli-Curci, when asked about husband; Praise for Mary Garden," *The Akron Beacon Journal,* January 22, 1921, p.1 (cover).
- "'It hurt me when I saw other women with their husbands,' is tragedy of Mrs. Derr, held for murder," *The Akron Beacon Journal,* September 23, 1921, p.1 (cover).
- "Joe Kirkwood comes within a stroke of equalling the record," *The Akron Beacon Journal,* September 10, 1921, p.7.
- "Lions begin to look little bored from overwork in film comedies," *The Akron Beacon Journal,* January 12, 1921, p.14.
- "Mid-season 'Joy Night' by Goodyear Three Arts club, pleasing performance," *The Akron Beacon Journal,* February 19, 1921, p.10.
- "Movie version of 'The Misleading Lady' preserves admirably contents of play," *The Akron Beacon Journal,* April 15, 1921, p.18.
- "'Passion' at Waldorf and Empress and 'Kismet' at Allen prove worth while screen events; Draw large crowds," *The Akron Beacon Journal,* March 28, 1921, p.10.
- "Pretty girls and elaborate costumes feature Follies," *The Akron Beacon Journal,* April 7, 1921, p.12.
- "'Take It From Me,' lively musical comedy, opens season at Grand," *The Akron Beacon Journal,* September 20, 1921, p.14.
- "'The Mistress of Shenstone,' fine example of emotional repression," *The Akron Beacon Journal,* April 6, 1921, p.12.
- "Theda Bara is favorite of Jane Lee as screen heroine," *The Akron Beacon Journal,* January 26, 1921, p.10.
- "Three-star laugh show at Waldorf," *The Akron Beacon Journal,* January 5, 1921, p.10.
- "'We believe Marie,' declares brother of accused woman," *The Akron Beacon Journal,* August 12, 1921, p.1 (cover).
- "Women don't like to do domestic work; They want to get out and rub elbows with business world," *The Akron Beacon Journal,* March 11, 1921, p.16.

1922

- "Loves infant she disowns as not hers," *The Ogden Standard-Examiner*, October 19, 1922, p.1 (cover).
- "Two women fill New York's lunch basket with 35,000 sandwiches," *The Pittsburgh Press*, November 21, 1922, p.34.

1923

- "23-year-old 'mother' of 128 babies gives up pleasures to head an orphanage," *Lancaster New Era,* January 26, 1923, p.20.
- "30,000 ready for game of 'war': Uncle Sam is host to army of summer soldiers," *Stevens Point Journal,* June 26, 1923, p.5.
- "$4,000,000 secret: Hidden in grave, where Czar's jewels may be buried," *Public Opinion*, February 13, 1923, p.2.
- "Alimony for men," *Lansing State Journal,* January 1, 1923, p.8.
- "All the sights from soup to nuts – life made easy!" *Salt Lake Telegram,* March 5, 1923, p.14.
- "Artist wields brush with her teeth," *Saskatoon Daily Star (Canada)*, December 12, 1923, p.2.
- "Beer is the New Jersey woman's platform," *The Buffalo Times,* September 5, 1923, p.3.
- "'Beer Pail' is her platform: Woman out for Mayor says old time bucket preferable to flask," *News-Democrat,* October 7, 1923, p.13.
- "Braves jungle with powderpuff," *The Tennessean,* May 6, 1923, p.54.
- "Broadway bows to 5-year-old: Edwin Mills," *Lansing State Journal,* May 17, 1923, p.15.
- "Cello's 4 feet tall; she's 3; yet she is musical prodigy," *Reading Times,* February 27, 1923, p.8.
- "Childhood dreams make $50,000 a year for 24-year-old girl designing ruffles," *Arizona Republic,* November 4, 1923, p.38.
- "Does sex pit sway murder juries? Yes, say lawyers," *The Independent-Record,* March 26, 1923, p.8.
- "Flapper, new problem of the industry: says women will fight over the eight hour day," *Salisbury Evening Post,* March 23, 1923, p.10.
- "Flapper wives kill of grocers and delicatessen king's get rich," *Princeton Daily Clarion,* August 6, 1923, p.6.
- "Girl of ten writes love rhymes to red-head; world of letters aroused by her genius," *The Sheboygan Press,* December 18, 1923, p.12.
- "Governor Smith's 'premier' talks of 'petticoat politics'," *Star-Gazette,* August 16, 1923, p.11.
- "Heartache isle! Curran to relieve immigrants' dread," *The Bee,* July 23, 1923, p.2.

- "Hoboes of United States claim rights to higher education," *Battle Creek Enquirer*, January 2, 1923, p.8.
- "Kilbane's line of chatter won't fiz on modest young French ring hero, cause he doesn't savee English: Lady writer interviews the French featherweight champion and finds that he likes sleep, won't eat chicken, has a piece of a rib for a jaw and is a nice man," *The Victoria Daily Times (Canada)*, April 14, 1923, p.10.
- "Lost: the Typical American girl?" *Lansing State Journal*, September 21, 1923, p.1-2 (cover story).
- "Made $200,000 out of $100; woman tells how she did it," *Salisbury Evening Post*, January 15, 1923, p.2.
- "Mother is proud of teacher who uses cigarettes: Scores men as being old fashioned; defends her daughter," *News-Democrat*, December 2, 1923, p.13.
- "Mrs. Hall's own detectives track slayers in famous church murder," *The Sheboygan Press*, June 9, 1923, p.8.
- "No more sleep! A shot of electricity will take its place, says inventor," *Muncie Evening Press*, October 16, 1923, p.3.
- "Paddock says one born fast on feet," *Idaho Evening Times*, May 3, 1923, p.6.
- "'Potatoes did it,' says girl who danced for twenty-seven hours," *Battle Creek Enquirer*, April 8, 1923, p.8.
- "Speedy interview given girl scribe by dash champion," *Santa Ana Register*, May 2, 1923, p.20.
- "Squirrels in the Movies? Certainly," *The Evening Tribune*, January 5, 1923, p.8.
- "Tut power in new jazz: Egyptian King will have an influence in the coming months," *The Daily Chronicle*, March 15, 1923, p.8.
- "Who will get Gould fortune: Children of two wives facing tangle over estate of $50,000,000," *The Richmond Item*, April 3, 1923, p.12.
- "Woman politician wants to give up job so that she can accomplish more good," *Messenger-Inquirer*, January 7, 1923, p.13.
- "Women going to bow-wows, says girl novelist: Nineteen-year-old writer enters hot debate with judge on immortality of sex," *Wisconsin State Journal*, October 7, 1923, p.2.
- "Women of France and Wales give tip to American wives," *The Independent-Record*, June 22, 1923, p.7.
- "Women who smoke must obey edict of experts who originate styles," *Arizona Republic*, April 16, 1923, p.9.

1924

- "Akron man started Chautauqua, who has become one of the great American institutions," *The Akron Beacon Journal*, July 14, 1924, p.1 (cover).

- "'Art exhibits can be made appealing to all' asserts new director of Akron Art Institute," *The Akron Beacon Journal,* August 2, 1924, p.1 (cover).
- "Catholic, Jew, Protestant join to bring children back in fold," *News-Democrat,* March 16, 1924, p.13.
- "'Don't star at anyone,' says dwarf, who attracts attention of hundreds of persons," *The Akron Beacon Journal,* November 6, 1924, p.1 (cover).
- "Girl bandits keep police on the jump as they vie with men in many crimes," *The Brooklyn Citizen,* January 27, 1924, p.13.
- "Here is what Akron Chinese residents think of revolution that ravishes their native land," *The Akron Beacon Journal,* October 17, 1924, p.19.
- "'I wish Christmas would come oftener' says little girl as she clasps doll tightly to her," *The Akron Beacon Journal,* December 25, 1924, p.13.
- "Lotta Crabtree, actress who left $4,000,000 to charity, once owned downtown block here, *The Akron Beacon Journal,* September 30, 1924, p.1 (cover).
- "Merely a page of life wherein husband disproves gossips and returns to home," *The Akron Beacon Journal,* September 8, 1924, p.1 (cover).
- "This little world: the color of Chinatown, past and present," *The Town Talk,* January 31, 1924, p.4.

1927

- "Children's home youngsters go to Cleveland to see real rodeo as guests of Veterans," *The Akron Beacon Journal,* May 18, 1927, p.25.
- "Old-time circus men in reunion at Akron," *The Akron Beacon Journal,* May 21, 1927, p.15.
- "Recommends bicycling as aid to good health: Opera singer, visiting Akron, remembered by many as woman who posed as 'The Greatest Mother in the World'," *The Akron Beacon Journal,* March 12, 1927, p.1 (cover).

XIV

Index of names

Index of names, places and important topics of the 1920's

www.ingramcontent.com/pod-product-compliance
Lightning Source LLC
Chambersburg PA
CBHW030634150426
42811CB00048B/106